Lecture Notes in Computer Science 13333

Founding Editors

Gerhard Goos
Karlsruhe Institute of Technology, Karlsruhe, Germany

Juris Hartmanis
Cornell University, Ithaca, NY, USA

Editorial Board Members

Elisa Bertino
Purdue University, West Lafayette, IN, USA

Wen Gao
Peking University, Beijing, China

Bernhard Steffen
TU Dortmund University, Dortmund, Germany

Moti Yung
Columbia University, New York, NY, USA

More information about this series at https://link.springer.com/bookseries/558

Abbas Moallem (Ed.)

HCI for Cybersecurity, Privacy and Trust

4th International Conference, HCI-CPT 2022
Held as Part of the 24th HCI International Conference, HCII 2022
Virtual Event, June 26 – July 1, 2022
Proceedings

 Springer

Editor
Abbas Moallem
San Jose State University
San Jose, CA, USA

ISSN 0302-9743   ISSN 1611-3349 (electronic)
Lecture Notes in Computer Science
ISBN 978-3-031-05562-1   ISBN 978-3-031-05563-8 (eBook)
https://doi.org/10.1007/978-3-031-05563-8

This Springer imprint is published by the registered company Springer Nature Switzerland AG
The registered company address is: Gewerbestrasse 11, 6330 Cham, Switzerland

Foreword

Human-computer interaction (HCI) is acquiring an ever-increasing scientific and industrial importance, as well as having more impact on people's everyday life, as an ever-growing number of human activities are progressively moving from the physical to the digital world. This process, which has been ongoing for some time now, has been dramatically accelerated by the COVID-19 pandemic. The HCI International (HCII) conference series, held yearly, aims to respond to the compelling need to advance the exchange of knowledge and research and development efforts on the human aspects of design and use of computing systems.

The 24th International Conference on Human-Computer Interaction, HCI International 2022 (HCII 2022), was planned to be held at the Gothia Towers Hotel and Swedish Exhibition & Congress Centre, Göteborg, Sweden, during June 26 to July 1, 2022. Due to the COVID-19 pandemic and with everyone's health and safety in mind, HCII 2022 was organized and run as a virtual conference. It incorporated the 21 thematic areas and affiliated conferences listed on the following page.

A total of 5583 individuals from academia, research institutes, industry, and governmental agencies from 88 countries submitted contributions, and 1276 papers and 275 posters were included in the proceedings to appear just before the start of the conference. The contributions thoroughly cover the entire field of human-computer interaction, addressing major advances in knowledge and effective use of computers in a variety of application areas. These papers provide academics, researchers, engineers, scientists, practitioners, and students with state-of-the-art information on the most recent advances in HCI. The volumes constituting the set of proceedings to appear before the start of the conference are listed in the following pages.

The HCI International (HCII) conference also offers the option of 'Late Breaking Work' which applies both for papers and posters, and the corresponding volume(s) of the proceedings will appear after the conference. Full papers will be included in the 'HCII 2022 - Late Breaking Papers' volumes of the proceedings to be published in the Springer LNCS series, while 'Poster Extended Abstracts' will be included as short research papers in the 'HCII 2022 - Late Breaking Posters' volumes to be published in the Springer CCIS series.

I would like to thank the Program Board Chairs and the members of the Program Boards of all thematic areas and affiliated conferences for their contribution and support towards the highest scientific quality and overall success of the HCI International 2022 conference; they have helped in so many ways, including session organization, paper reviewing (single-blind review process, with a minimum of two reviews per submission) and, more generally, acting as goodwill ambassadors for the HCII conference.

This conference would not have been possible without the continuous and unwavering support and advice of Gavriel Salvendy, founder, General Chair Emeritus, and Scientific Advisor. For his outstanding efforts, I would like to express my appreciation to Abbas Moallem, Communications Chair and Editor of HCI International News.

June 2022   Constantine Stephanidis

HCI International 2022 Thematic Areas and Affiliated Conferences

Thematic Areas

- HCI: Human-Computer Interaction
- HIMI: Human Interface and the Management of Information

Affiliated Conferences

- EPCE: 19th International Conference on Engineering Psychology and Cognitive Ergonomics
- AC: 16th International Conference on Augmented Cognition
- UAHCI: 16th International Conference on Universal Access in Human-Computer Interaction
- CCD: 14th International Conference on Cross-Cultural Design
- SCSM: 14th International Conference on Social Computing and Social Media
- VAMR: 14th International Conference on Virtual, Augmented and Mixed Reality
- DHM: 13th International Conference on Digital Human Modeling and Applications in Health, Safety, Ergonomics and Risk Management
- DUXU: 11th International Conference on Design, User Experience and Usability
- C&C: 10th International Conference on Culture and Computing
- DAPI: 10th International Conference on Distributed, Ambient and Pervasive Interactions
- HCIBGO: 9th International Conference on HCI in Business, Government and Organizations
- LCT: 9th International Conference on Learning and Collaboration Technologies
- ITAP: 8th International Conference on Human Aspects of IT for the Aged Population
- AIS: 4th International Conference on Adaptive Instructional Systems
- HCI-CPT: 4th International Conference on HCI for Cybersecurity, Privacy and Trust
- HCI-Games: 4th International Conference on HCI in Games
- MobiTAS: 4th International Conference on HCI in Mobility, Transport and Automotive Systems
- AI-HCI: 3rd International Conference on Artificial Intelligence in HCI
- MOBILE: 3rd International Conference on Design, Operation and Evaluation of Mobile Communications

List of Conference Proceedings Volumes Appearing Before the Conference

1. LNCS 13302, Human-Computer Interaction: Theoretical Approaches and Design Methods (Part I), edited by Masaaki Kurosu
2. LNCS 13303, Human-Computer Interaction: Technological Innovation (Part II), edited by Masaaki Kurosu
3. LNCS 13304, Human-Computer Interaction: User Experience and Behavior (Part III), edited by Masaaki Kurosu
4. LNCS 13305, Human Interface and the Management of Information: Visual and Information Design (Part I), edited by Sakae Yamamoto and Hirohiko Mori
5. LNCS 13306, Human Interface and the Management of Information: Applications in Complex Technological Environments (Part II), edited by Sakae Yamamoto and Hirohiko Mori
6. LNAI 13307, Engineering Psychology and Cognitive Ergonomics, edited by Don Harris and Wen-Chin Li
7. LNCS 13308, Universal Access in Human-Computer Interaction: Novel Design Approaches and Technologies (Part I), edited by Margherita Antona and Constantine Stephanidis
8. LNCS 13309, Universal Access in Human-Computer Interaction: User and Context Diversity (Part II), edited by Margherita Antona and Constantine Stephanidis
9. LNAI 13310, Augmented Cognition, edited by Dylan D. Schmorrow and Cali M. Fidopiastis
10. LNCS 13311, Cross-Cultural Design: Interaction Design Across Cultures (Part I), edited by Pei-Luen Patrick Rau
11. LNCS 13312, Cross-Cultural Design: Applications in Learning, Arts, Cultural Heritage, Creative Industries, and Virtual Reality (Part II), edited by Pei-Luen Patrick Rau
12. LNCS 13313, Cross-Cultural Design: Applications in Business, Communication, Health, Well-being, and Inclusiveness (Part III), edited by Pei-Luen Patrick Rau
13. LNCS 13314, Cross-Cultural Design: Product and Service Design, Mobility and Automotive Design, Cities, Urban Areas, and Intelligent Environments Design (Part IV), edited by Pei-Luen Patrick Rau
14. LNCS 13315, Social Computing and Social Media: Design, User Experience and Impact (Part I), edited by Gabriele Meiselwitz
15. LNCS 13316, Social Computing and Social Media: Applications in Education and Commerce (Part II), edited by Gabriele Meiselwitz
16. LNCS 13317, Virtual, Augmented and Mixed Reality: Design and Development (Part I), edited by Jessie Y. C. Chen and Gino Fragomeni
17. LNCS 13318, Virtual, Augmented and Mixed Reality: Applications in Education, Aviation and Industry (Part II), edited by Jessie Y. C. Chen and Gino Fragomeni

39. CCIS 1582, HCI International 2022 Posters - Part III, edited by Constantine Stephanidis, Margherita Antona and Stavroula Ntoa
40. CCIS 1583, HCI International 2022 Posters - Part IV, edited by Constantine Stephanidis, Margherita Antona and Stavroula Ntoa

http://2022.hci.international/proceedings

Preface

The cybersecurity field, in all its dimensions, is exponentially growing, evolving and expanding. New security risks emerge continuously with the steady increase of internet interconnections and the development of the Internet of Things. Cyberattacks endanger individuals and companies, as well as vital public services and infrastructures. Confronted with spreading and evolving cyber threats, the system and network defenses of organizations and individuals are falling behind, as they often fail to implement and effectively use basic cybersecurity and privacy practices and technologies.

The 4th International Conference on HCI for Cybersecurity, Privacy, and Trust (HCI-CPT 2022), an affiliated conference of the HCI International Conference, intended to help, promote and encourage research in this field by providing a forum for interaction and exchanges among researchers, academics, and practitioners in the fields of HCI and cyber security. The conference focused on HCI principles, methods and tools in order to address the numerous and complex threats which put at risk computer-mediated human-activities in today's society, which is progressively becoming more intertwined with and dependent on interactive technologies.

In this regard, and motivated by recent worldwide developments driven by the ongoing pandemic, such as increased usage of internet and IoT services for remote working, education, shopping, and health management, papers accepted in this year's proceedings have emphasized issues related to user privacy and data protection, as well as the impact of the pandemic in the field of cybersecurity. Furthermore, they focus on two major factors that are decisive for the acceptability of solutions in the field, namely trustworthiness and usability. Finally, innovative authentication methods and tools have been proposed in the papers, as well as cyber-defense and protection approaches.

One volume of the HCII 2022 proceedings is dedicated to this year's edition of the HCI-CPT Conference and focuses on topics related to user privacy and data protection, trustworthiness and user experience in cybersecurity, multi-faceted authentication methods and tools, HCI in cyber defense and protection, studies on usable security in intelligent environments, as well as the impact of the Covid-19 pandemic on cybersecurity.

Papers of this volume are included for publication after a minimum of two single–blind reviews from the members of the HCI-CPT Program Board or, in some cases, from members of the Program Boards of other affiliated conferences. I would like to thank all of them for their invaluable contribution, support and efforts.

June 2022   Abbas Moallem

4th International Conference on HCI for Cybersecurity, Privacy and Trust (HCI-CPT 2022)

The full list with the Program Board Chairs and the members of the Program Boards of all thematic areas and affiliated conferences is available online at

http://www.hci.international/board-members-2022.php

HCI International 2023

The 25th International Conference on Human-Computer Interaction, HCI International 2023, will be held jointly with the affiliated conferences at the AC Bella Sky Hotel and Bella Center, Copenhagen, Denmark, 23–28 July 2023. It will cover a broad spectrum of themes related to human-computer interaction, including theoretical issues, methods, tools, processes, and case studies in HCI design, as well as novel interaction techniques, interfaces, and applications. The proceedings will be published by Springer. More information will be available on the conference website: http://2023.hci.international/.

General Chair
Constantine Stephanidis
University of Crete and ICS-FORTH
Heraklion, Crete, Greece
Email: general_chair@hcii2023.org

http://2023.hci.international/

Contents

Trustworthiness and User Experience in Cybersecurity

Multi-faceted Authentication Methods and Tools

HCI in Cyber Defense and Protection

Studies on Usable Security in Intelligent Environments

The Impact of the Covid-19 Pandemic on Cybersecurity

User Privacy and Data Protection

Intermediate Help with Using Digital Devices and Online Accounts: Understanding the Needs, Expectations, and Vulnerabilities of Young Adults

Hanieh Atashpanjeh[1]([⊠]), Arezou Behfar[1], Cassity Haverkamp[2],
Maryellen McClain Verdoes[2], and Mahdi Nasrullah Al-Ameen[1]

[1] Department of Computer Science, Utah State University, Logan, USA
{hanieh.atashpanjeh,abehfar,mahdi.al-ameen}@usu.edu
[2] Department of Psychology, Utah State University, Logan, USA
cassity.haverkamp@aggiemail.usu.edu, maryellen.mcclainverdoes@usu.edu

Abstract. With the revolution in digital technologies, users face challenges to learn, understand, and use modern devices and online services. Thus, they seek intermediate help, i.e., assistance from others to avail the benefits of technological advancement. The prior studies showed that people with special needs, including the users with visual impairments, and older adults ask for help from their caregivers as they encounter problems with technology use. However, there is a gap in existing literature to systematically investigate the expectations, and challenges of users in availing help from others with using digital devices (e.g., computers, mobile phones) and online accounts. We addressed this gap in our work, where we focused on the young adults. The findings from our study unpacked the contexts of availing intermediate help with using devices and accounts, where we identified the corresponding challenges, concerns, and the security and privacy risks of users.

Keywords: Intermediate help · Digital devices and online accounts · User needs and behavior · Security and privacy vulnerabilities

1 Introduction

The technological advancements play a major role in modern civilization [29], where digital devices (e.g., computers, mobile phones) and online services have become an integral part of our day-to-day life. To avail the benefits of digital technologies to the desired extents, it is crucial that the end users have a clear understanding of how to use, and interact with digital devices and online accounts; what to expect from these technologies; and how to deal with unexpected situations in the course of using devices and accounts [3,7,11,16]. In these

---

H. Atashpanjeh and A. Behfar—contributed equally to this paper

A. Moallem (Ed.): HCII 2022, LNCS 13333, pp. 3–15, 2022.
https://doi.org/10.1007/978-3-031-05563-8_1

contexts, the rapid advancement of technology could pose challenges for users to learn, understand, and use modern devices and online services [3,6,26].

Prior studies focused on the people with special needs to understand their difficulties with using technologies, including the people with visual impairments [1,2,13], and older adults [17,23]. A few studies [21,28] investigated the authentication behavior of the people with certain disabilities. In a recent study [5], the authors pointed to the intermediate help (i.e., assistance from others) as one of the reasons why people share their computers and smartphones. In another study [16], Kocabas et al. found that asking for help from experts is one of the contingency plans of users in case they lose access to their devices or accounts. However, there is a dearth of systematic investigation in existing literature to gain in-depth understanding on the needs, expectations, and challenges of users in the process of availing intermediate help with using digital devices (e.g., computers, mobile phones) and online accounts. We addressed this gap in our work, where we focused on the young adults. In particular, we investigated the following research questions:

RQ1. What are the contexts and reasons for availing intermediate help with using digital devices (e.g., computers, smartphones) and online accounts?

RQ2. What are the challenges, concerns, and risks of users in getting intermediate help?

To address the above research questions, we conducted semi-structured interviews with 40 participants in the USA. The findings from our study unfold the contexts where the young adults ask for help with technology use, including for setup and configuration of devices, to comprehend the changes in features and services, to address usability and technical issues, and for remote communication. Our analysis shed light on the taxonomy of their expectations and challenges in availing help from different entities. We identified the security and privacy risks associated with intermediate help, where most participants reported sharing their passwords with the help-givers. Taken together, our study contributes to advance the HCI and Security community's understanding of the needs, expectations, and challenges of young adults in availing intermediate help, and the corresponding security and privacy risks.

2   Related Work

In this section, we provide an overview of the findings from prior work in the realm of intermediate help with technology use.

The study of Kiesler et al. [15] showed that professional support services underestimate the actual needs of technical assistance for an individual, where over 70% of household members asked for help from family members, especially from teenagers to address the issues with using computers and Internet at home. In another study [25], Poole et al. found that in organizational settings, people asked for help with technology use either based on the physical proximity to the help-giver, or waited until their preferred colleague would be available to help.

The study of Al-Ameen et al. [5] found that their less-educated, or older participants availed help from their social circles in creating and managing online accounts, including social media accounts. In the process of getting help, users share their passwords; the authors argued that the relationship between peers might change over time that could be concerning to them who had shared their sensitive information with others [5]. The study of Singh et al. [28] examined the sharing of authentication secrets with family members as a way of helping to manage financial activities, where almost all of their participants reported sharing their bank PINs. The authors also found that certain types of disabilities required their participants to get help during the face-to-face interaction with bank tellers and retail clerks [28].

The study of Wahidin et al. [30] focused on the needs of intermediate help with technology use for the people with visual impairments, where they interviewed five professional workers to understand their challenges and barriers with using technologies at the workplace. The findings from this study [30] point to the complexities and usability issues with using assistive technology, and shed light on the needs of collaboration between individuals with visual impairments and their sighted colleagues. In a separate study with visually impaired participants [2], Akter et al. investigated the privacy risks of their participants around technology use, and found that they were vulnerable to sharing sensitive data with the people they asked for help.

The study of Hayes et al. [13] aimed to understand how the individuals with visual impairments protect their digital privacy and security. The authors identified that their participants were not aware of the malicious applications on their personal computers [13]. In the work settings, participants reported concerns that the assistive technology, like an enlarged screen could make the sensitive information vulnerable to shoulder-surfing attacks [13].

Our Study. While prior studies investigated the taxonomy of intermediate help with technology use by different groups of users, including less-educated population, older users, and people with visual impairments, there is a dearth in existing literature to understand the needs, expectations, and vulnerabilities of young adults in availing intermediate help with using digital devices and online accounts. We addressed this gap in our work.

3   Methodology

We conducted semi-structured interviews (audio-recorded) with 40 participants (age range: 18–39; women: 50%) in the USA. We followed the guideline of Erikson [12] in choosing the age range for young adults. Most of our participants are from a non-Computer Science background, including majors in Psychology, Health Science, History, Finance, Biology, Parks and Recreation, Communicative Disorders, Nursing, Architecture, and Fine Arts (see Table 1 for details). To recruit participants, we leveraged the online platform developed and maintained by our university for human-subject studies. We also reached out to the participants through email listservs of the local community.

Table 1. Demographics of participants

PID	Gender	Age-range	College major
P1	F	30–34	School counseling med
P2	F	18–24	Human development and family studies
P3	F	18–24	Human biology
P4	M	25–29	N/A
P5	M	18–24	Computer science
P6	F	18–24	Parks and rec
P7	F	18–24	N/A
P8	M	18–24	History
P9	M	18–24	Psychology
P10	F	18–24	Communicative disorders
P11	F	18–24	Exploratory
P12	M	25–29	Technology systems
P13	M	18–24	Business management
P14	F	18–24	ELED
P15	M	18–24	Pre-Business
P16	F	18–24	Psychology
P17	M	25–29	Nursing
P18	M	18–24	Biology
P19	M	18–24	Psychology
P20	F	18–24	Human Dev. studies
P21	F	18–24	Psychology
P22	F	18–24	Health science
P23	F	18–24	Prephysical therapy
P24	F	18–24	Psychology
P25	F	18–24	Undecided (Exploratory)
P26	F	18–24	History
P27	F	18–24	Finance
P28	F	18–24	N/A
P29	F	18–24	Art
P30	M	18–24	Biological engineering
P31	N/A	18–24	General technology
P32	M	18–24	Computer science
P33	M	18–24	Business
P34	M	18–24	Landscape architecture
P35	M	18–24	N/A
P36	F	18–24	Accounting & Math
P37	M	18–24	Bio engineering
P38	M	18–24	Computer science
P39	M	35–39	Civil engineering
P40	M	25–29	Computer science

In preparing the questionnaire for an interview, the authors of this paper conducted several rounds of focus group discussion. We also gathered feedback from colleagues at our labs. We improved the structure and clarity of the questionnaire based on our focus group discussion, and the feedback from our lab members. Our study was approved by the Institutional Review Board (IRB) at our university.

3.1 Procedure

At the beginning of the study, participants were presented with an Informed Consent Document (ICD). As they agreed to ICD, we asked them a set of interview questions. During the study, participants were asked about the contexts and reasons for availing intermediate help, their relationship and interaction with the persons they ask for help, and their expectations and challenges around getting help. We asked them about the needs of, and concerns about sharing authentication secrets in the process of availing intermediate help. At the end, participants responded to a set of demographic questionnaires. On average, each session took between 25 and 40 min. Each participant was compensated with a $15 Amazon.com gift card.

3.2 Analysis

We transcribed the audio recordings. We then performed thematic analysis on our transcriptions [8–10]. Each transcript was coded by two independent researchers, where they read through the transcripts of the first few interviews, developed codes, compared them, and then iterated again with more interviews until we had developed a consistent codebook. Once the codebook was finalized, two researchers independently coded the remaining interviews. After all the interviews had been coded, both researchers spot-checked the other's coded transcripts and did not find any inconsistencies. Finally, we organized and taxonomized our codes into higher-level categories.

4 Results

In this section, we report the findings from our study. Based on the frequency of comments in participant responses, we employ the following terminology for consistency: a few (0–10%), several (10–25%), some (25–40%), about half (40–60%), most (60–80%), and almost all (80–100%).

4.1 Intermediate Help: Contexts and Reasons

Setup and Configuration. Setting up a modern device can be complicated for users due to the abundance of features that require configuration before they can start using them. In our study, we found that several participants need intermediate help to understand and navigate through the initial steps involved in setting up and configuring a device. They often ask others for help to create a mental model of the system, comprehend how it operates, and resolve the configuration settings. For instance, one of our participants (P13) suffering from visual impairment reported the challenges in understanding how to configure privacy settings of the software that assist him with reading and writing. He mentioned, *"...I need to build up understanding [of] these vision software such as 'Jaws' and 'ZoomText'...I recently got help to configure them in a way that's not intruding in my PC..."*

Our participant, P1 reported suffering from General Anxiety Disorder, which could impair the ability of memorization and recall [14]. As a part of her professional duties, P1 has to set up devices for her colleagues, including projectors, and printers. She referred to the differences in setup interface of these devices requiring her to memorize the configuration steps for each interface separately. As a result, sometimes she fails to recall the setup procedures and has to ask others for help.

A few of our participants reported availing intermediate help to get started with using emerging technologies (e.g., virtual reality, augmented reality), where P18 mentioned, *"...for the virtual reality, I asked how to learn, how to get started...I want to get pointed in the right direction first. So usually I ask people to help me out in getting started, and then I take over from there."*

Variations and Changes in Features. The modern devices and applications employ varying settings, features, and interaction techniques in providing services to the end users. In these contexts, a few participants expressed their frustration on how the variations in features and user interfaces, often from the same service providers pose challenges for them to adopt to the technology landscapes. Our participant, P39 mentioned, *"Like my laptop I guess is the technology that I asked for help with. Just because there's a lot of programs on a computer and, even within Microsoft, there's a ton. So, I don't necessarily know how those work plus, like, within your settings of the computer, there's a ton of stuff you can do...I'm not really too tech-savvy with any of that."*

A few of our participants reported confusions in understanding the new features offered by online services due to the 'novelty effect', and lack of available help from service providers on how to navigate through, and get benefited from their updated features. While referring to the need of assistance in order to understand and use the new online services for students at his university, P34 said, *"...that one [student's online account] is really confusing to me. I'm getting a hang of it."*

Usability of Technologies. One of our participants mentioned his brother's disability that causes difficulty in typing, and thus, he has to avail help from others. The small key-size on the current on-screen keyboard in mobile phones makes it challenging for his brother to type; he added, *"...I kind of wish they made it [key on on-screen keyboard] bigger, it was like, okay, maybe you have to scroll back and forth to get from one end to the other but then they're huge and you can use those"*.

Our participant, P9 suffers from Auditory Processing Disorder, which causes difficulty in following long conversations [24]. As a result, P9 has to seek intermediate help to comprehend the contents of online videos (e.g., Youtube tutorials, often used for academic learning), where many online videos do not incorporate subtitles, and the ones that do – are sometimes, incorrect or incomplete. He mentioned, *"I definitely think incorporating a caption device into sort of any smartphone would be awesome. Um, YouTube has recently changed their, um, use of their caption thing...which is cool, but also, one, you get like incorrect ones sometimes...and two, they're not on everything [every video]."*

Technical Issues. Several participants reported encountering technical issues while using computers and Internet at home that they had to ask for intermediate help. The error message on a computer informs users about the state of an operation that might have gone wrong. However, interpreting those message and translating them into appropriate actions emerge as a challenge for end users. For instance, one of our participants (P15) reported, *"Usually when there's like an error that pops up on a computer and I don't know, I usually have no idea what the error is, I always need someone to help me with that."*

Our participant, P38 referred to the trouble in using his computer due to a malfunctioning sound driver. In another instance, P20 had to ask for help in resolving the Internet connectivity issue, as he said, *"...some sort of internet connection issue where it's not obvious to me, I asked for help with an obscure thing that I don't understand."*

Remote Communication. A few of our participants reported difficulties in hearing that require them to ask for assistance for telephone communication. One of them (P17) who suffers from Enlarged Vestibular Aqueduct (EVA) – a condition caused by a malformation in the inner ear that leads to loss of hearing [20], said, *"My disability is being deaf. Sometimes I can't understand when there is a phone call, I can't call people very well...I asked others for help is like hearing certain things."* Another participant (P9) who seeks for help to use mobile devices for remote communication, mentioned, *"I have auditory processing disorder, and I have a hard time hearing people over the phone like it gets all garbled or like they speak really quiet so I often have someone else make the phone calls for me."*

4.2   Intermediate Help: Sharing Authentication Secrets

Most of our participants reported that they had shared their passwords with others in the process of availing intermediate help. Below, we present our findings on sharing authentication secrets while getting help with using digital devices (e.g., computers, mobile phones) or online accounts.

Digital Devices. While availing intermediate help with the use of digital devices (e.g., computers, mobile phones), our participants shared the passwords of their devices with family members, friends, and co-workers. In a few other cases, participants had to share their password with IT experts; one of them mentioned, *"My phone and my computer in order for like IT people to get access to it...they make you write down your password..."*

Several participants are comfortable to share passwords only with their family members. In availing help from friends, participants reported sharing their passwords based on needs; P13 mentioned, *"I shared with him [participant's friend] my computer password because he was helping me [to] figure out a software issue that he knew more about."* In this context, our participant, P8 has let his friends have their fingerprints recorded on his mobile phone for biometric authentication, so that his friends do not have to ask for password every time P8 needs help from them.

A few participants have distinct sharing preferences based on the contents stored in their devices, where they are more cautious in sharing the password for a device that contains documents and information pertaining their professional duties. For instance, P1 reported, *"Everyone knows the password to my phone like something will happen and I will be like, can you help me, and they will just log in. Um, computer wise I try not to share it [password] cause there is work stuff on there so there is stuff that I don't want just anyone looking at or getting into. For my phone...I will just share it with whoever I'm asking for help with whether that be a coworker or a friend or if I'm in a class and I'm like, this is broken can you help. With computer...I typically just log in and then have them once I log in."*

Online Accounts. Our participants reported sharing passwords for different online accounts, including bank, email, social media, and university accounts. Several of them rely on their parents to manage their financial activities; they shared the passwords for their banking accounts with their parents to avail assistance in this regard. A few participants shared the password for social media account with their family members, where P5 mentioned, *"When I first set up my Facebook account I needed help for that. So, my sister knew my password..."*

For most of our participants, the online platform for academic work (e.g., college account) offered the first technological freedom as they started using technology for their career, beyond the online experiences with games and entertainment. In this context, they reported difficulties in understanding and using the online platforms for academic activities, and found themselves underprepared to confidently use the system. Thus, they asked for help from their family members and shared with them the password for their college account.

We found instances of sharing the password for email account with friends in the process of getting intermediate help for account creation, and recovery. One of our participants (P9) reported sharing the authentication secret for her university account with her friend to avail help with filling up an online form.

4.3 Intermediate Help: Challenges and Concerns

In our study, we identified the challenges and concerns of participants in asking for help with technology use. Sometimes, the peers whom our participants ask for help do not have necessary technical skills although participants might expect them to fix the problems with their devices or accounts. Also, a help-giver may assume that the one asking for help already has a basic understanding of the technological issue, and thus, the solutions provided by them could be difficult for the help-seeker to implement; P1 said, *"I'll ask questions and they will assume that I half know the answer where I don't know anything..."*

Some of our participants reported being hesitant to ask for help because of their self-esteem, especially in cases, where they consider the problem with their device or account might appear very simple to the help-giver that the help-seeker do not want to appear inept to them in addressing such a problem. A few participants reported concern that asking for help from the same person multiple times might annoy them, and thus, they frequently change the source of availing intermediate help. P14 mentioned, *"...you don't like...going to the same person because you don't wanna be like...the one feeling unintelligent and so that's where big barrier comes in. Like I know there's some people who are really smart but I'm kind of hesitant to approach them because...I don't like to keep bugging them..."*

One of our participants (P9) suffering from Auditory Processing Disorder (APD) needs to ask for help to make a phone conversation on his behalf, which in some cases, leads him to share sensitive personal information with the persons he asks for help, like in a scenario where he needs to contact his physician over phone. He also reported his discomfort in asking for help, especially in cases where he is unsure of whether the help-giver would understand his circumstances caused by APD. He mentioned, *"I probably would be concerned asking someone who's not like a family member, just because it kind of, it comes off weird, if I'm just like, I can't make this call. 'Will you make this phone call?' - It makes it sound like I'm a wimp instead of like I actually can't do this...I don't think I'd ask just anyone for help."*

While asking for help over phone to fix issues with their devices or online accounts, a few participants faced challenges in following the instructions from a help-giver; P8 mentioned, *"...a lot of the times they [help-giver] are like, 'You need to click this.' And I'm like I don't even see that button."* In some cases, getting assistance over phone might not be possible due to the physical environment; a few participants mentioned that they needed to make a phone call for availing intermediate help, but could not do so because of being in a public library at that time.

Our participant, P2 reported challenges in availing help over chat messages as she suffers from dyslexia – a learning disorder that involves difficulty in reading [27]. Another participant (P13) mentioned difficulty in getting assistance over the medium that involves reading, where he reported suffering from Optic Nerve Hypoplasia – a condition that causes abnormal eye movement, and in turn, makes reading difficult for a user [19].

5 Discussion

In our study, we unpacked the contexts, challenges, and vulnerabilities of young adults as they avail intermediate help with technology use. In light of our findings, we believe that the service providers for digital devices and online accounts could play an important role in minimizing user needs of asking for help. In this regard, we present our recommendations below.

5.1 Multiple Modes of Communication

Our results show that users face challenges to communicate over telephone due to Auditory Processing Disorder, while users who experience difficulty in reading (e.g., due to dyslexia) find it hard to avail help over chat messages. Thus, the service providers should offer multiple modes of communication and let their customers choose the one they prefer when they need to avail help with technology use. We identified instances where participants faced difficulties in following the instructions from a remote help-giver whom they communicated over telephone. In such cases, allowing users to share their computer screen could let the service providers better help their customers.

5.2 Tutorials: Usability, Efficacy, and Inclusiveness

The usable, effective, and inclusive tutorials could help users to address the technical issues with their devices and accounts. In such cases, using graphical medium (e.g., video tutorial) instead of just plain text would contribute to user comprehension [4,18,22]. The tutorials should be well structured – accommodating different modules each focusing on a particular technical issue users might experience. The digital tutorials should aim to help users building an accurate mental model of the system (e.g., computer, mobile phone), and provide an interaction-based learning interface to let users reflect on their acquired knowledge before they implement that learning to fix the issues with their devices or accounts. In this way, end users could better help themselves in solving the issues with technology use, and in turn, avoid challenges and privacy risks associated with getting help from other entities.

The service providers should consider including subtitles with their video tutorials, so that their tutorials are comprehensible to the people with certain disabilities (e.g., Auditory Processing Disorder). Further, we emphasize on the dynamic and regular update of tutorials as the features and scopes of digital systems and online services continue to change, and accommodate solutions to the problems that were not covered before in the tutorials but reported by users in their communication with the service providers.

5.3 Ergonomic Design

The design of technology should be inclusive that addresses the needs of end users. The findings from our study show that users with the disability that causes difficulty in typing, find it hard to use the on-screen keyboard in their mobile phones due to the small key-size. We emphasize that the manufacturers of digital devices should include the users with special needs in their human-subject studies aimed to identify and fix the problems with user interaction, and leverage those insights in enhancing the inclusiveness of their technology design.

6 Limitations and Conclusion

We interviewed 40 participants in our study, where we followed the widely-used methods for qualitative research [8–10], focusing in depth on a small number of participants and continuing the interviews until no new themes emerged (saturation). We acknowledge the limitations of such study that a different set of samples might yield varying results. Thus, we do not draw any quantitative, generalizable conclusion from this study. In addition, self-reported data might have limitations, like recall and observer bias.

Despite these limitations, our study unpacks the contexts where young adults seek assistance with technology use; we identified their challenges, and concerns while availing intermediate help. Our findings also shed light on the security and privacy risks due to sharing authentication secrets in the process of getting help from others. In our future work, we would conduct a large-scale survey with the participants from diverse demographics and literacy levels to attain quantitative and more generalizable results.

References

1. Ahmed, T., Hoyle, R., Connelly, K., Crandall, D., Kapadia, A.: Privacy concerns and behaviors of people with visual impairments. In: Proceedings of the 33rd Annual ACM Conference on Human Factors in Computing Systems, pp. 3523–3532 (2015)
2. Akter, T., Dosono, B., Ahmed, T., Kapadia, A., Semaan, B.: I am uncomfortable sharing what i can't see: privacy concerns of the visually impaired with camera based assistive applications. In: 29th USENIX Security Symposium, pp. 1929–1948 (2020)
3. Al-Ameen, M.N., Chauhan, A., Ahsan, M.M., Kocabas, H.: A look into user's privacy perceptions and data practices of IoT devices. Inf. Comput. Secur. (2021)
4. Al-Ameen, M.N., Fatema, K., Wright, M., Scielzo, S.: Leveraging real-life facts to make random passwords more memorable. In: Pernul, G., Ryan, P.Y.A., Weippl, E. (eds.) ESORICS 2015. LNCS, vol. 9327, pp. 438–455. Springer, Cham (2015). https://doi.org/10.1007/978-3-319-24177-7_22
5. Al-Ameen, M.N., Kocabas, H., Nandy, S., Tamanna, T.: we, three brothers have always known everything of each other: a cross-cultural study of sharing digital devices and online accounts. Proc. Priv. Enhancing Technol. **2021**(4), 203–224 (2021)
6. Al-Ameen, M.N., Kocabas, H.M.: A first look into users' perceptions of digital medicine technology. In: Conference Companion Publication of the 2020 on Computer Supported Cooperative Work and Social Computing, pp. 203–207 (2020)

7. Al-Ameen, M.N., Tamanna, T., Nandy, S., Kocabas, H.: Understanding user behavior, information exposure, and privacy risks in managing old devices. In: Moallem, A. (ed.) HCII 2021. LNCS, vol. 12788, pp. 281–296. Springer, Cham (2021). https://doi.org/10.1007/978-3-030-77392-2_18

8. Baxter, K., Courage, C., Caine, K.: Understanding Your Users: A Practical Guide to User Research Methods, 2nd edn. Morgan Kaufmann Publishers Inc., San Francisco (2015)

9. Boyatzis, R.E.: Transforming Qualitative Information: Thematic Analysis and Code Development. sage, Thousand Oaks (1998)

10. Braun, V., Clarke, V.: Using thematic analysis in psychology. Qual. Res. Psychol. **3**(2), 77–101 (2006)

11. Dror, I.E., Mnookin, J.L.: The use of technology in human expert domains: challenges and risks arising from the use of automated fingerprint identification systems in forensic science. Law Probab. Risk **9**(1), 47–67 (2010)

12. Erikson, E.H.: Childhood and Society. WW Norton & Company (1993)

13. Hayes, J., Kaushik, S., Price, C.E., Wang, Y.: Cooperative privacy and security: Learning from people with visual impairments and their allies. In: Fifteenth Symposium on Usable Privacy and Security, pp. 1–20 (2019)

14. Johnson, S.U., Ulvenes, P.G., Øktedalen, T., Hoffart, A.: Psychometric properties of the general anxiety disorder 7-item (GAD-7) scale in a heterogeneous psychiatric sample. Front. Psychol. **10**, 1713 (2019)

15. Kiesler, S., Zdaniuk, B., Lundmark, V., Kraut, R.: Troubles with the internet: the dynamics of help at home. Hum.-Comput. Interact. **15**(4), 323–351 (2000)

16. Kocabas, H., Nandy, S., Tamanna, T., Al-Ameen, M.N.: Understanding User's behavior and protection strategy upon losing, or identifying unauthorized access to online account. In: Moallem, Abbas (ed.) HCII 2021. LNCS, vol. 12788, pp. 310–325. Springer, Cham (2021). https://doi.org/10.1007/978-3-030-77392-2_20

17. Kropczynski, J., Aljallad, Z., Elrod, N.J., Lipford, H., Wisniewski, P.J.: Towards building community collective efficacy for managing digital privacy and security within older adult communities. Proc. ACM Hum.-Comput. Inter. **4**(CSCW3), 1–27 (2021)

18. Kumaraguru, P., Sheng, S., Acquisti, A., Cranor, L.F., Hong, J.: Teaching Johnny not to fall for phish. ACM Trans. Internet Technol. (TOIT) **10**(2), 1–31 (2010)

19. Lambert, S.R., Hoyt, C.S., Narahara, M.H.: Optic nerve hypoplasia. Surv. Ophthalmol. **32**(1), 1–9 (1987)

20. Madden, C., Halsted, M., Benton, C., Greinwald, J., Choo, D.: Enlarged vestibular aqueduct syndrome in the pediatric population. Otol. Neurotology **24**(4), 625–632 (2003)

21. Marne, S.T., Al-Ameen, M.N., Wright, M.K.: Learning system-assigned passwords: a preliminary study on the people with learning disabilities. In: SOUPS (2017)

22. Mayer, R.E., Anderson, R.B.: The instructive animation: helping students build connections between words and pictures in multimedia learning. J. Educ. Psychol. **84**(4), 444 (1992)

23. Mentis, H.M., Madjaroff, G., Massey, A., Trendafilova, Z.: The illusion of choice in discussing cybersecurity safeguards between older adults with mild cognitive impairment and their caregivers. Proc. ACM Hum.-Comput. Inter. **4**(CSCW2), 1–19 (2020)

24. Moore, D.R., Ferguson, M.A., Edmondson-Jones, A.M., Ratib, S., Riley, A.: Nature of auditory processing disorder in children. Pediatrics **126**(2), e382–e390 (2010)

25. Poole, E.S., Chetty, M., Morgan, T., Grinter, R.E., Edwards, W.K.: Computer help at home: methods and motivations for informal technical support. In: Proceedings of the SIGCHI Conference on Human Factors in Computing Systems, pp. 739–748 (2009)
26. Seng, S., Al-Ameen, M.N., Wright, M.: A first look into users' perceptions of facial recognition in the physical world. Comput. Secur. **105**, 102227 (2021)
27. Shaywitz, S.E.: Dyslexia. N. Engl. J. Med. **338**(5), 307–312 (1998)
28. Singh, S., Cabraal, A., Demosthenous, C., Astbrink, G., Furlong, M.: Password sharing: implications for security design based on social practice. In: Proceedings of the SIGCHI Conference on Human Factors in Computing Systems, pp. 895–904 (2007)
29. Sjøberg, S.: Science and technology education: current challenges and possible solutions. Innovations Sci. Technol. Educ. **8**, 296–307 (2002)
30. Wahidin, H., Waycott, J., Baker, S.: The challenges in adopting assistive technologies in the workplace for people with visual impairments. In: Proceedings of the 30th Australian Conference on Computer-Human Interaction, pp. 432–442 (2018)

Improving Consumer Data Privacy Protection and Trust in the Context of the Digital Platform

Cong Cao$^{(\boxtimes)}$ ⓘD, Miaomiao Zheng, and Linyao Ni

Zhejiang University of Technology, Hangzhou, China
congcao@zjut.edu.cn

Abstract. In response to the full impact and the fair playing field of digital and cybersecurity, strong multilateral cooperation among politicians and businesses is needed in the global markets. Trust plays an important role in bridging the digital divide. Trust has long been key to social development and economic growth, and this is even more true in the digital economy of the Internet era. Most existing research on the relationship between consumers and trust has focused on specific scenarios. This paper explores the broad perspective of the digital economy and the development of digital society, taking the users of digital platforms as the research object. It then presents a model for a new trust system in the digital economic era that incorporates individual risk perception, enterprise reputation and structural guarantee mechanisms. This study uses partial least squares structural equation modelling (PLS-SEM) to evaluate the study model and hypotheses. The results, which use data from 146 samples, show that structural guarantee systems play an important role in effectively reducing personal risk perception and increasing trust intention. At the same time, the certifications and institutions of enterprises, along with third-party insurance plans, are important pieces of a structural security system. The results of this paper will further expand the application of consumer trust behaviour theory to the digital economy. These findings can also help companies build better relationships with consumers, promoting trust and increasing the options for potential business transactions.

Keywords: Online trust · Data privacy · Digital platform · Consumer behaviour · Protection framework

1 Introduction

With the acceleration of the digital process and of the integration of online and offline products, new forms of consumption are developing rapidly. As Internet platforms become more efficient at collecting personal data and people pay more attention to data security, there has also been increased attention on ways to build digital trust and strengthen the construction of credit systems in the digital environment [1, 2]. In a traditional industrial society, no business can succeed without trust. Similarly, in the Internet era, trust is the cornerstone of economic and social development [3, 4]. The digital economy driven by the information revolution has somewhat diluted the need for traditional everyday communication, transforming traditional trust relationships, which were based on interpersonal communication, into new digital trust relationships. Individual records on digital platforms constitute series of data which have shaped a new type of trust relationship in today's digital society [5, 6]. This change has also impacted traditional trust relationships.

Scholars have also examined ways to build trust in the digital economy. The current study focuses on two aspects of this topic. First, some scholars have explored ways to improve the mechanisms of existing digital platforms, such as reputation management and information display, to reduce consumers' perception of risk [7–11]. Second, others have explored methods for evaluating the security of digital enterprises, such as web page characteristics, individual consumer characteristics, and institutional characteristics [12–16]. However, most previous studies focus on the action mechanism and effect of individual governance strategies, but fail to conduct a comprehensive deconstruction of digital trust systems. It is difficult for such approaches to create a unified theoretical framework or to provide effective guidance to help enterprises build trust with potential consumers.

Therefore, using the digital economy and the development of digital society as a framework, this paper defines digital trust as an expansion of interpersonal trust and institutional trust. It is a new trust relationship based on two-way interactions that take place in digital space via digital technology.

In recent years, the rise of the digital economy has redefined the value of data. On the one hand, data has become a key factor in the creation and development of enterprises. On the other hand, the demand for fast, convenient, shared, intelligent modern services for using personal data is constantly increasing. The era of open, shared data has greatly enhanced the value of data. At the same time, attention to data security issues is increasing, and personal privacy faces unprecedented threats [17–19]. Balancing privacy protection with the need to share data has become an important issue in global governance. To this end, this paper examines the following research questions:

RQ1. What factors determine users' trust behaviour in the digital economy?
RQ2. How do these factors affect users' intention to trust?

To answer these questions, this study explores the formation and mechanisms of user trust in digital platforms using a combination of quantitative and qualitative analyses. This paper introduces a model for a new trust system for the digital economy that incorporates individual risk perception, enterprise reputation and structural guarantees. The PLS-SEM analysis of 146 samples shows that structural guarantees can reduce individual perception of risk and increase users' trust in enterprises and digital platforms. This paper also examines the main factors in the construction of structural security systems, namely certification, institution, and insurance. The results of this empirical study show that enterprises' reputations can significantly increase potential consumers' trust, but even a perfect structural guarantee cannot improve an enterprise's reputation. The results of this study enrich existing theoretical approaches to digital trust in the digital economy and can also help guide enterprises' future operations.

The article is organized as follows. First, the factors that impact trust behaviour are summarized; the research framework of the study is then described, and the corresponding research hypotheses are presented. Next, the quantitative PLS-SEM analysis of the questionnaire data is described, and the study model and hypotheses are evaluated and tested. The next section provides a qualitative analysis of respondents' comments, which were collected during in-depth interviews. This qualitative analysis was conducted to explore the mechanisms by which different factors impact trust behaviour. Finally, this paper presents the conclusions, theoretical and practical significance, and limitations of the study and outlines possible directions for future research.

2 Research Background and Hypotheses Development

In online business, trust is a key element of trade and exchange relationships [16]. Many consumers distrust unfamiliar digital platforms [20], and platform structural guarantee mechanisms, such as laws, governments, and contract effectiveness, can play a role as guarantees, easing the relationship between a platform and its users. Higher trust in these structural guarantees leads to greater consumer trust in online enterprises [21]. Therefore, we propose the following hypothesis:

H1. The stronger the structural guarantees of a digital platform, the more consumers trust that platform.

Risk perception refers to a user's subjective judgment of the characteristics and severity of the possible risks of using a digital platform. Consumers who are highly sensitive to risk inevitably resist disclosing personal information and engaging in online trading; they may even take evasive action [22]. Hanif and Lallie [23] examined the engagement of UK users over age 55 with an online banking application (app). Users' engagement with the app showed that their perception of the risks related to data storage, authentication and other issues impacted their sense of security, thereby impacting the likelihood that they would use the app. Therefore, we propose the following hypothesis:

H2. The higher the consumers' perception of risk, the weaker their intention to trust digital platforms.

Reputation is the assessment of a business's social attractiveness [24]. In addition to a company's products and services, factors such as its protection of consumer rights and interests, attention to employees' rights and interests, investment in environmental protection and support for public welfare impact its reputation. It is widely accepted that companies with good reputations will not risk damaging their reputation to pursue short-term gains at their customers' expense [25]. McKnight, et al. [26] further find that reputation positively impacts consumer preferences and choices. Consumers usually view reputation as an important reference factor for judging whether a business is trustworthy. Therefore, we propose the following hypothesis:

H3. The better the reputation of the digital platform, the more consumers will trust that platform.

To encourage trust in an asymmetric information environment, digital platforms inform consumers about relevant contracts, agreements, rules, third-party endorsements and other security guarantees; these elements comprise the structural guarantee mechanisms of the digital platform [26]. A perfect structural guarantee mechanism means that users' privacy and funds are fully protected and that reasonable network transactions are fully supported by relevant contracts and laws. When choosing among digital platforms with the same amount of information disclosure, users prefer platforms with high structural supports, as these ease concerns about information asymmetry [27]. Therefore, we propose the following hypothesis:

H4. The stronger the structural guarantee capabilities of a digital platform, the lower the consumers' perception of risk.

Structural guarantees can restrain enterprises' behaviour through mandatory terms and institutions, and they can reduce risk and increase user confidence. Enterprises can also use strong structural guarantee systems to strengthen their reputations. Such systems can promote consumer recognition of a company's business capabilities and reputation, thereby improving the company's reputation among larger groups of consumers [28]. Shao, et al. [29] further find that the construction of a structural guarantee is a crucial link in establishing the reputation of a digital platform. Therefore, we propose the following hypothesis:

H5. The stronger the structural guarantee capabilities of a digital platform, the better its reputation.

The institution of a digital platform refers to the provisions formulated by that platform to protect the rights and interests of both the platform and its users during transactions. In other words, the system is the code of conduct followed by both the platform and its users [30]. A perfect digital platform should include at least four institutions [31]. First, it must include a feedback mechanism, which is used to collect user perceptions of and suggestions for the platform. Second, it should include a security hosting service. Third, the platform should entrust some of the technical work of security to trusted third parties, such as the third-party payment services provided by Alipay and WeChat. Fourth, additional assistance services are typically used to reduce the risks to a user's person and property in case of an emergency; an example is the emergency contact settings provided by the Didi Chuxing platform. In digital economic activities, institution norms are an important part of an enterprise's structural guarantees, which can effectively regulate the enterprise's behaviour. Therefore, we propose the following hypothesis:

H6. The more perfect a digital platform's institution is, the greater its ability to provide structural guarantees.

Digital platforms often use additional insurance to reduce consumer risk. If a user suffers losses due to using the platform's products or services, this insurance enables the platform to compensate the user for these losses [31]. In business activities in the digital economy, insurance helps enterprises reduce their risks and protects the rights and interests of consumers by enhancing a platform's structural ability to protect consumers.

For example, the return insurance provided by the B2C e-commerce platform enriches the company's structural guarantee capabilities, optimizes the user experience during returns and exchanges, and reduces the company's operating expenses [32]. Therefore, we propose the following hypothesis:

H7. The more comprehensive a digital platform's insurance is, the greater its ability to provide structural guarantees.

Certification of a digital platform is an additional measure for guaranteeing that its products, services and management systems comply with local regulations [33]. From the first computers, which were only used for basic operations, to today's system of online communication, online payment and online entertainment, the Internet has become an indispensable part of our lives. However, this increasing dependence on the Internet has also led to correspondingly increasing network security risks [34]. Authentication services on digital platforms can help protect users from these risks. Incorporating services and technologies that are certified by third-party institutions can improve an enterprise's structural guarantees [35]. Therefore, we propose the following hypothesis (Fig. 1):

H8. The more perfect the certification of a digital platform, the greater its ability to provide structural guarantees.

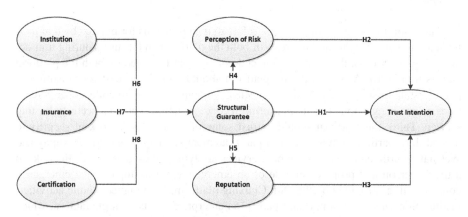

Fig. 1. Proposed research model and hypotheses

3   Research Design and Methodology

This study uses a combination of quantitative and qualitative analyses to answer the two research questions. First, a new trust system model for the digital era was established through a literature review and an analysis of second-hand data. Secondly, data were collected through a questionnaire survey. These data were then analysed using PLS-SEM to explore the influence of different factors on user trust intention. Finally, in-depth interviews were conducted to explore users' perceptions of risk and trust in digital platforms and the mechanisms of factors that impact user trust in online platforms.

The questionnaire used in this study was created based on previously published tools; appropriate adjustments were made to address the characteristics of current digital platforms. In the initial scale, all items except demographic about respondents used a seven-point Likert scale; with 1 for 'strongly disagree' and 7 for 'strongly agree.' Before the formal survey was conducted, we invited 20 college students to participate in a pilot study on a voluntary basis to test and improve the items of the questionnaire.

Most survey participants were college students; they all participated on a voluntary basis, and they received no compensation for participation. A total of 191 completed questionnaires were collected. After some questionnaires were eliminated due to too short answering time or too concentrated options, 146 valid questionnaires were included in the analysis. The participants' demographic characteristics are shown in Table 1: 55.5% are males; most (72.5%) are aged 18 to 34 years; 76.7% have at least a bachelor's degree; and 47.3% shop more than ten times a month.

Table 1. Demographic profile of respondents, N = 146.

Measure	Category	N	Percent
Gender	Male	81	55.5%
	Female	65	44.5%
Age	18–24	23	15.7%
	25–29	56	38.4%
	30–34	27	18.5%
	35–39	22	15.1%
	40–44	13	8.9%
	Over 45	5	3.4%
Education	College	34	23.3%
	Undergraduate	73	50.0%
	Postgraduate	39	26.7%
Online shopping frequency	At least once a month	0	0.0%
	2–5 times a month	34	23.2%
	6–10 times a month	43	29.5%
	More than 10 times a month	69	47.3%

PLS has strong explanatory power for small sample sizes, and the data need not be normally distributed for this kind of analysis [36, 37]. Furthermore, this approach can easily cope with reflective and formative measurement models without identification [38]. Therefore, in the present study, PLS was used to analyse the data and test the hypotheses. Although PLS has good explanatory power when the sample size is small, a large sample size increases the validity of the model. In general, the minimum sample size for a PLS analysis is at least ten times the largest number of predictors for any dependent variable in the model [36]. Since the largest number of indicators for a single variable in our model is seven, the minimum sample size is 70. Therefore, 146 valid samples met the minimum sample size for a PLS analysis.

4 Results

First, the reliability and validity of different constructs in the model were tested by evaluating the measurement model. Second, the relationships of different constructs with the predictive power of the model were examined by evaluating the structural model.

4.1 Measurement Model

In this study, composite reliability (CR) and Cronbach's α (CA) were used to test internal consistency and reliability. Outer loadings were used to test indicator reliability. As can be seen from Table 2, the CR and CA of all latent variables are greater than 0.8, and the outer loadings of all measurement indicators on their belonging constructs are greater than 0.850, indicating that the measurement model used in this study has good reliability [39].

Table 2. Descriptive statistics for the constructs.

	CA	CR	AVE
Trust Intention (Trust)	0.946	0.965	0.902
Structural Guarantee (Struc)	0.927	0.948	0.820
Perception of Risk (Risk)	0.860	0.915	0.781
Reputation (Reput)	0.972	0.982	0.947
Institution (Insti)	0.914	0.946	0.853
Insurance (Insur)	0.905	0.940	0.840
Certification (Certi)	0.847	0.907	0.765

In this study, the convergence validity of the measurement model was assessed by Average Variance Extracted (AVE), and the discriminant validity of the model was assessed by Fornell-Larcker indexes and cross loadings. As shown in Table 2, the AVEs of all the constructs in the measurement model were greater than 0.5, indicating good convergence validity [39]. In addition, the outer loading of each indicator on its belonging construct is greater than the cross loading of that indicator on the other constructs (Table 3). Meanwhile, as shown in Table 4, the AVE square root of each construct in the model is greater than the corresponding correlation values with other constructs. These results indicate that the measurement model used in this study has sufficient discriminant validity [40].

Table 3. Factor loadings and cross loadings.

	Trust	Struc	Risk	Reput	Insti	Insur	Certi
Trust.1	**0.954**	0.648	−0.709	0.273	0.481	0.089	0.778
Trust.2	**0.943**	0.624	−0.685	0.348	0.439	0.055	0.797
Trust.3	**0.953**	0.657	−0.702	0.309	0.525	0.121	0.795
Struc.1	0.668	**0.907**	−0.667	0.080	0.619	0.307	0.677
Struc.2	0.610	**0.908**	−0.576	0.059	0.676	0.346	0.691
Struc.3	0.587	**0.902**	−0.576	0.041	0.660	0.422	0.668
Struc.4	0.584	**0.906**	−0.584	0.049	0.601	0.378	0.650
Risk.1	−0.688	−0.600	**0.894**	−0.087	−0.296	−0.177	−0.608
Risk.2	−0.649	−0.585	**0.880**	−0.008	−0.365	−0.194	−0.555
Risk.3	−0.611	−0.577	**0.878**	0.020	−0.290	−0.169	−0.522
Reput.1	0.295	0.055	0.006	**0.974**	0.186	−0.263	0.353
Reput.2	0.338	0.094	−0.059	**0.977**	0.207	−0.264	0.370
Reput.3	0.317	0.033	−0.030	**0.968**	0.173	−0.278	0.347
Insti.1	0.458	0.656	−0.337	0.159	**0.923**	0.286	0.513
Insti.2	0.521	0.661	−0.331	0.238	**0.938**	0.324	0.565
Insti.3	0.425	0.638	−0.326	0.140	**0.910**	0.274	0.501
Insur.1	0.107	0.367	−0.161	−0.238	0.290	**0.927**	0.240
Insur.2	0.096	0.383	−0.222	−0.243	0.288	**0.913**	0.204
Insur.3	0.051	0.349	−0.176	−0.278	0.302	**0.910**	0.149
Certi.1	0.731	0.634	−0.505	0.357	0.458	0.109	**0.866**
Certi.2	0.752	0.661	−0.595	0.331	0.491	0.183	**0.891**
Certi.3	0.699	0.651	−0.569	0.274	0.546	0.275	**0.867**

Note: Bold number indicate outer loading on the assigned constructs

Table 4. Correlations among constructs and the square root of the AVE.

	Trust	Struc	Risk	Reput	Insti	Insur	Certi
Trust	**0.950**						
Struc	0.677	**0.906**					
Risk	−0.735	−0.664	**0.884**				
Reput	0.327	0.064	−0.030	**0.973**			
Insti	0.507	0.706	−0.359	0.194	**0.924**		
Insur	0.093	0.400	−0.204	−0.275	0.319	**0.917**	
Certi	0.831	0.742	−0.637	0.367	0.570	0.217	**0.875**

Note: Bold number represent the square roots of the AVEs

4.2 Structural Model

This study used bootstrapping in SmartPLS 3.3.7 to conduct a t-value significance test of the path coefficient. The original sample size is 146, and the maximum number of iterations (bootstrap subsamples) is 5,000 [41]. The path coefficient and the results of the significance test are shown in Fig. 2. These results show that system, certification, insurance, risk perception, structural protections and word of mouth significantly affect users' trust in digital platforms.

R^2 reflects the degree to which an exogenous latent variable explains an endogenous latent variable; an R^2 over 0.67 indicates strong explanatory power [42]. In this model, the R^2 of 'consumer trust intention' is 0.689, indicating that the proposed model has good explanatory power.

5 Discussion

In the present study, second-hand data and the results of previous studies were used to develop a new model for trust systems in the digital economy based on the user perspective. This model incorporates the factors of reputation, risk perception and structural guarantees. Next, 146 valid samples were collected, and these data were used to evaluate the research model and hypotheses via PLS-SEM. The results suggest that the trust intentions of digital platform users are mainly co-affected by individual risk perception, the reputation of the platform and the structural guarantees of the external environment. Institution, certifications and insurance also significantly improve consumers' trust in structural guarantees. High-quality structural protection reduces consumers' perception of risk. However, users' comments for digital platforms are not significantly impacted by structural guarantee factors.

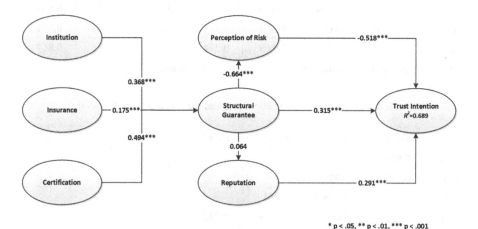

Fig. 2. Path coefficients and significance test results.

After we completed the quantitative data analysis, we randomly selected ten participants to take part in in-depth interviews; these interviews were used to explore the mechanisms that impact the formation of trust and risk behaviour. All interviewees stated that a sound structural security system can significantly reduce their risk perception and strengthen their trust. For example, interviewee 3 described the interaction between risk perception and structural security as follows: '*For me, the stronger the digital security system, especially on digital platforms, the safer I assume my digital information and personal privacy will be. These external supports reduce my expectation of data leakage and alleviate my perception of the risks, thus enhancing my trust in the platform.*'

Respondents believe that certification is an important factor in structural guarantee systems. Certification is an important tool to help consumers to identify trustworthy enterprises; it can help consumers avoid being deceived by illegal enterprises in unfamiliar environments. Interviewee 6 explained, '*On unfamiliar digital platforms, if enterprises display authentication logos for security or privacy, I feel much more confident about using them. I think that for enterprises, reliable certification institutions can reduce their business risks and prevent illegal behaviours. Viewing the information in this kind of authentication helps me understand the company's digital structural security and enhances my trust in them.*'

In addition, a company's institution is another important structural guarantee mechanism for protecting consumers from data losses and privacy breaches. For example, interviewee 1 said. '*The platform's rules and regulations reflect the importance they attach to personal data and privacy and also explain how they handle relevant information. Disclosing this makes it easier for me to understand how they will treat my personal information.*' Interviewee 7 added, '*I think the government should provide more standardized texts in the laws and strengthen publicity so that ordinary consumers can more easily understand their rights and the obligations and responsibilities of enterprises.*' Based on respondents' feedback and explanations, we find that, on the one hand, users think that institutional disclosure can effectively restrain enterprises' behaviour. On the other hand, consumers also expect the description of terms in the institution to be concise and to clearly explain how the platform obtains and uses data.

According to the research model developed in the present study, although insurance can improve a company's structural guarantees, it has less impact than certification and institutional factors. Interviewee 5 explained, '*Today, many platforms provide extra guarantees or insurance services. When something goes wrong, these third-party institutions can help deal with it and reduce my losses to a certain extent.*' Interviewee 2 further pointed out that '*such insurance services often charge extra fees, and communication and handling problems may be complicated. For example, I may buy additional insurance when I post a package. If there is a problem, the platform will have me contact the third-party insurance agency myself, which often increases the cost of communication.*' Interviewee feedback indicated that, although additional insurance mechanisms can transfer risks away from consumers, the current service experience and quality of these services do not fully meet consumer expectations. This may be an aspect that enterprises need to address in the future.

Although structural security can reduce consumers' risk perception, we found that has no significant impact on reputation. According to interviewee 4, '*The reputation of the platform mainly reflects the accumulation of its previous business transactions; it is not affected by structural guarantees. Improving a company's reputation is a gradual process; it changes slowly due to consumers' perceptions of service quality and satisfaction.'* Interviewee 9 added, *'I think a good reputation increases my trust in the enterprise, but better structural guarantees do not significantly improve its reputation. Because I think a company's reputation is based on consumers' comprehensive evaluation of its current status.'* This finding suggests that enterprises need to actively maintain their reputations. Once consumers form their perceptions of an enterprise, it is not easy to change these perceptions, at least not quickly.

6 Conclusion

In today's digital economy, trust is more important than ever. Building a new digital trust system requires positive interactions among enterprises, platforms, governments and users. An exclusive focus on business ethics cannot completely prevent crises of credibility. Furthermore, exclusive reliance on strict regulatory structures may inhibit business innovation. Relying solely on the application of emerging technologies will lead to new ethical problems. Therefore, the construction of trust in the digital economy requires cooperation and co-construction by academics and industrial leaders.

Digital trust is the foundation of development and innovation in the digital economy. Digital trust is the basic prerequisite for individuals and organizations to participate in digital economic transactions. This paper has analysed 146 empirical data samples using PLS-SEM and finds that, in the development of digital platforms, institution, certification and insurance are important factors in the establishment of structural security. Reputation and structural guarantees are the core elements of trust in the digital economy. Digital trust helps reduce user perception of risks, promote the formation of data factor markets, and promote the development of the digital economy. This study identifies strong structural guarantees to be those based on institution, certification and insurance. This approach enhances the establishment of digital trust relationships, effectively manages user risks, and can be used to establish a new model for trust systems in the digital economy.

This study contributes to existing theories on online trust and addresses a gap in the study of the relationships of trust and support systems with the digital economy. The quantitative analysis conducted here reveals the influence of several factors on user trust in digital platforms. The present study uses in-depth interviews and qualitative analyses to explain users' decisions related to trust and risk in the digital economy. This study is also useful for practitioners, as it provides a solid theoretical foundation that companies can use to develop effective structural guarantees for online platforms. This can effectively promote consumer trust in enterprises, thus increasing potential transaction volume.

Although this study's exploration of the factors that influence user trust in the digital economic environment is useful, the study is inevitably limited by its design and methods. First, although the study met the minimum sample size for a PLS-SEM analysis, further research with a larger sample would improve the model's measurement accuracy [36]. Moreover, since most participants in this study were undergraduate students, these findings cannot be generalized to other consumer groups. Future studies should collect similar data from different consumer groups to further test the model presented here.

In addition, the current study does explore differences in user behaviour in different national and cultural contexts. Therefore, future studies should collect data from users in different countries and regions to explore whether culture and customs impact users' risk perception and trust intention. Finally, this study does not examine the possible modifying effect of product type (including whether products are virtual or physical) on user behaviour in the digital economy. Future studies can explore whether user perceptions and behaviour are impacted by product type.

Acknowledgments. The work described in this paper was supported by grants from the Zhejiang University of Technology Humanities and Social Sciences Pre-Research Fund Project (GZ21731320013), and the Zhejiang University of Technology Subject Reform Project (GZ21511320030).

References

1. Salam, A.F., Lyer, L., Palvia, P., Singh, R.: Trust in e-commerce. Commun. ACM **48**(2), 72–77 (2005)
2. Kim, D.J., Ferrin, D.L., Rao, H.R.: A trust-based consumer decision-making model in electronic commerce: the role of trust, perceived risk, and their antecedents. Decis. Support Syst. **44**(2), 544–564 (2008)
3. Mou, J., Shin, D.-H., Cohen, J.F.: Trust and risk in consumer acceptance of e-services. Electron. Commer. Res. **17**(2), 255–288 (2017). https://doi.org/10.1007/s10660-015-9205-4
4. Monsuwé, T.P.Y., Dellaert, B.G.C., de Ruyter, K.: What drives consumers to shop online? A Literature review. Int. J. Serv. Ind. Manage. **15**(1), 102–121 (2004)
5. Lee, M.K., Turban, E.: A trust model for consumer internet shopping. Int. J. Electron. Commer. **6**(1), 75–91 (2001)
6. Cen, Y., et al.: Trust relationship prediction in Alibaba E-commerce platform. IEEE Trans. Knowl. Data Eng. **32**(5), 1024–1035 (2020)
7. Kim, Y., Peterson, R.A.: A meta-analysis of online trust relationships in E-commerce. J. Interact. Mark. **38**, 44–54 (2017)
8. Urban, G.L., Amyx, C., Lorenzon, A.: Online trust: state of the art, new frontiers, and research potential. J. Interact. Mark. **23**(2), 179–190 (2009)
9. Wang, Y.D., Emurian, H.H.: An overview of online trust: Concepts, elements, and implications. Comput. Hum. Behav. **21**(1), 105–125 (2005)
10. Zhao, S., Fang, Y., Zhang, W., Jiang, H.: Trust, perceived benefit, and purchase intention in C2C E-commerce: an empirical examination in China. J. Glob. Inf. Manage. **28**(1), 121–141 (2020)
11. Fang, Y., Qureshi, I., Sun, H., McCole, P., Ramsey, E., Lim, K.H.: Trust, satisfaction, and online repurchase intention: the moderating role of perceived effectiveness of E-Commerce institutional mechanisms. MIS Q. **38**(2), 407–427 (2014)
12. Patton, M.A., Josang, A.: Technologies for trust in electronic commerce. Electron. Commer. Res. **4**(1–2), 9–21 (2004). https://doi.org/10.1023/B:ELEC.0000009279.89570.27
13. Kimery, K.M., McCord, M.: Third-Party Assurances: The Road to Trust in Online Retailing, p. 10 (2002)
14. Belanger, F., Hiller, J.S., Smith, W.J.: Trustworthiness in electronic commerce: the role of privacy, security, and site attributes. J. Strateg. Inf. Syst. **11**(3), 245–270 (2002)
15. Kaplan, S.E., Nieschwietz, R.J.: A Web assurance services model of trust for B2C e-commerce. Int. J. Account. Inf. Syst. **4**(2), 95–114 (2003)

16. McKnight, D.H., Chervany, N.L.: What trust means in E-Commerce customer relationships: an interdisciplinary conceptual typology. Int. J. Electron. Commer. **6**(2), 35 (2001)

17. Martin, K.D., Borah, A., Palmatier, R.W.: Data privacy: effects on customer and firm performance. J. Mark. **81**(1), 36–58 (2017)

18. Bansal, G., Zahedi, F.M., Gefen, D.: Do context and personality matter? trust and privacy concerns in disclosing private information online. Inf. Manage. **53**(1), 1–21 (2016)

19. Antoniou, G., Batten, L.: E-commerce: protecting purchaser privacy to enforce trust. Electron. Commer. Res. **11**(4), 421–456 (2011). https://doi.org/10.1007/s10660-011-9083-3

20. Shao, Z., Yin, H.: Building customers' trust in the ridesharing platform with institutional mechanisms. Internet Res. **29**(5), 1040–1063 (2019)

21. Minton, E.A.: Believing is buying: religiosity, advertising skepticism, and corporate trust. J. Manage. Spirituality Relig. **16**(1), 54–75 (2019)

22. Liu, M., Bi, J., Yang, J., Qu, S., Wang, J.: Social media never shake the role of trust building in relieving public risk perception. J. Clean. Prod. **282**, 124442 (2021)

23. Hanif, Y., Lallie, H.S.: Security factors on the intention to use mobile banking applications in the UK older generation (55+). A mixed-method study using modified UTAUT and MTAM - with perceived cyber security, risk, and trust. Technol. Soc. **67**, 101693 (2021)

24. Doney, P.M., Cannon, J.P.: An examination of the nature of trust in buyer-seller relationships. J. Mark. **61**(2), 35 (1997)

25. Bögel, P.M.: Company reputation and its influence on consumer trust in response to ongoing CSR communication. J. Mark. Commun. **25**(2), 115–136 (2019)

26. McKnight, D.H., Choudhury, V., Kacmar, C.: The impact of initial consumer trust on intentions to transact with a web site: a trust building model. J. Strateg. Inf. Syst. **11**(3–4), 297–323 (2002)

27. Hasan, R., Shams, R., Rahman, M.: Consumer trust and perceived risk for voice-controlled artificial intelligence: the case of Siri. J. Bus. Res. **131**, 591–597 (2021)

28. Koufaris, M., Hampton-Sosa, W.: The development of initial trust in an online company by new customers. Inf. Manage. **41**(3), 377–397 (2004)

29. Shao, Z., Zhang, L., Brown, S.A., Zhao, T.: Understanding users' trust transfer mechanism in a blockchain-enabled platform: a mixed methods study. Decis. Support Syst. 113716 (2022)

30. Lu, B., Wang, Z., Zhang, S.: Platform-based mechanisms, institutional trust, and continuous use intention: The moderating role of perceived effectiveness of sharing economy institutional mechanisms. Inf. Manage. **58**(7), 103504 (2021)

31. Levantesi, S., Piscopo, G.: Mutual peer-to-peer insurance: the allocation of risk. J. Cooperative Organ. Manage. **10**(1), 100154 (2022)

32. Ren, M., Liu, J., Feng, S., Yang, A.: Pricing and return strategy of online retailers based on return insurance. J. Retail. Consum. Serv. **59**, 102350 (2021)

33. Furnell, S., Helkala, K., Woods, N.: Accessible authentication: Assessing the applicability for users with disabilities. Comput. Secur. **113**, 102561 (2022)

34. Sule, M.-J., Zennaro, M., Thomas, G.: Cybersecurity through the lens of digital identity and data protection: issues and trends. Technol. Soc. **67**, 101734 (2021)

35. Chang, Y., Wong, S.F., Libaque-Saenz, C.F., Lee, H.: The role of privacy policy on consumers' perceived privacy. Gov. Inf. Q. **35**(3), 445–459 (2018)

36. Chin, W.W., Newsted, P.R.: Structural equation modeling analysis with small samples using partial least squares. In: Hoyle, R. (ed.) Statistical strategies for small sample research, pp. 307–341. Sage Publication, Beverly Hills, CA (1999)

37. Chin, W.W.: The partial least squares approach for structural equation modeling. In: Modern Methods for Business Research. (Methodology for Business and Management), pp. 295–336. Lawrence Erlbaum Associates Publishers, Mahwah (1998)

38. Chin, W.W., Marcolin, B.L., Newsted, P.R.: A partial least squares latent variable modeling approach for measuring interaction effects: results from a Monte Carlo simulation study and an electronic-mail emotion/adoption study. Inf. Syst. Res. **14**(2), 189–217 (2003)

39. Bagozzi, R.P., Yi, Y.: On the evaluation of structural equation models. J. Acad. Mark. Sci. **16**(1), 74–94 (1988). https://doi.org/10.1007/BF02723327

40. Fornell, C., Larcker, D.F.: Evaluating structural equation models with unobservable variables and measurement error. J. Mark. Res. **18**(1), 39–50 (1981)

41. Hair, J.F., Ringle, C.M., Sarstedt, M.: PLS-SEM: indeed a silver bullet. J. Market. Theor. Pract. **19**(2), 139–152 (2011)

42. Hair, J.F., Black, W.C., Babin, B.J., Anderson, R.E.: Multivariate Data Analysis: a Global Perspective, 7th (edn.). Upper Saddle River, N.J.: Pearson Education (2010)

Secure Interoperation of Blockchain and IPFS Through Client Application Enabled by CP-ABE

Ruichen Cong[1], Yixiao Liu[1], Yenjou Wang[1], Kiichi Tago[2],
Ruidong Li[3], Hitoshi Asaeda[4], and Qun Jin[5]([⊠])

[1] Graduate School of Human Sciences, Waseda University, Tokorozawa, Japan
`carriecong@moegi.waseda.jp`
[2] Department of Information and Network Science, Chiba Institute of Technology,
Narashino, Japan
[3] Faculty of Electrical, Information and Communication Engineering,
Institute of Science and Engineering, Kanazawa University, Kanazawa, Japan
[4] National Institute of Information and Communications Technology (NICT),
Tokyo, Japan
[5] Faculty of Human Sciences, Waseda University, Tokorozawa, Japan
`jin@waseda.jp`

Abstract. In recent years, personal health data can be collected via
wearable devices and sensors and used for healthcare services improvement through data sharing. To share sensitive personal health data
securely, many frameworks and approaches using blockchain-based systems have been proposed. However, the issue of letting individuals control
and manage their data with privacy-preserving is still to be solved. In this
paper, we propose a new model of Individual-Initiated Auditable Access
Control (IIAAC) enabled with blockchain, CP-ABE (Ciphertext-Policy
Attribute-Based Encryption) and IPFS (Inter-Planetary File System) for
privacy-preserved data sharing. We describe the system architecture, its
main components for our proposed model, and the protocols to make
blockchain and IPFS interoperate with each other via a client application, including key generation, data publication, and data retrieval. We
further build an experiment environment to evaluate the performance of
our proposed model and architecture. Experiment results demonstrate
the feasibility of our proposed model and system architecture for privacy-
preserved data sharing.

Keywords: Blockchain · CP-ABE · IPFS · Fine-grained access
control · Privacy protection · Data sharing

1 Introduction

Wearable devices and sensors may collect different types of data for various
purposes with the rapid development of Internet of Things (IoT) technology.
A large amount of collected data can be used for service improvement in many

© The Author(s), under exclusive license to Springer Nature Switzerland AG 2022
A. Moallem (Ed.): HCII 2022, LNCS 13333, pp. 30–41, 2022.
https://doi.org/10.1007/978-3-031-05563-8_3

situations through data sharing. In particular, the Multi-Access Edge Computing (MEC) driven by 5G has made it possible to serve people for higher levels services in the healthcare area [1,2]. It can quickly and accurately monitor the state of personal health, such as heart rate, blood pressure, and sleep quality. In recent years, various types of data have been utilized to take proactive approaches to healthcare services [3]. These data related to a person's health and daily behavior are called Personal Health Data (PHD) [4]. The key features of blockchain [5], such as decentralization and immutability, have made it so popular for sharing and using PHD securely and efficiently. However, storing a large amount of data in the blockchain is inefficient.

To solve this problem, in our previous study [6], a new model of Individual-Initiated Auditable Access Control (IIAAC) for privacy-preserved IoT data sharing and utilizing is proposed, which is enabled by blockchain, Inter-Planetary File System (IPFS) and Ciphertext-Policy Attribute-Based Encryption (CP-ABE). We defined the system requirements to share sensitive data and designed the system architecture and the detailed procedures as well. We further compared our proposed model with related work in terms of functions and features. It showed that individual-initiated features and enhanced privacy protection with strict audits are two major advantages in our proposed IIAAC.

In this paper, we focus on secure interoperation of blockchain and IPFS through client application enabled by the CP-ABE encryption mechanism. We use Hyperledger Fabric, which is a consortium blockchain-based framework, and incorporate CP-ABE, which works as a key server to enable fine-grained access control according to the access policy and attribute level. We further propose a new model to use a client application to make Hyperledger Fabric and IPFS to interoperate each other. In such a way, it is easy for users to execute and manage user authentication, access policy setting, data publication and retrieval. It can be expected to provide an alternative approach to secure interoperation of blockchain and IPFS through client application enabled by CP-ABE for trusted data sharing. Furthermore, we build an experiment environment to evaluate the performance and verify the feasibility of IIAAC in the proposed architecture.

The remainder of this paper is organized as follows. In Sect. 2, related work on blockchain, IPFS and CP-ABE are overviewed, and privacy protection issues on data sharing are identified. In Sect. 3, we present the system architecture through client application and the detailed procedures. In Sect. 4, we describe the experiment environment for performance evaluation, and discuss the results. Finally, this paper is summarized, and future directions are highlighted in Sect. 5.

2   Related Work

In this section, we briefly introduce blockchain, IPFS, CP-ABE, and previous related research works conducted in the area of privacy-preserved data sharing based on blockchain platforms.

In 2008, Satoshi Nakamoto proposed Bitcoin, a virtual currency network that uses blockchain as the core technology [7]. Blockchain is a peer-to-peer distributed ledger and decentralization is one of the main features. Each node in the system has the same position; there is no supernode; and each node supervises and maintains the distributed ledger cooperatively. The blockchain incorporates numerous mature technologies such as consensus algorithms, cryptographic principles, and distributed storage to maintain the security and integrity of data recorded on the blockchain. On the other hand, there is a limitation on-chain storage. As blockchain grows, the amount of communication on the network and data stored as transaction history will increase. Therefore, blockchain is inefficient for storing a large amount of data.

To solve this problem, many frameworks and approaches using IPFS as off-chain storage in blockchain-based application systems have been proposed [8–10]. IPFS[1] is a peer-to-peer distributed file system, created by Juan Bennet at Protocol Labs in 2015. In IPFS, the corresponding hash value of data will be the same if the data is the same. Therefore, the problem of data redundancy in the network caused by repeated data storage can be solved. In this sense, IPFS is an appropriate storage platform for storing large amounts of data.

Since each node on the blockchain holds the same ledger and stores the same data, the data on the blockchain is transparent and cannot be tampered with. However, with the development of blockchain applications, various types of data are stored on the blockchain, such as personal health data. Personal health data is sensitive since it involves individual privacy, so it is not suitable for storing on the blockchain in plaintext.

To share sensitive data securely, Kumar and Dakshayini [11] proposed secure sharing of health data using Hyperledger Fabric, a consortium blockchain-based framework, among medical organizations. In this framework, to share the encrypted medical data among two medical organizations, one organization must send the access request for viewing the patient's medical data to the other organization. If the access request is approved, the patient's medical data can be obtained and decrypted by the organization. However, it is not flexible and efficient that the access requests must be approved case by case. Furthermore, the limitation of on-chain storage shows that it is inefficient to store large amounts of data on the blockchain. On the other hand, the scenario is described only for sharing data among different hospitals and does not consider sharing data initiated by individuals.

To let individuals manage their data initiatively, Saini et al. [12] developed an access control model for the medical system to secure the sharing of electronic medical records (EMRs) using smart contracts. In our previous study [4,6], we proposed an individual-centric architecture for privacy-preserved sharing and use of personal health data, which included a combination of off-chain cold storage and hot storage to let individuals own and manage their data. We further proposed Individual-Initiated Auditable Access Control (IIAAC) in a consortium blockchain-based system incorporating CP-ABE [13] and IPFS. Based on previous work, this study focuses on secure interoperation of blockchain and IPFS through client application enabled by the CP-ABE encryption mechanism.

---

[1] https://ipfs.io/.

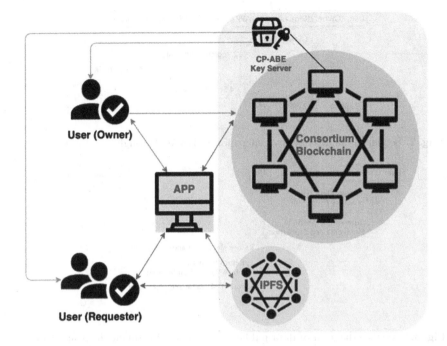

Fig. 1. System architecture through client application

3   Interoperation of Blockchain and IPFS Through Client Application

3.1   System Architecture

In this section, we describe the system architecture through a client application and discuss the detailed procedure in our proposed model. The system architecture considered in our proposed model mainly consists of components, such as consortium blockchain, IPFS distributed file system, CP-ABE encryption mechanism, client application, and two categories of users as shown in Fig. 1.

3.2   Protocols for IIAAC

In this section, we introduce the protocols including key generation, data publication and data retrieval of our system. The detailed procedures are shown in Figs. 2, 3 and 4. It shows the interoperation between blockchain and IPFS through a client application. In Fig. 2, the protocol is initiated by the user, which sends an attribute to CP-ABE server through the client application for authentication. After receiving the attribute, the CP-ABE key server generates the secret key (SK) for the user and sends it back to the user. In Fig. 3, the owner user sets the access policy and encrypts the data, and then the ciphertext is generated. Thereafter, the keywords for the data are specified as meta-data

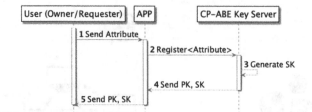

Fig. 2. Sequence diagram of key generation in IIAAC through client application

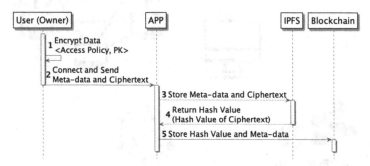

Fig. 3. Sequence diagram of data publication in IIAAC through client application

and the ciphertext is stored in IPFS through the client application. Then, IPFS returns the hash value, which will be published to the blockchain through the application. In Fig. 4, the requester user connects to the application and requests data access via blockchain. If the attribute of requester user satisfies the access policy the owner user set, the protocol retrieves the hash value in the blockchain and returns it to the requester through the application. After that, the ciphertext corresponding to the hash value is returned from IPFS and decrypted using the requester's secret key. However, if the attribute of the requester user does not satisfy the access policy, the ciphertext cannot be decrypted and the procedure is aborted.

4   Experiments and Discussions

4.1   Experiment Overview

The first experiment is designed to evaluate the case of off-chain storage on IPFS that interoperates with blockchain for data publication and retrieval in terms of the time of data uploading and downloading. To reduce the storage on blockchain, the encrypted PHD and the meta-data of PHD are stored in IPFS. The hash-value corresponding to the PHD is returned from IPFS. Thereafter, the hash-value is stored in blockchain. One of the main goals for interoperation of blockchain and IPFS is to improve the data storing efficiency. In this experiment, it is measured in terms of the processing time for data upload and download to

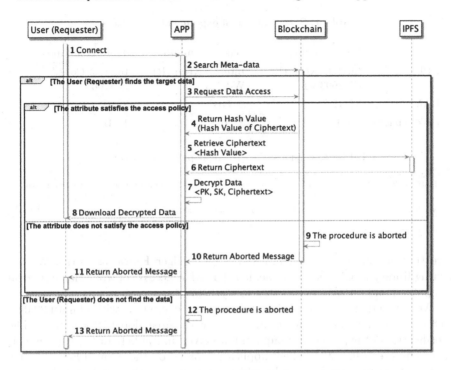

Fig. 4. Sequence diagram of data retrieval in IIAAC through client application

be completed. We test the time of data uploading and downloading, which is an important indicator to measure the latency of the system. In addition, we measure the simulated transactions per second (TPS) in the blockchain network.

The second experiment is conducted to test the encryption and decryption algorithms for CP-ABE in terms of the computation time. In this experiment, we compare the computation time for CP-ABE by different numbers of attributes.

To implement the experiments, we construct a Hyperledger Fabric network with multiple nodes. For deploying Fabric networks, we use the SOLO ordering mechanism, which involves a single ordering node. We build the experiment environment based on the Airmed Foundation's Node.js Terminal[2] to evaluate performance, which provides two ways to publish and retrieve data: one uploads data files with asymmetric encryption using PKI, and another one is without encryption. We implement the CP-ABE mechanism to have fine-grained access control according to the predetermined access policy and attribute levels. In addition, Mocha Test framework[3] is used to test the functions on the Airmed Foundation terminal and monitor and collect the experiment data. Tape[4], a lightweight tool to test the performance of Hyperledger Fabric, is used to mea-

---

[2] https://github.com/the-chain/airmedfoundation-terminal/.

[3] https://mochajs.org/.

[4] https://github.com/Hyperledger-TWGC/tape/.

Table 1. Specifications of experiment computers

	First computer	Second computer	Third computer
CPU	Intel ® Xeon (R) E5-2603 v4	Intel ® Xeon (R) W-2223	Intel ® Core TM i7-8700
RAM	32 GB	32 GB	8 GB
Disk capacity	2 TB	2 TB	1 TB

Table 2. Versions of experiment platforms and tools

Platforms/tools	Hyperledger fabric	IPFS	Node.js	Golang	Docker-container	Docker-compose	Charm	Python
Version	v 1.4.4	v 0.4.19	v 8.15.0	v 1.13.8	v 20.10.11	v 1.29.2	v 0.5.0	v 3.9.4

sure transactions per second (TPS) in Hyperledger Fabric networks. We use pairing library in Charm[5] to implement CP-ABE access control scheme in local computers, and CP-ABE is written in Python.

We stimulate three nodes separately on three computers with ubuntu 20.04.3 LTS 64bit version. The networks are linked with three global IP addresses. The specifications of experiment computers are given in Table 1. In the experiment, each computer runs as the client application based on the Airmed Foundation's Node.js Terminal simultaneously, which interoperates Hyperledger Fabric network and IPFS node. The versions of experiment platforms and tools are listed in Table 2.

A local IPFS node is launched in each computer, and a private IPFS network including three nodes is constructed. The first computer is responsible for uploading data to the IPFS network and generating transactions in the Hyperledger Fabric. The other two computers are responsible for retrieving and downloading data. The first computer can find and connect to the other two computers in the cluster after creating a private IPFS network on each computer. After the first computer as the primary system uploads the data, the data is stored in the IPFS node. The other two nodes in the other two computers can quickly access and download data.

4.2 Experiment Results

In this section, we present the experiment results. Figure 5 and Fig. 6 show the average upload time for publishing data in different sizes. In order to reduce the impact of network latency, we measure the time to upload data of 0.1 MB, 5 MB, 10 MB and 15 MB for 100× in two different periods, and then calculate the average upload time.

From Fig. 5, we can see that a linear trendline can be drawn to represent the increasing time to upload data of larger size. It takes about 69 ms to upload the

---

[5] https://jhuisi.github.io/charm/.

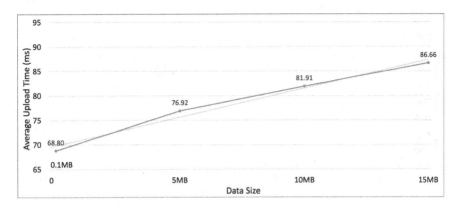

Fig. 5. Average upload time for data of different sizes (1)

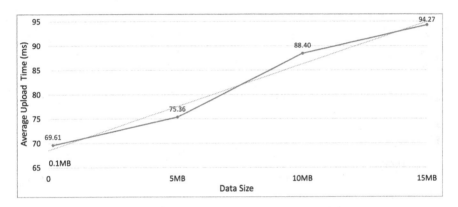

Fig. 6. Average upload time for data of different sizes (2)

data of small size (0.1 MB), which can be regarded as an initialization time for uploading. After that, from the data size of 5 MB, the uploading time increases with the data size, about 5 ms per 5 MB. Figure 6 shares a similar linear trendline with Fig. 5, though the average upload time for each different data size is somewhat different.

In addition, we observed some outliers of upload time in the experiments. More specifically, in the 100 tests for the first period, there were two outliers for 0.1 MB and six outliers for 5 MB (two to three times the normal value). For the second period, four outliers for 10 MB and five outliers for 15 MB (the same two to three times the normal value) were observed.

Then, we measure the time of data downloading from IPFS in different data sizes. Similarly, we measure the time to download data of 0.1 MB, 5 MB, 10 MB, and 15 MB for 100× in two different periods, and then calculate the average download time. The results are shown in Fig. 7 and Fig. 8. The same as in Figs. 5 and 6, a linear trendline was drawn to represent the increasing time to download

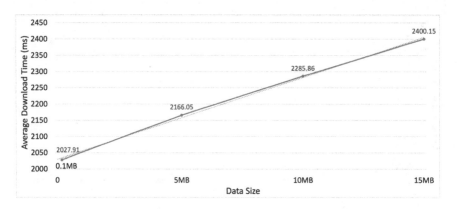

Fig. 7. Average download time for data of different sizes (1)

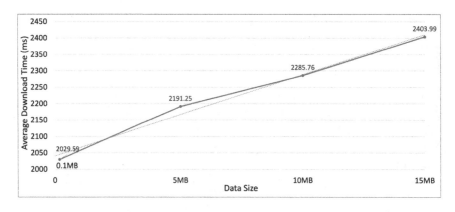

Fig. 8. Average download time for data of different sizes (2)

data of larger size. However, we can see from the figures that it takes much longer time to download data than to upload them. It took about 2028 ms to download data of 0.1 MB, and then the downloading time increases with the data size, about 120 ms per 5 MB. On the other hand, no outliers were observed for data downloading. We will investigate this outlier phenomenon in our future work.

Furthermore, we measure the simulated transactions per second (TPS) in Hyperledger Fabric networks. In our experiment, we set the number of transactions in the system to 40000. As shown in Fig. 9, the first block is generated in 240 ms, and the other blocks are generated in 50 to 100 ms. The total duration is 4 min and 17 s. The results show that 4000 blocks (each block is of ten transactions) were generated, and processed consistently at about 156 transactions per second (TPS). The processing time per block decreases and stabilizes gradually with the processing of transactions.

In addition, we implemented the CP-ABE scheme using Python on the first computer. In the experiment, the attributes number of access policy is initiated

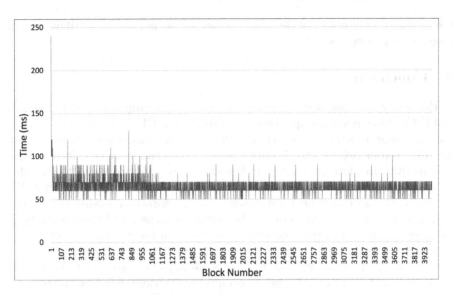

Fig. 9. Block processing time in hyperledger fabric

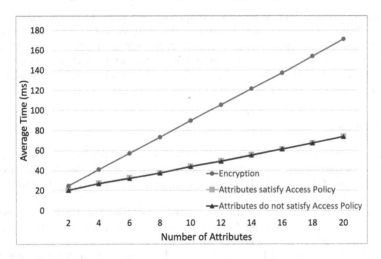

Fig. 10. Execution time of encryption and decryption in CP-ABE

from 2 to 20 with an interval of 2. The results are obtained for an average of 100 times of executions. We set two patterns for decryption: attributes that satisfy the access policy and attributes that do not satisfy the access policy. As shown in Fig. 10, the simplest access policy we set, which the number of attributes is 2, takes a specific initialization time on the encryption and decryption processes, about 20 ms. Then, the average times increase linearly with the number of attributes growing, about 18 ms per two attributes in the encryption process and about 8 ms per two attributes in the decryption process. It coincides with the increased complexity of the access policy as the number of attributes in an access policy increases.

5 Conclusion

In this study, we proposed a new model for secure interoperation of blockchain and IPFS through a client application enabled by the CP-ABE encryption mechanism. The proposed new model and architecture can be expected to provide an alternative approach for trusted data sharing. In this paper, we described the system architecture through a client application and the protocols with the detailed procedures, including key generation, data publication and data retrieval. We further built the experiment environment for performance evaluation for our proposed model and architecture. The results demonstrated the feasibility of the proposed model in the blockchain-based system for privacy-preserved data sharing.

For our future work, we plan to have a full implementation of the proposed model and architecture and conduct comprehensive experiments with comparison to the baselines to evaluate the scalability and effectiveness.

Acknowledgement. The work was supported in part by 2020-2021 Waseda University-NICT Matching Funds Program, 2020-2021 Waseda University Grants for Special Research Projects (Nos. 2020C-385, 2020R-056 and 2021C-292), 2020-2025 JSPS A3 Foresight Program (Grant No. JPJSA3F20200001), and 2021 Waseda University Advanced Research Center for Human Sciences Project (Support for Formation of Research Center of Excellence).

References

1. Hewa, T., Braeken, A., Ylianttila, M., Liyanage, M.: Multi-access edge computing and blockchain-based secure telehealth system connected with 5G and IoT. In: Proceedings of the 2020 IEEE Global Communications Conference (GLOBECOM), pp. 1-6 (2020)
2. Porambage, P., Okwuibe, J., Liyanage, M., Ylianttila, M., Taleb, T.: Survey on multi-access edge computing for internet of things realization. IEEE Commun. Surv. Tutor. **20**(4), 2961–2991 (2018)
3. McGhin, T., Choo, K.K.R., Liu, C.Z., He, D.: Blockchain in healthcare applications: research challenges and opportunities. J. Netw. Comput. Appl. **135**, 62–75 (2019)
4. Ito, K., Tago, K., Jin, Q.: i-Blockchain: a blockchain-empowered individual-centric framework for privacy-preserved use of personal health data. In: Proceedings of the 2018 9th International Conference on Information Technology in Medicine and Education (ITME), pp. 829–833 (2018)
5. Li, R., Asaeda, H.: A blockchain-based data lifecycle protection framework for information-centric network. IEEE Commun. Mag. **57**(6), 20–25 (2019)
6. Cong, R., Liu, Y., Tago, K., Li, R., Asaeda, H., Jin, Q.: Individual-initiated auditable access control for privacy-preserved iot data sharing with blockchain. In: Proceedings of the 2021 IEEE International Conference on Communications Workshops (ICC Workshops), pp. 1–6 (2021)

7. Nakamoto, S.: Bitcoin: a peer-to-peer electronic cash system. https://bitcoin.org/bitcoin.pdf. Accessed 7 Feb 2022
8. Liu, S., Hong, T.: A consortium medical blockchain data storage and sharing model based on IPFS. In: Proceedings of the 4th International Conference on Computers in Management and Business (ICCMB), pp. 147–153 (2021)
9. Kumar, S., Bharti, A.K., Amin, R.: Decentralized secure storage of medical records using blockchain and IPFS: a comparative analysis with future directions. Secur. Priv. 4(5), e162 (2021)
10. Tang, J., Jia, T., Chen, H., Wei, C.: Research on big data storage method based on IPFS and blockchain. In: Proceedings of the 2020 2nd International Conference on Video, Signal and Image Processing (VSIP 2020), pp. 55–60 (2020)
11. Kumar, N., Dakshayini, M.: Secure sharing of health data using hyperledger fabric based on blockchain technology. In: Proceedings 2020 International Conference on Mainstreaming Block Chain Implementation (ICOMBI), pp. 1–5 (2020)
12. Saini, A., Zhu, Q., Singh, N., Xiang, Y., Gao, L., Zhang, Y.: A smart-contract-based access control framework for cloud smart healthcare system. IEEE Internet Things J. 8(7), 5914–5925 (2021)
13. Bethencourt, J., Sahai, A., Waters, B.: Ciphertext-policy attribute-based encryption. In: Proceedings of the 2007 IEEE Symposium on Security and Privacy (SP 2007), pp. 321–334 (2007)

Mental Models of the Internet and Its Online Risks: Children and Their Parent(s)

Alexandra Mai[1,2(✉)], Leonard Guelmino[1], Katharina Pfeffer[1,2],
Edgar Weippl[2,4], and Katharina Krombholz[3]

[1] Vienna University of Technology, Vienna, Austria
[2] SBA Research, Vienna, Austria
amai@sba-research.org
[3] CISPA Helmholtz Center for Information Security, Saarland, Germany
[4] University of Vienna, Vienna, Austria

Abstract. Today, children have access to the Internet from an early age and are therefore considered digital natives. This paper investigates how children (aged five to eight) and their parents perceive and deal with the Internet and the privacy and security risks of being online. Therefore, we extended prior studies of Internet mental models of children. We used a two-fold study design by including drawing tasks in addition to a verbal interview. The drawings allowed us to uncover the tacit knowledge underlying children's and parents' mental models.

So far, research focused mainly on the threat models of "being online", while our study has a more holistic view, investigating general perceptions of the Internet in-depth. In contrast to prior studies, which were mainly conducted outside of Europe with highly-educated participants, we recruited participants in Central Europe with a diverse educational background.

We found that children's mental models start to take shape beyond physically tangible components between the age of seven to eight years. Hence, we argue that it is important to educate children about the Internet as well as security and privacy issues before that age. For younger children, we suggest using secure and privacy-preserving applications, as they are not yet able to grasp the bigger picture.

Keywords: Internet mental models · Children and parents study · Usable security

1 Introduction

The global Internet population continues to grow daily and already has more than 4.5 billion active users [18]. Today's children grow up in a digital world. In contrast to their parents, they do not know a world without the Internet. From a very early age, many of them experience video streaming on their parents' smartphones/tablets/smart TVs, digitized toys, or computer/console games [16]. Despite

© The Author(s), under exclusive license to Springer Nature Switzerland AG 2022
A. Moallem (Ed.): HCII 2022, LNCS 13333, pp. 42–61, 2022.
https://doi.org/10.1007/978-3-031-05563-8_4

a supposedly low level of direct interaction that children have with these devices, their privacy and security can be violated. For instance, incidents were reported where (default) settings allowed toys to unintentionally record children [24].

Using the Internet usually requires little technical knowledge about its components and how they interact with each other. However, in order to correctly assess one's own security and privacy on the Internet when using common applications (e.g., browsers, messaging applications) and behave accordingly, it is important to have at least a basic understanding of the system. This becomes especially crucial when security breaches or other problems occur (e.g., leaked passwords [13]).

Multiple studies investigated Internet mental models of teenagers and adults, however less research was done in the area of young children and their respective parents. Livingstone [22] found that children value their privacy both in offline and online communication with their peers, when seeking advice and when forming relationships. Therefore, it is important to respect and protect their desire for privacy. This paper takes a first step in this direction, by examining children's mental model of the Internet. Based on those findings, we provide advice on how to enhance i) privacy and security settings and ii) raise children's awareness.

The purpose of our study was to investigate the Internet mental models of children and their parents in Central Europe, in order to validate and extend prior studies by Kumar et al. [21] and Zhang-Kennedy et al. [37]. To deepen previous findings, we used drawing tasks and scenarios to elicit mental models of the Internet, which are often based on tacit knowledge. This hard-to-express form of knowledge is generated by individual experiences and assumptions, which strongly influence behavior [19].

One of our main goals was to examine whether the education of the parents influences the children's view and awareness of the Internet and its risks. We were particularly interested in aspects, that potentially interfere with a secure and privacy-preserving Internet usage of children. Furthermore, we aimed to understand the European context, as prior work was conducted mostly in countries outside the European Union (e.g., Australia and the U.S.).

In particular, we sought to answer the following research questions:

(RQ1) How do children and their parents perceive the Internet with its actors, components, and connections?
(RQ2) Are the mental models of children and their respective parent(s) similar?
(RQ3) Do children recognize potential security and privacy risks when using the Internet?

To answer these questions, we conducted 26 semi-structured interviews with 13 families in the metropolitan and suburban area of Austria. We used thematic analysis and iteratively conducted the interviews until we reached theoretical saturation.

Our findings suggest that children's mental models of the Internet deepen between the age five and eight. In this process, they switch from simple, physically tangible descriptions (e.g., a TV or smartphone), to elaborations that go beyond them (e.g., describing that the Internet represents knowledge). We found that the risk awareness also depends on the children's age. The reason for this is, on the one hand, that their parents shield and protect them from risks. On the other hand, the superficiality of their mental models is also a barrier to developing risk perception. Furthermore, we discovered that parents were more aware of security and privacy risks than children. However, most parents were not concerned about their own privacy, but more about their child's safety on the Internet. These concerns, however, restricted the privacy and freedom of children in some cases.

This paper is organized as follows: In Sect. 2, we provide background information and related work. Our used methodology, including the study design is described in Sect. 3. We present our findings in Sect. 4, followed by its discussion in Sect. 5. The limitations are discussed in Sect. 6 and in Sect. 7 we conclude our work and provide information about planned future work in this area.

2   Related Work

In this section, we examine related studies on Internet mental models as well as threat models of Internet related actions/devices from a children's and an adolescent's perspective. An overview of those studies can be found in Fig. 1, indicating the age, the number of participants, and the type of study.

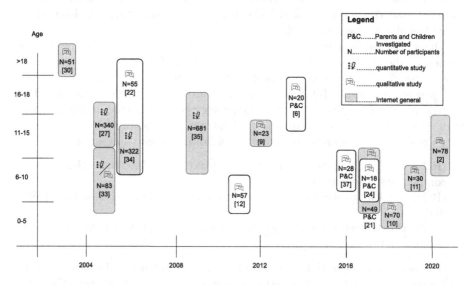

Fig. 1. Overview of relevant children/adolescents mental model studies on the Internet and online threats/privacy perceptions

2.1 Internet Mental Models

Thatcher and Greyling [30] conducted the first study about mental models of Internet users in 1998 with university students in South Africa. They created a questionnaire including a drawing task to explore their participants' understanding of the structure and functionality of the Internet. A methodologically similar study investigated the mental models of primary and high school students [27] in Greece.

Yan investigated in three large-scale studies [33–35] the effects of age and experience on the technical and social understanding children and adolescents have of the Internet. Hereby, he found that children have limited resources for their understanding of the Internet, which has implications on their Internet experience/usage and their perception of Internet related devices (e.g., PC, telephones, TV). Diethelm et al. [9] conducted a study with secondary school students and found metaphors for Internet education at that age.

In 2017, Kumar et al. [21] conducted an Internet mental model study with highly educated U.S. families (children aged five to eleven). The interviews were semi-structured, with hypothetical scenarios to make it easier for the children to imagine potential risks. They found that children have some strategies to avoid certain security or privacy risks, however they still heavily relied on parental support. The study with the smallest children (4–5) was conducted by Edwards et al. [10] to identity everyday concepts which can be used for Internet education. Eskelä-Haapanen and Kili [11] focused their study on the trustworthiness of information which can be obtained from the Internet. The most recent study was presented in 2021 by Brodsky et al. [2] which focused on the Generation Z and the influential factors of age and usage. Thereby, they found no significant differences, however determined that most participants described the Internet as ubiquity.

2.2 Privacy and Security Perceptions of Internet Related Actions/Devices

Livingstone [22] gave insights into children's understanding and interpretation of privacy. Ey and Cupit [12] conducted group interviews with children to investigate their strategies when facing online threats. Their results showed that the children were able to handle dangerous situations appropriately, if they received Internet related education, otherwise they had difficulties to identify the potential dangers.

Cranor et al. [6] explored the boundaries of teens' privacy when using online services in comparison to their parents. They revealed that parents and their teenage children have different privacy concepts, as parents made incorrect analogies between the real and the digital world.

Zhang-Kennedy et al. [37] studied the perceived mobile threat models of parents and their children (aged seven to eleven) in Canada. They identified different threat models and found that parents perform different protection strategies to protect their children from exposure.

McReynolds et al. [24] uncovered both, children's and parents' mental models of online toys and their expectations. They found that children were not aware of their toys' connection to the Internet. Most of the parents had privacy concerns about the toys recording their child, however, there were also some which approved the possibility to oversee their children's activities.

Our work differs in comparison to the aforementioned studies primarily in that we assessed the general perception of the Internet and its components and actors from both children and their parents. Based on those perceptions, we studied the connection of mental models and experienced risks as well as the prevention mechanisms used. To further extend the current base of knowledge, we also studied different levels of educational background and conducted our study in a different cultural background (Central Europe), which has so far been understudied.

3   Methodology

In the following, we describe the methodology used to recruit our participants and to collect and analyze our data.

3.1   Ethics

We followed our organizational guidelines as we unfortunately do not have an institutional review board. The guidelines require us to preserve the participants' privacy by limiting the amount of sensitive data that we collect to a minimum. Before conducting the interviews, we explained the purpose of the study and asked the parents to sign (for in-person interviews) or orally consent (for online interviews) to our data handling procedure. Our data handling procedure strictly follows the EU's General Data Protection Regulation (GDPR) [5].

Some of our study participants were children. It was particularly important to us to treat them with respect and give them the feeling that they are in a protected environment. Therefore, we tried to adapt the study design as much as possible to their needs. The children did not have to read anything as we worked with visual material and asked all the questions verbally.

3.2   Recruitment

It was our goal to recruit a diverse sample in regards to the participants' educational background and gender. We approached potential participants via social media as well as local pre-schools, following prior studies [6,12]. Furthermore, we used personal contacts and the referral principle to reach new participants. We distributed a short recruitment description of our study without disclosing the concrete purpose of our study. To describe our research project, we used the wording *digital media usage today* to not reveal too much information of our study beforehand and thus, prevent participants from reading up information

Table 1. Demographics of our study participants (26 interviews from 13 families)

	Parents	Children
Age		
Min–Max	35–44	5–8
Median	40	6.5
Gender		
M	30%	46%
W	70%	54%
Highest Education		
Pre-School	–	40%
Primary School	–	60%
A-Level/Apprenticeship	50%	–
Graduate education	50%	–

that could distort our study results. We chose the families based on the parents' educational background, in order to ensure a diverse sample.

We performed the selection of participants in three rounds. In the beginning, we recruited five families (10 interviews) with parents without a university degree and explored the data we gathered through an initial open coding process. Based on those findings, we extended our recruiting strategy to higher educated participants in order to broaden our insights by including a more diverse sample (10 interviews). In the third round, we collected six additional interviews from three families, with one seven-year and two eight-year-old children, as we noticed an explanation shift (from physical tangible components to more technical and intangible awareness) in understanding between seven- and eight-year-old children which we wanted to further analyze.

Hence, we ended with a total sample of 26 participants from 13 families. The demographics of our final dataset can be found in Table 1.

3.3 Study Design and Procedure

We constructed a semi-structured interview guideline and a short pre-study questionnaire (see Appendix A.1) containing closed-ended questions. The pre-study questionnaire covered the participants' demographics and their Internet usage. The interview guideline was used to understand the mental models of children and their parents about the Internet and its related threat landscape. In line with other mental model studies from usable security [20,23,36] and HCI [21,24] we used a drawing exercise besides a verbal interview to elicit the mental models. Our interview consisted of three drawing scenarios, which were guided by some questions to support the participants. The interview guidelines for parents and children differed only marginally, as we did not make any adjustments apart from using child-friendly language. The study materials used, such as pens and pictures, were also the same for both groups.

The drawing tasks covered three main themes: i) General Internet functionality, ii) specific types of activities the child performs on the Internet (e.g., watching a video), and iii) privacy and security concerns. The drawing tasks were used to help our participants visualize and organize their thoughts. To avoid misinterpretations of the drawings, we asked the participants to think-aloud and explain their pictures while drawing. Based on the verbal explanation and the drawings, we got comprehensive insights into the mental models of the participants.

The opening question of our semi-structured interview was *"Do you know the (term) Internet?"*. In the *first scenario* we asked the participants to describe the Internet's functionality and its main components and actors. Depending on the participants' answers to this question, we asked follow-up questions concerning the components and actors which they mentioned, and about connections between them. To conclude the first scenario, we asked for security and privacy risks the participants could think of.

The *second scenario* covered the setting of watching and streaming videos on YouTube. To facilitate immersion into the scenario, we provided a picture of the YouTube Kids page with two thumbnails of different videos (see Appendix Fig. 5a). After providing the picture, we asked our participants what they believe to happen when searching for and clicking on the displayed video. If participants encountered a mental block or did not mention where the video comes from and where it is stored, we asked specifically about this. To lead the participants to security and privacy aspects of the Internet, we asked them about their opinion of who can view the video(s) and who knows if someone watched a specific video.

In our *third scenario*, we investigated instant messaging. Similar to the second scenario, we showed a picture to accentuate the scenario (see Appendix Fig. 5b). To not exclude children who were not yet able to read, the picture we provided, both, for parents and children, only depicted emojis in the messages. We asked the participant to imagine sending a message to his/her relative. Based on this scenario, they were asked to draw the communication between them and their messaging partner. For assistance and to gather more in-depth information, we asked about their thoughts of the connections, potential message loss, and the people who can read them.

We did not directly ask the children about security or privacy threats, since we assumed based on prior studies [32, 37] that they are not familiar with such terms. Instead, we gave them hints by asking questions about mean or scary people or inappropriate behavior they experienced. Thereby, we reused the vocabulary used by the children in the pilot study, to ensure familiarity and to avoid interviewer bias.

Pilot-Study. Before conducting our study, we tested our interview design by interviewing two families (four interviews) as a pilot-study. Thereby, we found two improvements of the initial study design. Each scenario of our initial design consisted of two to three questions, without any further prescribed guidelines and inspirational cues for the participants. Furthermore, we provided only a single pen for the drawing task.

In our pilot-study, the participants seemed to be overwhelmed with the vague questions and no further guidance. During the first interview, we discovered that when the interviewer asked more specific follow-up questions, the participants felt more comfortable and expressed their thoughts more easily. Therefore, we extended our initial set of questions with four concrete questions for each scenario. Although the study design had been changed, by adding questions to the study design, we decided to integrate two interviews into our final set of data, as the interviewer asked those questions during the pre-study.

After the pilot-study, it became apparent that providing further coloring material would be beneficial. This was especially true for the children, as they felt slightly irritated by the fact that there was only one choice of color. As we aimed to encourage the creativity of the participants, we decided to provide more colors for our main study. To better distinguish between the general mental model and the threat model, we decided to provide the color red only when the participant started to elaborate security and privacy risks.

Interview Procedure. We interviewed 26 participants of 13 different families in the metropolitan and suburban area of Austria. 12 interviews were conducted in person and 14 via Skype, due to the ongoing Covid-19 pandemic at the time the study was conducted. The in-person interviews were performed at the participants' home to ensure a comfortable setting for the children. All participants agreed to being recorded, enabling us to transcribe them afterwards. Furthermore, we took pictures of the drawings for data analysis.

In the beginning, we briefed the parent-child pairs about the procedure, asked for their consent, and afterwards conducted the interviews with parents and children separately. However, we asked the parents to be nearby when interviewing their children to make the children feel more at ease. Therewith, we targeted at enabling the children to speak more freely, but still have the possibility to engage with their parents, if they felt uncomfortable. We interviewed the children first and then their parents, to prevent children from picking up words or content from their parents during the interview, and simply repeating them. One study was an exception as it was conducted the other way round, however the child did not stay in the same room to prevent any bias. The average interview lasted 25 min, whereby the interviews with children were shorter (average 15 min) than those with parents (average 30 min). As compensation, the parent-child pairs received a €10 gift voucher at the end of the interview.

3.4 Data Analysis

We recorded all interviews and transcribed them afterwards. Based on these transcriptions, two authors followed a thematic analysis [3] approach and coded and searched for re-occurring themes in two different rounds. During this process, the authors discussed their findings and codes until final agreement on the codebook was reached (inter-rater reliability Cohen's Kappa [4] $\kappa = 0.72$).

Our codes are related to the Internet itself (including its actors, components and their connections), the risks the participants faced (e.g., inappropriate content or unauthorized access to smartphones) and prevention strategies to avoid these (e.g., YouTube Kids or other filter mechanisms). The high level themes of our codebook are shown in Fig. 2.

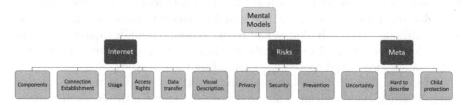

Fig. 2. Overview of main themes of our codebook

4   Findings

In the following, we describe our findings related to our participants' perceptions of the Internet and security and privacy risks while performing online actions. We present the qualitative insights and tendencies we encountered alongside with the participants' drawings and direct quotes.

To better understand our participants' knowledge and perceptions, we asked about their general Internet usage and technical understanding. An overview of their answers can be found in Table 2. We found that the majority of our parent participants used at least four Internet services regularly. In contrast, children used fewer online services. Only in the case of watching videos online, the children showed more activity than their parents. In Table 2, we marked some fields as "-" not applicable in the column of the children. In particular, we did not ask directly about privacy concerns, but used a more children-friendly wording. For email and banking services, we assumed that children do not use them on their own or don't possess one [8].

Both children and parents claimed to have an average knowledge of online devices and the Internet. However, only four participants learned specifically about the Internet during their education. Therefore, the knowledge was either self-taught or taught by reference persons (for children their caregivers), as indicated by the participants' statements about asking help from others.

4.1   Internet - Mental Models

To explore our participants' understanding of the Internet and thereby answer RQ1, we prepared open-ended questions in our interview guidelines and asked the participants to draw simultaneously to their explanations. We noted that four children (C4, C7, C8, C9) between five and six were not familiar with the term 'Internet', which made it difficult for them to directly talk about it. However,

Table 2. Participants Internet usage and knowledge based on Q6–Q8 from the pre-study questionnaire

	Parents		Children	
	Average	Median	Average	Median
Internet services				
Social Media	3.1	2.5	1.8	1
Videos	3.8	4	4.2	4.5
Online Shopping	3.5	4	1.9	1.5
Instant messaging	4.9	5	1.7	1
Video chatting	2.4	2	2.8	1
Email	4.5	5	–	–
Online Banking	3.6	3.5	–	–
Games	–	–	2.4	1
Privacy Concerned[a]	3.5	3.5	–	–
Self-Assessment skills				
Knowledge smartphone/tablets	3.2	3	3.2	3
Internet education	2.4	2	1.2	1
Asking help from others	3.1	3	4.2	4.5
Participant helps others	2.4	2	–	–

based on the two scenarios, we discovered that they did use some of the services on the Internet, but did not associate the word with them. For example, one five-year old child stated, that they are still able to watch videos on YouTube without the Internet (C8).

In comparison, seven and eight year old children did link their explanation of the Internet to their individual activities, such as playing games and watching videos. One child stated without further direct explanation:

"That it [the Internet] is not good for children." (C3)

We found, based on the remainder of the interview, that C3 had a bad experience with a YouTube video that showed content that was not suitable for children. One eight year old child articulated a quite concrete perception of the Internet:

"I imagine the Internet as a world, where I can do things, ask questions, and so on." (C1)

Another eight year old child stated that:

"It [the Internet] is everywhere.... and everyone with a Laptop or a smartphone can use it." (C12)

C1, C12 explained and drew the Internet as an earth where many (unknown) people are connected to each other and therefore, had a very similar mental model as three adults.

Another popular depiction of the Internet among our children participants were power poles or boxes which connect the user to the Internet. Three children (age seven and eight) used those visual representations. One child explained while drawing their picture (see Fig. 3):

"[The Internet] is back there by the Internet box. It has to charge a bit, the Internet, so you have to turn up the power beforehand so that it works." (C6)

We clustered the mental representations of the Internet verbalized and drawn by our participants in three categories based on how they are influenced by the knowledge of safety and privacy (see Sect. 4.2) of the participants:

- Activity/Interfaces: In this category participants first and foremost mentioned activities, which they perform while being online (e.g., finances, online shopping, social media, emails, games, videos). Thereby, they drew either user interfaces of the device they use or the activities themselves (three adults, nine children). Furthermore, especially the younger children explained their activities (watching a video or playing a game) in much detail about its content. The parents also mentioned activities, however explained in more detail, what they were doing and knew that they were actively engaging with the Internet and its information/resources.
- Earth/Worldwide: Participants in this category explained the Internet as an earth, which has global connections. The communication is possible in all directions (four adults, two children).
- Network/Technology: The participants mentioned or drew (via cable/WIFI etc.) connected components within a network which they are a part of. These components include smartphones, laptops and servers (four adults, two children).

The categories of mental models we defined are not mutually exclusive, as the mental model of one participant can contain parts of other categories. However, we made the assignment based on the study transcripts and in the case of several possible assignments, decided on the category based on the participant's drawing.

4.2   Online Risks - Mental Models

In this section we describe the findings of perceived security and privacy risks from the children's and parents' perspective.

Children. We asked children and parents about privacy and security risks. However, for children we refrained from using these words in the interviews since we assumed that they might not understand them. Instead, we used more

Fig. 3. Internet depiction of participant C6 with a (Internet) box.

tangible wording such as "bad guys on the Internet" or "people that want to steal your information".

In order to answer RQ2 and RQ3, we asked several times throughout the interview about threats which may jeopardize privacy and security of the participants. Thereby, we found that the children in our *Activity/Interface* category (age five to seven) showed little concern, when asked about mean, unfriendly, or unpleasant people or incidents. They either were unsure (three children), did not answer (one child), said there are no bad people on the Internet (two children), or told about videos that were "not good/nice" (three children). Furthermore, two children (age seven) mentioned risks related to their health.

"If you look too long, you get a headache." (C3)

It was interesting to observe that the youngest children assumed that only they and their mothers or families know when they do things on the Internet. In comparison, the older four children in the category explained that there are other people who see that you are watching a video, for example, by "a thumbs up" or the number of viewers.

The two children (age seven to eight) in the category *Earth/Worldwide* had a somewhat deeper understanding of the potential dangers of the Internet in comparison to the first category. They also emphasized that beside their parents, friends or people e.g., uploading the Videos know their actions. Furthermore, one child (age seven) noticed that:

"My dad said no (bad) person can change the message...Only if my grandma deletes it unintentionally [laughs]" (C11)

In the category *Network/Technology* we experienced the most knowledgeable children. The two children (age eight) mentioned during their interview that a bad person could be in the system. One of them even called that person a "Hacker", however they could not elaborate what this person could do in more detail. Furthermore, both were aware that their online activity can be noticed by other people. One specified who knows about their online activity:

> *"Beside my parents...Magenta knows the videos I watch...and Steam also knows the games I play"* (C13)

Especially the younger children had a very sparse understanding of online risks. Their threat models about the Internet were always connected to personal experiences. Only two older children (age eight) had an awareness of hackers or other bad people. Furthermore one child articulated that once their computer was broken due to a bad program which made their screen blue.

> *"We had a program on our computer which programmed everything blue and than it was broken."* (C11)

Parents. When asked about differences between security and privacy, eight parents gave a correct explanation, whereas five parents had a hard time distinguishing between these terms and/or used them as synonym (three of the Activity/Interfaces category, two of the Earth/Worldwide category).

Adults articulated a lot of potential risks. Figure 4 highlights the threats and how many participants mentioned them. The most mentioned and discussed risk from all participants, parents and children, were video-integrity exploits. Thereby, inappropriate content is disguised as being child-friendly. This phenomenon surfaced in 2017 and is known by the neologism *Elsagate* [1]. Ishikawa et al. [17] and Papadamou et al. [26] presented two studies to detect the disturbing content. However, until now no technical solution was found in order to

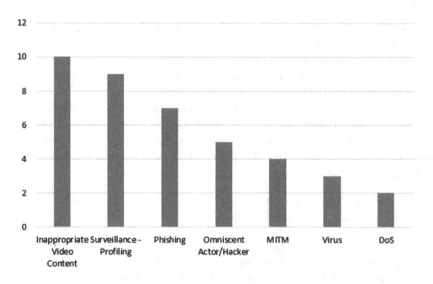

Fig. 4. Perceived security and privacy threats of adult participants

protect the children. Therefore, the parents of our study developed their own mitigation strategies (e.g., pre-watching the video).

In general, the parents related to category *Activity/Interfaces* expressed the least risk awareness among our adult participants. Beside inappropriate video contents they mentioned device theft (as it is not directly related to the Internet, we categorized it as "Other") and some sort of surveillance. The parents in this category have often stressed that they do not know or simply do not understand the Internet and its risks. Therefore, they could not answer more specific questions about where the videos are located or who sees/hears someone's activities.

In the category *Earth/Worldwide* the participants' risks perceptions were also centered around themselves and their close ones. In addition to the above described risks those parents expressed experience with phishing or similar social engineering mails/messages. Furthermore, one parent mentioned a hacker:

"My phone number is online available, so the [hacker] could also possibly hack/access my cell phone" (P12)

The parents of category *Network/Technology* all identified some sort of omniscient actor or hackers which can interfere with all systems, as nothing is completely secure. In line with the findings of Krombholz et al. [20] also two parents (one in this category and one from the Earth/Worldwide) mentioned that messages via Signal or WhatsApp can also be interfered/altered (although both messenger services are end-to-end encrypted). The parents of this category described risks from a more technical perspective, by mentioning viruses which infect systems or Monster-In-the-Middle (MITM) and Denial of Service (DOS) attacks. Technical details were provided only by parents which were professionally involved with technical aspects of the Internet.

The majority of all adult participants agreed on the privacy invasion of the Internet, however felt powerless against this transparency of the human being. They stated that they can only try not to provide even more additional information.

Besides a high risk awareness, eight participants stated that they don't think that neither their privacy nor their security are in direct threat.

"I can't control it [...], but I think, with a small fish like me they have nothing to get anyway-so they won't care." (P5)

Although many participants expressed the opinion that most attacks are unlikely, five explicitly mentioned that they take precautions. Those were either related to the use of well-known and trusted services (e.g., password managers, antivirus software, firewall, etc.), or resulted in them not putting too much private information on the Internet and storing passwords securely.

4.3   Child-Parent Pairs

In order to answer RQ2 we compared the mental models of all our child-parent pairs. Thereby we found that the mental models of the children are more sparse and differ greatly in their drawn and mentioned components. Only one child-parent pair was in the same category (CP11) namely *Network/Technology*. Interestingly, the other children in the categories *Network/Technology* and *Earth/Worldwide* had respectively the opposite category of their parents. We think, this may be due to the fact that the other parent has taken over the part of the upbringing/parenting or because the children imagine things differently and deem other aspects more important. Four children mentioned that one or both parents explained to them incidents which occurred on the Internet and told them about some other online risks (e.g., bad/inappropriate content, IT viruses, hackers), which was also confirmed by the statements of the respective parents.

5   Discussion of Findings

We found that children's mental models shift from activity based mental models of the Internet to more technical components and even tangible components between the age of seven to eight years, which is in line with children's cognitive development [7,15,31]. In line with the findings of Zhang-Kennedy et al. [37] and Kumar et al. [21] we found that parents are concerned with the security and privacy of their children and therefore, actively or passively mediate their actions. The younger children indicated that they used the Internet only when adults are around. In comparison, children aged eight years felt more secure and told us, that they use the Internet mostly on their own. Five of them also possessed their own smartphone. Most parents confirmed that their children have to ask them for permission to use the services of Internet.

Kumar et al. [21] found that parents saw security and privacy as a future concern, which is why they did not explain threats to their children, but rather blocked specific applications or protected information with passwords without further communication with their children. Opposed to Kumar et al., we found that the reason why some parents refrained from discussing threats with their children was that they perceived security and privacy threats as unlikely and only as hypothetical possibilities. However, we also discovered that four of our parent participants did not coincide with this approach. They stated that they actively engaged with their child(ren) in order to explain security and privacy risks to them.

"I see it [something inappropriate] and then I can block it and we can talk about it." (P8)

As the interviews with the children confirms the parental education and explanation of possible risks is important for the children, as they remember incidences vividly. Furthermore, some children stated explicitly that their parents did not educate them or just said they have to ask permission to use the Internet but the children were unsure what could happen and why.

We found that all children were able to articulate visual details from videos and games or could describe details about the interfaces of the Internet tools/devices. Therefore, we argue that child friendly designs and visualizations should be used to educate the children about the Internet and its related security and privacy risks. Yan [35] revealed a lack of education material for children. Therefore, we suggest on the one hand to further enhance online activities for children in order to make them inherently secure and privacy protecting and include visual cues designed especially for children (similar to the HTTPS security indicator) in the interfaces. On the other hand, we encourage parents, legal guardians, and teachers to actively educate children. Concretely, we recommend:

- Privacy and Security Enhancing Systems: The systems (mostly smartphone, tablets and televisions) and the applications children use should preserve their privacy and security. The parental control of browsers is one example of such an mechanism. However, as some parents mentioned, their children manage to overcome/disable such systems, as they knew their passwords/had one account. Therefore, a solution could be that a fingerprint/face recognition of a child could enable a different user account with different settings than their parents'. In the children settings e.g., no purchases should be allowed (without parental authorization) and contents should be restricted based on certain (parental) defined rules.
- Visual Interface Cues: The children from our study remembered certain visual cues in great detail (e.g., thumbs up symbol). Therefore, we suggest to add e.g., smileys or colorful borders to videos which have been screened for child-friendliness or which indicate whether they are scary or otherwise inappropriate for children. With the help of such cues, children can easily decide themselves whether they want to watch certain content or not.
- Education: In order to educate the children about the Internet we think their should be two approaches. First, the general education about the Internet and its risks should be performed with the help of visual supports [14,29] as the children are very influenced by them. Thereby books [25] or videos can help to provide the children with necessary information, while still being fun to watch for children. It would be great if some child favorite series would also create content with such information. Second, there should be an incident-related education, as we found that children remember them well. It has been shown by Rader et al. [28] that anecdotal stories about security incidents help adults to learn secure Internet behavior. Thus, we assume that also children's thinking and behavior about security risks on the Internet could be impacted by such stories, when they are tailored to their knowledge levels. Therefore, parents can either relate on their own knowledge and experiences, or retell stories they heard in the news or from friends. Possibly, books with visual representations or pictures in newspapers could be used for visualization. Both forms of education can either be performed by teachers, supervisors or the parents/legal guardians.

6   Limitations

We conducted our study with a relatively small sample and limited geographic diversity, therefore our study provides some qualitative insights, which need to be further investigated in a larger study. Our recruiting area was limited to one country as the first interviews were conducted in person. Furthermore, our sample is biased towards female parents (70% of our adult participants). Naturally, our methodology has its limitations, as the data is self-reported and, in comparison to quantitative studies, our results cannot be used for statistical analysis. Finally, the presence of some parents during their children's interviews, when conducted online, may have had an impact on their responses. However, we are confident that the children's comfort to answer questions honestly outweighs the potential parental bias, which is why we opted for this setting.

7   Conclusion and Future Work

With our work we explored the Internet mental models of children and their parents as well as related security and privacy concerns. Thereby, we found that the age of the children and their education (through parents and school) have a relevant influence on their perception of the Internet and its possibilities and dangers. Our results suggest that the comprehension and knowledge of this intangible technology deepens between the ages of five and eight. As future work, it remains to quantify our findings related to the influence of age by conducting a larger study with closed-ended questions. We are confident that our results can inform the design of future child-friendly Internet services and the way this topic is addressed in education.

Acknowledgments. This material is based upon work partially supported by the *Industry-related Dissertation* funding program. SBA Research (SBA-K1) is a COMET Centre within the framework of COMET - Competence Centers for Excellent Technologies Programme and funded by BMK, BMDW, and the province of Vienna. The programs are both managed by FFG.

A   Appendix

A.1   Pre-study Questionnaire

1. Age
2. Gender
3. Highest completed education
4. Do after-school care/grandparents or others look after your child regularly? If yes, how often?
5. Are you professionally involved with technical aspects of the Internet (IT related fields)?
6. How applicable are the following statements?
Never(1), Rarely(2), Sometimes(3), Often(4), Daily(5)
I use the following Internet services: [*only asked parents]

- *Social Media (Facebook, Xing, Instagram, etc.)*
- *VOD (YouTube, Netflix, Amazon Prime Video, etc.)*

- *Online Shopping (Amazon, ebay, willhaben, etc.)*
- *Instant messaging (WhatsApp, Facebook Messanger, Viber, etc.)*
- *Online video chat services (Skype, Facetime, etc.)*
- **Email*
- **Online banking*
- *Games (just asked during the children's interview)*

7. I am concerned about my privacy and the security of my data when using any of the services listed above. [only asked parents explicitly]
Not at all(1)—I am very concerned (5)
8. How much do the following statements apply to you?
Does not apply(1)—Applies very much (5)

- *I am experienced with technical devices such as computers, smartphones and tablets.*
- *I learned about the Internet in the course of my education.*
- *I often ask other people for help when I have problems with my computer/smartphone/tablet.*
- *I am often asked by other people for help when they have problems with their computer/smartphone/tablet.*

A.2   Pictures for Scenarios

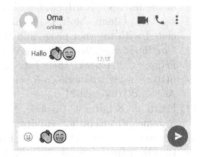

(a) Scenario 2   (b) Scenario 3

Fig. 5. Pictures shown during user study

References

1. Brandom, R.: Inside elsagate, the conspiracy-fueled war on creepy Youtube kids videos. https://www.theverge.com/2017/12/8/16751206/elsagate-youtube-kids-creepy-conspiracy-theory. Accessed 17 Nov 2020

2. Brodsky, J.E., Lodhi, A.K., Powers, K.L., Blumberg, F.C., Brooks, P.J.: "It's just everywhere now": middle-school and college students' mental models of the internet. Human Behav. Emerg. Technol. **3**(4), 495–511 (2021)
3. Clarke, V., Braun, V.: Thematic analysis. In: Michalos, M.C. (ed.) Encyclopedia of Critical Psychology, pp. 1947–1952. Springer, Heidelberg (2014). https://doi.org/10.1007/978-94-007-0753-5_3470
4. Cohen, J.: A coefficient of agreement for nominal scales. Educ. Psychol. Measur. **20**(1), 37–46 (1960)
5. Consulting, I.: General Data Protection Regulation GDPR. https://gdpr-info.eu/. Accessed 14 Jan 2021
6. Cranor, L.F., Durity, A.L., Marsh, A., Ur, B.: 'Parents' and 'teens' perspectives on privacy in a technology-filled world. In: 10th Symposium On Usable Privacy and Security (SOUPS' 14), pp. 19–35 (2014)
7. Damon, W., Lerner, R.M., Kuhn, D., Siegler, R.S.: Handbook of Child Psychology, Cognition, Perception, and Language. Wiley, Hoboken (2006)
8. Dell'Antonia, K.: When should a child get an e-mail account? https://parenting.blogs.nytimes.com/2013/01/11/when-should-a-child-get-an-e-mail-account/. Accessed 08 Feb 2021
9. Diethelm, I., Wilken, H., Zumbrägel, S.: An investigation of secondary school students' conceptions on how the internet works. In: Proceedings of the 12th Koli Calling International Conference on Computing Education Research, pp. 67–73 (2012)
10. Edwards, S., Nolan, A., Henderson, M., Mantilla, A., Plowman, L., Skouteris, H.: Young children's everyday concepts of the internet: a platform for cyber-safety education in the early years. Br. J. Educ. Technol. **49**(1), 45–55 (2018)
11. Eskelä-Haapanen, S., Kiili, C.: 'It goes around the world'-children's understanding of the internet. Nordic J. Digit. Literacy **14**(3–04), 175–187 (2019)
12. Ey, L.A., Glenn Cupit, C.: Exploring young children's understanding of risks associated with internet usage and their concepts of management strategies. J. Early Childhood Res. **9**(1), 53–65 (2011)
13. Fripp, C.: Check this list: 3.2 billion leaked usernames and passwords. https://www.komando.com/security-privacy/3-billion-leaked-passwords/777661/. Accessed 10 Feb 2021
14. Fruth, J., Schulze, C., Rohde, M., Dittmann, J.: E-learning of IT security threats: a game prototype for children. In: De Decker, B., Dittmann, J., Kraetzer, C., Vielhauer, C. (eds.) CMS 2013. LNCS, vol. 8099, pp. 162–172. Springer, Heidelberg (2013). https://doi.org/10.1007/978-3-642-40779-6_14
15. Gelman, S.A., Martinez, M., Davidson, N.S., Noles, N.S.: Developing digital privacy: children's moral judgments concerning mobile GPS devices. Child Dev. **89**(1), 17–26 (2018)
16. Holloway, D., Green, L., Livingstone, S.: Zero to eight: young children and their internet use (2013)
17. Ishikawa, A., Bollis, E., Avila, S.: Combating the Elsagate phenomenon: deep learning architectures for disturbing cartoons. arXiv preprint arXiv:1904.08910 (2019)
18. Johnson, J.: Global digital population as of October 2020. https://www.statista.com/statistics/617136/digital-population-worldwide/. Accessed 08 Jan 2021
19. Kearney, A.R., Kaplan, S.: Toward a methodology for the measurement of knowledge structures of ordinary people: the conceptual content cognitive map (3CM). Environ. Behav. **29**(5), 579–617 (1997)

20. Krombholz, K., Busse, K., Pfeffer, K., Smith, M., von Zezschwitz, E.: "if https were secure, i wouldn't need 2FA"-end user and administrator mental models of https. In: 2019 IEEE Symposium on Security and Privacy (S&P'19), pp. 246–263. IEEE (2019)
21. Kumar, P., Naik, S.M., Devkar, U.R., Chetty, M., Clegg, T.L., Vitak, J.: 'No telling passcodes out because they're private' understanding children's mental models of privacy and security online. In: Proceedings of the ACM on Human-Computer Interaction 1(CSCW), pp. 1–21 (2017)
22. Livingstone, S.: Children's privacy online: experimenting with boundaries within and beyond the family (2006)
23. Mai, A., Pfeffer, K., Gusenbauer, M., Weippl, E., Krombholz, K.: User mental models of cryptocurrency systems-a grounded theory approach. In: Sixteenth Symposium on Usable Privacy and Security (SOUPS' 20), pp. 341–358 (2020)
24. McReynolds, E., Hubbard, S., Lau, T., Saraf, A., Cakmak, M., Roesner, F.: Toys that listen: a study of parents, children, and internet-connected toys. In: Proceedings of the 2017 CHI Conference on Human Factors in Computing Systems, pp. 5197–5207 (2017)
25. Oy, H.R.: Hello Ruby Books Series. http://www.helloruby.com/books. Accessed 12 Dec 2021
26. Papadamou, K., et al.: Disturbed Youtube for kids: characterizing and detecting inappropriate videos targeting young children. In: Proceedings of the International AAAI Conference on Web and Social Media, vol. 14, pp. 522–533 (2020)
27. Papastergiou, M.: Students' mental models of the internet and their didactical exploitation in informatics education. Educ. Inf. Technol. 10(4), 341–360 (2005)
28. Rader, E., Wash, R., Brooks, B.: Stories as informal lessons about security. In: Proceedings of the Eighth Symposium on Usable Privacy and Security, pp. 1–17 (2012)
29. Sharp, D.L., Bransford, J.D., Goldman, S.R., Risko, V.J., Kinzer, C.K., Vye, N.J.: Dynamic visual support for story comprehension and mental model building by young, at-risk children. Educ. Technol. Res. Dev. 43(4), 25–42 (1995). https://doi.org/10.1007/BF02300489
30. Thatcher, A., Greyling, M.: Mental models of the internet. Int. J. Ind. Ergon. 22(4–5), 299–305 (1998)
31. Vygotsky, L.S.: The Collected Works of LS Vygotsky: Problems of the Theory and History of Psychology, vol. 3. Springer, Heidelberg (1997)
32. Wolfe, M.: Childhood and privacy. In: Altman, I., Wohlwill, J.F. (eds.) Children and the Environment, pp. 175–222. Springer, Boston (1978). https://doi.org/10.1007/978-1-4684-3405-7_6
33. Yan, Z.: Age differences in children's understanding of the complexity of the internet. J. Appl. Dev. Psychol. 26(4), 385–396 (2005)
34. Yan, Z.: What influences children's and adolescents' understanding of the complexity of the internet? Dev. Psychol. 42(3), 418 (2006)
35. Yan, Z.: Limited knowledge and limited resources: children's and adolescents' understanding of the internet. J. Appl. Dev. Psychol. 30(2), 103–115 (2009)
36. Zeng, E., Mare, S., Roesner, F.: End user security & privacy concerns with smart homes. In: Symposium on Usable Privacy and Security (SOUPS'17) (2017)
37. Zhang-Kennedy, L., Mekhail, C., Abdelaziz, Y., Chiasson, S.: From nosy little brothers to stranger-danger: children and parents' perception of mobile threats. In: Proceedings of the The 15th International Conference on Interaction Design and Children, pp. 388–399 (2016)

Privacy and Customer's Education: NLP for Information Resources Suggestions and Expert Finder Systems

Luca Mazzola[1](✉)(iD), Andreas Waldis[1](iD), Atreya Shankar[1], Diamantis Argyris[1], Alexander Denzler[1], and Michiel Van Roey[2]

[1] School of Information Technology, HSLU - Lucerne University of Applied Sciences and Arts, Suurstoffi 1, 6343 Rotkreuz, Switzerland
{luca.mazzola,andreas.waldis,atreya.shankar,diamantis.argyris,
alexander.denzler}@hslu.ch
[2] Profila GmbH, Seeburgstrasse 45, 6006 Luzern, Switzerland
info@profila.com

Abstract. Privacy is one of the key issues for citizen's everyday online activities, with the United Nations defining it as "a human right in the digital age". Despite the introduction of data privacy regulations almost everywhere around the globe, the biggest barrier to effectiveness is the customer's capacity to map the privacy statement received with the regulation in force and understand their terms. This study advocates the creation of a convenient and cost-efficient question-answering service for answering customers' queries on data privacy. It proposes a dual step approach, allowing consumers to ask support to a conversational agent boosted by a smart knowledge base, attempting to answer the question using the most appropriate legal document. Being the self-help approach insufficient, our system enacts a second step suggesting a ranked list of legal experts for focused advice. To achieve our objective, we need large enough and specialised dataset and we plan to apply state-of-the-art Natural Language Processing (NLP) techniques in the field of open domain question answering. This paper describes the initial steps and some early results we achieved in this direction and the next steps we propose to develop a one-stop solution for consumers privacy needs.

Keywords: Privacy · Data privacy regulation · Natural language processing · Consumers' privacy · Read and retrieve in open domain question answering

1 Introduction

Privacy is one of the key issues for citizen's everyday online activities. Online Privacy Literacy (OPL) is a recent approach to estimate knowledge about privacy rights, considering declarative and procedural aspects of preventive and corrective protective strategies [14]. The most important finding in this study,

A. Moallem (Ed.): HCII 2022, LNCS 13333, pp. 62–77, 2022.
https://doi.org/10.1007/978-3-031-05563-8_5

is the fact that an increase in theoretical users' knowledge does not reflect a reduction of their concerns, but rather ends up in an increased interest in understanding and fully exploiting the protective measures offered by relevant laws and regulations. This is also reflected in the higher consideration given to privacy protection from government and non-governmental institution, such as the United Nations [10], defining it as "a human right in the digital age" in the context of the current pervasive datafication. Despite the introduction of data privacy regulations almost everywhere around the globe, the biggest barrier to effectiveness is the customer's capacity to map the privacy statement received with the regulation in force and understand their terms.

The matter is twofold: on one side this is a complete switch of paradigm from the social network approach, where a service is offered to people free-of-charge because the business model came from the usage of consumers' personal information. On the other side, the content of companies' privacy policies and notices (at least, at the European level) are mainly guided by the GDPR; which is a legislative text and therefore uses typical juridical organisation of information and legal jargon, which makes comprehension by non-experts difficult. These two factors produce a barrier when a consumer would like to decide if a specific privacy-related contract is compatible with their desired level of privacy. Despite some analyses of GDPR effects such as the *"right to explanation"* [23], no major developments have concentrated on the education and explanation of privacy terms for general consumers, but only on the raised awareness. This mismatch between the risk realisation and the practical applicability of the tools provided by the legal framework has brought a sense of frustration for consumers as described in [20] with comments such as *"[the law] is not clear and simple to me while you come across it all the time and it impacts your data"*. As such, there is a need for immediate consumers' support while dealing with personal-data collection, storage and usage, in order to provide remediation actions for this tension and, thus, a more relaxed interaction with personalisation approaches. Figure 1 gives a graphical overview of this initial step.

2   Idea

While interacting with websites or registering for services, customers usually encounter privacy contracts stating the terms of agreement. Due to the complexity of these documents, customers usually accept these terms without understanding them completely. Our objective is to support customers' comprehension of such privacy contracts. By helping the average customer in understanding these contracts, we hope to foster more awareness regarding data privacy and individual rights regarding personal data usage. A natural interaction with the knowledge base is a precondition for the a positive usability by the average citizen. Conversational agents, that enhances traditional chatbots by adding contexts and users' goals, are well-known for their ability to guide the user towards the required information. They were already adopted successfully in context such as cybersecurity [9], health [13], and agriculture [11].

Fig. 1. Project graphical abstract: a customer is dealing with a privacy related agreement online and cannot fully understand the terms and conditions. Before approving it, they would like to clarify some aspects, using a conversational agent, that can point to the better suited document in a Q&A collection.

As part of this objective, our idea is to develop a smart Knowledge Base (KB) composed of documents that can be matched with the specific question a user has. This will work as the intelligence behind a simple conversational agent which we propose as a self-help tool. This should be able to solve the most common and standard questions, but will likely fail for more specific needs.

Figure 2 presents the case where the smart KB alone is inadequate in resolving customer doubts (a), either by not finding a fit-enough answer in the Q&A or by receiving a negative feedback from the customer on the provided answers set. In this situation, the system can propose to provide suggestion for legal scholars that can analyse the remaining open points and provide the user with a personalised answer. Specifically, the same knowledge base (b) will be employed to find matches between the question and human experts' profiles (c) resulting in a ranked list of specialised legal scholars and their rates (d), amongst which the customer can choose to receive a tailor-made interpretation (e). This can provide a rapid and low-cost option to clarify specific questions. Additionally, user feedback regarding the perceived quality of answers and experts suggested will be collected to internally improve performance and experts' profiles. Our final vision is to provide a one-stop-solution for every user's privacy-oriented questions.

The creation of the smart KB and its matching algorithm will be based on Natural Language Processing (NLP) in order to support the adoption of natural language in the interaction with the user, and to naturally support a conversational agent interface.

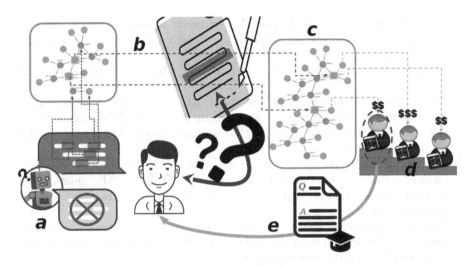

Fig. 2. Expert support: a request to the conversational agent is failed or not satisfactory (**a**), so the system uses the smart KB (**b**) to checks amongst the available experts (**c**) a pool of suitable professionals to answer the specific question, considering both its depth and breath. As results, a ranked list of professional is returned to the consumer together with the fees required by each of them (**d**). The customer can then select the preferred one, pay the fees and receive the qualified answer to his question (**e**). The answer is then stored and its evaluation is used to update the expert's profile for the following interactions.

Requirements Elicitation

The main aspects such a one-stop solution should provide were identified as from the following list, that will be refined and extended during the project development:

1. The knowledge base (KB) should include documents of different origin and scope, and should consider their legal relevance and normative strength in the analysis. The main identified categories are:
   (a) Legislative acts (at different level: international, European, national)
   (b) Juridical acts (Court & Administrative cases)
   (c) Regulatory (such as guidelines and recommendations advises from Data Protection Agencies (DPA))
   (d) Consumer organisations
   (e) Online Publications of Legal Research (both professional and non-professional)
   (f) Company Policies
2. An abstraction layer should be included in the KB, to recognise concepts included in documents and natural language statements and their relationships, thus homogenising their internal representation

3. The abstraction layer should provide a granular approach [19], in order to allow the joint consideration of specificity (depth) and coverage (breath) of a given input

4. Should be possible to extend the smart KB, by adding/updating data at all levels.

5. The underlying technology for the smart KB should offer a standardised and repeatable automated way to regenerate it, and should require minimal human intervention in the process (thus banning any rule-based approach for document analysis)

6. The produced inference process on users input should privilege the run-time efficiency, to allow scalability of the solution. The offline KB update could be more computationally expensive, but should be possible to run it without putting offline the service

7. The newly produced legally qualified content by human experts should be indexed and be available for the conversational agent, thus extending dynamically and focused the coverage of the KB

8. The KB should be usable to profile legal scholars based on their specialisation and to rank them as the better suited to answer a specific user request, based on the matching on depth and breath of the knowledge required fro answering with the expertise offered by the human expert

Additionally, the KB will be initially developed using the English language only, but should be possible to include multilingualism in a further stage. This is important for integration of European privacy-regulations, but also for countries with more than a single official language, such as Switzerland, were we plan to start from.

Based on these requirements, the following steps were taken, as described next. Section 3 report the results of the manual data collection, whether in Sect. 4 the automatic process of company privacy policy gathering and validation is described. Those two parts form the base for the initial KB and abstraction layer creation, as from the requirements [1–3]. Regarding requirements [5,6], Sects. 5 and 6 provide some initial exploration and potential directions for further research. Section 7 depicts some of the open issue still to be solved to provide a one-stop solution for a privacy-related expert finder. Eventually, the steps already taken and the future direction towards a usable system are sketched in Sect. 8, that concludes our contribution.

3   Manual Data Collection

AS stated before, currently we focus only on English based documents. The first part of the data collection was performed manually by experts. This part concentrates equally on all categories listed within the Requirement 1, with a particular attention in having an overall coverage of all levels. Table 1 resume the result of the manual data collection process.

An observation is that category (a) has a finite number of documents, being legislative acts privacy-relevant a bounded set, given a specific scope and language. Juridical acts (b) increases in time, but in a slow way, being official

Table 1. Manual data collection results, as from requirement [1] in Sect. 2.

ID	Category	#Subcategory	#Documents (EN)
(a)	Legislation	9	78
(b)	Juridical acts	9	189
(c)	Regulatory	6	123
(d)	Consumer organisations - guidelines	5	48
(e)	Online Legal Research	6	209
	≫ (e.1) *Professional*	*3*	*132*
	≫ (e.2) *Non-professional*	*3*	*77*
(f)	Privacy Company Policies[a]	4	256
TOTAL		**39**	**903**

[a] These policies appear in the website of the companies, and they represent a manually selected set of highly relevant companies operating on the Swiss/European market, in particular Germany, Austria and Switzerland (DACH).

acts that requires a significant official tribunal involvement. Thus, at a specific moment in time, the coverage that can be guaranteed in the manual data collection appears to be sufficient. A similar reasoning applies for Regulatory (C) and Consumer Organisation Guidelines (d). Category (e) of Online Legal Research (professional and non), these are User Generated Content (UGC) and we plan to not rely too much on them, at least at the beginning. Eventually, for Privacy Company Policies (f) an initial set of highly relevant document was compiled, retrieved and saved by hand in the project repository, but due to the cost of this data collection, an automatic process was implemented, as described in the next section.

4 Company Privacy Policies

As part of our approach in building a smart KB, we ascertained a need to develop a larger database of company privacy policies. This database could be used for several purposes, such as training language models and learning privacy-related concepts in real-world data, that will not be possible on the amount of privacy policy collected with the manual approach (∼250). Upon literature review, we found a few studies which developed a similar privacy policy database [1,2,15]. [2] is a relevant study which used historical data from the *Wayback Machine* to crawl privacy policy data. While useful, our objective required a slightly different approach since we require recently crawled privacy policies rather than historical ones.

Adapting our approach from [2], we first needed to identify a catalogue of companies with their respective web domains, headquarter locations and rough sizes. While [2] used the Alexa Rank[1] to identify domains for crawling, we

---

[1] https://www.alexa.com/topsites.

decided to use the 7+ Million Company data set[2] to start our crawling process. This was mainly because the 7+ Million Company data set offered metadata on companies that other sources did not. Upon retrieving this data set, we filtered the entries and kept company data where web domains and headquarter locations were available. Following this initial filtering, we crawled company domains using the following two distinct approaches.

4.1 Raw Crawl

We coin the crawling first approach as *Raw Crawl*. For this approach, we visited each company's domain and searched the raw web pages for certain regular expressions. In case this page was in the English language, we searched for terms such as *"privacy"* and *"data protection"*. In case this page was not in English, we used separate regular expressions, such as *"en"* and *"eng"*, to attempt to find an English language version of the page. All scraped results were saved in a SQLite database.

4.2 Search Engine

We coin the second crawling approach as *Search Engine*. Here, we utilised the crawling power of search engines in order to find respective privacy policies. Specifically, we used the DuckDuckGo[3] search engine API to search for and retrieve company's privacy policies. This had an added benefit of providing cleaner data. Similar to the first approach, we saved all scraped results in a SQLite database.

4.3 Policy Classifier

While crawling and scraping data from the web, it is common to encounter noise in the form of unintended documents and languages. While there exist several ways to mitigate such noise, we decided to follow a pre-tested approach from [2]. This approach involves utilising a Random Forests (RF) privacy policy classifier, which essentially classifies a given document as a privacy policy or

Table 2. Hyperparameters used for our Random Forests privacy policy classifier

Hyperparameter	Value	Description
Minimum DF	0.1	Minimum document term frequency for consideration
N-gram range	1–4	Word-level N-gram ranges used as inputs
Maximum depth	15	Maximum depth of each decision tree
Minimum leaf samples	3	Minimum number of samples at each leaf node
Estimators	200	Number of decision trees in the forest

---

[2] https://www.kaggle.com/peopledatalabssf/free-7-million-company-dataset.
[3] https://duckduckgo.com/.

Table 3. Summary statistics from our two crawling strategies; "en" refers to English language documents; filtered policies refer to policies which exceeded a classifier probability threshold of 0.75

Approach	# Companies	# Policies	# Policies [en]	# Filtered policies [en]
Raw Crawl	655'374	746'345	634'950	475'726
Search Engine	5'404	5'404	5'355	3'057
TOTAL	660'778	751'749	640'305	478'783

not given a certain confidence threshold. Similar to [2], we trained a Random Forests ensemble classifier [3] on annotated privacy policies retrieved from the study's publicly available data sources. For training this classifier, we utilised word-level TF-IDF features and hyperparameters as mentioned in Table 2. Our best privacy policy classifier achieved a precision and recall of 98.9% and 89.5% respectively at a probability threshold of 0.75. We used this aforementioned classifier threshold to partition our scraped data such that we only kept privacy policies of high quality.

4.4 Manual Evaluation

In order to test the RF classifier, and our assumption that only good quality privacy policy will get accepted with this setting, we performed a short manual evaluation. First we created for classes of outcome, based on the achieved probability closeness to the threshold:

- STRONG REJECT: documents with probabilities significantly inferior to the threshold ($p \ll 0.75$)
- WEAK REJECT: documents not in the previous class and presenting probabilities inferior but close to the minimum level ($0.75 - \epsilon < p < 0.75$)
- STRONG ACCEPT: documents with probabilities significantly superior to the threshold (close to the unit) ($p \gg 0.75 \implies p \simeq 1$)
- WEAK ACCEPT: documents not in the previous class and presenting probabilities superior but close to the minimum level ($0.75 \leq\, < p < 0.75 + \epsilon$)

We then sample 14 documents for each category and asked four users (u1 .. u4) to evaluate the documents as valid privacy policy (1) or not (0). The results of this evaluations are reported in the Table 4. This result clearly shows a strong agreement between the annotators themselves, as well as between the annotators and the RF model.

Table 4. Classifier manual evaluation: all the documents accepted by the RF are also accepted by the human evaluators, while some of the documents (close to the probability threshold) will be rejected even if a human user could accept them as valid.

Category	Evaluation	U1	U2	U3	U4
STRONG REJECT	1	0	0	0	0
	0	14	14	14	14
WEAK REJECT	1	0	1	1	3
	0	14	13	13	11
WEAK ACCEPT	1	14	14	14	14
	0	0	0	0	0
STRONG ACCEPT	1	14	14	14	14
	0	0	0	0	0

4.5   Results

Table 3 shows the results of our two crawling approaches. We utilised the *Raw Crawl* approach more frequently than the *Search Engine* approach due to rate limiting from the latter which slowed down our overall crawls. In total we were able scrape ~660K companies and obtain ~480K filtered English-language privacy policies; specifically those whose classifier probabilities exceeded our preset threshold of 0.75. In addition, we were able to obtain privacy policies from various European languages such as Dutch, French and German as a side-effect of our crawling approaches. These additional languages could potentially be used for downstream multi-lingual privacy analysis tasks.

5   Question Answering

Another essential aspect of our smart KB involves gathering real-world questions and answers related to privacy. This data could be used to train and evaluate our language models in the legal privacy domain. To do this, we first identified two important data sources for questions and answers; namely Law Stack Exchange and Reddit. In the next subsections, we describe these sources and our crawling approaches further.

5.1   Law Stack Exchange

Law Stack Exchange[4] is a subset of Stack Exchange where questions and answers are limited to the legal domain. We found this to be a good source of questions and answers for our smart KB. To crawl this data source, we simply utilised the Stack Exchange Data Dumps[5] and extracted data containing any of the

---

[4] https://law.stackexchange.com/.
[5] https://archive.org/details/stackexchange.

Table 5. Summary statistics from our Law Stack Exchange and Reddit question answering data

Source	# Questions	# Answers	Answers per question
Law Stack Exchange	1'349	1'988	1.47
Reddit	45'742	190'666	4.17
TOTAL	47'091	192'654	4.09

"gdpr", *"privacy"*, *"data-protection"*, *"data-ownership"*, *"ccpa"*, *"confidentiality"*, *"coppa"*, *"ferpa"*, *"can-spam-act-of-2003"* and *"tcpa"* tags into a SQLite database.

5.2 Reddit

Reddit is another source of useful questions and answers in the privacy domain. Based on our analysis, we found the *"gdpr"*, *"privacy"*, *"europrivacy"*, *"privacylaw"*, *"netneutrality"* and *"eff"* subreddits to be most useful for our smart KB. We utilised `pushshift.io`[6] to retrieve submissions and comments from the aforementioned subreddits and extracted this information into the same SQLite database.

5.3 Results

Table 5 shows a summary of the questions and answers extracted from Law Stack Exchange and Reddit. We can observe that Law Stack Exchange has fewer overall questions and answers, as well as answers per question, compared to Reddit. The difference could be attributed to Reddit being a more conversational platform with several exchanges per question compared to Law Stack Exchange being more formalised.

5.4 Unsupervised ML Evaluation

Before fine-tuning language models on our question answering data, we ran unsupervised evaluation on these questions and answers using pre-trained language models. This would give us a baseline as to how well various language models perform. For simplicity, we performed unsupervised evaluation only on the Law Stack Exchange data set. Our methodology for unsupervised evaluation is as follows:

1. Encode all questions and answers based on the specific model to get vector representation with 768 dimensions
2. Calculate the cosine similarity of each question-answer pair

---

[6] https://github.com/pushshift/api.

Table 6. Unsupervised question answering evaluation for Law Stack Exchange

Language model	Evaluation mode	K-candidates	Accuracy
SBERT (all-mpnet-base-v2) [16]	Local	1	**0.844**
		2	0.979
		3	0.991
		4	0.999
		5	1.000
	Global	1	**0.607**
		2	0.746
		5	0.838
		10	0.896
		20	0.931
Legal-BERT (legal-bert-base) [6]	Local	1	0.815
		2	0.973
		3	0.991
		4	0.997
		5	0.999
	Global	1	0.086
		2	0.116
		5	0.166
		10	0.210
		20	0.262

3. Evaluate local (find best answer from one thread) and global (find best answer from all answers of the data set) by selecting a set of K candidate answers
4. Calculate the accuracy depending on whether the target answer is within the first K candidates

Table 6 shows a summary of unsupervised evaluations for SBERT [16] and Legal-BERT [6]. Here, we observe that SBERT outperforms Legal-BERT for both the local and global evaluation modes. This also makes sense since SBERT is trained to produce reasonable sentence representation and is partly fine-tuned on QA data. This provides us with interesting insights, since we simultaneously require the legal language understanding of Legal-BERT and the question-answering capacity of SBERT. A combined approach towards our smart KB will likely involve combining the training approaches for SBERT and Legal-BERT.

Table 7. Macro-F_1 evaluation scores for ECtHR-A, ECtHR-B, SCOTUS and EUR-LEX

Model	ECtHR-A	ECtHR-B	SCOTUS	EUR-LEX
Legal-BERT (Small) [6]	**0.626**	**0.694**	**0.597**	0.482
Distil-BERT (Base) [17]	0.611	0.691	0.559	**0.515**
Mini-LM [24]	0.551	0.610	0.455	0.356
BERT-Tiny [22]	0.440	0.504	0.357	0.250

Table 8. Macro-F_1 evaluation scores for LEDGAR, UNFAIR-ToS and CaseHOLD

Model	LEDGAR	UNFAIR-ToS	CaseHOLD
Legal-BERT (Small) [6]	**0.820**	**0.817**	**0.729**
Distil-BERT (Base) [17]	0.815	0.794	0.686
Mini-LM [24]	0.796	0.132	0.713
BERT-Tiny [22]	0.733	0.111	0.662

5.5   Potential Bias

As per Table 6, we observed that SBERT had a significantly higher global unsupervised performance than Legal-BERT. To investigate causes, we looked into potential biases in the input data that could assist SBERT. We found that several answers had parts of the question quoted in them. We suspected these quotations to be forms of bias that could have contributed to the high performance of SBERT. An open task in question answering is to investigate how strongly the quotes in answers bias existing language models.

6   LexGLUE

An important part of developing our smart KB is to develop appropriate benchmarks for evaluation. Recent developments in NLP show a shift towards multi-task benchmarks for evaluating language models. As our focus is in the legal and privacy domain, we decided to use the LexGLUE benchmark from [8] as a starting point for benchmarking our smart KB. LexGLUE consists of 7 English language tasks from the legal domain; namely ECtHR-A [4], ECtHR-B [7], SCOTUS [18], EUR-LEX [5], LEDGAR [21], UNFAIR-ToS [12] and CaseHOLD [25].

Due to limited resources, we decided to start testing small and medium-sized Transformer language models on the LexGLUE benchmark. We envisioned these models as potential candidates for our smart KB. Tables 7 and 8 summarise the results of four smaller-sized models on the LexGLUE benchmark. Here, we can observe the Legal-BERT (small) performs the best on all tasks except EUR-LEX. After computing these scores, we reported these test results to [8] in order to support their benchmarking of multiple models.

While LexGLUE represents a comprehensive benchmark for evaluating our smart KB, we strongly believe in the creation of more appropriate benchmarks for our use-case. Since our smart KB is envisioned to perform open domain read-and-retrieve along with basic reading comprehension tasks, we would need to augment our evaluation benchmark with such tasks.

7   Expert Finder

As described in Sect. 2, the smart KB can cover the most general cases, where an answer is already present and the level are satisfactory for the consumer's needs. Anyway, when the system is unable to provide an answer or the user is not satisfied with the focus or precision of the reported resources, a second level support will be proposed to the user, involving the expertise of legal scholars, and some personalised fees to be paid for the service. In order to provide the best match (not always the most expert person in the subject asked, but with the right combination of proficiency focus and depth) the proposed solution will use again the granular knowledge base to map contributions of participating layers into juridical profiles comparable with questions characterisation. Thus, the same smart KB can be adopted to overcome the major barriers present in current expert finder systems, namely:

1. Explicit declaration of skills and knowledge by experts can be biased
2. Lack of consideration for different areas of expertise and different levels of knowledge
3. Classification of questions with regard to content has to be done manually and is a very complex/time-consuming task for users
4. Knowledge evolves over time, and capturing this evolution explicitly is problematic
5. Difficulty in determining which legal domain a question fits in, leading to sub-optimal forwarding of questions to experts
6. The cost of answering a question is fixed instead of being related to the complexity of the question

Our system will solve those issue, by moving the experts profile creation from an explicit, manually-declared process to an implicit, automatically-tracked approach. On top of it, time evolution will be considered, as newly provide answers from legal scholars will be used to align their internal characterisation in terms of both expertise focus and depth. Eventually, consumer's feedback will be used to build a reputation system, that will cooperate with the expert profiles to determine their positioning in the ranked list suggested to the user.

8   Conclusion

This positional paper advocates the creation of a convenient and cost-efficient question-answering service for answering customers' queries on data privacy.

It proposes a dual step approach: first by developing a conversational agent supported by a smart knowledge base which attempts to answer the question using the most appropriate legal document. In case the first step is insufficient, our system enacts a second step and suggests a ranked list of legal experts for focused advice. All of the matching will be supported by a granular knowledge base, enabling semantic matching between consumer's questions and privacy related documents or legal scholars providing the second-level support under the payment of fees personalised based on the specificity and coverage of the asked support.

To create the smart KB, after identifying some initial long-term requirements, we started classifying and collecting relevant documents. After manually retrieving most part of the stable and accessible sources, we turned to crawling and scraping companies' privacy policies along with real-world questions and answers from Law Stack Exchange and Reddit, to create a large enough dataset to be usable for Machine Learning approaches. We have also performed unsupervised ML evaluation on the Law Stack Exchange, which showed promising results for SBERT. Finally, we ran the LexGLUE benchmark on small and medium-sized language models. The results of this benchmark showed promising results for Legal-BERT. We determined that our smart KB would need to utilise training procedures from both SBERT and Legal-BERT.

To create our expert finder system, we first identified significant issues that we would need to overcome. With these open issues listed, we will start developing the expert finder in the next steps.

Acknowledgement. The research leading to this work was partially financed by *Innosuisse* - Swiss federal agency for Innovation, through a competitive call. The project 50446.1 IP-ICT is called *P2Sr Profila Privacy Simplified reloaded: Open-smart knowledge base on Swiss privacy policies and Swiss privacy legislation, simplifying consumers' access to legal knowledge and expertise.* (https://www.aramis.admin.ch/Grunddaten/? ProjectID=48867). The authors would like to thanks all the people involved on the implementation-side at Profila GmbH (https://www.profila.com/) for all the constructive and fruitful discussions and insights provided about privacy regulations and consumers' rights.

References

1. Ahmad, W., Chi, J., Tian, Y., Chang, K.W.: PolicyQA: a reading comprehension dataset for privacy policies. In: Findings of the Association for Computational Linguistics: EMNLP 2020, pp. 743–749. Association for Computational Linguistics (2020). https://www.aclweb.org/anthology/2020.findings-emnlp.66
2. Amos, R., Acar, G., Lucherini, E., Kshirsagar, M., Narayanan, A., Mayer, J.: Privacy policies over time: curation and analysis of a million-document dataset. In: Proceedings of The Web Conference 2021, WWW '21, p. 22. Association for Computing Machinery (2021). https://doi.org/10.1145/3442381.3450048
3. Breiman, L.: Random forests. Mach. Learn. **45**(1), 5–32 (2001). https://doi.org/10.1023/A:1010933404324

4. Chalkidis, I., Androutsopoulos, I., Aletras, N.: Neural legal judgment prediction in English. In: Proceedings of the 57th Annual Meeting of the Association for Computational Linguistics, pp. 4317–4323. Association for Computational Linguistics, Florence, Italy (2019). https://doi.org/10.18653/v1/P19-1424. https://aclanthology.org/P19-1424

5. Chalkidis, I., Fergadiotis, M., Androutsopoulos, I.: MultiEURLEX - a multi-lingual and multi-label legal document classification dataset for zero-shot cross-lingual transfer. CoRR abs/2109.00904 (2021). https://arxiv.org/abs/2109.00904

6. Chalkidis, I., Fergadiotis, M., Malakasiotis, P., Aletras, N., Androutsopoulos, I.: LEGAL-BERT: the muppets straight out of law school. In: Findings of the Association for Computational Linguistics: EMNLP 2020, pp. 2898–2904. Association for Computational Linguistics (2020). https://doi.org/10.18653/v1/2020.findings-emnlp.261

7. Chalkidis, I., Fergadiotis, M., Tsarapatsanis, D., Aletras, N., Androutsopoulos, I., Malakasiotis, P.: Paragraph-level rationale extraction through regularization: a case study on European court of human rights cases. In: Proceedings of the 2021 Conference of the North American Chapter of the Association for Computational Linguistics: Human Language Technologies, pp. 226–241. Association for Computational Linguistics (2021). https://doi.org/10.18653/v1/2021.naacl-main.22. https://aclanthology.org/2021.naacl-main.22

8. Chalkidis, I., et al.: LexGLUE: a benchmark dataset for legal language understanding in English. CoRR (2021). arXiv: 2110.00976

9. Franco, M.F., Rodrigues, B., Scheid, E.J., Jacobs, A., Killer, C., Granville, L.Z., Stiller, B.: SecBot: a business-driven conversational agent for cybersecurity planning and management. In: 2020 16th International Conference on Network and Service Management (CNSM), pp. 1–7. IEEE (2020)

10. Gstrein, O.J., Beaulieu, A.: How to protect privacy in a datafied society? A presentation of multiple legal and conceptual approaches. Philos. Technol. **35**(1), 1–38 (2022). https://doi.org/10.1007/s13347-022-00497-4

11. Jain, M., Kumar, P., Bhansali, I., Liao, Q.V., Truong, K., Patel, S.: FarmChat: a conversational agent to answer farmer queries. In: Proceedings of the ACM on Interactive, Mobile, Wearable and Ubiquitous Technologies, vol. 2, no. 4, pp. 1–22 (2018)

12. Lippi, M., et al.: CLAUDETTE: an automated detector of potentially unfair clauses in online terms of service. Artif. Intell. Law **27**(2), 117–139 (2019). https://doi.org/10.1007/s10506-019-09243-2

13. Meier, P., Beinke, J.H., Fitte, C., Behne, A., Teuteberg, F.: FeelFit - design and evaluation of a conversational agent to enhance health awareness. In: Krcmar, H., Fedorowicz, J., Boh, W.F., Leimeister, J.M., Wattal, S. (eds.) Proceedings of the 40th International Conference on Information Systems, ICIS 2019, Munich, Germany, 15–18 December 2019. Association for Information Systems (2019). https://aisel.aisnet.org/icis2019/is_health/is_health/22

14. Prince, C., Omrani, N., Maalaoui, A., Dabic, M., Kraus, S.: Are we living in surveillance societies and is privacy an illusion? An empirical study on privacy literacy and privacy concerns. IEEE Trans. Eng. Manag. 1–18 (2021). https://doi.org/10.1109/TEM.2021.3092702

15. Ravichander, A., Black, A.W., Wilson, S., Norton, T., Sadeh, N.: Question answering for privacy policies: combining computational and legal perspectives. In: Proceedings of the 2019 Conference on Empirical Methods in Natural Language Processing and the 9th International Joint Conference on Natural Language Processing (EMNLP-IJCNLP), pp. 4949–4959. Association for Computational Linguistics, Hong Kong (2019). https://doi.org/10.18653/v1/D19-1500. https://www.aclweb.org/anthology/D19-1500

16. Reimers, N., Gurevych, I.: Sentence-BERT: sentence embeddings using Siamese BERT-networks. In: Proceedings of the 2019 Conference on Empirical Methods in Natural Language Processing. Association for Computational Linguistics (2019). https://arxiv.org/abs/1908.10084

17. Sanh, V., Debut, L., Chaumond, J., Wolf, T.: DistilBERT, a distilled version of BERT: smaller, faster, cheaper and lighter. CoRR abs/1910.01108 (2019). http://arxiv.org/abs/1910.01108

18. Spaeth, H., et al.: Supreme court database code book (2020). https://scdb.wustl.edu

19. Stalder, F., Denzler, A., Mazzola, L.: Towards granular knowledge structures: Comparison of different approaches. In: 2021 IEEE 19th World Symposium on Applied Machine Intelligence and Informatics (SAMI), pp. 261–266. IEEE (2021)

20. Strycharz, J., Ausloos, J., Helberger, N.: Data protection or data frustration? Individual perceptions and attitudes towards the GDPR. Eur. Data Prot. L. Rev. **6**, 407 (2020)

21. Tuggener, D., von Däniken, P., Peetz, T., Cieliebak, M.: LEDGAR: a large-scale multi-label corpus for text classification of legal provisions in contracts. In: Proceedings of the 12th Language Resources and Evaluation Conference, pp. 1235–1241. European Language Resources Association, Marseille (2020). https://aclanthology.org/2020.lrec-1.155

22. Turc, I., Chang, M., Lee, K., Toutanova, K.: Well-read students learn better: the impact of student initialization on knowledge distillation. CoRR abs/1908.08962 (2019). http://arxiv.org/abs/1908.08962

23. Wachter, S., Mittelstadt, B., Russell, C.: Counterfactual explanations without opening the black box: automated decisions and the GDPR. Harv. JL Tech. **31**, 841 (2017)

24. Wang, W., Wei, F., Dong, L., Bao, H., Yang, N., Zhou, M.: MiniLM: deep self-attention distillation for task-agnostic compression of pre-trained transformers. CoRR abs/2002.10957 (2020). https://arxiv.org/abs/2002.10957

25. Zheng, L., Guha, N., Anderson, B.R., Henderson, P., Ho, D.E.: When does pretraining help? Assessing self-supervised learning for law and the CaseHOLD dataset. CoRR abs/2104.08671 (2021). https://arxiv.org/abs/2104.08671

Improving Rank-N Identification Rate of Palmprint Identification Using Permutation-Based Indexing

Mizuho Yoshihira[1], Ayumi Serizawa[1], Ryosuke Okudera[1], Yumo Ouchi[1],
Yuya Shiomi[1], Naoya Nitta[2], Masataka Nakahara[2], Akira Baba[2], Yutaka Miyake[2],
Tetsushi Ohki[1], and Masakatsu Nishigaki[1(✉)] ⓘ

[1] Shizuoka University, Hamamatsu, Shizuoka, Japan
nisigaki@inf.shizuoka.ac.jp
[2] KDDI Research, Inc, Fijimino, Saitama, Japan

Abstract. Biometric information can have high similarity among different people but high variability within the same person. Therefore, it is difficult to identify a person or distinguish between two people based on biometric information. One way to address these issues is to use certain biometric information as pivots to define the feature space of biometric information. However, previous research has not sufficiently examined methods for selecting these pivots. In this study, schemes for pivot selection and robust palmprint identification are proposed that can improve the rank-N identification rate.

Keywords: Biometric recognition · Palmprint identification · Permutation-based indexing

1 Introduction

Biometric information has advantages over other sources of personally identifiable information as it cannot be forgotten or lost. Further, biometric recognition is convenient because it does not require a password. Therefore biometric recognition has been used not only for smartphone login but also as a means of identity confirmation for purposes such as access control and payment systems. Several different approaches have been proposed with different modalities such as fingerprints, face, and iris [1]. This study is focused on palmprint identification as it is superior in terms of availability, i.e., biometric information can be obtained in a contactless manner via a camera built into a smartphone, social acceptability, i.e., the psychological burden caused by privacy concerns regarding the acquisition of biometric information is lesser than it would be for faces, and convenience, i.e., it can identify a person without the need to enter a user ID.

Figure 1 shows a pipeline for simple palmprint identification. In the enrollment phase, the users present their biometric information, i.e., their palmprint image, which is then enrolled into the database as a *template*. In the identification phase, the biometric information is obtained as a *query* from the user in the same manner as in the enrollment phase, and the system compares the query with the templates enrolled within the database.

A. Moallem (Ed.): HCII 2022, LNCS 13333, pp. 78–93, 2022.
https://doi.org/10.1007/978-3-031-05563-8_6

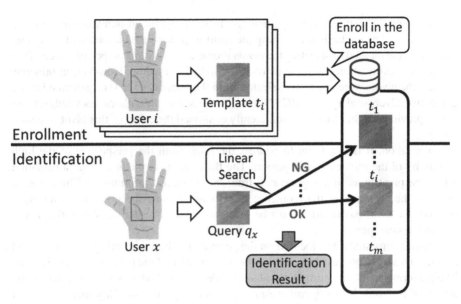

Fig. 1. A scheme for simple palmprint identification.

An issue with biometric recognition is that it can be difficult to distinguish between two people because biometric information generally has *high similarity* among different people and *high variability* within the same person (see Fig. 2). The conventional feature space defined for representing various types of images, such as dogs, bicycles, teacups, etc., cannot be sufficiently capable of distinguishing the differences in the biometric information between users. Furthermore, there is a general issue of the time required for the biometric identification increasing as the number of enrollees (templates) increases.

To resolve these issues, the *pivot-based indexing method* has been proposed to define the feature space of the biometric information using certain templates as *pivots*, i.e., representative points for calculating the distance to a template or a query [2–4]. Maeda et al. proposed a method of defining biometric features using a set of matching scores referred to as a *matching score vector* between each pivot and templates or query, where the pivots are a subset of the templates randomly selected from the enrolled templates [2]. The matching score vector can aid in finding a more similar template to the query in a step-by-step manner. Using this method, the user (template) that is most similar to the query can be identified in less time than that required for a linear search. Murakami et al. proposed to reduce the time required for the biometric identification by sorting the templates in order of similarity using a similarity search [3, 4]. The templates can be quickly sorted in order of similarity using a ranked matching score vector as an index referred to as a *permutation-based index*. The performance of the biometric identification might improve by comparing the query with the templates in order of similarity. and therefore, Murakami et al.'s pivot-based indexing method is known as the *permutation-based indexing method*.

Due to the high similarity of the biometric information, using a feature space with poor discriminability of the biometric information may affect the accuracy and speed of the biometric identification significantly. In the pivot-based indexing method, the pivots are used as the basis for forming the feature space of the biometric information. Therefore, the method of selecting the pivots is crucial to improve the performance of the biometric identification using the pivot-based indexing method. However, in previous studies, the pivots were randomly selected from the templates [2, 3] or generated using generative adversarial networks (GANs) [4]. To the best of the authors' knowledge, there are no previous studies that have sufficiently examined the effect of this pivot selection process.

In addition, it is important to address the issue from the perspective of the high variability of the biometric information. The fluctuations in the biometric information affect the pivot-based index generated from the biometric information. Therefore, to improve the accuracy of the biometric identification using the pivot-based indexing method, the pivot-based index must be made robust against the variability that exists within the same person.

Initially, this study was focused on the permutation-based indexing method [3] and two schemes were proposed to improve the performance of the palmprint identification. The performance of the permutation-based indexing method was evaluated using the aspect of the *rank-N identification rate*, the percentage of possibility that the correct template is contained within the top N ranks of the sorted templates. This paper is organized as follows. An account of the previous studies on pivot-based indexing methods is presented in Sect. 2. The proposed methods that improve the permutation-based indexing method by introducing the two schemes are explained in Sect. 3. The experimental settings and the experimental results are discussed in Sect. 4 and 5, respectively. Finally, Sect. 6 contains the conclusions derived from this study.

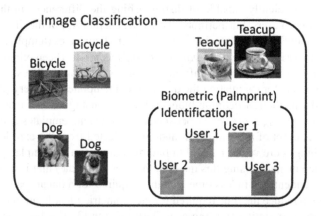

Fig. 2. Image classification and biometric identification.

2 Related Works on Pivot-Based Indexing Methods

A naive biometric identification method involves linear search, in which the verification, that is, the one-to-one matching between a query and a template, is performed starting from the top of the database storing all the enrollees' templates. However, with this strategy, the expected number of comparisons increase linearly with the number of enrollees (templates) [1]. Various solutions have been proposed to reduce the number of such comparisons by dividing the templates into several clusters [5, 6] or by sorting the templates in order of similarity [2, 3]. The former approach has limits in terms of scalability as the number of templates belonging in a cluster could still become large as the number of enrollees increase.

For the latter approach, the sorting accuracy depends on how the feature space of the biometric information is defined. There is no known general method to determine the feature space deductively; however, it has been shown that using certain biometric information as reference points or a basis (referred to as pivots) is effective [2, 3]. This is because the biometric information of another person will have a higher matching score, within the range below the threshold, when the similarity between the biometric information is slightly high, and a lower matching score when the similarity is completely low. In this study, these have been referred to as the *pivot-based indexing methods*.

2.1 Matching Score Vector for Biometric Identification

Maeda et al. proposed a method for defining a feature space of biometric information using a randomly selected subset of enrolled templates as pivots [2]. The comparison score set or the matching score vector between the pivots and biometric information was used as the biometric feature. The number of comparisons and the response time of the biometric identification could be greatly reduced compared to a linear search using the matching score vector to select a template with a higher correlation as the next template to be compared, as depicted in Fig. 3. To the best of the authors' knowledge, this study constitutes the first attempt to define biometric features based on comparisons with each pivot.

2.2 Permutation-Based Indexing

Murakami et al. proposed a method that uses the templates of certain enrollees as the pivots and characterizes the biometric information according to the order of the magnitude of comparison with each pivot, as shown in Fig. 4 [3]. This method is an example of applying permutation-based indexing, which is known as an efficient similarity search method for images and documents, for biometric identification [3,7, 8].

In the enrollment phase, the indexes are created from the templates using the pivot, and they are enrolled in the database. In the identification phase, a permutation-based index of a query is first calculated, and then the templates with the highest similarity are retrieved from the database and matched in order of similarity.

The similarity between the two indexes π_a and π_b is calculated using the Spearman Rho correlation coefficient, as shown in Eq. 1. m is the number of elements of each pivot, and $\pi(i)$ denotes the i th element in the permutation-based index π.

$$s(\pi_a, \pi_b) = \sum_{i=1}^{m} |\pi_a(i) - \pi_b(i)|^2 \tag{1}$$

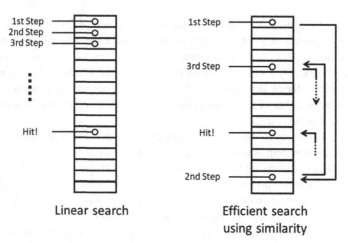

Fig. 3. Linear search and efficient search using similarity. (Quoted from [2], with certain modifications.)

In Reference [3], the identification algorithm is multiplexed by combining the permutation-based indexing with the score level fusion technique in the Bayes decision rule to achieve efficient multimodal biometric identification. Moreover, instead of randomly selecting the pivots from the templates, a method for generating them using generative adversarial networks (GANs) has been proposed [4]. However, as the purpose of the current method is to prevent privacy leakage from templates used as pivots, the generation of pivots that improve identification accuracy has not been considered.

3   Proposed Methods

3.1   Challenges Identified Within Previous Studies with Approaches for Improvement

In the existing pivot-based indexing methods [2–4] described in Sects. 2.1 and 2.2, the method of selecting the pivots which are the basis for forming the feature space of the biometric information has a significant impact on the identification accuracy and speed. However, in all the existing methods, the pivots are selected randomly, and the pivot selection method is put down as a future concern. To be precise, in reference [2] the number of pivots is analyzed theoretically; however, the selection of the pivots is based on the most accurate from the combinations chosen at random. In addition, the existing methods do not emphasize on the robustness of the pivot-based index against the variability of the biometric information within the same person.

In this study, two schemes are proposed for constructing pivots with efficient properties in terms of spatial separability of the pivots (Sect. 3.2) and robustness of the permutation-based index (Sect. 3.3). The nature of the biometric information, which is both (i) highly similar between different people and (ii) highly variable within the same person, renders biometric identification difficult. The former scheme aims to move the biometric features of different people away from each other, which contributes to

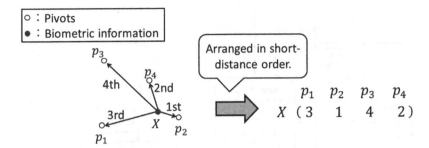

Fig. 4. A scheme for creating a permutation-based index from a template and pivots.

improving the pivot-based indexing method from the viewpoint of nature (i). The latter scheme aims to absorb the variations within the biometric features of the same person, which contributes to improving the pivot-based indexing method from the viewpoint of nature (ii).

The aim of this study is to improve the rank-N identification rate of palmprint identification using permutation-based indexing. The pipeline for the improved palmprint identification is shown in Fig. 5.

3.2 PCA-Based Pivot Orthogonalization

To improve the spatial separability of the pivots, pivot orthogonalization based on principal component analysis (PCA) is proposed, to efficiently select the pivots that improve the rank-N identification rate of palmprint identification. Specifically, the templates (palmprint images of the enrollment phase) of all enrollees are subjected to two-dimensional PCA to generate a sequence of the principal component images, and the first p members of the sequence are used as pivots. In this study, $p = 30$ was set throughout the preliminary experiments. This scheme has been referred to as *PCA-based pivot orthogonalization*.

PCA is a popular technique used to find an optimal representation of data. However, it has not yet been applied to pivot selection for palmprint identification using permutation-based indexing method. The orthogonalization of the pivots, that is, the basis that forms the feature space of the biometric information, is expected to increase the discriminability of the biometric information. Thus, improvements in the feature space property can be achieved using PCA-based pivot orthogonalization.

3.3 Index-Based Template Selection

To improve the robustness of the permutation-based index generated based on the biometric information, a scheme was adopted in which multiple palmprint images were obtained from each user at the time of enrollment, and the palmprint image with the most stable permutation-based index was selected as the template of the user. This scheme is referred to as the *index-based template selection*.

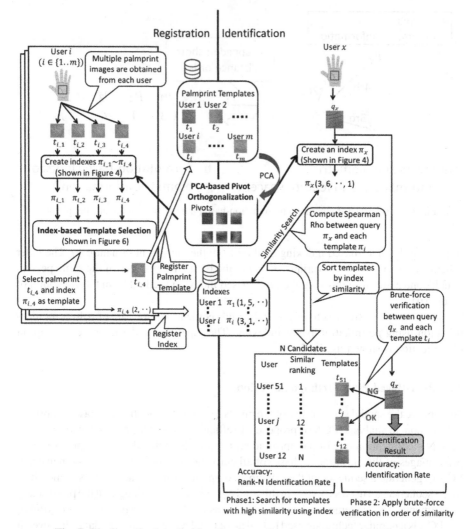

Fig. 5. Pipeline of palmprint identification using permutation-based indexing.

The specific procedure for the index-based template selection is as follows. First, t palmprint images (templates) $T_{u,1}, \cdots, T_{u,t}$ are obtained from any user u for enrollment and the permutation-based index $\pi_{T_{u,i}}$ is created for each palmprint image $T_{u,i}$. Next, using Eq. (2), the permutation-based index $\pi_{T_{u,s}}$ is chosen from $\{\pi_{T_{u,1}}, \cdots, \pi_{T_{u,t}}\}$ which minimizes the sum of the distances between the permutation-based indexes. The index $\pi_{T_{u,s}}$ and the corresponding palmprint image $T_{u,s}$ are registered as user u's template.

$$\pi_{T_s} = \underset{\pi_{T_j} \in \{\pi_{T_1}, \cdots, \pi_{T_t}\}}{\arg\min} \sum_{\substack{i=1 \\ i \neq j}}^{t} S(\pi_i, \pi_j) \tag{2}$$

Equation (2) selects the palmprint image closest to the center (on the distance scale of Eq. (1)) from t palmprint images of candidate within the same person. This contributes to creating a template that is robust against the high variability within the same person introduced with each palmprint image acquisition. Thus, improvement of the rank-N identification rate can be achieved by the index-based template selection. Figure 6 shows a schematic of the index-based template selection.

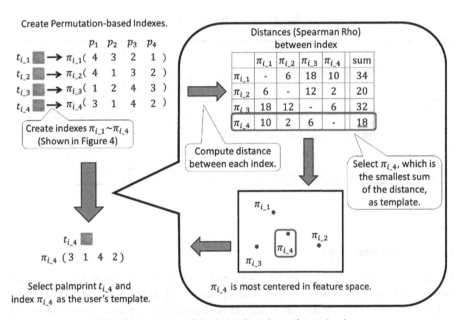

Fig. 6. A scheme of the index-based template selection.

4 Experiments

4.1 Experimental Patterns

To evaluate the effectiveness of the PCA-based pivot orthogonalization and index-based template selection proposed herein, the rank-N identification rate is compared with the five evaluation patterns, A through E, as shown in Table 1.

When a query (a palmprint image for identification) is entered into the palmprint identification system, the templates of all enrolled users (all palmprint images enrolled in the palmprint identification system) are sorted in order of similarity to the query. Pattern A is sorted using the existing permutation-based indexing method as described in Sect. 2.2. Patterns B and C modify pattern A by applying PCA-based pivot orthogonalization scheme and index-based template selection, respectively. Pattern D is the proposed method, in which both schemes are applied together to pattern A.

Pattern E is the control group, and band-limited phase-only correlation (BLPOC) [9] in low resolution is used to sort the templates of all the enrollees in order of similarity to the query. More specifically, the center region 128×128 [px] of the palmprint image was cropped and the matching score calculated using the BLPOC algorithm for palmprint recognition proposed in [10] with only the center $k \times k$ of the frequency domain. Through preliminary experiments, $k = 32$ was empirically adopted for speed and accuracy (hereafter referred to as "32-BLPOC"). The matching score is used as the similarity.

Table 1. Evaluation patterns.

	Template Sorting Method	Apply	
		PCA-based Pivots Orthogonalization	Index-based Template Selection
A	Permutation-based Indexing		
B		✓	
C			✓
D		✓	✓
E	BLPOC in low resolution		

4.2 Experimental Steps

As explained in Sect. 3.1, the pipeline from enrollment to identification in the proposed method (pattern D) is shown in Fig. 5. The pipelines for pattern C, B, and A differ from that for pattern D only by the difference between having or not having the PCA-based pivot orthogonalization, index-based template selection, and both together, respectively. The pipeline for pattern E includes a procedure for sorting the templates with a low-resolution BLPOC in a brute-force manner, instead of using the pivots and indexes.

These pipelines are composed of two stages: template sorting and exact matching. The performances of patterns A to E were evaluated for each stage. In the first stage, the rank-N identification rate for patterns A to E was calculated by applying the sorting method for each pattern and evaluating whether the template for the query user x is included within the top N positions of the resulting sorted templates. In the second stage, the identification accuracy of patterns A to E was calculated by repeatedly performing a one-to-one comparison (known as *verification* in biometric recognition) of the query and template, starting from the top of the sorted templates, and evaluating whether the identified user is determined to be user x. For this comparison in the proposed experiment, the BLPOC algorithm was used for palmprint recognition [10]. Further, the time required to sort the templates and for the one-to-one comparison after sorting were compared.

4.3 Experimental Environment

The execution environment used for the experiment is shown in Table 2.

Table 2. Execution environment.

CPU	Intel Core i7-11375H 3.3 GHz
RAM	LPDDR4X-4266 16 GB
OS	Ubuntu 20.04 LTS
Container engine	Docker 20.10.5
Language	Python 3.6.9

4.4 Dataset and Preprocessing

Ten palm images from both hands of 523 users (523 users $\times$ 2 hands $= 1,046$ enrollees) were acquired. Each of the ten palm images was divided into two groups in order of acquisition; five images were prepared as templates for registration and five images as queries for identification.

The palmprint images were created by performing the following preprocessing on all the palm images. Figure 7 shows examples of the palm and palmprint images used in this study.

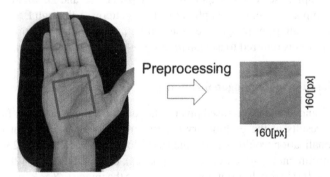

Fig. 7. Examples of palmprint images used in the evaluation experiments.

1. Apply the procedures used in [11] for cutting out the palmprint region of interest (ROI) in the palm image.
2. Resize the ROI of the palmprint to 160 × 160 [px].
3. Convert RGB color space to YUV color space and create a 160 × 160 [px] grayscale image with only Y values as a palmprint image.

4.5 Matching Score-based Template/Query Selection

As described in Sect. 4.4, in this experiment, five palmprint images were provided per user for enrollment and five for identification.

In the enrollment phase, for each user, the image closest to the center (in terms of the distance measure of the verification algorithm) was selected from the five enrollment images using Eq. (3), and this image was enrolled in the identification system database as the template for the user. This operation is referred to as *matching score-based template selection*.

$$q_s = \underset{q_j \in \{q_1, \cdots, q_v\}}{\arg \max} \sum_{\substack{i=1 \\ i \neq j}}^{v} M\left(q_i, q_j\right) \tag{3}$$

Here, $q_1, \cdots, q_v$ is the biometric information, and M is the verification algorithm. In this experiment, $v = 5$ was used and M is 32-BLPOC.

Owing to the use of matching score-based template selection, the palmprint images selected as templates are robust against the high variability within the same person. In other words, matching score-based template selection has a purpose similar to index-based template selection as described in Sect. 3.3, in that it increases the robustness of the biometric information. However, the difference is that index-based template selection contributes to a more stable permutation-based index, whereas the matching score-based template/query selection contributes to a more stable extraction of the palmprint images. Notably, the verification (one-to-one matching between a query and a template) is performed in the second stage of all the patterns A through E. In other words, it is necessary for all patterns A to E to choose a robust palmprint image in the enrollment phase. Hence, index-based template selection is applied to only patterns C and D, whereas matching score-based template selection is applied to all the patterns A through E.

This type of palmprint image selection can be applied in the identification phase, too. This operation is referred to as *matching score-based query selection*.

4.6 PCA-Based Pivot Orthogonalization

For patterns B and D, the PCA-based pivot orthogonalization was applied. In this study, based on the results of the preliminary experiments, it was decided that PCA-based pivot orthogonalization would be performed as follows. For each of the 5,230 palmprint images for enrollment (1,046 enrollees × 5 images), cut out the center 128 × 128 [px] from the 160 × 160 [px] palmprint image and reduce the image to 8 × 8 [px] to create an intermediate image. The results of the PCA for all the intermediate images are 64 basis images (8 × 8 [px]). The 30 basis images from the 1st to the 30th principal components were used as the pivots, as depicted in Fig. 8.

To calculate the matching score between a palmprint image (160 × 160 [px]) and each pivot (8 × 8 [px] base image), firstly, an intermediate image of the palmprint image was created in the same manner by cutting out the center 128 × 128 [px] and reducing the image to 8 × 8 [px]. Secondly, the normalized cross correlation (NCC) between this intermediate image and the basis image was calculated, and the NCC score was used as the matching score between the palmprint image and the base image.

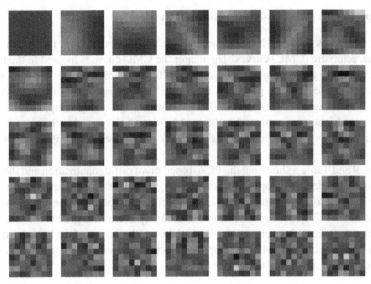

Fig. 8. Image obtained through the principal component analysis of a template. (Image size 8 × 8[px], from the 1st to the 30th principal components)

4.7 Index-Based Template Selection

For patterns C and D, index-based template selection was applied. In this case, five palmprint images were prepared for the enrollment of all users, therefore, $t = 5$ in Eq. (2) of Sect. 3.3.

In the case of a server-client identification system, the palmprint images captured by the client was sent to the server, and a palmprint identification was executed in the server. By capturing a series of images for the sequence of actions when the user presents his palm, the client device could capture multiple palmprint images. Therefore, the client device can always perform matching score-based template/query selection and send only the most stable palmprint image to the server. As matching score-based template/query selection is an operation that is completed within the client device, it can be used for both the enrollment and identification phases. Conversely, to perform the index-based template selection, the matching score with each pivot must be calculated. As the pivots are stored on the server, the client alone cannot perform the index-based template selection. Although it is possible to execute an index-based template selection on the server side by sending all the palmprint images captured by the client device to the server in the enrollment phase, the intention is to minimize the communication between the client and server during every identification transaction. Therefore, the index-based template selection is applied only during the enrollment phase.

5 Results

5.1 Experiments on Rank-N Identification Rate

Figure 9 compares the rank-N identification rate of patterns A to E using cumulative match characteristic (CMC) curves. The nearer the CMC curve is located to the top, the more accurate the performance. The rank-1 /5/20 identification rates for each pattern are shown in Table 3. Here, pattern E is a brute force comparison of the query to all the templates using a low-resolution BLPOC, involving sorting templates in a time-consuming and foolproof manner. In other words, pattern E is possibly the most accurate, and the question is in what manner the accuracy of patterns A through D approaches that of pattern E.

Figure 9 and Table 3 show that the PCA-based pivot orthogonalization and the index-based template selection proposed in this paper contribute to the improvement of the rank-N identification rate of palmprint identification using permutation-based indexing. The effect of the PCA-based pivot orthogonalization (pattern B) is greater than that of the index-based template selection (pattern C), and the combined use of the PCA-based pivot orthogonalization and index-based template selection (pattern D) achieves an accuracy that greatly surpasses that of pattern A.

Table 3. Comparison rank-1/5/20 identification rate for each pattern.

Pattern	Rank-1 identification rate [%]	Rank-5 [%]	Rank-20 [%]
A	26.77	45.32	62.43
B	67.11	79.64	87.09
C	29.06	48.66	67.21
D	71.89	84.23	91.20
E	97.99	98.95	99.52

5.2 Experiments on the Identification Accuracy and Required Time

The identification accuracy and time required for patterns A to E were evaluated in terms of speed and the number of comparisons. For the evaluation, the number of times the verification (one-to-one matching) was terminated was fixed to ensure that the success rate of identification for all the patterns would be 98%. Table 4 shows the results of the number of times the verification was repeated to find the identified person (average

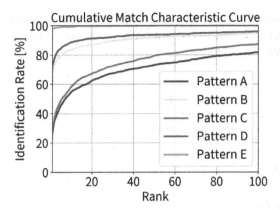

Fig. 9. Comparison of the rank-N identification rate for each pattern with the CMC curves.

number of verifications) and the time required to find the identified person (average time required and maximum time required).

The average number of verifications in Table 4 further confirms that the efficiency of the palmprint identification improved in order of the index-based template selection (Pattern C), PCA-based pivot orthogonalization (Pattern B), and the combination of both methods (Pattern D), which was consistent with the results of Fig. 9 and Table 4. The average processing time in Table 4 shows that patterns A through D outperform the control group (pattern E) in terms of processing speed.

For a more precise comparison of the processing speed, the breakdown of the average time required for patterns D and E is shown in Fig. 10. Pattern E is a brute force comparison of the query to all the templates using a low-resolution BLPOC. As shown in Table 4, the average number of verifications in pattern E can be suppressed by sorting the templates over time to ensure high quality sorting. With the improvement in the permutation-based indexing in this study, Pattern D succeeded in significantly reducing the time required to sort the templates; however, the quality of sorting was not at par with that of pattern E, which is the reason for the average number of verifications in pattern

Table 4. Performance comparison when the identification success rate was set to 98%.

Pattern	A	B	C	D	E
Number of times to terminate verifications	724	705	525	508	4
Average number of verifications	70.64	30.45	48.35	21.01	1.068
Standard deviation of the number of verifications	147.25	113.44	102.32	81.26	0.4333
Average processing time [s]	0.2764	0.1307	0.1932	0.09371	0.6405
Standard deviation of the average processing time [s]	0.5375	0.4201	0.3692	0.2931	0.02961
Maximum processing time [s]	2.6613	2.6590	1.8980	1.8529	0.9067

D being greater. However, the reduction in the processing time required for sorting was overwhelming, therefore, pattern D consumed approximately 1/6th of the time required for the entire identification process.

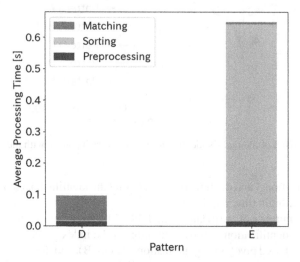

Fig. 10. Comparison of average processing time between patterns D and E.

6   Conclusion

In this study, a method to improve the accuracy of template retrieval by applying PCA-based pivot orthogonalization to palmprint identification using permutation-based indexing to improve the spatial separability of pivots was proposed. Furthermore, the application of index-based template selection to multiple permutation-based indexes obtained from multiple biometric records was suggested to improve the robustness of permutation-based index. The results confirmed that the proposed methods improved the rank-N identification rate and reduced the time required for palmprint identification.

References

1. Bolle, R.M., Connell, J.H., Pankanti, S., Ratha, N.K., Senior, A.W.: Guide to Biometrics. Springer, New York (2004). https://doi.org/10.1007/978-1-4757-4036-3
2. Maeda, T., Matsushita, M., Matsushita, K.: Identification algorithm using a matching score matrix. IEICE Trans. Inf. Syst. **E84-D**(7), 819–824 (2001)
3. Murakami, T., Takahashi, K.: Fast and accurate biometric identification using score level indexing and fusion. In: The IEEE/IAPR International Joint Conference on Biometrics, Washington, D.C., pp. 1–8 (2011)
4. Murakami, T., Fujita, R., Ohki, T., Kaga, Y., Fujio, M., Takahashi, K.: Cancelable permutation-based indexing for secure and efficient biometric identification. IEEE Access **7**, 45563–45582 (2019)

5. Kamei, T., Mizoguchi, M.: Fingerprint preselection using eigenfeatures. In: IEEE Computer Society Conference on Computer Vision and Pattern Recognition, Santa Barbara, California, pp. 918–923 (1998)
6. Germain, R.S., Califano, A., Colville, S.: Fingerprint matching using transformation parameter clustering. IEEE Comput. Sci. Eng. **4**(4), 42–49 (1997)
7. Chávez, E., Figueroa, K., Navarro, G.: Effective proximity retrieval by ordering permutations. IEEE Trans. Pattern Anal. Mach. Intell. **30**(9), 1647–1658 (2008)
8. Amato, G., Savino, P.: Approximate similarity search in metric spaces using inverted files. In: The 3rd International Conference on Scalable Information Systems (InfoScale '08), Brussels, Belgium, pp. 1–10 (2008)
9. Ito, K., Nakajima, H., Kobayashi, K., Aoki, T., Higuchi, T.: A fingerprint matching algorithm using phase-only correlation. IEICE Trans. Fundam. Electron. Commun. Comput. Sci. **E87-A**(3), 682–691 (2004)
10. Ito, K., Iitsuka, S., Aoki, T.: A palmprint recognition algorithm using phase-based correspondence matching. In: 16th IEEE International Conference on Image Processing (ICIP), Cairo, Egypt, pp. 1977–1980 (2009)
11. Nitta, N., Nakahara, M., Baba, A., Miyake, Y.: A method for estimating palmprint regions using skeletal information in palmprint authentication. In: Symposium on Cryptography and Information Security (SCIS 2021), vol. 3F3-2, pp. 1–6 (2021). (in Japanese)

Securing Software Defining Network from Emerging DDoS Attack

Temechu G. Zewdie and Anteneh Girma[(⊠)]

University of the District of Columbia, Washington, DC 20008, USA
temechu.zewdie@udc.edu

Abstract. Software-Defined Network (SDN) is a way to manage networks that separate the control plane from the forwarding plane [1]. The cloud provides a powerful computing platform that enables individuals and organizations to perform different tasks on the internet. Nowadays, many types of attacks compromise SDN in a Cloud computing platform. Out of these attacks, this research will focus on Distributed Denial of Service (DDoS) in IP trace.

DDoS attacks can have a significant impact against single tenanted architectures [2]. Thus, securing such a system is not trivial, but we can maximize the security level of a computing environment. This paper proposes a new solution approach that can be identifying, manage, and mitigate DDoS attacks. Besides, create a threat information database that will use as a reference for further investigation.

Finally, the proposed solution does not consider all types of DDoS attacks and AI/Machine learning detection solutions for attack detection and mitigation.

Keywords: Security · Software-defined network · Cloud computing · Distributed Denial of service attack

1 First Introduction

According to The Open Web Application Security Project (OWASP), the Denial of Service (DoS) attack focused on making a resource (site, application, and server) unavailable for the purpose it was designed [3]. Researchers proved that the goal of a DDoS attack is to cut off users from a server or network resource by overwhelming it with requests for service [4]. DDoS attacks continue to grow in frequency, volume, and severity as the technology grows. As Kaspersky research Lab reports, a DDoS attack can cost a company over $1.6 million. It is a staggering sum for any company precisely with financial damage to businesses can be severe [4].

Arbor Networks Inc is a leading provider of network security and management solutions for enterprise and service provider networks. In their report, Many world-leading financial service institutions and banks experienced significant outages and slowdowns due to politically motivated DDoS attacks [5]. Nowadays, even if many different DDoS detection and protection solutions providers exist, the DDoS attack has simultaneously grown its frequency, complication, and attack [6].

© The Author(s), under exclusive license to Springer Nature Switzerland AG 2022
A. Moallem (Ed.): HCII 2022, LNCS 13333, pp. 94–103, 2022.
https://doi.org/10.1007/978-3-031-05563-8_7

Therefore, from such an incident and attack, we realized that there should be an alternative and better detection and mitigation techniques has been done to address the DDoS attack problem. Thus, our solution approach is designed based on SDN-based solutions that can be scale-up for wide area networks.

1.1 Problem Statements

Software-defined network (SDN) and Cloud computing are emerging technology that has a lot of benefits for end-customer, high-end machines, infrastructure, storage, and high availability of a system with a competitive advantage [7]. Security is the availability of network service, the integrity system, and confidentiality. Data are an obstacle to SDN networks in cloud computing success [8].

Nowadays, several attacks compromise the SDN network in a cloud. Out of these attacks, denial of Service that has been coming from ping flood and Smurf, exploit ICMP, and Distributed Denial of Service (IP traceback) are the significant ones that affect SDN network in a cloud [9]).

In this regard, this research will review the details of security issues and find out a critical challenge. Security Information and Event Management (SIEM) helps monitor the network for malicious activities [10], and the main challenge of SIEM solutions is identifying the legitimate resource request from a threat. But the algorithm or a design correlated to the data is poorly designed to detect a threat.

Furthermore, as a FireEye survey, 37 percent of respondents receive more than 10,000 alerts each month. Of those alerts, 52 percent were false positives, and 64 percent were redundant alerts [11].

Once we identified the problem, the next issue will be mitigating and taking necessary action. Moreover, the most solution has not a treat management database that can capture the signatures for further investigation and research on DDoS attacks.

1.2 Our Proposal

Our proposed detection and mitigation solution can assure the security of Software-Defined Networking from Distributed Denial of Service attacks in a cloud computing platform.

In our solution approach works in the following manner. First, a request is coming to our system. Then, a suggested system keeps information of the attacker such as login id, IP address, and mac address of the requester. If ID, IP address, and mac address is new or not kept before in our threat database, our proposed system is considered a legitimate user.

Next, if a request existed in a treat database, the proposed system would check the database whether this request is coming within a given period not for more than ten times in a consecutive minute. If it is less, this request is legitimate and can grant access to exploit the resources.

However, if a request attempt is more than ten times within a given minute, our proposed system will consider as a treat. The new proposed system automatically denied access and registered all the pertinent information in our treat database for further investigation and research.

1.3 Contribution

During our study, we observed several SIEM solutions (like Hobbit, Nessus) works to identify incidents and Prevent SDN from distributed denial of service attacks in the cloud computing platform. The following are our research contributions,

- Introduce a new solution or a way of distinguishing a capturing a DDoS attack in SDN network
- Propose a new Solution to mitigate a detected attack and secure the SDN based cloud platform
- Create a threat information database that can use as a reference and further investigation from the previous attempts

In the next section, we review the current state-of-the-art (related work) to gain further knowledge about Software-Defined Networking (SDN), Distributed Denial of Service attack, and cloud computing. Then, the paper will discuss the methodology and Proposed Solution. Finally, analysis and discussion, conclusion, and future work will execute respectively.

2 Related Work

More recent work that merges in this field will be reviewed and highlighted in this section.

2.1 Themes on Software-Defined Networking Concept and Architecture

With numerous SDN-enabled devices in development and production, software-defined networking (SDN) is rapidly moving from vision to reality [12]. SDN architecture broadly consists of three layers, i.e., Application layer, control, and infrastructure [13].

The application layer is an open area to develop an innovative application as possible by leveraging all the network information about network topology, state, network statistics, etc. [13].

The Control layer is the land of the control plane where intelligent logic in SDN controllers would reside to control network infrastructure [13]. Here in this layer, a lot of business logic is being written in the controller to fetch and maintain different types of network information, state details, topology details, statistics details, and more [13].

The infrastructure layer comprises various networking equipment that forms the underlying network to forward network traffic [13]. It could be a set of network switches and routers in the data Centre. This layer would be the physical one over which network virtualization would be laid down through the control layer (where SDN controllers sit and manage the underlying physical network) [13] (Fig. 1).

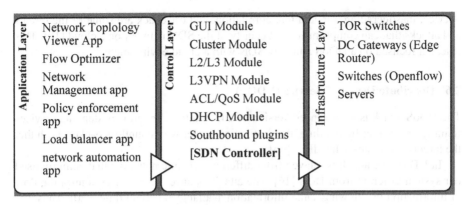

Fig. 1. SDN architecture and components [13]

2.2 Theme on SDN Security

Security is needed everywhere, and it needs to design and build secured architecture to the respective platform as needed. Security is all about the availability of network service, the integrity of a system, and the confidentiality of data [14]. According to Krishna and Sreeniv, Software-defined networking (SDN) brings numerous benefits by decoupling the control plane from the data plane; there is a contradictory relationship between SDN and distributed denial-of-service (DDoS) attacks [15].

2.3 Theme on Cloud

Clouds provide a powerful computing platform that enables individuals and organizations to perform various tasks. For instance, the use of online storage space, adoption of business applications, development of customized computer software, and creation of a "realistic" network environment is typical examples of cloud computing [16]. Despite its benefits, this multitenant cloud environment presents severe security threats and privacy vulnerabilities to both the cloud infrastructure and cloud users [17].

2.4 Theme on Cloud Security

Cloud computing represents an exciting computing paradigm shift in information technology. Security and privacy perception are primary obstacles to its wide adoption [17]. A cloud computing infrastructure includes a cloud service provider, which provides computing resources to cloud end users who consume those resources [17].

2.5 Security Threats and Attacks on Cloud

Threat: is an actor who wants to attack assets in the cloud [16] or any circumstance or event that can adversely impact organizational operations [18]. Meanwhile, an attack is an attempt to gain unauthorized access to system services, resources, or information or any attempt to compromise system integrity [14]. Eavesdropping, alteration, denial of

Service, masquerading, repudiation, correlation, and traceback are some of the threats and attacks that can compromise the Security of the SDN network on a cloud [19]. This research focused on a DDoS attack in SDN with a cloud environment.

2.6 Distribute Denial of Service (DDOS)

The DDoS attack is an advanced version of a DoS attack. In terms of denying services running on a server by flooding, the destination server with countless packets such that the target server cannot handle it [16].

In DDoS, the attack is relayed from different dynamic networks that compromised our system different from DOS [16]. The attackers have the power to control the flow of information by allowing some information available at certain times [20]. Thus, the amount and type of information available for public usage are clearly under the attacker's control [20]. According to new research by Qiao Yan and F. Richard Yu, there will be Possible DDoS attacks on SDN and available solutions [21] (Table 1).

Table 1. Possible DDoS attacks on SDN and available solutions [21]

Possible DDoS attacks	Attack implementation methods	Available solutions
Application layer DDoS attacks	By attacking application	FortNOX
	By attacking North bounded API	
Control layer DDoS attack	By attacking controller	Transport Layer Security (**TLS**) FortNOX AVANT-GUARD
	By attacking northbound API	
	By attacking southbound API	
	By attacking westbound API	
	By attacking eastbound API	
Infrastructure layer DDoS attacks	By attacking switch	Transport Layer Security (**TLS**) AVANT-GUARD
	By attacking southbound API	

2.7 DDOS Attack Over Time

DDoS attacks over time will dramatically increase, which means a lot of sites will tend to compromise [22] (Fig. 2).

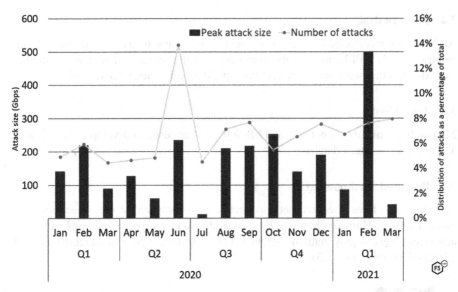

Fig. 2. DDoS attack trend for 2020 [22]

3   Methodology

In this section, the researcher will discuss in-depth specific procedures for collecting and analyzing data. Based on the collected data, the researcher addresses the objective of the research.

3.1   Document Analysis

Secondary data from documents, such as articles, IT Security Policies, Procedures, guidelines, and Reports of IT of DDOS attack specifically focused on SDN in the cloud computing environment.

3.2   Interview and Focus Group Discussion

Primary data will collect from selected professionals. Interview and focus group discussions had conducted with various expert staff. The discussion focused on how frequently DDoS attacks hit their environment and managed. These will find information on how DDoS attacks undergoing SDN in cloud computing environment-related challenges.

3.3   Empirical Study

In this research, an empirical study will be conducted to answer specific issues Such as DDoS attacks across the SDN-based cloud system and identify the DDoS attacks across the SDN in a cloud environment. Moreover, it asses' different ways or algorithms that can easily identify DDoS attacks and mitigation techniques and overall impact on the entire system's security.

3.4   Data Analysis

All information collected from document review, interview, focus group discussion, and empirical study will be used in the final output of the research. The analysis method carried out in this study will comprise both qualitative and quantitative [24].

3.5   Tools Used

Microsoft visual studio (.net 6.2) and MSSQL2014 are used to develop the application and manage the attack database.

3.6   Proposed Methodology

SDN Seems to have a secured network architecture compared to the conventional IP-based networks. However, SDN itself is vulnerable to many types of network intrusions and faces severe deployment challenges [1]. The following proposed architecture will address the problem (Fig. 3).

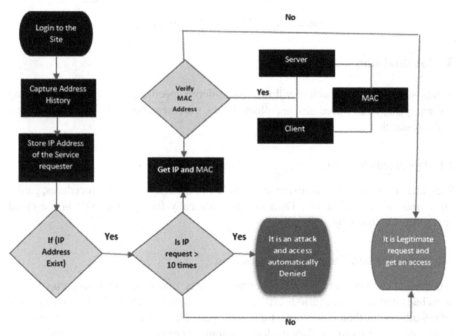

Fig. 3. Proposed architecture

4   Result and Discussion

In this experiment, we can identify the incidents, detect the attack and classify these attacks whether they are legitimate or not. Then, managing the incident and capturing all signatures for further reference are steps that we are performed.

In the first step, we tested the proposed solution by several lists of attackers. Then, a proposed solution updates users' profile and device information such as Mac address and IP Address. Based on the IP Address, each time the user arrives at the application is analyzed. When the new user enters into the application continuously, the new proposed system will determine whether the captioned traffic is a DDoS attack or not.

Correspondingly our experiment checks the coming traffic IP Address. If it is a new IP address and not stored before in our temp database, such a request is considered legitimate traffic, and the system will offer access to explore the required resources. In the meantime, If the request fulfilled all the priors' criteria, then the number of attempts will be the next value the system checked. Suppose the incoming request (Traffic) hits the server within 5 second more than ten times; the proposed system will not grant access to explore the required resources because such traffic is considered an attack. If it is considered an attack, our system right away records the captioned traffics its' all metadata in our log capturing database for further investigation and research. But if it is less than ten times, our new system will consider the incident legitimate and grant access.

Hence, our proposed solution can prevent the system from DDoS attacks, increase efficiency, and ensure the system's performance. Finally, we can also enrich our database for malicious request information from future attacks.

5 Conclusion and Recommendation

Software-defined networking (SDN) is an architecture that aims to make networks agile and flexible in prioritizing, deprioritizing, or even blocking specific types of packets with a granular level of control and security. When we come to cloud computing, it is a multi-tenant architecture that can manage traffic loads flexibly and more efficiently [28].

Nowadays, an acute cyber threat in the SDN-based cloud environment increased rapidly, in which distributed denial-of-service (DDoS) attack is one of the most damaging cyber-attacks. This paper proposes an efficient solution to tackle DDoS attacks in the SDN-based cloud environment.

This paper deeply examines how a DDoS attack happens in Software-Defined Networking with a Cloud computing platform and proposes a solution to protect a Software-Defined Networking with a Cloud computing environment from a DDoS attack.

Finally, the proposed solution can identify the attack, mitigate the attack, and create a threat database for further reference and investigation.

6 Future Work

Currently, many attacks compromise the SDN network in a cloud computing environment. This paper only examines and considers Distributed Denial of Service attacks with IP traceback. Still, other types of attack such as ping flood and Smurf exploit ICMP are not exhaustively examined. Moreover, the proposed solution is not considered a Machine learning technique to detect and classify DDoS attacks.

References

1. Scott-Hayward, S., O'Callaghan,G., Sezer, S.: SDN security: a survey (2013). http://tarjom efa.com/wp-content/uploads/2017/08/7602-English-TarjomeFa.pdf. Accessed 08 Aug 2019
2. Joshi, B., Vijayan, A.S., Joshi, B.K.: Securing cloud computing environment against DDoS attacks. In: International Conference on Computer Communication and Informatics, Coimbatore (2012)
3. OWASP: Open Web Application Security Project, OWASP (2019). https://www.owasp.org/index.php/Denial_of_Service. Accessed 1 July 2019
4. Kaspersky: Distributed denial of service: anatomy and impact of DDoS attacks (2019). https://usa.kaspersky.com/resource-center/preemptive-safety/how-does-ddos-attack-work. Accessed 01 July 2019
5. Shackleford, D.: DDoS attacks inans customer report, June 2013. http://pages.arbornetw orks.com/rs/arbor/images/IANS%20Arbor%20Networks%20Custom%20Report%20(2).pdf. Accessed 10 July 2019
6. Bawany, N.Z., Shamsi, J.A., Salah, K.: DDoS attack detection and mitigation using SDN: methods, practices, and solutions. Arab. J. Sci. Eng. **42**(2), 425–441 (2017). https://doi.org/10.1007/s13369-017-2414-5
7. Sharma, R.: A review on cloud computing- an emerging technology, June 2013. https://www.ijser.org/researchpaper/A-Review-on-Cloud-Computing-An-Emerging-Technology.pdf. Accessed 07 June 2019
8. Jain, R., Paul, S.: Cloud networking and communications, November 2013. https://www.cse.wustl.edu/~jain/papers/ftp/net_virt.pdf. Accessed 01 June 2019
9. Goodrich, M.T., Tamassia, R.: Introduction to Computer Security, in Computer Security, pp. 256–263. Library of Congress, Boston (2011)
10. Majeed, A., Rasool, R., Ahmad, F., Alam, M., Javaid, N.: Near-miss situation based visual analysis of SIEM rules for real time network security monitoring. J. Ambient. Intell. Humaniz. Comput. **10**(4), 1509–1526 (2018). https://doi.org/10.1007/s12652-018-0936-7
11. Francis, R.: CSO, 3 May 2017. https://www.csoonline.com/article/3191379/false-positives-still-cause-alert-fatigue.html. Accessed 28 Aug 2019
12. Scott, S., O'Callaghan, G., Sezer, S.: SDN security: a survey, August 2019. http://tarjomefa.com/wp-content/uploads/2017/08/7602-English-TarjomeFa.pdf. Accessed 06 June 2019
13. Arora, H.: Software Defined Networking (SDN) - Architecture and role of OpenFlow (2019)
14. Cyber Security Review, 16 Nov 2018. https://cybersecurityreviews.net/2018/11/16/a-quick-guide-to-important-sdn-security-issues/. Accessed 06 June 2019
15. Reddy, V.K., Sreenivasulu, D.: Software-defined networking with DDoS attacks in cloud computing, December 2016. http://ijitech.org/uploads/523416IJIT13210-702.pdf. Accessed 29 Aug 2019
16. Kayode, A., Adesola, O.: Threat handling and security issue in cloud computing. Int. J. Sci. Eng. Res. **6**(11), 1371–1385 (2015)
17. Ren, K., Wang, C., Wang, Q.: Security challenges for the public cloud. IEEE Internet Comput. **16**(1), 69–73 (2012). https://doi.org/10.1109/MIC.2012.14
18. NIST. https://nvlpubs.nist.gov/nistpubs/ir/2013/NIST.IR.7298r2.pdf. Accessed 08 June 2019
19. Goodrich, M.T., Tamassia, R.: Introduction to Computer Security. Library of Congress, Boston (2011)
20. Paul, V., Prasadh, K.: Scattered alter position attacker detection of app-DDoS attacks, DDoS attacks with gaussian-polynomial distribution model. Int. J. Comput. Sci. Eng. (IJCSE) **3**(4), 1 (2014)
21. Qiao Yan, F., Richard, Y.: Distributed denial of service attacks in software-defined networking with cloud computing. IEEE Commun. Mag. **53**(4), 52–59 (2015)

22. Warburton, D.: DDoS attack trends for 2020, 07 May 2021. F5. https://www.f5.com/labs/art icles/threat-intelligence/ddos-attack-trends-for-2020

23. Jackson, B.: Kinsta, 20 May 2019. https://kinsta.com/blog/ddos-attack/. Accessed 01 Aug 2019

24. Zewdie, T. G.: International Conference on Human-Computer Interaction. In: HCI International 2020 – Late Breaking Posters, Copenhagen (2020)

25. Phan, T., Park, M.: Efficient distributed denial-of-service attack defense in SDN-based cloud. IEEE **7**, 18701–18714 (2019)

26. ONF: Open Network Foundation (2019). https://www.opennetworking.org/sdn-defini tion/. Accessed 01 June 2019

27. Feghali, A., Kilany, R., Chamoun, M.: SDN security problems and solutions analysis. In: International Conference on Protocol Engineering (ICPE) and International Conference on New Technologies of Distributed Systems (NTDS) (2015)

28. Litemind. https://litemind.com/problem-definition/. Accessed 01 July 2019

29. ThousandEyes, (2018). https://marketo-web.thousandeyes.com/rs/thousandeyes/images/Tho usandEyes_White_Paper_DDoS_Attack_Analysis.pdf. Accessed 29 Aug 2019

Trustworthiness and User Experience in Cybersecurity

User Experience, Knowledge, Perceptions, and Behaviors Associated with Internet of Things (IoT) Device Information Privacy

Maria Chaparro Osman(✉) [ID], Andrew Nakushian [ID], Summer Rebensky [ID], Tricia Prior [ID], and Meredith Carroll [ID]

Florida Institute of Technology, Melbourne, FL 32901, USA
mchaparro2016@my.fit.edu

Abstract. Internet of Things (IoT) devices are becoming ubiquitous in the 21st-century world. Most individuals have interacted with at least one device such as an Alexa, Ring doorbell, or Nest thermostat. Many of these devices have access to personal information; however, the information security of these devices and the privacy of the personal information stored on these devices is not well understood by users. A survey was conducted to examine users' experience, knowledge, perceptions, and behaviors associated with those devices' privacy and security. The survey results revealed that participants perceive there is a risk with their IoT devices, however, there are two key issues that prevent them protecting themselves. First, they appear to have limited cybersecurity knowledge, including limited knowledge of who is accessing their data and for what purpose. Second, they do not always take the necessary precautions due to the inconvenience of such actions. These findings demonstrate that the privacy paradox is prevalent among users of IoT devices.

Keywords: Internet of Things · Privacy · Smart home · Survey · Privacy paradox

1 Introduction

Internet of Things (IoT) devices are becoming ubiquitous in the 21st-century. IoT is defined by Suresh (2014) as "a connection between humans – computers [via the internet] – things (p. 2, [1])." In simpler terms, IoT devices are everyday items that are connected to the internet. Examples of IoT devices include but are not limited to smartphones, smart thermostats, smart doorbells, and smartwatches. These devices present privacy and security challenges. Privacy refers to any rights the user has to control the collection, storage, and use of their personal information, while security refers to how the personal information on that device is protected against misuse [2]. As these connected devices gain popularity and acceptance into society, users' understanding of their device's privacy affordances is important to maintaining the security of users' information. Research has shown that many IoT device users do not recognize the risk to their privacy that their IoT devices pose [3]. Additionally, users have been shown to trust

A. Moallem (Ed.): HCII 2022, LNCS 13333, pp. 107–123, 2022.
https://doi.org/10.1007/978-3-031-05563-8_8

device manufacturers to protect their privacy [4]. A study by the Pew Research Center, a non-partisan data-driven social science/public policy research institute in the United States, found that the median score on a cybersecurity knowledge quiz administered to American adult internet users was only 5 out of 13 (equivalent to a score of 38%) [5]. This finding suggests that the cybersecurity/internet privacy knowledge of the general public is limited. Given the increase in IoT devices and their adoption by the public, this lack of knowledge is a concern.

When it comes to privacy, users have expressed that ensuring their information stays private is incredibly important [6]. However, many users' actions often do not reflect the level of importance they assign to privacy [6]. The disparity between users expressing concern for maintaining their privacy and actions taken is known as the privacy paradox. A clear example of the privacy paradox in action is the idea that social media networks are known to collect personal information, people do not want their information collected, yet individuals still use these services [7]. Many reasons have been cited for the privacy paradox, such as privacy calculus [8, 9], decision bias, e.g., overconfidence bias [8], lack of personal experience with information security breaches, social influence, e.g., pressures from people around them [8, 10], desire to enhance IoT device functionality [11], time [12], and privacy fatigue [13]. Privacy fatigue is the idea that while users may say that they care about their privacy, they do not take action because the requirements to secure their online data are too burdensome [13]. The participants end up feeling resigned to the fact that their data could be leaked [13, 14]. Users have cited complicated language as a reason for experiencing privacy fatigue. The language commonly used by cybersecurity experts is too difficult for everyday users to understand, prompting users to disregard privacy controls altogether [14]. Users have also admitted to sacrificing privacy for convenience, such as not using antivirus software because it is expensive [4, 15]. While users may indicate that they care about their privacy and protecting their data, their actions often show that they do not like to take actions that may be inconvenient.

Other key factors that influence user behaviors related to information security include perceived susceptibility and safeguard cost-effectiveness. Users who perceive themselves as susceptible, understand their device's privacy limitations, and consider implementing safeguards to be useful are less likely to have their private data breached [16]. On the other hand, a user experiencing privacy fatigue could experience a psychological distancing from security responsibility and safe behaviors [17]. Psychological distancing could put a user at great risk of having their privacy compromised. Understanding how users perceive their susceptibility to having their privacy breached is essential to promoting internet safety.

To better understand all of the factors contributing to users' perceptions of their IoT devices and their lack of action, it is important to identify which safe practices users already take while considering their existing awareness and attitudes [4]. Based on this, recommendations for increasing privacy-related actions while mitigating deterrents such as privacy fatigue can be generated. The purpose of the current study was to examine, by administering a user survey, individuals' perceptions, knowledge, experiences, and behaviors related to IoT device information security and associated privacy implications, to understand how to encourage users to utilize industry-recommended best practices to maintain the security of their information.

2 Methods

2.1 Participants and Sample

The survey sample consisted of 179 participants. Recruitment of participants took place through a STEM University in the Southeast United States. The participants were recruited from the university's student and faculty population via email list services, class distributions, Sona Systems®, and by asking participants to pass the survey link on to friends and colleagues. Additionally, the survey was distributed via the social media networking site LinkedIn. Although 179 participants completed the study, responses associated with 40 participants were removed. Twenty-six participant responses were not included as less than 20% of the questionnaire was completed. Ten participant's responses were removed for completing the survey in less than 3 min, the baseline time. The baseline completion time was developed during pilot testing, based on the number of questions in the survey, as it would not be feasible for an individual to have completed the survey in less than three minutes. Four participant responses were removed due to not properly completing the survey leading to a final sample of 139 participant responses. The final sample was comprised of 91 (65%) males and 47 (34%) females between the ages of 18 – 77. One participant did not specify their biological sex. When examined by generation, 47 (34%) participants were considered Generation Z (born in 1997 or later), 18 (13%) were considered millennials (born between 1981 and 1996), 20 (14%) were considered Generation X (born between 1965 and 1980), and 7 (5%) were considered Baby Boomers (born between 1945 and 1964). One-hundred two (51%) of the participants were active college students, 26 (13%) had commercial sector jobs, 25 (12.5%) worked in academia, 16 (8%) were Reserve Officers' Training Program (ROTC) cadets, 12 (6%) had past military experience, 7 (3.50%) were active-duty military, 7 (3.5%) were employed within the government, and 5 (2%) were civilian employees of the military. The occupational status question was a multi-select question, that is participants could choose one or more statuses, depending on how many applied to them. For example, a participant could simultaneously be a college student and have past military experience. Participation in the study was voluntary; extra credit was offered to students who participated through university courses. This study was reviewed and approved by the Institutional Review Board (IRB). All participant responses were kept confidential.

2.2 Survey Instrument

The survey study was a mixed-methods survey design delivered via Qualtrics software. The survey gathered a combination of quantitative data and qualitative data to obtain richer information about user behaviors. The questions were not forced response questions, and participants could answer or skip whatever questions they chose. The survey was divided into the following sections: (a) demographics questions, (b) experience questions, (c) knowledge questions, (d) perception questions, and (e) safe behaviors questions. The survey took approximately 20 min to complete. The data presented in the following sections are associated with a subset of these areas, focusing on user perceptions, knowledge, experience, and behaviors. The relevant sections are discussed in further detail below.

Demographics Questions The demographics section gathered information about age, biological sex, race, nationality, employment status, household composition, and military experience.

Experience Sections The experience sections of the survey examined device use and event experience. The device use section gathered information about the participants' use and experience with different types of IoT devices. Participants were first asked to answer for what purpose they used IoT devices in three categories, including smart home, which consisted of devices such as smart doorbells and virtual home assistants, smart mobiles: smartphones, smart wearables, and tablets, and computer: laptops and desktops. Due to the ability of computers to connect to the internet they, at a basic level, qualify as IoT devices. Although computers are not typically included in modern IoT literature they were included as point of comparison. Participants were then asked to rate their experience with each device from 1= no experience to 4 = extensive experience. An area for additional comments was included if a participant felt they wanted to add more information or clarify.

The event experience section examined whether the participants or anyone close to the participants had ever experienced an event in which their data was accessed and utilized without their consent. These questions were multiple choice. The participants were then asked to elaborate using open-ended response questions if they had experience with their data being accessed without their consent or were unsure whether it had happened. The participants were also asked if they felt their level of trust changed following an event in which their data was accessed without their consent. This item was scored on a five-point Likert type scale with response choices from 1- Strongly decreased to 5- Strongly increased.

Knowledge Questions The system knowledge section gathered participants' knowledge of what kind of third parties (e.g., internet service providers, device manufactures, the government) accessed data from the devices. Participants were asked what type of data they thought that third-party entities were accessing and for what purposes the collected data is used.

The information security knowledge section consisted of two parts. The first gathered responses related to what participants believed would indicate unauthorized access to their IoT devices; this used two open-ended response questions that asked what would indicate that one of the users' devices was being accessed by an outside party and how they could prevent someone from accessing their information without their consent. A dichotomously scored (Yes/No) question asked if participants would change how they interacted with the device if someone accessed it without their consent. They were then given an open-ended text box to explain why. The second part examined participants' knowledge of cybersecurity using questions developed by the Pew Research Center related to knowledge of cybersecurity terminology and concepts [5].

Perception Questions The users' perceptions of the security of their IoT devices were collected using Likert-type items. Participants were asked to what degree they trust the information security of the collected data and how concerned the participants are about the information security of the collected data. Trust and concern were measured on five-point Likert- type scales, from 1-did not trust and not at all concerned, to 5-completely trust and extremely concerned, respectively. Participants were given a space for additional comments if they felt they could not express their response to the other questions in the section.

The questionnaire also gathered participants' perceptions of the susceptibility of their IoT devices to being accessed without their consent using Likert-type items. Participants were then asked what they perceived the risks to be of their data being accessed or utilized without their consent. The participants were then asked to rate the susceptibility of each type of device (smart home, smart mobile, and computer) to being accessed without their consent using a Likert-type scale that ranged from 1-not at all susceptible to 5-completely susceptible.

Safe Behavior Questions The safe behaviors section examined what features (i.e., crash reports, location services, etc.) and security practices (e.g., two-factor authentication, antivirus) participants use. Participants were also asked whether they connect to public WIFI. This question was dichotomously scored (Yes/No).

2.3 Procedure

Potential study participants were provided a link to the survey via email or social media site. Upon clicking the link, they were presented with the informed consent form explaining the purpose of the study and their right to end the survey at any time free of consequences. After consenting, they were provided with a brief overview of the study and the types of relevant devices. They were informed that they had as much time as they needed to take the survey. When the participants completed the survey, they were allowed to provide an email address for any potential follow-up studies and prompted to submit the survey.

2.4 Data Analysis

The quantitative data were analyzed descriptively by obtaining response frequencies for each survey item. This allowed the researchers to identify trends in participants' perceptions, knowledge, experiences, and behaviors. The qualitative data was analyzed by categorizing the open-ended item responses into themes. This was done by reviewing responses for each qualitative question and extracting common themes. The themes were then reviewed, and similar themes were condensed. Each response was then categorized into one of the themes, allowing the researchers to obtain frequency counts of how many responses fit into each theme.

3   Results

3.1   User Experience

All the participants had experience with mobile devices and computers; however, only 92 (66%) participants owned smart home devices. Among the participants who owned smart home devices, the most frequently owned devices were streaming devices (75 participants, 82%), AI personal assistants (45 participants, 49%), and smart appliances (25 participants, 27%). When participants were asked about whether they had experienced a situation in which their data was accessed without their consent, 62 (45%) participants responded that they had experienced such an event. Thirty one (22%) participants responded that they had not experienced such an event, while 43 (31%) participants were unsure, and 3 (2%) participants did not respond (see Fig. 1). Sixteen (26%) of the participants who experienced an event in which their data was accessed without their consent expressed that their trust level did not change, and 12 (19%) expressed that their trust level actually increased after their data was accessed without their consent (see Fig. 2). Those who had an increase in trust commonly cited the company's actions such as bank notifications and changing their account as reasons for their increase in trust.

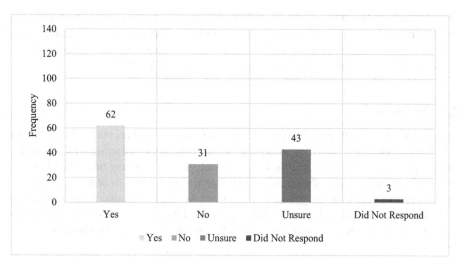

Fig. 1. Whether participant's had experienced their data being accessed without their consent

3.2 User Knowledge

Overall, a majority of the participants were aware of which third parties/service providers were accessing their data for all three device types. Participants were least familiar with which third parties were accessing their smart home device data, with 61 (44%) participants responding with unsure. More participants were familiar with what third parties were accessing their smart mobile device and computer data, with 31 (22%) and 34 (24%) participants responding unsure, respectively. The difference in the level of knowledge regarding data access between smart home, smart mobile, and computer devices was also present when participants were asked what types of data are being accessed. Fifty-six (40%) participants responded that they were unsure of what data is being accessed by their smart home devices, 22% of participants responded unsure for both smart mobile and computer devices with 31 and 30 participants responding,

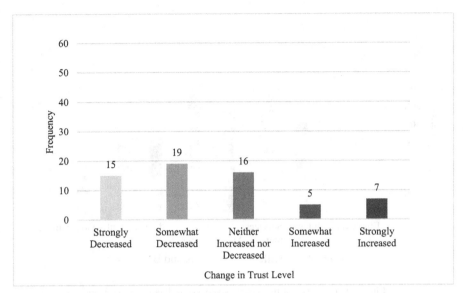

Fig. 2. Participants response to whether they felt a change in trust level occurred after experiencing their data being utilized or accessed without their consent.

respectively. Furthermore, 46 (33%) smart home, 21 (15%) smart mobile, and 24 (17%) computer users reported being unsure of the purposes for which their data is being accessed.

When asked how they would know that their devices were being accessed, 42 (30%) participants cited targeted advertisements, 33 (24%) participants cited alerts and notifications, and 32 (23%) participants cited devices acting abnormally. When asked which third parties they believed to be accessing their devices, 101 (72%) participants responded with the device manufacturer, and 89 (64%) responded with the internet service provider. When responses regarding who was accessing their data were broken down by generation, there are some apparent differences between the generational groups. The largest and most interesting difference was with respect to the government accessing their information. Forty-seven percent (8/17) of millennials believed that the government was accessing their information, compared to 22% (10/46) of Generation Z and 16% (4/25) of Baby Boomer and Generation X participants. There was also a noticeable difference between Generation Z and Boomers/Generation X regarding the perception that service providers were accessing their smart home devices. However, no statistical tests were conducted due to the disparate sizes of the generational groups. Overall, as a general trend for all categories except internet service providers, a higher percentage of millennials felt third parties (i.e., employers, device manufacturers, advertisement companies, government) were accessing their devices, compared to other generational groups. These results are shown in Fig. 3.

The average participant score on the five technical security questions taken from the Pew Research Center study was 58% (N =136). Twenty-four participants (approx. 17%) were only able to answer one question correctly, 66 participants (approx. 48%)

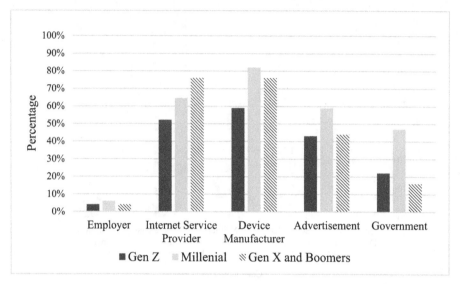

Fig. 3. Perceptions of third parties accessing data by generation

were only able to answer two to three questions correctly, and 49 participants (approx. 36%) were able to answer four to five of the questions. Table 1 presents a question-by-question breakdown of the percentage of participants that answered each question correctly in the present study compared to the Pew Research Study conducted in 2017. As a general trend, participants in the present study scored higher than the participants in the Pew Research Study. The most noticeable difference between the scores was regarding the Global Positioning System (GPS) tracking question. In the present study, 99 (73%) participants answered the question correctly, while in the original study, 548 (52%) answered the question correctly. The second most noticeable difference was in the https:// question, in which 73 (54%) of participants answered correctly in the present student versus 348 (33%) in the original study.

3.3 User Perceptions

Users indicated that they do not fully trust their devices. Of the 139 participants: 41 (29%) indicated that they do not trust, 46 (33%) indicated that they somewhat distrust, 27 (19%) indicated that they neither trust nor distrust, 24 (17%) indicated that they somewhat trust, and none indicated that they completely trust the information security of the data collected by their devices (see Fig. 4). Nearly all (96%) of the participants had some degree of concern regarding the security of their personal information.

When asked about the susceptibility of their devices to being accessed without their consent, AI home assistants had the highest frequency of "extremely susceptible" ratings, with 43 (31%) participants responding in that manner. The next highest was smart security cameras, where 39 (28%) participants rated the cameras as "extremely susceptible." Overall, 133 (96%) participants expressed some level of concern regarding the susceptibility of their IoT devices being accessed without their consent.

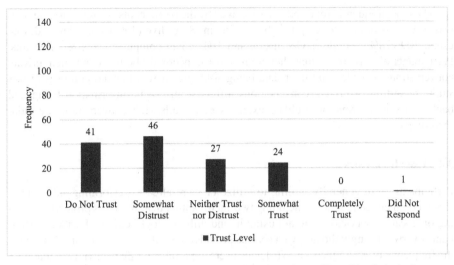

Fig. 4. Participants degree of trust in the security of the data collected by their devices

Table 1. Percentage of participants with each question correct

Question	All Wi-Fi traffic is encrypted by default on all wireless routers	What does the "https://" at the beginning of a URL denote, as opposed to http:// (without the "s")?	Turning off the GPS function of your smartphone prevents any tracking of your phone's location	If a public Wi-Fi network requires a password to access, is it generally safe to use that network for sensitive activities such as online banking?	What kind of information security risks can be minimized by using a Virtual Private Network (VPN)?
Pew Research	45% Correct	33% Correct	52% Correct	73% Correct	16% Correct
Current IoT Study	54% Correct	54% Correct	73% Correct	80% Correct	21% Correct

The most frequently reported risk perceived by the participants across all IoT devices was private information being tied back to them. Sixty-five (46%) smart home device users, 109 (78%) mobile device users, and 104 (75%) computer users reported this. Participants also reported that they were most concerned about having their private conversations recorded and their data being sold and shared. For the purposes of this study, recording of private conversations differs from private information being tied back as private information could be text messages/emails while conversations are audio recordings.

3.4   User Behaviors

Participants were generally willing to utilize or were already performing safe behaviors/recommended practices, including two-factor authentication, virus protection, turning off location services when not using it, and utilizing lock settings. Further, participants overwhelmingly did not want service providers to sell their data. Figure 5 presents the frequency of willingness of IoT device users to partake in safe behaviors to maintain their privacy. Of the 103 participants who said they were unwilling to have their data

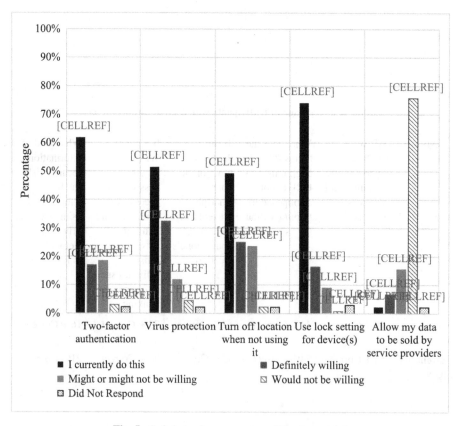

Fig. 5. Safe behaviors users are willing to partake

sold, most did not read the terms and conditions, which allows them to learn whether the service provider is selling their data. The participants who did not read the terms and conditions, for the most part, still enabled the features, see Fig. 6.

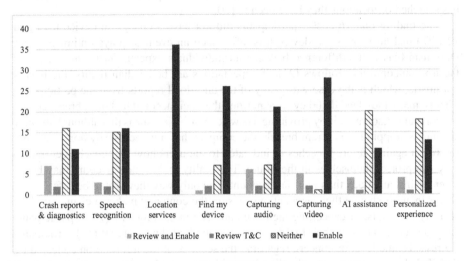

Fig. 6. Device features that are reviewed by the 103 participants who said they were unwilling to have their data sold.

The study found that overall participants do not read terms and conditions for various services/features. Seventy-two percent of participants responded that they do not read the terms and conditions for AI assistance. Additionally, 97 (70%) and 95 (60%) participants do not read the terms and conditions for speech recognition features of their devices and for location services, respectively. Furthermore, only 17 (12%) participants expressed that they would be more cautious if they experienced their device being accessed without their consent.

4   Discussion

4.1   User Experience

Overall, the survey found that smart home devices are not as prevalent as other devices such as cellphones and computers, which nearly every participant owned. Approximately two-thirds of the participants had smart-home devices, which may be due to the number of students who took the survey.

A plurality (62 participants, 45%) of participants said they had experienced their data being accessed without their consent, and results indicated that receiving targeted advertisements was the most common way participants could detect this. Seeing targeted advertisements for a product an individual may have discussed in front of an AI assistant is seemingly proof to many individuals that conversations are being recorded and this data is being provided to advertisers. However, this is not always the case, there are many methods used to provide ads. For example, the ad they were served that related to their conversation could have resulted from different machine learning and data mining techniques; due to the two individuals being close in proximity [18, 19]. Individuals who are in close proximity with eachother can recieve ads for products the other individual has searched or locations they have been to [20].

The finding that 16 (12%) participants did not have a change in device trust and 12 (9%) had an increase in device trust after such an event displays optimisim bias. Optimism bias is the difference between an individuals expectation for an event and the true outcome that follows [21]. If expectations are better than reality, the bias is optimistic, which is the case with many of the anecdotal reports from the participants. That is, many indictaed that they were notified that their account had been breached and the company resolved this by providing a new account. The issue is that although the new account is stopping the current breach, the company has not necessarily done anything to protect against future breaches or indicated to the users how the breach occurred so they can protect themselves in the future. The reality is their new account may be no safer against an attack than their last account. The only way they would be safer would be for them to change their own actions, ensure the company makes a change in their security protocols, or cancelling their account. The remaining 114 (79%) participants had a decrease in trust in their IoT devices. One-hundred-thirty-three (96%) participants expressed some level of concern regarding the security of the information collected by their IoT devices. However, only 17 (12%) said they would act in a more cautious way if their device was accessed without their consent. This indicates that while individuals may say they care about privacy, their actions suggest that they do not care enough to counteract the cost of taking the actions. This is in line with findings in the extant literature and supports the privacy paradox [22, 23].

4.2 User Knowledge

Another interesting finding was that participants scored an average of 58% on the cyber knowledge quiz. When compared with the Pew Research Center findings from 2017 the participants from the current study scored notably higher on each of the questions. For example, 99 (73%) participants from the present study knew that turning off the GPS function of a phone does not prevent tracking of the phone's location. In comparison, only 548 (52%) participants know that from the 2017 Pew Study [5]. A potential explanation for this finding is that the sample used in the current study has more knowledge of cybersecurity than the general population. This explanation is the most plausible explanation for this finding because most sample participants came from a STEM University. What is interesting about that demographic, though, was that despite the sample coming from a STEM university, the average score was less than 60%—indicating that even among more technical individuals, there is a notable lack of cybersecurity knowledge. Another plausible explanation is that, over the four years since the original study was conducted, the public has become more aware of cybersecurity issues because of heightened coverage by the media. Examples include the 2017 Equifax breach and the 2018 Marriot data breach.

4.3 User Perceptions

Although nearly three-quarters of the participants expressed that their biggest concern regarding risks to their privacy for both computers and mobile was private information being tied back to them, less than half responded the same for smart home devices. This is despite the fact that many smart home devices record audio and video information. A possible explanation for the disparity is that smart home device users lack the knowledge of the types of information their devices collect and what the service providers do with that information.

Interestingly, millennials were more likely to be concerned about the government accessing their private information than Generation Z or Generation X/Boomers. A potential explanation for this finding is the environment in which millennials grew up. Millennials grew up with the advent of modern technology but still remember a time before it was as ubiquitous as it is now. Additionally, millennials were in early to mid-adulthood in 2013 when Edward Snowden leaked information that the National Security Agency (NSA) in the United States was spying on American citizens' cell phone and internet data without a warrant or user consent [24, 25]. Many members of Generation Z were still children when this happened, and it may not have had the same breach of trust as it did with millennials. The finding that millennials perceive that the government is accessing their devices supports the idea that participants may lack knowledge of their system because they are more worried about a perceived threat than the actual present privacy threat.

4.4 User Behaviors

The majority of participants were using, or willing to use, safe behaviors to protect their personal information; participants who were willing to partake in safe device behaviors expressed that they would do it because it protects privacy, enhances security, and is beneficial for device performance. However, many participants expressed reasons for not being willing to take actions that seek to protect their privacy, including inconvenience, financial cost, and past negative experiences. These findings are in line with the extant research on privacy calculus [8]. Privacy calculus is the idea that the cost of taking privacy-enhancing actions outweighs the benefits. The presence of privacy calculus demonstrates that the privacy paradox is present among users of IoT devices because despite stating that they care about privacy, their actions illustrate otherwise [4].

The current study found that a large percentage of the participants did not read the terms and conditions for AI assistance, speech recognition, and location services. Previous research has shown that many users do not read the terms and conditions, especially if they require the user to access them separately [26]. As many IoT devices do not present the terms and conditions on the main setup screen, many users do not access this information and are therefore unaware of what the service provider does with their private data. Additionally, users tend not to read the terms and conditions of websites that they are familiar with, despite not knowing what the company is doing with their information [27]. In line with the privacy paradox, participants expressed that they were concerned with the security of their data but never actually researched who was accessing their information.

4.5 Recommendations

The data obtained in the current study resulted in the creation of a series of recommendations for the IoT device manufacturers. Specifically, the results of the user experience and knowledge questions, reveal the need for IoT device users to be informed and educated on their IoT devices' privacy, what constitutes as their data being accessed without their consent, and how to interact in a safer manner with their device.

The first way device manufacturers can increase user education is by making the navigation through the privacy policy part of the device set up and including call outs which summarize each section in laymens terms. The privacy language should be clear, concise, and free of technical jargon as the average resident of the United States reads at an 8th grade (ages 13–14) reading level; this means that instructions and privacy policies should be written at an 8th-grade reading level or lower [28]. If the language is presented in a more understandable and accessible way users will be able to not only be more educated on their device but understand how they can interact with their device to ensure the privacy of their data is at a level that matches their needs. To increase user's understanding of what third parties are accessing their devices, IoT device companies could provide users with a notification or list of which third parties are accessing data from the device. This would allow users to see exactly which service providers are accessing their personal information by default and who they have provided access to when accepting terms and conditions or downloading third party features. Furthermore, to ensure that users perform behaviors that are necessary to ensure that their privacy is at their desired level, companies should ensure the needed behaviors are quick and easy, or users will not perform them. For example, having to make multiple extra clicks or to an additional area to complete privacy enhancing behaviors is likely to cause users to ignore them [29]. Additionally, research has shown that when a task takes more than three clicks, users perceive that task as more difficult [30]. Because the extant literature explains that privacy fatigue sets in when users perceive tasks as difficult, it is important for interface designers to reduce the number of clicks required to complete privacy enhancing behaviors to three or fewer.

4.6 Limitations and Future Research

These findings must be interpreted with caution as the present study had several limitations. First, sample size was a large limitation as it was constrained by the available time and resources. Second, convenience sampling was used in an attempt to obtain as many data points as possible. Both of these factors limit the generalizability of the results. A third limitation of the study was that there was a great deal of missing data. The questions were not forced response questions, and as a result, some of the questions presented later in the questionnaire had fewer responses, likely from survey fatigue. Another limitation was that many of the questions referred to groups of devices (e.g., smart home devices), and this may have prevented finding variability in the data that might have been revealed asking about specific devices (e.g., responses associated with a smart vacuum are likely to be different than responses associated with a smart lock). Unfortunately, querying users about each specific device would have resulted in the survey length being prohibitive.

Future research should aim to increase the sample size and utilize alternative sampling procedures for the respondents so as to better respresent the target population. Future research also needs to be conducted to examine methods to effectively increase users' knowledge of what types of data are collected by their devices and who is accessing the data. If users have a better understanding of their IoT device security settings and associated implications, they may make more informed decisions regarding protecting their privacy. Research also should be conducted to address how to make behaviors necessary to protect user privacy less burdensome on users. Research has shown that privacy fatigue occurs when the measures to protect data are too costly [13].

5 Conclusion

In summary, a user survey regarding IoT user experiences, knowledge, perceptions, and behaviors revealed that a vast majority of participants expressed concerns regarding the privacy of the information that is being collected by their IoT devices. It was also revealed that a majority of participants do not read the terms and conditions for their devices, leaving participants unaware of what service providers and third parties are doing with their data. The survey also shows that there is a gap in the understanding of IoT device users regarding the privacy of the information collected by their devices. The scores on the cybersecurity knowledge questions demonstrated an overall lack of knowledge. Overall, users did not trust the privacy of their information, but in general, their levels of trust did not change when they had experienced a breach in their privacy. Additionally, only a small percentage of users expressed that they would take action if their privacy were breached, indicating that users may have resigned themselves to the fact that their data privacy may be breached. The resignation could mean that IoT device users are experiencing privacy fatigue [13]. The practical implications of this study are that IoT device users are at risk of using their devices in a manner that exposes them to a potential breach of privacy due to a lack of knowledge. Furthermore, there is a failure to take the steps that Device manufacturers could work towards resolving this issue by redesigning interfaces to be simpler, utilize jargon-free language and promote privacy-enhancing behaviors.

Disclosure This study was funded by the United States Office of Naval Research ONR FOA# N00014-19-S-F009. There were no conflicts of interest in this study.

References

1. Suresh, P., Daniel, J.V., Parthasarathy, V., Aswathy, R.H., Bajaj, K.: Cyberspace: Post-Snowden. Strategic Analysis, 4, 582 A state of the art review on the Internet of Things (IoT) history, technology and fields of deployment. In: 2014 International Conference on Science Engineering and Management Research (ICSEMR), pp. 1–8 (2014). https://doi.org/10.1109/ICSEMR.2014.7043637
2. Sattarova Feruza, Y., Kim, T.H.: IT security review: privacy, protection, access control, assurance and system security. Int. J. Multimedia Ubiquitous Eng. **2**(2), 17–32 (2007)

3. Acquisti, A., Brandimarte, L., Loewenstein, G.: Privacy and human behavior in the age of information. Science **347**(6221), 509–514 (2015)
4. Zheng, S., Apthorpe, N., Chetty, M., Feamster, N.: User Perceptions of Smart Home IoT Privacy (2018). https://doi.org/10.1145/3274469
5. Olmstead, K., Smith, A.: What the Public Knows About Cybersecurity. The Pew Research Center (2017)
6. Williams, M., Nurse, J.R.C., Creese, S.: Privacy is the Boring Bit: user perceptions and behaviour in the Internet-of-Things. In: 15th Annual Conference on Privacy, Security, and Trust (PST), pp. 181–18109 (2017). https://doi.org/10.1109/PST.2017.00029
7. Wu, P.F.: The privacy paradox in the context of online social networking: a self-identity perspective. J. Am. Soc. Inf. Sci. **70**(3), 207–217 (2019). https://doi.org/10.1002/asi.24113
8. Gerber, N., Gerber, P., Volkamer, M.: Explaining the privacy paradox: a systematic review of literature investigating privacy attitude and behavior. Comput. Secur. **77**, 226–261 (2018)
9. Rittenberg, L., Tregarthen, T.: Principles of Microeconomics. Saylor (2018)
10. Taddicken, M.: The 'privacy paradox' in the social web: the impact of privacy concerns, individual characteristics, and the perceived social relevance on different forms of self-disclosure. J. Comput.-Mediat. Commun. **19**(2), 248–273 (2014)
11. Aleisa, N., Renaud, K., Bongiovanni, I.: The privacy paradox applies to IoT devices too: a Saudi Arabian study. Comput. Secur. **96** 101897 (2020)
12. Kokolakis, S.: Privacy attitudes and privacy behaviour: a review of current research on the privacy paradox phenomenon. Comput. Secur. **64**, 122–134 (2017) https://doi.org/10.1016/j.cose.2020.101897
13. Choi, H., Park, J., Jung, Y.: The role of privacy fatigue in online privacy behavior. Comput. Hum. Behav. **81**, 42–51 (2018). https://doi.org/10.1016/j.chb.2017.12.001
14. Keith, M.J., Maynes, C., Lowry, P.B., Babb, J.: Privacy fatigue: the effect of privacy control complexity on consumer electronic information disclosure. In: International Conference on Information Systems (ICIS 2014), Auckland, New Zealand, December, pp. 14–17 (2014)
15. Kang, R., Dabbish, L., Fruchter, N., Kiesler, S.: My data just goes everywhere: user mental models of the internet and implications for privacy and security. In: 2015 Symposium on Usable Privacy and Security, pp. 39–52 (2015)
16. Rebensky, S., Carroll, M., Nakushian, A., Chaparro, M., Prior, T.: Understanding the last line of defense: human response to cybersecurity events. In: Moallem, A. (ed.) HCII 2021. LNCS, vol. 12788, pp. 353–366. Springer, Cham (2021). https://doi.org/10.1007/978-3-030-77392-2_23
17. Burns, A., Roberts, T., Posey, C., Bennett, R., Courtney, J.: Assessing the role of security education, training, and awareness on 'insiders' security-related behavior: an expectancy theory approach. In: 2015 48th Hawaii International Conference on System Sciences, pp. 3930–3940 (2015)
18. Tan, K.H., Zhan, Y.: Improving new product development using big data: a case study of an electronics company. RD Manage. **47**(4), 570–582 (2017)
19. Ribeiro-Navarrete, S., Saura, J.R., Palacios-Marqués, D.: Towards a new era of mass data collection: assessing pandemic surveillance technologies to preserve user privacy. Technol. Forecast. Soc. Chang. **167**, 120681 (2021)
20. Fan, C., Liu, Y., Huang, J., Rong, Z., Zhou, T.: Correlation between social proximity and mobility similarity. Sci. Rep. **7**(1), 1–8 (2017)
21. Sharot, T.: The optimism bias. Curr. Biol. **21**(23), R941–R945 (2011)
22. Norberg, P.A., Horne, D.R., Horne, D.A.: The privacy paradox: personal information disclosure intentions versus behaviors. J. Consum. Aff. **41**(1), 100 (2007)
23. Acquisti, A., Taylor, C., Wagman, L.: The economics of privacy. J. Econ. Lit. **54**(2), 442–492 (2016). https://doi.org/10.1257/jel.54.2.442

24. Wizner, B.: What changed after Snowden? A U.S. perspective. Int. J. Commun. [Online], 897+ (2017). https://link.gale.com/apps/doc/A504267253/LitRC?u=melb26933& sid=LitRC&xid=7bb84a74
25. Bajaj, K.: Cyberspace: post-Snowden. Strateg. Anal. **4**, 582 (2014)
26. Steinfeld, N.: "I agree to the terms and conditions": (How) do users read privacy policies online? An eye-tracking experiment. Comput. Human Behav. **55** 992–1000 (2016). https://doi-org.portal.lib.fit.edu/https://doi.org/10.1016/j.chb.2015.09.038
27. Milne, G.R., Culnan, M.J.: Strategies for reducing online privacy risks: why consumers read (Or don't read) online privacy notices. J. Interact. Mark. **18**(3), 15–29 (2004). https://doi.org/10.1002/dir.20009
28. Stossel, L.M., Segar, N., Gliatto, P., Fallar, R., Karani, R.: Readability of patient education materials available at the point of care. J. Gen. Intern. Med. **27**(9), 1165–1170 (2012). https://doi.org/10.1007/s11606-012-2046-0
29. Obar, J.A., Oeldorf-Hirsch, A.: The biggest lie on the Internet: ignoring the privacy policies and terms of service policies of social networking services. Inf. Commun. Soc. **23**(1), 128–147 (2020)
30. Jiménez Iglesias, L., Aguilar Paredes, C., Sánchez Gómez, L., Gutiérrez, M.P.-M.: User experience and media. The three click rule in newspapers' webs for smartphones. Revista Latina de Comunicacion Social, **73**, 595–613 (n.d.). https://doi.org/10.4185/RLCS-2018-1271

From Cybersecurity Hygiene to Cyber Well-Being

Shreya Gupta[1] and Steven Furnell[1,2]

[1] University of Nottingham, Nottingham, UK
steven.furnell@nottingham.ac.uk
[2] Nelson Mandela University, Gqeberha, South Africa

Abstract. End-user practices are widely recognized as a source of cybersecurity weaknesses, and yet efforts to support related awareness and understanding are often lacking in both the workplace and wider societal contexts. As a result, users are often expected to be cybersecurity-literate and to follow good cyber hygiene practices, without necessarily having an understanding or sufficient guidance on how to do so. This can be down to the fact that mainstream advice surrounding the definition for cyber hygiene is widely used but varies greatly in meaning- therefore can create confusion on what the user should prioritize. This paper investigates and defines the concept of cyber hygiene and uses this foundation as the basis for considering the notion of Cyber Well-being as a positive state that ought to be fostered amongst the user community. Rather than simply adopting the oft-taken stance that the user is a threat to technology, the aim behind Cyber Well-being is to consider the users' feelings as well as what they do to implement cyber hygiene. A total of 165 respondents were involved in order to understand varying interpretations of what good cyber hygiene looks like. A disconnect between theory and practice were apparent from later responses when respondents were asked about the issues that stood in the way of their cyber hygiene. The discussion also proposes how the findings can form the foundation for an accompanying tool that can assist users in practicing and tracking their cyber hygiene and may thereby foster confidence and support the formation of Cyber Well-being in their use of their technologies.

Keywords: Cybersecurity · Cyber hygiene · User awareness · Cyber well-being

1 Introduction

Cybersecurity is needed by individuals to protect and maintain various devices, but many users are not well-positioned to play their part in the process. Challenges can include a lack of knowledge or training, as well as an associated lack of confidence and comfort with the responsibilities. Despite this, users are still expected to succeed to a sufficient standard, which of course many do not. As a result, various past studies have tended to conclude that users are the biggest threat to technology, and this is arguably an unfair conclusion of they have effectively been set up to fail.

A. Moallem (Ed.): HCII 2022, LNCS 13333, pp. 124–134, 2022.
https://doi.org/10.1007/978-3-031-05563-8_9

The concept of cyber hygiene has a clear relationship to cybersecurity, insofar as the latter can be improved by practicing the former. However, while achieving and maintaining security is arguably in the user's interest, the task of doing so will be an easier and more agreeable task for some people than others. In some cases, the very fact of needing cybersecurity will make people feel uncomfortable, as it implicitly highlights the fact that they are under threat in some way. They can then become further concerned when trying to engage with the issue, thanks to the significant and potentially confusing volume of advice on offer [1]. Moreover, if they then feel that their cybersecurity is not sufficient or effective then they are likely to come away feeling concerned rather than protected. This realization gives us the basis for recognizing the notion of Cyber Well-being, which holds parallel to having good overall Well-being. It encompasses having a positive relationship with cybersecurity, which includes feeling in control and having sufficient knowledge.

With the above in mind, this paper examines users existing relationship with cybersecurity and cyber hygiene, and to consider steps that may be taken to improve the areas that may need to be fixed. The discussion begins with an examination of the existing notion of cyber hygiene, which proves to be widely mentioned by varyingly defined. This leads to discussion of some direct data collection work that was conducted in order to assess aspects of users' current relationship with cybersecurity, and how this impacts their both their hygiene practices and their feelings of resulting protection. This then informs the discussion that defines the notion of Cyber Well-being, and initial consideration of how users could be supported in achieving and maintaining this via the technology itself.

2   Interpretations of Cyber Hygiene

The term 'cyber hygiene' can be widely located in the literature, but the actual definitions of the concept and what it is considered to encompass can vary considerably [2]. This in turn presents a challenge in terms of understanding what actions users are expected to prioritize. Illustrating this point, Table 1 presents alternative definitions for 'cyber hygiene', drawing from a range of different sources. As is clear from the resulting set, while the term itself is widely utilized, there is an apparent lack of consistency in interpreting what it really means. Additionally, some framed from the perspective of the individual, whereas others associate the term with the organizational perspective.

While we are not seeking to add to the potential confusion by adding our own definition into the mix, in evaluating the existing definitions (and further details from the underlying sources from which they are taken) it is apparent that several further factors also emerge and recur between them, which are then varyingly considered to contribute to the interpretation of cyber hygiene:

- **Prior knowledge:** One must have previous knowledge of the practices, plus how and how often to implement them. Many definitions assume the user has this when it is evident that they do not.
- **Repetition:** Implies the reoccurrence of an action.
- **Habit:** Implies that something is often second nature to someone. A habitual event is one in which we do with a regular tendency.

Table 1. Alternative definitions of cyber hygiene.

Source	Definition
[3]	"follow best practices for security and protect their personal information"
[4]	"the adaptive knowledge and behavior to mitigate risky online activities that put an individual's social, financial, and personal information at risk"
[5]	"a set of practices organizations and individuals perform regularly to maintain the health and security of users, devices, networks and data"
[6]	"the practices and steps that users of computers and other devices take to maintain system health and improve online security. These practices are often part of a routine to ensure the safety of identity and other details that could be stolen or corrupted. Much like physical hygiene, cyber hygiene is regularly conducted to ward off natural deterioration and common threats"
[7]	"follow best practices for security and protect their personal information"
[8]	"the adaptive knowledge and behavior to mitigate risky online activities that put an individual's social, financial, and personal information at risk"
[9]	"a set of practices organizations and individuals perform regularly to maintain the health and security of users, devices, networks and data"
[10]	"the practices and steps that users of computers and other devices take to maintain system health and improve online security. These practices are often part of a routine to ensure the safety of identity and other details that could be stolen or corrupted. Much like physical hygiene, cyber hygiene is regularly conducted to ward off natural deterioration and common threats"
[11]	"follow best practices for security and protect their personal information"
[12]	"the adaptive knowledge and behavior to mitigate risky online activities that put an individual's social, financial, and personal information at risk"

- **Routine:** Implies an action is not a one-off event but has a sense of regularity and frequency. It may even be done in part of a particular order. This differs to habit, which is arguably a natural, almost unconscious tendency. A routine implies more regularity than a habit.
- **Consistency:** Something we do to form a habit; it implies a sense of steadiness.
- **Mitigation:** Reducing the severity of cyber harm or seriousness.
- **Maintenance:** Involves helping something be preserved; the act of preserving cyber safety.
- **Security:** The state of being free from damage or threat; arguably the main goal of cyber hygiene.
- **Practices:** There is a goal or ideology of cybersecurity, and this highlights the need for cyber hygiene practices to implement it and achieve it.
- **Protection:** Embodies defending rather than needing to deal with harm once it has already happened; taking measures of protection to prevent cyber harm.
- **Health:** This is an essential goal of cyber hygiene, and protection and mitigation measures are taken to achieve it.

While all of these factors can have a role to play in understanding cyber hygiene, the feasibility of practicing it is also related to other practical considerations. In particular, the way in which related cybersecurity features are presented can different significantly across different devices and operating systems. For example, settings can differ in terms of location, wording and capability, which can mean learning and becoming familiar with multiple ways to achieve the same ends. Furthermore, certain devices may have fewer options than others, meaning that some practices cannot be transferred at all. As a result, even if users are keen on operating securely, the ways of doing so may not be obvious or feel intuitive, and instead of being protected people feel overwhelmed by the effort and/or complexity, and good practice becomes neglected as a regular need and duty.

3 Exploring End-Users' Cybersecurity Understanding and Behaviors

Having identified the varying interpretations of what good cyber hygiene should look like, the research conducted a survey of end-users to further explore understanding and behaviors in practice. However, rather than directly phrasing questions in relation to cyber hygiene, issues were presented in the terms of cybersecurity as this was considered likely to be a better recognized point of reference. Questions were asked in order to gain an idea of a user's attitudes towards cybersecurity, as well as to help understand and develop the notion of Cyber Well-being.

The survey was distributed through Facebook and LinkedIn, with the hope that those who shared it would enable it to be further exposed within their networks of different skill sets and backgrounds to allow more diversity. The short timeframe of the parent research project meant that there was relatively limited time for data collection, and the questionnaire was live for two working weeks in early August 2021. At the point of closure, a total of 165 participants responded, comprising 108 female, 55 male and 2 non-binary. While the skew towards female respondents (65%) may cause resultant bias in the results it is also an interesting sample base, insofar as women have been identified as having the worst cyber hygiene within prior reports [13].

The main survey questions began by asking the respondents to rate their feelings and understanding around cybersecurity based upon the following four questions:

- *Do you consider yourself to be comfortable with the concept of Cybersecurity?* This is valuable to understand as a foundation, in the sense that if people feel comfortable with cybersecurity, it could imply a better basis for cyber hygiene.
- How *important do you believe it is to maintain your cybersecurity?* This gives an insight into how much people would value cyber hygiene measures.
- Do you feel committed to maintaining your cybersecurity (i.e. the effort you are prepared to make for it)? This gives an insight into likely behaviours.
- Do *you understand what measures to take to maintain your cybersecurity?* This provides an indicator of whether users are suitably positioned to act upon the issue.

The results are depicted in the series of charts in Fig. 1, and it is notable that there is a distinct difference between how the concept is regarded and what is really known

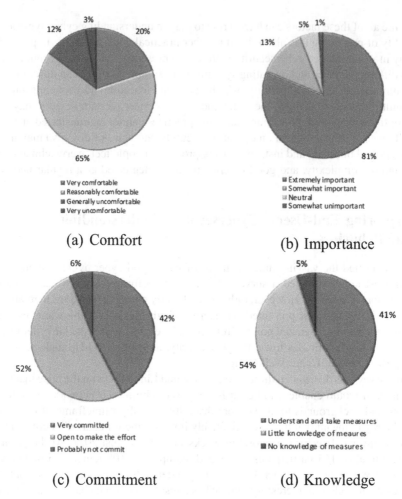

Fig. 1. Feelings and understanding around cybersecurity.

about it. Respondents in general were clearly comfortable with the concept, claimed to recognize its importance, and suggested that they were committed to making a related effort. However, their actual knowledge of what to do appeared to be somewhat adrift from the other responses.

The extent of self-declared behavior was further explored across a set of ten hygiene-related practices, as listed in Fig. 2. This revealed some significant variations in what the respondents claimed to do (and perhaps serves to highlight some of the practical difference between being very committed and prepared to make the effort from Fig. 1c). For example, while 89% claimed to avoid clicking suspicious links, there was significant fallaway in the responses to other issues, such as enabling two-factor authentication (63%), checking privacy settings (56%), performing regular malware scans (50%) and encrypting stored data (32%). While the individual measures were not assessed on a per device basis, respondents were asked about the general extent to which they took measures on different types of device. Perhaps unsurprisingly, the practices were most common on traditional computers (desktops/laptops), with almost a quarter saying they always or often did things here, and only 2% suggesting they never did so. The story on mobile devices (smartphones/tablets) was a little less positive, with around 60% always or often following the practices, and 3% never doing so. However, it was most starkly different with smart devices (e.g. smart TVs, smart speakers), where less than a quarter indicated frequent use of the measures and a third claimed never to use them. In one sense, this reflects that certain measures are not as readily available on smart devices, but it will also be likely to reflect a different usage culture that builds around different devices, with security *needs* being more readily recognized in some contexts than others.

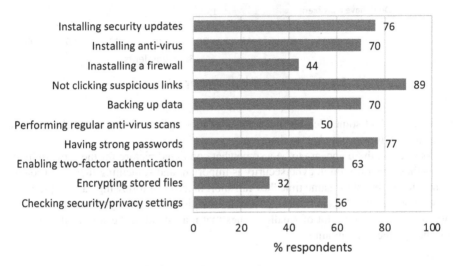

Fig. 2. Use of cybersecurity measures.

Interestingly, the results told a rather different story when the respondents were asked to rate the importance of the same measures. For instance, three quarters of users indicated encrypting their files as being of either high or medium priority, even though only a third actually did it. Similarly, while performing regular malware scans was rated as high or medium priority by over 80% of respondents, while only half had claimed to actually do it. Potential reasons for this disconnect between theory and practice were apparent from later responses when respondents were asked about the issues that stood in the way of their cyber hygiene. The findings, as depicted in Fig. 3, suggest that there many users face a range of practical barriers, which in turn create a gap between where they are and where they would like to be.

The final area that was explored in relation to current activities and practices was the extent to which respondents considered themselves to be aware of the status of cybersecurity on their devices. This was interesting from the perspective of knowing whether the devices have a way of showing this to users already, or if users are cyber literate enough to draw the conclusion for themselves. Based on the three levels of awareness offered as options, only 27% considered themselves to be fully aware, 56%

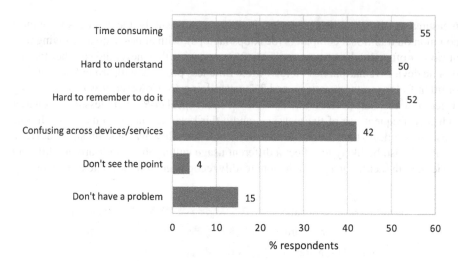

Fig. 3. Obstacles to implementing cybersecurity.

felt that they had some idea but not a lot, and 17% indicated that their cybersecurity status generally was not clear to them.

As a result, there appears to be a somewhat conflicted picture for the same individuals – they generally think cybersecurity is important and something they feel broadly committed to, but at the same time they fall short in terms of following various practices for various reasons. This in turn suggests that investigating cyber hygiene is a necessary measure, as there are a lot of smaller issues that may stand in the way of the average user being able to maintain it.

4   Towards Establishing Cyber Well-Being

Cyber Well-being is resulting notion that is intended to shift the dynamic and way we look at cybersecurity, focusing on the user's perspective and recognizing their comfort, control and knowledge surrounding cybersecurity. Rather than simply adopting the oft-taken stance that the user is a threat to technology, the aim behind Cyber Well-being is to consider the users' feelings as well as what they do to implement cyber hygiene. It represents their relationship with their cybersecurity, the intentionally adopts a perspective that is user-centered in terms of supporting rather than blaming them. With this in mind, we argue that a user is likely to have good Cyber Well-being if they:

- feel comfortable with terminology surrounding cybersecurity;
- don't feel anxious or overwhelmed with cyber hygiene;
- regularly implement cyber hygiene measures;
- feel in control of their cybersecurity;
- have sufficient knowledge to implement the basic cyber hygiene measures that is suited to their lifestyle and cybersecurity demands;
- have an overall positive attitude towards cybersecurity.

Given that users may have varying responses to each of these considerations, the resulting notion of Cyber Well-being (as with Well-being in more general terms) ends up being a spectrum rather than a clear-cut breakpoint in the categorization of good or bad. However, the overall sense of it can be generally good or generally bad, and those falling into the latter have the chance to improve matters by taking certain precautions. From the survey it was indicated that 20% were very comfortable with the concept of cybersecurity whereas 65% were reasonably comfortable. It is still possible to have a credible sense of Cyber Well-being without having the top band of comfort – it can be said you do not need to be an expert on cybersecurity to have a good relationship with cybersecurity – it can be as simple as maintaining your devices' cyber hygiene and feeling positive and confident towards it. Feeling engagement and control over their own cybersecurity is something that many people will not achieve instantly but it can be something they can work towards. The more they implement cyber hygiene measures, the more they would naturally get comfortable with it.

Of course, all of the above still raises the question of how to prompt and support the engagement that is needed. Anticipating this requirement, the final part of the survey had explored respondents' feelings about the potential for an assistive tool to support them in regularly implementing cyber hygiene and working towards the goal of good Cyber Well-being. A number of related ideas were identified and posed to respondents as potential features that a tool could offer. They were then asked to rate the perceived utility of each option. The results are presented in Table 2, noting of course that these are based on the respondents' perception of what the feature would be rather than having had any related experience of how it would be in practice.

Table 2. Opportunities for supporting Cyber Well-being

Potential features	Not useful	Somewhat useful	Neutral	Useful	Very useful
Clearly displaying your cybersecurity status level	1%	6%	11%	38%	44%
Providing tips on how to maintain your security (using clear, easy to understand language)	2%	13%	6%	41%	38%
Notifying you to implement cybersecurity measures at convenient times (i.e. when you do not appear to be busy with other activities)	2%	18%	7%	49%	24%
Informing you of the regularity of your different cybersecurity habits (i.e. how often you take different measures)	3%	9%	13%	53%	22%

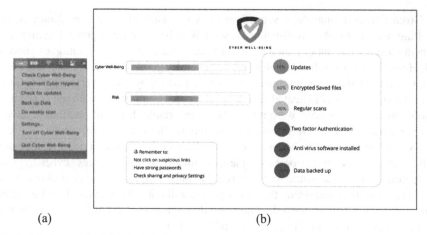

(a)   (b)

Fig. 4. Mock-ups of a Cyber Well-being (a) nav bar option and (b) desktop application dashboard.

It is clear from the positive responses that these features are perceived to offer value and so it was relevant to consider how they could feed forward into a tool that could support the user in practice. While the timeframe of the project did not enable any full-scale implementation activities, initial efforts were nonetheless made to consider how such a tool may look in practice. A resulting mock-up is depicted in Fig. 4 and shows several elements that could usefully form part of an actual implementation. In Fig. 4a illustrates the addition of a Cyber Well-being indicator in the navigation bar. Once clicked this offers several options, with the middle segment containing cyber hygiene measures, which can be prioritized so that users see the most relevant ones. Selecting the option to Check the Cyber Well-being would then bring up the dashboard interface depicted in Fig. 4b, which then offers a number of elements to communicate further details to the user:

- **Cyber Well-being gradient:** To display the user's overall Cyber Well-being status, based the aggregation of other sub-components. As it is evident from the data that managing cybersecurity can be confusing across devices, it would be desirable to have the ability to combine and report status information from across the user's different devices as a single, harmonized status value rather than having a series of distinct values for each device.
- **Dynamic list:** Shown on the right of the image, this list would adjust based on the user's engagement with the tasks required of them. In the illustration presented, updates have been completed the least and are therefore at the top of the list to denote something that needs to be looked at immediately.
- **Traffic light system:** A traffic light system on the individual cyber hygiene measures represents the level of completeness for each measure. Green signifies that an aspect is under control, yellow indicates some more work to be done on these related measures and red highlights aspects requiring urgent action. The percentage would represent how much that specific cyber hygiene measure is completed. Drilling down further into each indicator could then indicate which device(s) were contributing to the ratings.

Referring back to the set of defining characteristics for Cyber Well-being, Table 3 summarizes how they would potentially be supported by a full implementation of such a tool.

Table 3. Opportunities for tool-supported Cyber Well-being

Cyber Well-being characteristic	Potential for tool-based support
Feel comfortable with terminology surrounding cybersecurity	Provide a clear guide and index on cybersecurity terminology
Not to feel anxious or over-whelmed with cyber hygiene	Clear language and visuals, combined with intelligently issued notifications, can help to make the tool non-threatening and balance inter-actions to the lifestyle of the user
To regularly implement cyber hygiene measures	Given that time consuming nature of tasks was seen as a major obstacle, having timed notifications may have to structure and regularize the activity
To feel in control of their cybersecurity	A clear dashboard with key aspects in one place can help users to manage and feel informed and hence more in control
To have sufficient knowledge to implement the basic cyber hygiene measures that is suited to their lifestyle and cybersecurity demands	Helping the user to prioritize what they feel is important to them. This can be done in the settings of the app, as different lifestyles have different cyber demands
To have an overall positive attitude towards cybersecurity	Help to eliminate the obstacles that come with cybersecurity, al-lowing people to have an overall positive attitude

5 Conclusion

Examining the understanding of cybersecurity and the adoption of related cyber hygiene practices helps to give an insight into why some aspects are failing, and provides a foundation for the notion of Cyber Well-being to developed. Users can face many issues, and the current research further suggests that many are not equipped to implement cyber hygiene. It is often not a question of lacking technology, but rather lacking the surrounding understanding, opportunity and motivation to engage with it. The recognition of Cyber Well-being is specifically acknowledging the user's role, not just as agent to enable cybersecurity but also as a party who needs to feel benefit and reassurance from it.

For this concept to be taken further, there needs to be the correct tools in place for both achieving the necessary cyber hygiene practices, and also enabling users to measure and recognize their resulting Cyber Well-being. The related results and mock-up from this study give an initial insight into what can be offered, and offer a foundation for further work in this direction.

References

1. Redmiles, E., et al.: A comprehensive quality evaluation of security and privacy advice on the web. In: Proceedings of the 29th USENIX Security Symposium, 12–14 August 2020, pp. 89–108 (2020)
2. Vishwanath, A., et al.: Cyber hygiene: the concept, its measure, and its initial tests. Decis. Support Syst. **128**, 113160 (2020)
3. Cain, A.A., Edwards, M.E., Still, J.D.: An exploratory study of cyber hygiene behaviors and knowledge. J. Inf. Secur. Appl. **42**, 36–45 (2018)
4. Neigel, A.R., Claypoole, V.L., Waldfogle, G.E., Acharya, S., Hancock, G.M.: Holistic cyber hygiene education: Accounting for the human factors. Comput. Secur. **92**, 101731 (2020)
5. Irei, A.: What is cyber hygiene and why is it important? TechTarget SearchSecurity. https://www.techtarget.com/searchsecurity/definition/cyber-hygiene. Accessed 4 Feb 2022
6. Brook, C.: What is Cyber Hygiene? A Definition of Cyber Hygiene, Benefits, Best Practices, and More. Digital Guardian, 6 October 2020 (2020)
7. Tunggal, A.T.: What is Cyber Hygiene and Why is it Important? UpGuard. 24 August 2021. https://www.upguard.com/blog/cyber-hygiene. Accessed 4 Feb 2022
8. NortonLifeLock: Good cyber hygiene habits to help stay safe online. https://uk.norton.com/internetsecurity-how-to-good-cyber-hygiene.html. Accessed 4 Feb 2022
9. Trevors, M., Wallen, C.M.: Cyber Hygiene: A Baseline Set of Practices. Software Engineering Institute Carnegie Mellon University (2017). https://resources.sei.cmu.edu/asset_files/Presentation/2017_017_001_508771.pdf
10. RSI Security: Why is Cyber Hygiene Important? IS CYBER HYGIENE IMPORTANT? 4 September 2019 (2019). https://blog.rsisecurity.com/why-is-cyber-hygiene-important/
11. Ja, A.: The importance of cyber hygiene in cyberspace. Infosec Institute, 30 April 2015 (2015). https://resources.infosecinstitute.com/topic/the-importance-of-cyber-hygiene-in-cyberspace/
12. LIFARS: The importance of Cyber Hygiene, 14 July 2020 (2020). https://lifars.com/2020/07/the-importance-of-cyber-hygiene/
13. Gratian, M., Bandi, S., Cukier, M., Dykstra, J., Ginther, A.: Correlating human traits and cyber security behavior intentions. Comput. Secur. **73**, 345–358 (2018)

Lessons Learned and Suitability of Focus Groups in Security Information Workers Research

Julie M. Haney$^{(\boxtimes)}$ ⓘ, Jody L. Jacobsⓘ, Fernando Barrientos, and Susanne M. Furmanⓘ

National Institute of Standards and Technology, Gaithersburg, MD 20899, USA
{julie.haney,jody.jacobs,susanne.furman}@nist.gov
https://csrc.nist.gov/usable-cybersecurity

Abstract. Security information workers (SIW) are professionals who develop and use security-related data within their jobs. Qualitative methods – primarily interviews – are becoming increasingly popular in SIW research. However, focus groups are an under-utilized, but potentially valuable way to explore the work practices, needs, and challenges of these professionals. Based on our experience with virtual focus groups of security awareness professionals, this paper documents lessons learned and the suitability of using focus groups to study SIW. We also suggest ways to alleviate concerns SIW may have with focus group participation. These insights may be helpful to other researchers embarking on SIW research.

Keywords: Security information workers · Focus groups · Methodology · Security · Usability

1 Introduction

Security information workers (SIW)[1] are professionals who develop and use security-related data within their jobs. Some SIW are employed in largely technical roles, such as: IT professionals who implement and manage security systems and processes; developers who build software that implements security mechanisms; analysts who collect and investigate security data; Chief Information Security Officers (CISOs) and other security managers; and consultants who facilitate the adoption of security best practices and technologies [1]. Other SIW may have less-technical roles, for example, security policy makers, security communicators, or educators who instruct their students about safe online practices.

---

[1] The term "security information worker" does not describe a formalized cybersecurity work role (e.g., like those described in the National Initiative for Cybersecurity Education Workforce Framework for Cybersecurity [24]), but rather encompasses a range of professionals handling security information.

A. Moallem (Ed.): HCII 2022, LNCS 13333, pp. 135–153, 2022.
https://doi.org/10.1007/978-3-031-05563-8_10

Conducting research with SIW participants allows for discovering work practices, challenges, and needs to aid in the development of tools, techniques, and other support mechanisms that are usable and valuable to SIW and their stakeholders. Qualitative methods – largely interviews – have become increasingly popular when studying these workers [10]. Focus groups are a less-frequently used qualitative method but can be valuable for studying SIW (e.g., as employed in [4,13]). While other cybersecurity researchers have shared lessons learned in their experiences with surveys, interviews, and field observations of SIW (e.g., [28,30,36]), none have discussed how *focus groups* might be appropriate for studying SIW.

In this paper, we document lessons learned from our experiences with virtual focus groups of United States (U.S.) government security awareness professionals – those tasked with training their organization's workforce on security best practices – as part of a mixed-methods research project. We then discuss the suitability of using focus groups to study SIW, including potential benefits, disadvantages, challenges, and recommendations for offsetting hesitations SIW may have with focus group participation. These insights may be helpful to other researchers embarking on SIW research.

2   Background

2.1   Focus Groups

Focus groups are a research methodology typically having five characteristics: "(1) a small group of people, who (2) possess certain characteristics, (3) provide qualitative data (4) in a focused discussion (5) to help understand the topic of interest" [15]. Differing from other group interactions (e.g., meetings or a single group interview with a project team) in which consensus or recommendations are the goal, *multiple* focus groups are conducted to discover a range of perspectives. Data from the groups are then compared and contrasted. Although often conducted similarly, we also differentiate academic research focus groups (the topic of this paper) from marketing focus groups in which the goal is to understand people's behaviors and preferences related to consumer products.

Common Uses and Benefits. Focus groups are especially useful in exploratory research to discover people's perceptions and feelings about a topic of interest [29]. Focus group data can be used for a variety of purposes, including guiding program or policy development, gaining an understanding of behaviors, and capturing organizational concerns and issues.

Focus groups can also be valuable in mixed-methods research when used as either a precursor to quantitative surveys of larger samples [15] or as an aid in the interpretation of data collected in a survey [29]. When used as a precursor (as is this case in our experience), the interactive nature of focus groups can facilitate the development of survey questions and procedures by providing an understanding of how people think and talk about specific topics, identifying concepts that are of particular importance to participants, and soliciting ideas for survey recruitment [7,20,22].

Criticisms. Despite their strengths, several criticisms have been directed at focus groups. Because focus groups bring participants together in a non-probabilistic, artificial setting, focus group participants may intellectualize and present themselves as rational and thoughtful. However, in reality, behaviors may be unconscious, irrational, or driven by emotion [15,27]. Participants' responses may also be influenced by group dynamics and pressure to conform to the opinions of others [7]. Moreover, in cases in which groups are too large and the topic is complex, there is a fear of discussions becoming superficial [15].

Several measures can be taken to counter these potential pitfalls [7,15]. Focus groups can be paired with other methodologies (e.g., field observations or surveys) to capture real-world behaviors and validate findings. Furthermore, moderators have an important role in creating an open, welcoming environment in which participants feel safe to express their true thoughts. Moderators also should carefully monitor group dynamics to ensure a small number of individuals do not dominate the conversation. Limiting group size can help to ensure participants have adequate opportunity to express their thoughts.

It also should be noted that group dynamics and influence may not necessarily be a negative aspect of focus groups. Rather, observations of these interactions can actually be quite insightful as they may mimic participants' daily conversations with others [7].

2.2   Focus Groups in Security Information Workers Research

Focus group methods are infrequently found in formal, academic cybersecurity research. Fujs et al. [10] identified 160 papers describing qualitative research related to cybersecurity (not limited to studies involving SIW) from 2017-2019, classifying only 11 as using focus groups. However, the authors' definition of focus group is arguable in that they binned group interviews with only two individuals and workshops into the focus group category. Therefore, there may have been fewer focus group studies than the 11 reported.

Fewer examples can be found when applied specifically to research involving SIW. Bada et al. [4] conducted focus groups of security professionals to better understand the relationship between cybersecurity awareness-raising campaigns and the cybersecurity capacity maturity of six African nations. Kumar et al. [16] conducted focus groups with primary school teachers to identify, in part, how educators could best communicate security and privacy information to students. Gorski et al. [13] utilized four in-person focus groups of software developers in a participatory design study related to security warnings for cryptographic libraries. This was the only paper related to focus groups and SIW we found that described the methodology and focus group protocol development in detail. However, we discovered no papers that discuss lessons learned after the use of focus groups to study SIW.

3   Study Methodology

As a basis for our lessons learned and position on suitability for SIW research, we first provide an overview of how focus groups were employed in our research study. The study protocol was reviewed by the National Institute of Standards and Technology (NIST) Research Protections Office and determined to be exempt human subjects research.

3.1   Study Overview

Security awareness training can be a first step towards helping employees recognize and appropriately respond to security issues, with a goal of achieving long-term behavior change [35]. However, security awareness programs may face a multitude of challenges, including lack of resources and appropriately trained staff, a poor reputation among the workforce for training being a boring, "check-the-box" exercise, and a tendency to measure success based on training completion rates rather than workforce behavior change [3,25,37]. Moreover, it is unclear if these challenges apply to U.S. government (federal) organizations. To address this uncertainty, we conducted a two-phased, mixed-methods study leveraging both qualitative and quantitative methods to better understand the needs, challenges, practices, and necessary competencies of federal security awareness teams and programs.

Focus groups of 29 federal security awareness professionals were a first phase that informed a follow-on, predominantly quantitative survey completed by 96 security awareness professionals. A focus group methodology was selected as our qualitative phase for several reasons. Beyond the utility of informing the survey, since one of the goals of our study was to identify potential ways in which information could be shared more effectively across the community, we believed it would be valuable to observe how ideas emerged during group discussion. Focus groups would also serve a practical purpose as we had an abbreviated timeline in which to collect and analyze data. Our study results were going to inform the revision of a government security awareness guidance document set to commence around the same time as our study. Wanting to provide input earlier rather than later in the revision process and factoring in the time to design and execute a follow-on survey, we saw focus groups as being more efficient as compared to individual interviews.

3.2   Focus Group Design

When designing the study, we consulted seven subject matter experts (SMEs) who were veteran security awareness professionals or past and current coordinators of federal security collaboration forums that address security awareness topics. The SMEs provided input into the study's overall direction, focus group questions, and participant recruitment strategies.

We selected a multiple-category design for the focus groups, which involved focus groups with several types of participants to allow for comparisons across or within categories [15]. Based on SME discussions, we decided on three categories: 1) department-level organizations (e.g., U.S. Department of Commerce), 2) sub-component agencies, which are semi-autonomous organizations under a department (e.g., NIST is a sub-component under Department of Commerce), and 3) independent agencies, which are not in a department (e.g., General Services Administration). In the Executive Branch of the U.S. government, there are 15 departments, over 200 sub-components, and just over 100 independent agencies.

In deciding how many groups to conduct, we consulted the focus group methodology literature. In a multiple-category design, it is suggested that 3-4 focus groups per category are usually sufficient to reach data saturation, but there may be categories consisting of small populations for which fewer groups may suffice [15]. As such, we aimed for three groups each for the independent and sub-component categories. Since there are only 15 government departments from which to recruit, having two groups of those working at the department level was deemed to be acceptable. Furthermore, Guest et al. [14] found that about 80% of all data saturation occurs after 2 - 3 focus groups, with 90% occurring after 3 - 6 groups. Because we observed that many of the same themes identified during analysis occurred regardless of organization category, we felt relatively confident that we had likely reached a high level of data saturation with our eight groups.

To develop the focus group instrument, we followed the suggested process for creating a questioning route outlined in Krueger and Casey [15]. This route includes: an easy-to-answer, opening question; an introductory question that gets people thinking about the topic; a transition question that prompts participants to go into more detail about their experiences with the topic; key questions, which are the core of the discussion; and ending questions that allow participants to voice their thoughts on critical aspects of the topic and suggest other significant topics related to but not explored during the group. Appendix A contains the focus group script with labels for each type of question.

3.3   Data Collection

Focus group participants were selected to represent the diversity of federal agencies. We identified prospective participants via several avenues: recommendations from the SMEs; researchers' professional contacts; an online cybersecurity mailing list of small federal agencies; speakers and contest participants/winners from the last three years of the Federal Information Security Educators (FIS-SEA) conference [21]; and LinkedIn and Google searches. Invitations were sent via email. Participants had to be federal employees and have knowledge of the security awareness programs in their organizations either because they had security awareness duties or oversaw the programs.

We held the focus groups in December 2020 and January 2021. While focus groups are often conducted in-person, because of the pandemic and distributed locations of federal security awareness professionals across the U.S., we ran all focus groups using a virtual meeting platform. To maximize discussion time during the actual focus groups, we held a 15-minute meeting with each participant individually in the days preceding their focus group to test and troubleshoot their meeting connection and review the informed consent form. Participants were also provided the opportunity to ask questions. Prior to the focus group, each participant had to return their digitally signed consent form via email to the research team.

In all, we conducted eight focus groups with 29 total participants. Focus group sessions lasted 60-75 minutes, with each having 3-5 participants. Three focus groups consisted of 12 representatives from independent federal agencies. Two focus groups (each with 3 people) were with representatives from department-level agencies. The third set consisted of three focus groups with 11 representatives from 10 department sub-component agencies (in one group, two individuals from the same agency attended).

Three research team members managed the focus groups. The principal investigator served as the moderator for all groups. The moderator shared a slide presentation that displayed questions as they were being asked. To begin the focus groups, she welcomed participants and briefly discussed tips to help the conversation (e.g., "This is a confidential discussion," "There are no wrong answers" and "When not talking, please mute yourself."). Then she asked each question, probed further to clarify or get more details on responses as appropriate, and facilitated discussion. Another team member acted as the assistant moderator and helped participants with technical issues via chat and email. Finally, a note taker captured the main points of the groups' conversations as a backup in the event that the recording failed or was corrupted.

All focus groups were audio recorded and transcribed. Participants also completed an online survey to gather demographic and organizational information. To ensure anonymity and to be able to confidentially link data between the focus groups and demographic survey, each participant was assigned a reference code, with individuals from independent agencies identified as N01–N12, department-level organizations as D01–D06, and sub-components as S01–S11.

3.4   Data Analysis

Data analysis started with coding [6], which involved categorization of focus group data. Initially, each of the four members of the research team individually coded a subset of three transcripts (one from each category of focus group) using an *a priori* code list based on the focus group questions and then added new codes as needed. The research team met several times to discuss codes and develop a codebook (a list of codes to be used in analysis). As part of the final codebook, all codes were "operationalized," which involves formally defining each code to ensure understanding among all coders. Coding continued until all transcripts were coded by two researchers, who met to discuss code application and resolve differences. The entire research team convened to discuss overarching themes identified in the data and areas of interest to include in the subsequent survey.

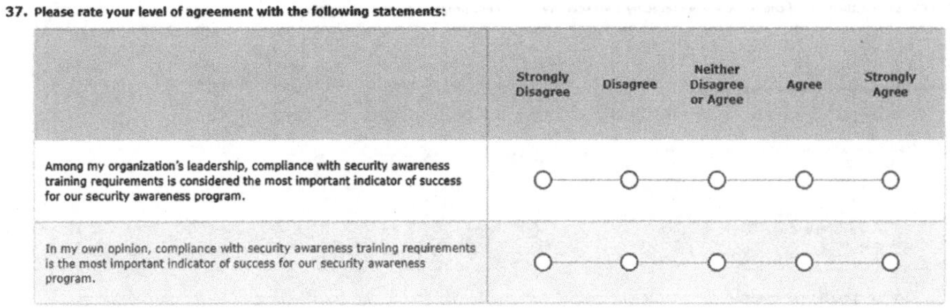

37. Please rate your level of agreement with the following statements:

	Strongly Disagree	Disagree	Neither Disagree or Agree	Agree	Strongly Agree
Among my organization's leadership, compliance with security awareness training requirements is considered the most important indicator of success for our security awareness program.	○	○	○	○	○
In my own opinion, compliance with security awareness training requirements is the most important indicator of success for our security awareness program.	○	○	○	○	○

Fig. 1. Survey question about compliance as an indicator of success for a security awareness program

3.5 Informing a Survey

Focus group data informed the development of a predominantly quantitative survey that was distributed to a larger number of security awareness professionals. The following describes several ways in which the survey was influenced.

We discovered areas of particular importance or divergence among focus group participants that were incorporated as questions in the survey. For example, we observed a tension among participants with respect to the success of the security awareness program being determined by compliance with training mandates (measured by training completion rates) versus actual impact on employees' behaviors. Thus, we developed a question to gauge this sentiment among surveyed organizations (see Fig. 1). As another example, focus group participants identified several significant challenges their security awareness programs face. In the survey, we developed corresponding questions that asked participants to rate the level of challenge they encountered (5-point Likert scale ranging from "Very challenging" to "Not at all challenging") for each of those challenge items (see Fig. 2 for an example).

Focus group data also informed possible answer choices for a number of questions. For instance, when asking what happens when employees do not complete their awareness training on time, we included answer options based on examples provided to us by focus group participants (see Fig. 3).

4 General Lessons Learned

Before addressing the suitability of focus groups for SIW research, we first discuss general lessons learned in our experience with virtual focus groups.

4.1 Differences from Interviews

Given that the moderator utilizes a semi-structured questioning approach, one might think that focus groups are similar to interviews. However, even though our research team had extensive prior experience with interviews, we discovered that focus groups were quite different than interviews in several respects.

27. Please rate the level of challenge encountered by your security awareness program for the following:

	Very challenging	Moderately challenging	Somewhat challenging	Not at all challenging	Does not apply
Providing security awareness information in an engaging way.	O	O	O	O	O
Customizing security awareness information to people with varying needs and levels of IT and security knowledge.	O	O	O	O	O
Communicating security awareness information to a distributed work force.	O	O	O	O	O
Finding existing security awareness materials to use.	O	O	O	O	O
Ensuring security awareness materials are 508 compliant.	O	O	O	O	O

Fig. 2. Example survey question about challenges encountered in the security awareness program

17. What happens to employees who do not complete their required training by the deadline? Check all that apply.

☐ They receive an email reminder.

☐ Their supervisor is contacted.

☐ Their account is disabled/suspended.

☐ Their annual performance rating is negatively impacted.

☐ Nothing

☐ Other:

Fig. 3. Survey question about consequences for not completing training

Recruitment Effort. We found that recruitment and scheduling were more labor-intensive as compared to interviews. There were significant challenges coordinating the schedules of participants to find blocks of time in which at least three people (plus the researchers) were available, especially since some participants had demanding jobs (e.g., CISO). When prospective participants responded affirmatively to our email invitation, to determine availability, we sent them a link to an online scheduling application with several possible dates and times for the focus groups. However, less than half used the application, resulting in our research team having to follow up with additional emails to coordinate.

Level of Detail. Focus groups do not afford the in-depth data often collected via individual interviews. Because more people have to provide input in an allotted time frame, fewer questions can be asked, and follow-on probes to gather more information may be limited. For example, in several of our focus groups, we had to skip a question due to time constraints, forcing us to follow up with participants via email to obtain responses. Therefore, there should be careful consideration on whether focus groups can provide the level of detail required for the study investigation and how many questions can be answered to the desired depth. In our case, because of the abbreviated timeline and main intent of data informing a follow-on survey that could validate initial findings, we felt that the data we collected was sufficient, especially with the five focus groups that were able to be scheduled for more than one hour. However, if conducted as a standalone study, the data might not have been enough to reach solid conclusions.

Group Dynamics. Unlike individual interviews, focus groups require careful moderation to navigate group dynamics and ensure all participants have an opportunity to share. We did indeed encounter dominant personalities whose responses had to be politely curtailed and more passive participants who had to be encouraged to offer input. In one of our early focus groups, we observed the participants falling into a round-robin pattern with one participant frequently going last and often agreeing with prior responses, e.g., "Similar to what others say, we do the same within our phishing program" (N01) and "I agree with both of those points" (N01). Therefore, we tried to encourage that participant to answer first in subsequent questions.

Despite several challenges, we discovered benefits of the group format. Participants became fellow questioners when someone would say something that piqued interest or needed clarification. During one of the independent agency focus groups, a participant posed a question to another based on a prior comment: "When you disable people [for not completing their training on time], is that done automatically or is that a manual process at your agency?" (N09). During another focus group, several participants said that they track user incidents as a way to measure the effectiveness of their programs. However, S04 said that he was struggling to understand how they relate incidents to training and asked his fellow participants for clarification. One participant provided an explanation and examples of what his organization does. Not only did this explanation aid the questioner, but it contributed additional data for our research purposes.

Comments could also aid in recall or trigger additional comments that might not have otherwise come out in individual interviews. For example, in one focus group, even though N01 had already provided a response to a question, another participant's comment about "stars" being awarded to employees who demonstrate good security behaviors prompted her to interject and spend an additional minute and a half sharing her organization's approach to incentives.

4.2 Virtual Focus Groups

We found that *virtual* focus groups necessitated adjustments to address challenges arising beyond those typically encountered in traditional, in-person groups.

Less is Better. Because of shorter attention spans and competing distractions when engaging in virtual meetings [17], it is recommended that virtual focus groups should involve fewer participants (as compared to the 5-8 people typical for in-person groups) as well as shorter blocks of time (60–90 min versus 2 h when in-person) [34]. To that end, we scheduled focus groups of 3-5 participants lasting at most 75 min. The short, individual meeting with each participant prior to their group allowed us to proactively address administrative and logistical items, freeing up time for more discussion during the actual focus groups.

Selecting a Usable Meeting Platform. We gave careful consideration to the selection of a virtual meeting platform. We desired an application that would be either familiar to most participants or easy-to-learn, required minimal set up (e.g., quick installation of a client) or could be accessed via a browser, allowed for recording, permitted participants to be viewed anonymously (e.g., by changing their display name and turning off the camera), and offered alternative connection options (e.g., dial-in by phone). We also wanted a platform in which we could share presentation slides to serve as a guide and reminder to participants about the current question being discussed. We ultimately selected Webex given that this platform was widely used within the government and met our criteria.

Expecting the Unexpected. In-person focus groups tend to be held in more controlled, predictable settings. However, the online aspect of virtual focus groups introduces new, and sometimes unexpected, challenges. Pre-group meetings with participants afforded an opportunity to guide participants through the use of the platform and troubleshoot technical difficulties. We also encouraged participants to join the group several minutes early in case extra help was needed. However, due to busy schedules, many participants were not able to join early, and several participants still encountered technical issues such as poor connections or speakers or microphones failing to work. To aid these participants, the assistant moderator acted in a troubleshooting role, conversing privately with participants experiencing issues using the meeting chat function or, in some cases, via email.

We also experienced two instances in which unexpected guests initially joined the meeting. In both cases, focus group participants had invited other coworkers to observe. However, because these coworkers had not signed the informed consent, we had to politely ask them to leave the meeting. Although we had previously mentioned that all participants had to sign the informed consent prior to the focus groups, in retrospect, we should have emphasized that the form covered the individual, not the organization.

Moderating Differently. The moderation of virtual focus groups can be especially challenging. Since most of our participants opted to not turn on their cameras, the lack of visual cues and delays in audio or video made turn-taking more difficult for participants and put the moderator at a disadvantage. For example, the moderator could not tell when someone gave an indication they wanted to say something and could not gauge participants' reactions to questions or others' responses. To address these issues, the moderator kept her camera on so as to allow participants to see her own visual cues. She also demonstrated patience when waiting for participants to respond, allowing for several seconds of silence to provide participants adequate time to think through their responses.

5   Suitability for Studying Security Information Workers

In addition to providing general lessons learned, we contribute a discussion on virtual focus group benefits and disadvantages that may be unique to studying SIW or similar populations.

5.1   Benefits

Overcoming Recruitment Challenges. Security information workers are traditionally difficult to recruit [5,28,36]. However, focus groups may provide some benefits that help overcome recruitment challenges.

Accommodating Time and Environment Constraints. SIWs are often overworked with busy schedules and may be part of a specialized and distributed workforce [5,9]. Although full ethnographic, in situ investigations (e.g., [30]) may provide the most comprehensive insights into the work of SIW, these types of studies may be impractical or impossible for a number of reasons, including resources required (for both the research team and the workers) and the sensitivity of SIW work environments that may necessitate significant relationship and trust building to access [9,23,30].

We found that shorter, virtual focus groups (versus in-person sessions) were less intrusive and more palatable considering these workers' time and location constraints. Given our own externally-driven time constraints, the focus groups allowed for gathering input from participants much more efficiently than would have been the case with interviews, allowing us to develop and launch our follow-on survey within our targeted time frame.

Information Sharing as an Incentive to Participate. Given their constraints, SIW must also be properly incentivized to participate. When discussing the challenge of recruiting security professionals, researchers have emphasized the importance of demonstrating the value of participation and addressing reciprocity (what the participant receives in return) [5,28]. It is common for researchers to extol the value of their research for the social good in recruitment materials, e.g., "Results will inform security awareness training program guidelines to aid federal organizations in the development of effective security awareness programs." However, a more individualized benefit should also be provided.

Offers of monetary compensation for those who participate, though common, may not be enough. Research institutions typically offer smaller amounts (e.g., $20–$25 for an hour-long interview [2]) not commensurate with the $50+ an hour earned on average by SIW in the U.S. [32,33]. In our situation, since we work for a government agency and recruited government employees, we were not able to offer any monetary incentive.

Instead, we found that the very nature of focus groups provided a personal, and perhaps more attractive, incentive to participate. Since information sharing is a natural and important way of working in the security community [8,19], the opportunity to hear about others' experiences during a focus group provided immediate benefit to participants and their organizations versus waiting for results to be captured in a report that may be published many months later.

In our study, we observed multiple participants commenting on the value of hearing what other organizations were doing. For example, at the end of their respective focus groups, a security awareness program lead of a large independent agency stated, "I've picked up some good tidbits from everybody else in the phone call today that I can go back and probably implement immediately" (N08), and a trainer in a sub-component agency remarked, "It's been very interesting to hear everyone's perspectives" (S06). After one participant talked about his organization's security day events in which they bring in external speakers, a CISO complimented the approach: "I'm totally borrowing that idea" (N06). Several participants even exchanged email addresses after their focus groups to continue their discussions.

Navigating a Specialized Field. The security community has its own specialized language, acronyms, and jargon, even more so for specialties within the field and certain sectors like the government. This language may be unfamiliar to researchers with no first-hand experience in the particular security field under investigation. Because of this lack of familiarity, researchers may find it difficult to sort through large amounts of data to find what will be of greatest interest to the community under study [36]. However, focus groups may be particularly valuable in countering this SIW research challenge as they allow experts in the field to self-identify areas of interest. What matters most to SIW comes out naturally and with more passion in group discussions.

We experienced these benefits first-hand. Although two members of our research team had security backgrounds, neither were overly familiar with the terminology used to describe federal security awareness programs and policies nor the unique challenges faced by these programs. We found that the focus groups aided our understanding of the specialized language of federal security awareness professionals, helped us identify areas of interest and particular challenge, and allowed us the opportunity to observe how professionals working in this field interact and communicate. These insights were vital to the creation of the follow-up survey and will greatly inform recommendations resulting from the study as well as how and where we present our findings to be of most value to the federal security awareness community.

5.2   Disadvantages and Challenges

There are also potential downsides to using focus groups with SIW and situations in which they are not appropriate.

Sensitive Topics. Some security topics may not be appropriate for group sharing, or SIW may be reluctant to share information that may reflect poorly on their organizations or themselves [5,18]. For example, in their work studying security practitioners, multiple research groups found that disclosure of organizational security procedures and tools was viewed as being sensitive since these were often proprietary or related to vulnerabilities that are usually closely-held secrets [5,9,12]

Security Mindsets. Security information workers often possess a "security mindset" in which they tend to think like a cyber attacker or adversary [26]. This "peculiar mix of curiosity and paranoia that turns life into a perpetual game of 'what if' questions" [31] may result in SIW being hesitant to participate in recorded virtual meetings or trust other focus group participants. Moreover, SIW may be wary of the researchers or the legitimacy of the study invitation. For example, in our study, despite sending our recruitment invitations from a government email address, one individual requested we send a digitally signed email from our institution to prove that we were not scammers before he would respond any further.

5.3 Mitigating Concerns

There were several mitigations we found effective in alleviating SIW concerns about participating in focus groups.

Establishing Credibility and Rapport. In countering potential mistrust of researchers among SIW, participation rates have been found to rise with the authority and credibility of the requestor [28]. In our experience, our affiliation with an institution having a positive reputation in the security field was helpful for persuading security awareness professionals to participate. The researchers' own security backgrounds further aided in putting people at ease as they believed they were talking to others with similar mindsets. This was also observed in Botta et al. [5] in which the lead researcher had experience as a security practitioner.

Efforts to build rapport with our participants were also valuable in creating a safe, open environment in which participants felt comfortable sharing their honest thoughts and experiences. We began these efforts during the individual, pre-focus group meetings described earlier that allowed us to meet participants before the group. We found that participants were more willing to turn on their cameras for these shorter meetings than in the actual focus groups, providing the opportunity to match names to faces. We were also able to communicate what participants should expect given that many had never participated in a focus group and were not sure what other types of people would be participating. Participants could also ask questions, which assured them that they and their concerns were important to the research team. Rapport-building continued during the focus groups, as the moderator encouraged and thanked participants for their responses throughout the sessions, and followed up afterwards with another "thank you" via email. Overall, the study afforded a way to network and establish relationships that continued after the focus groups, as demonstrated by several participants continuing communications with the research team in the months following.

Demonstrating Protective Measures. To encourage participation in virtual SIW studies, researchers need to explicitly address participant concerns when collecting data online, including how they are protecting security and confidentiality and minimizing harm to participants [11].

Clearly Communicate Protective Measures. Details about how participant identities and data will be protected should be included in the informed consent form. In countries or institutions in which informed consent is not required, researchers should still take care to clearly communicate these protections in writing. The importance of this communication was highlighted in other SIW studies. For example, Botta et al. [5] discussed their rigorous data protection procedure and how they relayed that to their interview participants. In their focus groups, Gorski et al. [13] described how they required focus group participants to sign a consent form detailing data protection practices that included anonymization of identities and destruction of audio recordings and personally identifiable information at the close of the study.

We followed a similar approach. As described previously, the informed consent was reviewed thoroughly during the pre-group meetings, and each participant had to sign and return the consent prior to their focus group. In the informed consent, we were specific about the measures we were taking, which included:

- the use of participant codes (e.g., D04) to link data
- our practice of redacting all names of people and organizations from the transcripts should they accidentally be mentioned
- at the end of the study, destruction of recordings and documents linking participant names and participant codes
- how and where data would be securely stored and transmitted (e.g., on a secured government server, transmitted via an encrypted, secure file transfer application)
- who has access to study data
- the voluntary nature of participation and the participant's right to withdraw from the study at any time
- a participant's right to ask that certain comments they made be removed from the research record
- how data would be reported in aggregate with care not to identify any individuals or organizations

At the conclusion of the pre-focus group meetings, multiple participants commented that they felt more comfortable with the study due to our discussion about the security and privacy procedures.

Use Secure Technologies that Support Participant Preferences. Using a secure virtual meeting platform that allows for individual privacy is another important mitigation to alleviate SIW concerns. We selected a platform that had no known vulnerabilities or privacy concerns at the time and which would allow participants options for anonymity, such as turning off cameras or changing display names. Most participants elected to keep their cameras off, and several changed their display names to be first name only. Furthermore, introductions at the beginning of the focus groups were not recorded, and participants could choose to not reveal their names or organizations to others during that time. This anonymity option was employed by one participant, who wished for her organization to remain anonymous due to political sensitivities.

We also allowed for options for completing the online demographic survey to accommodate participant preferences. The survey was implemented in Google Forms. However, we provided an alternative if a participant's organization blocked access to Google Workspace or if they felt uncomfortable entering their information online. We sent participants a Microsoft Word version of the survey that they could complete and securely transmit back via encrypted email or a secure file sharing application. Four participants took advantage of this option.

6   Conclusion

Focus groups are a rarely-used research method for studying security information workers. While not appropriate in all situations, focus groups can be a valuable way to collect data efficiently while capitalizing on the security community's proclivity to information sharing. Moving from in-person to virtual focus groups can provide even more benefits, as these reduce the time commitment for busy SIW and allow for the inclusion of individuals from multiple locations. When employing focus groups, careful consideration should be made to address potential SIW security and privacy concerns to encourage participation and ensure a positive participant experience.

Disclaimer
Certain commercial companies or products are identified in this paper to foster understanding. Such identification does not imply recommendation or endorsement by the National Institute of Standards and Technology, nor does it imply that the companies or products identified are necessarily the best available for the purpose.

Appendix A Focus Group Script

Moderator Introduction and Ground Rules
Welcome to our focus group! I'd like to start off by thanking each of you for taking time to participate today. We'll be here for about *[insert time]* at most. It may be less than that, but we want to allow plenty of time for discussion.

I'm going to lead our discussion today. I will be asking you questions and then moderating our discussion. *[Research team members]* are part of the research team and will be assisting me by taking notes and jumping in with follow-up questions when appropriate.

I'd like to go over a few items that will allow our conversation to flow more freely. *[Share PowerPoint presentation that summarizes ground rules.]*

1. This is a confidential discussion without fear of reprisal or comments being taken out of context. We told you how we are going to protect your confidentiality, and we ask the same of you with respect to others in the group here today.
2. If you don't understand a question or need clarification, please ask.
3. You don't have to answer every question, but we'd like to hear from each of you today as the discussion progresses. There are no "wrong answers," just different opinions and experiences.
4. We'll do our best with turn-taking. Unmute and jump in or click the "raise hand" icon next to your name in the Participants panel.
5. When not talking, please mute yourself to cut down on background noise and feedback.
6. Turning on your camera is optional but can help with conversational cues, but there's no pressure to turn it on.
7. Chat is available if you'd like to share a link or resource with the group or have any technical issues. But if you'd like to say something that contributes directly to the conversation, please say it out loud so that we can capture it on the recording.

Introduction of Participants
Opening question: First, we'll do some introductions. These will NOT be recorded. I'll go around to each of you. Please tell everyone your name, organization, and your role with respect to security awareness.

Focus Group Questions
I'm now going to start recording this session. *[Advance through slides for each question.]*

1. ***Introductory question:*** When I say "security awareness and training," what does that mean to you? What comes to mind?
2. ***Transition question:*** Tell me about your organization's approach to security awareness and training. This can include general security awareness for the workforce as well as awareness for specialized job roles.
3. ***Key question:*** How do you decide what topics and approaches to use for your security awareness program?
   (a) *[Probe for sub-components]* What kind of guidance/direction, if any, does your department provide? How much leeway do you have to tailor the training to your own organization?
   (b) *[Probe for department-level agencies]* What kind of guidance/direction, if any, do you push down to sub-components within your department?

4. **Key question:** What's working well with your program?
5. **Key question:** What's not working as well and why? What are your challenges and concerns with respect to security awareness in your organization?
6. **Key question:** How do you determine the effectiveness of your program, if at all?
7. **Key question:** If you could have anything or do anything for your security awareness program, what would that be?
   (a) *[Probe]* What would you do to solve the challenges you currently experience?
   (b) *[Probe]* What kinds and formats of resources and information sharing would be most beneficial?
8. **Key question:** What knowledge, skills, or competencies do you think are needed for those performing security awareness functions in your organization?
9. **Ending question:** If you had one or two pieces of advice for someone just starting a security awareness program in an agency like yours, what would that advice be?
10. **Ending question:** Recall that the purpose of our study is to better understand the needs, challenges, practices, and professional competencies of federal security awareness teams and programs. This understanding will lead to the creation of resources for federal security awareness professionals.
11. **Ending question:** Is there anything else that we should have talked about, but didn't?

Closing

I will now end the recording. That concludes our focus group. Thanks for attending and talking about these issues. Your comments have been very insightful.

Just a few reminders. If you want something that you said removed from the research record, please let us know. Also, if you think of anything else you didn't get a chance to talk about, feel free to email us.

We really appreciate your participation and thank you again for your time. Have a wonderful day!

References

1. 7th Workshop on Security Information Workers. https://security-information-workers.org/ (2021)
2. Acar, Y., Stransky, C., Wermke, D., Mazurek, M.L., Fahl, S.: Security developer studies with Github users: Exploring a convenience sample. In: Proceedings of the 13th Symposium on Usable Privacy and Security (SOUPS 2017). pp. 81–95 (2017)
3. Bada, M., Sasse, A.M., Nurse, J.R.: Cyber security awareness campaigns: Why do they fail to change behaviour? (2019). https://arxiv.org/ftp/arxiv/papers/1901/1901.02672.pdf
4. Bada, M., Solms, B.V., Agrafiotis, I.: Reviewing national cybersecurity awareness in Africa: An empirical study (2019)
5. Botta, D., Werlinger, R., Gagné, A., Beznosov, K., Iverson, L., Fels, S., Fisher, B.: Studying IT security professionals: Research design and lessons learned (2007)

6. Corbin, J., Strauss, A.: Basics of Qualitative Research: Techniques and Procedures for Developing Grounded Theory, 4th edn. Sage Publications, Thousand Oaks (2015)
7. Cyr, J.: The unique utility of focus groups for mixed-methods research. Polit. Sci. Politics **50**(4), 1038 (2017)
8. David, D.P., Keupp, M.M., Mermoud, A.: Knowledge absorption for cyber-security: The role of human beliefs. Comput. Hum. Behav. **106**, 106255 (2020)
9. Dykstra, J., Paul, C.L.: Cyber operations stress survey (COSS): Studying fatigue, frustration, and cognitive workload in cybersecurity operations. In: 11th USENIX Workshop on Cyber Security Experimentation and Test (CSET 18) (2018)
10. Fujs, D., Mihelič, A., Vrhovec, S.L.: The power of interpretation: Qualitative methods in cybersecurity research. In: Proceedings of the 14th International Conference on Availability, Reliability and Security, pp. 1–10 (2019)
11. Galloway, K.L.: Focus groups in the virtual world: implications for the future of evaluation. New Dir. Eval. **131**(2011), 47–51 (2011)
12. Goodall, J.R., Lutters, W.G., Komlodi, A.: I know my network: collaboration and expertise in intrusion detection. In: Proceedings of the 2004 ACM Conference on Computer Supported Cooperative Work, pp. 342–345 (2004)
13. Gorski, P., Leo, P., Acar, Y., Iacono, L.L., Fahl, S.: Listen to developers! A participatory design study on security warnings for cryptographic APIs. In: Proceedings of the 2020 CHI Conference on Human Factors in Computing Systems, pp. 1–13 (2020)
14. Guest, G., Namey, E., McKenna, K.: How many focus groups are enough? Building an evidence base for nonprobability sample sizes. Field Methods **29**(1), 3–22, 106255 (2017)
15. Krueger, R.A., Casey, M.A.: Focus Groups: A Practical Guide for Applied Research. Sage, Thousand Oaks (2015)
16. Kumar, P.C., Chetty, M., Clegg, T.L., Vitak, J.: Privacy and security considerations for digital technology use in elementary schools. In: Proceedings of the 2019 CHI Conference on Human Factors in Computing Systems, pp. 1–13 (2019)
17. Malhotra, A., Majchrzak, A., Rosen, B.: Leading virtual teams. Acad. Manage. Perspect. **21**(1), 60–70 (2007)
18. Mathew, A., Cheshire, C.: Risky business: Social trust and community in the practice of cybersecurity for internet infrastructure. In: Proceedings of the 50th Hawaii International Conference on System Sciences, pp. 2341–2350 (2017)
19. Mermoud, A., Keupp, M.M., Huguenin, K., Palmié, M., David, D.P.: To share or not to share: A behavioral perspective on human participation in security information sharing. J. Cybersecurity **5**(1) (2019)
20. Nassar-McMillan, S.C., Borders, L.D.: Use of focus groups in survey item development. Qual. Rep. **7**(1), 1–12, 106255 (2002)
21. National Institute of Standards and Technology: FISSEA - Federal Information Security Educators (2021). https://csrc.nist.gov/projects/fissea
22. O'Brien, K.: Using focus groups to develop health surveys: An example from research on social relationships and AIDS-preventive behavior. Health Educ. Q. **20**(3), 361–372, 106255 (1993)
23. Paul, C.L.: Human-centered study of a network operations center: Experience report and lessons learned. In: Proceedings of the 2014 ACM Workshop on Security Information Workers, pp. 39–42 (2014)

24. Petersen, R., Santos, D., Smith, M.C., Wetzel, K.A., Witte, G.: NIST Special Publication 800–181 Revision 1: Workforce Framework for Cybersecurity (NICE Framework) (2020). https://nvlpubs.nist.gov/nistpubs/SpecialPublications/NIST. SP.800-181r1.pdf
25. SANS: 2021 SANS security awareness report: Managing human cyber risk (2021). https://www.sans.org/security-awareness-training/resources/reports/ sareport-2021/
26. Schneier, B.: The security mindset (2008). https://www.schneier.com/blog/ archives/2008/03/the_security_mi_1.html
27. Sim, J.: Collecting and analysing qualitative data: Issues raised by the focus group. J. Adv. Nurs. **28**(2), 345–352, 106255 (1998)
28. Smith, E., Loftin, R., Murphy-Hill, E., Bird, C., Zimmermann, T.: Improving developer participation rates in surveys. In: Proceedings of the 6th International Workshop on Cooperative and Human Aspects of Software Engineering (CHASE), pp. 89–92 (2013)
29. Stewart, D.W., Shamdasani, P.N.: Focus Groups: Theory and Practice, vol. 20. Sage, Thousand Oaks (2014)
30. Sundaramurthy, S.C., McHugh, J., Ou, X.S., Rajagopalan, S.R., Wesch, M.: An anthropological approach to studying CSIRTs. IEEE Secur. Priv. **12**(5), 52–60, 106255 (2014)
31. The State of Security: The security mindset: the key to success in the security field, November 2015. https://www.tripwire.com/state-of-security/off-topic/the-security-mindset-the-key-to-success-in-the-security-field/
32. U.S. Bureau of Labor Statistics: Information security analysts (2021). https:// www.bls.gov/ooh/computer-and-information-technology/information-security-analysts.htm
33. U.S. Bureau of Labor Statistics: Software developers, quality assurance analysts, and testers (2021). https://www.bls.gov/ooh/computer-and-information-technology/software-developers.htm
34. UX Alliance: Conducting remote online focus groups in times of COVID-19, April 2020. https://medium.com/@UXalliance/conducting-remote-online-focus-groups-in-times-of-covid-19-ee1c66644fdb
35. Wilson, M., Hash, J.: NIST Special Publication 800–50 - Building an information technology security awareness program (2003). https://nvlpubs.nist.gov/nistpubs/ Legacy/SP/nistspecialpublication800-50.pdf
36. Witschey, J., Murphy-Hill, E., Xiao, S.: Conducting interview studies: Challenges, lessons learned, and open questions. In: Proceedings of the 1st International Workshop on Conducting Empirical Studies in Industry (CESI), pp. 51–54 (2013)
37. Woelk, B.: The successful security awareness professional: Foundational skills and continuing education strategies (2015). https://library.educause.edu/~/media/ files/library/2016/8/erb1608.pdf

A Survey of User Experience in Usable Security and Privacy Research

Danielle Jacobs[1]([✉])[iD] and Troy McDaniel[2][iD]

[1] School of Computing and Augmented Intelligence, Arizona State University,
Tempe, AZ 85281, USA
danielle.r.jacobs@asu.edu
[2] The Polytechnic School, Arizona State University, Mesa, AZ 85212, USA
troy.mcdaniel@asu.edu

Abstract. Today people depend on technology, but often do not take
the necessary steps to prioritize privacy and security. Researchers have
been actively studying usable security and privacy to enable better
response and management. A breadth of research focuses on improving the usability of tools for experts and organizations. Studies that look
at non-expert users tend to analyze the experience for a device, software,
or demographic. There is a lack of understanding of the security and privacy among average users, regardless of the technology, age, gender, or
demographic. To address this shortcoming, we surveyed 47 publications
in the usable security and privacy space. The work presented here uses
qualitative text analysis to find major themes in user-focused security
research. We found that a user's misunderstanding of technology is central to risky decision-making. Our study highlights trends in the research
community and remaining work. This paper contributes to this discussion by generalizing key themes across user experience in usable security
and privacy.

Keywords: Cybersecurity · Human factors · Information security ·
Privacy · Usability

1 Introduction

Modern technology allows users to be connected, and as a result, so much of daily
life depends on technology. This dependency is deepening as smart connected
devices continue to drive transformative changes to the digital age, putting individuals' privacy at risk. The risk to users is sizeable, covering the gamut from
company data breaches, hardware-level vulnerabilities that leak passwords, to
poor security hygiene that gives information away. Moreover, the widespread
adoption of technology increases these risks, as demonstrated by the recent
upsurge in cybercrime [33]. The field of usable security and privacy was developed
in response to ubiquitous technology's emerging threats. According to NIST, the

The authors thank Arizona State University and the National Science Foundation for
their funding support under Grant No. 1828010.

A. Moallem (Ed.): HCII 2022, LNCS 13333, pp. 154–172, 2022.
https://doi.org/10.1007/978-3-031-05563-8_11

research aims to "make it easy to do the right thing, hard to do the wrong thing, and easy to recover when the wrong things happen" [51]. Furthermore, we want to design technology, especially security and privacy-focused solutions, to be user-friendly. A cross-discipline approach helps to inform solutions. This area's interdisciplinary research spans hardware, software, human-computer interaction, psychology, economics, and more. Such collaborative research builds a collation to understand better the dynamics of technology, end-users, security, and privacy.

An integrative approach to user-centered privacy and security is not new. By the 1980s, researchers were applying human factors to privacy and security [22]. With nearly 40 years of progress, it is essential to pause and examine the efforts. There is a myriad of publications to survey. Understanding the gaps, current state, and everyday experiences of the user can provide a foundation for continued progress. The scope of current work is prodigious, partly due to the decades of work and multi-disciplinary methods. The usability of technology has been an evolving process. In the late 1980s, Karat studied security usability through the lifecycle of a tool's development [22].

Today, looking at the existing work, we see a variety of tools and technologies. Researchers have sought to understand how the privacy and security of everyday tools can better address issues faced by users. This includes determining cognitive models users create when engaging with tools and highlighting existing knowledge gaps. Overall we see the main focus of current work centered around certain groups of users or technology applications. A large subsection of this work includes deep dives into studying experts, resulting in the identification of themes as part of a qualitative review of nearly 70 publications to better capture how researchers define the field [28]. More specific to end-users, we see some work describing how users react to vulnerabilities, focusing on novice users' processes [5,39]. Surveying the current publications for usable security and privacy, we found a heavy focus on organizations, specialists, specific demographics, or particular technologies. We may understand how security researchers and experts define the risks and the field of study. However, there has been no effort to generalize a user's understanding of usable security and privacy.

This review dives deep into existing literature to extract and analyze how novice users perceive security and privacy. First, we will investigate the findings from the literature to find common themes in user experience across technology. Next, we will apply a qualitative data analysis technique to identify the end-user-specific themes. In analyzing the data, we will answer questions around the research community and user experience. Finally, this review highlights emerging trends and questions in the area. We seek to answer the following research questions (RQ) to guide our research:

RQ1 [User Experience and Risk]: *What user behaviors put users more at risk, and what do users believe places them most at risk?*
We found several responses, thoughts, and situations users shared across the surveyed studies. Diving deeper into what was reported in the citations, we found that misunderstandings and design issues cause risky behaviors.

We document examples of risky behavior across the literature through the coding process and showcase examples. In our findings, the misconception of technology, tool design, and trust leads users to make more risky decisions.

RQ2 [Trends and Challenges]: *What are emerging trends and challenges to the field?*
There are several common approaches to study usable security and privacy. Our results show surveys, interviews, and user experiments are the most common methods applied to research. We also illustrate trends in researched topics across the papers. Three topics are explored the most: warnings, phishing attacks, and passwords. More recent publications suggest an emerging trend in the heterogeneity of user groups, as articles consider different demographics. This highlights the communities' realization that security and privacy tools need to meet a diverse population. Furthermore, we report on the challenges and future work based on the surveyed literature. These challenges are reported as a series of themes. We find that there are discrepancies between future work and challenges. Finally, in looking at the remaining gaps, we discuss the most cited obstacles and emerging issues that remain.

2   Related Work

Here we briefly review the current topics covered around usable privacy and security. Finally, we describe how our work is different from work that has come before.

2.1   Usable Security and Privacy Work

Work in usable security and privacy has been around since the 1980s. In the 90s, Whitten and Tygar looked at how the usability of PGP 5.0 prevents the average person from adopting encryption software [56]. With the threat landscape growing for cyber physical systems, corporations, and governments, a plethora of work has looked at cybersecurity from the perspective of a larger system [15,35,52]. In this context, usability is especially important for response and operations.

For example, Kokulu et al. investigated Cybersecurity Operations Centers (SOC) to find common operational bottlenecks that can be addressed to improve a SOC's effectiveness [23]. In other recent papers, researchers apply situational awareness to the cybersecurity incident responders [2]. Others have sought to integrate usability to develop better tools for security response, making analysis easier [18]. This shows the diversity of current work. While there is vast work on improving security usability for specialists and organizations, another breadth of research focuses on the everyday user.

Prior work has sought to understand users' perceptions and experiences with data usage. Work that focuses on user experience has converged on understanding difficulties users have with integrating security and privacy into everyday life.

For example, Schufrin et al. created TransparencyVis to allow users to visualize how personal data is used online [47]. Instead of looking at data for privacy, some work has focused on a specific technology's usable security and privacy. Sunshine et al. set out to understand how helpful SSL warnings are to users [53]. In addition, several recent works examine factors that influence security behaviors. Pearman et al. looked at the challenges in adopting password managers [36]. Ray et al. built from Pearman et al.'s work and examined challenges facing password managers for older adults [38]. Similarly, researchers have examined the impact of specific demographics in usable security and privacy [31,42,50]. Usable security and privacy research ranges from visualizations to user's mental models. Motivated by a citizen-centered, end-user-centered approach, this paper focuses specifically on research that targets the average user.

Qualitative Coding. Lennartsson et al. perform a literature review of what usable security means to the research community to capture this breadth better [28]. In this piece, Lennartsson et al. apply qualitative coding to a large sample size of usable security and privacy research to identify novel themes that impact usability for security-related topics. We expect to see some differences and similarities for our user experience-focused analysis. This is because our survey paper specifically focuses on the everyday end-user and our research questions.

Framework. Prior work has examined the human factors surrounding everyday users' reactions to vulnerabilities [39]. Rebensky et al. focused on two areas. First is the stages of human response to cybersecurity events. The second is factors that influence human response to cybersecurity events. This resulted in formalizing developed cybersecurity response factors.

Contribution. Our research contrasts with prior work by expanding the meta-analysis. A key contribution to the field is our assessment of trends, challenges, and future opportunities. In addition, we seek to better understand the themes reported around user experience and other aspects of existing work.

3   Methods

This analysis explores usable security and privacy research around the everyday user. By understanding the trends, patterns, user-oriented results, and remaining gaps, researchers can direct efforts toward solving remaining challenges. End-user-centered research is a broad field. Therefore, this paper excludes citations concentrating on organizational and security experts to narrow the scope and provide a survey paper centered on everyday users. The motivation of this survey is first to examine research from the lens of a security researcher and second from the perspective of a human factors researcher. The selected literature reflects this prioritization; most citations are from security conferences and workshops, followed closely by leading human-computer interaction conferences and workshops. Literature was found and pulled through IEEE Xplore, ACM Digital Library, SpringerLink, and Onesearch databases. Our search included a particular focus on top security conferences and workshops such as USENIX Security Symposium, IEEE Symposium on Security and Privacy, and Symposium on Usable Privacy and Security. To include human systems research, the selection also comprises usable security papers from the Conference on Human Factors in Computing Systems and Human Computer Interaction International. As of early 2022, this survey was accurate based on access time. Due to the breadth of research in Usable Security and Privacy, this is not a comprehensive review of these topics; but, through the content provided, shows the common themes, trends, and challenges of the field.

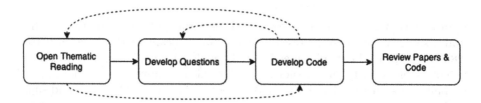

Fig. 1. Flow diagram of the methods and approach taken in this survey paper. The dashed lines indicate a repeated process, while the solid lines indicate the main process flow.

This paper seeks to apply qualitative meta-data analysis techniques to survey usable security and privacy work. For this approach the team used QSR International's Nvivo Software [29]. We followed the electric coding methods discussed by Saldaña that allows multiple methods [46]. Figure 1 details the process that was followed in this user-focused survey. Documents were collected based on the inclusion criteria. Then, open thematic reading of literature generated common themes. The open reading, focused on user-centered security studies, resulted in detecting trends, user perception, and challenges remaining in the field. Some of the challenges identified are directly discussed in the citations. At the same time, other challenges became apparent by the lack of inclusion in the sources. Themes found in initial readings provided content that spurred questions this survey seeks to investigate further. After developing the questions for this survey, we developed a codebook to answer the questions. Open coding ensured we captured any additional themes or findings. Coding is an iterative process, with re-reading, updating, and reviewing. Figure 1 captures this by including dotted lines between steps that occurred multiple times. Finally, we are left with a qualitatively led process to answer the user-centered questions (Table 1).

Table 1. Table of 47 publications analyzed

No.	Reference
1	Acquisti et al. (2017) [1]
2	Benenson et al. (2015) [3]
3	Bilogrevic et al. (2021) [4]
4	Bravo-Lillo et al. (2011) [5]
5	Bravo-lillo et al. (2013) [6]
6	Chassidim et al. (2020) [7]
7	Chin et al. (2012) [8]
8	Consolvo et al. (2021) [9]
9	Downs et al. (2006) [10]
10	Egelman, S. & Peer, E (2015) [12]
11	Egelman et al. (2008) [11]
12	Emami-Naeini et al. (2020) [13]
13	Emami-Naeini et al. (2019) [14]
14	Forget et al. (2019) [16]
15	Frik et al. (2019) [17]
16	Halevi et al. (2013) [19]
17	Haney et al. (2021) [20]
18	Ion et al. (2015) [21]
19	Komanduri et al. (2011) [24]
20	Kondracki et al. (2020) [25]
21	Krombholz et al. (2019) [26]
22	Lebeck et al. (2018) [27]
23	Lennartsson et al. (2021) [28]
24	Mayer et al. (2021) [30]
25	McDonald et al. (2021) [31]
26	Mendel (2019) [32]
27	Naqvi et al. (2019) [34]
28	Pearman et al. (2019) [36]
29	Rader et al. (2012) [37]
30	Ray et al. (2021) [38]
31	Rebensky et al. (2021) [39]
32	Redmiles, E.M. (2019) [40]
33	Redmiles et al. (2018) [44]
34	Redmiles et al. (2019) [41]
35	Redmiles et al. (2016) [42]

(*continued*)

Table 1. (*continued*)

No.	Reference
36	Redmiles et al. (2020) [43]
37	Reeder et al. (2018) [45]
38	Schufrin et al. (2020) [47]
39	Shen et al. (2021) [48]
40	Sheng et al. (2010) [49]
41	Simko et al. (2018) [50]
42	Sunshine(2009) [53]
43	Venkatadri et al. (2018) [54]
44	Wash, R. & Rader, E. (2015) [55]
45	Whitten, A. & Tygar, J.D. (1999) [56]
46	Wu et al. (2018) [57]
47	Zeng et al. (2017) [58]

4   Limitations

Our study encounters sample size issues and methodological limitations when analyzing literature using qualitative meta-analysis. First, the sample size of the literature could be more exhaustive. We selected based on inclusion in security and privacy conferences or human-computer interaction conferences, but this alone can yield more papers. Papers in the survey also needed to include emphasis on non-expert users. To ensure that our sample size was adequate for the analysis of user interactions, we coded to saturation [46]. Using the open code approach, we reached a point where several new articles yielded no more codes for our focus area of user experience.

A best practice for developing qualitative codes is to utilize multiple researchers. First, multiple researchers help to ensure agreement and validity of the codebook. Then, the agreement is evaluated using statistics, such as kappa coefficient [46]. This was not possible for this study, but our analysis can assure validity because the codebook reached saturation.

Finally, another limitation to this survey focusing on user perceptions, interactions, and experience within the privacy and security field, is the divergence between a citations' age and current trends in the area. We hypothesize that changes in user technological expertise, increased reliance on online activities during COVID-19, and other population trends could lead to older publications with results that may no longer be as accurate. For example, a finding in one of the evaluated papers could indicate that the median population sampled does not use 2-Factor Authentication (2FA). If the users were sampled today, we may find that more recent events, such as increase in remote work, have cause greater 2FA adoption.

5   Results

We analyzed a total of 47 papers taken from both the security and privacy domain and human-computer interaction discipline. Documents were found by an extensive search and determined acceptable for inclusion if they (1) discussed security and privacy-related research for non-expert users (2) came from a conference or publication identified for inclusion. After collecting a sizeable pile of material to analyze, we followed the steps outlined in Fig. 1. One researcher read documents to develop initial questions. She returned to the first article and started an open coding process when this was complete. If a theme occurred multiple times, it became part of the codebook. The goal was to find consistent themes across all the documents in several areas: user experience, trends, and challenges. This included more initial codes such as demographics, discussion of ethics, hypotheses, qualitative coding, methods, tools, and technology. A second read-through narrowed the code structure; iterative reading brought some distinctions in results that impacted the code structure. For instance, it became apparent that the trends fit into two main categories: Technology and Methods. Similarly, our hope to identify challenges and new directions lead to two separate code classifications: Challenges and Future Work. We can better determine what challenges remain without recommendations for future work in separating the two. The remaining content of this section focuses on the codebook and data obtained in the qualitative analysis.

5.1   User Experience

One of the questions we sought to answer focused on user risk. First, we wanted to understand better how user risk is framed across technology and demographics. For example, what user-oriented themes surface across all publications surveyed regardless of technology, age, gender, or demographic-specific challenges? Understanding this can help answer the questions around user behavior and beliefs that impact risk. Our qualitative approach provides an answer by identifying themes that reflect user experience. In the open-coding, we developed a code structure shown in Table 2. Misconception is a common theme in 20 of the publications. Surprisingly, Habituation and Personality appeared to be the least common. Trade-offs, which we expected to be widely shared only appeared in 8 of the publications. To demonstrate the frequency of themes, Table 2 includes the paper count for each topic in descending order.

5.2   Trends

We focused on discovering trends through qualitative analysis. User Experiments, Surveys, and Mental Models wove through the existing literature, tie the works together. As a result, Methods became a shared theme. Table 3 lists the methods we recorded in the qualitative analysis. In reading, we saw papers look at various topics, including Chrome alerts, Secure-Socket Layer (SSL) warnings, and Password Managers. We sub-coded Technology and Tools to capture what exactly studies reported. Table 3 lists the technology and tools that were common across the survey analysis.

5.3   Future Work and Challenges

The codes for challenges are listed in Table 4. Future work required adjustment; the themes still are broad enough to have multiple papers assigned to the code but more detailed to sufficiently represent the content discussed. The themes around challenges and future work were separated for analysis. During the open coding process, many of the difficulties identified mapped to specific items as future work. Figure 2 shows how the challenges mapped to specific future work themes reported. In this figure, we tried to reflect the relationship between two themes by color. Themes that did not have an item in the other column are gray to indicate no relationship. If we take one of the future work items, for example, Assist Users with Defaults, we see many challenges it addresses. In this example, adding defaults can help habituation by avoiding overexposing users to warnings. Similarly, the concept of designing smart user defaults is a part of improving user interface design and access control mechanisms. Interdependencies and the rapid change of technology are two challenges mentioned by more than one publication but are not addressed in the themes that emerged around future work. We find some future work that, while important, does not reflect the most common challenges reported in our survey.

Table 2. Themes found in the user-centered analysis along with count of papers that reported on theme

Themes	Publication count
Misconceptions	20
Tool Improvements	14
Trust	13
Knowledge & Skill	12
Timeliness	10
Advice	9
Trade-off	8
Security and Privacy Settings	7
Threats	7
Lack of Information	5
Dependency	5
Data Collection	5
Habituation	5
Personality	2

Table 3. The trends found in methods and technology application across the 47 papers surveyed

Technology and Tools
Browsers
Mobile device
Phishing attacks
Messages and Warnings
IoT
Labels
Social Media
Passwords
HTTPS
Augmented Reality
Data
Password Managers
Authentication

Methods
Experiment
Interview
Literature Survey
Mental Model
Modes and Frameworks
Survey
Themes

Table 4. The trends found in challenges and future work across the 47 papers surveyed

Challenges
One-Size Fits All
Habituation
Trade-off
Rapid Change of Technology
Knowledge & Skill
Inform
User Interface Design
Access Control
Misconceptions
Ecosystem Inter-Dependencies
Data Format and Storage
Unknowns for Certain Demographics

Future Work
Assist Users with Defaults
Mental Models
Understand Trade-offs
Design Warnings to Inform
Communicate Data Collection
Improve Security Education
Examine from New Perspectives
More Analysis of 2FA Adoption
Legal Actions
Standardize Interfaces
Better Measurements

6 Discussion

We have so far presented results that follow immediately from our data. In this section, we will answer the two research questions based on the findings of this survey and discuss key discoveries from the results of the qualitative analysis.

6.1 RQ1 [User Experience and Risk]: *What User Behaviors put Users More at Risk, and What Do Users Believe Places them Most at Risk?*

There is a relationship between risky behaviors, users' beliefs, and misconceptions. Our results indicate that the risky behaviors, beliefs, and misconceptions

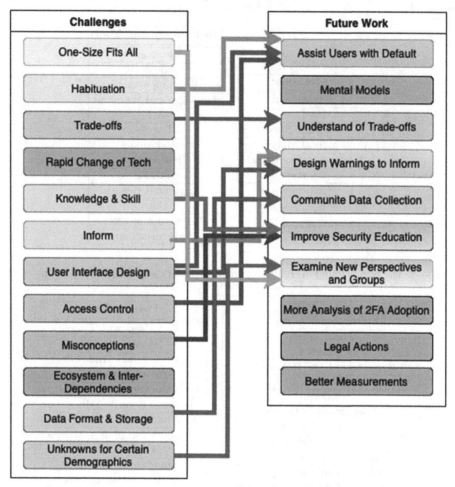

Fig. 2. Relationship between common challenges and commonly identified future work in the surveyed publications

are integral to the user experience. Our analysis found that the motivation for risky behaviors stemmed from misconceptions, lack of knowledge, or design flaws. Users engage in risky behaviors when the security and privacy solutions are not friendly. This was especially true for password management. Pearman et al. found that people who do not use password management tools "indicated multiple risky password habits, including heavy reuse of passwords and few or no unique passwords" [36]. Permissions, access control, and settings seemed to be a continuous challenge for users. Many users did not make changes when the interface did not work intuitively or provide users with the most secure options. Shen et al. reported on this relationship: "Users may notice unexpected permissions after reviewing their permission settings yet few of them (two out of 20) regularly review their permission settings" [48]. Reviewing permissions requires users to be active and mindful of settings. Even if users find unwanted settings, they rarely seek to change things.

In fact, according to the literature surveyed, it may be best to remove users' need to act when it comes to security-related decisions. Offering security and privacy features as defaults can avoid dangerous actions. Forget et al. and Sunshine et al. conducted two different investigations. Still, both found that users tend to make risky decisions, and removing security maintenance from the user can offer better protection. The thematic analysis by Forget et al. suggests that users who did not actively manage settings by resorting to defaults were more secure [16].

Similarly, in looking at warnings, Sunshine et al. and Bravo-Lillo et al. found that removing users' interactions with warnings and, instead, providing filtering methods to protect the user would increase security [5,53]. Users need assistance to avoid risky decisions. Poor decisions occur due to a lack of urgency and an incorrect understanding. When examining user response to unauthorized account access, Redmiles found that users were slow to act [40].

In the same publication, user beliefs factored into the response, "Collectivist cultural identity appears to influence both participants' threat models and support sources. Participants from more collectivistic cultures (Vietnam, Brazil, and India) were more concerned about someone they knew gaining access to their account than an unknown 'hacker'" [40]. End users develop models of threats, and these models influence their reaction. When users have misconceptions of the model, they take riskier actions. Wash et al. report on this: "Many participants reported weakly held beliefs about viruses and hackers, and these were the least likely to say they take protective actions" [55]. This often comes from a lack of knowledge or understanding of the technology. Many of the citations surveyed here report how users make risky decisions when they do not completely understand the meaning of warnings. For example, in the case of website security, Downs et al. found that "most participants had seen lock images on a web site, and knew that this was meant to signify security, although most had only a limited understanding of what that meant or how to interpret" [10]. Understanding what a user interface is communicating can help users create a more accurate understanding of what is risky and what is not risky.

Recent research exploring different populations and user groups has found design and mental models critical for users to make secure decisions and avoid unnecessary risk. In this survey, we found publications that looked at three distinct user groups: older adults [17,38], refugees [50], and sex workers [31]. These unique groups had increased dependencies on technology that could increase risks to the user. For example, the adults in care facilities often become dependent on the technology to ensure safety. A participant in Frik et al.'s study summarizes this, "'You cede a lot of your personal privacy rights when you move into a place like this, in exchange for services being rendered to you'" [17]. Older adults encounter other dependencies that increase risks, such as dependencies on family or limited resources. In the literature surveyed we found that older adults rely on close individuals to help with security settings. In some cases, we also find that older adults are more limited in resources and rely more on recycled devices or public computers. All these actions put increased risk on privacy and security [17].

Refugees experience similar, if not at times more polarizing, dependencies. For example, refugees are often dependent on their case manager [50]. Another issue facing refugees is that technology solutions to provide security do not consider challenges for this user group. Simko et al. provide the example of password questions. Password questions do not accurately reflect experiences that refugees can relate and, therefore, answer [50]. Sex workers face similar limitations with technology that can force them to make riskier decisions by avoiding secure payment options [31]. In the cited work, sex workers report understand the risks and opt to avoid using the technology due to the limitations.

User behaviors are, in a way, responses to nudges and cues. Acquisti et al. argue that importance of understanding nudges in decision-making can help to provide avenues for safer security and privacy [1]. From our survey, we find that the risky behaviors users take result from poor user interfaces and incomplete understandings of security. With misconceptions and insufficient nudges, users will be inclined to move toward decisions that increase risk. Whether users are aware of the risks, security and privacy measures should be available and designed for all user groups. Without inclusive design, those most at risk of threats will be unprotected.

6.2   RQ2 [Trends and Challenges]: *What are Emerging Trends and Challenges to the Field?*

Trends. Interviews, surveys, and experiments were the most common methods in the publications analyzed. Our coding found 17 publications used interviews, 21 used surveys, and 18 used experiments. These methods are essential for collecting user information. In an analysis of user responses, Redmiles et al. found that survey data and measurements of users do not always match; however, reporting bias can be improved through filtering and weighting survey data [41]. These methods are tried and true across various fields and are likely to continue being heavily relied upon in the usable security and privacy space. Table 3 lists the themes that emerged for methods during this survey.

Table 3 also includes the results for technology and tools. Warnings and phishing are some of the best-studied areas [6,10,11,16,45,53,57]. However, we see emerging technology becoming more prominent. Emerging technology publications in this review included IoT and Augmented Reality [13,14,20,27,58]. Among other notable trends is a renewed focus on at-risk users. Since demographics is not a tool or technology, it was not captured as a theme in Table 3, but the increase in research is apparent. Our analysis found recent reports looked at specific demographics, such as older adults or refugees. This suggests a growing interest in the research community to better understand diverse users.

Challenges and Future Work. We examined challenges and future work through thematic analysis. Despite nearly 40 years of research, usable security and privacy still faces obstacles. Many of the impediments can be summarized by usability or user awareness. In our analysis of thematic codes, we found areas that were identified for future research or categories that represent unaddressed challenges. For example, security settings may not transfer between devices in modern IoT ecosystems. Users must learn new interfaces and constantly update settings for every new device. The lack of standardization is a challenge that more than one publication discussed. However, none of the items under future work in Fig. 2 reflect this gap. Future work identifies other areas that need development, even if the corresponding challenge did not emerge in the open coding process. We highlight obvious gaps and remaining work in the field here through the themes identified in Fig. 2.

One remaining challenge that became apparent in the survey is the limitation of data. Some authors reported limitations around measurements; better measurements mean researchers can sufficiently capture user experience [44]. After reading through the publications presented here, we expand upon the need to have more data and measurements. Trends and well-established challenges implore researchers to continue toward inclusive design, but gaps remain.

Currently, we can evaluate mental models, technology, user interface (UI) designs, but the research community lacks an understanding of how users have changed over time. We expect to see changes in users; we hypothesize that this change can be due to increased technology adoption and improved usable security and privacy. Some of the studies in this paper are nearly 20 years old, while others are recent. In this survey, it became apparent that there are limits on measuring how users' risks have evolved. We can look at how the research trends have changed over time, but this speaks more to what the research community is focusing on rather than what changes users are experiencing. Table 2 shows the challenges and remaining work identified in the publications examined. After analyzing the trends and challenges, we believe there is also a need to expand user data collection for usable security and privacy and possible metrics to evaluate the data. In future work, our team hopes to investigate this specific challenge. Data can enable us to answer questions about user experience over time or after a significant event, like COVID-19.

7 Conclusion

So much work in usable privacy and security focuses on technology and application. Our goal is to step outside the application and away from expert users to help generalize findings for novice users. Through reading and qualitative analysis, we find that there are many shared methods, trends, and challenges among the surveyed publications. This paper delivers a systematic literature survey of user experience and remaining work. We demonstrate common themes reported in the 47 publications and we devise risky behaviors common to non-experts. Our survey paper dives into the remaining gaps identified in current work and extrapolates other challenges. By presenting generalizable end-user-specific themes, we portray similarities between existing work. We have an opportunity to build upon existing work, emerging trends, and remaining questions in the field to better incorporate users in the design and development of privacy and security features.

References

1. Acquisti, A., et al.: Nudges for privacy and security. ACM Comput. Surv. **50**(3), 1–41 (2017). https://doi.org/10.1145/3054926
2. Albanese, M., et al.: Computer-aided human centric cyber situation awareness. In: Liu, P., Jajodia, S., Wang, C. (eds.) Theory and Models for Cyber Situation Awareness. LNCS, vol. 10030, pp. 3–25. Springer, Cham (2017). https://doi.org/10.1007/978-3-319-61152-5_1
3. Benenson, Z., Lenzini, G., Oliveira, D., Parkin, S., Uebelacker, S.: Maybe poor Johnny really cannot encrypt. In: Proceedings of the 2015 New Security Paradigms Workshop, pp. 85–99. ACM, New York, September 2015. https://doi.org/10.1145/2841113.2841120. https://dl.acm.org/doi/10.1145/2841113.2841120
4. Bilogrevic, I., et al.: "Shhh... be quiet!" reducing the unwanted interruptions of notification permission prompts on chrome. In: USENIX Security Symposium (2021)
5. Bravo-Lillo, C., Cranor, L.F., Komanduri, S.: Bridging the gap in computer security warnings: a mental model approach. IEEE Secur. Priv. **9**, 18–26 (2011)
6. Bravo-lillo, C., Cranor, L.F., Downs, J., Reeder, R.W., Schechter, S.: Your attention please designing security-decision UIs to make genuine risks harder to ignore. In: Symposium On Usable Privacy and Security (2013). https://www.microsoft.com/en-us/research/publication/your-attention-please-designing-security-decision-uis-to-make-genuine-risks-harder-to-ignore/
7. Chassidim, H., Perentis, C., Toch, E., Lepri, B.: Between privacy and security: the factors that drive intentions to use cyber-security applications. Behav. Inf. Technol. **40**(16), 1769–1783 (2020). https://doi.org/10.1080/0144929X.2020.1781259
8. Chin, E., Felt, A.P., Sekar, V., Wagner, D.: Measuring user confidence in smartphone security and privacy. In: Proceedings of the 8th Symposium on Usable Privacy and Security, SOUPS 2012, p. 1. ACM Press, New York (2012). https://doi.org/10.1145/2335356.2335358. http://dl.acm.org/citation.cfm?doid=2335356.2335358
9. Consolvo, S., Kelley, P.G., Matthews, T., Thomas, K., Dunn, L., Bursztein, E.: "Why wouldn't someone think of democracy as a target?": security practices & challenges of people involved with U.S. political campaigns. In: Proceedings of the 30th USENIX Security Symposium, pp. 1181–1198 (2021). https://www.usenix.org/conference/usenixsecurity21/presentation/consolvo
10. Downs, J.S., Holbrook, M.B., Cranor, L.F.: Decision strategies and susceptibility to phishing. In: Proceedings of the Second Symposium on Usable Privacy and Security - SOUPS 2006, vol. 149, p. 79. ACM Press, New York (2006). https://doi.org/10.1145/1143120.1143131
11. Egelman, S., Cranor, L.F., Hong, J.: You've been warned: an empirical study of the effectiveness of web browser phishing warnings. In: Conference on Human Factors in Computing Systems - Proceedings, pp. 1065–1074. ACM Press, New York (2008). https://doi.org/10.1145/1357054.1357219. http://portal.acm.org/citation.cfm?doid=1357054.1357219

12. Egelman, S., Peer, E.: Predicting privacy and security attitudes. ACM SIG-CAS Comput. Soc. **45**(1), 22–28 (2015). https://doi.org/10.1145/2738210.2738215. https://dl.acm.org/doi/10.1145/2738210.2738215

13. Emami-Naeini, P., Agarwal, Y., Faith Cranor, L., Hibshi, H.: Ask the experts: what should be on an IoT privacy and security label? In: Proceedings - IEEE Symposium on Security and Privacy 2020-May, pp. 447–464 (2020). https://doi.org/10.1109/SP40000.2020.00043

14. Emami-Naeini, P., Dixon, H., Agarwal, Y., Cranor, L.F.: Exploring how privacy and security factor into IoT device purchase behavior. In: Conference on Human Factors in Computing Systems - Proceedings, pp. 1–12 (2019). https://doi.org/10.1145/3290605.3300764

15. Es-Salhi, K., Espes, D., Cuppens, N.: RIICS: risk based IICS segmentation method. In: Zemmari, A., Mosbah, M., Cuppens-Boulahia, N., Cuppens, F. (eds.) CRiSIS 2018. LNCS, vol. 11391, pp. 143–157. Springer, Cham (2019). https://doi.org/10.1007/978-3-030-12143-3_13

16. Forget, A., et al.: Do or do not, there is no try: user engagement may not improve security outcomes. In: 12th Symposium on Usable Privacy and Security, SOUPS 2016, pp. 97–111 (2019). https://www.usenix.org/conference/soups2016/technical-sessions/presentation/forget

17. Frik, A., Nurgalieva, L., Bernd, J., Lee, J.S., Schaub, F., Egelman, S.: Privacy and security threat models and mitigation strategies of older adults. In: Proceedings of the 15th Symposium on Usable Privacy and Security, SOUPS 2019, pp. 21–40 (2019)

18. Gove, R.: Automatic narrative summarization for visualizing cyber security logs and incident reports. IEEE Trans. Vis. Comput. Graph. **28**(1), 1182–1190 (2022). https://doi.org/10.1109/TVCG.2021.3114843

19. Halevi, T., Lewis, J., Memon, N.: A pilot study of cyber security and privacy related behavior and personality traits. In: Proceedings of the 22nd International Conference on World Wide Web - WWW 2013 Companion, pp. 737–744. ACM Press, New York (2013). https://doi.org/10.1145/2487788.2488034. http://dl.acm.org/citation.cfm?doid=2487788.2488034

20. Haney, J., Acar, Y., Furman, S.: "It's the company, the government, You and I": user perceptions of responsibility for smart home privacy and security. In: 30th Security Symposium (Security 21) (2021)

21. Ion, I., Reeder, R., Consolvo, S.: "...No one can hack my mind": comparing expert and non-expert security practices. In: Proceedings of the 11th Symposium on Usable Privacy and Security, SOUPS 2015, pp. 327–346 (2015)

22. Karat, C.M.: Iterative usability testing of a security application. Proc. Hum. Factors Soc. Annual Meeting **33**(5), 273–277 (1989). https://doi.org/10.1177/154193128903300508

23. Kokulu, F.B., et al.: Matched and mismatched SOCs: a qualitative study on security operations center issues. In: Proceedings of the ACM Conference on Computer and Communications Security, pp. 1955–1970 (2019). https://doi.org/10.1145/3319535.3354239

24. Komanduri, S., et al.: Of passwords and people: measuring the effect of password-composition policies. In: Conference on Human Factors in Computing Systems - Proceedings, pp. 2595–2604. ACM, New York, May 2011. https://doi.org/10.1145/1978942.1979321. https://dl.acm.org/doi/10.1145/1978942.1979321

25. Kondracki, B., Aliyeva, A., Egele, M., Polakis, J., Nikiforakis, N.: Meddling middlemen: empirical analysis of the risks of data-saving mobile browsers. In: Proceed-

ings - IEEE Symposium on Security and Privacy 2020-May, pp. 810–824 (2020). https://doi.org/10.1109/SP40000.2020.00077

26. Krombholz, K., Busse, K., Pfeffer, K., Smith, M., von Zezschwitz, E.: "If HTTPS were secure, I wouldn't need 2FA" - end user and administrator mental models of HTTPS. In: 2019 IEEE Symposium on Security and Privacy (SP), vol. 2019-May, pp. 246–263. IEEE, May 2019. https://doi.org/10.1109/SP.2019.00060. https://ieeexplore.ieee.org/stamp/stamp.jsp?tp=&arnumber=8835228

27. Lebeck, K., Ruth, K., Kohno, T., Roesner, F.: Towards security and privacy for multi-user augmented reality: foundations with end users. In: Proceedings - IEEE Symposium on Security and Privacy 2018-May, pp. 392–408 (2018). https://doi.org/10.1109/SP.2018.00051

28. Lennartsson, M., Kävrestad, J., Nohlberg, M.: Exploring the meaning of usable security - a literature review, October 2021. https://doi.org/10.1108/ICS-10-2020-0167

29. QIP Ltd.: Nvivo (2020). https://www.qsrinternational.com/nvivo-qualitative-data-analysis-software/home

30. Mayer, P., Kastel, S., Zou, Y., Schaub, F., Aviv, A.J.: "Now I'm a bit angry:" individuals' awareness, perception, and responses to data breaches that affected them. In: USENIX (2021)

31. McDonald, A., Barwulor, C., Mazurek, M.L., Schaub, F., Redmiles, E.M.: "It's stressful having all these phones": investigating sex workers' safety goals, risks, and practices online. In: Proceedings of the 30th USENIX Security Symposium, pp. 375–392 (2021)

32. Mendel, T., Toch, E.: My Mom was getting this popup. Proc. ACM Interact. Mob. Wearable Ubiquit. Technol. **3**(4), 1–20 (2019). https://doi.org/10.1145/3369821. https://dl.acm.org/doi/10.1145/3369821

33. Naidoo, R.: A multi-level influence model of COVID-19 themed cybercrime. Eur. J. Inf. Syst. **29**(3), 306–321 (2020)

34. Naqvi, B., Seffah, A.: Interdependencies, conflicts and trade-offs between security and usability: why and how should we engineer them? In: Moallem, A. (ed.) HCII 2019. LNCS, vol. 11594, pp. 314–324. Springer, Cham (2019). https://doi.org/10.1007/978-3-030-22351-9_21

35. Nyre-Yu, M., Sprehn, K.A., Caldwell, B.S.: Informing hybrid system design in cyber security incident response. In: Moallem, A. (ed.) HCII 2019. LNCS, vol. 11594, pp. 325–338. Springer, Cham (2019). https://doi.org/10.1007/978-3-030-22351-9_22

36. Pearman, S., Zhang, S.A., Bauer, L., Christin, N., Cranor, L.F.: Why people (don't) use password managers effectively. In: Proceedings of the 15th Symposium on Usable Privacy and Security, SOUPS 2019, pp. 319–338 (2019). https://www.usenix.org/conference/soups2019/presentation/pearman

37. Rader, E., Wash, R., Brooks, B.: Stories as informal lessons about security. In: Proceedings of the 8th Symposium on Usable Privacy and Security, SOUPS 2012, p. 1. ACM Press, New York (2012). https://doi.org/10.1145/2335356.2335364. http://dl.acm.org/citation.cfm?doid=2335356.2335364

38. Ray, H., Wolf, F., Kuber, R., Aviv, A.J.: Why older adults (don't) use password managers. In: Proceedings of the 30th USENIX Security Symposium, pp. 73–90, 2021. www.usenix.org/conference/usenixsecurity21/presentation/ray

39. Rebensky, S., Carroll, M., Nakushian, A., Chaparro, M., Prior, T.: Understanding the last line of defense: human response to cybersecurity events. In: Moallem, A. (ed.) HCII 2021. LNCS, vol. 12788, pp. 353–366. Springer, Cham (2021). https://doi.org/10.1007/978-3-030-77392-2_23

40. Redmiles, E.M.: 'Should i worry?' A cross-cultural examination of account security incident response. In: Proceedings - IEEE Symposium on Security and Privacy, vol. 2019-May, pp. 920–934 (2019). https://doi.org/10.1109/SP.2019.00059
41. Redmiles, E.M., Kross, S., Mazurek, M.L.: How well do my results generalize? Comparing security and privacy survey results from MTurk, web, and telephone samples. In: Proceedings - IEEE Symposium on Security and Privacy, vol. 2019-May, pp. 1326–1343 (2019). https://doi.org/10.1109/SP.2019.00014. https://ieeexplore.ieee.org/stamp/stamp.jsp?tp=&arnumber=8835345
42. Redmiles, E.M., Malone, A.R., Mazurek, M.L.: I think they're trying to tell me something: advice sources and selection for digital security. In: Proceedings - 2016 IEEE Symposium on Security and Privacy, SP 2016, pp. 272–288 (2016). https://doi.org/10.1109/SP.2016.24
43. Redmiles, E.M., et al.: A comprehensive quality evaluation of security and privacy advice on the web. In: Proceedings of the 29th USENIX Security Symposium, pp. 89–108 (2020)
44. Redmiles, E.M., Zhu, Z., Kross, S., Kuchhal, D., Dumitras, T., Mazurek, M.L.: Asking for a friend: evaluating response biases in security user studies. In: Proceedings of the 2018 ACM SIGSAC Conference on Computer and Communications Security, pp. 1238–1255. ACM, New York, October 2018. https://doi.org/10.1145/3243734.3243740
45. Reeder, R.W., Felt, A.P., Consolvo, S., Malkin, N., Thompson, C., Egelman, S.: An experience sampling study of user reactions to browser warnings in the field. In: Conference on Human Factors in Computing Systems - Proceedings, vol. 2018-April, pp. 1–13. ACM, New York, April 2018. https://doi.org/10.1145/3173574.3174086
46. Saldaña, J.: The Coding Manual for Qualitative Researchers. Sage (2009)
47. Schufrin, M., Reynolds, S.L., Kuijper, A., Kohlhammer, J.: A visualization interface to improve the transparency of collected personal data on the internet. In: 2020 IEEE Symposium on Visualization for Cyber Security, VizSec 2020, pp. 1–10 (2020). https://doi.org/10.1109/VizSec51108.2020.00007. https://transparency-vis.vx.igd.fraunhofer.de/
48. Shen, B., et al.: Can Systems Explain Permissions Better? Understanding Users' Misperceptions under Smartphone Runtime Permission Model. Security (2021)
49. Sheng, S., Holbrook, M., Kumaraguru, P., Cranor, L.F., Downs, J.: Who falls for phish?: a demographic analysis of phishing susceptibility and effectiveness of interventions. In: Proceedings of the 28th International Conference on Human Factors in Computing Systems, CHI 2010, vol. 1, p. 373. ACM Press, New York (2010). https://doi.org/10.1145/1753326.1753383. http://portal.acm.org/citation.cfm?doid=1753326.1753383
50. Simko, L., Lerner, A., Ibtasam, S., Roesner, F., Kohno, T.: Computer security and privacy for refugees in the United States. In: 2018 IEEE Symposium on Security and Privacy (SP), vol. 2018-May, pp. 409–423. IEEE, May 2018. https://doi.org/10.1109/SP.2018.00023. https://ieeexplore.ieee.org/stamp/stamp.jsp?tp=&arnumber=8418616. https://ieeexplore.ieee.org/document/8418616/
51. National Institute of Standards and Technology: Usable Security & Privacy—NIST. https://www.nist.gov/programs-projects/usable-security-privacy
52. Stevens, R., Votipka, D., Redmiles, E.M., Mazurek, M.L., Ahern, C., Sweeney, P.: The battle for New York: a case study of applied digital threat modeling at the enterprise level. In: Proceedings of the 27th USENIX Security Symposium, pp. 621–637 (2018). https://www.usenix.org/conference/usenixsecurity18/presentation/stevens

53. Sunshine, J., Egelman, S., Almuhimedi, H., Atri, N., Cranor, L.F.: Crying wolf: an empirical study of SSL warning effectiveness. In: Proceedings of the 18th USENIX Security Symposium, pp. 399–416 (2009)
54. Venkatadri, G., et al.: Privacy risks with Facebook's PII-based targeting: auditing a data broker's advertising interface. In: Proceedings - IEEE Symposium on Security and Privacy 2018-May, pp. 89–107 (2018). https://doi.org/10.1109/SP.2018.00014
55. Wash, R., Rader, E.: Too much knowledge? Security beliefs and protective behaviors among United States internet users. In: Proceedings of the 11th Symposium on Usable Privacy and Security, SOUPS 2015, pp. 309–325 (2015)
56. Whitten, A., Tygar, J.D.: Why Johnny can't encrypt: a usability evaluation of PGP 5.0. In: 8th USENIX Security Symposium (1999)
57. Wu, Y., Gupta, P., Wei, M., Acar, Y., Fahl, S., Ur, B.: Your secrets are safe: how browsers' explanations impact misconceptions about private browsing mode. In: The Web Conference 2018 - Proceedings of the World Wide Web Conference, WWW 2018, pp. 217–226 (2018). https://doi.org/10.1145/3178876.3186088
58. Zeng, E., Mare, S., Roesner, F.: End user security & privacy concerns with smart homes. In: Proceedings of the 13th Symposium on Usable Privacy and Security, SOUPS 2017, pp. 65–80 (2017). https://www.usenix.org/conference/soups2017/technical-sessions/presentation/zeng

Are HTTPS Configurations Still a Challenge?: Validating Theories of Administrators' Difficulties with TLS Configurations

Alexandra Mai[1,2(✉)], Oliver Schedler[3], Edgar Weippl[2,4],
and Katharina Krombholz[3]

[1] Vienna University of Technology, Vienna, Austria
`amai@sba-research.org`
[2] SBA Research, Vienna, Austria
[3] CISPA Helmholtz Center for Information Security, Saarland, Germany
[4] University of Vienna, Vienna, Austria

Abstract. HTTPS has been the standard for securing online communications for over 20 years. Despite the availability of tools to make the configuration process easier (e.g., Let's Encrypt, Certbot), SSL Pulse scans show that still more than 50% of the most popular websites are poorly configured, which emphasizes room for improvement. Although a few recent studies looked at the remaining challenges for administrators in configuring HTTPS from a qualitative perspective, there is little work that produced quantitative results. Therefore, we conducted a survey with 96 experienced administrators (as opposed to a student sample) to investigate to which extent configuration problems revealed in prior studies actually exist in the wild. Our results confirm that Let's Encrypt and ACME clients, such as Certbot, simplify configuration and maintenance for administrators, thus increasing the security of HTTPS configurations. Moreover, we extend the current body of work by examining the trust administrators put into Let's Encrypt and Certbot. We found that trust and usability issues are currently barriers to the widespread adoption of Certbot.

Keywords: HTTPS · Usable security · Quantitative administrator study

1 Introduction

Communication has increasingly shifted from the analogue to the digital realm, currently exacerbated by the pandemic as real-world contacts are limited. Cryptographic protocols like TLS (*Transport Layer Security*) form the basis of secure digital communication since they protect sensitive information against unauthorized modification, processing, destruction, or access. HTTPS is the current

A. Moallem (Ed.): HCII 2022, LNCS 13333, pp. 173–193, 2022.
https://doi.org/10.1007/978-3-031-05563-8_12

standard to guarantee secure communication between a client and a web server. Every day, TLS is used several million times by different applications such as email, websites, or messengers. However, to guarantee the security benefits of this protocol, it must be configured and maintained correctly by an administrator, which has shown to be prone to human error [6,21,34]. Free of charge tools such as Let's Encrypt and Certbot were introduced so that administrators are not anymore required to understand the full complexity of the cryptographic protocols. Let's Encrypt [2] is a certificate authority that issues cost-free certificates. Certbot is an Automatic Certificate Management Environment (ACME), which supports web administrators in generating and securely extending certificates and therewith, makes the process of configuring HTTPS more user-friendly. Several publications [7,13] indicate an upward trend in HTTPS adoption and configuration security, but there is still potential for improvement, as many configurations remain insecure. Based on the Qualys SSL Lab Report of November 2021[1], about half of their scanned websites currently provide inadequate security.

Over the last years, several studies highlighted challenges of the HTTPS configuration process and the substantial impact of flawed configurations on security and privacy [5,9,27,31]. Moreover, studies that shed light on the perspective of developers and administrators have increased in the last few years. Those user studies used different qualitative methods, such as qualitative interviews and lab studies, to explore the challenges of the HTTPS deployment process.

We use the theories developed from previously conducted user studies to formulate our research questions. In this paper, we quantify the configuration problems revealed in prior studies through two administrator studies. To reach high external validity and get a realistic picture of the current situation, it was especially important to us to find participants who are actively configuring or maintaining web servers. We extend the body of knowledge on administrator studies by (i) providing numbers that show the extent to which challenges discovered in prior studies (still) exist and (ii) investigating usability challenges with HTTPS configurations in a professional setting.

Therewith, we answer the following research questions:

(RQ1) To which extend do the configuration problems revealed in prior studies actually exist in the wild?

(RQ2) Do web administrators trust HTTPS and the currently available configuration software (e.g., Let's Encrypt, Certbot)?

(RQ3) What usability issues occur when using Certbot in a professional setting?

Therefore, the main contributions of this paper are to:

- validate results of earlier qualitative studies with a quantitative survey,
- extend the body of administrator-studies and,
- investigate remaining usability issues with the usage of Certbot.

---

[1] SSL Pulse—monitoring Alexa's top million websites for the quality of SSL and TLS support https://www.ssllabs.com/ssl-pulse/.

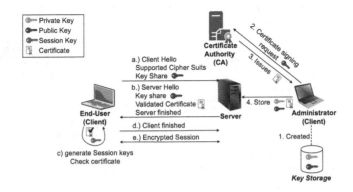

Fig. 1. How to generate a certificate (1.-4.) and establish a encrypted communication session using TLS1.3 (a.-g.)

The remainder of the paper is organized as follows: In Sect. 2, we provide background information and related work. Our methodological approaches of both study designs and recruitment processes are described in Sect. 3. We present our results and statistical analysis in Sect. 4, followed by a discussion in Sect. 5. In Sect. 6, we present the limitations of our study and Sect. 7 concludes the paper.

2 Background and Related Work

Two decades ago, the Transport Layer Security (TLS) protocol was introduced to guarantee data privacy and integrity of communication between a client and a server. Today, TLS is commonly used as the security layer in the HTTPS (**HTTP** over TLS) protocol.

An abstract depiction of HTTPS can be found in Fig. 1. The certificate binds the public key to the identity of the server, which is verified by a challenge-response protocol (between step 2. and 3.). To establish a secure communication channel over TLS (1.3) between a client and a server, the client initializes a session by sending a "Client hello", the clients supported cipher suits and its key share. Then, the server answers with a return message which includes: i) a hello message, ii) the server key share, iii) the verified certificate and iv) the finished message[2]. Afterwards the client generates the session key with the servers key share and checks the certificate. If the certificate is valid, the clients also sends a finished message (encrypted with session key) to the server and after that the communication takes place within an encrypted session.

Although HTTPS is the most widely used standard [13] for secure Internet communication, there are still many faulty configurations [10] in the wild. Over the last years, several studies highlighted open challenges with HTTPS and the

---

[2] The finished message is a protected/encrypted with the just negotiated algorithms, and keys. It serves as a "checksum" for the other party before other (sensitive) information is shared via the session.

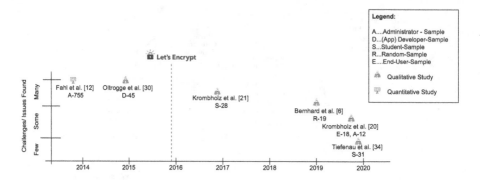

Fig. 2. Overview of administrator studies on HTTPS over time and their abstracted amount of reported challenges.

impact that insecure configurations have on security and privacy [9,11]. In the following, we discuss the related work from the administrators' perspectives.

Within the last six years, SSL and TLS user studies focused on the administrators' point of view. Figure 2 presents an overview of these user studies, which sample sizes were used, and how many challenges were found. The found challenges/issues are calculated based on the described results of the user studies (Few: <25%; Some: ~25–50%; Many: >50% of the participants faced challenges).

Fahl et al. [12] conducted a large-scale study with administrators to determine the reasons for non-validating security-critical X.509 certificates[3]. Their results showed that one third accidentally misconfigured the certificates and two thirds intentionally used non-validating certificates. Reasons for the use of non-validating certificates were that sites were either no longer in use or not designed to be accessible for users.

Oltrogge et al. [30] studied the applicability of certificate pinning for non-browser software. They found that pinning is considered very complex among developers, which results in poor adoption. Therefore, they implemented a web application that supports the developers by guiding them through a pinning-protected TLS implementation. However, users were still facing difficulties to deploy pinning correctly.

In 2017, Krombholz et al. [21] identified major pitfalls administrators face during the TLS deployment. They revealed that the configuration procedure is too complex and identified protocol components that are difficult to understand even for experts who managed to deploy valid configurations. In general, their results suggest that administrators heavily rely on online sources that, depending on their quality, often lead to faulty deployments.

The introduction of Let's Encrypt paved the way for the widespread use of encrypted communication [4]. However, still some challenges remained, that had to be overcome. Manousis et al. [27] found that only half of the domains, that

---

[3] X.509 is a standard format of public key certificates used e.g., for TLS, which specifies an identity and a public key and is either self-signed or signed by a certificate authority (CA).

were configured with Let's Encrypt certificates, had a valid LE certificate. Thus, they revealed that automation does not fully release administrators from the burden of dealing with the complexity of the protocol.

Bernhard et al. [6] extended the study of Krombholz et al. [21] with a more diverse sample and Let's Encrypt. Hereby, they confirmed the difficulty of the deployment process and confirmed that participants were not able to successfully deploy HTTPS. In order to understand the challenges faced by developers, Krombholz et al. [20] conducted a qualitative study with a focus on the general understanding of the HTTPS protocol. They investigated the mental models of 12 administrators and 18 end-users and found that many administrators only have a sparse understanding of the protocol, its components, and how they interact with each other. Tiefenau et al. [34] showed the positive effect of the improved usability through Certbot (and Let's Encrypt) on the security of HTTPS.

Our work differs in comparison to the aforementioned studies primarily in that we quantitatively assessed the (remaining) usability issues and administrators' trust in Let's Encrypt and Certbot. Besides, our work provides high external validity by capturing an actual set of web server administrators (responsible for certificate managing, set-up of TLS etc.), in comparison to a student sample. Therewith, we extend the current literature of developer studies with a real-world sample.

3 Methodology

In the following, we describe the methodology used to design, collect and analyze the data obtained from our studies.

3.1 Small-Scale Study

Following Jensen and Laurie [17], we conducted a small-scale study, to flexibly explore the problem space before designing our online survey. Although some studies qualitatively investigated the administrative point of view [6,20,21,34], we replicated and challenged those results as the technology and the frameworks investigated in those studies have changed over time. In 2018 the latest version of TLS (1.3) became available and since 2021 versions older than TLS1.2 are deprecated. Furthermore, ACME clients such as Certbot have been revised several times and new ACME clients were released (e.g., Caddy2) in the last five years. We developed a questionnaire to shed light on administrators knowledge of the interplay between certificates, encryption and keys. The questionnaire consisted of 31 questions (26 closed-ended and 5 open-ended questions), asking for demographic data, experiences with web server software and TLS knowledge. At the end of the questionnaire, we asked the participants how they thought the TLS set-up process could be improved. The answers were coded by two researchers individually and discussed afterwards until agreement on all coding conflicts was reached. The inter-rater reliability (Krippendorff's Alpha value [19] of $\alpha = 0.87$) indicates a high level of agreement.

Table 1. Descriptive quantitative analysis demographics (N = 16)

Demographic	Participants (%)
Gender	
Male	11 (75%)
Female	2 (13%)
Prefer not to say	2 (13%)
Age	
18–32	5 (31%)
33–42	6 (38%)
23–52	3 (19%)
>52	2 (13%)
Highest completed education	
High school	2 (13%)
Bachelor degree	4 (25%)
Master degree	8 (50%)
Other	2 (13%)

For this study, we recruited $N = 16$ administrators from one company in Central Europe (demographics can be found in Table 1), with more than 250 employees. The participants were web administrators, either configuring the company's web servers (including certificate management), or working as consultants for clients. The study took place on two different days, in a laboratory environment provided by the company with a supervisor to ensure equal conditions. The online questionnaire was distributed directly on-site by the supervisor. If there were any questions, there would have been pre-made aids, which the supervisor could have given, but they were not used.

Study Findings. We first asked the participants' knowledge about certificates and their connection to keys with open questions, followed by closed-ended questions. When asked with an open question, 11 participants (69%) managed to correctly describe the purpose of a certificate (i.e., it is required for the proof of the server's identity during the authentication process and needed to establish a secure communication session). The rest of the participants either described only parts of the certificates' purpose (3; 19%) or mixed things up (2; 12%)). In line with findings by Krombholz et al. [20], two (12%) participants tended to confuse authentication and encryption. In the context of certificates and security indicators, four participants explicitly mentioned issues with (blind) trust which one have to put into the protocol. They explained that administrators have to trust the authenticity of the CA's certificates and end-users have to trust the security indicators indicating the trustworthiness of a website.

When asking them about keys and public-key cryptography (e.g., "How would you describe public key cryptography?"), ten (63%) participants were able to explain this type of encryption correctly and three (19%) only explained parts of it. The remaining participants either stated that they did not know (1;

6%) or confused public and private keys (2; 12%), which could lead to severe problems (i.e., leaked information and insecure communication).

Besides the general functionality of the TLS protocol, we asked questions about the configuration and used technologies. 14 participants (88%) used a traditional CA (e.g., GoDaddy or Comodo), 12 participants (75%) obtained their certificate from a local self-maintained CA, and only one participant used Let's Encrypt. According to 13 participants (81%), the choice of certificate origin (i.e., which CA was used) was prescribed by the employer or client, the rest stated that they did not know (19%).

We discovered that 6 participants (38%) still recommend outdated and insecure TLS/SSL protocols and are not sure which mechanisms are currently state-of-the-art (e.g., forward secrecy) to ensure strong security. The test rating of SSL Labs[4] for the company's server configuration is in line with these findings as it only gets a B due to insecure settings (e.g., support of old protocols).

To get a better understanding of the problems with the TLS configuration, we asked our participants directly about the difficulties they encountered during HTTPS configuration. The majority (14; 88%) stated, that they had no problems, and only two (12%) stated that they did. Occurring problems were on the one hand that the Microsoft-ISS registry settings did not have the appropriate setting levels and on the other hand, our participants missed deactivating fallbacks to older (TLS/SSL) versions. Their suggestions for improvement were staff training on state-of-the-art technologies, stricter (company) rules on HTTPS usage, and automatic configuration checks (ciphers, TLS versions).

3.2 Quantitative Study Design

We opted for an online survey to get quantitative insights into the HTTPS configuration process from the administrators' point of view. The first study (see Sect. 3.1) informed the survey questions and answer possibilities. Therefore we rephrased, deleted and added survey questions based on findings in the first study. For example, we added closed-ended knowledge questions followed up by open-questions to provide the participants the possibility to express their thoughts in more detail. The answers of the first study where participants mentioned issues with trust, gave us the impulse to investigate the administrators' trust in HTTPS, Let's Encrypt and Certbot. We used English as the language for the questionnaire, as it is the working language in many IT-related jobs.

The survey consisted of a maximum of 47 questions, some of which were follow up questions: (i) 28–34 closed-ended questions (multiple- and single-choice, 5 point likert scale) and, (ii) 9–13 open questions

We made most of the open questions optional to answer in order to not discourage the participants. In this study, too, the answers were coded by two researchers and then discussed until agreement was reached (Krippendorff's

---

[4] https://www.ssllabs.com/ssltest/ - a service which analyses the configuration, the security and the supported TLS versions.

Table 2. Demographics of 96 study participants

Gender	Female (5%)	Male (76%)	Non-Binary (2%)	Not disclosed (16%)	Self-described (1%)
Age	18–24 (7%)	25–34 (42%)	35–44 (36%)	45–54 (12%)	>55 (2%)
Country working in	USA (28%) NA (4%)	Austria (24%)	Germany (20%)	Rest Europe (17%)	Others (7%)
Education	No schooling (1%) Master (32%)	High school (18%) Professional degree (1%)	College (8%) PhD (5%)	Technical training (3%)	Bachelor (31%)
Profession	Programmer (30%) Web Admin (4%)	System Admin (19%) Tester (2%)	IT Consultant (11%) Other (19%)	IT Architect (9%)	Manager (6%)
# Web server	1 (12%)	2–5 (36%)	6–10 (15%)	>10 (37%)	

Alpha value [19] of $\alpha = 0.83$). The survey was hosted on soscisurvey.de [14] and took on average 30 min to complete.

We tested our online survey design in two rounds of pilot studies with 19 participants (10 security researchers and 9 administrators) who gave feedback. We checked the comprehension of the questions as well as their order and removed unclear phrasing as far as possible.

Recruitment. A common challenge when conducting an expert (administrator) study, is to acquire a satisfactory number of participants. In contrast to most previous studies in the area of HTTPS usability for administrators, we did not recruit computer science students but instead opted for administrators with HTTPS configuration experience. Although there are several studies [3,33,35] that indicate that students can be representative for administrators and developers, this has not yet been confirmed in the area of HTTPS configuration. Therefore, we recruited participants with professional knowledge of the HTTPS configuration and maintenance process. We only included administrators who maintained at least one web server within the 2020, in order to get an optimal view of current administrators' challenges and also, to avoid fading knowledge.

Following Pfeffer et al. [32] and Krombholz et al. [20], we distributed our survey via Twitter, LinkedIn, Facebook, Reddit, and sent it out via mailing lists. As it was particularly difficult to reach female administrators, we joined channels on social media and mailing lists that were primarily for women. To increase the response rate and as compensation for the participation, we announced a lottery [15,22] consisting of four gift vouchers valued €50 each.

Sample Validity. To ensure statistical power, we calculated the effective sample size by following best practices for quantitative studies [24,25]. We chose a significance level of 5%, a 95% confidence interval, and a power of 80%, which led us to a minimum sample size of $N > 91$.

Altogether, we received 212 responses. From the total responses, we filtered out unfinished questionnaires, data sets with incorrectly answered sanity questions, and inconsistently filled out check-up questions. Furthermore, we calculated the average time spent per question in order to avoid automatic or random completion of the questionnaire. Our final sample consists of $N = 96$ participants, which exceeds our calculated minimum sample size. The demographics of our final data set can be found in Table 2.

Data Analysis. We used four different approaches to analyze our data:

- *Descriptive Analysis:* to summarize all data according to frequencies, central tendencies, and dispersion or variation.
- *Exploratory Data Analysis:* to find relationships and patterns among our data from a bird-eye view (e.g., by visualizing the data).
- *Statistical Tests:* to investigate the correlation between different variables (pair-wise χ^2 or Fishers' exact tests F, with expected frequencies <5, for nominally scaled single choice and multiple choice[5] questions, including an interpretation of the effect size Cramér's V [18]). Thereby, we rejected the null hypothesis of independence if $p < 0.05$, within a 95% confidence interval.
- *Open-Coding:* to analyze the qualitative data (open questions), we coded these questions, by extracting recurring themes and statements. We provide some of the answers for illustration and better insight (see Sect. 4).

3.3 Ethical Considerations

Our organization, unfortunately, has no ethical review board but established a series of guidelines that have to be followed when conducting user studies. Each data set was stored anonymously with an assigned ID. The email addresses collected for the lottery were stored separately from their corresponding data sets. At the beginning of the questionnaire, we informed the participants which personal data will be collected and how they will be stored, strictly following the EU's General Data Protection Regulation (GDPR[6]).

4 Results

In the following, we present the results of our quantitative online study, by providing both quantitative and qualitative insights. We analyzed the dataset based on our hypothesis that Let's Encrypt positively influence administrators' experiences, as prior studies showed [6,12,21,34]. Furthermore, we investigated whether there are correlations or differences in our data that can be explained by other (demographic) characteristics (besides different CA usage), but did not find any, except for the company size (small <50; large >50). Therefore, we present our results with a focus on: i) company size of administrators' current employer (small <50 vs. large >50) and ii) usage of Let's Encrypt vs. others.

---

[5] We applied the Holm-Bonferroni correction [16] to counteract the multiple comparisons problem for multiple-choice questions.

[6] https://gdpr-info.eu/.

4.1   General TLS/HTTPS Knowledge

We asked the administrators how they acquired their knowledge, in order to understand different influencing factors. All participants stated, that they acquired it through online research. Almost 60% relied exclusively on online sources and one-fifth additionally on information gathered from colleagues. 18% received training of web server configurations for TLS through education or specific seminars. Only a minority of 6% obtained their knowledge from company specifications such as from configuration frameworks and their documentation. One administrator described the learning process as "failure, lots of failures". Thereby, we found no significant difference between large and small companies (χ^2: $p > .08$) and Let's Encrypt and other CA users (χ^2: $p > .2$).

Furthermore, we explicitly asked whether public and private keys play a part in HTTPS. 90% of the participants answered correctly, others either stated the absence of knowledge (5%) or answered incorrectly (5%). Thereby, we found significant differences with large effect size V between Let's Encrypt and other CA users (F: $p < .03$), as Let's Encrypt users answered it more correctly than the other users. Between small and large companies, we did not find any significant differences (χ^2: $p > .05$). When asked with an open question how the keys are used, about one-third could explain neither the role of them in the encryption/decryption process nor their connection to certificates. Interestingly, the statements about the precise connection(s) between the keys and TLS were answered correctly by a much larger proportion ($>75\%$) of the participants. Only the statement "TLS uses (PKI) certificates to authenticate parties communicating" led to some confusion. In fact, 48% marked it as wrong and 52% as correct. Some of the participants noted in the "Other" option that they were confused although they provided a correct explanation. Thus, we rated these answers as correct (in total 76% answered correctly).

4.2   Configuration and Maintenance

The services configured and maintained by the administrators are equally distributed between company internal, external, and private services. For work-related server configurations, most of the administrators used NGINX (60%), followed by Apache (48%). Microsoft ISS and Caddy2 were used by one-fifth each; HaProxy and Traefik were mentioned in the "Other" option. Internal web servers of the company were only used by 10% of the participants.

We also asked our participants which software they (would) use privately. Hereby, 60% answered NGINX. Less than a third (29%) would use Apache for private web server configurations. 28% of the participants selected Caddy2 and below 10% other software. Thereby, we observed no significant differences between private and professional server-software usage and the company size (χ^2: $p > .2$).

In order to authenticate the HTTPS server, a certificate or another validation mechanism is used. Most participants (91%) use a free-of-cost alternative for obtaining certificates, such as Let's Encrypt (at least for some of their certificates). From these participants, around one-third exclusively uses Let's Encrypt. The second most used certificate source is a local self-governing CA (41%). However, these CAs are used only in combination with another certificate source. Traditional CAs, external providers such as Cloudflare, or self-signed certificates, are used by less than a third. Altogether, 20% of the administrators were obliged by their company to choose a specific certificate origin. We found significant differences concerning the obligation to use specific certificate origins depending on the CA usage (χ^2: $p < .03$, $V > .27$ [medium]). Let's Encrypt users are not obliged by their company to use them in comparison to other CA users. Furthermore, our results show a significant difference between the company size (F: $p < .01$) and the obligation of specific certificate origins, whereby large companies more often specify the place of origin.

The vast majority (84%) of the participants used an ACME client, to obtain certificates of Let's Encrypt. The usage of Let's Encrypt and Certbot is allowed by over two-thirds of the companies. We found a significant difference between large and small companies (F: $p < .02$), whereby small companies are more open to their usage. Altogether, 15% of the participants stated that it is prohibited by their company to use them, mostly due to mandatory software (company internal) or customer guidelines. About 82% of those using these tools reported that they changed their (working) routine. The other participants felt uncertain (11%) or were sure that they did not influence their workflow (7%).

The most important factors influencing the working process were on the one hand the automation and the associated security that comes certain ACME clients, and on the other hand, the free-of-cost certificates which are easy to handle (even when using multiple certificates). Our participants perceived the higher update frequency both as positive, when used within an automation framework such as Certbot, and negative when used without one. Without an automation framework, the renewal process must be either self-automated or handled manually each time. In this context, one administrator stated:

"Although there is the automatic [certificate] renewal (cronjob), it happens that certificates expire, leading to broken services." (P11)

The confidence in the security of most of our participants' configurations is very high (85%) with strong differences between Let's Encrypt and other CA users (χ^2: $p < .03$, $V > .28$ [medium]). In fact, Let's Encrypt users were not that confident about the security of their website. The main reason given by those participants was that they did not achieve an A grade in a TLS/SSL-test.

Certificates have different levels of validation, depending on the type of service they are used for. There are three different types:

- Domain Validation (DV): the CA verifies the owner of the certificate who has control over the domain (low-level validation).
- Organization Validated (OV): the CA verifies the organization and its rights to use the domain (medium level validation).
- Extended Validation (EV): the CA verifies the legal identity of the organization (high-level validation).

Administrators argued that the validation decision is often based on a cost-benefit factor. On the one hand, websites need to appear trustworthy in order for web users to trust their integrity. On the other hand, stronger validation is (more) expensive and often provides no noticeable benefit for the consumer. We found a significant difference between our participants' usage of CAs (F: $p < .04$) and their required certificate validation levels. We attribute this to the fact that Let's Encrypt does not provide EV and OV, as those validations require additional human interaction. Administrators using OV were required to do so due to company policies or customer requirements. The vast majority of administrators agreed that DV is the most important one (81%), as without it TLS would lose its meaning. The requirement of OV is stated by 16%, followed by 9% reporting a need for EV. 12% stated that they do not know which kind of validation they need and 3% were unwilling to disclose the requirements or answered that it depends on the use case.

TLS Deployment. During the set-up of TLS, several configurations can be made which influence the security and compatibility of the web server. Two-thirds of the participants have actively switched off HTTP as part of the TLS configuration in order to guarantee a connection via HTTPS. Most web server frameworks provide the administrator with certain software defaults, however, nearly two-thirds (64%) stated that they changed them. The answers to the question of why they have changed the default settings were mostly, that the default settings often do not meet the security standards of the administrators (73%) or the companies (17%).

"No sane defaults, those defaults prevent desirable security properties." (P3)

The answers significantly differ between the different company sizes (χ^2: $p < .03$, $V > .28$ [medium]), as administrators of large companies, changed the default settings more often. Many changed the allowed ciphers and TLS versions to either stricter or looser settings depending on their requirements. Hereby, some explicitly stated that they enabled older versions for increased compatibility, thereby accepting the greater security risk. Furthermore, some enabled forward secrecy and HSTS headers to harden security and OCSP stapling to reduce costs for validation. Many changes were motivated by recommendations of Mozilla or various SSL/TLS scanners and guidelines such as bettercrypto.org.

In a professional environment, security audits help to reduce the risks of vulnerabilities. Half of the participants stated that their company performed audits when an exploit was found, 26% performed regular security audits, and 21% perform audits before live deployment.

Problems. In order to investigate the problems administrators currently face, we asked them to elaborate on their experiences. Slightly more than half (57%) of the participants reported, that they had no problems during the configuration.

The remaining participants (43%) stated, that they had experienced at least some problems.

"No [problems] when setting up standard web servers, but lots when setting up custom stacks." (P71)

These challenges were mostly experienced by administrators, who did not use Certbot (60%) (χ^2: $p < .03$, $V > .27$ [medium]). The main challenges were caused by compatibility issues (23%), errors with the certificate chain (12%), the certificates order as well as trust issues with other (self-signed) certificates (9%). Those issues often appeared due to operating systems that were too old or clients which did not support new TLS versions. Also, errors from former administrators (5%) were mentioned, as some forgot to send the certificate chain when configuring the TLS server, which can lead to issues finding the correct root. Another problem for some administrators was poorly designed error messages, which were not perceived as helpful, as well as error reports, which did not show up in the console. In order to generate a (valid) certificate, the administrator needs to send a certificate signing request. However, if one puts a wrong value into the request or forgets information, the issued certificate is faulty.

4.3   Trust

The confidence a person places in a technology (i.e., trust) is an important factor for its adoption. Due to the complexity of trust establishment with multiple factors involved, in this paper we only focus on self-reported trust users put in HTTPS, the security indicator, Let's Encrypt, and Certbot. Therewith, we do not intend to simplify the concept of trust, but rather provide the first impetus to examine its influence on the use and configuration of HTTPS.

In order to enable HTTPS, some sort of authentication (via a CA) is necessary. We asked our participants whether they trust in the security of the HTTPS communication channel, the security indicator of web browsers (lock symbol), and the CA Let's Encrypt as well as the ACME client Certbot. The results of these questions are summarized in Table 3.

In general, the trust of our participants in **HTTPS** was very high. Reasons for that were the strong cryptography used in state-of-the-art TLS versions, its open-source nature, and the strong community behind it. The main argument against trust in HTTPS was that there are still too many poorly configured web servers in the wild. We found that administrators of larger working environments have higher trust in the security of HTTPS than those of smaller ones (χ^2: $p < .02$, $V > .28$ [medium]). We explain this by their increased use of (higher) security standards and certificate validations (see Sect. 4.2), which strengthens the security of their HTTPS servers. One participant stated:

"It's the best we have. It's probably not 100% secure, but it's secure enough for my purposes". (P55)

Our participants' trust in **Let's Encrypt** was even higher than in HTTPS. Thereby Let's Encrypt users have more trust in it than users of other CAs. This can be explained by the fact that the use of technology can strongly influence trust [23,29].

Some participants said, that although Let's Encrypt might not be technically different from other CAs, its non-technical features surpass others. These include its open-source nature, the expert community supporting it, the non-profit motive, the documentation, and the transparency when incidents happen. However, some administrators reported that a problem with the free CA is the (ab)use of its certificates for phishing websites, as confirmed by media reports [8].

Table 3. Results for trust questions

Trust in	Yes	No	I don't know
HTTPS	80%	13%	7%
Security indicator	69%	23%	8%
Let's Encrypt	90%	4%	6%
Certbot	57%	6%	37%

Certbot's tasks range from certificate ordering to domain validation and automatic certificate renewal. The open source ACME client Certbot it is trusted 30% less than Let's Encrypt. The trust in Certbot depends on whether administrators use Let's Encrypt or other CAs as we observed significant differences between those two characteristics (χ^2: $p < .01$, $V > .33$ [medium]). The reasons to trust this ACME client are very similar to those of Let's Encrypt. For Certbot's default usage, root privileges are required, which is not appreciated by some of our participants. Furthermore, one participant stated

"I don't trust it to not completely trash my server configuration. (Which has happened.)" (P8)

The **security indicators** in the browsers are not trusted by 23% of the administrators. Again, problems with phishing websites were mentioned. Moreover, participants complaint about pre-installed (rogue) root certificates, which are distributed in operating systems, although a green lock symbol still appears.

"The lock symbol is one of the things you should check, but not the only one. [It's] not good enough as a single factor of trust"

5   Discussion

In this section, we discuss our results and compare them to the results of previously conducted studies. Thereby, we will go into detail about current the administrators' knowledge of TLS, their confidence in the technology (and their skills/knowledge), and their challenges with HTTPS. With our study, we quantify prior findings and show that administrators choose outdated TLS-versions or weak ciphers due to various reasons and that although Certbot provides high usability there are some adoption/usage barriers.

5.1   Knowledge of Certificates and Keys

Certificates have an essential role in the configuration of TLS, therefore administrators must understand their basic concept and functionality. We found that the majority of our participants were able to correctly answer our questions (both open- and closed-ended) related to keys and how they interact with certificates.

In contrast to our findings, Krombholz et al. [20] found in their study that administrators did not mention and thereby not acknowledge the existence of keys, while explaining HTTPS. Furthermore, they found that although the administrators mentioned some protocol components and commands, less than half of them talked about server authentication and its link to end-to-end encryption. We theorize that these "knowledge gaps" arose because they did not explicitly ask for explanations of fixed keywords, such as *certificates*, *public* and *private keys*. In comparison, we specifically asked about these components and thus, we were able to query the (possibly) passive knowledge of the administrators. In line with Krombholz et al. [20], we found knowledge gaps of the administrators related to how the server and the CA interact, confusions of encryption and authentication, and a negative perception of HTTPS and the security indicator.

5.2   Trust

As mentioned in Sect. 4.3, trust is a very complex concept and until now, to the best of our knowledge, no study did investigate the confidence of administrators in HTTPS and its most widely used configuration software. We closed this gap with our study and will discuss our drawn insights in the following. However, we do not claim exhaustiveness and emphasize the need for future in-depth investigations on this topic. Our results suggest that administrators have high trust in the compound protocol HTTPS. Furthermore, we can conclude that administrators are very satisfied with the use of Let's Encrypt, due to its automation and transparency in case of security breaches. Moreover, we found that they put high trust in Let's Encrypt's free CA. In contrast, Certbot is currently not very trusted among administrators. Reasons might include that (i) using Certbot is not necessary to obtain a free Let's Encrypt certificate and therefore, it is not that well known, (ii) users had negative experiences with its auto-configuration functionality (see Sect. 4.3, quote of participant P8) and (iii) it requires root privileges in its standard-setting putting users off.

Recommendation 1: *To overcome entry barriers, we suggest providing a slimmed-down version of Certbot, which among others does not require root-privileges in its standard settings.*

5.3   Let's Encrypt and Certificate Validation

The introduction of Let's Encrypt made it possible to secure connections to web servers using HTTPS without any financial burden. Due to its open-source code, the strong community of experts behind it and its popularity, more than 150 M

Let's Encrypt certificates have been issued so far. We found that the use of Let's Encrypt is generally supported by the majority of companies, but is somewhat more common among smaller companies. The free creation of certificates means that even smaller websites, regardless of whether they are created for business or private use, can offer HTTPS connections. To provide more security by limiting the damage of key compromise and misissuance, the lifetime of Let's Encrypt certificates is set to 90 days. However, the short(er) lifetime also poses some challenges for the administrators. Our results show that although there is the possibility to automatically update certificates, some participants do not do so since they consider it as an additional burden. Users are encouraged by Let's Encrypt to automate the certificate renewal process [1], however, for some web servers, this needs to be done manually or by changing the default settings. Some administrators (5%) forgot to automate their certificate renewal process, which could result in invalid certificates and broken services.

Recommendation 2: Therefore, a suggestion for improvement would be to automatically enable the renewal process for all ACME clients and web servers and visually alert the administrator when this option is not enabled.

The validation levels of certificates and their security guarantees were known by most of our participants. However, still, 12% did not know which validation their certificate provides. A possible reason for this knowledge gap could be that those administrators used Let's Encrypt, which only provides DV, hence no in-depth knowledge of certificate validation is needed by its users. When using Certbot, manual DV or an appropriate DNS plugin is the only way to obtain wildcard certificates[7]. Unfamiliarity of the validation guarantees of a certificate, which we discovered by 12% of our participants, could lead to wrong decisions for web servers with higher certificate requirements.

Recommendation 3: In order to overcome this lack of knowledge, we suggest to visually or textually emphasize the validation provided within the process of certificate generation in the ACME client.

5.4 HTTPS Challenges

Although many participants are well aware of the security risks of older TLS versions, there are still many websites allowing older (i.e., insecure) versions. Fahl et al. [12] found that two-thirds of their participants deliberately used non-validating certificates due to compatibility issues or because their web server was used exclusively for testing purposes. Furthermore, some web servers were not intended to be publicly accessible and their administrators were not even aware of the fact, as they could only be found with the help of a web crawler.

In our study, one-fifth of the administrators reported using certificates with poor security settings since they were forced to do so to support old servers and operating systems, or company or client requirements. We argue that the

---

[7] A certificate that contains a wildcard character (*) which can be used for multiple sub-domains of a domain.

discrepancy between the higher number of insecure servers found in Fahl et al.'s study and ours might have two main reasons: i) we did not crawl the internet and therefore, our data solely relies on self-reporting, and ii) the introduction of Let's Encrypt and Certbot (or other ACME clients) helped administrators to freely and correctly configure their certificates. Fahl et al. revealed as part of their findings a wish list of administrators in order to make the configuration process of X.509 certificates for HTTPS web servers easier. Let's Encrypt has realized this wish list.

Challenges regarding the TLS deployment process with an Apache web server were first investigated by Krombholz et al. [21] whose work was later extended by Bernhard et al. [6]. Both found that the process is very complex and only a part of their participants was able to deploy a secure configuration. Bernhard et al.'s comparison between Let's Encrypt and manual deployment methods suggests more effective HTTPS deployments when using Let's Encrypt, which takes less time and achieves slightly better SSL Lab grades. We observed that administrators using Let's Encrypt felt less confident that their website is configured in a secure way in comparison to other CA users. In line with Krombholz et al.s' results, we found that one-third of the administrators did not strictly enforce HTTPS, 7% had problems with properly securing their communication (usage of weak ciphers), and 5% perceived error messages as too generic and unclear.

Tiefenau et al. [34] concluded that Certbot is an asset in the field of fast, easy, and secure TLS configuration. One of the remaining weaknesses they mentioned is its transparency. We cannot quantify this with our study as no administrator explicitly mentioned it. However, we found that some participants mentioned that it is sometimes difficult to change (standard) settings as it is unclear what current setting include.

Recommendation 4: Therefore, we suggest providing an "advanced" option, which allows the user to change settings in more detail and get a clear overview of current settings.

Some participants indicated that they reviewed their website with a rating tool, such as SSL Labs, to determine if they have configured it securely.

Recommendation 5: Since there are still some websites with insufficient TLS security, we suggest that ACME clients like Certbot automatically perform a rating during the configuration process. This way administrators can actively decide if they are satisfied with the rating and the associated settings.

5.5 Administrator vs. Student Sample

Computer science students are often used as a convenience sample for expert users [3, 21, 28, 35]. Since related work used different methodologies than us (quantitative vs. qualitative) and had different technical assumptions/conditions, we cannot make direct comparisons. However, in the following, we discuss interesting observations obtained from triangulating our findings.

In order to get the most accurate picture of the problems faced by administrators, it is necessary to understand their prerequisites. Students have a different demographic distribution compared to administrators. On average, the administrators in our sample are ~15 years older. Furthermore, not all student participants of prior studies (30–40%) had experience with the work of a system administrator or the configuration process of TLS.

Although we found similar results compared with previous user studies which used student samples, there is no conclusive evidence that administrators can be replaced by students. In fact, we found additional results including the need for "advanced" settings in ACME clients, the barrier of requested root privileges of Certbot (in its standard settings), and the confidence in Let's Encrypt and Certbot. Therefore, we conclude that in order to get an accurate picture of the specific challenges faced by professional administrators, a convenient sample of computer science students should not be used as a substitution.

However, we argue that student samples can be helpful for the detection of difficulties with HTTPS in a broader sense, since Let's Encrypt and ACME clients enable anyone to configure HTTPS due to reduced complexity and no financial cost.

6   Limitations

Our sampling strategy allowed us to recruit a diverse sample of web server administrators with experience in the deployment or maintenance of HTTPS. Despite our recruiting strategy, our sample still has limitations, as our participants work mostly in Central Europe or the US. Therefore, we can't generalize our results as they might be influenced by cultural factors, such as privacy and security awareness in different countries. Although we managed to recruit some female participants (5%), this number is still slightly below the average in IT engineering jobs [26]. However, we found no dedicated studies on the gender distribution of system administrators, making it difficult to judge the representativeness of our sample. Naturally, our quantitative survey approach also has its limitations as the data is self-reported and could have been distorted by participants looking up information during answering the questionnaire. We tried to minimize this risk by asking knowledge questions and evaluating the average time taken by participants to answer them as described in Sect. 3.2.

7   Conclusion

We closed the gap between prior qualitative studies and real-world administrators' challenges by conducting a descriptive quantitative analysis and an online survey. Therefore, we recruited administrators who configured or maintained at least one web server at the time of the study to ensure that the experience with the servers and frameworks used is up to date. Our results quantify the participants' trust in HTTPS and the problems they faced during configuration. Therewith, we confirmed that some administrators still choose weak ciphers for their encryption or old TLS versions due to compatibility reasons. Furthermore, although the usability of Certbot is very high, the need for root privileges in the default setting was stated as a barrier for usage. Many web servers and ACME clients automated a number of their services to reduce their complexity. Therefore, further studies have to be conducted with currently underinvestigated tools (e.g., NGINX and Caddy), to examine their influence in the handling and security of HTTPS. Furthermore, the very complex factor of trust and its influence on the HTTPS configuration process must be examined more in-depth in future work to ensure secure online communication.

Acknowledgment. This material is based upon work partially supported by the *Industry-related Dissertation* funding program. SBA Research (SBA-K1) is a COMET Centre within the framework of COMET - Competence Centers for Excellent Technologies Programme and funded by BMK, BMDW, and the province of Vienna. The programs are both managed by FFG.

References

1. Aas, J.: Why ninety-day lifetimes for certificates? https://letsencrypt.org/2015/11/09/why-90-days.html. Accessed 08 Jan 2021
2. Aas, J., et al.: Let's encrypt: an automated certificate authority to encrypt the entire web. In: ACM SIGSAC Conference on Computer and Communications Security (CCS 2019), pp. 2473–2487 (2019)
3. Acar, Y., Backes, M., Fahl, S., Kim, D., Mazurek, M.L., Stransky, C.: You get where you're looking for: the impact of information sources on code security. In: IEEE Symposium on Security and Privacy (S&P 2016), pp. 289–305. IEEE (2016)
4. Aertsen, M., Korczyński, M., Moura, G.C., Tajalizadehkhoob, S., van den Berg, J.: No domain left behind: is let's encrypt democratizing encryption? In: Applied Networking Research Workshop, pp. 48–54 (2017)
5. Akhawe, D., Amann, B., Vallentin, M., Sommer, R.: Here's my cert, so trust me, maybe? Understanding TLS errors on the web. In: 22nd International Conference on World Wide Web, pp. 59–70 (2013)
6. Bernhard, M., Sharman, J., Acemyan, C.Z., Kortum, P., Wallach, D.S., Halderman, J.A.: On the usability of https deployment. In: 2019 CHI Conference on Human Factors in Computing Systems, pp. 1–10 (2019)
7. Chan, C., Fontugne, R., Cho, K., Goto, S.: Monitoring TLS adoption using backbone and edge traffic. In: IEEE INFOCOM 2018-IEEE Conference on Computer Communications Workshops (INFOCOM WKSHPS), pp. 208–213. IEEE (2018)
8. Cimpanu, C.: 14,766 Let's Encrypt SSL Certificates Issued to PayPal Phishing Sites. https://www.bleepingcomputer.com/news/security/14-766-lets-encrypt-ssl-certificates-issued-to-paypal-phishing-sites/. Accessed 11 Dec 2020
9. Clark, J., Van Oorschot, P.C.: SoK: SSL and https: revisiting past challenges and evaluating certificate trust model enhancements. In: IEEE Symposium on Security and Privacy (S&P 2013), pp. 511–525. IEEE (2013)
10. Durumeric, Z., Kasten, J., Bailey, M., Halderman, J.A.: Analysis of the https certificate ecosystem. In: Conference on Internet Measurement, pp. 291–304 (2013)
11. Durumeric, Z., et al.: The security impact of https interception. In: Network and Distributed System Security Symposium (NDSS 2017) (2017)

12. Fahl, S., Acar, Y., Perl, H., Smith, M.: Why eve and Mallory (also) love webmasters: a study on the root causes of SSL misconfigurations. In: ACM Symposium on Information, Computer and Communications Security, pp. 507–512 (2014)

13. Felt, A.P., Barnes, R., King, A., Palmer, C., Bentzel, C., Tabriz, P.: Measuring https adoption on the web. In: 26th USENIX Security Symposium (USENIX 2017), pp. 1323–1338 (2017)

14. GmbH SS: SoSci Survey - the Solution for Professional Online Questionnaires. https://www.soscisurvey.de/. Accessed 08 Jan 2021

15. Harris, I.A., Khoo, O.K., Young, J.M., Solomon, M.J., Rae, H.: Lottery incentives did not improve response rate to a mailed survey: a randomized controlled trial. J. Clin. Epidemiol. **61**(6), 609–610 (2008)

16. Holm, S.: A simple sequentially rejective multiple test procedure. Scand. J. Stat. (1979)

17. Jensen, E., Laurie, C.: Doing Real Research: A Practical Guide to Social Research. Sage (2016). ISBN 978-1446273883

18. Kim, H.Y.: Statistical notes for clinical researchers: chi-squared test and Fisher's exact test. Restorative Dentistry Endod. **42**(2) (2017)

19. Krippendorff, K.: Content Analysis: An Introduction to It's Methodology, pp. 241–243. SAGE Publications (2004)

20. Krombholz, K., Busse, K., Pfeffer, K., Smith, M., von Zezschwitz, E.: "If HTTPS were secure, I wouldn't need 2FA"-end user and administrator mental models of HTTPS. In: IEEE Symposium on Security and Privacy (S&P 2019) (2019)

21. Krombholz, K., Mayer, W., Schmiedecker, M., Weippl, E.: "I have no idea what I'm doing"-on the usability of deploying HTTPS. In: 26th USENIX Security Symposium (USENIX 2017), pp. 1339–1356 (2017)

22. Laguilles, J.S., Williams, E.A., Saunders, D.B.: Can lottery incentives boost web survey response rates? Findings from four experiments. Res. High. Educ. **52**(5), 537–553 (2011)

23. Lee, J.H., Song, C.H.: Effects of trust and perceived risk on user acceptance of a new technology service. Soc. Behav. Personal. Int. J. **41**(4), 587–597 (2013)

24. Lenth, R.V.: Some practical guidelines for effective sample size determination. Am. Stat. **55**(3) (2001)

25. Lipsey, M.W.: Design Sensitivity: Statistical Power for Experimental Research. Sage (1989). ISBN 978-0803930636

26. Liu, S.: Software developer gender distribution worldwide as of early (2020). https://www.statista.com/statistics/1126823/worldwide-developer-gender/. Accessed 10 Jan 2021

27. Manousis, A., Ragsdale, R., Draffin, B., Agrawal, A., Sekar, V.: Shedding light on the adoption of let's encrypt. arXiv preprint arXiv:1611.00469 (2016)

28. Naiakshina, A., Danilova, A., Tiefenau, C., Smith, M.: Deception task design in developer password studies: exploring a student sample. In: Fourteenth Symposium on Usable Privacy and Security (SOUPS 2018), pp. 297–313 (2018)

29. Nor, K.M., Pearson, J.M.: The influence of trust on internet banking acceptance. J. Internet Banking Commer. **12**(2), 1–10 (1970)

30. Oltrogge, M., Acar, Y., Dechand, S., Smith, M., Fahl, S.: To pin or not to pin-helping app developers bullet proof their TLS connections. In: 24th USENIX Security Symposium (USENIX 2015), pp. 239–254 (2015)

31. Parsovs, A.: Practical issues with TLS client certificate authentication. In: Network and Distributed System Security Symposium (NDSS 2014), vol. 14, pp. 23–26 (2014)

32. Pfeffer, K., et al.: On the usability of authenticity checks for hardware security tokens. In: 30th USENIX Security Symposium (USENIX 2021) (2021)
33. Redmiles, E.M., Malone, A.R., Mazurek, M.L.: I think they're trying to tell me something: advice sources and selection for digital security. In: IEEE Symposium on Security and Privacy (S&P 2016), pp. 272–288. IEEE (2016)
34. Tiefenau, C., von Zezschwitz, E., Häring, M., Krombholz, K., Smith, M.: A usability evaluation of let's encrypt and certbot: usable security done right. In: ACM SIGSAC Conference on Computer and Communications Security (CCS 2019), pp. 1971–1988 (2019)
35. Yakdan, K., Dechand, S., Gerhards-Padilla, E., Smith, M.: Helping Johnny to analyze malware: a usability-optimized decompiler and malware analysis user study. In: IEEE Symposium on Security and Privacy (S&P 2016), pp. 158–177. IEEE (2016)

Towards the Improvement of UI/UX of a Human-AI Adversarial Authorship System

Sadaira Packer[(✉)], Cheryl Seals, and Gerry Dozier

Auburn University, Auburn, AL 36849, USA
{smp0043,sealscd,doziegv}@auburn.edu

Abstract. AuthorCAAT (Author Cyber Analysis & Advisement Tool) is a tool created to aid users in protecting their online privacy by assisting them in altering their writing style through Adversarial Authorship. There have been several iterations of AuthorCAAT that were all tested for efficiency, but not for usability. In this work, we conduct a preliminary study on AuthorCAAT-V to determine any features that need improvement to inform our iterative design decisions for an Adversarial Authorship framework JohariMAA. We plan to develop JohariMAA to adapt to the evolving authorship attribution field and be accessible to a broad audience. Our usability assessment of AuthorCAAT reveals issues involving task complexity, usability, user experience, and user interface efficiency. We discuss potential design decisions for JohariMAA planned to alleviate these issues.

Keywords: Human-AI collaboration · Adversarial authorship · AuthorCAAT · Usability

1 Introduction

Social media usage is at an all-time high and is continuing to grow. KEPIOS reported that the number of social media users has increased from 4.2 billion to 4.62 billion over this past year [16]. The increasing use of social media and the Internet means participating in mass information sharing, thus sacrificing personal privacy. As a result, we are vulnerable to threats to privacy and security caused by our willingness to surrender a large amount of information about ourselves through our emails, status updates, and comments without a second thought about these likely threats.

Some people may use public and private profiles online to separate their professional lives from their personal opinions, but this is not necessarily enough to keep the two separate. The writing style of a user is a behavioral biometric that can be traced back to a specific author with the use of authorship attribution techniques [24]. The ease of attaining our identities through our writing style can cause serious problems when an employee casually discusses their employer

© The Author(s), under exclusive license to Springer Nature Switzerland AG 2022
A. Moallem (Ed.): HCII 2022, LNCS 13333, pp. 194–205, 2022.
https://doi.org/10.1007/978-3-031-05563-8_13

in a negative light and shares it through their private profiles. Another issue could occur if an employee shares information regarding ethical issues within their workplace. This sharing information about issues in the workplace can potentially be traced back to the employee by gathering all of the emails from a company's employees and using that data to perform authorship attribution. In addition, this process can be used to deter people from whistle-blowing or advocating for better practices within their company.

Biometric data storage has proven to have unintended consequences. For example, organizations can use fingerprinted data to target people with malicious advertising as another example of how an organization can utilize your biometrics against you. In 2020, the average number of social media accounts per person was 8.4 [10]. Fingerprinted user accounts can be linked across various sites, their likes, dislikes, and opinions can be analyzed and used to target them with specific information. This targeted information can range from innocuous things like an ad for a television series to more harmful things like disinformation surrounding politics or public health.

AuthorCAAT is a tool that was created to protect the online identity of users [8]. While AuthorCAAT has shown to be an effective tool for anonymization [1], there are issues pertaining to its usability. AuthorCAAT relies heavily on the user's input for the anonymization process. The user is responsible for configuring the anonymization process by making a series of choices per mutation iteration. The process can be very long and repetitive for the user, causing fatigue and frustration.

To combat the negative qualities of AuthorCAAT, we are developing the Adversarial Authorship framework JohariMAA (Johari Window Model for Adversarial Authorship). JohariMAA aims to maintain the effectiveness of AuthorCAAT while offering a more pleasant user experience. JohariMAA will be a system that can adapt to the ever-changing authorship attribution methods.

JohariMAA's ability to manipulate the features of one's writings can aid in the protection of one's privacy and make it more difficult for bad actors to target them maliciously. Without the ability to pinpoint exactly what an individual's thoughts and opinions are, it becomes far more difficult for someone to be completely surrounded by the disinformation. This can help cut down on the successful spread of fake news, which is a serious problem in our society today. In this paper, we analyze the issues within AuthorCAAT and use those problem points to inform the design choices of JohariMAA.

2   Related Work

When adding the element of artificial intelligence to a program, it is important to take into account how it affects the user experience. In [25] they examined the effect of having artificial intelligence involved at varying amounts in a program called DuetDraw, where a user collaborates on drawings with artificial intelligence. The researchers tested four experimental conditions where two different communication styles (detailed or basic instructions) were paired up with two different initiative styles (lead or assist). The participants preferred detailed instructions over the basic instruction when paired with both initiative styles. They also found that most users wanted to take the lead. The users felt that the AI should perform the more repetitive tasks. The setup that did not include AI had the best predictable, comprehensible, and controllable scores. The detailed instruction style performed better than the basic instruction style in these categories.

In [30] the relationship between controllability and accuracy is explored by varying the accuracy of the AI and the controllability of the crane movement in a crane simulator. The participants had three possible rectification approaches: manual controls, automation, or both manual controls and automation. They found that users preferred to move the crane manually even when the controllability was low and less time-efficient than the autonomous option.

Adversarial stylometry is the altering of one's writing style in order to evade authorship attribution [3,24]. The three forms of adversarial stylometry are imitation, obfuscation, and translation. Anonymouth is a framework that performs adversarial stylometry through helping one to make their writings anonymous by offering suggestions to alter the document [21]. Suggestions are made to the user based on the target values created from calculating the features of the sets of samples belonging to the user and other authors. Users could only make the changes suggested by the Basic 9 feature set, as the Writeprints (Limited) feature set's suggestions were too complex. Larger feature sets are more difficult to use because the changes they suggest are not easy for a user to apply.

Adversarial Authorship does not just focus on stylometric features but goes beyond them to include other types such as psychometric features. AuthorCAAT performs Adversarial Authorship. AuthorCAAT is an instance of a $(1 + 1)$ Interactive Evolutionary Computation (IEC) [2,9,11,32,33] that allows a human to interactively evolve adversarial text. IEC involves a human's subjective evaluation in the optimization of a system. IEC is useful for problems that may not be easily evaluated with a fitness function, such as design and music generation problems. Adversarial text helps to preserve privacy and anonymity. The goal of AuthorCAAT is to conceal the author's identity through the creation of adversarial text and preserve the context of the original text. The first version of AuthorCAAT utilized iterative language translation (ILT) and iterative paraphrasing as mutation methods [8,19]. The languages used for translations were English, Spanish, and Chinese.

AuthorCAAT-II included AuthorWebs [7]. AuthorWebs are developed through Entropy-Based Evolutionary Clustering (EBEC). An AuthorWeb is made up of authors, their writing samples, and vectors of the features extracted from the writing samples. They are used to visualize nodes with arcs directed to and from them. The arcs represent writing samples, where each node represents an author. Each arc is directed towards the node that it is closest to the extracted feature vector. The arcs directed to a node are called an author cluster. In AuthorCAAT-II, users can select which author cluster that they would like to right towards or away from.

AuthorCAAT-III introduced ILT hill-climbing to the IEC process as an additional mutation method [13]. The languages used for translation are Spanish, Chinese, Japanese, Korean, Russian, Arabic, French, and German. In ILT hill-climbing, ILT is done with all eight languages for a number of iterations. After these iterations, the resulting translation closest to the selected author target is presented to the user. The user can select this translation to replace the current text or modify the current text and resubmit it to the ILT hill-climbing process.

The feature sets available are character unigrams, sentiment analysis [23, 28, 29, 36, 38, 39], linguistic inquiry and word count (LIWC) [26, 34], topic model [20], bag of words, and stylometry. AuthorCAAT-V uses GEFeS (Genetic & Evolutionary Feature Selection) for off-line feature selection. GEFeS allows for the evaluation of various subsets of a feature set in order to determine the best features for a specific dataset [6, 12, 37]. AuthorCAAT-V also utilizes a linear support vector machine because it has been shown to perform well in [15] and [14] when used with multiple feature sets.

In [1] AuthorCAAT-V was used to create 25 adversarial texts. Three other author masking techniques (Castro [5], Mihaylova [22], and Rahgouy [27]) were also used individually and combined in a system called AIM-IT to create sets of adversarial texts. Castro uses a simple method for masking the original text in an attempt to shorten it. This is primarily done through contraction replacement, synonym substitution, and sentence simplification. Mihaylova targets many different style indicators typically used in author identification. The authors present three main categories: text transformations, noise, and general transformations. Text transformation consists of methods such as adding or removing punctuation, splitting or merging sentences. Noise consists of replacing American English words with their British English counterparts and vice versa and adding or removing function words at beginnings of sentences. The general transformation consists of techniques like contraction replacement and replacing possessive phrases using regular expressions. These techniques are utilized to push the features of a specified text toward the average of a specified training corpus. Rahgouy is a method similar to Mihaylova. Rahgouy used word replacement, phrase replacement, contraction replacement, and either sentence splitting or merging, to transform their text samples.

The adversarial texts were then classified by four authorship attribution systems (keselj03 [17], teahan03 [35], koppel11 [18], and a CNN [31]). AuthorCAAT-V had a greater accuracy reduction in three of the four authorship attribution systems than the other four author masking techniques. We then took the adversarial texts that were created with AuthorCAAT-V and ran them through AIM-IT. Combining AIM-IT with AuthorCAAT-V yielded the greatest reduction in accuracy overall for three of the four classifiers. We have explored the efficiency of the AuthorCAAT system versions, and the work discussed in this paper will analyze and evaluate the usability of the user interface and user experience of the AuthorCAAT systems. This research will support the design and development of JohariMAA with the hope of usage by a broader audience to mask their identity through Adversarial Authorship.

3   Further Development of AuthorCAAT

AuthorCAAT-VI is similar to AuthorCAAT-V except for the addition of a paraphraser, three authorship attribution systems, and the ability to upload a dataset to use as the set of authors for the background dataset. AuthorCAAT-VI does not utilize GEFeS; all features are used. The process begins with constructing a parent text and then selecting an 'Author Target' from the set of authors in the dataset that is loaded into AuthorCAAT-VI. Once a target has been selected, the user chooses either to move towards the target or away from the target based on several operations: (1) iterative language translation (ILT) hill-climbing, (2) paraphrasing, or (3) two way language translation.

In ILT hill-climbing, a parent text (PT) is translated (two-way translation) into a foreign language and then back into English. The languages used are Spanish, Chinese, Japanese, Korean, Russian, Arabic, French, and German. The best result produced by the translation process is selected as the child text (CT) for the next iteration through the languages. The paraphrasing operator takes submits the PT to a paraphrasing method and the resultant text becomes the CT. For two-way translation, a user will first select a language and then translate from English into this language and then back to English.

When the user selects the CT, it then becomes the new PT. However, if the user is not satisfied with the CT, they may choose another operator to create a new CT or modify the PT and then select another operator. The user repeats this evolutionary process until an adversarial text is developed that evades the selected authorship attribution system.

We tried incorporating the three author masking techniques used in AIM-IT into AuthorCAAT after seeing how well the adversarial texts performed in [1] when they were generated in AuthorCAAT-V and then processed through AIM-IT. AuthorCAAT-VII adds Castro, Mihaylova, and Rahgouy to the list of operations that the user can choose from to create the CT. We attempted to add Castro, Mihaylova, and Rahgouy into the hill-climbing also but this addition resulted in the hill-climbing taking several minutes longer to run due to each author masking techniques taking over a minute to run individually. They also did not improve the quality of the texts that were created with the hill-climbing. So not only did adding Castro, Mihaylova, and Rahgouy increase the time it took do a single run of hill-climbing, it prolonged the overall time it took to use the system because the hill-climbing would need to be ran more times to get a suitable CT. We added the paraphraser into the hill-climbing, because it has a similar run time as the languages and the CT that is generated is not negatively affected by its addition.

3.1   Limitations

AuthorCAAT was developed to support our research in Adversarial Authorship, but not designed to support broader population that is unfamiliar with the area. The development focused on achieving anonymity, and we did not formally study tool usability. The user interface of AuthorCAAT-VII consists of three windows.

In the main window, the user enters the text and interacts with the system to assist in the anonymization process. The author scores window visually represents the parent text's similarity to each of the 25 authors from the background dataset based on the selected feature set. The authorship attribution window is where the user has the option to check the anonymity of their text against three authorship attribution systems: keselj03, koppel11, teahan03. AuthorCAAT currently has ten buttons, three drop-down menus, and three windows. All of these components can be a bit overwhelming for the user. There are no indicators to let the user know how to use the program properly. The buttons for steepest ascent and steepest descent hill-climbing are labeled with abbreviations. SAHC and SDHC are not common abbreviations, which may cause some users frustration as they may not know the purpose of these buttons.

4   Examining the Usability of AuthorCAAT

We conducted a preliminary study on AuthorCAAT-V. For the study we used AuthorCAAT-V because it is the last stable version and proved effective in performing Adversarial Authorship [1]. As shown in Fig. 1, AuthorCAAT-V does not include the authorship attribution window that is included in AuthorCAAT-VII. We asked participants to use AuthorCAAT-V to create an adversarial text. We gave a set of instructions to the participants that guided them through their usage of AuthorCAAT-V. Participants began the process within an initial text sample from the CASIS dataset [24]. The experimental process is to modify this text sample with the aid of AuthorCAAT interactively. After the experiment, a survey was completed consisting of the ten questions from the System Usability Scale [4] and asked participants about any issues encountered when using the program. Figure 2 depicts the process of operating AuthorCAAT-V.

Our study gave us a more in depth look at the usability issues within AuthorCAAT. One of the issues users experienced was the program failing. When this would happen the user would only be able to identify the cause of the error if they ran the program from the command line because AuthorCAAT would just stop responding without any error messages. This would cause the user to have to close the program and restart it.

Some users still experienced confusion about the process of using AuthorCAAT even though instructions were given and were unable to complete the task of creating adversarial text. There were ten steps included within the instructions to run AuthorCAAT. Some of the steps are not as straightforward as others. For example, after users enter the text that they would like to anonymize and choose which feature set they would like to utilize, they must look at the 25 author scores and select an author target that they would like their text to mimic. This choice is entirely up to the user. While there is not necessarily a correct choice, there can be choices that are unhelpful in the anonymization process. For example, if a chosen target is too far away from the original, getting the text identified as the chosen author's target could be impossible. But this could also be the case if the choice is too close to the original author. This part of the process is a bit

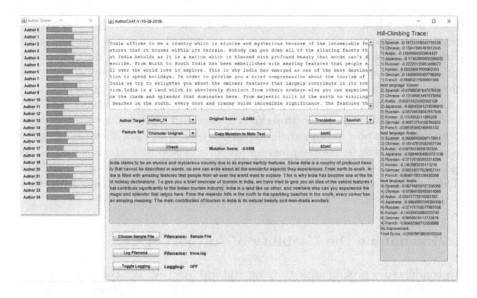

Fig. 1. The GUI of AuthorCAAT-V.

of trial and error. The user picking an unhelpful choice leads to prolonging their time spent using the program. One user reported spending over three hours trying to create the adversarial text before giving up. Some of the other decisions left up to the user include the mutation method and whether or not they will accept the resulting text as their new PT. All of these decisions made by the user influences the process significantly. The more unhelpful choices the user makes, the longer the process takes. The longer the process takes, the more fatigued the user becomes. To give the users a better chance of creating adversarial text, and doing so in a reasonable amount of time, we need to reduce the potential for unhelpful choices.

5   Designing JohariMAA

After examining the feedback from users, we now explore possible designs for JohariMAA. Improving the flow of information is a key factor in improving how the user experiences a program. Using either multiple pages or combining and simplifying options to reduce the clutter should make it easier for a user to understand how to properly use the program. Displaying every option at once can be confusing for the user, especially when there is no clear labeling to show the order that the steps are to be completed. Giving only the necessary information and steps in a program like JohariMAA will make learning the program easier for the user.

The design will also need to include several other features that were missing from AuthorCAAT, such as displaying error messages and better error handling. Having a tutorial option and tooltips can assist with the learnability of the

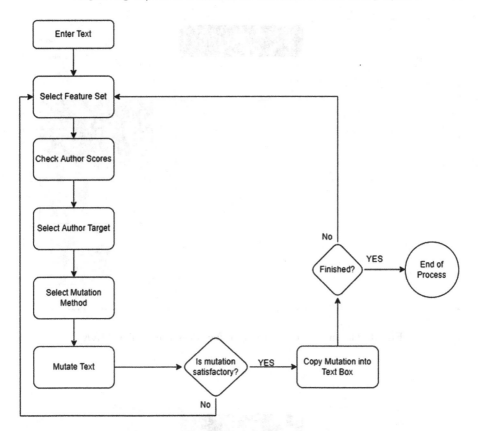

Fig. 2. A flowchart depicting the process of operating AuthorCAAT.

program. Instead of displaying the hill-climbing trace to notify the users that the mutation process is in progress, we can display processing messages. The user experience would benefit from a reduction in choices for the author target. This could be done by presenting the user with a reduced set of potential author targets based on the feature set that they select. Another possibility to explore is getting rid of the choice entirely and just running the mutation function for each author target in the reduced set and presenting the user with the mutated text for each option.

Figure 3 shows a potential design for JohariMAA. This design consists of a text box where users can enter their text and view the mutated texts by using the tabs labeled for each mutation. The tabs for the mutated text will appear dynamically depending on how many mutations the user chooses to create. Once a tab is selected for the mutated text there will be an option to move that text to the parent tab. To the right of the text box is three buttons that each expand into a panel of more options and information about each step of the process. Above this set of buttons is a menu button. The menu button gives users access to options like downloading the adversarial text and instructions for

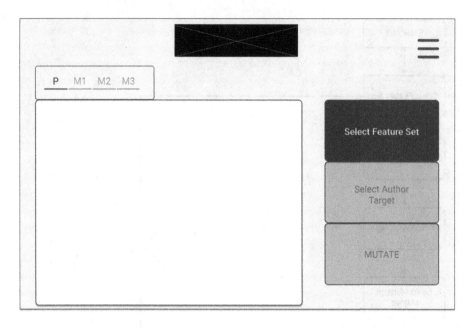

Fig. 3. The main view of the interface design for JohariMAA.

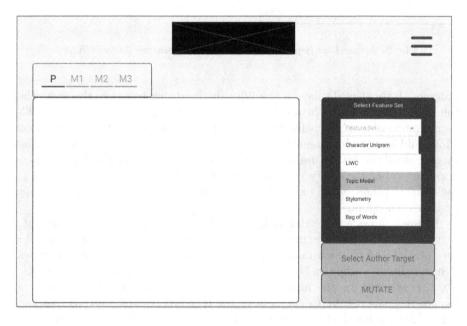

Fig. 4. JohariMAA interface design depicting the select feature set button expanding into a dropdown menu.

the program. A user can only select a step in the process if the previous step has been configured (e.g. a user can only select author target(s) if they select a feature set first). The buttons that are unavailable for use will be denoted by being a lighter color. When you click the first button it expands into a panel that shows a dropdown bar consisting of all the available feature sets (see Fig. 4). After making the feature set selection, the panel collapses back into a button, and the button for the next step is then available to be selected. These are some of the potential design choices that are meant to lead the user through the process without them having to guess what step is next. The options are concealed for each step until they are in use to minimize interface clutter.

6 Conclusion

AuthorCAAT was developed with the hopes of providing a tool that could aid in the preservation of online anonymity by allowing users to alter their writing style interactively. After several versions, we have developed a system that can efficiently conceal one's identity with respect to several authorship attribution algorithms. We are creating a framework, JohariMAA, with the same goal of preserving online anonymity. The framework will be able to adapt to the evolving authorship attribution algorithms. In this paper, we began working towards the development of JohariMAA by evaluating AuthorCAAT where we discovered several issues such as error handling and task complexity. We then propose design ideas for JohariMAA that would offer an improved user interface, and therefore an improved user experience. In future work, we plan on applying our design ideas to JohariMAA before doing usability testing.

References

1. Allred, J., Packer, S., Dozier, G., Aykent, S., Richardson, A., King, M.: Towards a human-AI hybrid for adversarial authorship. In: 2020 SoutheastCon, pp. 1–8. IEEE (2020)
2. Back, T., Hammel, U., Schwefel, H.P.: Evolutionary computation: comments on the history and current state. IEEE Trans. Evol. Comput. 1, 3–17 (1997)
3. Brennan, M., Afroz, S., Greenstadt, R.: Adversarial stylometry. ACM Trans. Inf. Syst. Secur. 15(3), 1–22 (2012)
4. Brooke, J., et al.: SUS-a quick and dirty usability scale. Usability Eval. Ind. 189(194), 4–7 (1996)
5. Castro-Castro, D., Ortega, R., Muñoz, R.: Author masking by sentence transformation. In: CLEF (Working Notes) (2017)
6. Davis, L.D., Mitchell, M.: Handbook of Genetic Algorithms (1991)
7. Day, S., Brown, J., Thomas, Z., Gregory, I., Bass, L., Dozier, G.: Adversarial authorship, author webs, and entropy-based evolutionary clustering. In: International Conference on Computer Communications and Networks (2016)
8. Day, S., Williams, H., Shelton, J., Dozier, G.: Towards the development of a cyber analysis & advisement tool (CAAT) for mitigating de-anonymization attacks. In: Modern Artificial Intelligence and Cognitive Science Conference, vol. 1584, pp. 41–46 (2016)

9. De Jong, K., Spears, W.: On the state of evolutionary computation. In: Fifth International Conference on Genetic Algorithms (1993)
10. Dean, B.: Social network usage & growth statistics: How many people use social media in 2022? https://backlinko.com/social-media-users
11. Dozier, G.: Evolving robot behavior via interactive evolutionary computation: from real-world to simulation. In: ACM Symposium on Applied Computing (2001)
12. Dozier, G., et al.: GEFeS: genetic & evolutionary feature selection for periocular biometric recognition. In: 2011 IEEE Workshop on Computational Intelligence in Biometrics and Identity Management (CIBIM), pp. 152–156. IEEE (2011)
13. Faust, C., Dozier, G., Xu, J., King, M.C.: Adversarial authorship, interactive evolutionary hill-climbing, and author CAAT-III. In: 2017 IEEE Symposium Series on Computational Intelligence, SSCI 2017 (2017)
14. Gaston, J., et al.: Authorship attribution via evolutionary hybridization of sentiment analysis, LIWC, and topic modeling features. In: 2018 IEEE Symposium Series on Computational Intelligence (SSCI), pp. 933–940. IEEE (2018)
15. Gaston, J., et al.: Authorship attribution vs. adversarial authorship from a LIWC and sentiment analysis perspective. In: 2018 IEEE Symposium Series on Computational Intelligence (SSCI), pp. 920–927. IEEE (2018)
16. Kemp, S.: Tiktok gains 8 new users every second (and other mind-blowing stats). https://blog.hootsuite.com/simon-kemp-social-media/
17. Keselj, V., Peng, F., Cercone, N., Thomas, C.: N-gram-based author profiles for authorship attribution. In: Proceedings of the Conference Pacific Association for Computational Linguistics, PACLING, vol. 3, pp. 255–264 (2003)
18. Koppel, M., Schler, J., Argamon, S.: Authorship attribution in the wild. Lang. Resour. Eval. 45(1), 83–94 (2011)
19. Mack, N., Bowers, J., Williams, H., Dozier, G., Shelton, J.: The best way to a strong defense is a strong offense: mitigating deanonymization attacks via iterative language translation. Int. J. Mach. Learn. Comput. 5, 409 (2015)
20. McCallum, A.K.: Mallet: a machine learning for language toolkit (2002). http://Mallet.Cs.Umass.Edu
21. McDonald, A.W.E., Afroz, S., Caliskan, A., Stolerman, A., Greenstadt, R.: Use fewer instances of the letter 'i': toward writing style anonymization (2012)
22. Mihaylova, T., Karadzhov, G., Nakov, P., Kiprov, Y., Georgiev, G., Koychev, I.: Su@ pan'2016: author obfuscation. In: CLEF (Working Notes), pp. 956–969 (2016)
23. Narayanan, M., et al.: Adversarial authorship, sentiment analysis, and the author-web zoo. In: 2018 IEEE Symposium Series on Computational Intelligence (SSCI), pp. 928–932. IEEE (2018)
24. Neal, T., Sundararajan, K., Fatima, A., Yan, Y., Xiang, Y., Woodard, D.: Surveying stylometry techniques and applications. In: 2016 IEEE European Symposium on Security and Privacy (EuroS P) (2017)
25. Oh, C., Song, J., Choi, J., Kim, S., Lee, S., Suh, B.: I lead, you help but only with enough details: understanding user experience of co-creation with artificial intelligence. In: Proceedings of the 2018 CHI Conference on Human Factors in Computing Systems, pp. 1–13 (2018)
26. Pennebaker, J., Boyd, R., Jordan, K., Blackburn, K.: The development and psychometric properties of LIWC. University of Texas at Austin (2015)
27. Rahgouy, M., Giglou, H.B., Rahgooy, T., Zeynali, H., Khayat, S., Rasouli, M.: Author masking directed by author's style (2018)
28. Riloff, E., Wiebe, J.: Learning extraction patterns for subjective expressions. In: Proceedings of the 2003 Conference on Empirical Methods in Natural Language Processing, pp. 105–112 (2003)

29. Riloff, E., Wiebe, J., Wilson, T.: Learning subjective nouns using extraction pattern bootstrapping. In: Proceedings of the Seventh Conference on Natural Language Learning at HLT-NAACL 2003, pp. 25–32 (2003)
30. Roy, Q., Zhang, F., Vogel, D.: Automation accuracy is good, but high controllability may be better. In: Proceedings of the 2019 CHI Conference on Human Factors in Computing Systems, pp. 1–8 (2019)
31. Shrestha, P., Sierra, S., González, F.A., Rosso, P., Montes-Y-Gómez, M., Solorio, T.: Convolutional neural networks for authorship attribution of short texts. In: Proceedings of the 15th Conference of the European Chapter of the Association for Computational Linguistics: Volume 2, Short Papers, pp. 669–674 (2017)
32. Spears, W.M., De Jong, K.A., Bäck, T., Fogel, D.B., de Garis, H.: An overview of evolutionary computation. In: Brazdil, P.B. (ed.) ECML 1993. LNCS, vol. 667, pp. 442–459. Springer, Heidelberg (1993). https://doi.org/10.1007/3-540-56602-3_163
33. Takagi, H.: Interactive evolutionary computation: fusion of the capabilities of EC optimization and human evaluation. In: IEEE (2001)
34. Tausczik, Y.R., Pennebaker, J.W.: The psychological meaning of words: LIWC and computerized text analysis methods. J. Lang. Soc. Psychol. **29**, 24–54 (2010)
35. Teahan, W.J., Harper, D.J.: Using compression-based language models for text categorization. In: Croft, W.B., Lafferty, J. (eds.) Language Modeling for Information Retrieval, pp. 141–165. Springer, Heidelberg (2003). https://doi.org/10.1007/978-94-017-0171-6_7
36. Wiebe, J., Wilson, T., Cardie, C.: Annotating expressions of opinions and emotions in language. Lang. Resour. Eval. **39**(2), 165–210 (2005)
37. Williams, H.C., Carter, J.N., Campbell, W.L., Roy, K., Dozier, G.V.: Genetic & evolutionary feature selection for author identification of html associated with malware. Int. J. Mach. Learn. Comput. **4**, 250 (2014)
38. Wilson, T., et al.: OpinionFinder: a system for subjectivity analysis. In: HLT/EMNLP 2005, pp. 347–354 (2005). https://doi.org/10.3115/1225733.1225751
39. Wilson, T., Wiebe, J., Hoffmann, P.: Recognizing contextual polarity in phrase-level sentiment analysis. In: Proceedings of Human Language Technology Conference and Conference on Empirical Methods in Natural Language Processing, pp. 347–354 (2005)

Multi-faceted Authentication Methods and Tools

Bu-Dash: A Universal and Dynamic Graphical Password Scheme

Panagiotis Andriotis[1,2]($\boxtimes$) (ID), Myles Kirby[1], and Atsuhiro Takasu[2] (ID)

[1] University of the West of England, Bristol BS16 1QY, UK
panagiotis.andriotis@uwe.ac.uk
[2] National Institute of Informatics, Tokyo 101-8430, Japan

Abstract. Biometric authentication gradually replaces knowledge-based methods on mobile devices. However, Personal Identification Numbers, passcodes, and graphical password schemes such as the Android Pattern Unlock (APU) are often the primary means for authentication, or they constitute an auxiliary (or backup) method to be used in case biometrics fail. Passcodes need to be memorable to be usable, hence users tend to choose easy to guess passwords, compromising security. The APU is a great example of a popular and usable graphical password scheme which can be easily compromised, by exploiting common and predominant human behavioristic traits. Despite its vulnerabilities, the scheme's popularity has led researchers to propose adjustments and variations that enhance security but maintain its familiar user interface. Nevertheless, prior work demonstrated that improving security while preserving usability remains frequently a hard task. In this paper we propose a novel graphical password scheme built on the foundations of the well-accepted APU method, which is usable, inclusive, universal, and robust against shoulder surfing and smudge attacks. Our scheme, named `Bu-Dash`, features a dynamic user interface that mutates every time a user swipes the screen. Our pilot studies illustrate that `Bu-Dash` attracts positive user acceptance rates and maintains acceptable usability levels.

Keywords: Smudge attacks · Android pattern · User authentication · Shoulder surfing

1 Introduction

User authentication on mobile devices is a ubiquitous task performed daily by millions of users. Personal Identification Numbers (PIN) have been widely used during mobile computing's adolescence, but after 2010 we have seen a remarkable variety of proposals that aim to replace 4- or 6-digit PIN screen lock methodologies (alphanumeric, graphical, biometrics, implicit authentication). Android developers were among the first that attempted to introduce a graphical-based method for user authentication on mobile devices proposing the APU scheme during 2008 [13]. Earlier studies have shown that the APU is still utilized by at least 25% of Android users [13,24].

© The Author(s), under exclusive license to Springer Nature Switzerland AG 2022
A. Moallem (Ed.): HCII 2022, LNCS 13333, pp. 209–227, 2022.
https://doi.org/10.1007/978-3-031-05563-8_14

The proliferation of biometric methods is evident nowadays due to the increased usability they offer, urging users to replace traditional text or graphical passwords (knowledge-based) with fingerprint and face identification methods [36] (biometric-based). However, although biometrics seems to be the preferred user authentication methodology, there still exists the need to set up a secondary password on the device in case the biometric sensor fails. Therefore, text or graphical-based passcodes are still necessary to ensure smooth and untroubled authentication for mobile device users.

Prior work on text-based authentication investigated the transition from 4- to 6-digit PIN passcodes and concluded that longer PINs attain only marginally improved security [32]. The transition from 4-digit to longer passcodes was the only notable security upgrade of this knowledge-based user authentication method for mobile devices. On the other hand, several graphical password schemes have been proposed aiming to provide more usable and secure solutions for mobile devices [14,17,34].

Focusing particularly on the APU, the addition of password meters as an improvement towards raising users' security awareness has been studied extensively [2,27,28], but such solutions have not been considered yet for inclusion by the industry. In addition, research has shown that similarly to the extension of the 4- digit to 6-digit format for passcodes [24], strategies like the expansion from the standard 3×3 to a 4×4 grid, do not offer significant security enhancements [4]. Other proposals include node re-arrangement [29], system-guided contact point selection [9], or dual super-imposed input on the same 3×3 grid [13] aiming to prevent or minimize threats from shoulder surfing attacks. The common characteristic of these methods is their intention to propose (mainly minor) structural interventions to the original APU scheme that will not drastically affect users' familiarity with the interface, avoiding users' frustration and disapproval.

Despite the plethora of proposals to improve graphical passwords against smudge [6] and shoulder surfing attacks [16], to the best of our knowledge, there is no research work that attempts to assess the feasibility of using a methodology which is based on the implementation of a dynamic grid. In this paper we introduce Bu-Dash, a proof of concept based on design principles found in the APU and in gaming platforms[1].

Initially inspired from the *Morse code* and its use of dots (or Bullet points •) and Dashes (−) to create an encoded vocabulary/lexicon to be used in telecommunications, we envisioned a passcode scheme that comprises shapes/symbols instead of alphanumerical characters. However, because the use of only two symbols in a password would introduce security issues (i.e., limited password space), we propose to utilize additional symbols as the passcodes' potential building blocks: ○, □, −, △, ×. These shapes should probably look familiar to gamers[2], or other broader audiences[3]. Their selection was based on research which demon-

---

[1] https://www.playstation.com/en-gb/legal/copyright-and-trademark-notice/.

[2] We utilized Google's "Material Icons" as the password building blocks in this research work: https://fonts.google.com/icons.

[3] We refer to viewers of the popular series "Squid Game".

strates that these are the least complex shapes in a series of different candidates [10].

Additionally, to defend from shoulder surfing and mainly smudge attacks, we propose a novel approach in designing graphical password schemes. Instead of forming the password by swiping a finger on the nodes of a static grid, we propose the use of a dynamically changing grid. Bu-Dash is based on the popular APU 3×3 node interface which is well-known to mobile device users. However, instead of having static nodes (i.e., •), Bu-Dash's grid is dynamic, featuring randomly assigned shapes in its nodes (○, □, −, △, ×). The shapes keep changing every time users move their fingers on the grid making the scheme more robust to shoulder surfing and smudge attacks, without drastically affecting its usability. In summary, this paper makes the following contributions:

- We propose a novel graphical password scheme based on Android's popular 3 × 3 node interface that is secure against smudge attacks.
- We develop a mobile application to showcase the Bu-Dash system and collect preliminary feedback from mobile device users.
- We conduct a series of pilot studies with users who volunteered to participate and comment on the feasibility of introducing such a scheme.
- We report early results that show usability is not drastically reduced due to the introduction of a shifting grid on the scheme's interface.

2   Related Work

Graphical passwords for mobile devices have been introduced as a more usable solution for user authentication because graphical information is more memorable by humans [11]. Prior work on Android patterns however investigated users' biases and habits when interacting with the 3×3 node interface and found favorable starting/ending points and N-grams [3], which are sometimes related to the influence of human factors such as users' handedness [1]. The APU security was quantified by Uellenbeck et al. [30] who found that, in theory, APU selection is as diverse as selecting a 3-PIN password [13]. The lack of APU's passcode diversity due to human aspects was also confirmed by Aviv et al. [4] in an online study, and more extensively by Loge et at. [23] whose work showcased users' poor security perceptions when forming passcodes in different contexts (e.g., authentication in banking or shopping apps). The APU has been also studied as an attack surface with research focusing basically on side channel and guessing attacks. Aviv et al. [6] showed that smudges (unintentionally residing on mobile devices' screens) can eventually aid guessing attacks against users' passwords. Andriotis et al. [3] combined insights retrieved from collected passcodes and performed an *in situ* lab study, experimenting with guessing attacks. At a later work, they commented on the feasibility of performing successful guessing attacks on the APU using common knowledge [1]. Android patterns are also susceptible to shoulder surfing [5] and video-based attacks [33]. However, the APU scheme remains popular among Android users [24] drawing researchers' attention.

The lack of diversity in choosing Android patterns and the influence of human biases in the scheme's security have led researchers to propose a variety of solutions aiming to make the APU more robust to smudge attacks [15,20,26] and shoulder surfing [12]. Another strand of research proposes the use of password meters to diversify input and enhance awareness [2,27,28]. Other proposals incorporate dual input on the same 3 × 3 framework [13], feature extended 4 × 4 grid interfaces [4], utilize background images and animations to enhance passcode selection [35], employ assisted pattern formation [9], or integrate blocklists [25] to enable a more diverse pattern selection and incommode guessing attacks. Most of these solutions do not alter radically the well-known 3 × 3 interface, but they attempt to include small adjustments in the user authentication experience keeping the main grid in a static state. Tupsamudre et al. [29] propose an alternate circular layout (namely "Pass-O") simplifying the APU drawing rules. Their usability evaluation shows that users tend to create shorter and less complex passwords under the Pass-O scheme [31].

Alternative layouts and dynamic grids have been proposed in the past for *PIN-based* authentication aiming to minimize the influence of shoulder surfing attacks. However, floating [17] or rotating [8] grids result in longer login times than conventional text-based systems, and gesture-based proposals such as "SwiPIN" [34] might require long training periods for the user to become familiar with. Other proposals include the use of colors and shapes in the user authentication process. "Chameleon" is a hybrid scheme using a mixture of digits, colors and shapes but it is not clear whether it can fit in small screens like these used on smartphones [18]. Some of the shapes used in this work (○, □, △) are similar to those we utilize for the Bu-Dash scheme. Similar symbols with the ones we use in our paper are also incorporated in Lee's work [22]. Finally, similar to our scheme, "SteganoPIN" [21] and "SwitchPIN" [19] are using dynamic interfaces that randomly assign digits on 3 × 3 grids. The SteganoPIN creators however state that their system is more appropriate for ATM and PoS systems rather than mobile devices.

In this paper we propose Bu-Dash, the first graphical password scheme for mobile devices that adopts concepts from aforementioned work, but aims to present a more usable and simple authentication process. We assume that the scheme aims to protect against a non-targeted attacker that performs a physical observation (not video-, or camera-based) attack. Similarly to the APU concept, attackers are only able to perform an "online" attack, meaning that they have limited attempts to guess the passcode before the device gets locked.

3   Proposed Scheme

Our proposed scheme adopts design concepts from the APU and uses symbols as the building blocks of the password (Fig. 1). We use the familiar 3 × 3 grid setting from Android and the method of forming the password by swiping the finger among different nodes on the grid. However –different from Android which uses a static grid– we propose the use of a dynamic grid that keeps changing

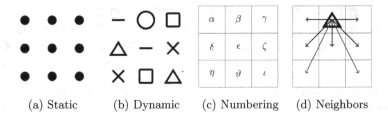

| (a) Static | (b) Dynamic | (c) Numbering | (d) Neighbors |

Fig. 1. The Android pattern lock screen grid (**a**), and an instance of the ever-changing Bu-Dash grid (**b**). Part (**c**) shows the nomenclature for the nodes' positions and Part (**d**) demonstrates eligible moves to neighbor nodes from position β. Blue color indicates "knight moves" [5]. (Color figure online)

when the users swipe their fingers (Fig. 1b, 2). We believe that this addition to the password scheme will make the authentication process more resistant to shoulder surfing attacks. The `Bu-Dash` grid is not static and it does not feature only bullet points as nodes (like the Android's grid, see Fig. 1a). The `Bu-Dash` grid is dynamic and it includes 5 different shapes as nodes (Fig. 1b). The nodes (shapes) are randomly chosen and fetched by the system when the password scheme launches and they keep changing when users swipe their fingers to select the next node in the password chain. We implemented the following guidelines to assist users to get familiar with `Bu-Dash` passwords.

- The password is formed as a sequence of shapes from the following set of symbols: $\{\bigcirc, \square, -, \triangle, \times\}$
- *Length*: The preferred password must be 4–9 shapes long.
- *Diversity*: The preferred password must contain at least 2 different shapes.
- Passwords are formed when users swipe their fingers on a 3×3 grid that keeps changing when they visit a new position.
- *Allowed moves*: Users are allowed to swipe their fingers in the neighbor nodes only, therefore "jumps" to a distant node are not feasible (e.g. from β to θ in Fig. 1c), unless they chose a "knight move" [5], (as seen in Fig. 1d).
- Users are allowed to revisit a node on the grid as many times they need.

Figure 2 shows an example of a user forming the following password to unlock a device: $\triangle - \times -$.

4 Methodology

First, we conducted an online survey requesting respondents (Android and iOS users) to provide a `Bu-Dash` password that they would use on their devices. The request was to provide an *"easy-to-use and secure password"*. In this digital "pen-and-paper" study, participants were not interacting with a device. They were asked to envision a *usable* and *secure* `Bu-Dash` password based on the constrains mentioned in Sect. 3. They also had the chance to view a short video that

(a) Initial   (b) 1st Node   (c) Change   (d) 2nd Node   (e) Change   (f) 3rd Node   (g) Change   (h) 4th Node

Fig. 2. Example: Forming the password $\triangle - \times - :$ The starting grid (a) shows the 5 shapes in random order. Users can place their fingers to any node featuring the $\triangle$ shape (b) and the node will become visited. At that moment, the shapes on the grid change randomly (c) and the user tries to reach the next shape of the password, which is $-$ (d) swiping to position β. The $-$ is reached and the grid changes again (e). The same process continues until the full password is formed (f–h). Notice the variety of options the user has to visit positions ζ or η in (e), and positions γ, θ, or ι in (g).

was explaining how the scheme works and showing an example about how they can swipe their fingers on the dynamic grid to form a password. We did not show any examples about how to form a certain password aiming to avoid introducing unwanted biases. Our primary intention was to gather information about how intelligible the proposed scheme is. Additionally, we asked the participants if they would prefer this scheme over the traditional APU. In this paper we refer to this group of participants as the "**Survey**" group *(n = 65)*. The survey was communicated to a diverse mix of students and staff via emails and announcements in the learning platform of our Institution. We received responses from 85 individuals (who joined anonymously), but only 65 consented in participating and answered all given questions. As an incentive for their participation, individuals were included in a raffle to win vouchers.

At a second phase, we assessed users' interactions with the proposed scheme. We developed an application, titled "Bu-Dash", which was distributed via the Google Play app store in the "Education" category. The application was featuring the Bu-Dash password grid and captured initially participants' input. The application was later updated to acquire very basic usability features at the latter stages of our experiments. We released the first edition of the Bu-Dash application on Google Play and asked a small group *(n = 14)* of Android users (utilizing the same communication channels as previously) to interact with the Bu-Dash grid and provide passwords they would use on their devices. We refer to these respondents as the "**Pilot**" group in this work.

Participants were asked to download our application on their Android devices and then launch it. The application asked them to provide basic demographics (gender, age, education), and answer some generic, multiple-choice questions (mobile OS they use, if they were familiar with the APU, and which kind of authentication they use on their devices). Afterwards, participants viewed a set of instructions about how to create a Bu-Dash password. It should be noted that the sequence of shapes was randomized every time the user was looking at the instructions. We followed this strategy to assess if provided passwords were affected by the first shape the users were seeing in the instructions. Finally, respondents were asked to form their preferred Bu-Dash password on their devices. Mimicking the same process while forming an APU passcode, the application was asking the participants (as a final step) to re-enter and confirm their **Bu-Dash** password. Additionally, users had the choice to be included in a raffle to win vouchers and then exit the application.

The application was updated at a later stage as we were aiming to review usability characteristics of the proposed scheme. We added a "Memory Game" to the application and asked a different group of participants to play. Users had the choice to play any of the "Easy", "Medium", "Hard" levels. The rules of the game were simple. After viewing the formation of (let's say) an "Easy" password on the **Bu-Dash** grid (i.e., a sequence of 4 shapes: ×○×□), they were asked to re-enter this password. They were also given the chance to watch again the password formation on their screens as many times as they wanted. The "Medium" password consisted of 6 shapes and the "Hard" one consisted of 9 shapes. We did not use any complexity metrics [2] for this task, because our primary goal was to figure out if users would be able to recall at least a 4-node password. Therefore, we were aiming to assess the *short-term memorability* of the scheme. In this paper we refer to these participants as the auxiliary or "**Aux**" group *(n = 18)*.

5   Results

First, we present results derived from the "Survey" group, comprising individuals that did not have access to the Bu-Dash application via their devices. Then, we discuss outcomes derived from two different user groups (namely "Pilot" and "Aux") of our Bu-Dash application which utilized the proposed password scheme. Our aim is to identify common traits (if any) and attempt an initial assessment of **Bu-Dash**'s usability features.

5.1   Password Space

Looking at the **Bu-Dash** password design constrains we recall that the passcode must be at least 4 shapes long and its length can be up to 9 nodes. There are 5 different available shapes to choose from and there must be at least 2 different shapes in the password. Neighbor nodes can be visited as many times as necessary to form the password and the system ensures that there always exists at least one available shape (from the set of the 5) in the neighborhood of a visited node. This means that there exist $5 \cdot 5 \cdot 5 \cdot 5 - 5 = 620$ different 4-node **Bu-Dash** passcodes. Similarly, there are $\underbrace{5 \cdot 5 \cdot 5 \ldots 5 \cdot 5}_{9 \ nodes} - 5 \approx 1.9M$ different combinations to form a 9-node passcode. We exclude those combinations that contain the same symbols in each passcode, e.g., those similar to ○○○○ for a 4-node passcode. Thus, we have more than 2.4M unique passcodes under this scheme (i.e., 2,441,220). Therefore, **Bu-Dash**'s password space is more than 6 times bigger than the one defined by the APU scheme (which has 389,112 unique passcodes [1,28]). However, the APU has a wider space (if we consider that options are equiprobable) when we focus on passwords with 4–6 nodes.

5.2 "Survey" Group

Most participants in the treatment group were undergraduate students (72%). In the "Survey" group most respondents identified as males (66%), and iOS users (78%), but the majority (94%) was familiar with the APU. In this survey we were basically targeting respondents that did not have access to the Bu-Dash application; this explains the prevalence of iOS users in the sample. Most participants (94%) said they use a passcode on their devices and the majority (72%) prefer biometric authentication methods (Fingerprint/Face ID). After providing basic demographics, the participants saw a sequence of the available Bu-Dash shapes (○–△□×) and instructions about how to form a *valid* Bu-Dash password. We then asked them the following open-ended questions:

- **Q1**: "Write down the passcode you chose (C for circle, D for dash, T for triangle, S for square, X for X), e.g. CDCDCC".
- **Q2**: "Would you use the "Bu-Dash" passcode scheme on your device? Which scheme you would use: a) Android Pattern Lock, or b) Bu-Dash? Please explain why.

Below we discuss insights resulted from their responses.

The Bu-Dash Scheme is Comprehensive. Although we did not offer any mechanisms to validate correct formation and input of the provided Bu-Dash passwords, invalid entries were not identified **(Q1)**. Thus, we deduce that the scheme is intelligible and the provided instructions are sufficient and comprehensive.

Password Characteristics. We gathered statistics from the acquired passwords, and we discuss them here (see Table 1). We mentioned previously that participants saw a sequence of the shapes they should use to create their Bu-Dash passwords and we said that the circle was the first symbol in the sequence: (○–△□×). This might have created a bias towards starting their passwords with a ○, because 22 participants (i.e., approximately 1/3) created a password featuring a ○ as a starting point. In the next sections we discuss how we managed to overcome this issue by randomizing the shapes we show first in the tutorial part of the Bu-Dash application. Additionally, we noticed that the – and the × symbols were the least favorite to start a password in this sample of users. We also estimated how many times the distinct shapes appear in the set and we report that their frequency is almost uniform (with approximately 51 appearances each). Finally, □ and – appear to be used less frequently than the other symbols, with 46 and 44 appearances, respectively.

We also gathered frequency analysis results (see Table 2). Most participants created a password with 6 nodes (18 respondents) and 21 respondents used 4 shapes in their passwords. One can deduce that the "Survey" participants were mostly focused on the proposal of a secure password because they did not have the opportunity to actually use the Bu-Dash scheme on their devices. Therefore, we report the following attributes of the provided password set. For the length of

Table 1. Password characteristics of "Survey" password set

Password characteristics	O	□	–	△	×
N^o of passwords starting with shape	**22**	14	8	12	9
N^o of times appeared in password set	51	46	44	51	51

Table 2. Frequency analysis of "Survey" password set

Password length frequency			Shapes used per password		
Length	Freq.	%	Shapes N^o	Freq.	%
4	12	18.46%	2	8	12.31%
5	10	15.39%	3	19	29.23%
6	**18**	**27.69%**	4	**21**	**32.31%**
7	12	18.46%	5	17	26.15%
8	5	7.69%	Length: $\mu = 6.185$, $\sigma = 1.580$		
9	8	12.31%	Shapes: $\mu = 3.723$, $\sigma = 0.992$		

the passwords we have $\mu = 6.185$ and $\sigma = 1.580$ (μ: mean, σ: standard deviation). The median value of the password length is 6 and the median value of the number of shapes per password is 4.

Qualitative Study - Biometrics Prevalence. Finally, we taxonomized respondents' answers to **Q2** in a qualitative codebook. Recall that the majority of respondents are iOS users (51 respondents) and they utilize biometric authentication on their devices. However, 23 people in the sample (of 65) expressed positive views regarding the use of a Bu-Dash password on their devices (e.g., **P51**: *"Yes, because you could easily remember the shapes"*). Additionally, 6 participants did not use a strong positive word (i.e., "Yes", "Definitely", etc.) and they were taxonomized as neutral. However, they eventually expressed a positive attitude towards the proposed scheme: e.g., **P42**: *"On a mobile device I would try it out. I like the idea that it moves about"*. Positively inclined respondents basically commented on the usability and security that Bu-Dash provides: **P61**: *"Yes, it provides improved security for my device and is easy"*, and: **P41**: *"Cause it the same concept as using numbers its secure and easy to remember"*.

Negative answers for using Bu-Dash were basically focused around users' convenience with current methods and biometric authentication (13 users). However, we should recall that knowledge-based methods are still important, because they are required as a complimentary method of authentication, in case the device remains idle for a long time (or after it restarts), or in case the biometric sensors fail (especially in the COVID era, when users wear face masks in closed spaces, thus methods such as "FaceID" are not –currently– usable). Although **Q2** requested from users to choose whether they would use a Bu-Dash or an APU password, several participants seem they would not give up the convenience provided by biometrics. This was made clear in their responses: e.g., **P49**: *"No, because Face ID is much faster"*. However, if we ignore these responses (given that they did not comment on their preference between the APU or Bu-Dash, but they just advocated for biometrics) we can see that the same amount of people in our sample are positively (29), or negatively (28) inclined to use Bu-Dash. *Note:* Considering that 6 participants expressed a neutral view but they were eventually more keen to adopt the proposed scheme: e.g., **P52**: *"Maybe, it seems like an interesting and puzzling way to make your phone secure"*.

5.3   "Pilot" Group

Similar to the "Survey" group, participants in the "Pilot" group of users were mostly undergraduate students (79%), identified as males (71%), using biometric authentication (57%) and their main device was running Android (79%). This group was the first to use the Bu-Dash scheme on their devices; therefore, insights from provided passwords are very useful to understand the usability and security of the scheme. We gathered their responses to compare them with our initial results derived from the "Survey" group.

Starting Point. In Sect. 5.2 we discussed the possible bias our survey instructions might have introduced regarding the starting point of the provided passwords. The Bu-Dash's application instructions however were illustrating the shapes in random order every time they were fetched, aiming to eliminate similar biases. Furthermore, we tracked the sequence of shapes shown in the instructions during our experiments and compared them with the provided passwords from the users. The results demonstrate that only 2 of the 14 users provided a password that started with the same shape as the one that was firstly depicted in the instructions. Therefore, we believe that our updated tutorial instructions do not subconsciously introduce biases. Additionally, Table 3 shows that the majority of the "Pilot" participants preferred to start their password with a ×. Furthermore, the × is the most common symbol that appeared in this password set.

Using the Bu-Dash Grid. A comparison between Table 4 with the results reported in Sect. 5.2 shows that although users envision and formulate on paper long and complex passwords (length: $\mu = 6.185$; shapes included: $\mu = 3.723$) aiming to advance security, they eventually end up with shorter and less complex passwords (length: $\mu = 5.214$; shapes included: $\mu = 2.786$) the first time they formulate a Bu-Dash "phrase" on their devices (median length: 5; median N^o of shapes 2.5). This is a common trend in grid-based password authentication [2]. Thus, in this treatment we can see that most respondents created a password with 4 nodes and half of the participants used 2 different shapes only. However, we advocate that the dynamic grid and the randomized order of the Bu-Dash starting grid are adequate to minimize shoulder surfing and smudge attacks. Additionally, although the majority of participants in this group provided shorter passwords, we believe that the proposed scheme is more secure compared to the APU. Recent research illustrated [1] that due to common biases when users

Table 3. Password characteristics of "Pilot" password set

Password characteristics	○	□	–	△	×
N^o of passwords starting with shape	3	2	1	0	**8**
N^o of times appeared in password set	8	7	5	6	**13**

Table 4. Frequency analysis of "Pilot" password set

Password length frequency			Shapes used per password		
Length	Freq.	%	Shapes N^o	Freq.	%
4	6	**42.86%**	2	7	**50.00%**
5	3	21.43%	3	3	21.43%
6	3	21.43%	4	4	28.57%
7	0	0%	5	0	0%
8	2	14.28%	**Length:** $\mu = 5.214$, $\sigma = 1.424$		
9	0	0%	**Shapes:** $\mu = 2.786$, $\sigma = 0.893$		

form APU passcodes (e.g. starting from top left), its available password space decreases dramatically (more than 90% for 4-node passcodes). Additionally, it is more feasible to extract parts of an APU password via observation (and then perform a guessing attack) because an attacker can easily recall edges that link nodes, making the whole password less secure. On the contrary, Bu-Dash nodes are not visually linked with edges, thus an attacker cannot easily infer the next node in the password if a node is known.

To conclude, Tables 3 and 4 showcase that the most favorite shape to begin a Bu-Dash passcode in this treatment was the ×. This shape also appears often in the password set along with ○. The least used symbol in the "Pilot" password set is the –. Additionally, as stated in the previous paragraphs, users in this treatment valued usability more than security and preferred less busy passcodes compared to the "Survey" participants.

5.4 "Aux" Group

The "Aux" treatment contained mainly participants identified as males (78%), Android users (83%), familiar with the APU (89%), using biometric authentication on their devices (67%). 56% were undergraduate students and the rest had at least one University degree. Results derived from this group's provided data (Tables 5 and 6) confirm that when respondents use the Bu-Dash grid, they seem they choose shorter and less complex passcodes (length: $\mu = 4.833$; shapes included: $\mu = 2.778$). Median values for length is 4 and for the number of included shapes is 3.

Table 5. Password characteristics of "Aux" password set

Password characteristics	○	□	–	△	×
N^{o} of passwords starting with shape:	3	2	0	5	**8**
N^{o} of times appeared in password set:	**14**	6	5	12	13

Table 6. Frequency analysis of "Aux" password set

Password length frequency			Shapes used per password		
Length	Freq.	%	Shapes N^{o}	Freq.	%
4	10	**55.6%**	2	6	33.33%
5	5	27.78%	3	10	**55.56%**
6	1	5.55%	4	2	11.11%
7	0	0%	5	0	0%
8	2	11.11%	**Length:** $\mu = 4.833$, $\sigma = 1.295$		
9	0	0%	**Shapes:** $\mu = 2.778$, $\sigma = 0.647$		

Frequency Analysis. Tables 5 and 6 confirm trends we saw in the "Pilot" treatment. × is the most preferred starting shape in this treatment too (44.4%). Since this is not a large scale study (we report preliminary results here) we can only note that this finding might introduce security concerns related to the available password space, similarly with the APU scheme as commented in Sect. 5.3. However, provided data from participants that interacted with the Bu-Dash grid (both from "Pilot" and "Aux" treatments) show that 68.75% of users that formed a short Bu-Dash code (4-nodes), preferred to include at least 3 shapes in their passcode. Therefore, we can see from these data that users value security when forming easy-to-use passcodes aiming to add more shapes in the sequence. Additionally, similar to Sect. 5.3, "Aux" data show that the – is the least used shape in the password set.

Commonly Used Passwords. Another noteworthy finding is that we did not encounter any particular passcode to be prevalent in the whole password set (Survey-Pilot-Aux, namely *S.P.A.*). We recognize that reported results come from a limited sample of participants ($n = 97$) and that diversity in the provided passcodes should be expected. However, only 5 different passcodes were seen to exist -twice- in the provided data. These are as follows: △○××, ×○×□, ○□△×○, ×××□□□, ×△×△×△×△.

Preliminary Usability Assessment. We asked the "Aux" Group's respondents to participate in a Memory Game that was added in the final iteration of our experiments. As explained in Sect. 4, respondents were asked to play a Memory Game which featured 3 complexity levels ("easy", "medium", "hard"). We did not explicitly tell them how many levels they should attempt to play. As

Table 7. Memory game completions

Level	Attempted	Completed	Average attempts to completion	Failed/no completion	Failure rate
Easy	18	17	1.13	1	5.6%
Medium	12	8	1.88	4	33.3%
Hard	5	3	2.67	2	40.0%

we did not use any complexity metrics to assess how difficult it would be for an individual to memorize these passcodes, we randomly formulated one 4-node, one 6-node, and one 9-node passcode as an "easy", "medium", and "hard" Bu-Dash password, respectively. Participants would choose the level of complexity they would like to play, and then they would see the password while it was formed on their screens. There was no limit on how many times they would watch the tutorial. Afterwards, they had to recall and form that password on the Bu-Dash grid. The Bu-Dash application logged how many times they tried to play a game and if they successfully recalled the passcode. Results are as follows (see Table 7).

Most participants in the "Aux" Group attempted to play the *Easy* game, but only 8 and 5 tried to solve the *Medium* and *Hard* levels, respectively. Seventeen users watched and successfully completed the *Easy* challenge; the average number of attempts to completion was approximately 1.13 attempts. Two participants of this group were considered as outliers and were excluded from the former estimation as they seemed they did not manage to complete the challenge after a reasonable number of attempts (more than 10 attempts each). The *Medium* challenge was undertaken by 12 individuals, and 8 of them successfully completed it with an average of 1.88 attempts. The *Hard* challenge was attempted by only 5 respondents; 3 of them successfully formed the –admittedly– challenging to recall password with an average of 2.67 attempts. These numbers confirm the expectation that when a password becomes longer, it eventually gets less usable and difficult to recall. However, there exist passcodes like the following one that are long, but very memorable: ×××□□□○○○. Thus, password length is not the only feature that contributes to complexity. Further experiments are needed to properly assess long-term memorabiltiy and the effects of password length in the password's complexity.

6 Discussion

We envisioned an authentication system that would be easy to comprehend and adopt, and at the same time, it would be secure against smudge attacks and shoulder surfing. We believe that Bu-Dash is a universal scheme because it can be employed for user authentication in various settings. It can be utilized on smartphones and tablets, or it can be adjusted to work on even smaller screens (e.g., smartwatches). Our proposed method can be fit for use on portable computers (using a trackpad, or the mouse) and desktops. It is also *universal* because its building blocks are common shapes that can be recognized and used easily by any human. Therefore, there are no language, or other cultural, or education burdens that could discourage people from using it.

Its dynamic 3×3 interface ensures that users will not feel unfamiliar with the authentication process. Bu-Dash works similarly with the APU, requiring users to swipe their fingers on the mobile device screen in order to form the password. Compared to the APU, it has less restrictions (for example, a node can be visited as many times as needed) and its password space is 6 times larger. Our online survey indicated that the scheme is comprehensive and easy to perceive because respondents ("Survey" Group), did not provide any invalid passwords when asked to create one after reading our basic instructions.

By looking at the passwords provided by participants from groups "Pilot" and "Aux" (they actually interacted with Bu-Dash on their devices providing valuable, real world data) we can infer that the scheme provides the opportunity to diversify users' input compared to the APU. We did not find several repeating passcodes, but we recognize that our sample is not extended enough. However, we only saw a few trends in the sample that might be linked with human habits; e.g., the preference in using × as a starting point, or the fact that – seems to be the least favorite shape to use in general. Additionally, our analysis demonstrated that when participants were asked to form a Bu-Dash passcode on their devices, they chose *shorter* passcodes aiming probably to make them more memorable and usable. However, early indications show that while they were choosing short passcodes, they also aimed to *add complexity* to the passcode using at least three shapes.

In this paper we report preliminary usability results. Although our data are credible (because they come from users that interacted with our scheme on their actual devices), we cannot confirm if they generalize well. This is a limitation of this paper. The collected Bu-Dash passcodes, derived by 97 participants in different settings, along with their associated metadata might provide a good first impression of how users would utilize the scheme, but there needs to be a longitudinal and large-scale study that would confirm the results provided in this paper. The collection of a larger dataset in the future will enable us also to perform a more robust security analysis using metrics, such as α-*guesswork* ($\tilde{G}_\alpha$) or β-*success rate*, as proposed by Bonneau [7]. In this work we talked about the password space defined by the Bu-Dash scheme and we mentioned that it is larger from the one defined by the APU. However, the set of unique Bu-Dash passcodes with a shorter length is smaller than the one in the APU scheme. As discussed in Sect. 5, Android pattern formation is usually driven by human habits and biases, significantly shortening the password space. We advocate that Bu-Dash is a secure authentication method because it uses a dynamic grid which is randomly initialized every time it is launched.

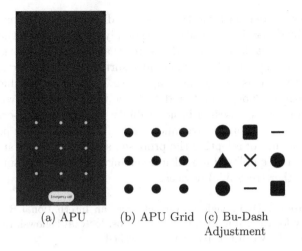

(a) APU   (b) APU Grid   (c) Bu-Dash
                                Adjustment

Fig. 3. Potential adjustments in the use of the Bu-Dash scheme.

Furthermore, in Fig. 3 we propose an adjustment for the Bu-Dash scheme that adhere to the APU design concepts. Figure 3b shows the current static APU grid embedded in any Android version. Our analysis and results are based on data derived from volunteers that engaged with the Bu-Dash grid as shown in Fig. 2. However, Fig. 3c features a more precise adaptation of the Bu-Dash scheme to the APU design concept. It would be useful as future work to see if there exist any significant implications if the latter design prevails as a preferred visual improvement. Additionally, it would be interesting to see how additional variations of our proof of concept would affect usability and security (e.g., utilizing more than 5 symbols as building blocks, although this change might require further adjustments to the design constrains).

Ethical Considerations Volunteers provided informed consent before participating in the study. No identifiable data were stored and we cannot foresee any ethical issues deriving from our research, as it relates and presents a proof of concept which is not employed yet as a real authentication system on the participants' mobile devices. All volunteers were encouraged to uninstall our Bu-Dash application when they concluded their participation.

7   Conclusion

We presented a novel graphical password scheme, named Bu-Dash. Bu-Dash's users create passcodes comprising sequences of simple shapes in an intuitive manner. We conducted a series of studies asking volunteers to interact with Bu-Dash and gathered data that allow us to report a positive attitude towards adopting the scheme as a primary authentication method for mobile devices.

Preliminary results demonstrate the scheme's diversity and its extended password space. The dynamic grid features randomly mapped edges that constitute the basis of the Bu-Dash scheme and ensures that the authentication process is secure against smudge attacks and shoulder surfing. However, we noticed some human biases against using specific shapes (e.g., –) and we concluded that the users in our sample mostly preferred to start their passcodes with a certain symbol (×). Finally, we assessed basic usability features and reported that the scheme seems to be comprehensive, and usable. To conclude, this paper demonstrated the feasibility of adopting the proposed scheme as a user authentication method that can be employed in multiple settings, ranging from smartphones to desktops, and other (portable) devices.

Acknowledgement. Dr Panagiotis Andriotis was an International Research Fellow of Japan Society for the Promotion of Science (Postdoctoral Fellowships for Research in Japan (Standard)) when this paper was published.

References

1. Andriotis, P., Oikonomou, G., Mylonas, A., Tryfonas, T.: A study on usability and security features of the Android pattern lock screen. Inf. Comput. Secur. **24**(1), 53–72 (2016). https://doi.org/10.1108/ICS-01-2015-0001
2. Andriotis, P., Tryfonas, T., Oikonomou, G.: Complexity metrics and user strength perceptions of the pattern-lock graphical authentication method. In: Tryfonas, T., Askoxylakis, I. (eds.) HAS 2014. LNCS, vol. 8533, pp. 115–126. Springer, Cham (2014). https://doi.org/10.1007/978-3-319-07620-1_11
3. Andriotis, P., Tryfonas, T., Oikonomou, G., Yildiz, C.: A pilot study on the security of pattern screen-lock methods and soft side channel attacks. In: Proceedings of the Sixth ACM Conference on Security and Privacy in Wireless and Mobile Networks, WiSec 2013, pp. 1–6. ACM, New York (2013). https://doi.org/10.1145/2462096.2462098
4. Aviv, A.J., Budzitowski, D., Kuber, R.: Is bigger better? Comparing user-generated passwords on 3×3 vs. 4×4 grid sizes for Android's pattern unlock. In: Proceedings of the 31st Annual Computer Security Applications Conference, ACSAC 2015, pp. 301–310. Association for Computing Machinery, New York (2015). https://doi.org/10.1145/2818000.2818014
5. Aviv, A.J., Davin, J.T., Wolf, F., Kuber, R.: Towards baselines for shoulder surfing on mobile authentication. In: Proceedings of the 33rd Annual Computer Security Applications Conference, ACSAC 2017, pp. 486–498. Association for Computing Machinery, New York (2017). https://doi.org/10.1145/3134600.3134609
6. Aviv, A.J., Gibson, K., Mossop, E., Blaze, M., Smith, J.M.: Smudge attacks on smartphone touch screens. In: Proceedings of the 4th USENIX Conference on Offensive Technologies, WOOT 2010, pp. 1–7. USENIX Association (2010)
7. Bonneau, J.: The science of guessing: analyzing an anonymized corpus of 70 million passwords. In: 2012 IEEE Symposium on Security and Privacy, pp. 538–552 (2012). https://doi.org/10.1109/SP.2012.49
8. Chen, Y.L., Ku, W.C., Yeh, Y.C., Liao, D.M.: A simple text-based shoulder surfing resistant graphical password scheme. In: 2013 International Symposium on Next-Generation Electronics, pp. 161–164 (2013). https://doi.org/10.1109/ISNE.2013.6512317

9. Cho, G., Huh, J.H., Cho, J., Oh, S., Song, Y., Kim, H.: SysPal: system-guided pattern locks for Android. In: 2017 IEEE Symposium on Security and Privacy (SP), pp. 338–356 (2017). https://doi.org/10.1109/SP.2017.61

10. Dai, L., Zhang, K., Zheng, X.S., Martin, R.R., Li, Y., Yu, J.: Visual complexity of shapes: a hierarchical perceptual learning model. Vis. Comput. **38**, 419–432 (2021)

11. De Angeli, A., Coventry, L., Johnson, G., Renaud, K.: Is a picture really worth a thousand words? Exploring the feasibility of graphical authentication systems. Int. J. Hum.-Comput. Stud. **63**(1), 128–152 (2005). https://doi.org/10.1016/j.ijhcs.2005.04.020. https://www.sciencedirect.com/science/article/pii/S1071581905000704. HCI research in privacy and security

12. De Luca, A., et al.: Now you see me, now you don't: protecting smartphone authentication from shoulder surfers. In: Proceedings of the SIGCHI Conference on Human Factors in Computing Systems, CHI 2014, pp. 2937–2946. Association for Computing Machinery, New York (2014). https://doi.org/10.1145/2556288.2557097

13. Forman, T., Aviv, A.: Double patterns: a usable solution to increase the security of Android unlock patterns. In: ACSAC 2020, pp. 219–233. Association for Computing Machinery, New York (2020). https://doi.org/10.1145/3427228.3427252

14. Gugenheimer, J., De Luca, A., Hess, H., Karg, S., Wolf, D., Rukzio, E.: ColorSnakes: using colored decoys to secure authentication in sensitive contexts. In: Proceedings of the 17th International Conference on Human-Computer Interaction with Mobile Devices and Services, MobileHCI 2015, pp. 274–283. Association for Computing Machinery, New York (2015). https://doi.org/10.1145/2785830.2785834

15. Kabir, M.M., Hasan, N., Tahmid, M.K.H., Ovi, T.A., Rozario, V.S.: Enhancing smartphone lock security using vibration enabled randomly positioned numbers. In: Proceedings of the International Conference on Computing Advancements, ICCA 2020. Association for Computing Machinery, New York (2020). https://doi.org/10.1145/3377049.3377099

16. Khan, H., Hengartner, U., Vogel, D.: Evaluating attack and defense strategies for smartphone PIN shoulder surfing, pp. 1–10. Association for Computing Machinery, New York (2018). https://doi.org/10.1145/3173574.3173738

17. Kim, S.H., Kim, J.W., Kim, S.Y., Cho, H.G.: A new shoulder-surfing resistant password for mobile environments. In: Proceedings of the 5th International Conference on Ubiquitous Information Management and Communication, ICUIMC 2011. Association for Computing Machinery, New York (2011). https://doi.org/10.1145/1968613.1968647

18. Ku, W.C., Liao, D.M., Chang, C.J., Qiu, P.J.: An enhanced capture attacks resistant text-based graphical password scheme. In: 2014 IEEE/CIC International Conference on Communications in China (ICCC), pp. 204–208 (2014). https://doi.org/10.1109/ICCChina.2014.7008272

19. Kwon, T., Na, S.: SwitchPIN: securing smartphone pin entry with switchable keypads. In: 2014 IEEE International Conference on Consumer Electronics (ICCE), pp. 23–24 (2014). https://doi.org/10.1109/ICCE.2014.6775892

20. Kwon, T., Na, S.: TinyLock: affordable defense against smudge attacks on smartphone pattern lock systems. Compute. Secur. **42**, 137–150 (2014). https://doi.org/10.1016/j.cose.2013.12.001. https://www.sciencedirect.com/science/article/pii/S0167404813001697

21. Kwon, T., Na, S.: SteganoPIN: two-faced human-machine interface for practical enforcement of pin entry security. IEEE Trans. Hum.-Mach. Syst. **46**(1), 143–150 (2016). https://doi.org/10.1109/THMS.2015.2454498

22. Lee, M.K.: Security notions and advanced method for human shoulder-surfing resistant pin-entry. IEEE Trans. Inf. Forensics Secur. **9**(4), 695–708 (2014). https://doi.org/10.1109/TIFS.2014.2307671

23. Loge, M., Duermuth, M., Rostad, L.: On user choice for android unlock patterns. In: European Workshop on Usable Security, ser. EuroUSEC, vol. 16 (2016)

24. Markert, P., Bailey, D.V., Golla, M., Dürmuth, M., Aviv, A.J.: This pin can be easily guessed: analyzing the security of smartphone unlock pins. In: 2020 IEEE Symposium on Security and Privacy (SP), pp. 286–303 (2020). https://doi.org/10.1109/SP40000.2020.00100

25. Munyendo, C.W., Grant, M., Philipp Markert, P., Forman, T.J., Aviv, A.J.: Using a blocklist to improve the security of user selection of Android patterns. In: Seventeenth Symposium on Usable Privacy and Security (SOUPS 2021). USENIX Association, August 2021. https://www.usenix.org/conference/soups2021/presentation/munyendo

26. Schneegass, S., Steimle, F., Bulling, A., Alt, F., Schmidt, A.: SmudgeSafe: geometric image transformations for smudge-resistant user authentication. In: Proceedings of the 2014 ACM International Joint Conference on Pervasive and Ubiquitous Computing, UbiComp 2014, pp. 775–786. Association for Computing Machinery, New York (2014). https://doi.org/10.1145/2632048.2636090

27. Song, Y., Cho, G., Oh, S., Kim, H., Huh, J.H.: On the effectiveness of pattern lock strength meters: measuring the strength of real world pattern locks, pp. 2343–2352. Association for Computing Machinery, New York (2015). https://doi.org/10.1145/2702123.2702365

28. Sun, C., Wang, Y., Zheng, J.: Dissecting pattern unlock: the effect of pattern strength meter on pattern selection. J. Inf. Secur. Appl. **19**(4), 308–320 (2014). https://doi.org/10.1016/j.jisa.2014.10.009. https://www.sciencedirect.com/science/article/pii/S2214212614001458

29. Tupsamudre, H., Banahatti, V., Lodha, S., Vyas, K.: Pass-O: a proposal to improve the security of pattern unlock scheme. In: Proceedings of the 2017 ACM on Asia Conference on Computer and Communications Security, ASIA CCS 2017, pp. 400–407. Association for Computing Machinery, New York (2017). https://doi.org/10.1145/3052973.3053041

30. Uellenbeck, S., Dürmuth, M., Wolf, C., Holz, T.: Quantifying the security of graphical passwords: the case of Android unlock patterns. In: Proceedings of the 2013 ACM SIGSAC Conference on Computer and Communications Security, CCS 2013, pp. 161–172. Association for Computing Machinery, New York (2013). https://doi.org/10.1145/2508859.2516700

31. Vaddepalli, S., Nivas, S., Chettoor Jayakrishnan, G., Sirigireddy, G., Banahatti, V., Lodha, S.: Passo - new circular patter lock scheme evaluation. In: 22nd International Conference on Human-Computer Interaction with Mobile Devices and Services, MobileHCI 2020. Association for Computing Machinery, New York (2020). https://doi.org/10.1145/3406324.3417167

32. Wang, D., Gu, Q., Huang, X., Wang, P.: Understanding human-chosen PINs: characteristics, distribution and security. In: Proceedings of the 2017 ACM on Asia Conference on Computer and Communications Security, ASIA CCS 2017, pp. 372–385. Association for Computing Machinery, New York (2017). https://doi.org/10.1145/3052973.3053031

33. Ye, G., et al.: A video-based attack for Android pattern lock. ACM Trans. Priv. Secur. **21**(4) (2018). https://doi.org/10.1145/3230740

34. von Zezschwitz, E., De Luca, A., Brunkow, B., Hussmann, H.: SwiPIN: fast and secure PIN-entry on smartphones, pp. 1403–1406. Association for Computing Machinery, New York (2015). https://doi.org/10.1145/2702123.2702212

35. von Zezschwitz, E., et al.: On quantifying the effective password space of grid-based unlock gestures. In: Proceedings of the 15th International Conference on Mobile and Ubiquitous Multimedia, MUM 2016, pp. 201–212. Association for Computing Machinery, New York (2016). https://doi.org/10.1145/3012709.3012729

36. Zimmermann, V., Gerber, N.: The password is dead, long live the password – a laboratory study on user perceptions of authentication schemes. Int. J. Hum.-Comput. Stud. **133**, 26–44 (2020). https://doi.org/10.1016/j.ijhcs.2019.08.006. https://www.sciencedirect.com/science/article/pii/S1071581919301119

A Preliminary Investigation of Authentication of Choice in Health-Related Mobile Applications

Oluwadamilola Arinde[✉], Jinjuan Feng, and Ziying Tang

Towson University, Towson 21252, USA
ogbenr1@students.towson.edu

Abstract. User authentication is a security measure that involves authenticating the identity claimed by a user before granting access to a system or an application. Even though there are numerous studies that examined users' experiences with a variety of authentication methods, very few have focused on the approach of granting users the freedom to select one or more authentication methods of their own choice. Initial work in this area suggested that the 'Authentication of Choice" (AoC) approach has the potential to serve as a usable and secure authentication solution on mobile devices. However, the studies only evaluated the AoC approach on the Android platform when users executed tasks with low security and privacy concerns. To address this gap, we investigated the 'Authentication of Choice' approach in mobile health apps that potentially involve more sensitive information. An online longitudinal study was conducted with 30 participants to assess three authentication processes. The result of the study provides insight into how users interact with and perceive the AoC approach in the context of mobile health apps.

Keywords: Authentication of Choice · Usability · Security

1 Introduction

User authentication involves authenticating the identity claimed by a user before granting access to a system or an application. An effective user authentication method is of paramount importance to prevent illicit access to any information service especially health-related applications. Even though there exist many studies that examined users' experiences with these authentication methods, very few studies have focused on the approach that grants users the freedom to select one or more authentication methods of their own choice. Oluwafemi and Feng (2020) conducted studies to understand how users perceive the 'Authentication of Choice' (AoC) approach in the context of mobile applications [1]. The results suggested that the AoC approach has the potential to serve as a usable and secure authentication solution on mobile devices. However, this work only evaluated the AoC approach on the Android platform when users executed tasks with low security and privacy concerns. User perception about an authentication approach might differ when the nature of the tasks involves more sensitive information such as those supported in health applications. In this paper, we report a study that aims to investigate

© The Author(s), under exclusive license to Springer Nature Switzerland AG 2022
A. Moallem (Ed.): HCII 2022, LNCS 13333, pp. 228–240, 2022.
https://doi.org/10.1007/978-3-031-05563-8_15

the 'Authentication of Choice' approach in the context of mobile health apps. A cross-platform mobile app called "HealthyCog" was developed with five commonly adopted authentication methods. We conducted an online longitudinal study with 30 participants to assess the performance and user perception of the AoC approach in the context of mobile health apps. The study adopted a 'within-group' design with three types of authentication processes: alphanumeric password, Single Factor AoC, and Multi-Factor AoC. The results suggest that there is potential to adopt the authentication of choice approach on health-related mobile applications to improve user experience and security.

2 Related Work

2.1 Traditional Authentication Methods

In access control, validation is the initial phase and usually employs authentication mechanisms that employ three types of factors: something you know (knowledge factor), something you have (possession factor), and something you are (inherent factor) [2].

Knowledge Factor Authentication. This method requires users to input a piece of information the user knows before granting them access to the system [2]. The information is usually a secret that should be known by the user only and is often referred to as a password. Password methods are the most widely used authentication methods because they are relatively easy to implement and do not have high operating costs compared to the other authentication methods. Despite the success in its adoption, it's being associated with security issues [2]. The security level of password is low as it can face multiple attacks such as brute force attacks and other threats emerging from improper storage of the passwords [3]. Another problem with this method is if a user chooses a weak password, then attackers can easily gain access to the systems. On the other hand, if a user chooses a strong password, they may not be able to remember it and may have to write it down, causing security risks.

Possession Factor Authentication. This method is based on a physical object that the user possesses. This object could be a mobile device, a token, or a smart card. For mobile app authentication, applications can have the secret information stored on the hardware of the device such as on the SIM card, or the secret information can be received through the mobile device SMS operation [3]. Receiving secret information via SMS is the more frequently used method and the secret information passed is commonly referred to as One Time Password (OTP). Even though this approach is great in terms of usability, it also has its' drawbacks, one is possible network issues that could cause delayed delivery of the OTP. The device could also get stolen or lost. The OTP is commonly used in combination with knowledge factor authentication on mobile devices.

Inherent Factor Authentication. This method uses biometrics to gain access control. Biometrics involves measuring and analyzing the physiological or behavioral characteristics of a person [4]. Examples include fingerprint, face, voice, signature, etc. Biometric authentication has several advantages over knowledge or possession factor authentication Because a person's biometrics cannot be forgotten and is highly unlikely to get lost or stolen [5]. One of the challenges of biometrics is that it may be inaccessible for people with specific types of disabilities. Biometrics can also fail [5], falsely rejecting a valid user, or falsely accepting an invalid user.

2.2 Multiple Factor Authentication

The traditional security procedure for user authentication is based on only one factor, referred to as Single-factor authentication (SFA) [6]. The most popular SFA method is the Knowledge factor authentication, particularly "passwords". The SFA is widely used but has several problems associated with it [7]. made an argument in their study that despite the popularity of SFA methods, they are not strong enough to provide the needed level of security to the system. This claim was further supported in several other studies [8]. According to a survey [6], the strength of user authentication can be greatly improved if two or more factors are used instead of single-factor authentication. From the previous review of the single-factor authentication methods, it is established that each authentication method has limitations and relying completely on only one of these methods may not be the best decision.

Multi-factor Authentication (MFA). MFA was subsequently proposed to provide a higher level of security and continuously promote the protection of information systems and applications from unauthorized access by combining two or more distinct and different categories from the authentication factors [9]. This additional step provided an improved level of security since the authentication process can rely on the security strength of the combination of different factors. An instance of MFA that requires three authentication factors is when a user must input a password (knowledge factor), scan their fingerprint (Inherent factor), and input a One-Time Password (possession factor) before having access to the system.

While multi-factor authentication improves the security of the authentication system, it may interfere with the usability of the system. One of the challenges is the user's lack of motivation [10] because some users believe that multi-factor authentication is making the system more complex to use. Another study [11] classifies the usability challenges from three perspectives: task efficiency, task effectiveness, and user preference. Task efficiency deals with how long it takes to register and get a user authenticated. Task effectiveness is the number of logins attempts to gain access into the system while user preference is to determine if users prefer a particular authentication combination factor over another. Researchers proposed that the usability of multi-factor authentication can be improved if different authentication factors are collected simultaneously or at the same time [12].

2.3 Authentication of Choice

To design a usable and secure system [13], suggests that researchers need to go beyond using human-centered design techniques and adopt design techniques that give users the ability to make decisions. One of Ben Schneiderman's golden rules of interface design:

support of internal locus of control addresses the concept of user decision-making design approach. There is a sense of satisfaction that comes with users knowing they are thought of during the design process and given the freedom to make choices in an application [14]. suggests user interface be designed in such a way that users feel more responsible and accountable for their actions. If this is apparent in the interface, users will less likely misuse their access rights to the system. As we have established that there is no perfect authentication method in terms of usability and security, there is no one authentication method that can accommodate all users. It will be challenging to design an authentication method that is universally accessible for the users without the knowledge of the users' abilities and disabilities [15]. Users may also have a preferred authentication method depending on their physical abilities and cognitive skills [16, 17] proposed a choice-based authentication approach that can address the issues with current authentication methods including security issues, usability issues, and universal access.

As discussed before, multiple factors authentication might increase the burden on users in terms of time, difficulty, and complexity and therefore, negatively affecting user perception and adoption. If users are granted the freedom to choose their preferred authentication method(s) during the process, it might alleviate the negative impact of added time and complexity.

2.4 Security and Usability of Mobile Health Applications

Technology has been adopted in different industries now as it is proven to improve industries and business successes. This is also true in the health sector and the trend is strengthening during the global pandemic. The pandemic has forced the healthcare industry to integrate technology now more than ever for the good of the industry and all stakeholders. Mobile health applications are growing exponentially as it is useful in telehealth that requires remote patient monitoring.

According to a study conducted by Statista, as of the first quarter of 2021, there were 53,054 mHealth apps [18] available in the Google Play store and 53,979 in the App Store [19]. Statista also shows that based on the apps downloaded from both App stores, there was a 65% global growth in the medical apps downloaded from January 2020 to July 2020. The growth in the USA is 30% while South Korea had the highest growth of 135%.

The growth of mobile health apps has led to increasing challenges in the protection of sensitive data that can be collected during the use of the app. The government compliances (e.g., Health Insurance Portability and Accountability Act (HIPPA)) that need to be met in terms of the data collected, security in form of the authentication methods used in gaining access to the app, the usability of the app itself are some of the challenge's that developers face.

There are reportedly increasing vulnerabilities in the mobile health apps available. An assessment by Intertrust highlights major security gaps in mHealth apps, one of them indicates 71% of tested mHealth apps have a high-level security vulnerability [20]. One of the high-level security vulnerabilities is the possibility of a data breach due to weak data encryption on the apps, another one is 81% data leakage from COVID-tracking applications [20]. With such security issues, it is understandable how the key focus in the development of mHealth apps is security. The balance of security and usability in these applications is crucial for successful adoption and high-quality service.

3   Methods

The goal of this online longitudinal study is to examine the performance and user perception of different authentication methods when using the Authentication of Choice approach in the context of mobile health-related applications. The study adopted a within-group design with three conditions for authentication:

- Alphanumeric password: Participants signed up and logged in with email and password
- Single-factor AoC: Participants chose one authentication method out of five options (alphanumeric passwords, pin, phone One Time Password (OTP), facial recognition, and fingerprint authentication)
- Multi-factor AoC: Participants chose two authentication methods of their choice from the five options listed above.

3.1   Participants

30 participants took part in the study. The age of participants varies, with 19 participants in the age range of 18–30 years, 10 in the range of 31–40 years, and 1 above 40 years. The participants included 13 females and 17 males. 17 participants used iPhones and 13 used Android phones. 15 of the participants were college students in the Computer Science and Information Technology field of study, while the remaining 15 participants were professionals working in various fields such as IT, healthcare, engineering, and business. No financial incentive was provided for participating in the study.

3.2   HealthCog Application

An application named "HealthyCog" was developed for the purpose of this study. The application is a cross-platform application that can be used on both iOS and Android platforms. The app presents five authentication methods that are commonly adopted in commercial mobile devices:

- Alphanumeric email and password
- Personal Identification Number (PIN)
- One-Time-Password (OTP) via SMS
- Facial recognition
- Fingerprint recognition

The application design followed general usability guidelines and underwent several rounds of testing based on feedback from the users. Users can create three types of accounts on the application using the same email:

– Type 1: Alphanumeric email and password
– Type 2: Single-factor authentication of choice with five options
– Type 3: Multi-factor authentication of choice (Two) with five options

The home page and the registration page of the application are demonstrated in Fig. 1 below.

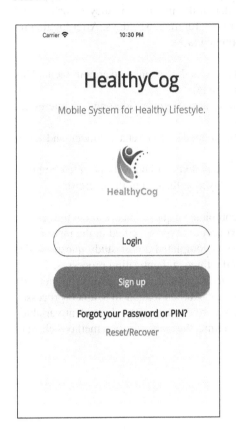
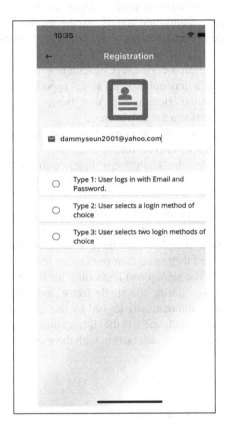

(a) Home page   (b) Registration

Fig. 1. Home page and registration page of the HealthyCog app

3.3 Procedure

The study was conducted online. Participants were recruited by sending flyers out to college students via the school email system and a WhatsApp community group. An informed consent form was sent out via email to all who responded. After providing consent to take part in the study, Instructions for the study environment and procedure were sent out to participants via email. A demographic questionnaire was completed at the beginning of the study. Each participant used the app for a period of 3 weeks, interacting with one authentication process during each week. The order of the three authentication conditions was counterbalanced among the participants to control the learning effect.

During the study, participants first installed the 'HealthyCog' app from the App Store or Google Play Store depending on if they had an iOS or an Android phone. Following successful installation, each participant created an account on the app. The type of account created depended on the order in the instructions they received. The participants then logged into the account every day for the next 7 days. After logging in, they completed one of the following health-related tasks:

- Select the 'HealthyCog ChatBot' function and schedule a tentative appointment (This is a fictional task; no actual appointment is made)
- In the 'HealthyCog Arm' function, watch an arm exercise video and, if interested, perform the arm exercise
- In the 'Med Reminder' function, add a fictional medication, set a reminder, and select a time interval for the reminder
- Visit the 'Daily Steps' function to activate the pedometer and walk for a few minutes if able to. The number of steps taken is displayed at the end of the exercise.

At the end of the first week, participants completed a questionnaire about the session via Google Form before switching to the next account type specified in the instruction. After completing all three sessions, participants completed a post-study questionnaire where they rated their preference for each of the three authentication processes.

The signup and login time for the three conditions and the authentication methods chosen during the single-factor and multi-factor Authentication of Choice processes were automatically logged by the app into a secure database. The dependent variables for the study include the sign-up time, the login time, the authentication methods chosen, and the user satisfaction with the methods.

4 Results

4.1 Login Time

Based on the login duration logged in the database, the multi-factor authentication condition took the longest time with an average of 12.6 s, the password method had an average login time of 11.75 s while the single-factor condition had an average time of 7.6 s. Figure 2 shows the average login time of the three conditions in seconds. A One-Way Repeated Measures Analysis of Variance (ANOVA) test suggests that there is a significant difference at the $p < .05$ level between the three conditions $(F (2,87 = 4.12, p < 0.05))$. Participants spent a significantly longer time logging into the application using the Alphanumeric password and the multi-factor AoC process than the single-factor AoC process. There is no significant difference in the login time between the alphanumeric passwords condition and the multi-factor AoC condition.

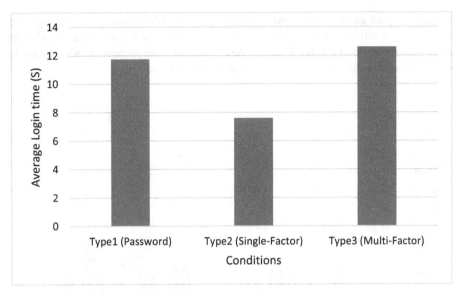

Fig. 2. Average login time of the three conditions in seconds

4.2 Authentication Method Chosen for AoC

Table 1 illustrates the number and percentage of participants who chose each authentication method under the single-factor AoC and multi-factor AoC conditions. In the multi-factor AoC condition, each participant chose 2 methods. Therefore, the total number of participants choosing all methods is 60 and the total percentage of participants is 200%.

Table 1. Number and percentages of participants who chose each method under Type 2 and Type 3 conditions.

Authentication Method	Type 2	Type 3	Type 2%	Type 3%
Password	2	7	6.6%	23.3%
Pin	14	23	46.6%	76.7%
OTP	3	10	10%	33.3%
Fingerprint	6	11	20%	36.7%
Face Recognition	5	9	16.6%	30%
Total	30	60	99.8%	200%

As illustrated in Table 1, the PIN authentication method is the most frequently chosen method in both conditions at 46.6% and 76.7% respectively. For single-factor AoC, the second most frequently chosen method was the Fingerprint at 20%, and Face Recognition comes third at 16.6%. The SMS OTP was chosen by 3 participants while the Password method was the least chosen method by 2 participants. Similar results in the ranking were observed for multi-Factor AoC except that OTP was the third most frequently chosen while Face recognition was the fourth. Figure 3 illustrates the percentage of participants who chose each authentication method under both conditions.

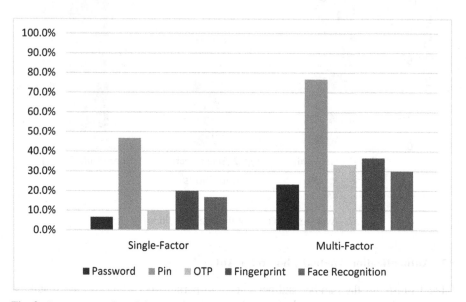

Fig. 3. Percentages of participants who chose each method under Type 2 and Type 3 conditions

4.3 Preferred Authentication Process

In the post-study questionnaire, we asked the participants to rank their preference towards the three authentication processes. Table 2 illustrates how the participants ranked each process.

Table 2. Number and percentages of participants who ranked each of the three conditions as their first, second, and third choice.

Rank	Alphanumeric Password number (%)	Single-Factor number (%)	Multi-Factor number (%)	Total
First	1 (3.3%)	18 (60%)	11 (36.7%)	30
Second	6 (20%)	11 (36.7%)	13 (43.3)	30
Third	23 (76.7%)	1 (3.3%)	6 (20%)	30
Total	30	30	30	

60% of the participants ranked the single-factor AoC as their first choice. 36.7% chose the multi-factor AoC as their first choice, only 3.3% chose the alphanumeric password condition. For the second choice, 43.3% chose the multi-factor AoC as their second choice, 36.7% selected single-factor AoC as their second choice, and 20% selected alphanumeric as the second choice. The least preferred process of the three is the alphanumeric password at 76.7%, multi-factor at 20%, and single-factor at 3.3%. A Chi-Square test suggests a significant difference at $p < .001$ level in the participants' ranking between the three conditions (X^2 $(4, N = 30) = 43.8, p < 0.001$). Figure 4 shows the number of participants who ranked each of the three conditions as their first, second, and third choice.

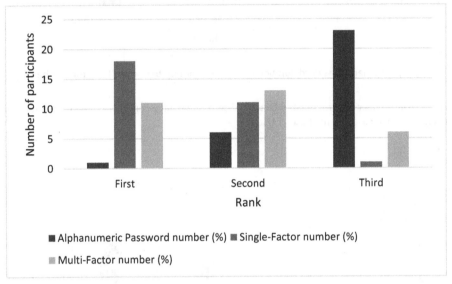

Fig. 4. The number of participants who ranked each of the three conditions as their first, second, and third choice.

Participants were also asked to rank their preferences of the three conditions based on the ease of use and perceived security. In terms of ease of use, 96.7% of the participants chose the single-factor AoC as the most preferred while 83.3% selected the alphanumeric password authentication as the less preferred. Regarding security, 86.7% of participants chose multi-factor AoC as the most secure and 90% chose alphanumeric password as the least secure. Figures 5 and 6 show the number of participants who ranked each of the three conditions as their first, second, and third choice based on the Ease of Use and Security respectively.

In the post-study questionnaire, participants were asked to select an option from strongly agree (5), agree (4), neutral (3), disagree (2), and strongly disagree (1) for questions related to security improvement, login time, difficulty to use, and memorability regarding the three conditions. 97% of the participants strongly agreed that multi-factor AoC improved security. Only 13% agreed that the multi-factor AoC took too much

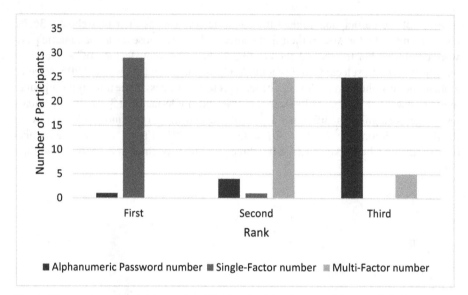

Fig. 5. The number of participants who ranked each of the three conditions as their first, second, and third choice based on the Ease of Use.

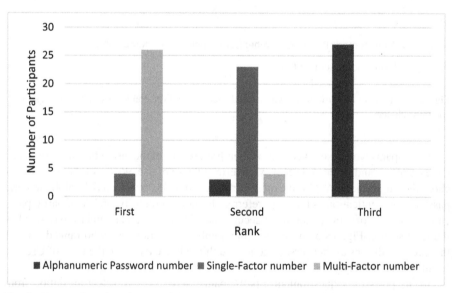

Fig. 6. The number of participants who ranked each of the three conditions as their first, second, and third choice based on the Security.

time. Only 10% agreed that the multi-factor AoC was difficult to remember, and only 10% agreed that multi-factor AoC was difficult to use. Therefore, although most of the participants prefer the single-factor AoC process, their responses to these specific questions suggest that they are likely to adopt the multi-factor AoC approach if needed because most of them consider it to be the most secure of the 3 conditions with acceptable efficiency, memorability, and ease of use.

5 Discussions and Conclusions

The results suggested that when users are given the freedom to choose the authentication method(s) on health-related mobile apps, the single-factor Authentication of Choice is the most preferred among the three approaches and the PIN method is the most chosen method. Participants also perceived the single-factor Authentication of choice as the most preferred in terms of ease of use and the multi-factor authentication as the most preferred in terms of security. Multi-factor authentication was perceived as the second preferred condition after the single-factor condition. The alphanumeric password ranked the lowest in terms of general preference, ease of use, as well as security. Participants' preference towards the single-factor authentication of choice condition over the alphanumeric password condition suggests that participants like the freedom to choose an authentication method for their health-related mobile applications. Participants' preference towards the multi-factor AoC condition over the alphanumeric password condition could be attributed to the extra layer of security it provides. The result of this study is largely consistent with the finding of Oluwafemi and Feng (2020) on Authentication of Choice in general mobile applications. It suggests that there is potential to adopt the authentication of choice approach on health-related mobile applications to improve user experience and security.

Regarding limitations, the study only investigated a limited set of authentication methods and some commonly adopted techniques such as gesture passwords and location-based authentication were not examined. In addition, the participants of the study were primarily students or professionals who were experienced in using mobile devices in general and mobile authentication in particular. The finding may not be generalizable to senior people or those with limited experience in mobile devices or authentication. We are planning to include a broader set of authentication methods in future studies. We will also work with senior users to measure their performance and understand their perception of the authentication of choice approach.

Acknowledgments. We would like to thank all the participants for their time and effort taking part in the study.

References

1. Oluwafemi, J., Feng, J.: How users perceive authentication of choice on mobile devices. In: 13th International Conference on Advances in Computer-Human Interactions. pp. 345–351. ACHI, Spain (2020)

2. Nilesh, A., Salendra, P., Mohammed, F.: A review of authentication methods. IJSTR **5**(11), 246–249 (2016)
3. Lampson, B.: Computer security in the real world. IEEE Comput. **37**(6), 37–46 (2004)
4. Authentication Methods: https://www.uio.no/studier/emner/matnat/ifi/INF5261/v10/studen tprojects/authentication-methods/FinalReportAuthenticationMethods.pdf. Accessed 14 Jan 2022
5. Introduction to Biometrics Technologies and Applications: CyLab Carnegie Mellon https://users.ece.cmu.edu/~jzhu/class/18200/F06/L10A_Savvides_Biometrics.pdf. Accessed 16 Jan 2022
6. Madhuravani, B., Reddy, P., LalithSamanthReddy, P.: A comprehensive study on different authentication factors. IJERT **2**(10), 1358–1361 (2013)
7. Gunson, N., Marshall, D., Morton, H., Jack, M.: User perceptions of security and usability of single-factor and two-factor authentication in automated telephone banking. Comput. Secur. **30**, 208–220 (2011)
8. Riley, C., Buckner, K., Johnson, G., Benyon, D.: Culture & biometrics: regional differences in the perception of biometric authentication technologies. AI Soc. **24**(3), 295–306 (2009)
9. Abhishek, K., Roshan, S., Kumar, P., Ranjan, R.: A comprehensive study on multifactor authentication schemes. In: Meghanathan, N., Nagamalai, D., Chaki, N. (eds.) Advances in Computing and Information Technology, pp. 561–568. Springer, Berlin, Heidelberg (2013). https://doi.org/10.1007/978-3-642-31552-7_57
10. Das, S., Dingman, A., Camp, L.: Why Johnny doesn't use two factor a two-phase usability study of the FIDO U2F security key. In: International Conference on Financial Cryptography and Data Security (FC). (2018)
11. Aleksandr, O., Sergey, B., Niko, M., Sergey, A., Tommi, M., Yevgeni, K.: Multi-Factor Authentication, A Survey. Cryptography **2**(1) (2018) https://doi.org/10.3390/cryptography 2010001
12. Raja K.B., Raghavendra R., Stokkenes M., Busch M.: Multi-modal authentication system for smartphones using face, iris, and periocular. In: Biometrics (ICB). In: 2015 International Conference on, IEEE. pp. 143–150 (2015)
13. Cranor, L.F., Buchler, N.: Better together: usability and security go hand in hand. IEEE Secur. Priv. **12**(6), 89–93 (2014). https://doi.org/10.1109/MSP.2014.109
14. Vance, C., Paik, Y.: Forms of host-country national learning for enhanced MNC absorptive capacity. J. Manag. Psychol. **20**(7), 590–606 (2005)
15. Fairweather, P., Hanson, V., Detweiler, S., Schwerdtfeger, R.: From assistive technology to a web accessibility service. In: International Conference on Assistive Technologies (ASSETS). ACM. (2002)
16. Belk, M., Fidas, C., Germanakos, P., Samaras, G.: Security for diversity: studying the effects of verbal and imagery processes on user authentication mechanisms. In: Proceedings of the IFIP TC13 Conference on Human-Computer Interaction. pp. 442–459. South Africa (2013)
17. Hausawi, Y.M., Allen, W.H., Bahr, G.S.: Choice-based authentication: a usable-security approach. In: Stephanidis, C., Antona, M. (eds.) UAHCI 2014. LNCS, vol. 8513, pp. 114–124. Springer, Cham (2014). https://doi.org/10.1007/978-3-319-07437-5_12
18. Number of mHealth apps available in the Google Play Store from 1st quarter 2015 to 1st quarter 2021, https://www.statista.com/statistics/779919/health-apps-available-google-play-worldwide/, Accessed 17 Dec 2021
19. Number of mHealth apps available in the Apple App Store from 1st quarter 2015 to 1st quarter 2021, https://www.statista.com/statistics/779910/health-apps-available-ios-wor ldwide/, Accessed 17 Dec 2021
20. Intertrust Releases 2020 Security Report on Global mHealth App Threats, https://www.int ertrust.com/news/intertrust-releases-2020-security-report-on-global-mhealth-app-threats/, Accessed 17 Dec 2021

On-Demand Biometric Authentication for System-User Management

Isao Nakanishi[✉][iD]

Tottori University, Tottori 680-8552, Japan
nakanishi@tottori-u.ac.jp

Abstract. To realize a secure system-user management, continuous authentication must be implemented in the system. In addition, only limited biometrics that can be measured passively are applicable for continuous authentication. However, continuous authentication is a heavy processing load for the system. In this study, possible methods for conducting a continuous authentication are examined from the viewpoint of reducing the processing load, and two types of on-demand authentication approaches are confirmed to be effective.

Keywords: System-user management · Continuous authentication · Biometrics · On-demand authentication · Processing load

1 Introduction

In the transport systems involving many human lives, security systems handling confidential information, and online-learning systems for licenses and qualification purposes, it is extremely important to distinguish regular users of the system. In general, user authentication is performed only once when users begin to use a system, such as a log-in authentication using a password. However, if a regular user is replaced by a nonregular user after authentication, the nonregular user can easily use the system.

To prevent such spoofing, continuous authentication, in which users are constantly authenticated while using the system, is required. Therefore, continuous authentication is drawing research attention [1]. However, general passwords and ID cards cannot be used in continuous authentication because it is inconvenient for users to keep presenting them while using the system. Thus, biometrics is expected to be used in continuous authentication. However, if the conscious use of biometrics brings about the same level of inconvenience as passwords and ID cards, the use of only passively detectable biometrics that do not need to be consciously presented will be essential. Continuous authentication can be realized only when passively detectable biometrics are applied. Although such an affinity between biometrics and continuous authentication has also been pointed out in Ref. [2], a concrete proposal has yet to be examined.

A. Moallem (Ed.): HCII 2022, LNCS 13333, pp. 241–254, 2022.
https://doi.org/10.1007/978-3-031-05563-8_16

Initially, biometrics was expected to be a convenient authentication method because unlike passwords and ID cards, such information is never lost or forgotten [3]. However, passwords and ID cards are still used in our daily lives. Although there may be several reasons for this, one reason is that passwords and ID cards are sufficient for person authentication. In person authentication, security is always contrary to usability[1]. In ordinary circumstances, security never has a higher priority than usability. Ease of use is important for ordinary people. As an alternative to passwords and ID cards, biometrics must overcome the inconvenience of introducing a new method into people's lives, which is an ongoing problem. An aspect unique to biometrics, thereby validating its use, is continuous authentication.

The face, iris, and ear images are applicable as passively detectable biometrics that users are not required to consciously present. However, such features are exposed on the body surface; therefore, it is easy for others to capture them without knowledge of the user, and there is a risk that the authentication system using the modality will be counterfeited through the use of forgeries produced with the captured data. There is also a risk that they can be changed through plastic surgery. Moreover, there is a tendency for the face to be prohibited from use because it directly concerns the issue of privacy [4]. Therefore, the biometric modalities that are exposed on the body surface are ineligible for this study. Any vulnerability or risk has to be excluded in transport systems involving many human lives, security systems handling confidential information, and other areas.

There are also behavioral biometrics that are extracted for human actions such as moving, writing, speaking, and typing. However, biometrics based on actions differing from those applied by the system are excluded because they cannot be unconsciously presented. Assuming the use of a system, although a voiceprint or typing pattern is applicable, they are usable only when speaking or typing.

Therefore, there is no conventional biometrics suitable for contentious authentication. The author has noted continuous authentication as a killer biometrics application [5] and has therefore proposed the use of an intra-body (palm) propagation signal as passively detectable biometrics and evaluated its verification performance [6–10]. Moreover, the author has noticed brainwaves (electroencephalogram, EEG) as passively detectable biometrics and evaluated different verifications of their performance [11–16].

However, with continuous authentication, the authentication process is always being executed; therefore, if the application and authentication processes are executed on the same system, the processing load of the system will become heavy. In Ref. [1], the increase in power consumption from the authentication processing is also pointed out.

---

[1] If the threshold for determining whether a user of a system is genuine becomes high, the security of the system increases, whereas the usability is decreased because a user may be rejected many times even if the user is genuine.

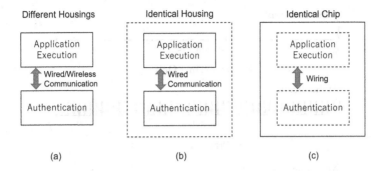

Fig. 1. System configuration.

Therefore, this study examines what types of methods are effective in realizing continuous authentication through the use of passively detectable biometrics for the purpose of reducing the processing load.

2   Assumed Authentication System

First, the relationship between the execution of an application and authentication processing is defined. People execute an application in a system, whereas authentication processing has no relation with the application execution. Therefore, it is natural to suppose that application execution and authentication processing are applied in different systems, as shown in Fig. 1(a). However, even if a user is determined to be non-regular by the authentication system, it is impossible to directly prevent a non-regular user from using the application system. The two separate systems exchange information using some means of communication. However, if the communication means are disconnected or a fake signal is inserted into the communication path, the application system cannot know that the user is non-regular. Even if the two systems are installed in a specific case (Fig. 1(b)), the same problem as in (a) may be caused in the inner cable connecting the two systems. To solve this problem, these two systems must be installed on a chip, as shown in (c). However, case (c) is unrealistic because it is necessary to prepare a dedicated chip for each application.

It is easy to realize these systems using software on a general-purpose CPU, and the disconnection problem in the communication path does not arise. Thus, in this study, it is assumed that the application and authentication are processed using software in a CPU. Therefore, less processing load is required for authentication.

3   Authentication of System User

Four types of authenticating users can be assumed in the system, as described in Fig. 2, where the horizontal axis represents the passage of time while using the system and small downward arrows indicate the authentication execution. The larger the number of the arrows, the heavier the processing load becomes.

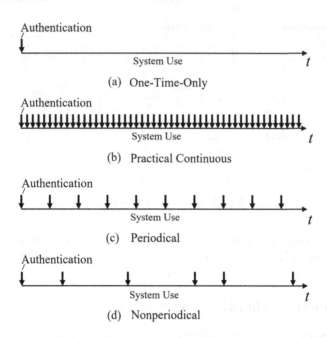

Fig. 2. Four types of authentication of system users.

3.1 One-time-only Authentication

Figure 2(a) shows the one-time-only (one-off) authentication, in which the authentication is executed only once when the user begins to use the system. Log-in authentication when starting the use of a computer or mobile device is a typical example. However, one-time-only authentication never prevents a spoofing in which a regular user is switched to a nonregular user after authentication. This spoofing is also called "section hijacking" [17, 18].

3.2 Continuous Authentication

To prevent such hijacking, continuous authentication, in which the users are continuously authenticated while using the system, is required. However, strictly speaking, the authentication is executed not in a continuous (analog) time but in a discrete time, as shown in Fig. 2(b), for instance, every frame (50 ms) [19], every second [17, 20], or every cycle for an instruction execution of the system [18, 21–23].

As the biometrics, a passively detectable face image and voiceprint were used, along with a fingerprint detected from a sensor equipped on a mouse for computer use [17, 19, 20]. In addition, soft biometrics (skin and clothes colors) extracted from images [18], touching actions on a smartphone display [21, 22], keystrokes when typing on a keyboard, and voiceprints when calling or conducting a voice-search on a web sites [23] were used.

In these studies, the reason why multiple biometrics were used is to deal with a case in which appropriate biometric data for authentication cannot be obtained when executing authentication. For instance, in authentication using face images, when a face is not facing the camera, an appropriate face image for matching cannot be obtained, and thus alternative biometrics are used. Moreover, when using the keystroke of a keyboard or a mouse operation as biometrics, even if they temporarily stop and their biometric data can no longer be obtained, the prior obtained authentication score (reliability) is maintained despite its decrease over time. When the deceased score is less than the threshold determined in advance, the system usage is prohibited, and the user is re-authenticated.

It is important that the actions applied for using the system and authentication be identical. It is impossible or inconvenient to conduct an action that differs from that when using the system. In the following, it is not assumed that the system usage is interrupted, and biometric data are presented for authentication.

However, in addition to the application execution, a continuous authentication system operates without stopping, and thus its processing load increases. In Ref. [20], it was reported that the system overhead reaches up to 42% when authentication is applied every second.

4   Periodical and Non-periodical Authentication

To reduce the processing load, it is necessary to reduce the number of authentication executions while preventing spoofing.

4.1   Periodical Authentication

Instead of continuous authentication, it is conceivable to authenticate at regular intervals, as shown in Fig. 2(c). For convenience, this is called periodical authentication. In Ref. [24], the authentication using a face image was conducted at 30-s intervals, and thus, it is expected to reduce the processing load. However, the possibility of spoofing during the 30-s period is not considered. In addition, a problem in which the applicable biometric data cannot be obtained when executing the authentication, as mentioned above, is not considered.

4.2   Nonperiodical Authentication

Thus, it is conceivable that authentication is executed only when required and executable. This is called nonperiodic authentication, and can reduce the processing load, as shown in Fig. 2(d). However, the actual amount of reduced processing load depends on the authentication frequency.

To further discuss the reduction in the number of processes in a non-periodic authentication, Fig. 3 is presented, in which, similar to Fig. 2, the horizontal axis represents the passage of time while using the system, and the small downward arrows indicate the authentication execution. In addition, continuous operations in the system usage (for instance, typing or handling) and a break between them are distinguished as "Working" and "Break", respectively.

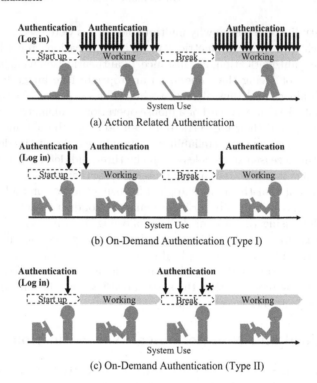

(a) Action Related Authentication

(b) On-Demand Authentication (Type I)

(c) On-Demand Authentication (Type II)

Fig. 3. Nonperiodical authentication.

4.3   Action-Related Authentication

Authentication that is triggered by the operation of a device is called action-related authentication herein, as shown in Fig. 3(a). In Refs. [25–27], the authors assumed operations when applying a keyboard and computer mouse or when touching a smartphone display. Although these studies may be classified as continuous authentication, in this study, they are treated separately because they differ from the way continuous authentication is approached.

Because action-related authentication is applied continuously during an operation, the effect of reducing the processing load depends on the operation frequency, although it is not considered to be high. In addition, there may be temporary breaks during an operation; therefore, a mechanism for maintaining the authentication score obtained before, as described in Sect. 3.2, is provided.

5   On-demand Authentication

The author proposed on-demand authentication [14, 28–31], in which authentication is applied when required and possible. Unlike action-related authentication, the frequency of authentication execution is low, which results in a reduction in the processing load. However, its realization has not actually been discussed. What type of situation describes "when authentication is required"?

5.1   Type I

The author proposed the use of an intra-body (palm) propagation signal [6–10], that is, the signal propagated between two electrode pairs on the body, as a type of biometrics. If the characteristics of the propagated signals differ from each other, the propagated signal can be used as a new biometric modality. Various systems are applied with the user touching or gripping a part of the system. If a detection mechanism of the intra-body propagation signal is equipped in the system, the propagated signal can be detected without any positive action; thus, it is a passively detectable biometric. On-demand authentication using such a biometrics is called Type I, as shown in Fig. 3(b).

Can it be assumed that a driver will be replaced with someone else when turning a handle? In addition, can it be assumed that a computer user will be replaced when typing on a keyboard or moving a mouse? The answer is clearly no. Therefore, it is not necessary to authenticate the user while touching the system[2]. This is an extremely important aspect of the present study.

In the case of action-related authentication, continuous action when using a mobile device is applied as a biometric; therefore, continuous authentication is required, which increases the processing load. By contrast, when not using continuous action as a biometric, it is not necessary to authenticate continuously even when using a system. This is a different aspect between action-related authentication and the proposed Type I authentication. When the use of the system is started, authentication is executed once, after which, or during a break, authentication is not conducted.

5.2   Type II

By contrast, it is possible for a user to be replaced with someone else during a break while at work[3]. Thus, it is proposed to avoid authenticating the user while using the system and instead to authenticate the user when a break is detected. This is considered Type II, as shown in Fig. 3(c).

This type is preferable to biometrics that use cognitive information, such as brain waves [11–16, 28–31]. In brain wave measurements, noise from body movements can be mixed into the waves, which becomes a problem. When using

---

[2] Even if the user changes into someone else after authentication, it is possible to deal with the spoofing by authenticating the user nonperiodically while increasing the frequency of the authentication, that is, applying a processing load. The authentication frequency should be determined by considering the increase in the processing load.

[3] The break is assumed to be temporal, for instance, a temporary interruption to think while using a computer, or a temporary stop at a traffic signal while driving. If the user leaves the system, it is considered that the work has been completed and a log-in authentication will be required again.

the response to stimulation in brain waves, the mixing of different stimuli must be avoided. As mentioned in the previous subsection, if it is not assumed that the user changes during a work period, it becomes sufficient to apply authentication during a break, which is convenient for preventing noise from being mixed into the brain waves.

However, it is unpredictable when a break will end, and the work will resume. When using passively detectable biometrics such as brain waves, it is unknown when authentication can be conducted. If authentication is applied after spoofing, it is possible to prevent such spoofing. Therefore, Type II has a deterrence against spoofing. However, if authentication is conducted only once during a break, the user is replaced with someone else as a sink-or-swim gamble, and the spoofing is not prevented after authentication. Thus, authentication must be conducted periodically or nonperiodically during a break with the proposed Type II approach.

Even so, the risk of user replacement after authentication just before resuming the work, as indicated by "*" in Fig. 3(c), cannot be completely eliminated. To eliminate this risk, a multimodal type combining Type I is required. In this case, authentication is conducted during both work and break periods, which results in an increase in the processing load.

5.3   Reduction of Processing Load

Based on the above discussion, on-demand authentication is the most effective method for reducing the processing load while preventing spoofing. However, the effect of reducing the processing load depends on the length of the work and break times. When the break time is longer than the work time, the processing load of Type II increases. By contrast, a lengthy work time results in a large processing load for Type I. Which type is suitable depends on the application? For instance, when users use an application while occasionally thinking, Type I is suitable. When users do nothing except use the application, then Type II is suitable. However, the above examination is based only on the frequency of the authentication execution. However, a processing load also occurs owing to the authentication itself. The actual processing load must be evaluated by combining the authentication frequency and amount of authentication processing.

5.4   Detection of Start/Break/End-of-work Times

In the proposed Types I and II approaches, it is necessary to accurately detect the start, pause, and end-of-work times. The trigger of the detection is the start, pause, or end of keyboard typing or mouse operation when using a computer. When driving, the start, pause, and end of driving are detected by pressing an accelerator pedal, pressing a brake pedal, and leaving the seat, respectively. These are detectable using pressure sensors and signal processing techniques, and their processing load is not large. In addition, in the case of driving. These triggers may be obtained from the driving control system of the car.

5.5 Working During Break Period

Next, let us examine a case of working during a break period. In this study, it is assumed that strict user management is required, such as transport systems involving many human lives, security systems handling confidential information, and online learning systems for licenses and qualifications. It is therefore unexpected for users to do the other work during their break period, for instance, when drinking, eating, calling of the phone, or chatting, among other cases. The user concentrates on conducting the original work (application) while using the system. A break is a temporary pause in work and not for carrying out other works. In the proposed Type II approach, it is assumed that the authentication is executed during the break, but it is not assumed that the user will conduct other tasks.

However, body movements are assumable during a break, which results in noise in the brain waves. Therefore, during body movements, authentication using brain waves should be avoided. However, if large body movements occur during a break, it may suggest that a regular user is trying to be replaced with someone else. Thus, by detecting body movements, authentication can be prohibited while the body is in motion. If such movement continues for more than a certain interval, a log-in authentication will be required again, assuming that spoofing has occurred.

6 Processing of On-demand Authentication

Based on the discussion thus far, the processing of the proposed on-demand authentication method is examined.

6.1 Type I

The processing flow of Type I is shown in Fig. 4. At first, the login authentication is performed[4]. After the login authentication, the system usage by the user is started. When detecting the beginning of a work period, authentication using passively detectable biometrics is applied. If the user is regarded as genuine, the user is permitted access to the system until the break period is detected. After the break, if the start of the work is detected again, authentication is resumed. However, if the end of the work is detected, the authentication process also ends.

---

[4] In on-demand authentication, passively detectable biometrics are also used for a login authentication, whereas action-related authentication requires the user to use other biometrics or a password/ID card for login authentication.

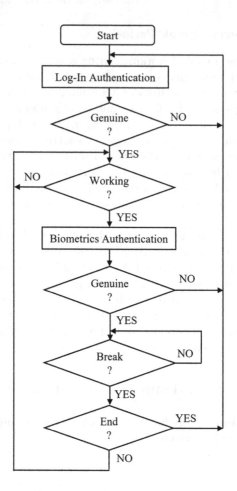

Fig. 4. Processing flow of Type I.

6.2 Type II

The processing flow for Type II is shown in Fig. 5. After login authentication and the start of system use, the user is permitted to use the system unless a break in work is detected. If a work interruption is detected and then the end of the work is also detected, the system use will be ended. If the end of the work is not detected, the interruption is regarded as a work break, and body movement detection is applied. If body-movement is not detected, the authentication is conducted. If the user is regarded as genuine, the user is permitted to use the system, and the interval for applying the next authentication is set, where a nonperiodic authentication is assumed to be conducted during the break. At the time set for the next authentication, the detection of the break restarts. However, if body movement is detected, authentication is not conducted. The detection of body-movement is continued within the allowable preset time. If the interval

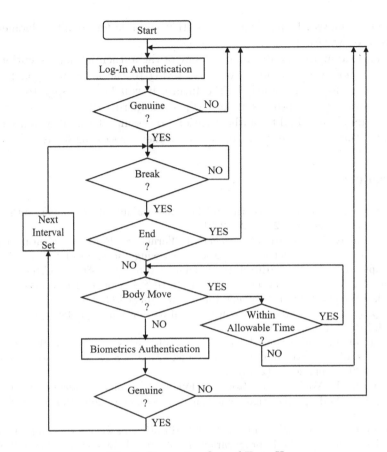

Fig. 5. Processing flow of Type II.

in which the authentication is not performed becomes larger than the allowable time, the system usage of the user is forcibly refused.

7   Conclusions

To prevent spoofing in system-user management, continuous authentication is required; however, this increases the processing load of the system. In addition, only passively detectable (consciously presentable) biometrics are applicable for continuous authentication.

In this study, from the viewpoint of reducing the processing load, we examined what type of method is effective in realizing continuous authentication using passively detectable biometrics. As a result, it was confirmed that the proposed on-demand authentication system is effective. Moreover, Type I, which applies authentication during work, and Type II, which conducts authentication during a break period, were proposed as on-demand authentication, and their feasibilities were evaluated. In particular, Type II is suitable for cognitive biometrics, such as brain waves.

In this examination, only the frequency of the authentication execution was considered; however, the processing load owing to the authentication process itself should also be included. In the future, it will be necessary to comprehensively evaluate the processing load when considering the authentication frequency and load required for authentication processing. It will also be necessary to build authentication systems and evaluate their processing loads.

References

1. Baig, A.F., Eskeland, S.: Security, privacy, and usability in continuous authentication: a survey. Sensors **21**, 1–26 (2021)
2. Abdulwahid, A.A., Clarke, N., Stengel, I., Furnell, S., Reich, C.: Continuous and transparent multimodal authentication: reviewing the state of the art. Cluster Comput. **19**, 455–474 (2016). https://doi.org/10.1007/s10586-015-0510-4
3. Jain, A., Bolle, R., Pankanti, S.: BIOMETRICS Personal Identification in Networked Society. Kluwer Academic Publishers, Norwell (1999)
4. EU privacy watchdogs call for ban on facial recognition in public spaces. Reuters Tech News, 21 June 2021
5. Nakanishi, I.: Unconscious biometrics for continuous user verification. In: Proceedings of the 8th International Conference on Signal Processing Systems (ICSPS2016), pp. 20–25 (2016)
6. Nakanishi, I., Yorikane, Y., Itoh, Y., Fukui, Y.: Biometric identity verification using intra-body propagation signal. In: Proceedings of 2007 Biometrics Symposium (2007)
7. Nakanishi, I., Sodani, Y., Li, S.: User verification based on the support vector machine using intra-body propagation signals. Int. J. Biometrics **5**(3/4), 288–305 (2013)
8. Inada, T., Sodani, Y., Nakanishi, I.: Intra-palm propagation signals as suitable biometrics for successive authentication. J. Comput. Technol. Appl. **7**(2), 65–72 (2016)
9. Nakanishi, I., Ogushi, I., Nishi, R., Murakami, T.: Effect of propagation signal and path on verification performance using intra-body propagation signals. In: Proceedings of 2017 International Conference on Biometrics Engineering and Application (ICBEA2017), pp. 80–84 (2017)
10. Fujita, K., Ishimoto, Y., Nakanishi, I.: Person verification using intra-palm propagation signals with a new phase spectrum. In: Proceedings of 12th International Conference on Knowledge and Smart Technology (KST2020), pp. 86–90 (2020)
11. Nakanishi, I., Miyamoto, C., Baba, C.: EEG based biometric authentication using new spectral features. In: Proceedings of 2009 IEEE International Symposium on Intelligent Signal Processing and Communication Systems (ISPACS2009), pp. 651–654 (2009)
12. Nakanishi, I., Baba, S., Miyamoto, C., Li, S.: Person authentication using a new feature vector of the brain wave. J. Commun. Comput. **9**(1), 101–105 (2012)
13. Nakanishi, I., Miyamoto, C., Li, S.: Brain waves as biometrics in relaxed and mentally tasked conditions with eyes closed. Int. J. Biometrics **4**(4), 357–372 (2012)

14. Nakanishi, I., Baba, S., Ozaki, K., Li, S.: Using brain waves as transparent biometrics for on-demand driver authentication. Int. J. Biometrics **5**(3/4), 321–335 (2013)
15. Nakanishi, I., Yoshikawa, T.: Brain waves as unconscious biometrics towards continuous authentication - the effects of introducing PCA into feature extraction. In: Proceedings of 2015 IEEE International Symposium on Intelligent Signal Processing and Communication Systems (ISPACS2015), pp. 422–425 (2015)
16. Nakanishi, I., Maruoka, T.: Biometrics using electroencephalograms stimulated by personal ultrasound and multidimensional nonlinear features. Electronics **9**(24), 1–18 (2020)
17. Zhang, S., Janakiraman, R., Sim, T., Kumar, S.: Continuous verification using multimodal biometrics. In: Proceedings of International Conference on Biometrics (ICB2006), pp. 562–570 (2006)
18. Niinuma, K., Park, U., Jain, A.K.: Soft biometric traits for continuous user authentication. IEEE Trans. Inf. Forensics Secur. **5**, 771–780 (2010)
19. Altinok, A., Turk, M.: Temporal integration for continuous multimodal biometrics. In: Proceedings of 2003 Workshop on Multimodal User Authentication, pp. 207–214 (2003)
20. Kwang, G., Yap, R.H.C., Sim, T., Ramnath, R.: An usability study of continuous biometrics authentication. In: Tistarelli, M., Nixon, M.S. (eds.) ICB 2009. LNCS, vol. 5558, pp. 828–837. Springer, Heidelberg (2009). https://doi.org/10.1007/978-3-642-01793-3_84
21. Frank, M., Biedert, R., Ma, E., Martinovic, I., Song, D.: Touchalytics: on the applicability of touchscreen input as a behavioral biometric for continuous authentication. IEEE Trans. Inf. Forensics Secur. **8**, 136–148 (2012)
22. Kumar, R., Phoha, V.V., Serwadda, A.: Continuous authentication of smartphone users by fusing typing, swiping, and phone movement patterns. In: Proceedings of 2016 IEEE 8th International Conference on Biometrics Theory, Applications and Systems (BTAS2016) (2016)
23. Crawford, H., Renaud, K., Storer, T.: A framework for continuous, transparent mobile device authentication. Comput. Secur. **39**, 127–136 (2013)
24. Crouse, D., Han, H., Chandra, D., Barbello, B., Jain, A.: Continuous authentication of mobile user: fusion of face image and inertial measurement unit data. In: Proceedings of 2015 International Conference on Biometrics (ICB2015) (2015)
25. Patel, V.M., Chellappa, R., Chandra, D., Barbello, B.: Continuous user authentication on mobile devices: recent progress and remaining challenges. IEEE Signal Process. Mag. **33**, 49–61 (2016)
26. Mondal, S., Bours, P.: A computational approach to the continuous authentication biometric system. Inf. Sci. **304**, 28–53 (2015)
27. Mondal, S., Bours, P.: A study on continuous authentication using a combination of keystroke and mouse biometrics. Neurocomputing **230**, 1–22 (2017)
28. Nakanishi, I., Miyamoto, C.: On-demand biometric authentication of computer users using brain waves. In: Zavoral, F., Yaghob, J., Pichappan, P., El-Qawasmeh, E. (eds.) NDT 2010. CCIS, vol. 87, pp. 504–514. Springer, Heidelberg (2010). https://doi.org/10.1007/978-3-642-14292-5_51
29. Nakanishi, I., Baba, S., Li, S.: Evaluation of brain waves as biometrics for driver authentication using simplified driving simulator. In: Proceedings of 2011 International Conference on Biometrics and Kansei Engineering (ICBAKE2011), pp. 71–76 (2011)

30. Nakanishi, I., Baba, S., Li, S.: Driver authentication using brain waves while route tracing as a mental task. In: Proceedings of the 6th International Conference on Security and Cryptography (SECRYPT2011), pp. 90–96 (2011)
31. Nakanishi, I., Fukuda, H. and Li, S.: Biometric verification using brain waves toward on-demand user management systems - performance differences between divided regions in alpha-beta wave band. In: Proceedings of the 6th International Conference on Security of Information and Networks (SIN2013), pp. 131–135 (2013)

PushID: A Pressure Control Interaction-Based Behavioral Biometric Authentication System for Smartwatches

Youngeun Song$^{(\boxtimes)}$ and Ian Oakley

Ulsan National Institute of Science and Technology, Ulsan, Republic of Korea
soyo61@unist.ac.kr

Abstract. Smartwatches support a wide range of functionality, including mediating access to sensitive data and services. However, securing access to them is difficult due to their small size—it is difficult, for example, to enter alphanumeric passwords accurately due to the limited space available to present a keyboard. Consequently, 4-digit PIN is commonly used to secure smartwatches, a technique widely acknowledged to be highly vulnerable to simple guessing attacks. To address these usability and security issues, we propose PushID, a new behavioral biometric technique for a smartwatch that combines four on-screen targets with five pressure levels to enable input of any one of 20 unique symbols from a single screen touch. In addition to this relatively large input space, PushID captures behavioral features during pressure input (e.g., finger touch profile, wrist motions) and uses this as a behavioral biometric. We report on a preliminary study of PushID and its security against random guessing attack: it achieves good usability for a single input (approximately 2 s) and high resistance to guessing (false-positive rates of 1.05%). We argue that pressure-based input can improve the security and maintain the usability of smartwatch lock systems.

Keywords: Smartwatch · Behavioral biometrics · Usability

1 Introduction

The Smartwatch market is steadily growing and is anticipated to achieve sales of 230.30 million units by 2026 [17]. The majority of smartwatches are currently paired with a smartphone to support all functionality. However, as devices become more advanced standalone functionality is starting to be introduced to support users during tasks such as exercise, situations in which users may prefer not to be encumbered by a smartphone. Building on this trend, in the future commercial smartwatches could provide a wide range of services in standalone settings such as collecting health data, storing personal messages, and processing payments. Due to the sensitive nature of these applications, we argue there is a need to secure access to standalone smartwatches.

However, the small size of these devices makes traditional knowledge-based authentication schemes, such as alphanumeric passwords, slow and awkward

A. Moallem (Ed.): HCII 2022, LNCS 13333, pp. 255–267, 2022.
https://doi.org/10.1007/978-3-031-05563-8_17

to enter. Simpler schemes such as Personal Identification Number (PIN) are more feasible but are widely acknowledged to be vulnerable to random guessing attacks [14]. Physiological biometrics-based authentication could be an alternative solution that can improve usability and security over such knowledge-based schemes—such systems have proven popular on smartphones. However, the sensors for established physiological biometrics, such as fingerprints, are hard to integrate into the small case of a smartwatch. As an alternative, researchers have proposed behavioral biometrics based on data from built-in smartwatch sensors such as the touch screen [14] or inertial motion unit [3] with promising results. Pressure-based input is another form of touch input that may lead to rich variations in behavioral characteristics. In addition, it can help support authentication by increasing the scope of different inputs that are available on small input areas—multiple pressure levels can be entered on each on-screen button. Reflecting these benefits, pressure has been proposed as a behavioral biometric feature during tap-based smartwatch authentication [14]. Additionally, explicitly controlling touch force has been used to enable pressure-based explicit authentication schemes on a smartphone [10, 16].

In this paper, we extend these approaches by proposing PushID, a smartwatch authentication system based on a novel pressure-based behavioral biometric. This paper presents the design of the scheme and results of a user study exploring its usability and security against random guessing attacks. PushID is based on features extracted from screen touches and wrist motion data in which users intentionally modulate the force they exert. Specifically, we extracted a total of 165 features from raw touch and wrist motion data while the participants generated, sustained, and released one of five discrete pressure levels on a wrist-mounted touch screen. We performed a simple empirical study (N = 30) to collect user behavior while operating PushID. The participants entered 20 randomly assigned PushID entries according to instructions provided during the study. We used this data to train recognizers for each participant and compared user verification performance in a simulated random guessing attack scenario in terms of False-Positive Rate (FPR), False-Negative Rate (FNR), and Equal Error Rate (EER). We also measured the completion time to input a single PushID entry to evaluate the usability of PushID.

The results indicate that the best verification performance of the PushID recognizer was as follows: mean FPR was 1.05%, mean FNR was 42.76%, and mean EER was 8.34%. In the case of FPR, PushID shows improved values compared to other behavioral biometric authentication schemes for smartwatches, such as the 21.65% reported for AirSign [3], and the 7.2% in Beat-PIN [8]. However FNRs, and correspondingly, EERs are higher compared to these closely related schemes [3, 7, 8, 14]. In terms of usability, participants took a mean of 2.09 s for each input, a good level of performance compared to both popular authentication schemes such as PIN (2.195 s) [14] or other behavioral biometrics-based authentication proposed for smartwatches [7, 8, 14].

Based on these results we argue that authentication via pressure-based behavioral biometrics (based on data captured when users are asked to input specific pressure levels) is a promising approach to smartwatch security that can enhance resistance to random guessing attacks while maintaining good authentication time.

2   Related Work

User authentication systems can be divided into two different modes [20]: identification and verification. In the case of identification, there is an assumption that multiple users share a device so the authentication task is to clarify the identity of the current user among the stored set of genuine users. On the other hand in verification, there is a single genuine user (a device or account owner) and the task is to verify whether or not the submitted data represents that captured from the genuine user or any other individual (e.g., another user or an imposter). In this paper, we consider only verification scenarios.

2.1   Behavioral Biometrics in Smartwatches

Biometric authentication, which identifies or verifies a user according to their sensed characteristics (either physiological or behavioral) is an important and popular authentication method that can achieve both strong security and good usability in platforms as diverse as smartphones and door locks. This method is known as a viable solution to memorability issues and has high resistance against guessing attacks compared to knowledge-based authentication, which authenticates an individual based on information that they know (e.g., a password or PIN). There are two different authentication methods—first, physiological biometrics, which is based upon the unique body features of an individual (i.e., fingerprint) and, second, behavioral biometrics, which authenticate an individual based on their unique activity patterns (e.g., typing patterns) [19]. Though physiological biometrics are well established in many devices, such as the fingerprint or face recognition systems that appear on smartphones, they are hard to implement on smartwatches [14] because they typically require specialized sensors (e.g., fingerprint readers, high-resolution cameras) they are difficult to integrate into small watch form factors. On the other hand, behavioral biometrics may be a more appropriate approach, as many smartwatches are already designed to accurately track the detailed activities of their user to support applications such as exercise or physiological monitoring.

We summarize previously reported verification performance for behavioral biometrics on smartwatches in Table 1. We express performance data in terms of *False Positive Rate* (FPR, the ratio of the number of accepted attempts by non-legitimate users to the total number of attempts by non-legitimate users), *False Negative Rate* (FNR, the ratio of the number of rejected attempts by legitimate users to the total number of attempts by legitimate users), and *Equal Error rate* (EER, the trade-off point where a recognizer is tuned to match FNR and FPR as equal). Various user behaviors, which can be captured by popular smartwatch sensors such as motion sensors or the touchscreen, have been studied

Table 1. Verification performance in random guessing attack for existing smartwatch authentication systems using behavioral biometrics. FPR (false positive rate), FNR (false negative rate), and EER (equal error rate) expressed in %.

Work	FPR	FNR	EER
Li and Xie [12]	0	22	NA
AirSign [3]	21.65	19.48	NA
VeriNet [13]	10.24	20.77	7.17
TapMeIn [14]	0.98	5.3	1.3

for biometrics. Specific modalities include arm gestures [12], mid-air gestures [3], wrist motion data during PIN input [13], and screen tapping rhythm [14]. Their performance is complex and reporting of metrics is not completely consistent. Nonetheless, it is obvious that attaining high performance, in terms of low EERs (or the combination of low FPRs and FNRs) is demanding: a majority of this work achieves scores of 20% or higher on at least one of these metrics. However, bucking this trend, TapMeIn [14] achieved 0.98% EER in response to random guessing attacks. To do this, TapMeIn extracted different touch features from a customized explicit authentication code—a passcode in the form of a rhythmical tapping pattern. This highlights the possible advantages of extracting behavioral features from novel touch actions beyond standard taps. We argue that the more expressive performance inherent in this type of input may help to increase the uniqueness of the behavioral biometrics that can be derived from a user's input.

Based on these arguments, we propose PushID to explore the value of the behavioral features extracted from both the touch screen (including touch force data) and 3-dimensional motion sensors (accelerometer and gyroscope to track wrist motion) while users explicitly perform a complex and dynamic input action; controlling specific forces during an entry of a single pressure-based input.

2.2 Pressure Input-Based Authentication

There have long been studies claiming that pressure input is expressive and precisely controllable [2]. Highly accurate pressure sensors are currently integrated into many commercial laptops and smartphones, while binary pressure sensors appear on smartwatches. We argue that pressure input is particularly useful in small form factor devices, which frequently suffer from fat-finger problems, because it can provide additional input options even when screen real estate is highly limited [16].

The potential of pressure-based input has been studied in various studies and showed diverse results. For instance, ForcePIN [10] is a PIN system that features two pressure levels, doubling the number of possible input symbols available. ForcePIN achieved a reasonable authentication time of 3.66 s to complete input of 4-digit passcodes. Pressure has also been studied in the area of touch-based behavioral biometrics. One noteworthy focus for this work is to improve the security of standard lock inputs. For example, De Luca et al. [4] collected touch-related features including location, size, speed, duration, and pressure during pattern lock input on a smartphone, and achieved 77% accuracy while performing authentication tasks. Salem and Obaidat [18] report the peak verification performance in this area—0.9% EER—in a study using 10-keystroke dynamics-related features, including pressure during the task of entering eight alphanumeric passwords. We assert these prior results indicate that pressure input tasks can generate data that is appropriate for verifying an individual using a behavioral biometric approach. The system we present in this paper borrows methods from much of the work reviewed in this section; it leverages the idea that pressure input can increase the expressivity of touch input on small screen wearables to create a behavioral biometric authentication system that provides a large number of attainable passcodes on a small input surface. The goal of this work is to retain authentication usability while improving resistance to random guessing attacks. We do this by investigating the efficiency (time to enter) and FPR, FNR, and EER of our proposed PushID system that is based on extracted touch and wrist motion behavioral features that occur during pressure input.

3   PushID System Design

3.1   Threat Model

PushID was designed to enhance resistance to random guessing attacks, a simple and common attack strategy. In this study, we set the attack scenario as that of an attacker who has gained a victim's device via methods such as theft and tries to unlock it without any preliminary knowledge related to the user or passcode [12]. We assume the attacker was not able to previously observe genuine unlock attempts.

3.2   PushID Interface

Existing commercial smartwatches, such as the Apple Watch First Generation and above, provide pressure input on their touch screen. However, they only support binary levels of touch force so app developers can not use multi-level pressure input at this time. Since this study required a platform that could measure detailed pressure, we used an iPhone X smartphone (iOS 12.1.4) that supports analog pressure measurements in place of a smartwatch—this device has also been widely used for research about touch force-based interaction [6,10]. In order to use the smartphone as a watch, we placed the phone on an armband and made a prototype to receive touch input from only a 24 by 30 mm area in the center of the screen. Emulating a watch with a smartphone in this fashion has been previously adopted for investigating the user experience of next-generation smartwatch interfaces [5]. Although the smartphone (174 g) and a smartwatch (e.g., Apple Watch 6's 30.5 g) are substantially different in weight, we believe these changes likely had a limited impact on the user behavior data we collected

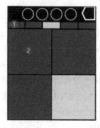 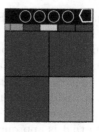

Fig. 1. GUI of PushID (left) showing touch force gauge (1) and buttons (2). Highlight items are in yellow. Example screen during input (right) showing red pressure cursor over first pressure level.

in this study. According to a study about physical loading on the wrist [9], significantly increased stress and fatigue appeared when participants wore a wrist-mounted wearable computer weighing more than 0.54 kg, and lifted their arm for more than 10 s. In the case of our study, the apparatus was about one-third of this weight limit and, generally, the authentication completion time was considerably shorter than 10 s. Accordingly, we do not believe the use of a phone in place of a watch invalidates the work we report. For the rest of this paper, we refer to our wrist-mounted prototype as a "watch".

Single PushID entries were achieved by pressing an on-screen button with a specific level of touch force. Figure 1 shows the current graphical user interface (GUI)—four large (12 by 12 mm) square buttons are provided and one of five pressure levels can be entered per button, so a total of twenty different input behaviors are available. We chose four targets because we want to provide users with large and easy-to-select targets and this design is used for prior research on smartwatch authentication with similar goals [15]. We picked five pressure levels based on prior work [6]—participants in this study indicated that the use of five discrete pressure levels led to high precision and accuracy.

We used the full touch pressure range that could be measured on the watch, but not all five pressure levels were equally divided; the interval of each pressure level was adjusted to improve selection performance following prior designs of five pressure level input systems [6]. Specifically, we reduced the intervals of highest and lowest pressure levels, as these levels have been reported to be easy to select [1]. There was no official way to convert the pressure values measured by iPhoneX to International System Units. Therefore, we first calculated the five pressure levels based on the values measured by the iPhone, and after obtaining a conversion formula through a calibration procedure using an electronic scale and a set of weights. This enabled converting the iPhone's sensor data into gram-force units. After this process the pressure levels were defined as (in gram-force): 0 to 54.85; 54.85 to 167.50; 167.50 to 280.16; 280.16 to 333.17 and; 333.17 to 392.81.

The graphic interface of PushID prompted users to select a yellow highlighted target button and pressure level. It showed the pressure levels as segments on a horizontal gauge (Fig. 1). When a user touched the screen, the touched button was displayed in green, and the current touch force was displayed as a red line that moved across along the gauge (and its segments) in real-time. The five different pressure levels were marked on the gauge. A pressure level was selected when the currently exerted pressure remained in the same pressure level for 300 milliseconds, a technique borrowed from prior work [6]. Progress during this pressure-dwell was marked by feedback in the form of the currently selected level filling up with a blue highlight; after 300ms it was full. If the correct pressure level was selected this highlight turned green, whereas it turned purple if the wrong pressure level was selected. The use of this pressure dwell enabled accurate selection of pressure levels during finger release as this process was rapid (less than 50 ms) and did not result in a selection of any new pressure levels. As this system has the potential to be combined with a knowledge-based authentication scheme in the future, the interface also contained graphic feedback for entering four entries as a set; the entry history was displayed using four circles, and it also supported the ability to modify entered entries with a delete button. These functions were not used in the current study.

3.3   System Overview

Like other behavioral biometric authentication technologies, PushID requires two separate processes: *Enrollment* and *Verification*. A summary of the overall system is shown in Fig. 2 and these two stages are briefly described below.

- *Enrollment*: If a genuine user successfully entered the target pressure level within the target button shown on the screen, a feature vector was calculated based on the behavioral data collected from the beginning of the touch to finger release of the screen. Then the system also generated feature vectors of attackers, that should be distinguished from the genuine user based on a random guessing attack scenario. Finally, the system finished pre-processing the genuine user data and attacker data and then trained a per-user recognizer for verification using machine learning techniques.
- *Verification*: If the genuine user or attacker succeeded in entering the target pressure level within the target button according to the instructions shown on the screen, a feature vector was calculated. Then the user-specific recognizer generated during *Enrollment* was used to judge whether the data represented the genuine user or an imposter.

During enrollment, the PushID system recorded touch screen data (X and Y coordinates of touchpoint, touch radius, and touch force) 100 Hz, and captured wrist-motion data from the watch inertial measurement unit (IMU) 250 Hz while genuine users entered a PushID item. Specifically, we logged acceleration and rotational velocity (gyroscope data) in X, Y, and Z axes.

In the feature extraction stage, a feature vector consisting of summary statistics of 12 variables derived from four distinct behavioral traits captured during input of a single PushID entry was created. These are touch (force, x-position, y-position, radius), acceleration (X, Y, and Z axes, and magnitude), and rotational

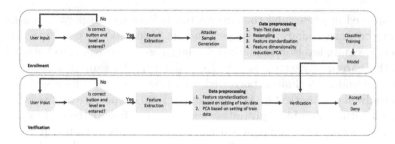

Fig. 2. Overview of PushID system implemented for this study

velocity (X, Y, and Z axes, and magnitude). The calculated summary statistics were: minimum, maximum, range, mean, and standard deviation. Additionally, frequency domain analysis was done via zero-padded Fast Fourier Transforms (FFT). We used the top four amplitudes and the top frequencies at which they occur as features. The highest amplitude frequency was always zero, so it was dropped as a feature. Moreover, we included skewness and kurtosis for all variables except positions of touch and radius since these variables exhibited very narrow deviations. Lastly, we included three features related to input time— touch duration in milliseconds and the number of samples of collected touch and wrist motion data. Each calculated feature value was also converted to a z-score according to the combination of button and pressure level selected; the mean and standard deviation of each feature per combination of button and pressure level were calculated from the full set of user data. In the end, a total of 165 features were created to form the feature vector from each input trial.

To train and test binary authentication classifiers to support user verification, it is also necessary to prepare the feature vectors of attackers. We applied two different methods for this. Firstly, we used the traditional method of extracting feature vectors from randomly sampled pre-collected data from other users. We created attacker feature vectors in the same way as in the case of genuine user data. Secondly, we synthesized feature vectors based on the distributions of individual feature values in the pre-collected user data set. This approach has been applied in prior work [14] and offers the advantage that it does not require storing any genuine data from other users. We generated 720 feature vectors using both of these methods and based on a set of 28 users data collected in an empirical study.

After preparing feature vectors for both a genuine user and attackers, the following pre-processing steps were applied:

1. Split data into train data and test data. We divided the feature vectors of the genuine user and the attackers into data for training a recognizer and data for evaluating verification performance. In the case of genuine user data, we use initial data for training to reflect a realistic unlock scenario during enrollment. We varied the set size of training data (nTrain) between 3 to 14

genuine user entries and sought to identify the optimal nTrain size, in terms of the verification performance of recognizers, via a grid-search procedure.

2. Re-sampling. We used the random re-sampling technique to match the amount of genuine user samples and attacker samples in the training data to reduce the influence of imbalanced classes on verification performance. The target re-sampling number of each class (nResampling) was varied from 20 to 720 in hops of 50 according to a grid-search procedure.

3. Feature standardization. The values of each feature were converted to a Z-score according to the statistical distributions in the training data.

4. Feature dimensionality reduction. As a large number of features can overestimate classification performance during training, we incorporated dimensionality reduction methods [20]. For this study, we used principal component analysis (PCA) and adjusted the retention percentage of variance explained by all of the selected components (PCATh) from 0.98 to 0.6 via grid-search.

After completing data pre-processing, two different types of classifiers were generated: one-class classifiers and binary classifiers. For both, we used a support vector machine (SVM) with a Radial Basis Function kernel, as this approach has been frequently used in behavioral biometrics research [20]. We applied a 10 fold cross-validation grid-search for tuning classifier hyperparameters [11].

The verification process determined whether a new PushID input was entered by a genuine user. Firstly the system checked whether the user correctly entered input according to guidance on screen. If this was correct. the feature vector was calculated for the input in the same way as during the enrollment process. Finally, this feature vector was submitted to the appropriate user classifier.

4 Data Collection Study

We performed an empirical study to explore the usability and security of PushID. We collected 551 valid PushID entries, and evaluated the verification performance of PushID in a simulated random guessing attack scenario. This study was approved by the local institutional review board (IRB).

4.1 Participants

A total of 30 participants (mean age = 23.07, $\sigma = 2.66$) were recruited through a post on a social media site for members of a local university. Among the participants, 18 were male and 12 were female. Left-handed people were excluded to increase the homogeneity of collected data. We recorded familiarity with smartphones, smartwatches, and pressure interaction on these devices via a questionnaire with 5-point Likert scales. Results indicated a high familiarity with smartphones ($\mu = 4.47$, $\sigma = 1.31$), a low familiarity with smartwatches ($\mu = 1.33$, $\sigma = 0.76$), moderate experience with pressure interaction with smartphones ($\mu = 2.27$, $\sigma = 1.51$) and low experience with pressure on smartwatches ($\mu = 1.27$, $\sigma = 0.69$). 5 USD in local currency was given as compensation for study participation. One participant showed low compliance with study instructions (in terms of accurate button and pressure level selection), so their data was excluded from all analyses. We report on data from the remaining 29 participants in this paper.

4.2 Procedure

The study was conducted in a silent laboratory environment while the participants sat in a chair without armrests. Each participant completed the below steps:

Instructions: The study started with a participant reading the study guide and then filling out the consent form. The participant could ask questions about the study at any time. The participant read paper guidelines about how to enter PushID items. The participant was guided to perform all input tasks as quickly and accurately as possible. Also, the participant had to keep their arm suspended in space while performing each input trial. There was no restriction on posture between trials; this minimized fatigue. In addition, we further reduced accumulated fatigue by mandating a break of at least 5 s after every 8 trials.

Input task: After receiving all the experimental instructions, participants put on the watch to perform the study input tasks. They achieved this by correctly selecting the yellow target button and the target pressure level displayed on the screen. The combination of target buttons and pressure levels were randomized for each trial, and each participant completed 19 trials.

4.3 Measures

To evaluate the usability of the PushID input task, *Input time*, the period between screen contact and release during each correct PushID entry was recorded. Based on collected behavioral data of the participants, verification FPR, FNR, and EER were explored for a wide set of classifier parameters using the grid-search procedures discussed in Sect. 3.3. This revealed how to generate a recognizer with the best possible EER.

5 Results and Discussion

In terms of usability measurements, the participants took a mean of 2.09 s ($\sigma = 1.68$) for each input. This represents an on par level of performance compared to both popular authentication schemes such as PIN (2.195 s) [14] and other behavioral biometrics-based authentication proposed for smartwatches [7,8,14]. In terms of resistance to random guessing attack, the best PushID recognizer used an nTrain of 14, nResampling of 520, and a PCATh of 0.98 with the binary classifier built using synthesized imposters—mean FPR was 1.05% ($\sigma = 0.76$), mean FNR was 42.76% ($\sigma = 22.50$), and mean EER was 8.34% ($\sigma = 8.06$). In the case of the real user imposter set, peak performance was achieved with nTrain of 14, nResampling of 720, and a PCATh of 0.98 with the binary classifier —mean FPR was 2.04% ($\sigma = 1.98$), mean FNR was 42.07% ($\sigma = 23.51$), and mean EER was 11.67% ($\sigma = 7.54$). Interpreting these results, we note that in the case of FPR, PushID shows improved values compared to other behavioral biometric authentication schemes for smartwatches, such as the 21.65% reported for Air-Sign [3], and the 7.2% in Beat-PIN [8]. However FNRs, and correspondingly, EERs are higher compared to these closely related schemes [3,8,14,21]. This result also showed a discussion point about the method to prepare imposter data to train and test the security of recognizers against random guessing attacks—the lower FPR when using synthesized imposter than real human data may mean that either the former method was effective at training the recognizer, or it led to weaker attacks than the latter one. Further work with collecting more user data is needed to systemically explore this point.

We can draw some wider conclusions from these results. The high FNR may occur because within-subject variability may be elevated by the fact that participants selected various random combinations of buttons and pressure levels. More consistent selections may lead to improved performance. Additionally, the high FNR values may be due to the limited size of train/test data in our current study; collecting an extended data set is a clear next step for this work. In addition, performance may be improved by considering multiple touch events, each featuring production of a different pressure level. Furthermore, PushID could also be combined with a knowledge-based authentication scheme involving entering a series of symbols each associated with a different button/pressure level combination. We see value in exploring these ideas in future work.

6 Conclusion

This paper proposes PushID, a behavioral biometric authentication system based on touch and motion traits extracted from five-level touch force input that seeks to achieve good usability and security as a lock system for a smartwatch. Our study indicates PushID ably resisted simulated random guessing attacks. Furthermore, it also achieves an input time that is on-par with other authentication techniques. We believe these results are promising and support the future development of the PushID pressure-based behavioral biometric concept as a viable smartwatch lock system.

Acknowledgement. This work was supported by the Basic Science Research Program through the National Research Foundation of Korea (NRF) funded by the Ministry of Science and ICT (2020R1F1A1070699).

References

1. Accot, J., Zhai, S.: Refining fitts' law models for bivariate pointing. In: Proceeding of The SIGCHI Conference on Human Factors in Computing Systems (2003). https://doi.org/10.1145/642611.642646
2. Brewster, S.A., Hughes, M.: Pressure-based text entry for mobile devices. In: Proceeding of the 11th International Conference on Human-Computer Interaction with Mobile Devices and Services (2009). https://doi.org/10.1145/1613858.1613870

3. Buriro, A., Van Acker, R., Crispo, B., Mahboob, A.: AirSign: a gesture-based smartwatch user authentication. In: 2018 International Carnahan Conference on Security Technology (2018). https://doi.org/10.1109/CCST.2018.8585571

4. De Luca, A., Hang, A., Brudy, F., Lindner, C., Hussmann, H.: Touch me once and i know it's you! implicit authentication based on touch screen patterns. In: Proceeding of the SIGCHI Conference on Human Factors in Computing Systems (2012). https://doi.org/10.1145/2207676.2208544

5. Gil, H., Lee, D., Im, S., Oakley, I.: TriTap: identifying finger touches on smartwatches. In: Proceeding of the 2017 CHI Conference on Human Factors in Computing Systems (2017). https://doi.org/10.1145/3025453.3025561

6. Goguey, A., Malacria, S., Gutwin, C.: Improving discoverability and expert performance in force-sensitive text selection for touch devices with mode gauges. In: Proceeding of the 2018 CHI Conference on Human Factors in Computing Systems (2018). https://doi.org/10.1145/3173574.3174051

7. Guerar, M., Migliardi, M., Palmieri, F., Verderame, L., Merlo, A.: Securing pin-based authentication in smartwatches with just two gestures. Concurr. Comput. Pract. Exp. **32**(18), e5549 (2020). https://doi.org/10.1002/cpe.5549

8. Hutchins, B., Reddy, A., Jin, W., Zhou, M., Li, M., Yang, L.: Beat-Pin: a user authentication mechanism for wearable devices through secret beats. In: Proceeding of the 2018 on Asia Conference on Computer and Communications Security (2018). https://doi.org/10.1145/3196494.3196543

9. Knight, J.F., Baber, C.: Assessing the physical loading of wearable computers. Appl. Ergon. **38**(2), 237–247 (2007). https://doi.org/10.1016/j.apergo.2005.12.008

10. Krombholz, K., Hupperich, T., Holz, T.: Use the force: evaluating force-sensitive authentication for mobile devices. In: Twelfth Symposium on Usable Privacy and Security (2016). https://www.usenix.org/conference/soups2016/technical-sessions/presentation/krombholz

11. scikit learn: 3.2. tuning the hyper-parameters of an estimator (2021). https://scikit-learn.org/stable/modules/grid_search.html. Accessed 27 Apr 2021

12. Li, Y., Xie, M.: Understanding secure and usable gestures for realtime motion based authentication. In: IEEE INFOCOM 2018-IEEE Conference on Computer Communications Workshops (2018). https://doi.org/10.1109/INFCOMW.2018.8406912

13. Lu, C.X., Du, B., Kan, X., Wen, H., Markham, A., Trigoni, N.: VeriNet: user verification on smartwatches via behavior biometrics. In: Proceeding of the First ACM Workshop on Mobile Crowdsensing Systems and Applications (2017). https://doi.org/10.1145/3139243.3139251

14. Nguyen, T., Memon, N.: Tap-based user authentication for smartwatches. Comput. Secur. **78**, 174–186 (2018). https://doi.org/10.1016/j.cose.2018.07.001

15. Oakley, I., Huh, J.H., Cho, J., Cho, G., Islam, R., Kim, H.: The personal identification chord: a four buttonauthentication system for smartwatches. In: Proceeding of the 2018 on Asia Conference on Computer and Communications Security (2018). https://doi.org/10.1145/3196494.3196555

16. Ranak, M.N., Azad, S., Nor, N.N.H.B.M., Zamli, K.Z.: Press touch code: a finger press based screen size independent authentication scheme for smart devices. PLOS One, **12**(10), e0186940 (2017). https://doi.org/10.1371/journal.pone.0186940

17. Reportlinker: global smartwatch market-growth, trends, covid-19 impact, and forecasts (2021–2026). yahoo!finance (2021). https://finance.yahoo.com/news/global-smartwatch-market-growth-trends-113500113.html

18. Salem, A., Obaidat, M.S.: A novel security scheme for behavioral authentication systems based on keystroke dynamics. Secur. Priv. **2**(2), e64 (2019). https://doi.org/10.1002/spy2.64

19. Shah, S.W., Kanhere, S.S.: Recent trends in user authentication-a survey. IEEE Access **7**, 112505–112519 (2019). https://doi.org/10.1109/ACCESS.2019.2932400
20. Teh, P.S., Zhang, N., Teoh, A.B.J., Chen, K.: A survey on touch dynamics authentication in mobile devices. Comput. Secur. **59**, 210–235 (2016). https://doi.org/10.1016/j.cose.2016.03.003
21. Zhang, H., Xiao, X., Ni, S., Dou, C., Zhou, W., Xia, S.: Smartwatch user authentication by sensing tapping rhythms and using one-class DBSCAN. Sensors **21**(7), 2456 (2021). https://doi.org/10.3390/s21072456

A Hand Gesture-Based Authentication Method that Makes Forgery Difficult

Hideaki Terui and Hiroshi Hosobe[✉] [iD]

Faculty of Computer and Information Sciences, Hosei University, Tokyo, Japan
hosobe@acm.org

Abstract. Physiological biometric authentication methods such as fingerprint, face, vein, and iris authentication have become or are becoming popular. Although these methods are highly accurate, they still have the problem of poor authentication due to noise and other disturbance in recognition. To alleviate this problem, behavioral biometric authentication also has been being studied. Among them, hand gesture-based authentication methods adopt the geometry and motion of hands and fingers. However, such hand gesture-based methods have the problem that they require larger movements than other authentication methods and are easily seen by third persons, which enables forgery. In this paper, we propose a hand gesture-based authentication method that incorporates dummy gestures to make forgery difficult. It allows increasing the number of gesture elements by inserting dummy gestures into real gestures during authentication. We show the results of an experiment that we conducted to examine whether the participants could insert dummy gestures and whether the dummy gestures could work as a countermeasure against forgery.

Keywords: Biometric authentication · Hand gesture · Forgery prevention

1 Introduction

Passwords are often used in authentication as a security measure. While passwords can be easily created, they have the disadvantage that they can be memorized by third persons. For this reason, physiological biometric methods such as fingerprint, face, vein, and iris authentication have become or are becoming popular. Although these methods are highly accurate, they still have the problem of poor authentication due to noise and other disturbance in recognition.

To alleviate this problem, behavioral biometric authentication also has been being studied. Along this line, researchers proposed hand gesture-based authentication methods adopting the geometry and motion of hands and fingers [2, 4, 5, 7–10, 17, 22, 25, 27, 30, 31, 34]. However, such hand gesture-based methods have the problem that they require larger movements than other authentication methods and are easily seen by third persons (sometimes called shoulder surfing [2]), which enables forgery.

© The Author(s), under exclusive license to Springer Nature Switzerland AG 2022
A. Moallem (Ed.): HCII 2022, LNCS 13333, pp. 268–279, 2022.
https://doi.org/10.1007/978-3-031-05563-8_18

In this paper, we propose a hand gesture-based authentication method that incorporates dummy gestures to make forgery difficult. It allows increasing the number of gesture elements by inserting dummy gestures into real gestures during authentication. In the experiment, we examined whether the participants could insert dummy gestures and whether the dummy gestures could work as a countermeasure against forgery. As a result, we found that it was not difficult to authenticate with dummy gestures. We also found that adding the average of 1.8 dummy gestures to four real gestures made it difficult to memorize the entire gestures.

The rest of this paper is organized as follows. Section 2 describes previous work related to our method, and Sect. 3 briefly explains preliminaries to our method. Section 4 proposes our method, and Sect. 5 gives its implementation. Section 6 presents the results of the experiment, and Sect. 7 discusses our method. Finally, Sect. 8 provides conclusions and future work.

2 Related Work

Many existing personal computers and mobile devices use text-based passwords and similar symbolic sequences such as PIN codes for user authentication. However, some users employ vulnerable passwords to easily memorize or enter the passwords. Google's Android introduced pattern lock [23], which allows users to draw patterns by connecting dots on touch screens instead of entering text passwords. Since Android's pattern lock uses only a small number of dots, they are essentially almost as simple as passwords. In addition, Ye et al. [33] showed the possibility of attacking pattern lock; they were able to infer correct patterns by analyzing videos for the motion of fingertips even if the videos had not directly captured the screens.

As an alternative to passwords, there has been research on biometric authentication [12,28,29] employing characteristics of users. Methods for biometric authentication can be roughly divided into two categories, the first one using physiological characteristics and the second one using behavioral characteristics. Physiological characteristics include, for example, fingerprints, faces, irises, and palm veins. In particular, fingerprint authentication is widely used in smartphones and tablets, and face recognition-based authentication has lately become popular. There has also been research on the use of the physiological characteristics of hands for biometric authentication [3]. For example, Jain et al. [11] showed the possibility of identifying persons by the geometry of hands.

The method that we propose in this paper falls in the second category of biometric authentication. Behavioral characteristics used in this category include, for example, pen pressures, keystrokes, and gaits [12,15,28,29,32]. Kholmatov and Yanikoglu [13] proposed an online signature verification method that used not only the form of a signature but also the number and the order of the strokes and the velocity and the pressure of the pen. Kim et al. [14] used the pressures of fingertips as behavioral characteristics, in particular, to solve the shoulder surfing problem in the context of collaborative tabletop interfaces. Ataş [1] proposed a biometric authentication method using the tremors of hands, and implemented it by using the Leap Motion Controller.

Our biometric authentication method uses hand gestures as behavioral characteristics. Such methods can be categorized into two, one using two-dimensional (2D) hand gestures, and the other using three-dimensional (3D) hand gestures [6]. Methods using 2D hand gestures for biometric authentication typically employ touch screens. Niu and Chen [18] proposed the use of gestures with taps on a touch screen for authentication. Sae-Bae et al. [20] proposed multi-touch gestures using a thumb and four fingers on a multi-touch screen, and studied particular 22 gestures. Sherman et al. [24] studied the use of free-form gestures for authentication.

Biometric authentication methods using 3D hand gestures can be further categorized into sensor- and camera-based methods [6]. Sensor-based methods typically use accelerometers. Guerra-Casanova et al. [8] proposed the use of an accelerometer-embedded mobile device to capture a 3D hand gesture like an in-air signature. Sun et al. [25] developed a biometric authentication system for smartphones that used on-phone accelerometers to capture 3D hand gesture signatures. It should be noted that such sensor-based methods do not consider the motion of fingers.

Camera-based biometric authentication methods perform image processing. Fong et al. [7] used the stationary images of 3D hand gestures that represented sequences of alphabets in a hand sign language. Aumi and Kratz [2] used a depth camera for authentication with 3D hand gestures for diagrammatic shapes such as a star and a spiral.

More recently, there has been research on camera-based methods using the Leap Motion Controller (LMC). We previously proposed an authentication method using three types of 3D hand gestures [9,10]. We particularly studied the use of the motion of fingertips and wrists for 3D gestures. We implemented the method by using LMC to capture 3D gestures.

Other researchers also used LMC for hand gesture-based authentication. Nigam et al. [17] used LMC to capture in-air signatures for authentication. Xiao et al. [31] also used LMC to handle in-air signatures. Chahar et al. [4] proposed "Leap password" consisting of six gestures using one of 10 fingers at a time. Chan et al. [5] used LMC for authentication using a circle-drawing gesture with one finger. Saritha et al. [22] also used LMC to treat circle-drawing, swipe, screen-tap, and key-tap gestures. Wong and Kang [30] proposed stationary hand gestures that used the free motion of fingers without the motion of hands, wrists, and arms; they implemented a biometric authentication method by using LMC. Zhao and Tanaka [34] proposed a hand gesture-based authentication method using LMC; it was capable of updating gesture templates to make it work for a long period. Wang and Tanaka [27] proposed a hand gesture-based authentication method based on machine learning; to ease the learning process, it incorporated data augmentation and incremental learning.

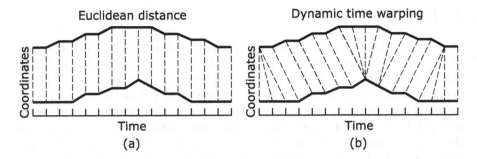

Fig. 1. Matching two data sequences by dynamic time warping.

3   Preliminaries

In this section, we briefly describe the Japanese fingerspelling alphabets, the Leap Motion Controller, and dynamic time warping, which we use for our hand gesture-based authentication method.

3.1   Japanese Fingerspelling Alphabets

Fingerspelling is a visual language that maps static hand gestures into alphabets. A hand gesture is made by extending or bending fingers and occasionally turning over the hand. Fingerspelling differs according to countries. The Japanese fingerspelling alphabets [19] are used in Japan.

3.2   Leap Motion Controller

The Leap Motion Controller [26] is a motion sensor specialized in hand gestures. It is equipped with a stereo infrared camera and an infrared light-emitting diode (LED). It computes the positional information of hands in the 3D space by lightening and capturing the hands with the LED and the stereo camera. It achieves the tracking speed of 120 fps and the tracking accuracy of 1/100 mm, and captures a stereo image each frame.

3.3   Dynamic Time Warping

Dynamic time warping [21] computes the matching of two data sequences in such a way that the distances between the matched points in the sequences are the shortest. As shown in Fig. 1(a), comparing two data sequences by simply using the same time points may yield large errors for parts of large movements. By contrast, dynamic time warping minimizes the errors by matching the time points as shown in Fig. 1(b).

4   Proposed Method

Our method allows a user to register a single sequence of gestures by combining gesture elements that were borrowed from the Japanese fingerspelling alphabets [19]. However, simply increasing the number of such gesture elements imposes a burden on the user. Therefore, to make the gesture sequence difficult for third persons to memorize and forge, our method allows the user to insert multiple dummy gestures into real gestures during authentication. Since human short-term memory has the capacity of 7 ± 2 [16], the additional dummy gestures make the entire gesture sequence more difficult for third persons to memorize and forge.

Dummy gestures should not be recognizable to third persons although the user needs to distinguish dummy gestures from real gestures for authentication. For this purpose, we introduce conditions that real gestures should satisfy, and allow the user to select a condition at the time of registering a gesture sequence. Specifically, we introduce the following 12 conditions for real gestures that we decided from the observation of the Japanese fingerspelling alphabets: (1) the palm directs downward and (2) upward; (3) the thumb extends and (4) bends; (5) the index finger extends and (6) bends; (7) the middle finger extends and (8) bends; (9) the ring finger extends and (10) bends; (11) the little finger extends and (12) bends.

Dummy gestures can be constructed by performing gestures that do not satisfy the condition selected by the user. It is not necessary to select gestures from the Japanese fingerspelling alphabets. For example, if the user selects the condition for real gestures that the thumb bends, then any gestures with the thumb extending will be recognized as dummy gestures and will be excluded from the authentication. The user can insert various dummy gestures such as the other finger bending and extending, which will make the condition difficult for third persons to recognize.

In authentication, the order of real gestures must be preserved, but dummy gestures can be inserted anytime. For example, let g_1, g_2, g_3, and g_4 be a sequence of real gestures and d_1, d_2, and d_3 be a sequence of dummy gestures. Then the following sequences P_1 and P_2 of seven gestures are legal:

$$P_1 = (g_1, d_1, g_2, g_3, d_2, d_3, g_4)$$
$$P_2 = (d_1, g_1, g_2, d_2, g_3, g_4, d_3).$$

By contrast, the following sequence P_3 of gestures is illegal because the order of the real gestures is not the same:

$$P_3 = (g_1, d_1, g_3, g_2, d_2, d_3, g_4).$$

5   Implementation

We implemented the proposed method as a prototype system in Java by using the Leap Motion Controller [26]. For dynamic time warping, we used Salvador

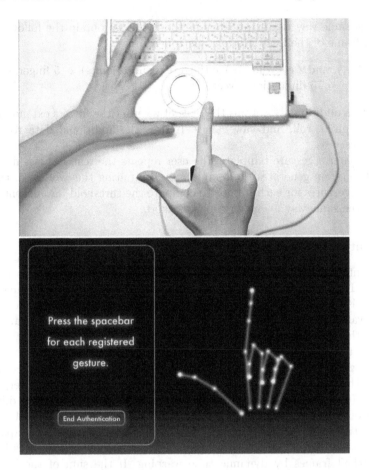

Fig. 2. Prototype system based on our hand gesture-based authentication method.

and Chan's implementation [21]. The system consists of approximately 1100 lines of code. Figure 2 shows the system that is performing the authentication of a user's gesture sequence.

5.1   Template Registration

The system first asks the user to register gesture templates. The user selects one from the 12 conditions for real gestures described in Sect. 4. The user selects four real gestures from the Japanese fingerspelling alphabets in such a way that they satisfy the selected gesture condition. We determined this number four of the real gestures, based on the preliminary experiment that we previously conducted.

In the same way as our previous method [10], we obtain the following data for each frame of the Leap Motion Controller:

(x, y, and z coordinates) × (fingertip and 4 joints) × (5 fingers)
= 75-dimensional vector.

The system additionally obtains the data of whether the fingers extend or bend, and their pitch, roll, and yaw values. It uses the additional data to identify dummy gestures.

To register a gesture template, the user repeats the real gestures five times. Then the system generates the template by computing the average of the data of the five gestures for each frame. To compute the threshold for authentication, we used the same way as our previous method.

5.2   Authentication

In authentication, the user performs dummy gestures in addition to four real gestures. To identify dummy gestures, the system records for each frame whether the hand is turned over or not and whether each finger extends or bends. It uses the roll value to judge whether the hand is turned over. It decides that a finger bends if the finger bends for 30% or more of the period of a gesture.

When the system does not regard an input gesture as a dummy, it compares the input gesture with the stored gesture templates. To handle difference in speed between the input gesture and the templates, we use our previous interpolation method [10] as well as dynamic time warping [21]. Also, we handle difference in positions between the input gesture and the templates by translating the input gesture to the initial positions of the templates. The system compares the input gesture with a template by computing the Euclidean distances between the matched frames by dynamic time warping. If the sum of the Euclidean distances is smaller than the predetermined threshold, the system accepts the input gesture.

6   Experiment

To evaluate the proposed method, we conducted an experiment. We particularly examined whether new users could perform hand gestures for authentication and whether dummy gestures could work as a countermeasure against gesture forgery.

6.1   Procedure

We recruited 12 participants who are all male and 22.0 years old on average (more specifically, one 24-year-old, one 23-year-old, seven 22-year-old, and three 21-year-old persons). We restricted them only to male to exclude the influence of the difference of hand geometry as much as possible. They all were new to hand gestures.

Table 1. Result of the questionnaire.

Question	Mean	Variance
1: Easiness of hand gesture-based authentication	2.7	1.7
2: Easiness of authentication with dummy gestures	2.9	1.7
3: Easiness of inserting dummy gestures	3.3	1.4
4: Appropriate number of dummy gestures	2.9	0.24
5: Number of dummy gestures that disabled memorizing	1.8	0.69

We asked each of them to select one from the 12 conditions. They started and finished each gesture element by extending all the fingers. They first selected four gesture elements (g_1, g_2, g_3, and g_4) from the Japanese fingerspelling alphabets, and registered a gesture template by repeating the gesture sequence five times. Then they authenticated the gesture sequence without dummy gestures five times. Next, they performed gestures by inserting two to six dummy gestures that occurred to them at that time. In addition, they watched the videos where another person was performing gestures, by which we investigated how many dummy gestures were needed to make them difficult to memorize.

After the experiment, we conducted a questionnaire. We asked them to answer the following three questions in Likert scale from 1 (very difficult) to 5 (very easy).

Question 1: Was the hand gesture-based authentication easy?
Question 2: Was the authentication with dummy gestures easy?
Question 3: Was it easy to insert dummy gestures by yourself?

We also asked them to answer the numbers of gestures for the following two questions.

Question 4: How many dummy gestures do you think are appropriate?
Question 5: How many dummy gestures disabled you from memorizing another person's gesture sequences?

6.2   Results

Table 1 shows the results of the questionnaire. The results of questions 1 and 2 indicate that the participants who were new to hand gestures were able to use our hand gesture-based authentication method. The result of question 3 indicates that it was not difficult for the participants to insert dummy gestures by themselves. According to the results of questions 4 and 5, they wanted to insert about three dummy gestures, but they were disabled by nearly two dummy gestures from memorizing gesture sequences.

Table 2 shows the result of the acceptance rates of the gestures of the participants. The rates varied according to the participants; while the rates for participant 2 were significantly low, the rates for participant 5 were comparatively high. The error rate for dummy gestures was 0.038% since 9 out of the 240 dummy gestures performed by the 12 participants were accepted.

Table 2. Acceptance rates of the gestures of the participants.

Participant	g_1 (%)	g_2 (%)	g_3 (%)	g_4 (%)	Mean (%)
1	40	60	70	70	60
2	0	0	10	20	7.5
3	0	90	70	20	45
4	30	30	10	60	33
5	90	80	70	30	68
6	40	40	60	0	35
7	30	30	100	0	40
8	100	80	60	20	65
9	30	10	40	0	20
10	20	10	30	90	38
11	0	0	70	90	40
12	20	80	30	20	38

7   Discussion

The result of question 1 indicates that the participants found it slightly difficult to perform the hand gesture-based authentication for the first time. However, as far as we observed the participants' behaviors during the experiment, they were able to perform hand gestures after practice. We think that, since the Japanese fingerspelling alphabets include hand gestures that appear in daily life, the participants were able to perform the gestures without much difficulty.

According to the result of question 2, the authentication with dummy gestures was easier than the hand gesture-based authentication. More specifically, some participants answered to question 2 that the authentication with dummy gestures was easy even if they answered to question 1 that the hand gesture-based authentication was difficult. We think that the authentication with dummy gestures is not difficult even for users who think of the hand gesture-based authentication as being difficult.

The result of question 3 indicates that the participants did not think that it was difficult to insert dummy gestures by themselves. We think that this is because of the simplicity of our method that specifies only one condition for real gestures and lets the users perform dummy gestures that do not satisfy the condition. A participant commented that it was easy to produce variations of gestures because only turning over the hand made a different gesture.

The result of question 5 indicates that inserting only 1.8 dummy gestures made it difficult for the participants to memorize entire gesture sequences. In other words, it was difficult to memorize a sequence of 5.8 gestures consisting of four real and 1.8 dummy gestures. Our experiment showed that the general capacity of 7 ± 2 of human short-term memory [16] was also true for gesture sequences. According to the result of question 4, the participants thought that adding 2.9 dummy gestures was appropriate. Therefore, we claim that performing seven gestures including three dummy gestures works as a countermeasure against gesture forgery.

As shown in Table 2, our system did not achieve high acceptance rates, compared to other related methods. There were few gestures that achieved the acceptance rates of 90% or more although it is difficult to simply compare the results because of the different gestures performed by the participants. We think that a cause for those low acceptance rates was that it was difficult for the participants to accurately perform each gesture while performing multiple gestures, compared to the case of performing only one gesture. In fact, we confirmed that the variance of the time for performing gestures in authentication was larger than that in registration, which means that the time for performing gestures in authentication largely varied.

8   Conclusions and Future Work

We proposed a hand gesture-based authentication method that incorporated dummy gestures to make forgery difficult. Although the acceptance rate of real gestures was not high, we showed that the method worked as a countermeasure against gesture forgery by incorporating 1.8 dummy gestures. Also, it effectively identified dummy gestures with the low error rate of 0.038%.

Our future work is to support an undo function; some participants commented that it was troublesome to perform gestures from the beginning when they made a single mistake while performing multiple gestures. Another future direction is to improve the acceptance rate of real gestures by using Wang and Tanaka's method [27].

Acknowledgement. This work was partly supported by JSPS KAKENHI Grant Number JP21K11836.

References

1. Ataş, M.: Hand tremor based biometric recognition using Leap Motion device. IEEE Access **5**, 23320–23326 (2017)
2. Aumi, M.T.I., Kratz, S.G.: AirAuth: evaluating in-air hand gestures for authentication. In: Proceedings of ACM MobileHCI, pp. 309–318 (2014)
3. Bača, M., Grd, P., Fotak, T.: Basic principles and trends in hand geometry and hand shape biometrics. In: New Trends and Developments in Biometrics, pp. 77–99. InTech (2012)
4. Chahar, A., Yadav, S., Nigam, I., Singh, R., Vatsa, M.: A leap password based verification system. In: Proceedings of IEEE BTAS, pp. 1–6 (2015)
5. Chan, A., Halevi, T., Memon, N.: Leap motion controller for authentication via hand geometry and gestures. In: Tryfonas, T., Askoxylakis, I. (eds.) HAS 2015. LNCS, vol. 9190, pp. 13–22. Springer, Cham (2015). https://doi.org/10.1007/978-3-319-20376-8_2

6. Clark, G.D., Lindqvist, J.: Engineering gesture-based authentication systems. IEEE Pervasive Comput. **14**(1), 18–25 (2015)
7. Fong, S., Zhuang, Y., Fister, I., Fister Jr., I.: A biometric authentication model using hand gesture images. Biomed. Eng. Online **12**(111), 1–18 (2013)
8. Guerra-Casanova, J., Sánchez-Ávila, C., Bailador, G., de Santos Sierra, A.: Authentication in mobile devices through hand gesture recognition. Int. J. Inf. Secur. **11**(2), 65–83 (2012)
9. Imura, S., Hosobe, H.: Biometric authentication using the motion of a hand (poster). In: Proceedings of ACM SUI, p. 221 (2016)
10. Imura, S., Hosobe, H.: A hand gesture-based method for biometric authentication. In: Kurosu, M. (ed.) HCI 2018. LNCS, vol. 10901, pp. 554–566. Springer, Cham (2018). https://doi.org/10.1007/978-3-319-91238-7_43
11. Jain, A.K., Ross, A., Prabhakar, S.: A prototype hand geometry-based verification system. In: Proceedings of International Conference on Audio- and Video-Based Biometric Person Authentication (AVBPA), pp. 166–171 (1999)
12. Jain, A.K., Ross, A., Prabhakar, S.: An introduction to biometric recognition. IEEE Trans. Circ. Syst. Video Technol. **14**(1), 4–20 (2004)
13. Kholmatov, A., Yanikoglu, B.: Identity authentication using improved online signature verification method. Pattern Recogn. Lett. **26**(15), 2400–2408 (2005)
14. Kim, D., et al.: Multi-touch authentication on tabletops. In: Proceedings of ACM CHI, pp. 1093–1102 (2010)
15. Mahfouza, A., Mahmouda, T.M., Eldinc, A.S.: A survey on behavioral biometric authentication on smartphones. J. Inf. Secur. Appl. **37**, 28–37 (2017)
16. Miller, G.A.: The magical number seven, plus or minus two: some limits on our capacity for processing. Psychol. Rev. **63**(2), 81–97 (1956)
17. Nigam, I., Vatsa, M., Singh, R.: Leap signature recognition using HOOF and HOT features. In: Proceedings of IEEE ICIP, pp. 5012–5016 (2014)
18. Niu, Y., Chen, H.: Gesture authentication with touch input for mobile devices. In: Prasad, R., Farkas, K., Schmidt, A.U., Lioy, A., Russello, G., Luccio, F.L. (eds.) MobiSec 2011. LNICST, vol. 94, pp. 13–24. Springer, Heidelberg (2012). https://doi.org/10.1007/978-3-642-30244-2_2
19. Ochiai, K., Kamata, K.: Description method of Japanese manual alphabet using image features. In: Proceedings of IEEE SMC, pp. 1091–1093 (1989)
20. Sae-Bae, N., Ahmed, K., Isbister, K., Memon, N.: Biometric-rich gestures: a novel approach to authentication on multi-touch devices. In: Proceedings of ACM CHI, pp. 977–986 (2012)
21. Salvador, S., Chan, P.: Toward accurate dynamic time warping in linear time and space. Intell. Data Anal. **11**(5), 561–580 (2007)
22. Saritha, L.R., Thomas, D., Mohandas, N., Ramnath, P.: Behavioral biometric authentication using Leap Motion sensor. Int. J. Latest Trends Eng. Technol. **8**(1), 643–649 (2017)
23. Shabtai, A., Fledel, Y., Kanonov, U.: Google Android: a comprehensive security assessment. IEEE Secur. Priv. **8**(2), 35–44 (2010)
24. Sherman, M., et al.: User-generated free-form gestures for authentication: security and memorability. In: Proceedings of MobiSys, pp. 176–189. ACM (2014)
25. Sun, Z., Wang, Y., Qu, G., Zhou, Z.: A 3-D hand gesture signature based biometric authentication system for smartphones. Secur. Comm. Netw. **9**(11), 1359–1373 (2016)
26. Ultraleap. Leap Motion Controller. https://www.ultraleap.com/product/leap-motion-controller/

27. Wang, X., Tanaka, J.: GesID: 3D gesture authentication based on depth camera and one-class classification. Sensors **18**(3265), 1–23 (2018)
28. Wayman, J., Jain, A., Maltoni, D., Maio, D.: An introduction to biometric authentication systems. In: Wayman, J., Jain, A., Maltoni, D., Maio, D. (eds.) Biometr. Syst., pp. 1–20. Springer, London (2005). https://doi.org/10.1007/1-84628-064-8_1
29. Wayman, J.L.: Fundamentals of biometric authentication technologies. Int. J. Image Gr. **1**(1), 93–113 (2001)
30. Wong, A.M.H., Kang, D.-K.: Stationary hand gesture authentication using edit distance on finger pointing direction interval. Sci. Prog. **2016**(7427980), 1–15 (2016)
31. Xiao, G., Milanova, M., Xie, M.: Secure behavioral biometric authentication with Leap Motion. In: Proceedings of ISDFS, pp. 112–118. IEEE (2016)
32. Yampolskiy, R.V., Govindaraju, V.: Taxonomy of behavioural biometrics. In: Behavioral Biometrics for Human Identification: Intelligent Applications, pp. 1–43. IGI Global (2009)
33. Ye, G., et al.: Cracking Android pattern lock in five attempts. In: Proceedings of NDSS. Internet Society (2017)
34. Zhao, J., Tanaka, J.: Hand gesture authentication using depth camera. In: Arai, K., Kapoor, S., Bhatia, R. (eds.) FICC 2018. AISC, vol. 887, pp. 641–654. Springer, Cham (2019). https://doi.org/10.1007/978-3-030-03405-4_45

VibroAuth: Authentication with Haptics Based Non-visual, Rearranged Keypads to Mitigate Shoulder Surfing Attacks

Manisha Varma[1], Stacey Watson[2], Liwei Chan[3], and Roshan Peiris[1(✉)]

[1] iSchool, Rochester Institute of Technology, Rochester, NY, USA
{mk2568,rxpics}@rit.edu
[2] University of Waterloo, Waterloo, Canada
stacey.watson@uwaterloo.ca
[3] National Chiao Tung University, Hsinchu, Taiwan

Abstract. PIN (Personal Identification Number) code entry is a widely used authentication method used on smartphones, ATMs, etc. However, it is typically subject to shoulder surfing attacks where, a bystander may observe the user's keypad during PIN code entry. To mitigate this issue, we present a novel method that uses non-visual keypads for entering PIN codes where, the numbers on the keypad are invisible and rearranged. The numbers are rearranged by shifting the rows/columns of the keypad and we use haptic patterns to privately convey the keypad layout information to the user. The results of our first study with 22 participants indicated that the participants could learn the haptic patterns relatively fast and use the non-visual keypads with high accuracy. Next, a security experiment with 12 participants discusses the effectiveness of our method in mitigating shoulder surfing attacks.

Keywords: Haptic · Authentication · PIN codes · Usable security · Mobile

1 Introduction

Authentication mechanisms or login methods, help users securely verify their identity and protect their private and sensitive data stored in their devices such as smart phones and laptops from unwanted access. Authentication mechanisms typically include methods such as the use of PIN (Personal Identification Numbers) codes, drawing patterns and biometrics (fingerprints, facial recognition) to lock and unlock the device and gain access to the data within [3,17]. In certain situations, these methods are also used in combination for "two-factor-authentication" where for example, a PIN code (*what a person knows*) and a fingerprint (*unique to the person*) are used as a two-step authentication mechanism [16].

PIN codes and drawing patterns methods are typically subject to *shoulder surfing attacks*, i.e., a third party may be able to obtain the entered PIN code

A. Moallem (Ed.): HCII 2022, LNCS 13333, pp. 280–303, 2022.
https://doi.org/10.1007/978-3-031-05563-8_19

Fig. 1. Shoulder surfing view of a user entering the PIN code using the VibroAuth mechanism. The numbers on the keypad are invisible and rearranged. The user determines the rearranged keypad layout by performing a *long-touch* gesture on a tile on the keypad to playback a haptic pattern that represents the number assigned to that tile. This number is used to identify the layout from the "Possible Keyboard Layouts" displayed on the top

or pattern by observing the user's device without the user's knowledge (looking over the shoulder or recording using a hidden camera) during the code entry. Biometric authentication mechanisms present a way to overcome this risk. However biometric methods too are subject to more complex modes of attacks such as replicating the biometric properties using 3D printed silicon artifacts [34]. Biometric methods presents a further danger since such biometrics of a person cannot be replaced [13,38].

From these authentication methods, PIN codes are widely adopted due to their simplicity to implement and use [9,37]. PIN codes are often used in smart phones as an alternative authentication mechanism especially during situational impairments such as sweaty fingers preventing fingerprint authentication [28] or masks preventing facial recognition authentication [12]. Therefore, due to the risk that shoulder surfing attacks present during the use of PIN codes in these situations, recent research has begun to explore novel and innovative alternative authentication methods such as gaze-based PIN code entry [20], graphical PIN code entry [10], 3D printed multi-factor authentication [27], magnetic gestural authentication [36] and haptic mechanisms [7,26,33].

In this paper, we expand this area of research by proposing a novel authentication method for smartphones that uses rearranged "non-visual" numerical keypad layouts for PIN code entry (Fig. 1). *Non-visual* denotes that the numbers on the keypad are hidden so that it is invisible for a shoulder surfing attacker. Users are presented with haptic patterns that allows them to determine the keypad layout from the several possible keypad layouts. Haptic patterns are used due to their ability to present information to the user in a "private" manner since the haptic sensation is typically felt only by the user of the device. Therefore, we present the following main contributions.

- We present a novel VibroAuth mechanism that uses dynamically arranged non-visual keypad layouts to prevent shoulder surfing attacks
- With a remote evaluation with 27 participants, we report on the users' ability to learn the haptic patterns and, evaluate seven different methods to present the dynamic keypad layouts in terms of their accuracy, time duration and qualitative feedback
- We evaluate the resilience of our method to shoulder surfing attacks with a security study with 12 participants.

2   Related Work

Recent research has considered many different approaches as alternative authentication mechanisms.

2.1   Alternative Authentication Methods

Eye gaze interactions have been widely used to provide alternative authentication mechanisms [14,20,21,41]. Kumar et al. [21] presented EyePassword, a system that allows the user to select the password or PIN code keys using eye gaze from an on screen keypad. In [14], three different eye gaze interactions methods for PIN-entry are evaluated. In addition, the authors investigate a new approach of gaze gestures and compare it to the well known classical gaze interactions. Sluganovic et al. [41] shows how the reflexive physiological behavior of human eyes can be used to build fast and reliable biometric authentication systems. This paper focuses on specific reflexive eye movements that can be actively triggered using a simple visual stimulus.

Eye gaze methods have also been used in combination with other methods as well for a multimodal approach. Here, such combinations have proven the resilience against shoulder surfing attacks since the shoulder surfer is required to observe both the eye movements of the user and the combined input technique. In [1] the authors investigate multiple authentication mechanisms that leverages gestures, eye gaze and a multimodal combination of such methods to study their resilience to shoulder surfing. [1] also experiment with fixed and randomized layouts of the keypads. In GazeTouchPIN [20], the authors propose a method where the user first touches a row that has the required digit and uses a left or right eye gaze movements to select a the correct digit.

Among other methods, in [2], the researchers introduce and propose a biometric encryption to mobile web services authentication based on iris. In MultiLock [4] researchers propose a passive, graded authentication system that allows a user to categorize applications into various security bins based on their sensitivity. As a gesture based approach, SWIPIN [45] proposes a system that allows input of traditional PINs using touch gestures such as up or down as an alternative authentication method. In addition, in [19], the authors present a waving gestures based authentication mechanism. In [27], authors have proposed 3D printed artefacts for two factor authentication. Work has also been performed to provide improved and secure authentication methods for blind users as well. In PassChords [5], the authors propose a multi touch approach while [43] proposes a mobile tactile aid based approach for eyes free interaction [44]

Besides novel code entry mechanisms for authentication, recent research has also focused on redesigning the keypads. For example, [42] and [35] have considered keyboard randomization to mitigate shoulder surfing attacks. In [35], authors explored ways to make PIN codes harder to read even if an attacker observes the entire input and output procedure of the PIN entry process.

2.2 Haptics Based Approaches

Bianchi et al., proposed a novel design for shoulder-surfing resistant authentication method based on tactile cues [6,8]. According to the research, users found it relatively easy to remember the tactile PIN codes. The future work for this research was to explore the memorability and learnability of tactile passwords. [6] presents the design and implementation of a novel input keypad which uses tactile cues as means to compose a password. In this system, passwords are encoded as a sequence of randomized vibration patterns, which makes it visually impossible for an observer to detect which items are selected. Similarly, in Vibrapass [15], the user's mobile phone directly communicates with the ATM machines. When the phone vibrates on command from the ATM, this method allows the user to enter a false character and mislead a potential shoulder surfer.

In contrast to all these methods, our approach mainly focuses on presenting a non-visual and rearranged keypad layout to the users so that a shoulder surfing attacker would not be able to identify the digits during PIN code entry. In addition, the keypad information is communicated to the user via haptic feedback mechanisms in private.

3 Threat Model

In our threat model, a user attempts to enter a PIN code on their smartphone. An observer (a shoulder surf attacker) observes them during the PIN code entry unobstructed using a camcorder. When the user senses the a the observer, they switch their PIN code entry using one of the several keyboard rearranging methods of the VibroAuth method.

4 VibroAuth Mechanism

The main concept of the VibroAuth mechanism is to present the users with a non-visual numerical keypad layout in which the numbers are rearranged according to pre-determined methods. In addition, the numbers on each tile of the keypad are invisible to ensure that a shoulder surfing attacker is unable to observe the keypad layout. The keypad layouts are determined by performing a *"long-touch"* (touch and keep touching the tile) on any key (tile) of the keypad which triggers a haptic pattern. Using this haptic pattern, the user is able to identify the number of that key, and thereby determine the correct keypad layout from a list of a possible keypad layouts. Once the keypad layout is determined, the user may follow the keypad layout and enter the relevant PIN number.

4.1   Keypad Design

The graphical representation of the keypad layout is similar to that of a slightly modified traditional numerical keypad layout as shown in Fig. 2(c): we added two extra zeros on the left and right side of the zero of a traditional numerical keypad to maintain uniform keypad layout (a tile layout of 3 columns × 4 rows). This keypad design includes two additional security measures in addition to the proposed non-visual rearranging of numbers approach. Firstly, while a shoulder surfer may still be able to identify the pattern of the user's finger movement, the design with additional zeros allows the user to potentially mislead the shoulder surfing attacker by selecting the left or the right zeros (if the PIN code contains a zero). Secondly, we removed any animations of the keypad tiles so that a shoulder surfer could find it difficult to observe when a tile was pressed. Here, an entry of a digit is only signified by the appearance of a corresponding dot on the PIN code display above the keypad (two dots just above the keypad in Fig. 1).

4.2   Presenting Rearranged Keypad Layouts

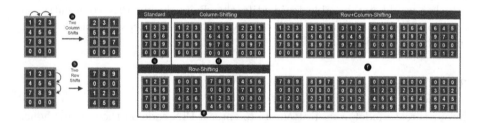

Fig. 2. (a) An example of shifting the first column by two columns shifts to the right in the column-shifting method. Subsequent columns are shifted (rotated if beyond the limit) in the same order (b) Similar example for the row-shifting method (c)–(f) All possible keyboard layouts for the row, column or row+column shifting methods. The relevant set of possible keyboards are shown to the user when entering the PIN code.

For rearranging the keypad, our main design consideration was that, the user should be able to determine the rearranged keypad with less effort and in a relatively quick manner.

To achieve this, we explore changing the keypad layout by shifting rows, columns or both. That is, the entire keypad is shifted by a random number of times in one direction using the pre-determined method (rows-shifting, column-shifting or rows+columns-shifting) starting from the traditional keypad layout (Fig. 2(a), (b)). This is done while maintaining the same tile layout and changing the invisible number assigned to each tile. For example, in the column-shifting method, the rows of the keypad are shifted by two times to the right resulting in the keypad layout depicted in Fig. 2(a). Therefore, column-shifting method provides three possible keypad layouts, row-shifting method provides four possible layouts, and row-column shifting provides twelve possible keypad layouts as shown in Fig. 2(c–f). The relevant possible keypad layouts are displayed to the user in the authentication interface (Fig. 1). The user is able to determine entire keypad layout by identifying a single digit on the keypad except, if the identified keys is a 0, the user will need to identify a second key as observed in Fig. 2 (since there are three zeros).

In addition, we introduce a *"touch-shifting"* method, in which the keypad is shifted again using the same shifting method every time the user enters a digit of the PIN code. If there is *no-touch-shifting*, the keypad layout will remain the same while entering the whole PIN code. Thus, the possible keypad layouts are the same whether using *touch-shifting* or not since they are dependent on the shifting method. For the scope of this work, we only consider *shifting* the entire set of rows/columns and not *rearranging* the rows/columns nor randomizing the number positions. This was so that the latter methods could lead to high number of possible keypad layouts increasing the time taken for authentication and adding to the cognitive loads of the user.

4.3   Haptic Patterns

We used haptic patterns to represent individual numbers so that by performing a *long-touch* gesture on any tile and feeling the haptic feedback from it, the user could determine the number assigned to it. In designing the haptic patterns, a main design consideration was to present simple and distinguishable haptic patterns that can be learned relatively fast by the user.

To achieve this we considered Morse Code to present the haptic patterns since previous research has shown that haptics can be used for learning Morse Code [40]. Morse Code presents a set of standardized combination sequences of *dot* and *dash* elements to represent characters including numbers. Dots are presented as one *time unit*, and a dash as three *time units*. In the context of this work, a time unit is the duration that a haptic vibration is presented to the user. In between two consecutive elements (dots and/or dashes), the vibration is absent for a duration of one time unit.

The Morse Code representation of numbers take a unique five-element format (five total dots and/or dashes). Here, a 0 is represented by five dashes, a 5 by five dots. Numbers 1–4 are started by the corresponding number of dots and the rest (of the five elements) are filled with dashes while numbers 6–9 are started with dashes and the rest are filled by dots as indicated in Fig. 3 (left). While Morse Code can represent the entire English alphabet and the numbers, our approach only requires the representation of the numbers 0–9. Therefore, to

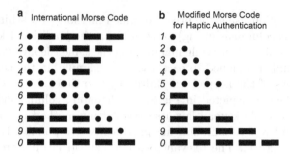

Fig. 3. Morse Code was adopted for designing the haptic vibration patterns (a) Standard Morse Code for numbers 0–9 that are used in the keypad (b) Modified Morse Code patterns for the VibroAuth method

address our design consideration to facilitate relatively fast learning, we modified the Morse Code such that the different elements at the end in the five elements of the standard Morse Code were removed resulting in the modified Morse Code patterns as shown in Fig. 3 (right). Here, while 0 and 5 remained the same, the rest included either only dots or dashes. Therefore, a user is only required to distinguish if the element of the number is a dot or a dash and subsequently count the number of elements to determine the number.

Our initial research focus is on using the VibroAuth mechanism for smartphone authentication. Therefore we utilized the vibrotactile devices of smartphones as our haptic devices. Through a brief pilot study and based on previous research [40], we set the duration of the *time-unit* as 200 ms for the haptic vibrations. Therefore, for example, actuating the number 2 in the VibroAuth approach would be presented as {vibrate (200 ms), no vibration (200 ms), vibrate (200 ms)}.

4.4   Authentication Method

The keypad is rearranged every time the user opens the PIN code entry screen. To enter a digit of the PIN code, the user essentially performs two gestures. First is a *long-touch* on any tile of the keypad which triggers the relevant haptic pattern (once the *long touch* is detected, the haptic pattern will continue to play even if the finger is removed from the tile). After identifying the number using this haptic pattern, the user may refer to the "Possible keypad Layouts" (Fig. 1) to determine the keypad layout. Once the layout is determined, the user may enter the correct digit using a *short-touch*. If the shifting-method is a *no-touch-shifting* method, the user may enter the subsequent digits using the same keypad layout. However, in the *touch-shifting* method, the user is required to repeat the above process before entering each digit.

4.5   Implementation

The implemented authentication interface is depicted in Fig. 1. Here the user sees a 3 × 4 keypad layout of tiles with the numbers invisible and a set of possible keypad layouts shown above. We used the Android[1] platform to implement the above concept on smartphone devices. Each tile is a TextView[2] that had event listeners to identify *long-touch* and *short-touch* events. The *long-touch* was implemented using Android's *setOnLongClickListener*[3] interface. With this interface, if the user touches a tile for more than 500 ms, the haptic vibration pattern is triggered. For the vibrations, we used Android's *Vibrator* class that uses the haptic vibration motor of the smartphone. The *short-touch* was implemented using Android's standard *setOnTouchListener*[4] interface.

5   Study 1: Evaluating Keypad Layout Shifting Methods

The main goal of this study was to evaluate the ability of the participants to use the different keypad layout shifting methods accurately (with the VibroAuth method) and, qualitatively assess their perceived usability and security of the proposed methods. In addition, we conducted a preliminary study to evaluate the ability of the participants to learn and recall the haptic patterns. Due to the COVID-19 situation both preliminary and the main studies were conducted in a single session in an online format.

5.1   Method

Apparatus. We designed an Android app that consists of both preliminary and main evaluations additionally with tutorials/practice screens for both. A tutorial to present and familiarize the users with the haptic patterns are shown in Fig. 4(a). Here, the participants are able to go to different numbers using the "NEXT" and "PREVIOUS" buttons. When the "VIBRATE" button is pressed, the corresponding haptic vibration pattern of that number is played. The Fig. 4(b) shows the evaluation of the haptic pattern recall ability. Here, the participant was presented with a random vibration pattern and was required to enter the corresponding number of the haptic pattern in the provided text box. The participant was able to repeat the haptic pattern if required by pressing the "VIBRATE" button. At the end of the evaluation the participant was provided with the correct answer percentage.

Figure 4(c) shows an example practice screen for practicing the row+column-shifting method. The practice screen is designed similar to the actual evaluation screen with additional options to help the participant familiarize with the shifting

---

[1] https://developer.android.com/.

[2] https://developer.android.com/reference/android/widget/TextView.

[3] https://developer.android.com/reference/android/view/View.
OnLongClickListener.

[4] https://developer.android.com/reference/android/view/View.OnClickListener.

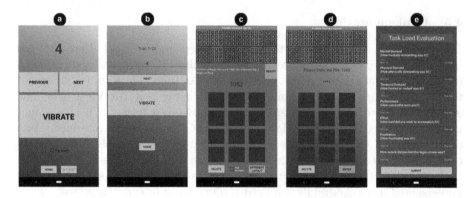

Fig. 4. Screenshots from the evaluation app (a) Example of a tutorial page to learn the haptic vibration patterns (b) Evaluation of the haptic vibration patterns (c) Practice screen for practicing PIN Code entry using the current shifting method (shows example is row+column shifting method) (d) Evaluation screen for the shifting method (e) Questionnaire screen for the qualitative evaluation after the evaluation of each shifting method

method. Here, an instruction box displays a brief description of the shifting method. The participant is free to try out haptic patterns and can enter numbers using the *long-touch* and *short-touch* gestures respectively. Any numbers that the participant enters are displayed visually above the keypad. The "See Numbers" checkbox at the bottom allows the participant to display the numbers on the keypad tiles (the participant is informed that this check box is not present in the evaluation screen). The "DIFFERENT LAYOUT" button allows the participant to change and try out different keypad layouts using the same shifting-method. The top of the screen displays "Possible Keypad Layouts" to help the participant determine the corresponding keypad layout by identifying a tile on the keypad. Once the participant is ready, clicking the "READY!" button takes them to the evaluation screen.

An example evaluation screen of the same row+column-shifting method is shown in Fig. 4(d). Here, the instruction box displays a random four-digit PIN code for the participant to enter using the current shifting method. Here too, the *long-touch* and *short-touch* gestures are used to determine the keypad layout and enter the PIN code digits (dots are shown as the digits are entered). Once the PIN code is entered, clicking the "ENTER" button will display the participant's answer and take them to a screen that displays a list of Likert scale questions (Fig. 4(e)).

For the purpose of the study, we recorded the data in a text file within the app on the participant's device. The recorded data includes: time taken to complete the tutorial and the preliminary evaluation, time taken to practice each login method, required/entered complete PIN code, and *long-touch/short-touch* details. To avoid any additional difficulty to the participant, at the end of the study, the data file was automatically attached to an email draft which the participant was prompted to send. (The email was not automatically sent and the participant was still required press "Send" to send it.)

Study Design. The preliminary study consisted of providing 20 randomly ordered haptic patterns (10 numbers repeated twice) and requiring the participant recall the corresponding number of each pattern. Each correct answer was counted as 1. The participant was required to score a minimum of 85% to move to the main study.

Table 1. Study design with two independent variables: *SHIFT* and *TOUCH*

		TOUCH	
		No-touch-shifting	Touch-shifting
3*SHIFT	Row	R	RTS
	Column	C	CTS
	Row+Colum	RC	RCTS

For the main study (evaluating the keypad layouts), we designed a within-subjects study with two independent variables (Table 1): *SHIFT* with three levels (Row-Shifting (*R*), Column-Shifting (*C*), Row+Column (*RC*)) and *TOUCH* with two levels (No-touch-shifting, Touch-shifting). In addition, a traditional keypad (Fig. 2(c)) with the numbers invisible (denoted as *NON*), was evaluated as the baseline condition for reference purposes. The dependent variables were the PIN code entry accuracy, the time taken to enter the PIN code and the qualitative feedback. The condition order was randomized for each participant. As the main task, the participant was required to enter a randomly generated four digit PIN code as accurately and fast as possible. Each condition repeated the task three times (three different randomly generated PIN codes). Therefore, each participant faced a total of 21 trials in the main study: 7 shifting-methods × 3 repetitions. The qualitative feedback was collected using the NASA TLX [18] questionnaire. In addition, this questionnaire included the question "How secure did you feel the login method was?" to measure the participants' perceived security level of each shifting-method (Fig. 4(e)).

Participants. We recruited 22 participants aged 20–29 (*M*: 23.05, *SD*: 2.42) through announcements in social media and local mailing lists (Originally we recruited 29 participants of which 5 participants' data was removed due to data collection issues and as outliers). The main selection criteria was that the participants had access to an Android phone since the app was developed only on the Android platform. Participants were rewarded with a cash payment of $15/h.

Procedure. Although we had planned for a face-to-face study, the entire study was shifted to an online format due to the COVID-19 situation. The procedures were approved by the institution's Institutional Review Board (IRB).

Once a suitable participant was recruited, the Informed Consent Form was emailed along with the study details. Participants were informed that they would be required to install an app that was developed by the authors on their phone. Once the Informed Consent was provided, the study session was conducted online on the Zoom video conferencing platform[5]. With the participant's consent, they were requested to share the screen of their smartphone during the Zoom session. At the beginning of the session, the participant was provided with a brief introduction of the research topic (shoulder surfing attacks, our approach, etc.) and a pre-study questionnaire that collected basic demographic information and information about their knowledge and understanding of shoulder surfing attacks. Next, the participant was provided with the Android Package (APK) file of the app with detailed installation instructions to install it on their own smartphones. The home screen of the app provided buttons to open the relevant screens for the preliminary study and the main study. Once the app was installed, the experimenter instructed the participant to open the haptic vibrations pattern tutorial (Fig. 4(a)).

After a brief explanation of how to operate the tutorial, the participant was allowed to take up to a maximum of 30 min to learn the haptic patterns. At any time before 30 min, the participant was allowed to start the haptic pattern recall study if they felt confident. If the participant scored less than the required 80%, they were allowed to redo the tutorial and study one more time. The 30 min and the one-time repeat limits were set due to the logistical limitations of the online study. However, all participants took a maximum of 15.4 min (M: 11.2 min, SD: 2.4) and scored above the required 80% in the first try.

After completing the preliminary study, the participant was instructed to open the main study which opens the practice screen of the shifting-method determined by the randomized condition order. Here, the participant was allowed to practice (without a time limit) to familiarize with the shifting method until they felt confident. In addition, the experimenter provided a sample PIN code for the participant to enter in order to familiarize with the method. Next, they completed the evaluation of that method (Fig. 4(d)) followed by the qualitative evaluation questionnaire (Fig. 4(e)). This process was repeated for all conditions. Upon completion of all seven conditions, the participant was prompted to send an email which had the data file of the experiment attached.

After finishing all conditions of the main experiment, the participant completed a post study questionnaire (to rate the difficulty/ease to learn/remember haptic patterns and usefulness of the "Possible Keyboard Layouts") and had a brief informal discussion with the experimenter. The whole experiment session took approximately 75–90 min.

---

[5] https://zoom.us/.

5.2   Results of Study 1

Pre-study Survey Results. The pre-study survey aimed to gain an understanding of the participants' knowledge and perceptions of the current authentication methods and their approaches to protect privacy and security. The participants used their own smartphones for the study that included different smartphone models of Samsung (9 participants), OnePlus (7 participants), Google Pixel (4 participants) and others (Motorolla, Xioami).

The survey reported that all participants had used smartphones for a minimum of 6 years (M: 8.7 SD: 2.6) and used biometric methods (fingerprint or facial recognition) as the main method to gain access to their smartphones. In addition, as the alternative/secondary authentication method, approximately 73.2% of the participants used PIN code entry, 24% used pattern unlock methods and the rest used other methods (password, iris unlock, etc.).

Next, 86% of the participants reported that they were aware of "shoulder-surfing-attacks" (this term was explained to the participants). 90% expressed that they may have been exposed to such a situation where someone has been watching their smartphones during authentication. 86% of the participants reported that they take preventive measures such as covering/hiding the screen during authentication and/or use privacy screens.

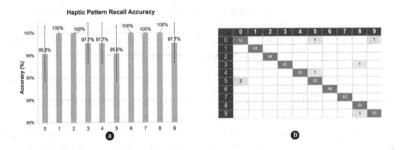

Fig. 5. Results of Preliminary Evaluation of Study 1 (a) Accuracy of recalling haptic patterns of numbers 0–9. Error bars indicate the 95% confidence interval (b) Confusion matrix for the numbers 0–9 indicated by the number of times a number was reported (44 indicates a 100% recall accuracy)

Preliminary Study Results. The results of the Preliminary Evaluation of Study 1 are shown in Fig. 5. Overall, the participants completed the preliminary study (both tutorial and the recall study) in approximately 12.3 min (SD: 2.6 min) with a maximum time of 15.4 min. The overall mean recall accuracy was 98.40% (SD: 6.1%). Here, 16 out of the 22 participants recalled the haptic patterns with a 100% accuracy. Numbers 0 & 5 had the lowest accuracy (M: 95.45%) with them being often recognized as the number each other (Fig. 5(b)).

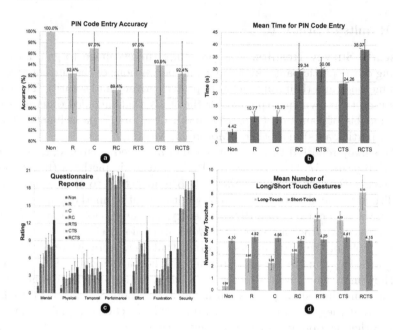

Fig. 6. Results of Main Evaluation of Study 1: (a) PIN code entry accuracy for each shifting method (b) Time taken for PIN code entry (c) Ratings for the NASA TLX & perceived security for each shifting method categorized by the questions. Error bars indicate the 95% confidence interval (Key: No-Shifting (*NON*), Row-Shifting (*R*), Column-Shifting (*C*), Row+Column (*RC*), Row-Touch-Shifting (*RTS*), Column-Touch-Shifting (*CTS*), Row+Column-Touch-Shifting (*RCTS*))

Results of the Main Study. The overall results of evaluating the authentication using different shifting-methods are shown in Fig. 6. The mean accuracy levels of entering the PIN codes using each method are shown in Fig. 6(a). The participants were able to enter the PIN codes with an overall accuracy of 94.6% (*SD*: 11.94%). The data was further analysed using 3×2 Repeated Measures ANOVA with the *SHIFT* and *TOUCH* as the independent variables (Table 1). No significant main effects were found *SHIFT* ($F(2,42) = 1.156, p = 0.324$), *TOUCH*($F(1,21) = 0.581, p = 0.451$) and *SHIFT*TOUCH* ($F(2,42) = .770, p = 0.470$).

The mean time taken to enter the PIN code using each method is shown in Fig. 6(b). The time data was further analysed using 3×2 Repeated Measures ANOVA with the *SHIFT* and *TOUCH* as the independent variables (Table 1). Sphericity violations were corrected with the Greenhouse-Geisser correction. Significant main effects were found in the *SHIFT* ($F(1.27, 26.737) = 18.994, p < .001$), and *TOUCH*($F(1,21) = 28.931, p < .001$). These main effects were not qualified by an interaction between *SHIFT*TOUCH*($F(1.31, 27.55) = 2.089, p = 0.156$).

Figure 6(c) indicates the mean ratings for each of the NASA TLX questionnaire categories (*Mental, Physical, Temporal, Performance, Effort, Frustration*)

Table 2. P values from pairwise comparisons for (a) PIN code entry time (b)-(f) qualitative ratings (Key: Row-Shifting (R), Column-Shifting (C), Row+Column-Shifting (RC), Row-Touch-Shifting (RTS), Column-Touch-Shifting (CTS), Row+Column-Touch-Shifting $(RCTS)$). $^* = p < 0.05$, $^{**} = p < 0.01$, $^{***} = p < 0.001$.

Comparison	P values							
	PIN code entry time (a)	Mental (b)	Physical (c)	Temporal (d)	Performance (e)	Effort (f)	Frustration (g)	Security (h)
R - C	1	0.719	0.887	0.189	0.447	0.195	0.792	0.758
R - RC	<.001***	0.01*	1	0.977	0.24	0.02*	0.009**	0.005**
R - RTS	<.001***	0.003**	0.092	0.337	0.553	0.005**	<.001***	0.014*
R - CTS	0.022*	0.005**	0.157	0.485	0.779	0.015*	0.032*	0.026*
R - RCTS	<.001***	<.001***	0.004**	0.67	0.67	<.001***	<.001***	<.001***
C - RC	<.001***	0.027*	0.649	0.22	0.141	0.031*	0.012*	0.001**
C - RTS	<.001***	0.002**	0.006**	0.302	0.583	0.003**	<.001***	0.002**
C - CTS	0.016*	0.002**	0.127	0.13	1	0.045*	0.011*	0.006**
C - RCTS	<.001***	<.001***	0.004**	0.231	0.291	<.001***	<.001***	<.001***
RC - RTS	1	0.19	0.021*	0.419	0.26	0.061	0.011*	0.977
RC - CTS	1	0.571	0.212	0.796	0.073	0.842	0.588	1
RC - RCTS	0.456	<.001***	0.006**	0.82	0.51	0.004**	<.001***	0.043*
RTS - CTS	1	0.613	0.749	0.243	1	0.086	0.019*	0.779
RTS - RCTS	0.579	0.002**	0.141	0.276	0.312	0.179	0.115	0.012*
CTS - RCTS	0.008**	<.001***	0.096	0.753	0.512	<.001***	0.031*	0.006**

and the perceived security (*Security*). All ratings were reported on a 21 point Likert scale as per [18]. Therefore, each category was individually analysed with a non-parametric two way Friedman's test with the *SHIFT* and *TOUCH* as the independent variables (Table 1). The analysis reported significant effects in *SHIFT* for the *Mental, Physical, Effort, Frustration* and *Security* categories. *TOUCH* reported significant effects in the same categories while no significant effects were found in *SHIFT*TOUCH* for all categories. Therefore, pairwise post hoc analyses were conducted on the *Mental, Physical, Effort, Frustration* categories using the Wilcoxon signed rank test with Bonferroni correction. The summarized p-value data are shown in Table 2 columns (b–f).

5.3   Discussion of Study 1

The preliminary study results indicated that the participants could learn the modified Morse Code based haptic patterns relatively quickly and easily. This is observed in the minimum accuracy reported at 95.5% for numbers 0&5 and the maximum time taken to complete the study at 15.4 min. Previous research that investigated learning Morse Code haptic patterns reported approximately four hours to learn the patterns [40]. However, it should be noted this study [40] was a *passive-haptic-learning* exercise where the participants learned the haptic patterns of the entire English alphabet (26 patterns) while engaged in a another task. In our study, the participants were engaged in the learning task for only the numbers 0–9 (10 patterns) through the tutorials and we shortened the haptic patterns from the original Morse Code patterns. In addition, all participants reached the minimum recall accuracy requirement of 80% in their first try (only 1 out of the 22 participants reported a below 90% recall accuracy). These observations were further reflected in the post study discussions: the participants rated the difficulty/ease of learning and remembering the haptic patterns at (M: 4.54, SD: 0.67) and (M: 4.3, SD: 0.72) respectively (1-very difficult, 5-very easy). However, in this study, these results are based on a *time unit* of 200 ms that was determined via a pilot study and previous research [40]. When asked about the vibration pattern speeds, a majority of the participants indicated that they were "fine" with the presented *time unit* while seven participants indicated that they would have preferred faster vibrations (lower *time unit*). One participant mentioned, *"The vibration patterns for numbers 1–8 were perfect. However for numbers 9 and 0 it felt as if it took a long time for the pattern to finish"*. Therefore, while the presented vibration patterns were useful in the scope of this study, further inquiry is required to find ideal timing levels. To address this, as one option, our future studies will investigate allowing the users themselves to set the *time units* based on their preference using a "slider" like interface.

In terms of the authentication interface (Fig. 4(d)), participants rated the usefulness of displaying the "Possible Keyboard Layouts" at (M: 4.8 SD:0.58) (1-extremely unuseful, 5-extremely useful). However, one participant indicated the preference for a bigger image while, two participants commented that there should be an option to hide the image so that they could use it hidden once they are more familiar with the different shifting-methods and the keypad layouts. In addition, our keypad logs indicated that as the first gesture, the participants mostly used the *long-touch* gesture either on the left top or the right top keypad tile to identify the keypad (approximately 84%). Here, the participants encountered number 0 approximately 12.2% of the time requiring an additional *long-touch* gesture to identify the keyboard. However, overall, the participants did not indicate any difficulty of having three zeros in the keypad in their feedback.

In the main study, the mean PIN code entry accuracy reported relatively high accuracy levels with the minimum (89.4%) reported for the *RC* shifting-method. Interestingly, although not statistically significant, the *touch-shifting* method of *RC* (*RCTS*) reported a higher level of mean accuracy in comparison to *RC*. In the post-study discussions, 2 participants indicated that *touch-shifting* methods required a higher level of attention to the frequent changes in the keypad layouts and therefore they were more engaged with the task minimizing errors. The NASA TLX categories also indicate this point where the *Mental* demand and the *Effort* required was higher for RCTS than RC. In addition, all participants indicated that both R and C shifting-methods were easier than the rest (besides the *NON*) while RCTS was selected as the most difficult. However, the *RCTS* was rated higher for the sense of perceived security (Fig. 6(d)-"Security") than both R and C methods. In addition, the statistically non-significant differences in the high ratings of the *Performance* category of NASA TLX indicates that the participants felt confident in their performance in using all different shifting methods.

While the participants were able to use the different shifting-methods with high accuracy, the time taken to enter a 4-digit PIN code was relatively high as well. Participants commented on this point where P26 said *"Purpose of enhanced security is fulfilled but it makes the overall process of just unlocking a phone a bit more frustrating given the case where we need to unlock our phones several times in a day"* and P6 said *"I would definitely prefer [the VibroAuth Method] to secure my complete phone, but seeing the time taken for authentication, it might be frustrating to use it every time you unlock your phone"*. This is a valid concern for authentication on a regularly used device such as a smartphone. As observed in Fig. 6(b), the mean time taken for the authentication procedure is 10 s or more (besides the NON condition). Previous research such as Gaze-TouchPIN [20] and haptics based PIN code entry methods such as Secure Haptic Keypad [6], Spinlock [7] and others [8,33] too reported approximately above 10 s for authentication. In our research, it should be noted that the lowest times reported (for accurate PIN entry) for R was 4.47 s, C was 4.25 s and RC was 6.83 s, while *touch-shifting* methods reported above 10 s with CTS reporting 9.65 s. Furthermore, there were 5 and 8 instances where the mean PIN code entry times that were less than 5 s for R and C methods respectively while, 3 instances reported less than 7 s for RC method. As discussed by authors of GazeTouchPIN, we too identify that this could be due to the novelty of an unfamiliar method to enter PIN codes. In our study, we provided sufficient time for the participant to practice the different shifting-methods and instructed them to proceed to the evaluation phase only when they are confident. However, participants spent approximately only 10 min on average on practicing a new shifting methods. As such, although the participants could enter the PIN code with a high accuracy, the longer times taken could be due to the participants' unfamiliarity of the method. Therefore, we identify the possibility that prolonged use of these methods would have resulted in faster PIN code entry times. This point could be further observed in the Fig. 6(d). Here, if a participant was fully familiar with the shifting method and used the top left/right keypad tile for the first *long-touch* gesture, the number of *long-touch* gestures required to identify the keypad layouts would be (to enter a 4 digit PIN code): 0 for Non; 1 for R and C; for RC; 4 for RTS and CTS; and 4 for $RCTS$ (if a 0 is encountered in these locations for R, RTS, RC or $RCTS$ shifting-methods an additional *long-touch* gesture is required). However, as observed in Fig. 6(d), the participants have performed few additional number of *long-touch* gestures than would have been ideally necessary. In their feedback, two participants mentioned that although they identified the keypad layout, sometimes they used a *long-touch* gesture before entering a digit to confirm their choice. Therefore, we aim to explore the prolonged use of this method in our future research.

From another perspective, as an alternative approach to address the longer PIN code entry times, P16 suggested that *"I think making it an optional login can be better because it might help us when we are out in public and can use the normal key pad login whenever we are not in public"*. Similarly, P6 mentioned *"I might use it to secure my confidential documents, banking apps etc. which*

I would not be using that frequently but I would want it to be secure". Thus, as suggested by the participants, these shifting-methods could be useful based on the context of the information being secured and their regularity of access. For example, a user may use a simpler mechanism (such as *NON*) for regular PIN code entry and more complex methods (such as R, C, RC or *touch-shifting* methods) to access seldom accessed but, more sensitive information (banking, etc.).

6   Study 2: Security Study

We conducted a separate observation attack based security study to evaluate the resilience of this method against shoulder surfing attacks. Due to the COVID-19 situation, this study too was conducted remotely on the Zoom videoconferencing platform.

6.1   Method

Participants. We recruited 12 participants (denoted as S1–S12) aged 22–32 (M: 26.91, SD: 3.03). We recruited participants who had participated in the previous study to ensure they had experience with the VibroAuth method. All participants were familiar with shoulder surfing attacks.

Fig. 7. Two videos were shown to the participants in Study 2 (a) PIN code entry using different shifting-methods (b) The entered PIN code was revealed after the participants guessed the PIN code (Close up view) (c) Results of the security study (Successful attack rates/guesses of the PIN code)

Procedure. At the beginning, the participants were re-introduced to our approach that discussed the shifting-methods, haptic patterns and the authentication procedure. To facilitate a remote study, the participants were then shown a slide deck consisting of pre-recorded videos of a user entering PIN codes using each of the different methods. Each video consisted of two clipped videos: the first showed a user entering a random PIN code (Fig. 7(a)) and the second revealed the entered PIN code (Fig. 7(b)). After the first video, the participant was required to guess the PIN code in three guesses and discuss their approach to guessing/hacking the PIN code. The participants were allowed to request to replay the video or keep/show the possible keyboard layouts if needed. The study took approximately 50–60 min to complete.

6.2   Results and Discussion of Study 2

The results are shown in Fig. 7(c). Here, most participants were able to guess the PIN codes in the *NON* condition where the keyboard layout is similar to the typical keyboard layout. Out of the rest of the shifting methods, successful attacks were reported only agains the *R* and the *C* methods with only a maximum of 8.6% success against the *C* condition.

An emerging theme in the participant feedback was that the absence of the animations made it difficult for some participants to identify the exact moment a number of the PIN code was entered. This was revealed in some of the feedback where participants mentioned that *"[NON condition] was not at all difficult, I knew which numbers were present because it was the standard layout"* while S2 mentioned *"There was no blinking or feedback [on the keypad] so it was difficult to understand"*.

As the strategy, the participants mainly followed the finger movement patterns of the user to identify the tiles which were touched to enter the digits (similar to typical shoulder surfing attacks). Based on these movements and the possible set of keypads, the participants mentioned that they could come up with a possible set of PIN code combinations to decode the entered PIN code. As observed in Fig. 7(c), this strategy was successful in the *R* and *C* methods to a certain extent. However, several participants mentioned that the absence of the keypad tile animations made identifying the key presses difficult (as motioned above). Therefore, this factor in combination with the rearranged keyboard layouts resulted in a lower rate of successful attacks against the *C* condition where, with a known finger movement pattern, three guesses would have sufficed for a successful attack (*C* condition has only three possible keyboard layouts).

While this strategy is feasible for the *R* and *C* methods, such a 'brute-force' type attack with the known possible PIN codes could be difficult for the *RC* and the *touch-shifting* methods. Here, even if the locations of each digit was seen by an attacker, *RC* method would result in 12 possible PIN codes while the number of possibilities exponentially increase for the *touch-shifting* methods: RTS: 64 ($4 \times 4 \times 4 \times 4$) possibilities, CTS: 27 ($3 \times 3 \times 3 \times 3$) possibilities, and $RCTS$: 20,736 ($12 \times 12 \times 12 \times 12$) possibilities. This is further seen in the results where the *touch-shifting* methods did not report any successful attacks. Thus, the increased number of possibilities could mean that this strategy could reach the maximum number of tries that would typically lock the smartphone semi-permanently (or even factory-reset newer smartphones) quite easily. In addition, it should be noted that our current study focused on only a 4-digit PIN code where as increasing the number of digits would increase the number of possible PIN codes for the *touch-shifting* methods significantly.

Furthermore, S5 mentioned *"The user long pressed for long enough, so I assumed it would be a 3 and followed the layout and listening to the vibrations would make it easier"*. Although their attack attempt in that instance was unsuccessful, we aim to address the observation of vibration patterns in our future research. We identify that randomizing the *time unit* values of the vibration patterns, auto-starting the vibrations of a known keypad tile and lowering vibration intensities (at random or overall to reduce vibration sounds) could potentially alleviate these observed issues.

7 Discussion, Limitations and Future Work

In summary, our user studies indicated that the users could use the VibroAuth method with relatively high accuracy (overall 95%). In addition, our second study identified that most methods were relatively resilient to shoulder surfing attacks with all *touch-shifting* methods reporting zero successful attacks and the C condition reporting the highest rate of success only at 8.6%. In contrast, we acknowledge that a main limitation of our method is that the time taken to complete an authentication procedure was relatively long. While similar haptic based PIN code entry methods [6–8,33] reported similar relatively high input times, this is possibly due to the complexity (multi-step process) of the process of the different shifting methods. In contrast, the participants felt more sense of security with the provided methods. As such, we identify potential usage scenarios for the VibroAuth method.

7.1 Potential Usage Scenarios

Based on the participant feedback, we intend to explore employing this method for situations that require varying levels of security as discussed in Sect. 5.3. In addition, using this method, the users could customize and choose the shifting methods actively based on the application (banking, etc.) or context (ex: R or C in a normal situation and select another method if the user feels a shoulder surfer is watching).

Another advantage of the VibroAuth method is that it could also be applied on devices such as the keypads of ATM machines or PIN code based door-locks where there might not be any screen based keyboards input. This method only requires a vibrotactile motor and the relevant driver circuitry as additional hardware. However, it should be noted that since many such devices may contain physical buttons, some security limitations may apply (ex. button presses may be visible).

7.2 Limitations and Future Works

There are few limitations in the current approach.

The current studies only explore the potential of *shifting* the rows and/or columns of the keypad. However, we intend to investigate few other methods to rearrange the keypads such as rotating the numbers 0–9 or randomizing the entire keypad. Both these methods could adopt the same principle and authentication method of VibroAuth. Here for example, while randomization could potentially increase the security, it could also add more task loads to the user requiring them to search for each individual key.

The current study (unintentionally) consisted of a participant demography of young adults who had used smart phones for a minimum of 6 years. Therefore, the study could not consider the potential accessibility issues of our approach. I.e., this method could have potential limitations for user groups such as older adults (complexity of the process for regular use), users that may have lower tactile sensitivity (to feel the haptic vibration patterns) or low-vision (to see the "Possible Keyboard Layouts"). Thus, a major portion of our future studies will focus on the accessibility aspects of this approach. Conversely, due to limited usability of existing authentication methods for blind users [5], we also intend to explore a variation of our approach for blind users with the use of vibrotactile feedback.

Both studies described in the paper were done in an online format due to the COVID-19 situation. Therefore, although intended, we could not conduct more "real world scenarios" as a part our studies. For example, the observed results in Study 1 could vary if the user was entering the PIN code while walking or while distracted by another task. Similarly, for Study 2, our intention was to have another participant observe a participant of Study 1 while a PIN code was being entered similar to a real shoulder surfing attack. Such real-world-like observations could provide more insights to this work.

Similarly, these studies were carried out in short-term scenarios (75–90 min) due to the same reason as above. In contrast, long-term study could provide more insights into the kinesthetic effects of the finger movements, improvements to the PIN code entry times, etc. Therefore, as a next step, this research requires a long term, in-the-wild type studies to observe such effects.

The current study only considers vibrotactile feedback as the haptic mechanism. However, the work is an aim in the direction of our 'wearable security' research direction which aims to use our wearable haptic feedback methods as such as wearable vibrotactile devices [24,25,39], thermal (haptic [11,29,31,32,46] and touch sensing [30]) and wearable soft haptic displays [22,23] due to their ability to provide private feedback suitable for haptics based authentication. As such, We believe that these explorations will potentially introduce and expand the field of haptic-based authentication methods.

In conclusion, this work presents VibroAuth, an alternative PIN code based authentication method that uses rearranged non-visual keypads for authentication. The keypads were rearranged by shifting the row and/or columns and the users are able to identify the rearranged keypad through haptic patterns. We also discuss an additional "touch-shifting" method that rearranges the keypad every time a digit of the PIN code is entered. A preliminary study revealed that the participants could learn our customized haptic patterns in a relatively fast manner. Results of Study 1 indicated that the participants could use our method system with relatively high accuracy (minimum reported accuracy was 89.4%) however, the time required was relatively high similar to previous haptics based PIN code entry methods. The second study with several participant discusses the main advantages and the resilience of our method against shoulder surfing attacks.

References

1. Abdrabou, Y., Khamis, M., Eisa, R.M., Ismail, S., Elmougy, A.: Just gaze and wave: exploring the use of gaze and gestures for shoulder-surfing resilient authentication. In: Proceedings of the 11th ACM Symposium on Eye Tracking Research & Applications, ETRA 2019. Association for Computing Machinery, New York (2019). https://doi.org/10.1145/3314111.3319837
2. Al-Hussain, A., Al-Rassan, I.: A biometric-based authentication system for web services mobile user. In: Proceedings of the 8th International Conference on Advances in Mobile Computing and Multimedia, MoMM 2010, pp. 447–452. Association for Computing Machinery, New York (2010). https://doi.org/10.1145/1971519.1971596
3. Al-Sada, M., Toyama, S., Nakajima, T.: A mobile VR input adaptation architecture. In: Proceedings of the 13th International Conference on Mobile and Ubiquitous Systems: Computing, Networking and Services, MOBIQUITOUS 2016, pp. 286–287. Association for Computing Machinery, New York (2016). https://doi.org/10.1145/2994374.3004073
4. Aras, S., Gniady, C., Venugopalan, H.: MultiLock: biometric-based graded authentication for mobile devices. In: Proceedings of the 16th EAI International Conference on Mobile and Ubiquitous Systems: Computing, Networking and Services, obiQuitous 2019, pp. 100–109. Association for Computing Machinery, New York (2019). https://doi.org/10.1145/3360774.3360781
5. Azenkot, S., Rector, K., Ladner, R., Wobbrock, J.: PassChords: secure multi-touch authentication for blind people. In: Proceedings of the 14th International ACM SIGACCESS Conference on Computers and Accessibility, ASSETS 2012, pp. 159–166. Association for Computing Machinery, New York (2012). https://doi.org/10.1145/2384916.2384945
6. Bianchi, A., Oakley, I., Kwon, D.S.: The secure haptic keypad: a tactile password system. In: Proceedings of the SIGCHI Conference on Human Factors in Computing Systems, CHI 2010, pp. 1089–1092. Association for Computing Machinery, New York (2010). https://doi.org/10.1145/1753326.1753488
7. Bianchi, A., Oakley, I., Kwon, D.S.: Spinlock: a single-cue haptic and audio PIN input technique for authentication. In: Cooper, E.W., Kryssanov, V.V., Ogawa, H., Brewster, S. (eds.) HAID 2011. LNCS, vol. 6851, pp. 81–90. Springer, Heidelberg (2011). https://doi.org/10.1007/978-3-642-22950-3_9
8. Bianchi, A., Oakley, I., Kwon, D.S.: Counting clicks and beeps: exploring numerosity based haptic and audio pin entry. Interact. Comput. **24**(5), 409–422 (2012). https://doi.org/10.1016/j.intcom.2012.06.005
9. Bonneau, J., Herley, C., van Oorschot, P.C., Stajano, F.: The quest to replace passwords: a framework for comparative evaluation of web authentication schemes. In: 2012 IEEE Symposium on Security and Privacy, pp. 553–567 (2012)
10. Bošnjak, L., Brumen, B.: Shoulder surfing: from an experimental study to a comparative framework. Int. J. Hum.-Comput. Stud. **130**, 1–20 (2019). https://doi.org/10.1016/j.ijhcs.2019.04.003, http://www.sciencedirect.com/science/article/pii/S1071581918305366
11. Chen, Z., Peiris, R.L., Minamizawa, K.: A thermal pattern design for providing dynamic thermal feedback on the face with head mounted displays. In: Proceedings of the Eleventh International Conference on Tangible, Embedded, and Embodied Interaction, TEI 2017, pp. 381–388. Association for Computing Machinery, New York (2017). https://doi.org/10.1145/3024969.3025060

12. Damer, N., Grebe, J.H., Chen, C., Boutros, F., Kirchbuchner, F., Kuijper, A.: The effect of wearing a mask on face recognition performance: an exploratory study (2020)
13. Datta, P., Bhardwaj, S., Panda, S.N., Tanwar, S., Badotra, S.: Survey of security and privacy issues on biometric system. In: Gupta, B.B., Perez, G.M., Agrawal, D.P., Gupta, D. (eds.) Handbook of Computer Networks and Cyber Security, pp. 763–776. Springer, Cham (2020). https://doi.org/10.1007/978-3-030-22277-2_30
14. De Luca, A., Weiss, R., Drewes, H.: Evaluation of eye-gaze interaction methods for security enhanced pin-entry. In: Proceedings of the 19th Australasian Conference on Computer-Human Interaction: Entertaining User Interfaces, OZCHI 2007, pp. 199–202. Association for Computing Machinery, New York (2007). https://doi.org/10.1145/1324892.1324932
15. De Luca, A., von Zezschwitz, E., Hußmann, H.: Vibrapass: secure authentication based on shared lies. In: Proceedings of the SIGCHI Conference on Human Factors in Computing Systems, CHI 2009, pp. 913–916. Association for Computing Machinery, New York (2009). https://doi.org/10.1145/1518701.1518840
16. Grassi, P.A., Fenton, J.L., Garcia, M.E.: Digital identity guidelines [including updates as of 12–01-2017]. Technical report (2017)
17. Harbach, M., De Luca, A., Egelman, S.: The anatomy of smartphone unlocking: a field study of android lock screens. In: Proceedings of the 2016 CHI Conference on Human Factors in Computing Systems, CHI 2016, pp. 4806–4817. Association for Computing Machinery, New York (2016). https://doi.org/10.1145/2858036.2858267
18. Hart, S.G., Staveland, L.E.: Development of NASA-TLX (task load index): results of empirical and theoretical research 52, 139–183 (1988). https://doi.org/10.1016/S0166-4115(08)62386-9, http://www.sciencedirect.com/science/article/pii/S0166411508623869
19. Hong, F., Wei, M., You, S., Feng, Y., Guo, Z.: Waving authentication: your smartphone authenticate you on motion gesture. In: Proceedings of the 33rd Annual ACM Conference Extended Abstracts on Human Factors in Computing Systems, CHI EA 2015, pp. 263–266. Association for Computing Machinery, New York (2015). https://doi.org/10.1145/2702613.2725444
20. Khamis, M., Hassib, M., Zezschwitz, E.V., Bulling, A., Alt, F.: GazeTouchPIN: protecting sensitive data on mobile devices using secure multimodal authentication. In: Proceedings of the 19th ACM International Conference on Multimodal Interaction, ICMI 2017, pp. 446–450. Association for Computing Machinery, New York (2017). https://doi.org/10.1145/3136755.3136809
21. Kumar, M., Garfinkel, T., Boneh, D., Winograd, T.: Reducing shoulder-surfing by using gaze-based password entry. In: Proceedings of the 3rd Symposium on Usable Privacy and Security, SOUPS 2007, pp. 13–19. Association for Computing Machinery, New York (2007). https://doi.org/10.1145/1280680.1280683
22. Kurogi, T., Yonehara, Y., Peiris, R.L., Fujiwara, T., Minamizawa, K.: Haptic plaster: soft, thin, light and flexible haptic display using DEA composed of slide-ring material for daily life. In: ACM SIGGRAPH 2019 Emerging Technologies, SIGGRAPH 2019. Association for Computing Machinery, New York (2019). https://doi.org/10.1145/3305367.3327983
23. Kurogi, T., Yonehara, Y., Sago, G., Shimada, M., Fujiwara, T., Peiris, R.L.: Small, soft, thin, lightweight and flexible tactile display enabling to provide multiple mechanical stimuli. In: Extended Abstracts of the 2020 CHI Conference on Human Factors in Computing Systems, CHI EA 2020, pp. 1–8. Association for Computing Machinery, New York (2020). https://doi.org/10.1145/3334480.3383010

24. Maeda, T., Peiris, R., Masashi, N., Tanaka, Y., Minamizawa, K.: HapticAid: wearable haptic augmentation system for enhanced, enchanted and empathised haptic experiences. In: SIGGRAPH ASIA 2016 Emerging Technologies, SA 2016. Association for Computing Machinery, New York (2016). https://doi.org/10.1145/2988240.2988253

25. Maeda, T., Peiris, R., Nakatani, M., Tanaka, Y., Minamizawa, K.: Wearable haptic augmentation system using skin vibration sensor. In: Proceedings of the 2016 Virtual Reality International Conference, VRIC 2016. Association for Computing Machinery, New York (2016). https://doi.org/10.1145/2927929.2927946

26. Malek, B., Orozco, M., El Saddik, A.: Novel shoulder-surfing resistant haptic-based graphical password. In: Proceedings of EuroHaptics, vol. 6, pp. 1–6 (2006)

27. Marky, K., Schmitz, M., Zimmermann, V., Herbers, M., Kunze, K., Mühlhäuser, M.: 3D-auth: two-factor authentication with personalized 3D-printed items. In: Proceedings of the 2020 CHI Conference on Human Factors in Computing Systems, CHI 2020, pp. 1–12. Association for Computing Machinery, New York (2020). https://doi.org/10.1145/3313831.3376189

28. Olsen, M.A., Dusio, M., Busch, C.: Fingerprint skin moisture impact on biometric performance. In: 3rd International Workshop on Biometrics and Forensics (IWBF 2015), pp. 1–6 (2015)

29. Peiris, R.L., Chan, L., Minamizawa, K.: Thermocons: evaluating the thermal haptic perception of the forehead. In: Proceedings of the 29th Annual Symposium on User Interface Software and Technology, UIST 2016 Adjunct, pp. 187–188. Association for Computing Machinery, New York (2016). https://doi.org/10.1145/2984751.2984762

30. Peiris, R.L., Nakatsu, R.: TempTouch: a novel touch sensor using temperature controllers for surface based textile displays. In: Proceedings of the 2013 ACM International Conference on Interactive Tabletops and Surfaces, ITS 2013, pp. 105–114. Association for Computing Machinery, New York (2013). https://doi.org/10.1145/2512349.2512813

31. Peiris, R.L., Peng, W., Chen, Z., Minamizawa, K.: Exploration of cuing methods for localization of spatial cues using thermal haptic feedback on the forehead. In: 2017 IEEE World Haptics Conference (WHC), pp. 400–405 (2017). https://doi.org/10.1109/WHC.2017.7989935

32. Peng, W., Peiris, R.L., Minamizawa, K.: Exploring of simulating passing through feeling on the wrist: using thermal feedback. In: Adjunct Publication of the 30th Annual ACM Symposium on User Interface Software and Technology, IST 2017, pp. 187–188. Association for Computing Machinery, New York (2017). https://doi.org/10.1145/3131785.3131819

33. Potocny, J., McNulty, S., Maiga, K., Zadeh, M.H.: On the incorporation of haptic effects in security authentication. In: 2015 IEEE International Conference on Systems, Man, and Cybernetics, pp. 469–473 (2015)

34. Ramachandra, R., et al.: Custom silicone face masks: vulnerability of commercial face recognition systems presentation attack detection. In: 2019 7th International Workshop on Biometrics and Forensics (IWBF), pp. 1–6 (2019)

35. Roth, V., Richter, K., Freidinger, R.: A pin-entry method resilient against shoulder surfing. In: Proceedings of the 11th ACM Conference on Computer and Communications Security, CCS 2004, pp. 236–245. Association for Computing Machinery, New York (2004). https://doi.org/10.1145/1030083.1030116

36. Sahami Shirazi, A., Moghadam, P., Ketabdar, H., Schmidt, A.: Assessing the vulnerability of magnetic gestural authentication to video-based shoulder surfing attacks. In: Proceedings of the SIGCHI Conference on Human Factors in Computing Systems, CHI 2012, pp. 2045–2048. Association for Computing Machinery, New York (2012). https://doi.org/10.1145/2207676.2208352

37. Salman, M., Li, Y., Wang, J.: A graphical pin entry system with shoulder surfing resistance. In: 2019 IEEE 4th International Conference on Signal and Image Processing (ICSIP), pp. 203–207 (2019)

38. Sarkar, A., Singh, B.K.: A review on performance, security and various biometric template protection schemes for biometric authentication systems. Multimed. Tools Appl. 1–56 (2020)

39. Schaack, S., Chernyshov, G., Ragozin, K., Tag, B., Peiris, R., Kunze, K.: Haptic collar: vibrotactile feedback around the neck for guidance applications. In: Proceedings of the 10th Augmented Human International Conference 2019, AH2019. Association for Computing Machinery, New York (2019). https://doi.org/10.1145/3311823.3311840

40. Seim, C., Reynolds-Haertle, S., Srinivas, S., Starner, T.: Tactile taps teach rhythmic text entry: passive haptic learning of Morse code. In: Proceedings of the 2016 ACM International Symposium on Wearable Computers, ISWC 2016, pp. 164–171. Association for Computing Machinery, New York (2016). https://doi.org/10.1145/2971763.2971768

41. Sluganovic, I., Roeschlin, M., Rasmussen, K.B., Martinovic, I.: Using reflexive eye movements for fast challenge-response authentication. In: Proceedings of the 2016 ACM SIGSAC Conference on Computer and Communications Security, CCS 2016, pp. 1056–1067. Association for Computing Machinery, New York (2016). https://doi.org/10.1145/2976749.2978311

42. Tan, D.S., Keyani, P., Czerwinski, M.: Spy-resistant keyboard: more secure password entry on public touch screen displays. In: Proceedings of the 17th Australia Conference on Computer-Human Interaction: Citizens Online: Considerations for Today and the Future, OZCHI 2005, pp. 1–10. Computer-Human Interaction Special Interest Group (CHISIG) of Australia, Narrabundah (2005)

43. Wolf, F.: Design of a tactile aid for non-observable mobile authentication to address observation attacks (2017)

44. Wolf, F., Kuber, R., Aviv, A.J.: Perceptions of mobile device authentication mechanisms by individuals who are blind. In: Proceedings of the 19th International ACM SIGACCESS Conference on Computers and Accessibility, ASSETS 2017, pp. 385–386. Association for Computing Machinery, New York (2017). https://doi.org/10.1145/3132525.3134793

45. von Zezschwitz, E., De Luca, A., Brunkow, B., Hussmann, H.: SwiPIN: fast and secure pin-entry on smartphones. In: Proceedings of the 33rd Annual ACM Conference on Human Factors in Computing Systems, CHI 2015, pp. 1403–1406. Association for Computing Machinery, New York (2015). https://doi.org/10.1145/2702123.2702212

46. Zhu, K., Perrault, S., Chen, T., Cai, S., Lalintha Peiris, R.: A sense of ice and fire: exploring thermal feedback with multiple thermoelectric-cooling elements on a smart ring. Int. J. Hum.-Comput. Stud. **130**, 234–247 (2019). https://doi.org/10.1016/j.ijhcs.2019.07.003, https://www.sciencedirect.com/science/article/pii/S1071581919300862

HCI in Cyber Defense and Protection

The Pitfalls of Evaluating Cyber Defense Techniques by an Anonymous Population

Asmaa Aljohani$^{(\boxtimes)}$ and James Jones

George Mason University, Fairfax, VA, USA
{aaljoha,jjonesu}@gmu.edu

Abstract. In this work, we report on the results of recruiting anonymous (yet qualified) participants from Prolific, a crowdsourcing platform, to engage in hacking experiments that involve defensive cyber deception. This work is part of a longitudinal study undertaken by the authors in [4] and is exploratory in nature due to the final sample size. While the sample size is small, our preliminary results revealed some consistency in the behavioral patterns (e.g., risk-seeking behavior) between our population and populations recruited through other means. We also analyzed and identified variables (e.g., prior CTF experiences, non-naivety) that could be used to qualify anonymous participants or predict participant retention in longitudinal studies. Moreover, this research provides insights into the intricacies (e.g., validity threats) of evaluating defensive techniques using an anonymous, crowdsourced population, highlighting opportunities for future research that could be a key to enriching autonomous cyber defense [32].

Keywords: Cybersecurity · Anonymous · Experiment · Deception · Crowdsourcing · CTF

1 Introduction

In the cyber world, avoiding all risks is impossible, which warrants incorporating approaches to mitigate threats or detect signs of intrusions. One such approach is cyber deception which presents attackers with a manufactured reality. The effectiveness of cyber deception has been addressed in the literature. However, the populations from which the participants were drawn, the designs, and/or the schemes of incentives employed in prior studies differ from this study. This work focuses on conducting malicious user experiments with anonymous, crowdsourced participants. Experimenting with such a population is crucial with respect to cyber defense evaluation because of the commonalities between crowdworkers and hackers. Both hackers and crowdworkers may be inclined to maximize their monetary rewards while minimizing the time and effort spent on a task [13,43]. Moreover, the majority of participants who qualified for our experiments were male and young participants, which also bears similarities to hacker populations [1]. While our sample is mainly composed of beginner hackers (aka script kiddies) and developers, an accumulation of small, discrete observations

A. Moallem (Ed.): HCII 2022, LNCS 13333, pp. 307–325, 2022.
https://doi.org/10.1007/978-3-031-05563-8_20

of hacking activities of unsophisticated hackers may uncover differences that can help inform models for more sophisticated attackers.

In previous work [4], we examined the suitability of two popular crowdsourcing platforms, Prolific and Amazon Mechanical Turk, to run hacking experiments and concluded that online recruitment for such experiments is challenging. Prolific participants, however, provided better quality data and were technically more qualified compared to MTurk participants due, in part, to the unique capabilities (e.g., a built-in custom pre-screening) provided by Prolific. As such, this paper outlines the results of running hacking experiments that involve defensive cyber deception on Prolific. The contributions of this research are as follows: (1) we analyzed and identified variables that could be used to qualify participants and predict participant success and/or retention across tasks, (2) we examined how an anonymous, crowdsourced population behaved when interacting with defensive cyber deception in light of what has already been observed in the literature, and (3) we outlined observations and gaps related to the design and execution of cyber defense evaluation studies on crowdsourcing platforms.

2 Review of Literature

2.1 Recruitment

Malicious user studies' participants are typically hired through the researcher's network, cybersecurity groups, universities, or crowdsourcing platforms. Researchers in [22] and [39] recruited professional red teamers or employees who have skills in red teaming, cyber operations, and systems administration. Other researchers recruited college students to investigate the effectiveness of cyber defensive techniques [3]. In [28,37], the authors evaluated the effectiveness of web-based deception by conducting CTF experiments in which participants were known to be familiar with IT and were part of organizations.

The researchers in [12,15,29,41] recruited anonymous participants from crowdsourcing platforms to study attackers' characteristics or behaviors. Aggarwal et al. [2] used mixed methods to recruit participants, one of which was Amazon Mechanical Turk. The recruitment procedure in [2] differed from prior studies in that the researchers screened participants based on their cybersecurity knowledge scores, as the task involved simulated hacking activities using the HackIT tool [3].

2.2 Assessing Knowledge, Skills, and Abilities

The measures used by researchers to determine if participants qualify for a certain task are typically tailored to the population from which the sample of participants is drawn. In [39], to screen participants who were known to have technical and relevant backgrounds, Shade et al. asked participants a few questions to gauge their familiarity with commands used to launch host-based attacks. Answers to the questions were collected via free-form text to assess the participants' abilities to complete a hacking task. Likewise, Ferguson-Walter et al. [22]

recruited professional red teamers who were asked to report on their areas and levels of expertise in cybersecurity. Most of the questions in Ferguson-Walter's study were self-rating.

Aggarwal et al. [2] conducted a screening test on basic cybersecurity knowledge to qualify participants recruited from multiple channels including MTurk for hacking experiments. It is unclear, however, how many MTurk participants were qualified for the experiments compared to those recruited from other channels and whether there was a difference in the knowledge score between the populations. Moreover, the researchers only assessed the participants' theoretical knowledge.

Self-rating or basic knowledge questions may be sufficient if the researcher is recruiting from a population known to be familiar with cybersecurity. However, the same approach is not suitable if the pool from which participants are drawn is anonymous. The reason is that when it comes to anonymous populations, the likelihoods of fraud and/or misunderstanding are higher. Moreover, self-rating measures may be susceptible to participants' biases and perceptions of their abilities.

To establish the foundation on which recruitment, research, or education of security professionals is based, researchers have utilized frameworks such as the National Initiative for Cybersecurity Education (NICE) Cybersecurity Workforce Framework [7,8,33]. In [7,8], Armstrong et al. explored the Knowledge, Skills, and Abilities important to perform Vulnerability Assessment and Management (VAAM) activities (e.g., penetration testing tasks) by interviewing attendees at major cybersecurity conferences (e.g., DEFCON and BlackHat). While it is crucial to pinpoint KSAs that are unique to penetration testing (hacking) tasks, with an anonymous population, these KSAs cannot be reliably assessed using self-rating scales unless mapped to knowledge and technical assessments [33] suitable for such a population.

Research studies on measuring cybersecurity knowledge and investigating how different populations with varying levels of knowledge and experiences approach cybersecurity tasks can be found in the literature focusing on usable security or threat hunting [5,9,30,34]. Ben-Asher [9], for instance, assessed theoretical and practical knowledge by gauging students and professionals' familiarity with technical terms and network security tools and by asking some general questions about security training, certification, and the amount of time spent working with security tools. Virtually no work has attempted to measure theoretical and technical security knowledge and investigate its impact on how anonymous, crowdsourced participants tackle hacking challenges. In our work, we explored ways to evaluate the knowledge and skill of an anonymous, crowd sourced population.

2.3 Web-Based Deception

The use of cyber deception to protect the web is not novel and has been evaluated by multiple researchers. Han et al. [28] evaluated the effectiveness of deception at detecting intruders but did not address how knowledge of deception may affect attackers' strategies. While the study conducted in [37] addressed how knowledge of deception could impact attackers' decision-making processes, as in [28], the population from which participants were drawn was known to be familiar with information technology. Although the researchers in [28,37] did not collect personally identifiable information, the fact that participants were part of an enterprise could have hindered the collection of sensitive information, including personality traits/cognitive biases. In a study conducted to understand cyber defense work [6], cybersecurity professionals cited lack of anonymity as a reason for not contributing to scientific studies. Armstrong et al. [6] stated that cybersecurity professionals prefer to maintain anonymity as a self-preservation measure. The platforms used in our research guarantee anonymity.

Our work also differs from previous studies in two ways. First, in [37], the researchers used a point-based system to reward participants, which might explain why 43% of the participants stated that knowing about deception did not influence their paths or attack strategies. A point-based system holds less weight compared to a monetary one. In our experiments, a monetary reward was given to participants for finding and submitting a flag. Attaching a financial incentive and/or a penalty to a hacking task can be a sufficient motivator of behavior change (i.e., increasing the tendency to behave maliciously or to carefully consider alternative paths). Second, the researchers in [37] also provided some hints to help participants complete the task, which is not reflective of a real-world hacking scenario.

3   Method

3.1   Testbed Specifications and Design

All hacking experiments were conducted on AWS EC2 instances. Because we collected participants' behavioral biometrics [31], traffic to the testbed was encrypted using an industry-standard encryption algorithm. This procedure was followed to protect participants' unique behavioral patterns. A load-balancer with sticky sessions enabled was also used in the main experiment to control participants access to the experimental conditions. The testbed was made accessible via Qualtrics and Prolific.

3.2   Participants

Recruitment. Participants were mainly recruited via Prolific [35]. However, because the number of qualified participants was small, we invited participants via the university's cybersecurity mailing list and social media to join the platform and to attempt the study. To maintain participants' anonymity and to prevent social desirability bias, direct communication with the researchers using any means that may expose personally identifiable information was discouraged. Because we invited participants from outside the platform, we modified the pre-screening requirements outlined in [4] by removing any restrictions on the number of approved tasks or the approval rate.

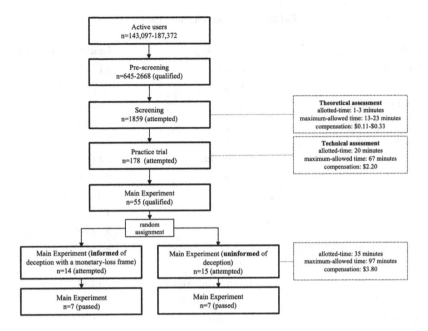

Fig. 1. Recruitment procedure on Prolific

The total number of participants who attempted the screening survey was 1859 participants, including participants from a previous study [4]. Twenty participants declined to attempt the screening survey, and 1211 participants did not have a cybersecurity background. 178 participants were invited to the practice trial (See Table 1), and 452 were excluded for either providing low-quality data/suspicious inputs or for misunderstanding the questions. We also excluded those who did not meet the criteria needed to proceed to the practice trial. The criteria were as follows: (1) a proficiency level in web security that is equal to or above basic knowledge, (2) at least, a year of experience in cybersecurity (with the exception that if a participant answered the knowledge question in a way that was indicative of a hacker's mindset, they were invited), and (3) correct answers to any of the knowledge questions. The knowledge questions were selected such that they could be answered in multiple correct ways (i.e., reflective of either a hacker's mindset or a developer's mindset). The knowledge questions consisted of simple and complex attack (filter evasion) scenarios to measure basic and advanced web-hacking knowledge. Participants who passed the practice trial, which consisted of a simple hacking challenge, were qualified for the main experiment (See Fig. 1 and refer to [4] for more details). Participants who attempted but did not pass the experiments were partially compensated based on their efforts.

Table 1. Sample characteristics

Category	Sub-categories	Count (percentage)
Gender	Female	34 (19%)
	Male	144 (81%)
Student status*	Yes	144 (81%)
	No	18 (10%)
Employment	Full-time	54 (30%)
	Part-time	29 (16%)
	Other	95 (54%)
Age	18–24	130 (73%)
	25–34	43 (24%)
	$\geq$35	5 (2%)
Years of formal/informal experience in cybersecurity	At least a year	81 (45%)
	2–4 years	84 (48%)
	5 or more years	8 (4%)
	No experience	5 (2%)
Subject	Computer Science	89 (50%)
	Computing(IT)	63 (35%)
	Engineering	26 (15%)
Number of approved tasks	0–59	72 (40%)
	$\geq$60	106 (60%)
Approval rate	Less than 95%	11 (6%)
	Greater or equal to 95%	167 (94%)
Proficiency-level in web security	Basic knowledge	33 (18%)
	Novice	78 (43%)
	Intermediate	48 (27%)
	Advanced	18 (10%)
	Expert	1 (0.5%)

* Data of sixteen participants was missing (expired).

3.3   Experiment Design

Main Experiment. All hacking experiments consisted of three parts: (1) pre-task guidelines and a questionnaire, (2) a hacking task, and (3) a post-task questionnaire. In the hacking task, participants were asked to find a vulnerability in our website and exploit it to access a flag, an HMAC of the participant's IP address. The goal of the main experiment was to observe participants' behavior across two different conditions: (1) informed about the possibility of deception with a monetary loss frame, and (2) uninformed about deception. The reason we used a monetary loss frame as opposed to a gain frame was that the framing effect is known to be more pronounced in the former (i.e., the loss frame is a stronger contributor to behaviour change [27]). In this experiment, participants were asked to complete the task individually and to keep the task confidential.

To run the experiment, participants were randomly assigned to one of two versions of the website. The only difference between the two versions was that only one website alerted participants to the possibility of deception and informed them of a possible monetary loss if they interacted with fake elements. A Web Application Firewall (WAF) module was used to log participants' interactions with deceptive elements and to cause delay or redirection. As part of the deception plan and in additional to the vulnerability used in the practice trial, we added other elements, including disallow entries in robots.txt, honey cookies, honey HTML elements, including hidden fields, commented URLs, and base64-encoded content, fake web vulnerabilities (e.g., SQL injection, directory traversal), secrets embedded in obfuscated JavaScript codes, and default usernames and passwords [24,25,28]. The fake vulnerabilities used in this experiment were classified into three categories: functional, functional but required more effort to exploit, and non-functional vulnerabilities (i.e., did not lead to any flag). Unbeknownst to participants, the vulnerabilities and monetary loss were fake.

4 Results and Analyses

4.1 Quantitative Analysis

Quantitative data analysis was performed using JASP software [40].

Predictors of Success in the Practice Trial. To determine if there was a difference between participants whose answers were reflective of an adversarial mindset (the knowledge score was coded as 1) and those who provided neutral answers (the knowledge score was coded as 0), we invited participants from both groups to attempt the practice trial. Participants' status in the practice trial was coded as 1 (approved) if they passed or 0 (not approved) if they failed. We also investigated if a participant's reported proficiency-level in web security or prior participation in capture-the-flag competitions could predict the participant's status in the practice trial.

No significant association was found between the way a participant answered the knowledge questions, participant's self-reported proficiency-level, or years of experience in cybersecurity and the participant's status in the practice trial (Refer to Table 2). We speculate that because there was no timing restriction placed on the knowledge section, some participants might have used outside resources to look up answers to the knowledge questions. However, participants who attempted the task took on average 4 min to submit the survey, which was slightly higher than the allotted time (3 min). As for the proficiency-scale, our finding confirms that self-rating scales are insufficient to assess participants' expertise because they can be influenced by participants' own biases and self-perceptions [19]. A significant relationship was found between the participants' self-reported answers on whether they had participated in capture-the-flag competitions and their status in the practice trial.

Table 2. Summary of test statistics - predictors of success in the practice trial

Variable	Test	Value	df	p
Knowledge score	X^2	1.197	1	.274
Proficiency-level in web security	Mann-Whitney	2977	–	.176
Years of experience in cybersecurity	Mann-Whitney	3233	–	.600
Participation in CTF competitions	X^2	5.964	1	.015
Participation in bug bounty programs	X^2	0.636	1	.425
Total number of participants	178			

Predictors of Success in the Main Experiment. A total number of 55 participants were qualified for the main experiment based on the theoretical and technical assessments detailed in [4]. We examined if participants' own classification of the hacking challenge and their performance in the practice trial, measured by the time spent until the flag was found (See Fig. 2), could predict their success in the main experiment. We found that participants' own classification of the difficulty level of the practice trial (e.g., easy, medium) to be not significantly associated with success in the main experiment (p = .306, a Fisher's exact test). Likewise, task performance in the practice trial was not a reliable predictor of success in the main experiment (OR = 1.001, p = 0.260). The conditions (informed/uninformed) to which participants were assigned were excluded from the logistic regression model, as no significant association was found between the groups and success in the main experiment.

Experience, Success, and Retention. We sought to investigate if the total number of tasks completed by participants could be used to predict if they were likely to return and complete subsequent experiments. Palan and Schitter [35] set the threshold that divides the Prolific population into experienced and inexperienced to 60 submitted tasks. The initial finding of their study was that participants with 60 or more previous submissions were more likely to return to subsequent studies. We used the same threshold to investigate if there is any association between the number of submitted tasks and participant retention across tasks. We analyzed the associations by considering only those who successfully completed the practice trial and the main experiment. The rationale behind this decision was that experienced participants might be more likely to persist and thus succeed. We found a significant association between the number of submitted tasks and success in the practice trial ($X^2(1, 178) = 4.263$, p = .039). No significant association with success in the main experiment was found ($X^2(1, 55) = 0.773$, p = .379). However, we found a significant association between the number of previously submitted tasks and whether a participant attempted the main experiment ($X^2(1, 55) = 6.490$, p = .011)—regardless of whether they succeeded or not. This indicates that the number of previous submissions may serve as a reliable indicator of participant retention in longitudinal studies.

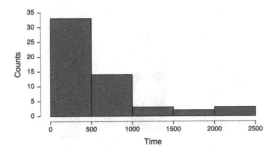

Fig. 2. Total time spent (sec) until the flag was found in the practice trial.

4.2 Qualitative Analysis

The main experiment was originally conducted to uncover any association between the conditions participants were randomly assigned to and the selected path to the flag (i.e., the selected vulnerability). More specifically, we were interested in understanding how the placement and type of vulnerabilities influence a hacker's decision, when correlated with factors such as the experimental conditions, personality traits, and cognitive biases, among other factors. However, because the number of participants who attempted the main experiment was insufficient to produce statistically significant findings, we only reported participants' comments on the hacking tasks along with our observations. The total number of participants who returned to the main experiment was 39 out of 55. Two participants declined to complete the task individually. Four participants returned the task. Thirty-two participants attempted the hacking challenge. Two participants were excluded from subsequent analyses because they were part of a pre-test. Outliers were also excluded from the analyses.

In the framing condition, the average time fourteen participants spent searching for vulnerabilities—regardless of whether a vulnerability was found or not—was ~34 min, and the average number of HTTP requests, including requests to non-functional URLs, made was 65 requests. In the no-framing condition, the average time fifteen participants spent searching for vulnerabilities was ~28 minutes (See Fig. 3), and the average number of HTTP requests made was 49 requests.

Results from controlled experiments conducted to evaluate network and host-based deception showed that participants, in the presence of deception—whether informed of it or not—took on average more time than those in the uninformed or no deception conditions [23,39]. Since the populations in prior studies were known to be familiar with IT or security and the experiments were conducted onsite, our goal was to investigate if the same could be observed in an anonymous qualified population recruited online. Moreover, while Ferguson-Walker et al. [22] offered compensation to participants, the compensation was not tied to task outcome, as was the case in our study. We found the average time taken by those in the informed condition to be higher than that of those in the uniformed condition, which is consistent with Ferguson-Walker et al.' findings [23].

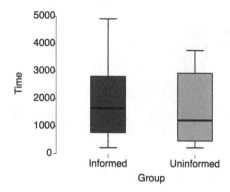

Fig. 3. Time spent (sec) searching for vulnerabilities by the informed and uninformed groups.

Task completion times on crowdsourcing platforms typically deviate from the normality assumption as noted in [30] and observed in our study. Moreover, given that the sample size of each group was small, we ran the Mann-Whitney U test and found the difference between the two groups to be statistically insignificant (p = .621). Although the average number of vulnerabilities, including functional and non-functional vulnerabilities, triggered by the informed group was larger than that of the uninformed group as found in [23], no significant difference was found. Besides the small sample size, other probable explanations for such results are discussed in the following subsections.

Uninformed of Deception. In this condition, three out of seven participants reported that they were uncertain about the path that led them to the flag. One reason was the number of possible paths that one could traverse. Unlike the previous study [4], in which the website consisted of a single login page, the attack surface in this study was larger. As such, a feeling of being overwhelmed was expressed by participants, *"I was overwhelmed by all the possible places to hide the flag. I hate time limits a LOT"* (P2).

Because there was no penalty associated with triggering vulnerabilities under this condition, a typical approach a participant would follow is to traverse every possible path until success is achieved, starting with the most familiar path (e.g., an HTML source code as in the practice trial). A participant reported, *"The vulnerability was due to the fact that the "Restricted area" link was commented, but the server-side action invoked by the link still existed on the server. I could not know in advance whether the server-side action was still enabled or not, that's why I was uncertain about my approach and trying was the only way to find out if I was right"* (P3). Another participant followed the same approach, *"I tried many false leads, some very promising - like a commented username and password, or a hidden field"* (P4).

The allotted time can be a tell-tale sign as to the challenge complexity and thus can become a confounding factor that influences participants' selection of vulnerabilities. In our experiments, participants considered the time limit as a determinant of task complexity, irrespective of the fact that the platform allowed them to complete the task in a much longer time. One participant stated, *"Since the time restriction was 35 min, I was certain, that the answer was hidden in some html comment"* (P5). While such a choice might have also been influenced by past experiences, it does show the influence of the allotted time on path selection, which may pose a significant ecological validity threat. It is important to note that on Prolific the amount of compensation a participant may receive— a minimum of \$6.50/h—is proportionate to the task completion time sets by the researcher, making it expensive to adjust the time if the researcher desires to limit or eliminate its effect on path selection.

Informed of the Possibility of Deception (a Monetary-Loss Frame). Participants in this group were presented with the following alert: *Caution: the website may contain fake vulnerabilities. If you triggered/interacted with a fake vulnerability, you risk losing up to 50% of your original reward.*

In this condition, all participants reported that they were uncertain about the path that led them to the flag. Frustration was also expressed, given the imposed time limit and the penalty associated with making wrong choices, *"No path ever guarentees a flag"* (P9).

Humans are boundedly rational, meaning their choices can be influenced by cognitive biases and heuristics. According to the Instance-Based Learning theory (IBL) [13,14], cognitive biases can lead to an irrational decision that is mostly influenced by past experiences. This theory might explain why participants took paths that they have had success with in the past while ignoring the substantial penalty associated with tripping over a fake element. For instance, a participant stated, *"I started to check website code and found/share.php. Don't know though if it is fake or real. Found username DeveloperQ and perhaps password which is Color9841#. It did not work though"* (P10). Another participant commented, *"I was checking the HTML Code of every subpage. I found commented a href on forgot password page which went to share.php page with a code"*. While such behavior can also be explained by the fact that participants were mostly beginners in web hacking, this pattern of behavior was repeated even though participants' responses indicated their familiarly with other sources of vulnerabilities *"Because when exploring web vulnerabilities there could exist several vulnerabilities, cookies, source code... But luckly it was in the source code"* (P13).

Moreover, studies have shown that in the presence of a time limit participants who were exposed to a loss-frame condition were more likely to exhibit risk-seeking behavior [27], as observed under this condition. This behavior is evidenced in the large number of vulnerabilities triggered by the informed group as compared to the uniformed one (See Fig. 4), which is also consistent with findings from [14,23]. Although our study design differs in some aspects (e.g., number of rounds), Cranford et al. [14] found that when monitoring probabilities were made available to participants, participants attacked more often, especially in later stages of the game.

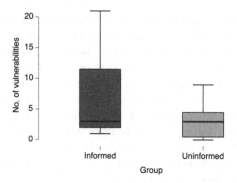

Fig. 4. Number of vulnerabilities triggered by the informed and uninformed groups.

We also suspect that some participants might have been less concerned about the penalty because the amount of compensation cannot be changed once the task is published. While it can be prorated if it falls below the minimum payment required, the amount of compensation cannot be deducted unless a special arrangement is made and agreed upon between the researcher and the participant. On Prolific, for instance, the researcher may ask the participant to return the task, after which the researcher could use the bonus payment feature to partially compensate the participant. While we informed participants of the possibility of deduction in the consent form, we found it necessary to be explicit about how the deduction will be processed.

5 Discussion

5.1 Lack of Validated Measures

One major hurdle in recruiting anonymous participants from crowdsourcing platforms is the lack of validated measures to accurately assess participants' skills and expertise in cybersecurity while weeding out fraudsters and minimizing the time needed to run studies. Moreover, the chance of participants misunderstanding research questions is higher on these platforms [17].

Validated psychometric tests or screening measures are typically developed by comparing inputs from experts with inputs from nonexperts as in [16]. There have been a few attempts to create psychometric tests to assess coding knowledge and expertise in software engineering [10,21]. One recent effort was made to develop and validate a 15-item psychometric self-efficacy scale to measure improvements in secure software development skills [42]. This scale is limited in that it relies on self-evaluation and was evaluated using data obtained partly from anonymous populations. Danilova et al. [16] developed and validated screening questions tailored towards crowd-sourced, anonymous developers to assess basic programming knowledge. Even though the authors in [16] did not assess security knowledge, the lessons drawn from their experiments may inform the design and validation of appropriate security assessment measures.

Lack of validated assessment measures leads to a considerably long recruitment time, as experienced in this study. To minimize the time and effort needed to construct, test, and validate a measure while increasing the credibility of research findings, it is generally recommended to use existing and already validated measures whenever possible [36]. In our study, we used theoretical and technical assessments to qualify anonymous participants. However, only a few variables, e.g., capture-the-flag experiences and participant non-naivety, predicted success and/or retention across tasks, emphasizing the need to develop and validate measures to properly qualify anonymous populations for hacking tasks.

5.2 Security Students vs Security Professionals

To investigate the external validity of research studies, researchers have attempted to compare the performance of professional and student populations. In the context of defensive cybersecurity, few studies on threat identification and vulnerability assessment compared students with professionals. Outcomes of such studies were conflicted but inconclusive. In a study aimed to analyze the impact of professional expertise on the accuracy of assessing vulnerabilities according to the Common Vulnerability Scoring System (CVSS), Allodi et al. [5] found no distinction between experienced security professionals and security students with respect to assessment accuracy. On the other hand, researchers in [9] found a difference between novices and experts based on responses to a security expertise questionnaire designed to investigate if knowledge of security led to a better detection of intrusion attempts. The authors stated that practical knowledge and expertise may improve threat detection performance, albeit based on the attack scenarios. Likewise, in usable security studies, Naiakshina et al. [34] performed direct comparisons between CS students, freelancers, and professional developers and concluded that findings from these comparisons, while informative, may not be definitive. More specifically, Naiakshina et al. [34] stated that differences between populations can be attributed to the context of comparison.

In our work, the majority of participants were identified as students. While there have been studies that involve security professionals performing hacking activities, a direct comparison between this study and what has already been reported in the literature cannot be made due to the differences in the studies' objectives and designs. How security professionals and students compare when performing offensive cybersecurity tasks remains an open question.

5.3 Data and Naivety of Crowdworkers

One major validity threat is the self-reported data. Although we excluded responses that we found suspicious or inconsistent, the exclusion process was subjective. While we mentioned in [4] that the built-in pre-screening can minimize response bias, self-reported data obtained using the custom pre-screening feature must also be scrutinized. We advise researchers, especially when conducting longitudinal studies, to collect and compare such data at different times to track inconsistencies (or regular changes). It is important to mention that while the platform encourages participants to keep their data up to date, there remains the possibility that a participant may choose not to, resulting in missing data.

Participant naivety (or non-naivety), measured by the number of previous submissions, can affect participants' engagement with a study. We noticed participants with a few or no approved task(s) were more likely to abandon the study if it was challenging. On the other hand, experienced participants who were more familiar with the platform's features (e.g., the maximum allowed time) were more likely to persist. Time limits can also influence how participants approach the task. For an experienced participant, a shorter task completion time may increase their tendency to traverse a familiar path as observed in our experiment. For a novice participant, a short time limit can cause stress, while a long time limit can result in an overestimation of task complexity. Both cases may lead to selective attrition or harm the validity of research results. For instance, any emotional response (e.g., frustration) a researcher may be interested in triggering and monitoring could thus be attributed not to the defensive technique but rather to external factors like the imposed time limit.

5.4 Maliciousness

Maliciousness is an attribute that is hard to investigate by interviewing professional hackers or observing real-world hackers, emphasizing the need for novel and feasible approaches to study its role in attackers' decisions. Multiple studies have addressed maliciousness [26] or identified the characteristics/motivations of individuals who are likely to behave maliciously on crowdsourcing platforms [18,38]. Schild et al. [38] studied maliciousness using cheating paradigms (e.g., the coin flip and Mind Game paradigms) and found that the approval rate and age or gender could be used as indicators of maliciousness. Schild et al. stated that young or male participants with low approval rates were more likely to behave maliciously. While there is a potential to investigate the role maliciousness (e.g., violating the rules) plays in attackers' decision-making, we found that relying on the aforementioned factors is limiting. Based on our experiments and with a 95% approval rate as the threshold [38], the percentage of qualified participants who had low approval rates was approximately 6%, which was not enough to make a strong inference. The percentage was much smaller when a 90% approval rate was considered as the threshold [20] to determine participants' characteristics (e.g., honesty). Based on our observations, we found low approval rates to be linked to poor performance as opposed to dishonesty. Given that our sample was skewed towards young and male participants, characteristics representative of hacker populations, other methods [11] may bear fruit when it comes to investigating how malicious attackers interact with deception and to establishing ground-truth data on malicious behavior.

5.5   Inviting Outsiders

Due to the small number of qualified participants, we reached out to security students outside the platform to join in and attempt the tasks. However, we could not reach the target sample size necessary for making robust conclusions. Reasons included the fact that participants were required to register and complete tasks irrelevant to the study and the lack of hands-on experience in offensive security. For instance, some participants stated they were more familiar with defensive cybersecurity (e.g., blue-team activities as opposed to red-team activities). The naivety of newly enrolled participants was also a factor in attrition among this population (discussed in Sect. 5.3).

6   Conclusion and Future Work

Testing the effectiveness of deceptive techniques is vital because they target characteristics (e.g., cognitive biases) that are less likely to change overnight compared to the ever-changing technical landscape. In this research, we analyzed a set of theoretical and technical assessment methods and identified variables that could be used to qualify or predict retention among anonymous participants. While it was shown that retention could be predicted simply by the number of tasks previously submitted by participants, qualifying anonymous participants for hacking tasks requires further research and refinement. Moreover, although we found some consistency in the behavioral patterns (e.g., the average task completion time) between our population and professional/unqualified populations involved in defensive cyber deception tasks, one should be cognizant of the confounding factors (e.g., time limits) that may have equally contributed to such behaviors. Identical behaviors (e.g., traversing familiar paths) and emotional responses (e.g., frustration) were also observed in both groups, which could be attributed to multiple factors, including the deceptive elements used. It should be noted that some of the confounders are features of the platform over which the researchers may have limited control. To conclude, future research in areas related to the evaluation of cyber defensive techniques by anonymous populations should include:

- developing and validating psychometric tests by utilizing frameworks such as the NICE Cybersecurity Workforce Framework. The study conducted by Armstrong et al. [7], which identified competencies required for penetration testing activities, may serve as a starting point.
- comparing how anonymous, professional, and student populations approach offensive tasks under similar settings.
- performing a systematic and statistical evaluation of confounding factors on crowdsourcing platforms in the context of defensive cyber deception.

Acknowledgment. We thank the participants who contributed to this study.

Ethics Statement. This study was carried out under the approval of George Mason University's Institutional Review Board. All participants gave their consent at each stage of the study. The protocol followed in this study was approved by George Mason University's IRB approval number: #1674586-3.

References

1. The 2020 Hacker Report. Technical report, HackerOne (2020)
2. Aggarwal, P., Du, Y., Singh, K., Gonzalez, C.: Decoys in cybersecurity: an exploratory study to test the effectiveness of 2-sided deception. arXiv:2108.11037 [cs], August 2021
3. Aggarwal, P., Gonzalez, C., Dutt, V.: HackIt: a real-time simulation tool for studying real-world cyberattacks in the laboratory. In: Gupta, B.B., Perez, G.M., Agrawal, D.P., Gupta, D. (eds.) Handbook of Computer Networks and Cyber Security, pp. 949–959. Springer, Cham (2020). https://doi.org/10.1007/978-3-030-22277-2_39
4. Aljohani, A., Jones, J.: Conducting malicious cybersecurity experiments on crowd-sourcing platforms. In: The 2021 3rd International Conference on Big Data Engineering (BDE 2021), p. 12. ACM (2021)
5. Allodi, L., Cremonini, M., Massacci, F., Shim, W.: Measuring the accuracy of software vulnerability assessments: experiments with students and professionals. Empir. Softw. Eng. **25**(2), 1063–1094 (2020). https://doi.org/10.1007/s10664-019-09797-4
6. Armstrong, M.E., Jones, K.S., Namin, A.S.: Framework for developing a brief interview to understand cyber defense work: an experience report. In: Proceedings of the Human Factors and Ergonomics Society Annual Meeting, vol. 61, no. 1, pp. 1318–1322 (2017). https://doi.org/10.1177/1541931213601812
7. Armstrong, M.E., Jones, K.S., Namin, A.S., Newton, D.C.: The knowledge, skills, and abilities used by penetration testers: results of interviews with cybersecurity professionals in vulnerability assessment and management. In: Proceedings of the Human Factors and Ergonomics Society Annual Meeting, vol. 62, no. 1, pp. 709–713 (2018). https://doi.org/10.1177/1541931218621161
8. Armstrong, M.E., Jones, K.S., Namin, A.S., Newton, D.C.: Knowledge, skills, and abilities for specialized curricula in cyber defense: results from interviews with cyber professionals. ACM Trans. Comput. Educ. **20**(4), 1–25 (2020). https://doi.org/10.1145/3421254
9. Ben-Asher, N., Gonzalez, C.: Effects of cyber security knowledge on attack detection. Comput. Hum. Behav. **48**, 51–61 (2015). https://doi.org/10.1016/j.chb.2015.01.039
10. Bergersen, G.R., Sjoberg, D.I., Dyba, T.: Construction and validation of an instrument for measuring programming skill. IEEE Trans. Softw. Eng. **40**(12), 1163–1184 (2014). https://doi.org/10.1109/TSE.2014.2348997
11. Chen, P., Sun, H., Fang, Y., Liu, X.: CONAN: a framework for detecting and handling collusion in crowdsourcing. Inf. Sci. **515**, 44–63 (2020). https://doi.org/10.1016/j.ins.2019.12.012

12. Cranford, E., Gonzalez, C., Aggarwal, P., Cooney, S., Tambe, M., Lebiere, C.: Adaptive cyber deception: cognitively informed signaling for cyber defense (2020). https://doi.org/10.24251/HICSS.2020.232

13. Cranford, E.A., Gonzalez, C., Aggarwal, P., Tambe, M., Cooney, S., Lebiere, C.: Towards a cognitive theory of cyber deception. Cogn. Scie. **45**(7) (2021). https://doi.org/10.1111/cogs.13013

14. Cranford, E.A., Gonzalez, C., Aggarwal, P., Tambe, M., Lebiere, C.: What attackers know and what they have to lose: framing effects on cyber-attacker decision making. In: 64th Human Factors and Ergonomics Society (HFES) Annual Conference, p. 5 (2020)

15. Curtis, S.R., et al.: The Dark Triad and strategic resource control in a competitive computer game. Pers. Individ. Differ. **168**, 110343 (2021). https://doi.org/10.1016/j.paid.2020.110343

16. Danilova, A., Naiakshina, A., Horstmann, S., Smith, M.: Do you really code? Designing and evaluating screening questions for online surveys with programmers. In: 2021 IEEE/ACM 43rd International Conference on Software Engineering (ICSE), pp. 537–548. IEEE, Madrid, May 2021. https://doi.org/10.1109/ICSE43902.2021.00057

17. Danilova, A., Naiakshina, A., Smith, M.: One size does not fit all: a grounded theory and online survey study of developer preferences for security warning types. In: Proceedings of the ACM/IEEE 42nd International Conference on Software Engineering, pp. 136–148. ACM, Seoul, June 2020. https://doi.org/10.1145/3377811.3380387

18. Dickinson, D.L., McEvoy, D.M.: Further from the truth: the impact of moving from in-person to online settings on dishonest behavior. J. Behav. Exp. Econ. **90**, 101649 (2021)

19. Dunning, D.: The Dunning-Kruger effect. In: Advances in Experimental Social Psychology, vol. 44, pp. 247–296. Elsevier (2011)

20. Ensor, T.M., Surprenant, A.M., Neath, I.: Increasing word distinctiveness eliminates the picture superiority effect in recognition: evidence for the physical-distinctiveness account. Mem. Cogn. **47**(1), 182–193 (2018). https://doi.org/10.3758/s13421-018-0858-9

21. Feigenspan, J., Kastner, C., Liebig, J., Apel, S., Hanenberg, S.: Measuring programming experience. In: 2012 20th IEEE International Conference on Program Comprehension (ICPC), pp. 73–82. IEEE, Passau, June 2012. https://doi.org/10.1109/ICPC.2012.6240511

22. Ferguson-Walter, K., et al.: The Tularosa study: an experimental design and implementation to quantify the effectiveness of cyber deception (2019). https://doi.org/10.24251/HICSS.2019.874

23. Ferguson-Walter, K.J., Major, M.M., Johnson, C.K., Muhleman, D.H.: Examining the efficacy of decoy-based and psychological cyber deception. In: 30th USENIX Security Symposium, p. 18. USENIX Association (2021)

24. Fraunholz, D., Reti, D., Duque Anton, S., Schotten, H.D.: Cloxy: a context-aware deception-as-a-service reverse proxy for web services. In: Proceedings of the 5th ACM Workshop on Moving Target Defense, pp. 40–47. ACM, Toronto, January 2018. https://doi.org/10.1145/3268966.3268973

25. Fraunholz, D., Schotten, H.D.: Defending web servers with feints, distraction and obfuscation. In: 2018 International Conference on Computing, Networking and Communications (ICNC), pp. 21–25. IEEE, Maui, March 2018. https://doi.org/10.1109/ICCNC.2018.8390365

26. Gadiraju, U., Kawase, R., Dietze, S., Demartini, G.: Understanding malicious behavior in crowdsourcing platforms: the case of online surveys. In: Proceedings of the 33rd Annual ACM Conference on Human Factors in Computing Systems - CHI 2015, pp. 1631–1640. ACM Press, Seoul (2015). https://doi.org/10.1145/2702123.2702443

27. Guo, L., Trueblood, J.S., Diederich, A.: Thinking fast increases framing effects in risky decision making. Psychol. Sci. **28**(4), 530–543 (2017). https://doi.org/10.1177/0956797616689092

28. Han, X., Kheir, N., Balzarotti, D.: Evaluation of deception-based web attacks detection. In: Proceedings of the 2017 Workshop on Moving Target Defense - MTD 2017, pp. 65–73. ACM Press, Dallas (2017). https://doi.org/10.1145/3140549.3140555

29. Katakwar, H., Aggarwal, P., Maqbool, Z., Dutt, V.: Influence of network size on adversarial decisions in a deception game involving honeypots. Front. Psychol. **11**, 535803 (2020). https://doi.org/10.3389/fpsyg.2020.535803

30. Layman, L., Diffo, S.D., Zazworka, N.: Human factors in webserver log file analysis: a controlled experiment on investigating malicious activity. In: Proceedings of the 2014 Symposium and Bootcamp on the Science of Security - HotSoS 2014, pp. 1–11. ACM Press, Raleigh (2014). https://doi.org/10.1145/2600176.2600185

31. Leiva, L.A., Vivó, R.: Web browsing behavior analysis and interactive hypervideo. ACM Trans. Web **7**(4), 1–28 (2013). https://doi.org/10.1145/2529995.2529996

32. Major, M.M., Souza, B.J., DiVita, J., Ferguson-Walter, K.J.: Informing autonomous deception systems with cyber expert performance data, p. 11, August 2021. http://arxiv.org/abs/2109.00066

33. Mäses, S., Maennel, O., Sütterlin, S.: Using competency mapping for skills assessment in an introductory cybersecurity course. In: Auer, M.E., Rüütmann, T. (eds.) ICL 2020. AISC, vol. 1329, pp. 572–583. Springer, Cham (2021). https://doi.org/10.1007/978-3-030-68201-9_56

34. Naiakshina, A., Danilova, A., Gerlitz, E., Smith, M.: On conducting security developer studies with CS students: examining a password-storage study with CS students, freelancers, and company developers. In: Proceedings of the 2020 CHI Conference on Human Factors in Computing Systems, pp. 1–13. ACM, Honolulu, April 2020. https://doi.org/10.1145/3313831.3376791

35. Palan, S., Schitter, C.: Prolific.ac-a subject pool for online experiments. J. Behav. Exp. Financ. **17**, 22–27 (2018). https://doi.org/10.1016/j.jbef.2017.12.004

36. Redmiles, E.M., Acar, Y., Fahl, S., Mazurek, M.L.: A Summary of survey methodology best practices for security and privacy researchers. Technical report (2017). https://drum.lib.umd.edu/bitstream/handle/1903/19227/CS-TR-5055.pdf

37. Sahin, M., Hebert, C., De Oliveira, A.S.: Lessons learned from SunDEW: a self defense environment for web applications. In: Proceedings 2020 Workshop on Measurements, Attacks, and Defenses for the Web. Internet Society, San Diego (2020). https://doi.org/10.14722/madweb.2020.23005

38. Schild, C., Lilleholt, L., Zettler, I.: Behavior in cheating paradigms is linked to overall approval rates of crowdworkers. J. Behav. Decis. Making **34**(2), 157–166 (2021). https://doi.org/10.1002/bdm.2195

39. Shade, T., Rogers, A., Ferguson-Walter, K., Elsen, S.B., Fayette, D., Heckman, K.: The moonraker study: an experimental evaluation of host-based deception (2020). https://doi.org/10.24251/HICSS.2020.231

40. Team, J.: JASP (Version 0.14.1) [Computer software] (2020). https://jasp-stats.org/

41. Veksler, V.D., Buchler, N., LaFleur, C.G., Yu, M.S., Lebiere, C., Gonzalez, C.: Cognitive models in cybersecurity: learning from expert analysts and predicting attacker behavior. Front. Psychol. **11** (2020). https://doi.org/10.3389/fpsyg.2020. 01049
42. Votipka, D., Abrokwa, D., Mazurek, M.L.: Building and validating a scale for secure software development self-efficacy. In: Proceedings of the 2020 CHI Conference on Human Factors in Computing Systems, pp. 1–20. ACM, Honolulu, April 2020. https://doi.org/10.1145/3313831.3376754
43. Votipka, D., Stevens, R., Redmiles, E., Hu, J., Mazurek, M.: Hackers vs. testers: a comparison of software vulnerability discovery processes. In: 2018 IEEE Symposium on Security and Privacy (SP), pp. 374–391. IEEE, San Francisco, May 2018. https://doi.org/10.1109/SP.2018.00003

The Dimensionality of the Cyber Warrior

Morgan L. Ferretti, Timothy Richards, Jessica G. Irons, and Kirsten Richards[✉]

James Madison University, Harrisonburg, VA 22807, USA
richa3ke@jmu.edu

Abstract. A cyber ready military is critical to national security. Yet, traditional kinetic warfare techniques for selecting and evaluating combatants do not necessarily apply directly to the abilities necessary to perform as an outstanding cyber warrior. Cyber warfare represents a fundamentally distinct form of warfare, and it is necessary to define the leadership competencies and skills required for cyber warfare to prepare for engagement in the multi-faceted cyberwarfare domain.

The cyber domain is multi-faceted and multi-disciplinary. It integrates the use of computer science, mathematics, economics, law, psychology, engineering, and others. We present an analysis of the skills required for cyber warrior readiness. In actuality, the cyber warrior of the future cannot be described as a single type of individual or single set of training. Rather, the cyber warfare theatre comprises a complex interplay of technologies, strategies, policies, and warriors with vastly varying skillset. Using current literature, we present a multi-dimensional view of cyber warfare abilities and propose evaluations for those abilities based on validated psychometric evaluations.

Keywords: Cyber Warrior · Traits · Military

1 The Cyber Domain

The cyber domain is multi-faceted and multi-disciplinary, integrating the use of computer science, mathematics, economics, law, psychology, engineering and more and impacting every facet of modern life from the use of electricity that powers millions of homes and businesses and the transportation network that moves millions of people daily to national security and military operations (Dawson and Thomson 2018). With growing interest and reliance on cyber systems, the need for resilient and effective cyber operations is increasingly apparent (Maybury, 2015). The cyber domain advances and diversifies quickly. This rapid development requires increased specialist responsibilities and roles at different levels of competence in short timeframes (Yamin and Katt 2019). Often, technology develops faster than the societal institutions that monitor these technologies (Leonard and Biberman 2007).

Perhaps because of swift advances in technology, cyber and related skills are inconsistently operationalized in the literature despite relevance to critical domains such as education and military operations (Leonard and Biberman 2007). For example, the phrases cyber domain, cyberspace, and cyber field are used interchangeably in the literature in

---

The original version of this chapter was revised: An error in the presentation of Kirsten Richards name and the affiliation has been corrected. The correction to this chapter is available at https://doi.org/10.1007/978-3-031-05563-8_32

A. Moallem (Ed.): HCII 2022, LNCS 13333, pp. 326–339, 2022.
https://doi.org/10.1007/978-3-031-05563-8_21

reference to the same construct. The Department of Defense (DOD) defines the cyber domain (and, presumably, cyberspace and cyber field) as a global domain within the information environment that encompasses an interdependent network of information systems, infrastructures and resident data, including the Internet, telecommunications networks, computer systems, embedded processors and controllers, and other related technologies (DOD 2017).

More specifically, the Department of the Army describes the cyber domain as a system composed of three layers: (1) the physical layer, which refers to hardware and infrastructure supporting our networks (i.e., the Internet) and the geographic location of the hardware, (2) the logical layer, which consists of all of the devices that are connected to each computer network (i.e., IP addresses), and (3) the social layer, which consists of the human and cognitive aspects, including the cyber professionals and people interacting within and between each network. (TRADOC 2010).

Though some research has investigated the social layer in both general cyberoperations and social network manipulation and psychological warfare in recent political unrest and intelligence analysis, there is lack of understanding with regards to the traits and learning abilities of the cyber domain professionals and work performance (Dawson and Thomson 2018). Existent work often focuses solely on technological aspects of the cyber domain (i.e., network intrusion detection sensors and algorithms, intelligent system designs, etc.), ignoring the critical roles that humans play (i.e., work performance) in cyber operations (Vieane et al. 2016); however, professionals in the cyber domain must understand both the technical and social aspects of the cyber domain, which includes complex human interactions (Garvin et al., 2013). Furthermore, it is necessary to understand the psychological and social traits and aptitudes that will support success in the cyber warfare theater. To mature the cyber domain generally and within the military, we must understand the roles, tasks, and responsibilities of human operators in these environments as this supports optimized selection of job roles within the cyber domain (Vieane et al. 2016).

Understanding human interactions and traits may help to better understand the cyber domain and its vulnerabilities (Arachchilage & Love, 2013; Shillair et al., 2015) as well as create a strong cyber defense. Cyber security is vital to defending the networks that encompass the cyber domain. Cyber security breaches are growing and are costly to the institutions attacked and to the national economy (Cashell et al. 2004). Cyber security is a high-ranking national priority that only becomes more essential as civilian and military infrastructure becomes more dependent on networked electronic systems.

Diverse job roles and descriptions comprise the operations that occur continuously throughout the cyber domain. Newhouse and colleagues (2016) describe various categories in the cyber security workforce framework, including designing and building secure information technology systems, investigating cyber-crimes and mitigating threats. The range of roles and tasks throughout the cyber domain highlight the need for identifying specific skills and traits that can predict uniquely optimal matches between job task and the individuals who perform them. It is important to evaluate the job categories of the cyber domain as well as the traits already identified and needed to assess cyber aptitudes. As such, a comprehensive and validated assessment of skills and traits is necessary, however, a comprehensive assessment does not yet exist.

1.1 Distinctions in Cyber Operations and Cyber Operators

As complexity of cyber infrastructure grows exponentially so do opportunities for threat and vulnerability (Dawson and Thomson 2018). The role of cyber operations in national security continues to expand and the U.S. military's ability to ensure robust cyber security is increasingly important (Li and Daugherty 2015). One process that will be critical for effective cyber warfare is distinguishing between cyber offensive and defensive strategies as well as identifying skills operators to carry out these strategies. The skills and traits of individuals that are best suited for effective execution of those strategies is likely to differ given the dissimilarity of the strategies. Each of these areas of operations encompasses unique and potentially contradictory requirements.

Brantley and Smeets (2020) discuss common distinctions that are made between three types of cyber operations: (1) defensive cyber operations, which are characterized by computer network actions to protect, monitor, analyze, detect, and respond to unauthorized activity; (2) cyber espionage operations, which are actions taken through the use of computer networks to gather data from target or adversary information systems or network; and (3) offensive cyber operations, which is use of computer networks to disrupt, deny, degrade, or destroy information resident in computers and computer networks, or the computers and networks themselves, or in basic, operations designed to achieve tangible effects. The noted types of cyber operations are based on the DOD's distinction between Computer Network Attack, Computer Network Defense and Computer Network Exploitation (Brantley & Smeets, 2020).

Butler (2013) identified the typical offensive cyber warrior as generally an anonymous hacker who attempts to remain undetected, while a defensive cyber warrior could be a network system administrator, an intrusion detection analyst, a software developer, or a private antivirus company. Butler (2013) also highlighted the differences between combatants in traditional, kinetic warfare and those of the cyber domain. In traditional warfare, offensive and defensive forces train similarly and directly interact in kinetic warfare in real time; however, Butler (2013) contended that cyber warfare works differently. Cyber offenders may spend months planning and preparing for an attack that takes seconds to execute while defensive forces spend their time either trying to make themselves less vulnerable to attack or responding after an attack to try to recover and/or mitigate damage. Additionally, cyber defense requires activities that may be viewed as mundane, such as software patching and password management (Slayton, R. 2021). The differences in combatants between cyber warfare and traditional warfare with respect to offensive and defensive strategies underscore the need for more research investigating the skills necessary to perform as a cyber warrior as they likely differ from traditional war combatants (Day 2020). Further, the divergent characteristics of cyber warfare and traditional warfare may indicate a need for a different set of leader competencies for the wing commanders of cyber warfare units (Day 2020). The creation of an aptitude battery for cyber security operators may require differentiation between potential for success in defensive and offensive capacities.

2 Cyber Operations in the Military

Over the past decade, the literature continues to emphasize that cyber operations have become an integral asset in U.S. and international military capabilities (Li and Daugherty 2015). Reliance upon data networks to conduct military operations presents new challenges to the competence profiles of military personnel. The entry of cyber warfare into military infrastructure is a new domain of warfare that is incredibly atypical in this space that requires an exhaustive assessment of beneficial skills (Heatherly and Melendez 2019). The emergence of the cyber domain as a new warfighting platform and the DOD's establishment of Cyberspace Command emphasizes the United States' intent to gain superiority in this emerging area as well as the rise of information technology and networking to the forefront of military thinking (Folks and Richard 2011). With the growth of the cyber domain, it is becoming increasingly acknowledged fact that militaries need a specific type of soldier trained for the cyber "battlefield" (Røisilien et al. 2014).

The military operations are increasingly dependent on computer network systems, which is a source of both strength and vulnerability. Though cyber operations play an important role in various operations throughout the military, they also create critical vulnerabilities to attack or exploit for our enemies. Enemies may have cyber offenders that attempt to deny, manipulate, disrupt, or destroy critical infrastructures and sensitive data through cyber-attack, which may have various impacts on the nation and its security. For example, the U.S Air Force depends on critical infrastructure and key resources for many of their military activities (Eom 2012), and attacks on this infrastructure may have various negative impacts on citizens. The priority for safe and secure systems must be balanced against the appeal of using information insecurity as a strategic asset.

According to Campbell (2015), careers in the cyber domain of the military can be distributed into 4 general categories: (1) attacking, (2) development, (3) defending, and (4) exploitation. The differences between roles and job tasks throughout the cyber sectors highlight the need for identifying skills required by each position. Several militaries, including the US, the UK, and Norway, have emphasized the need for a specific type of soldier that will have the cyber domain as their 'battlefield' and recent topics of interest include how to characterize this 'cyber warrior' and described the skills are needed to be successful in this role (Røislien 2014).

Dykstra and colleagues (2018) distinguish a subset of cyber operations called tactical cyber operations, in which cyber capabilities are used to achieve specific effects on a network. Another example is red team penetration testing, where an independent group plays the adversarial role and 'attacks' an organization to test that organization's defenses. Tactical cyber operations are unique in several respects. First, performance is highly dependent on speed and precision, similar to occupations, such as fighter pilots and surgeons. The longer operation, the greater the risk (i.e., increased likelihood of unintended detection on the network). Tactical operators require specialized skills and traits. For example, penetration testers have a breadth of expertise in network and software fundamentals, reconnaissance, exploitation, and adversarial thinking. Training for this type of work is extensive, expensive, and employee turnover is costly (Dykstra and Paul 2018). Taken together, the current literature, military needs, and job skills and roles collectively suggest the need for identification and assessment of key traits and skills necessary to succeed throughout the cyber domain.

3   Traits and Skills of the Successful Cyber Warrior

Requirements of cyber operators in the military surpass current abilities to produce qualified cyber warriors (Worley 2016; McGettrick 2013; Glass 2015). These needs could be mitigated by developing valid strategies that identify and assess knowledge, skills, and abilities (KSAs) most important to jobs in the cyber domain (Jones et al. 2018). The limited work done on KSAs of the cyber warrior stress the significance of technological competence but fail to acknowledge various human factors (e.g., Jeff & Boleng, 2008; Contiand and Raymond 2011). The importance of a sophisticated technological skill set is emphasized alongside assumptions that the competence of infantrymen – such as the ability to endure sleep deprivation or the importance of social network and trust – are of less relevance to cyber warriors. Though technological skillsets may be essential to successful military cyber operations, all character traits that may influence performance should be considered and analyzed, including social skillsets.

Fulp (2003) suggests a minimum set of core subject matter courses for cyber domain curricula: (1) discrete mathematics, (2) computer hardware/architectures, (3) programming, (4) operating systems, and (5) algorithms. These subject matters can be translated into skills that are potentially needed and assessed in cyber professionals and potential cyber workers. Dawson and Thomson (2018) suggest that there is little empirical information about what makes a good cyber professional and they propose the following characteristics for successful cyber professionals: (1) systematic thinkers, (2) team players, (3) proficient technical and social skills, (4) civic duty and trustworthiness, (5) continued learning, and (6) proficient communication skills. The characteristics are explained in more detail below:

1   **Systemic Thinkers.** Individuals in the cyber domain need to have an ability to step back from the specific piece of equipment on which they are working and consider the interconnections they may not physically be able to see or touch. For example, employees in the cyber domain need to understand the different systems that may be impacted by a single software upgrade (Cook, 2014).
2   **Team Players.** The magnitude of the complexity of the cyber domain increases the likelihood that a future cyber workforce is going to be working more in teams and less on their own. A current challenge with cyber security teams is that they tend to operate as a cluster of individuals in a group (Champion et al., 2014) rather than exhibiting cohesion and trust that involves a shared sense of identity (Gilson et al., 2015; Seong et al., 2015). The type of team that will develop in cyber operations is likely to be distinct from that of kinetic warfare (Conti and Raymond 2011). In the military context, cyber teams tend to be teams of diverse talents. Recent research has identified that cyber security teams are better able to solve complex tasks than individual analysts, potentially because of the range of expertise across analysts (i.e., Rajivan et al. 2013a, b; Rajivan, 2014; Rajivan and Cooke, 2018). Incident triage performance was highest in a group comprised of individual with heterogeneous

talents compared to a team with members of similar talents (Rajivan et al., 2013b). Though, this research emphasizes the need for the ability to work in teams, more research is needed to examine different organizations of teams or combinations of teams. An assessment of skills and aptitudes needed for the cyber force could assist in progressing this research.

3 **Technical and Social Skill.** Any future development of a cyber domain workforce must consider the additional competencies necessary to accomplish their tasks. For example, a cyber defense worker needs to consider all the ways they and their coworkers could be exploited by a malicious entity as well as be able to communicate the vulnerability in a way that is easily understood by laymen (Dawson and Thomson 2018).

4 **Civic Duty.** Insider threats are the largest vulnerability on any network and can do the irreparable damage. There is extensive research on values and vocational fit, however, the future cyber workforce must be loyal to the ideals of the country and organization to which he, she, or they belong(s) (Cook et al., 2012). Given the sensitivity of data to which the cyber workforce will have access, as well as the lack of knowledge of their superiors and their coworkers, the future cyber domain is going to have to engender trust within and amongst individuals that work in the domain (Knafo & Sagiv, 2004).

5 **Continued Learning.** Given that technology consistently changes, the future cyber workforce may be operating on outdated knowledge (Cook, 2014). Individuals in the cyber domain will have to constantly seek the latest information about security, network vulnerabilities, and capabilities (Champion et al., 2014). This will require a passion for learning and solving puzzles and a willingness to problem solve.

6 **Communications.** With limited evidence, Dawson and Thomson (2018) emphasize that not only will the future cyber workforce need increased emotional intelligence, but they will need to be able to communicate technical information to an audience that may not have a technical background. Cyber warriors will need to be able to discuss requirements with budget personnel to obtain new resources and be able to explain to their supervisor why a certain idea may be catastrophic.

Executive strategic leaders will require even more competence in both technical and leadership aspects of cyber operations (Day 2020). With no empirical studies in the literature focused on the leader competencies or developmental needs of Air Force cyber wing commanders, Day and colleagues (2020) showed a broad correlation to the Air Force foundational competencies with the following competencies: information seeking, communication, strategic thinking (planning), influence, creative thinking, resource management, leadership, initiative, fostering innovation, teamwork, and decision-making. Day and colleagues also highlighted a critical competency and developmental need for expertise, literacy, and currency in cyber law and legal and ethical boundaries for future cyber wing commanders. Conti and Raymond highlight the need for leaders with technical proficiency and the ability to instill a sense of trust and comradery without necessarily resorting to traditional physical hardship practices (Conti and Raymond 2011).

Recently, Jøsok and colleagues (2019) investigated how cyber defense operator's level of self-regulation can contribute to their performance in operations and hypothesized that higher levels of self-regulation predict higher levels of cognitive agility as measured by cognitive movement in The Hybrid Space conceptual framework. Twenty-three cyber cadets from the Norwegian Defense Cyber Academy (NDCA) completed self-regulation questionnaires (SRQs) and self-reported their cognitive location during a 4-day cyber defense exercise. Results indicated that higher levels of self-regulation were associated with displays of cognitive agility. Understanding factors that contribute to cyber operator performance are needed to improve education and training programs for military cyber personnel (Jøsok et al. 2019). The limited work done on KSAs that may be valuable for successful cyber professionals in the military context provide a starting point for assessment and analysis of potential measures that could be useful in predicting success of cyber warriors.

4 Assessment of Cyber Skills Aptitude

Research in the cyber domain generally operationalizes success using questionnaires, peer identification, or self-selection (Rajivan et al., 2017). Questionnaires typically operationalize success by using one or more of the following criteria: years of experience, job title, technical competency, and range of competencies (i.e., Ben-Asher & Gonzalez, 2015). Further, 40% of professionals felt that job experience was the highest contributor to positive performance over degree of knowledge/education (12%; Ben-Asher & Gonzalez, 2015). Many professionals reported anecdotally that those receiving on-the-job training and mentoring exhibited the highest performance benefits as measured by future career success. Similarly, Asgharpour and colleagues (2007) found that professionals who rated themselves as having higher levels of expertise tended to have a broader set of competencies compared to those with less self-professed expertise.

The increased utility of, and reliance on, the cyber domain in military operations has led to higher demand of technically qualified cyber personnel (Champion et al., 2014). This is demonstrated through investment in cyber defense units, cyber defense education (NATO 2016a), and the recognition of cyberspace as a domain of operations (NATO 2016b); however, cyber operator tasks, competence requirements, and performance are unsettled concepts that lack clear definition and guidelines to support selection, education, and training of this new category military personnel. While technical cyber competence is paramount to operate in the cyber domain, the soft skills and cognitive competencies have started to receive more attention. The following section provides information regarding measures or assessments that are already used in the literature or have been recommended for cyber force assessment.

- **National Initiative for Cybersecurity Education (NICE).** The Department of Homeland Security's National Initiative for Cybersecurity Careers and Studies (NICCS) developed a Cybersecurity Workforce Framework (NICE 2016) to provide a base set of work roles for the cyber workforce. Though this framework was developed to support US government hiring requirements and was not empirically justified, it is the most well-documented rostering of work roles in the cyber domain. This collection includes nine work-role categories, 31 specialty areas, and over 1000 types of knowledge, skills, and abilities (Dawson and Thomson 2018).

- **The Five-Factor Model (FFM).** The FFM has been broadly matched to vocational interests (Barrick et al., 2003). FFM describes five global characteristics of personality: (1) Extraversion, (2) agreeableness, (3) conscientiousness, (4) emotional stability, and (4) openness to experience. Combined with vocational interests, personality constructs may explain how our patterns of behavior and our likes and dislikes interact to account for vocational preferences and potentially work performance.

- **Holland Code Realistic, Investigative, Artistic, Social, Enterprising, and Conventional (RIASEC) Test.** The RAISEC model refers to six work environment types: realistic (systematic manipulation of machines or animals), investigative (curious, methodological, and precise), artistic (non-conforming and original), (4) social, (5) enterprising (achieving organizational goals and maximizing profit), and (6) conventional (filing, organizing and what is typically conceptualized as bureaucratic work; Barrick et al., 2003). Potentially, understanding the type of occupational work required of future cyber workers will provide valuable insight into selecting individuals with the potential to excel across the cyber domain (Dawson and Thomson 2018). Holland's vocational interests argues for creating a typology of personality and organizations which then can better predict which employees will remain with an organization as opposed to attrite (Holland,1996). Applying this strategy to the cyber domain may offer a better understanding of characteristics between people and occupations that are emerging (Dawson and Thomson 2018). Holland believes an employee's satisfaction with a job, as well as propensity to leave that job, depends on the degree of agreement between an individual's personality and their occupational environment (Barrick et al., 2003, p. 46).

- **Values and Vocations.** The influence of values on occupational interest, selection, and retention has been well documented throughout the organizational literature (Dawson and Thomson 2018). Values in this context refer to trans-situational constructs that orient behavior toward desired goals and outcomes (Bardi and Schwartz, 2003; Schwartz et al., 2012). Individuals are attracted to organizations that they believe reflect their values or are likely to match their interests. For the cyber domain, values are potentially even more important than in other professions for various reasons: (1) the technical knowledge that cyber professionals possess is likely much deeper than the average worker, which means they must be trusted with their employers' primary communications, logistics, human resource, and other critical infrastructure and resources; (2) by understanding the values that motivate individuals to select certain cyber occupations, we may be able steer potential professionals to occupations that best match their skill set; and (3) by finding those whose values do not match, we may be able to weed out potential threats (Cook et al., 2012).

- **Schwartz Values.** Schwartz values have been widely tested cross culturally and validated throughout the literature. Schwartz values map motivational aspirations and goals consisting of competing and complementary alignments (see Fig. 1; Bardi and Schwartz, 2003; Knafo and Sagiv, 2004; Schwartz et al., 2012). Schwartz's values may be used to distinguish the kinds of values within different workplace settings, such as differences between private sector and military employment. This could potentially be applied to distinguish between various jobs in the cyber domain of the military.

- **Situational Strength.** Any development of a cyber workforce must account for the breadth and variety of organizations encompassed in the cyber domain. Accounting for situational strength may fill in characteristic gaps that then better predicts workplace performance. Defining organizational context and situations as weak or strong may aid in identifying individuals who will be successful in different segments of the cyber domain beyond personality traits and organizational types (Cook et al., 2012; Judge and Zapata, 2015). Past research highlights the influence of the situation on individual behavior. To continue progressing the cyber workforce, accounting for both organizational context and situational strength is necessary. Accounting for the FFM/vocational types as well as organizational contexts may provide a more holistic prediction of future workplace performance. Organizational context may be expected to provide similar patterns of performance, regardless of individual differences.

5   Traits and Skills that Have not yet Been Assessed

Current literature primarily focuses on technical aspects of cyber workforce development, which fails to account for the entirety of characteristics that make up a cyber warrior. The current conceptualization of technical needs of the cyber domain are often viewed separately from the social aspects occurring in the domain, which creates disjointed spheres of knowledge (Shin et al., 2015), and therefore ignores important social and organizational influences that may dictate success or failure in everyday settings (Dawson and Thomson 2018). Social information is often seen as a data point for cyber-operations rather than an indicator for success in cyber workforce development (Dawson and Thomson 2018). The future development of any cyber work force that neglects the social aspect of human behavior on the network also neglects a critical component of cyber security. In contrast, the development of a future cyber workforce that accounts for both technical and social skills will be more likely to identify and understand expertise that enables true creativity and excellence in performance (Gates et al., 2014).

One reason for this gap in the literature may stem from the fact that educating cyber warriors is rather novel to the military sphere as well as the lack of a standardized conceptualization of the cyber domain (Røislien et al. 2014). Few, if any, comprehensive and thorough analyses of the cyber warrior have been conducted. Instead, social scientific research in the cyber domain has focused largely on more general and overall issues such as the interrelation between cyber security and national and international security, explorations of cyber power and cyber war (Conti and Raymond 2011). In summary, a consistently identified gap in the research regarding the cyber domain, where technical skills are being examined without the context of human factors such personality, social traits or aptitudes. Failing to acknowledge human factors creates an inadequate sphere of knowledge for identifying good cyber professionals (Dawson and Thomson 2018). A more holistically approach that encompasses human traits and the distinctive aspects with cyber warfare is necessary. Cyber defense competitions arising from U.S. service academy exercises may offer a platform for collecting data that can inform research that ranges from describing behaviors during certain challenging cyber situations to identifying ideal cyber warrior characteristics. This knowledge in turn could lead to better preparation of cyber warriors in military settings (Malviya et al. 2011).

Research on person-organization (P-O) fit argues that individuals select certain organizations based on how well they perceive it will match with their knowledges, skills, values, and interests (Cable and Parsons, 2001). From a P-O fit perspective, organizations look to hire individuals consistent with their organizational climate. One of the biggest challenges in recruiting a future cyber workforce is the great demand for skilled cybersecurity professionals. People hired into various positions must understand both the technical aspects of the cyber domain (Gates et al., 2014) and the social aspects of their jobs (Ono et al., 2011) as well as the situational dynamics within each organization (Meyer et al., 2010). This does not mean that it is impossible to identify individuals who will fit in multiple areas within the cyber domain; however, it suggests that it is likely not possible to create a cyber education or military training program that encompasses various sectors in the cyber domain. SThe implications for attraction, selection, and attrition models of person-organization fit suggest that like the cyber domain itself is both physical and logical, individuals drawn to the cyber workforce may be drawn to certain aspects of a specific segment of the industry. Identifying individual characteristics such as Big Five Personality traits as well as Organizational Types may help to identify individuals who may thrive in different segments of the cyber domain. Furthermore, being able to distinguish between operations in the cyber domain may also help provide clarity for what traits are likely to be necessary within specific areas within the cyber domain (Meyer et al., 2010).

6 Assessments that May Be Useful

There has been a long (Yerkes 1919) and continuing (e.g., Ackerman 1988; Ackerman and Cianciolo 2002; Carretta, Perry and Ree 1996) effort to identify the variables that predict skilled performance. Measures that might be useful in identifying potential cyber warriors are discussed in this section.

- **Fluid intelligence (G_f).** To measure the construct of general fluid abilities (Carroll, 1993), several tasks can measure a wide range of abilities: (1) Culture Fair Intelligence Tests 1 through 4 (Cattell, 1963), (2) Raven's Progressive Matrices Tests 1 and 2 (Raven, 1989), and the Shipley Institute of Living Scale Part 2 (Shipley, 1967). These measures are all well-established, culture-fair measures of G_f, with a minimal verbal component. Cattell's (1963) Culture Fair Intelligence Tests requires completion of a variety of nonverbal problem-solving tasks. Test 1 is pattern completion, Test 2 requires determining the abstract forms that do not belong to the sequence, Test 3 is a visual analogies task, and Test 4 requires application of derived rules to a novel situation. Raven's (1989) Progressive Matrices requires completion of two-dimensional pattern sequences. The Shipley (1967) Institute of Living Scale Part 2 requires recognition of patterns in verbal and nonverbal sequences.
- **Crystallized intelligence (G_c).** To measure the construct of general crystallized abilities, there are two measures of vocabulary: the Mill Hill Vocabulary Scale (Raven, 1989) and the Shipley (1967) Institute of Living Scale Part 1.
- **Short-term memory.** To measure the construct of short-term memory, there are two classic measures, Digit Span and Letter Span. In these tasks, participants repeated increasingly longer strings of either digits or letters.

- **Working memory.** To measure the construct of working memory capacity, there are two most widely recognized measures that utilize a dual task design: (1) Reading Span (participants read aloud a series of sentence–unrelated word pairs while trying to retain the words in memory in order to produce ordered serial recall when prompted; Daneman & Carpenter, 1980) and (2) Operation-Word Span (participants read equation-word pairs aloud while again trying to retain the words in memory; Turner & Engle, 1989).
- **Spatial working memory.** For spatial span ability, there are two tasks: (1) Rotation Span (Shah & Miyake, 1996) and (2) Matrix Span (Kaneet al., 2004). These tasks both measure the visuo-spatial abilities of working memory.
- **Closure flexibility (CF).** For closure flexibility, there are two measures: (1) the Group Embedded Figures Test (GEFT; Goodenough et al., 1991) and (2) the Closure Flexibility test (Thurstone, 1960). These measures both require a participant to detect a simple form embedded in a more complex one.
- **Cyber Operations Stress Survey (COSS).** Operator stress is a common, persistent, and disabling effect of cyber operations and an important risk factor for performance, safety, and employee burnout. COSS is a low-cost method for studying fatigue, frustration, and cognitive workload in real-time tactical cyber operation (Dykstra and Paul 2018).
- **NASA Task Load Index (TLX).** The NASA TLX is a popular subjective assessment used in engineering to measure cognitive workload along six dimensions on a 20-point unanchored scale (Hart 2006). These dimensions are mental demand, physical demand, time demand, subjective performance, frustration, and effort. The TLX is a well validated instrument and has been used in hundreds of studies of information technology (Dykstra and Paul 2018).
- **Openness Toward Organizational Change Scale (OTOCS).** Openness toward organizational change is central to employees' responses to organizations' strategic actions. Recent work has provided validity evidence based on relations to other variables, being negatively associated with burnout and positively associated with work engagement, job satisfaction and quality of work as well as examined the expected dimensionality, and showed acceptable levels of reliability (Sinval et al. 2021).

7   Conclusions and Future Directions

Dawson and Thomson (2018) emphasize the paucity of quantitative assessment regarding the cognitive aptitudes, work roles, or team organization required by cyber security professionals to be successful. The people who operate within the cyber domain need a combination of technical skills, domain specific knowledge, and social intelligence to be successful. One reason for this gap in the literature may stem from the fact that educating cyber warriors is rather novel to the military sphere. Additionally, there is a lack of standardized conceptualization of the cyber domain. This paper highlights the need for more empirical work that consistently defines the cyber warriors and examines the traits, skills, and measures that can be used to predict individuals' aptitudes for cyber operations within the military. It may also be necessary to differentiate based on specific operations, such as the traits for cyber offenders versus defenders. With growing interest and reliance on cyber systems, the need for resilient and effective cyber operations is increasingly apparent (Maybury, 2015). We have presented a dimensional analysis of the skills required for cyber warriors within the military, using past literature to describe potential traits, characteristics, and measures that may be useful in identifying cyber warriors. The cyber warrior of the future is not best described as the characteristics of a single individual. Rather, a thriving cyber domain workforce will be comprised of a cyber operator with varying skillsets, abilities, and aptitudes. Future research must differentiate between the various roles within the cyber field and seek to understand cyberwarriors in relationship to the complexity of the cyber security theater. Future work may also examine suggestions from cyber professionals in the field that account for offense and defense as well as the diversity of skillsets that is needed within the cyber warrior field to help further inform assessment and aptitudes to identify future cyber warriors.

References

Ackerman, P.L.: Determinants of individual differences during skill acquisition: Cognitive abilities and information processing. J. Exp. Psychol. Gen. **117**(3), 288 (1988)

Ackerman, P.L., Cianciolo, A.T.: Ability and task constraint determinants of complex task performance. J. Exp. Psychol. Appl. **8**(3), 194 (2002)

Brantly, A., Smeets, M.: Military operations in cyberspace. In: Handbook of Military Sciences, pp. 1–16 (2020)

Butler, S.C.: Refocusing cyber warfare thought. Air Univ Maxwell AFB AL Air Force Research Institution (2013)

Campbell, S.G., O'Rourke, P., Bunting, M.F.: Identifying dimensions of cyber aptitude: the design of the cyber aptitude and talent assessment. In: Proceedings of the Human Factors and Ergonomics Society Annual Meeting, vol. 59, no. 1, pp. 721–725. SAGE Publications, Los Angeles (2015)

Carretta, T.S., Perry, D.C., Jr., Ree, M.J.: Prediction of situational awareness in F-15 pilots. Int. J. Aviat. Psychol. **6**(1), 21–41 (1996)

Cashell, B., Jackson, W.D., Jickling, M., Webel, B.: The economic impact of cyber-attacks. Congressional research service documents, CRS RL32331 (Washington DC), 2 (2004)

Conti, G., Raymond, D.: Leadership of cyber warriors: Enduring principles and new directions. Military Academy West Point NY Department of Electrical Engineering and Computer Science (2011)

Dawson, J., Thomson, R.: The future cybersecurity workforce: going beyond technical skills for successful cyber performance. Front. Psychol. **9**, 744 (2018)

Day, A.E.: Leading Air Force Cyber Warriors: Cyber Wing Commander Competencies. Doctoral dissertation, Regent University (2020)

DOD Dictionary of Military and Associated Terms, 60, as of March 2017. http://www.dtic.mil/doctrine/new_pubs/dictionary.pdf

Dykstra, J., Paul, C.L.: Cyber operations stress survey (COSS): studying fatigue, frustration, and cognitive workload in cybersecurity operations. In: 11th USENIX Workshop on Cyber Security Experimentation and Test ({CSET} 18) (2018)

Eom, J.H., Kim, N.U., Kim, S.H., Chung, T.M. (2012, June). Cyber military strategy for cyberspace superiority in cyber warfare. In: Proceedings Title: 2012 International Conference on Cyber Security, Cyber Warfare and Digital Forensic (cybersec), pp. 295–299. IEEE (2012)

Folks, I.I., Richard, L.: Network Centric Warfare in the Age of Cyberspace Operations. ARMY WAR COLL CARLISLE BARRACKS PA (2011)

Fulp, J.D.: Training the cyber warrior. In: Irvine, C., Armstrong, H. (eds.) Security Education and Critical Infrastructures: IFIP TC11 / WG11.8 Third Annual World Conference on Information Security Education (WISE3) June 26–28, 2003, Monterey, California, USA, pp. 261–273. Springer US, New York, NY (2003). https://doi.org/10.1007/978-0-387-35694-5_24

Glass, B.: Job Market Intelligence: Cybersecurity Jobs, 2015. Burning Glass Technologies, Boston, MA (2015)

Hart, S.G.: NASA-task load index (NASA-TLX); 20 years later. In: Proceedings of the Human Factors and Ergonomics Society Annual Meeting, vol. 50, no. 9, pp. 904–908. Sage publications, Los Angeles, October 2006

Heatherly, C.J., Melendez, I.: Every soldier a cyber warrior. Cyber Defense Rev. 4(1), 63–74 (2019)

Jones, K.S., Namin, A.S., Armstrong, M.E.: The core cyber-defense knowledge, skills, and abilities that cybersecurity students should learn in school: results from interviews with cybersecurity professionals. ACM Trans. Comput. Educ. (TOCE) 18(3), 1–12 (2018)

Jøsok, Ø., Lugo, R., Knox, B.J., Sütterlin, S., Helkala, K.: Self-regulation and cognitive agility in cyber operations. Front. Psychol. 10, 875 (2019). https://doi.org/10.3389/fpsyg.2019.00875

Leonard, B., Biberman, J.: Utilizing multi-dimensionality in the workplace: a meta-study. Managerial Finance (2007)

Li, J.J., Daugherty, L.: Training cyber warriors: what can be learned from defense language training?. RAND NATIONAL DEFENSE RESEARCH INST SANTA MONICA CA (2015)

Malviya, A., Fink, G.A., Sego, L., Endicott-Popovsky, B.: Situational awareness as a measure of performance in cyber security collaborative work. In: 2011 Eighth International Conference on Information Technology: New Generations, pp. 937–942. IEEE, April 2011

McGettrick, A.: Toward curricular guidelines for cybersecurity: Report of a workshop on cybersecurity education and training. Association of Computing Machinery (ACM) (2013). https://www.acm.org/education/TowardCurricularGuidelinesCybersec.pdf

Moore, T., Friedman, A., Procaccia, A.D.: Would a 'cyber warrior' protect us: exploring trade-offs between attack and defense of information systems. In: Proceedings of the 2010 New Security Paradigms Workshop, pp. 85–94, September 2010

NATO. (2016, July 9). Warsaw Summit Communiqué. Retrieved from NATO HQ: http://www.nato.int/cps/en/natohq/official_texts_133169.htm

Newhouse, B., Keith, S.S., Witte, G.: NICE Cybersecurity Workforce Framework. National Institute of Standards and Technology, Gaithersburg (2016)

O'Connell, M.E.: Cyber security without cyber war. J. Conflict Secur. Law 17(2), 187–209 (2012)

Potter, L.E., Vickers, G.: What skills do you need to work in cyber security? A look at the Australian market. In: Proceedings of the 2015 ACM SIGMIS Conference on Computers and People Research, pp. 67–72, June 2015

Røislien, H.E., Lund, M.S., Knox, B.: Mapping the" Cyber Warrior": What Skill-Set Does the Cyber Warrior Need?. In: International Conference on Cyber Warfare and Security, p. 373. Academic Conferences International Limited (2014)

Samn, S.W., Perelli, L.P.: Estimating aircrew fatigue: a technique with application to airlift operations. School of Aerospace Medicine Brooks Afb tx (1982)

Sinval, J., Miller, V., Marôco, J.: Openness toward organizational change scale (OTOCS): validity evidence from Brazil and Portugal. PLoS ONE 16(4), e0249986 (2021)

Shoemaker, D., Kohnke, A., Sigler, K.: A guide to the National Initiative for Cybersecurity Education (NICE) cybersecurity workforce framework (2.0). Auerbach Publications (2018)

Slayton, R.: What Is a Cyber Warrior? The Emergence of US Military Cyber Expertise, 1967–2018 (Winter 2021). Texas National Security Review (2021)

Training, US Army, and Doctrine Command. Cyberspace Operations Concept Capability Plan 2016–2028 (2010)

Vieane, A., Funke, G., Gutzwiller, R., Mancuso, V., Sawyer, B., Wickens, C.: Addressing human factors gaps in cyber defense. In: Proceedings of the Human Factors and Ergonomics Society Annual Meeting, vol. 60, no. 1, pp. 770–773. SAGE Publications, Los Angeles, September 2016

Worley, C.: Hacking the skills shortage a study of the International shortage in Cybersecurity skills. In: Lewis, J.A. (Chair) Hacking the skills shortage A study of the International shortage in Cybersecurity skills [Video file]. Symposium conducted at the meeting of Center for Strategic & International Studies, Washington, DC (2016). https://www.csis.org/events/hacking-skills-shortage

Yamin, M.M., Katt, B.: Cyber security skill set analysis for common curricula development. In: Proceedings of the 14th International Conference on Availability, Reliability and Security, pp. 1–8 (2019)

Yerkes, R.M.: Report of the psychology committee of the national research council. Psychol. Rev. **26**(2), 83 (1919)

Exploring Rationality of Self Awareness in Social Networking for Logical Modeling of Unintentional Insiders

Florian Kammüller[1,2]([✉]) and Chelsea Mira Alvarado[1,2]

[1] Middlesex University London, London, UK
f.kammueller@mdx.ac.uk, CA936@live.mdx.ac.uk
[2] Technische Universität Berlin, Berlin, Germany

Abstract. Unawareness of privacy risks together with approval seeking motivations make humans enter too much detail into the likes of Facebook, Twitter, and Instagram. To test whether the rationality principle applies, we construct a tool that shows to a user what is known publicly on social networking sites about her. In our experiment, we check whether this revelation changes human behaviour. To extrapolate and generalize, we use the insights gained by practical experimentation. Unaware users can become targeted by attackers. They then become unintentional insiders. We demonstrate this by extending the Isabelle Insider framework to accommodate a formal model of unintentional insiders, an open problem with long standing.

Keywords: Self awareness in social networks · Unintentional insiders · Rational choice theory · Formal verification

1 Introduction

The privacy paradox [3] shows that humans can be on one side quite concerned about security and privacy in general but when it comes to their own behaviour they seem to ignore any caution and freely spread their private data into public cloud based social network services, like Facebook, Twitter or Instagram. Assuming that humans are rationally acting beings has led to quite successful models and prediction in economics using what is termed Rational Choice Theory (RCT) [43]. Sociologist have transferred RCT more generally to social interaction forming what is known as *exchange theory*. We want to test this theory on the privacy paradox and use the results to improve automated logical verification of social networks. We consider a dynamic system research approach more suitable. The Isabelle Insider framework permits modeling and analyzing dynamic state transition. Thus we can reason on actions and their effects. Methodologically, we thus follow the action research approach [39] interleaving empirical research with interventions, here, practical implementations and verification.

This paper first presents an empirical study on increasing privacy awareness for the construction of a social self awareness tool for social networks. It uses assumptions from RCT testing and highlighting the significance of applying this theory. RCT can be considered as a follow up theory of Max Weber's sociological explanation which has strongly inspired the human actor model of Isabelle's Insider framework. Consequently, it appears natural to use the RCT interpretation found in the empirical study to extend the human model in the Isabelle Insider framework. Moreover, it turns out that the RCT interpretation of social awareness allows to model unintentional insiders a challenge hitherto unanswered.

This paper first gives some background from sociology about RCT and the Isabelle Insider framework (Sect. 2). Section 3 presents the tool based study on privacy awareness in social networks and the influence of RCT giving some insights into the requirements, design, testing and evaluation of the tool and the key findings in the RCT interpretation with respect to privacy awareness. This section is based on the Bachelor of Science dissertation of one of the authors [1]. Section 4 then continues to transfer the experimental findings into extending the Isabelle Insider framework and illustrating them on the case study. The Isabelle sources are publicly available on github [22].

2 Background

2.1 Social Explanation and Rational Choice Theory

Rational choice theory is based upon the assumption that complex social phenomena can be explained by individual actions that constitute them. This philosophy now coined *methodological individualism* holds that: 'The elementary unit of social life is the individual human action. To explain social institutions and social change is to show how they arise as the result of the action and interaction of individuals' [9]. Seemingly very close to *methodological individualism*, is what was originally conceived by Max Weber [45,46] as 'understanding explanation' (*Verstehendes Erklären*) sketched in Fig. 1. Despite these similarities, RCT is more extreme in only considering rational actions. John Scott explains in his critical overview over RCT [43]: 'what distinguishes RCT [...] is that it denies the existence of any kind of action other than the purely rational [...]'. We draw from Scott's overview to contrast and provide the right context for our work. He quite critically highlights the limitations of RCT in particular when branching out from economics and applying RCT more generally to sociology. According to Scott, Homans [12] was a "pioneering figure" in establishing rational choice theory in sociology setting up the basic framework of *exchange theory* which can be understood as RCT for social interaction. In this framework, money and market mechanisms of economic theories are replaced by human resources as time, information, approval and prestige. Besides pioneering RCT, Homans additionally grounded exchange theory on assumptions that he drew from behaviourist psychology. While the methodological individualism of rational choice theories starts from individuals' actions and sees all social phenomena reducible to these actions, Homans went one step further into explaining them. For him it was necessary to reduce these actions to conditioned

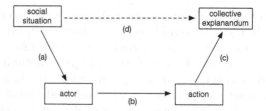

Fig. 1. Max Weber's sociological explanation model: a macro-micro-macro-level-transition explaining sociological phenomena by breaking down the global facts from the macro level (a) onto a more refined local view of individual actors at the micro-level (b). Finally those micro-steps are generalized and lifted back on the macro-level (c) to explain the global phenomenon (d).

psychological responses. In brief, human behaviour is like animal behaviour not free but determined by rewards and punishment. This reinforcement is called 'conditioning' and determines human behaviour. Behaviour can thus be studied purely externally and needs no inspection of internal mental states.

While others rejected Homans' claims about this explanation of human behaviour – and even Homans came to see it as inessential – for our formal model of awareness and unintentional insiders it is very helpful. In Sect. 4, when we formalize the taxonomy extracted from the experimental work into Isabelle, we model human behaviour in the sense of 'conditioning'. We actually do model the internal state of the actors although Homans considered this as unnecessary but our model permits dynamic state inspection including psychological disposition of human actors.

2.2 Isabelle Insider Framework

The Isabelle Insider framework [5,31] has also been inspired by Max Weber and methodological individualism. In mapping this fundamental philosophy to logic, this framework follows a common introductory textbook for sociologists by Hartmut Esser [10] written in the spirit of Popper's critical rationalism. This offers an approach to understand sociological experiments in a formal way using a logical view on explanation by the logicians Hempel and Oppenheim [11]. In addition, the Isabelle Insider framework uses a taxonomy provided in [41] which is founded on empirical and psychological studies of counterproductive workplace behaviour. In Sect. 4, we will in more detail present the details of how the human disposition and its effects to the environment are modeled in Isabelle and how this model is now extended to accommodate the unintentional insider.

Isabelle is an interactive proof assistant based on Higher Order Logic (HOL). Application specific logics are formalized into new theories extending HOL. They are called object-logics. Although HOL is undecidable and therefore proving needs human interaction, the reasoning capabilities are very sophisticated supporting "simple", i.e., repetitive, tedious proof tasks to a level of complete automation. The use of HOL has the advantage that it enables expressing even the most complex application scenarios, conditions, and logical requirements and HOL simultaneously enables the analysis of the meta-theory. That is, repeating patterns specific to an application can be abstracted and proved once and for all. An object-logic contains new types, constants, and definitions. These items reside in a theory file. For instance, the file `UnintentionalInsider.thy` contains the object-logic for unintentional insiders described in the following paragraphs. This Isabelle Insider framework is a *conservative extension* of HOL. This means that our object logic does not introduce new axioms and hence guarantees consistency. Conceptually, new types are defined as subsets of existing types and properties are proved using a one-to-one relationship to the new type from properties of the existing type.

We are going to use Isabelle syntax and concepts in the presentation of the Isabelle Insider framework and will explain them when they are used.

3   Social Networks and Privacy Awareness

3.1   Requirements Analysis and Design of Social Awareness Tool

A questionnaire was created in order to research about public attitudes to internet security amongst social media users. Quantitative and qualitative data are obtained through this method, allowing more time for analysis of the results and how the results can be used to create a prototype. Answers to 'How many different social media apps/websites do you use every day?', show that 84.6% of 39 responses use more than 3 different forms of social media every day. This shows the commonality and reliance of social media in everyday lives and how many different apps can hold information about you.

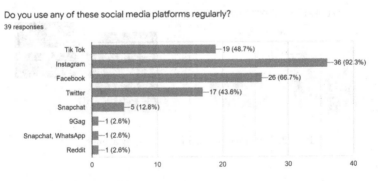

Do you use any of these social media platforms regularly?
39 responses

The above chart show the most common applications that people use, Instagram, Facebook and TikTok have shown to be the most common platforms. Each of which have shown to have breaches in misuse of personal data they have collected from their users.

How many people have their accounts on private? The majority, 56.4%, say that only some are private, meaning that the users have chosen to only privatise one or more of their accounts but have left others to be able to be accessed by the public. Are these users aware of how much information they have put out publicly? Surprisingly, the most common answers are completely aware or somewhat aware. Of the amount. 59% have said that they have knowledge of information they have posted publicly but leave room for uncertainty as to how much is actually available to the public. This shows a slight concern from users in their social media behaviour.

3.2   Testing and Evaluation

The left side of Fig. 2 shows the design of the search page which focuses on clear minimalistic esthetic to display clear concise information, which will be easily accessible by all. The website title placed at the top middle and highlights the purpose pf the website. The search bar is in the middle of the page, letting the user know that the tool only has one importance and should not show otherwise. The user will not be lost when navigating the website, easing user comfort. The bottom grey section reflects basic information on the importance of internet security and what the website aims to show. User inputs through the search bar and uses the search button. The right side of the figure displays what the user sees when they have searched a username. Profiles are created of the available information such as other social media accounts that are linked to the username searched. The profiles are highlighted by the black boxes they are in that contrast the white background, allowing less crowded visuals which may have disorientated people.

Fig. 2. Interface of social network awareness tool

For the implementation, we used opensource API's. An API is an application programming interface that allows computers to send signals and receive data in return. This enables specific queries and actions to be retrieved. APIs need keys allowing access to sensitive data whilst also protecting important and sensitive data that cannot be accessed by any user. All social networks allow developers to apply for API keys, allowing APIs to be used for projects. The API allowed us to retrieve that data necessary enabling to connect to the internet and use genuine social network server data. Users are able to search any username on any social network and retrieve related information. The API's proved to be the best solution for this project as we could acquire the necessary data and use it to create a summarized only profile. The results are thus inherently genuine reflecting real world scenarios.

3.3 Key Findings and RCT Interpretation of Privacy Awareness

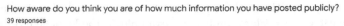

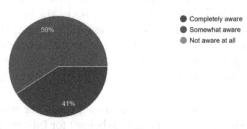

Most importantly, the last question investigates the issue of social media behaviours. It asks whether they would personally change their online behaviours if they were able to see what others could see about them. From responses to this question on the questionnaire, many have shown concern about what others could obtain from the information they post online and would immediately act on this by privatising their social media. Consequently, this shows the importance of a tool that helps people become more aware of their online behaviours.

It matches the rationality assumption of RCT and proves that creating awareness changes the users attitude. This creates a potential for improved privacy in social networks and how awareness could change the risk of attacks on privacy.

4 Modeling Unaware Social Network Users and Unintentional Insiders in Isabelle

The state based dynamic semantics of the Isabelle infrastructure framework allows expressing how awareness dynamically changes the global policy and thus how a change on awareness eliminates the risk. We also show how to integrate awareness into the notion of insiderness thus extending the Isabelle Insider framework to unintentional insiders based on the findings of our experiment with the social awareness tool.

4.1 Infrastructures, Policies, Actors in Isabelle

The Isabelle Infrastructure framework supports the representation of infrastructures as graphs with actors and policies attached to nodes. These infrastructures are the *states* of the Kripke structure.

The transition between states is triggered by non-parameterized actions get, move, eval, and put executed by actors. Actors are given by an abstract type actor and a function Actor that creates elements of that type from identities (of type string written ''s'' in Isabelle).

```
typedecl actor
type_synonym identity = string
consts Actor :: string ⇒ actor
```

Note that it would seem more natural and simpler to just define actor as a datatype over identities with a constructor Actor instead of a simple constant together with a type declaration like, for example, in the Isabelle inductive package by Paulson [42]. This would, however, make the constructor Actor an injective function by the underlying foundation of datatypes therefore excluding the fine grained modelling that is at the core of the insider definition: in fact, the core insider property UasI (see below) defines the function Actor to be injective for all except insiders and explicitly enables insiders to have different roles by identifying Actor images.

To represent the macro level view seeing the actor within an infrastructure, we define a graph datatype igraph (see below) for infrastructures. This datatype has generic input parameters that are going to be supplied as concrete parts of an application infrastructure on instantiation of an igraph. They represent the actual location graph, the actors in each locations, their roles, credentials and psychological disposition (see following subsection) and the locations' state.

```
datatype igraph = Lgraph (location × location)set
                        location ⇒ identity set
                        actor ⇒ (string list × string list)
                        actor ⇒ actor_state
                        location ⇒ string list
```

Consider here the social network case study as an example.

```
ex_graph ≡  Lgraph
  {(aphone,instagram), (bphone,instagram)}
    (λ x. if x = aphone then {''Alice''} else
    (if x = bphone then {''Bob''} else {}))
    ex_creds ex_locs
```

Policies specify the expected behaviour of actors of an infrastructure. Atomic policies of type apolicy describe prerequisites for actions to be granted to actors given by pairs of predicates (conditions) and sets of (enabled) actions:

```
type_synonym apolicy = ((actor ⇒ bool) × action set)
```

For example, the apolicy pair (λx. has (x, ''PIN''), {move}) specifies that all actors who know the PIN are enabled to perform action move.

Infrastructures combine an infrastructure graph of type igraph with a policy function that assigns local policies over a graph to each location of the graph, that is, it is a function mapping an igraph to a function from location to apolicy set.

```
datatype infrastructure = Infrastructure igraph
                         [igraph, location] ⇒ apolicy set
```

For our social network example, the initial infrastructure contains the above graph ex_graph and the local policies defined shortly.

```
sn_scenario ≡ Infrastructure ex_graph local_policies
```

The function local_policies gives the policy for each location x over an infrastructure graph G as a pair: the first element of this pair is a function specifying the actors y that are entitled to perform the actions specified in the set which is the second element of that pair.

```
local_policies G x ≡
case x of
   aphone ⇒ {(λ y. has G (y,''aPIN'')), {put,get,move,eval})}
 | bphone ⇒ {((λ y. has G (y,''bPIN'')), {put,get,move,eval})}
 | instagram ⇒ {(λ y. ∈ {Actor ''Alice'', Actor ''Bob''},
                          {put,get,move,eval})}
 | _ ⇒  {})
```

We define the behaviour of actors using a predicate enables: within infrastructure I, at location l, an actor h is enabled to perform an action a if there is a pair (p,e) in the local policy of l – delta I l projects to the local policy – such that action a is in the action set e and the policy predicate p holds for actor h.

```
enables I l h a ≡ ∃ (p,e) ∈ delta I l. a ∈ e ∧ p h
```

For example, the statement enables I l (Actor''Bob'') move is true if the atomic policy (λx. True, {move}) is in the set of atomic policies delta I l at location l in infrastructure I. Double quotes as in ''Bob'' create a string in Isabelle/HOL.

4.2   Modelling the Human Actor and Psychological Disposition

The human actor's level is modeled in the Isabelle Insider framework by assigning the individual actor's psychological disposition to each actor's identity.

```
datatype actor_state = State psy_state motivations
```

There are selector functions motivation and psy_state to project the components from an actor_state element. The psychological state of an actor is not determined using the formal system but we use here empirical facts as input as for example our own studies from Sect. 3 or other sociological findings, like [41]. The formal representation of *Psychological State* is a simple enumeration datatype distinguishing the "normal" state of happiness from one in which the actor is alerted or "suspicious".

```
datatype psy_states = happy | suspicious
```

The element on the right hand side are the two injective constructors of the new datatype psy_states. They are simple constants, modeled as functions without arguments. Motivation plays a vital role in RCT and as Homans observed the strongest one is that humans seek approval (which is only excluded by a state of mind that corresponds to complete detachment which we abbreviate as "zen").

datatype motivations = approval_hungry | zen

The types for psychological state and motivations allow defining the users state of unawareness by a predicate.

definition unaware :: actor_state ⇒ bool
  unaware a ≡ motivation a = {approval_hungry} ∧ happy = psy_state a

4.3   Privacy by Labeling Data and State Transition

The Decentralized Label Model (DLM) [40] introduced the idea to label data by owners and readers. We use this idea and formalize a new type to encode the owner and the set of readers of a data item.

type_synonym dlm = actor × actor set

Labelled data is then just given by the type dlm × data where data can be any data type.

The abstract state transition provided in the underlying Kripke structure theory is instantiated in the infrastructure model by an inductive definition of a state transition relation $\rightarrow_n$ over infrastructures. A set of inductive rules defines this transition relation $\rightarrow_n$ relative to characteristics of the current state. These characteristics can exploit the information encoded into the infrastructure as well as the enables predicate to express how the next infrastructure state evolves from the current one. We show here the rules for put and get as they suffice to illustrate how to model the social network application scenario.

The put pata rule assumes an actor h residing at a location l in the infrastructure graph G and being enabled the put action. In addition, the psychological state pgra G h needs to be unaware. Here we add the newly extended option for the human actor model to the semantic rule as precondition thus stating that only unaware users put their data onto the graph. If infrastructure state I fulfills those preconditions, the next state I' can be constructed from the current state by adding the data item ((Actor h, hs), n) at location l. The addition is given by updating (using :=) the existing data storage lgra G l at location l with the singleton set {((Actor h, hs), n)}. Note that the first component Actor h marks the owner of this data item as h.

```
put:
G = graphI I ⟹ h @_G l ⟹ enables I l (Actor h) put ⟹
unaware (pgra G h) ⟹
I' = Infrastructure
        (Lgraph (gra G)(agra G)(cgra G)(pgra G)
          ((lgra G)(l := (lgra G l ∪ {((Actor h, hs), n)}))))
        (delta I)
⟹ I →_n I'
```

The get data rule resembles the put data rule in many parts. However, here
an actor h accesses data in a remote location l' and adds it to the data in his
current location l. This copying of data is only permitted if the current location
l' of the data enables h to **get** and if the list of readers **hs** in the data item
((Actor h', hs), n) contains the entry Actor h or if the accessing actor is h
herself.

```
get_data:
G = graphI I ⟹ h @_G l ⟹ enables I l' (Actor h) get ⟹
((Actor h', hs), n) ∈ lgra G l' ⟹ Actor h ∈ hs ∨ h = h' ⟹
I' = Infrastructure
        (Lgraph (gra G)(agra G)(cgra G)(pgra G)
          ((lgra G)(l := (lgra G l ∪ {((Actor h', hs), n)}))))
        (delta I)
⟹ I →_n I'
```

The global policy is 'only the owner and friends can access the data on the cloud'
using for example the definition of friends as {''Alice'', ''Bob''}.

```
global_policy I a ≡  a ∉ friends
              ⟶ ¬(enables I instagram (Actor a) get)
```

We can prove that Bob is enabled to get (Alice's data) at instagram if Bob is
specified as a reader in an application scenario where Alice sets the label parameter **hs** in a put action accordingly. So, using the features of attack tree analysis
of the Isabelle Insider framework, we can formally prove such statements. However, we are interested in investigating negative effects of unawareness and how
a change of human behaviour may improve the situation. Therefore, we use the
representation of human factors and (malicious) Insiders in the Isabelle Insider
framework, integrating the existing notion of malicious insiders and extending
them to include also unintentional insiders.

4.4   Representing Human Factors and Insiders

The Isabelle Insider framework defines "[a]n insider [as] a trusted user of a system who behaves like an attacker abusing privileges thereby bypassing security
controls" [24]. This definition leads to the notion of an insider as an attacker
formally represented as an actor Eve who is a malicious "evil" actor outside
some set of actors within the system. Actors are represented as having a unique

identity as well as a role of actor which normally is the same as their identity unless impersonation happens. Insiderness is now represented by explicitly identifying the actor Eve with privileged users. Thus the malicious actor Eve can act like an inside actor. So far, the Isabelle Insider framework has rooted insiderness on a taxonomy from the insider threat literature based on psychological studies [41]. Thus, insiderness was uniquely determined by the description of an insider as a system actor turning bad as a consequence of susceptible dispositions and triggering events leading to a "tipping point".

Technically, we model this explicit yet flexible impersonation of privileged users inside the system by a function Actor that maps identities to roles. In places where an impersonation is deemed feasible the function may map the identity of the "evil" actor Eve to the same role as that of a privileged user inside the system. For all other identities that are not compromised the function actor maps these identities exclusively to roles in the system, that is, for these identities Actor is injective: $id_0 \neq id_1 \Rightarrow$ Actor $id_0 \neq$ Actor id_1.

Here, we want to extend this classical view of an intentional insider to that of an unintentional insider [44]. As Matt Bishop puts it "[i]n many cases, unintentional insider attacks are as dangerous as deliberate insider attacks; preventing them adds more complexity to an already, difficult problem. Any approach therefore must have not only a technical aspect (detecting the attack), but also a non-technical aspect (detecting the problem), which includes consideration of social, political, legal, and cultural influences, among others" [4].

We remain in the spirit of this design decision of representing the human actor but extend it with awareness and thus unintentional insiderness. In the following we retrace the steps of the formal insider model as originally conceived in the Isabelle Insider framework highlighting the additions and extensions to accommodate unintentional insiders.

4.5   Integrating Unaware with Malicious Insiders

For the integration of unintentional insiders with the existing the malicious insiders, e.g. [24], we extend the definitions of the types motivations and psy_state given in Sect. 4.2. The values for the malicious insider are based on a taxonomy from psychological insider research by Nurse et al. [41].

```
datatype psy_states = ... | depressed | disgruntled | angry | stressed
```

Another example is *motivation* for malicious insiders ranging far [41].

```
datatype motivations = ... | financial | political | revenge
                | fun | competitive_advantage | power | peer_recognition
```

The transition to become an insider is represented by a *catalyst* that tips the insider over the edge so he acts as an insider formalized as a "tipping point" predicate.

```
definition tipping_point :: actor_state ⇒ bool
tipping_point a ≡ motivation a ≠ {} ∧ motivation a ≠ {approval_hungry}
                ∧ happy ≠ psy_states a
```

To embed the fact that the attacker is an insider, the actor can then impersonate other actors. This assumption entails that an insider `Actor ''Eve''` can act like their alter ego, say `Actor ''Charlie''` within the context of the locale. This is realized by the predicate `UasI`.

```
UasI a b ≡ (Actor a = Actor b) ∧
          ∀ x y. x ≠ a ∧ y ≠ a ∧ Actor x = Actor y ⟶ x = y
```

Note that this predicate also stipulates that the function `Actor` is injective for any other than the identities `a` and `b`. This completes the Actor function to an "almost everywhere injective function". Insiderness can now be defined as a rule that is triggered by conditions that may be valid in a state of the infrastructure. For the malicious insider, this condition has been the "tipping point" for an actor's state (given here as the parameterized `as a`). To integrate insiderness to unintentional insiders, we simply add **unawareness** as an additional sufficient condition to the rule.

```
Insider a C as ≡ tipping_point (as a) ∨ unaware (as a)
               ⟶ (∀ b ∈ C. UasI a b)
```

Although the above insider predicate is a rule, it is not axiomatized. It is just an Isabelle definition, that is, it serves as an abbreviation. To use it in an application, like the auction protocol, we can use this rule as a local assumption in theorems or using the **assumes** feature of locales [32]).

Based on the state transition and the above defined `sn_scenario`, we define the first Kripke structure.

```
sn_Kripke ≡
Kripke { I. sn_scenario ⟶* I } {sn_scenario}
```

4.6   Attack: Eve Can Get Data

How do we find attacks? The key is to use invalidation [30] of the security property we want to achieve, here the global policy. Since we consider a predicate transformer semantics, we use sets of states to represent properties. The invalidated global policy is given by the following set `ssn`.

```
ssn ≡ {x. ¬ (global_policy x ''Eve'')}
```

The attack we are interested in is to see whether for the scenario

```
sn_scenario ≡ Infrastructure ex_graph local_policies
```

from the initial state `Isn ≡{sn_scenario}`, the critical state `ssn` can be reached, that is, is there a valid attack `(Isn,ssn)`?

For the Kripke structure

```
sn_Kripke ≡ Kripke { I. sn_scenario ⟶* I } Isn
```

we first derive a valid and-attack using the attack tree proof calculus.

$$\vdash \ [\mathcal{N}_{(\text{Isn,SN})}, \ \mathcal{N}_{(\text{SN,ssn})}] \oplus_{\wedge}^{(\text{Isn,ssn})}$$

The set SN is an intermediate state where Alice moves to instagram to then put her data ''Alice's_diary'' there.

The attack tree calculus [17] exhibits that an attack is possible.

sn_Kripke ⊢ EF ssn

The attack tree formalisation in the Isabelle Infrastructure framework provides adequacy, that is, Correctness and Completeness theorem for the relationship between attack trees and the CTL statement [17]. We can thus simply apply the Correctness theorem AT_EF to immediately prove CTL-EF statements. This application of the meta-theorem of Correctness of attack trees saves us proving the CTL formula tediously by exploring the state space in Isabelle proofs. Alternatively, we could use generated code for the function is_attack_tree in Scala [22] to check that a refined attack of the above is valid.

5   Conclusions

5.1   Related Work on Awareness

Awareness contributes to having knowledge of something; thus, security awareness could be considered as a cognitive behavioural response to security and understanding its consequences. Some studies investigate this possible understanding of internet and cyber security awareness, such as Bulgur [6]. Korovessis et al. [34] introduces a "toolkit approach to information security awareness and education", whilst focusing on organisations and the importance of user training by introducing a toolkit. Training in this sense, focuses on teaching skills to safeguard information. They completed a string of surveys, focus groups and interviews with different participant groups and ages to establish the effectiveness of the toolkit. Results showed that the prototype was successful in establishing awareness, however limitations were shown through the delivery of the approach as the kit was not accessible to everyone. Kruger and Kearney [36] establish a model prototype for assessing informational security awareness. The model focuses on knowledge, attitude, and behaviour. As stated by Lacey [38], the gap in internet security is not the technology, but fundamentally the awareness in people. The effectiveness of the approach is assessed by the resulting attitudes and behaviour to the topic.

Bada, Sasse and Nurse [2] also investigated through a psychological perspective where lack of motivation lead to poorly designed security systems and poor security compliance. The study results showed a raised awareness and had positive effects on creating a "security minded culture". By introducing human factors to awareness campaigns, the results deemed more positive, showing us that security awareness can be increased if the tool used is more personal and relatable. Bada, Sasse and Nurse [2] provide a literature based survey on the effectiveness of campaigns on human behaviour comparing cyber security awareness campaigns in Africa and UK. They review Dolan et al.'s nine critical factors which influence and change human behaviour. Although these factors provide an even finer granularity of categorizing human motivations, they are aligned with the psychological characterization by Homans [12] that we use as a basis for our model. While our work uses an experimental approach, their survey [2] also leads them to conclude that "security education has to be more than providing information to users - it needs to be targeted, actionable, doable and provide feedback". Our approach is aligned with their findings, since our security tool and modeling enables a "targetted, actionable, doable" analysis of a social network leading to feedback to the user.

Labuschagne et al. [37] proposed a game hosted by social networking sites to increase security awareness. The game uses social networks, something that is accessible by those at home and at work. Lack of security knowledge is what makes people vulnerable and unable to protect their information, an idea clearly stated by Kritzinger and von Solms [35], with internet becoming so involved in personal lives, it is paramount that the tools to raise awareness should be accessible to all. The approach utilises a medium that is popular, therefore accessible. Whilst a prototype has not been created, the approach must be analysed to see if it would utilise the increase of public awareness to internet security. In this scenario the game that is hosted by social media sites is an approach that would possibly be interacted with by the younger audience, producing a limitation as to its non-inclusive medium, leaving a numerous amount of the public not being educated to. Jemal Abwajy 2012 [18] concludes that combined delivery methods of text, video and game would be a more suitable approach to deliver security awareness, rather than individual as it creates an inclusive audience.

5.2   Related Work on Isabelle Insider and Infrastructure Framework

A whole range of publications have documented the development of the Isabelle Insider framework. The publications [29–31] first define the fundamental notions of insiderness, policies, and behaviour showing how these concepts are able to express the classical insider threat patterns identified in the seminal CERT guide on insider threats [7]. This Isabelle Insider framework has been applied to auction protocols [25, 26]. An Airplane case study [23, 24] revealed the need for dynamic state verification leading to the extension of adding a mutable state. Meanwhile, the embedding of Kripke structures and CTL into Isabelle have enabled the emulation of Modelchecking and to provide a semantics for attack trees [14–17, 20]. Attack trees have provided the leverage to integrate Isabelle formal reasoning for IoT systems as has been illustrated in the CHIST-ERA project SUCCESS [8] where attack trees have been used in combination with the Behaviour Interaction Priority (BIP) component architecture model to develop security and privacy enhanced IoT solutions. This development has emphasized the technical rather than the psychological side of the framework development and thus branched off the development of the Isabelle *Insider* framework into the Isabelle *Infrastructure* framework. Since the strong expressiveness of Isabelle allows to formalize the IoT scenarios as well as actors and policies, the latter framework can also be applied to evaluate IoT scenarios with respect to policies like the European data privacy regulation GDPR [18]. Application to security protocols first pioneered in the auction protocol application [25,26] has further motivated the analysis of Quantum Cryptography which in turn necessitated the extension by probabilities [13,19,21].

Requirements raised by these various security and privacy case studies have shown the need for a cyclic engineering process for developing specifications and refining them towards implementations. A first case study takes the IoT healthcare application and exemplifies a step-by-step refinement interspersed with attack analysis using attack trees to increase privacy by ultimately introducing a blockchain for access control [20]. This formalisation of secure distributed data labels has given rise generalising to sets of blockchain for Inter-clockchain protocols [28]. First ideas to support a dedicated security refinement process are available in a preliminary arxive paper [33] but the first to fully formalize the RR-cycle and illustrate its application completely is the application to the Corona-virus Warn App (CWA) [27].

5.3   Discussion and Outlook

We have presented a pragmatic action research study into awareness in social networks. User awareness interviews have given evidence to design, implement, and test a web-based tool enabling to show the user how much is known about her. This feedback leads users to be more cautious and not give private data to social networks. In our research, we have followed the action research methodology, that is, we have used quantitative and qualitative research with practical interventions which consisted in implementing a web application tool based on social network APIs for feedbacking to users what is visible of their data. In addition, we mechanized formal modeling and analysis for social network scenarios including human actors in Isabelle. For the latter application, we have used the Isabelle Insider framework to provide a dynamic logic model enabling (1) formally reproducing the experimental scenario and (2) embedding the notion of awareness in the general security notion of insiderness. We have thus linked up social network analysis to formal security engineering and provided a novel formal notion of unintentional insiderness.

References

1. Alvarado, C.M.: Privacy and risk on the internet: a social search tool for social networking users to increase self-awareness in information sharing. BSc CS dissertation, Middlesex University London (2021)
2. Bada, M., Sasse, A., Nurse, J.R.C.: Cyber security awareness campaign: why do they fail to change behaviour? In: International Conference on Cyber Security for Sustainable Society, pp. 118–131 (2015). arXiv:1901.02672
3. Barnes, S.B.: A privacy paradox: social networking in the United States. First Monday 11(9) (2006)
4. Bishop, M., Nance, K., Clark, J.: Inside the insider threat (introduction). In: Proceedings of the 50th Hawaii International Conference on System Sciences, p. 2637, January 2017

5. Boender, J., Ivanova, M.G., Kammüller, F., Primiero, G.: Modeling human behaviour with higher order logic: insider threats. In: STAST 2014. IEEE (2014). Co-located with CSF 2014 in the Vienna Summer of Logic

6. Bulgurcu, B., Cavusoglu, H., Benbasat, I.: Information security policy compliance: an empirical study of rationality-based beliefs and information security awareness. MIS Q. **34**(3), 523–548 (2010)

7. Cappelli, D.M., Moore, A.P., Trzeciak, R.F.: The CERT Guide to Insider Threats: How to Prevent, Detect, and Respond to Information Technology Crimes (Theft, Sabotage, Fraud). SEI Series in Software Engineering, 1st edn. Addison-Wesley Professional (2012)

8. CHIST-ERA. Success: Secure accessibility for the internet of things (2016). http://www.chistera.eu/projects/success

9. Elster, J.: The Cement of Society. Cambridge University Press, Cambridge (1989)

10. Esser, H.: Soziologie - Allgemeine Grundlagen. Campus (1993)

11. Hempel, C.G., Oppenheim, P.: Studies in the logic of explanation. Philos. Sci. **15**, 135–175 (1948)

12. Homans, G.: Social Behaviour: Its Elementary Forms. Routledge and Kegan Paul (1961)

13. Kammüller, F.: Formalizing probabilistic quantum security protocols in the Isabelle infrastructure framework. Informal Presentation at Computability in Europe, CiE (2019)

14. Kammüller, F.: Formal models of human factors for security and privacy. In: 5th International Conference on Human Aspects of Security, Privacy and Trust, HCII-HAS 2017. LNCS, vol. 10292, pp. 339–352. Springer (2017). Affiliated with HCII 2017

15. Kammüller, F.: Human centric security and privacy for the IoT using formal techniques. In: Nicholson, D. (ed.) AHFE 2017. AISC, vol. 593, pp. 106–116. Springer, Cham (2018). https://doi.org/10.1007/978-3-319-60585-2_12

16. Kammüller, F.: A proof calculus for attack trees in Isabelle. In: Garcia-Alfaro, J., Navarro-Arribas, G., Hartenstein, H., Herrera-Joancomartí, J. (eds.) ESORICS/DPM/CBT -2017. LNCS, vol. 10436, pp. 3–18. Springer, Cham (2017). https://doi.org/10.1007/978-3-319-67816-0_1

17. Kammüller, F.: Attack trees in Isabelle. In: Naccache, D., et al. (eds.) ICICS 2018. LNCS, vol. 11149, pp. 611–628. Springer, Cham (2018). https://doi.org/10.1007/978-3-030-01950-1_36

18. Kammüller, F.: Formal modeling and analysis of data protection for GDPR compliance of IoT healthcare systems. In: IEEE Systems, Man and Cybernetics, SMC 2018. IEEE (2018)

19. Kammüller, F.: Attack trees in Isabelle extended with probabilities for quantum cryptography. Comput. Secur. **87**, 101572 (2019)

20. Kammüller, F.: Combining secure system design with risk assessment for IoT healthcare systems. In: Workshop on Security, Privacy, and Trust in the IoT, SPTIoT 2019, Colocated with IEEE PerCom. IEEE (2019)

21. Kammüller, F.: QKD in Isabelle - Bayesian calculation. arXiv, cs.CR (2019)

22. Kammüller, F.: Isabelle Insider and Infrastructure framework with Kripke strutures, CTL, attack trees, security refinement, and examples including IoT, GDPR, QKD, and social networks (2021). https://github.com/flokam/IsabelleAT

23. Kammüller, F., Kerber, M.: Investigating airplane safety and security against insider threats using logical modeling. In: IEEE Security and Privacy Workshops, Workshop on Research in Insider Threats, WRIT 2016. IEEE (2016)

24. Kammüller, F., Kerber, M.: Applying the Isabelle insider framework to airplane security. Sci. Comput. Programm. **206**, 102623 (2021)
25. Kammüller, F., Kerber, M., Probst, C.: Towards formal analysis of insider threats for auctions. In: 8th ACM CCS International Workshop on Managing Insider Security Threats, MIST 2016. ACM (2016)
26. Kammüller, F., Kerber, M., Probst, C.: Insider threats for auctions: formal modeling, proof, and certified code. J. Wirel. Mob. Netw. Ubiquit. Comput. Dependable Appl. (JoWUA) **8**(1), 44–78 (2017)
27. Kammüller, F., Lutz, B.: Modeling and analyzing the corona-virus warning app with the Isabelle infrastructure framework. In: Garcia-Alfaro, J., Navarro-Arribas, G., Herrera-Joancomarti, J. (eds.) DPM/CBT -2020. LNCS, vol. 12484, pp. 128–144. Springer, Cham (2020). https://doi.org/10.1007/978-3-030-66172-4_8
28. Kammüller, F., Nestmann, U.: Inter-blockchain protocols with the Isabelle infrastructure framework. In: Formal Methods for Blockchain, 2nd Int. Workshop, Colocated with CAV 2020, Open Access series in Informatics. Dagstuhl publishing (2020, to appear)
29. Kammüller, F., Probst, C.W.: Invalidating policies using structural information. In: IEEE Security and Privacy Workshops, Workshop on Research in Insider Threats, WRIT 2013 (2013)
30. Kammüller, F., Probst, C.W.: Combining generated data models with formal invalidation for insider threat analysis. In: IEEE Security and Privacy Workshops, Workshop on Research in Insider Threats, WRIT 2014 (2014)
31. Kammüller, F., Probst, C.W.: Modeling and verification of insider threats using logical analysis. IEEE Syst. J. Spec. Issue Insider Threats Inf. Secur. Digit. Espionage Counter Intell. **11**(2), 534–545 (2017)
32. Kammüller, F., Wenzel, M., Paulson, L.C.: Locales a sectioning concept for Isabelle. In: Bertot, Y., Dowek, G., Théry, L., Hirschowitz, A., Paulin, C. (eds.) TPHOLs 1999. LNCS, vol. 1690, pp. 149–165. Springer, Heidelberg (1999). https://doi.org/10.1007/3-540-48256-3_11
33. Kammüller, F.: A formal development cycle for security engineering in Isabelle. arxiv preprint, http://arxiv.org/abs/2001.08983 (2020)
34. Korovessis, P., Furnell, S., Papadaki, M., Haskell-Dowland, P.: A toolkit approach to information security awareness and education. J. Cybersecur. Educ. Res. Pract. **2**(5) (2017)
35. Kritzinger, E., von Solms, S.: Cyber security for home users: a new way of protection through awareness enforcement. Comput. Secur. **29**(8), 840–847 (2010)
36. Kruger, H., Kearney, W.: A prototype for assessing information security awareness. Comput. Secur. **25**(4), 289–296 (2006)
37. Labuschagne, W.A., Burke, I., Veerasamy, N., Eloff, M.M.: Design of cyber security awareness game utilizing a social media framework. In: Information Security for South Africa, pp. 1–9 (2011). https://doi.org/10.1109/ISSA.2011.6027538
38. Lacey, D.: Managing the Human Factor in Information Security. Wiley, Hoboken (2009)
39. Lewin, K.: Aktionsforschung und minderheitenprobleme. In: Lewin, K. (ed.) Die Lösung sozialer Konflikte, pp. 278–298. Christian-Verlag, Bad-Neuheim (1948)
40. Myers, A.C., Liskov, B.: Complete, safe information flow with decentralized labels. In: Proceedings of the IEEE Symposium on Security and Privacy. IEEE (1999)
41. Nurse, J.R.C., et al.: Understanding insider threat: a framework for characterising attacks. In: IEEE Security and Privacy Workshops (SPW). IEEE (2014)
42. Paulson, L.C.: Proving properties of security protocols by induction. In: CSFW, pp. 70–83. IEEE Computer Society (1997)

43. Scott, J.: Rational choice theory. In: Understanding Contemporary Society: Theories of the Present, pp. 126–138. SAGE (2000)
44. C. I. T. Team: Unintentional insider threats: a foundational study. Technical report CMU/SEI-2013-TN-022, Software Engineering Institute, Carnegie Mellon University, Pittsburgh, PA (2013)
45. Weber, M.: Conceptual exposition. In: Economy and Society. Bedminster Press (1968)
46. Weber, M.: Wirtschaft und Gesellschaft. Grundriss der verstehenden Soziologie, 5th edn. Tübingen (1972)

Shaping Attacker Behavior: Evaluation of an Enhanced Cyber Maneuver Framework

Jennifer A. B. McKneely[1(✉)], Tara K. Sell[2], Kathleen A. Straub[1], Mika D. Ayenson[1], and Daniel Thomas[1]

[1] Johns Hopkins University Applied Physics Laboratory, Laurel, MD 20723, USA
`jennifer.mckneely@jhuapl.edu`
[2] Department of Environmental Health and Engineering, Johns Hopkins University, Baltimore, MD 21202, USA

Abstract. Recent cyberattacks highlight the limitations of perimeter-based defenses and the need for a multi-layered approach to cybersecurity. Modern cybersecurity best practices include elevated internal sensors and controls; however, these are reactive defensive measures. Cyber defenders need layered defenses to protect systems when perimeters are breached. Cyber maneuvers are a paradigm shift in cyber defense that incorporates proactive cyber actions that aim to achieve positional or temporal advantages over an adversary in the cognitive, technical, and physical domains. Cyber defenders can implement maneuvers by taking actions on the network to create situations where attackers become visible, detectable, and must reshape their planned attack steps impeding progress and mission success. Current cyber-defense frameworks primarily focus on the technical actions and response, with limited attention on adversary behavioral and cognitive effects. We discuss current frameworks and present an alternative enhanced cyber maneuver framework that integrates cognitive processing mechanisms through which an adversary's behavioral response can be shaped. Our enhanced framework provides a foundation with specific cyber maneuvers and actions mapped through the explanatory influence mechanisms and cognitive effects to shape the desired behavioral outcomes. We demonstrate the effect of proposed maneuvers on attacker behavior to validate the framework and mappings and the methodology for testing. In so doing, we define a cyber-maneuver framework that transcends cyber deception and Moving Target Defense and propose a methodology for cyber maneuver design and evaluation. Cyber maneuvers and the cognitive and behavioral responses they are designed to shape are described. We introduce and describe a preliminary study of an evaluation methodology that enables prediction and quantification of cyber maneuver effects.

Keywords: Behavior-based cybersecurity · Cognition in cyber

1 Introduction

1.1 Cyber Maneuvers

The highly visible SolarWinds Orion cybersecurity attack [1] of 2020 highlights that passive perimeter-based network defenses, while necessary, are insufficient in repelling

Advance Persistent Threats (APTs). Cyber defenders need a layered defense capability that not only strengthens the edges but provides for active mechanisms to detect and disrupt attackers when they are able to breach the perimeter defense. Cyber maneuver is an emerging concept of cyber operations that may be effective in bolstering network defenses.

Cyber maneuver's aim is to eliminate an adversary's advantage by introducing surprise, confusion, and disorder to distract and disrupt the adversary's cognitive processes [2, 3]. Cyber maneuvers span the full spectrum of offensive to defensive cyber operations and are implemented based on a mission's goal. Defensive cyber maneuvers intend to cause predictable behavioral responses that make an adversary more detectable and curtail their progress enabling defenders to proactively respond to attacks. They [3–5] shift the advantage from the adversary to the defender. Allen [2] defines cyber maneuvers as follows:

Cyber maneuvers are actions taken within and through cyberspace to achieve physical, technical, and cognitive positional and temporal advantages over an adversary.

Network defenders' physical advantages include access to friendly and adversary cyber capabilities. Technical advantages include having more capable cyber capabilities and methods of employment than the adversary. Cognitive advantages include, but are not limited to, superior situational awareness over the adversary and creating surprise, confusion, undermining their confidence, and manipulating their thoughts and actions.

Defensive cyber maneuvers are part of comprehensive protect, monitor, and respond approaches to cyber defense where actions are taken on the network to expose undetected adversaries by causing them to become visible and actionable, and to disrupt adversary missions by reshaping or curtailing adversary progress. Research into network-based defense approaches and software diversity show effectiveness but require defenders to notice and respond in less time than it takes an adversary to complete their already-in-progress attack [6]. Reports [7] show that 88% of data is stolen in mere minutes, meanwhile vulnerabilities can take days to mitigate. Mitigation is only possible after discovery which can take weeks or months to occur. These reactive cyber defense strategies are insufficient for today's evolving threat [5, 6]. Effective cyber defense requires cost-effective strategies that expose adversaries and interrupt them prior to exploitation.

Cyber defense frameworks typically focus on technology solutions; however, cyber defenses must extend beyond solely technology-focused solutions and integrate psychological operational strategies. Implementation of both technological advancements and the continuous, operational application of mental creativity and agility will help ensure cybersecurity success. In contrast to technical solution-oriented frameworks, we propose an enhanced cyber maneuver framework that applies proactive defensive actions to establish a positional advantage in the cognitive domain. The cognitive advantage stems from the defender's ability to measurably influence the adversary's cognitive processing to predictably shape their behavioral response. The cognitive advantage stems from the defender's ability to measurably influence adversaries' cognitive processes and emotional responses, including, but not limited to, increasing workload, frustration, reducing confidence, and shaping the adversaries' subsequent behavior in a predictable way.

2   Cyber Maneuver Frameworks

Maneuvers have shown to be beneficial in military operations [8]; they are conducted to trigger predictable, observable adversary actions. Research in cyber maneuver describes the technical or environmental implications of introducing cyber maneuvers [8, 9] or model specific responses to technical cyber defense solutions [10–14]. However, empirical support for the cognitive effects of defensive cyber maneuvers is limited.

Currently articulated cyber maneuver frameworks vary widely in the degree to which they invoke and leverage an adversary's cognitive or emotional response to achieve the desired goal. For instance, Brantly [15] operationalizes cyber maneuvers and describes their use to attain strategic and mission objectives within cyber and cross-domain operations. Lack of specificity in the mapping of cyber actions to behaviors limits the ability to directly plan cyber operations that target specific outcomes. CONCEAL, a deception planning framework proposed by Duan, Al-Shaer, Islam, and Jafarian [16], transforms situational input (e.g., constraints, system configurations, and host assignments) into deceptive host configurations designed to meet specific operational goals. Success criteria and effectiveness metrics are characterized in terms of technical considerations and risk. The framework does not incorporate consideration of how cognitive, mental, or workload effects associated with deception may drive attackers toward target beliefs or behaviors. Almeshekah and Spafford [17] present a more comprehensive explanation of adversary beliefs, limitations, and cognitive responses that mediate deception effectiveness within cyber deception but does not extend beyond this technical implementation; similar analysis can be applied in contexts without deception.

The defender's objective is behavioral—divert, delay, or defeat an attacker's progress. The means to affect behavior, though often underspecified, is cognitive manipulation by distracting, confusing, or frustrating the adversary. The enhanced cyber maneuver framework actively integrates cognitive considerations in terms of analyzing exploitable limitations (e.g., cognitive biases and processing limitations) and anticipating the adversary's cognitive or emotional response (e.g., increased frustration or decreased confidence) so as to predict the behavioral outcomes associated with specific maneuvers.

3   Enhanced Cyber Maneuver Framework

The enhanced cyber maneuver framework seeks to address the under specification of the impact on the humans-in-the-loop by explicitly representing humans and cognitive processing into the cyber maneuver concept. Similarities between deception and cyber maneuver [18] are leveraged and we incorporate findings from successful Psychological Operations (PSYOP) [19, 20] to integrate human limitations in cognitive processing and persuasion. These include leveraging cognitive biases, working memory and inhibition limitations, intuitive response to messaging, and natural tendencies to minimize mental effort and socially connect to others. Cyber maneuvers are designed to influence adversary behavior, much like PSYOP. However, the mapping of theories of persuasion and behavior change has yet to be done, which impacts the ability of cyber defenders to design and evaluate predictable cyber maneuvers prior to execution.

When considered through the lens of behavioral economics, cyberattacks can be reduced to a series of decisions. One decision, for instance, is an attacker must decide which network asset to pivot to next, or whether to remain stealthy. These decisions consist of value-based judgements in which risk is weighed against potential reward. Attacker decision-making is likely also influenced by contextual factors, including the stress and fatigue associated with offensive cyber operations (OCO) [21] and uncertainty associated with causes of system behavior [22].

Cyber defenders can leverage cognitive processing and heuristic decision-making theories when designing maneuvers to disrupt and shape judgements. The Elaboration Likelihood Model (ELM) [23] posits that people receive and interpret new information along one of two routes (central or peripheral) based on the motivation and capability of the receiver. Highly attentive receivers respond via the central route where they actively elaborate on new information, assessing, filtering, and scrutinizing that information before integrating it into their situational hypotheses and/or current belief model. In contrast, individuals with reduced cognitive capacity or interest process new information using peripheral route thinking, without active analysis, issue-relevant thinking, or elaboration. In the context of cyber engagement, an attacker employing central route thinking will carefully analyze a new event, explore alternative explanations, and may engage in additional data gathering (e.g., conducting additional scans) or even alter their attack in response to environmental change. In contrast, attackers driven by distraction to the more shallow, peripheral route thinking become more likely to accept the persuasive maneuver manipulation "at face value" and more susceptible to the errors inherent in heuristic decision-making.

Information load, when combined with pressure and uncertainty, can drive attackers toward peripheral thinking routes, which in turn drives attackers to invoke decision-making shortcuts or heuristics [24]. Heuristic decisions are faster, but prone to predictable errors known as cognitive biases. For example, confirmation bias occurs when decision-makers readily note and assimilate evidence confirming an existing hypothesis while actively ignoring counter evidence. Cyber maneuvers can be explicitly designed to leverage biases based on (1) understanding the range of known cognitive biases and processing limitations, (2) anticipating the adversary's attack goal, and (3) predicting their cognitive or emotional response to interference associated with the maneuver. In the context of confirmation bias, an effective maneuver would integrate system changes and generate system feedback consistent with the adversary's goals and the expected attack outcome. Cyber maneuver designers should seek to actively understand and exploit confirmation bias and other known biases when developing maneuvers.

Our enhanced cyber maneuver framework is based on Allen's [2] cyber maneuver concept, and is elaborated with desired human behavior and the cognitive mechanism by which that behavior would emerge (Fig. 1). In short, a maneuver planner starts by selecting the desired effect (e.g., keep the adversary busy) and the associated adversary behavior(s) that can lead to that end (e.g., detecting resulting anomalous network traffic). From there, the planner identifies a set of maneuvers and, within them, specific candidate cyber actions that might drive the target behavior. Lastly, a systematic mapping is done for each candidate action to its estimated associated influence or cognitive processing effect. This analysis should take into consideration general cognitive limitations (e.g., attention or working memory limits), processing or workload invoked by the maneuver (e.g., increased attention or memory load), emotional response evoked by the maneuver (e.g., increased frustration or decreased confidence), and emergent decision-making biases resulting from peripheral route thinking and heuristic decision-making (e.g., confirmation bias.) Using this systematic evaluation, maneuver planners can exclude, select, and prioritize tactics based on a holistic analysis of the cognitive effects that mediate the success of the maneuver. A planner must think like the adversary when designing the maneuver. The planner must assess alternative explanations for emerging system and information effects *from the adversary's perspective*, focus on the limitations and cognitive biases that drive adversaries toward assumptions and heuristic thinking, and design maneuvers to reinforce and exploit them.

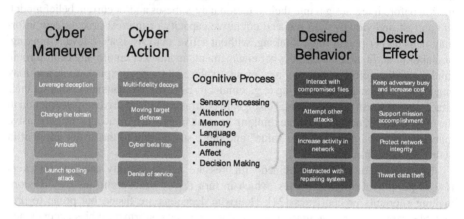

Fig. 1. Enhanced cyber maneuver framework

3.1 Categories of Maneuvers and Maneuver Actions

Cyber maneuvers were mapped by threat objectives and the cognitive mechanisms that mediate and shape adversary beliefs and behaviors (Table 1) to support cyber maneuver selection and operational planning. Specifying the cognitive mechanisms amplifies the role of human operators within the cyberattack system and facilitates verification testing prior to execution. The maneuvers presented here focus on defensive actions; however, the framework extends to offensive maneuvers, which will be added as the research and technology matures.

Table 1. Mapping defensive cyber maneuvers to desired effect and cognitive mechanisms

Cyber threat framework (objectives)	Cyber maneuver	Cyber action	Influence/cognitive mechanisms	Desired behavior	Desired effect
Expand/refine targeting/exfiltrate	**Ambush**	Dumb admin - makes apparent, but not real errors	• Confidence • Attention • Decision-making • Heuristics and bias	Adversary takes more detectable actions due to overconfidence	Detect previously undetected adversaries
Expand/refine targeting	**Herd**	Bandwidth reduction on selected high value assets	• Frustration • Attention • Increased workload • Decision-making • Heuristics and bias	Move to fake or low value asset	• Thwart data theft • Observe TTP
Hide	**Stimulate a Response**	Reboot	• Confusion • Frustration • Workload • Attention • Decision-making • Heuristics and bias	Increased activity in network	• Detect adversary • Deter future operations
		Rotate	• Confusion • Frustration • Workload • Attention • Decision-making • Heuristics and bias	Increased activity in network	• Detect adversary • Deter future operations
		Change credentials	• Confusion • Frustration • Workload • Attention • Decision-making • Heuristics and bias	Increased activity in network	• Detect adversary • Deter future operations
Establish initial control/expand/refine targeting	**Leverage Deception**	decoy assets	• Confusion • Attention • Decision-making • Heuristics and bias	Access fake systems Conduct operation exposing TTP	• Detect adversary • Distract from real assets, expose TTP
Expand/refine targeting/establish persistence		Decoy credentials	• Confidence • Attention • Decision-making • Heuristics and bias	Access fake systems Conduct operation exposing TTP	• Detect adversary • Expose TTP

(*continued*)

Table 1. (*continued*)

Cyber threat framework (objectives)	Cyber maneuver	Cyber action	Influence/cognitive mechanisms	Desired behavior	Desired effect
Alter system behavior/extract data/destroy HW/SW/data		Decoy content with/out beacons	• Confidence • Attention • Decision-making • Heuristics and bias	Exfiltrate fake content, confuse adversary as to content validity	Adversary unsure what content is real
Extract data		Decoy communications	• Confidence • Attention • Decision-making • Heuristics and bias	Cause adversary confusion as to real vs decoy traffic and assets	Cause adversary to wait longer to take an action
Expand/refine targeting	**Change the terrain**	• Moving target defense • Rotate memory address • Rotate MAC address	• Confidence • Frustration • Attention • Workload • Working memory • Decision-making • Heuristics and bias	Attempt other attacks	• Waste time • Waste resources,
Establish persistence	**Leverage Perishability**	Reduce persistence by changing configurations	• Uncertainty • Frustration • Workload • Working memory • Decision-making • Heuristics and bias	Frequently check implants, making more detectable	Make adversary more detectable and less effective
Establish initial control/alter system behavior/extract data	**Delay Adversary**	Reduce bandwidth selectively	• Frustration • Decision-making • Workload • Heuristics and bias	Increased time on network asset	• Detect adversary • Switch to a different target

4 Testing Cyber Maneuvers

Fundamental to the framework is the inclusion of a comprehensive methodology to evaluate maneuvers in a systematic and predictive manner. Maneuvers need to be tested via a repeatable method to empirically validate and verify the effects and cognitive processing that mediates them. Validating a cyber maneuver involves (1) defining the desired behavior; (2) mapping the cognitive mechanism(s) by which the behavior is shaped; (3) operationally defining metrics/measures to assess both the cognitive and technical effects; and (4) instrumenting an experimental environment that can execute the cyber maneuvers and capture the critical effects, behaviors, responses.

Evolving from technology focused solutions requires measurement of cyber maneuver effects on the behavioral responses and cognitive mechanisms through which they are shaped. Participant activity logs with timestamps for the virtual machines (VMs) can be used to capture behavior reflected in adversary traffic and host- and network-based traffic and actions analyzed to show what commands are used, when they are used, frequency of use, along with the load on the machine. These data provide indications of cyber maneuver effects by showing the visibility of the adversary (machine load changes) and behavioral responses (e.g., reattempt access) time synched with the cyber action. Cognitive processing can be captured using both subjective (e.g., self-report) and objective data. Self-report measures that gauge participant perceptions of mission progress and confidence can be collected during simulated attacks through scenario embedded queries. Additionally, post-run task related questions are useful to measure attacker workload, confusion, surprise, confidence, and frustration [25]. NASA Task Load Index (TLX) is a proven method of subjective cognitive workload that assesses six dimensions on a 20-point unanchored scale [26]. Objective workload can be assessed via portable measures of neural activity from brain imaging using functional Near-Infrared (fNIRS). fNIRS measures blood volume, flow, and oxygenation and, by extension, neural activity. An emerging body of literature indicates that fNIRS measures are sensitive to mental task load [27] and that specific patterns of neural activity observable with fNIRS are associated with psychological processes involved in influence (counter arguing, self-integration, self-affirmation, and narrative immersion) [28].

4.1 Pilot Study

This study was conducted in accordance with Johns Hopkins University's Institutional Review Board (IRB) under protocol IRB00214055.

We conducted a pilot study to demonstrate the ability to systematically evaluate the technical and cognitive effects of cyber maneuvers. The application of fNIRS to complex long duration tasks is relatively new and not yet proven in the cyber domain. We explored the feasibility of adding this measurement technique as a proof-of-principal. We developed and used a comprehensive virtual environment to conduct experiments evaluating various actions supporting the stimulate a response, herd, and leverage deception cyber maneuvers presented in Table 1. Cyber missions involve a series of actions to accomplish the objective (described in MITRE ATT&CK [29]) that extend over weeks, months, or longer. To allow for testing within a constrained period of time, experimental tasks were designed to be a subset of a typical cyberattack allowing for multiple trials of a specific task within a single test session. Our experiment was inspired by France's response to cyberattack during their 2017 elections that demonstrated that decoy content files that contain and, by exfiltration (exfil), disseminate misinformation can further increase confusion and uncertainty [30].

Study Design. We designed a two-session experiment to evaluate the *stimulate a response* and *leverage deception* cyber maneuvers. During Session 1, we evaluated the *stimulate a response* maneuver by challenging participants to exfiltrate as much content as possible from a target network over four Trials. *Stimulate a response* was implemented via two separate cyber actions: reboot and revert. These actions require aperiodic re-authentication, forcing participants to reinitiate access actions resulting in increased likelihood of detection and confusion, uncertainty, and frustration from lost effort. During Session 2, we evaluated both the *stimulate a response* maneuver/revert action and *leverage deception/decoy* action combination by challenging the participant to maliciously modify target website content over two Trials. To support the *stimulate a response maneuver*, the revert action reset the network to a previous, known state based on a predefined interval resulting in confusion, uncertainty, and frustration as a result of the lost effort. *Leverage deception* was deployed as both decoy systems and decoy content, which increases adversary visibility and wastes their time and resources. Note this preliminary study did not include cyber defenders who would conceptually receive an alert if decoy content/systems were interacted with. Additionally, this study was conducted as a pilot to demonstrate the ability to measure behavioral and cognitive effects on cyberttackers and is an early step to developing empirical approaches to more comprehensively integrate human considerations into cybersecurity. Therefore, we conducted the analysis as a case study approach conducting a deep dive on individual participant, including analysis of interview data. This will be used to hone data collection tools for use in follow-on experiments.

Participants. Ten male staff members of the Johns Hopkins University Applied Physics Laboratory (JHU/APL), recruited through purposeful sampling, volunteered to participate in both sessions. Six participants were under age 35, three between 35 and 49, and two over 50. Participants reported varying levels of cyber red teaming experience, as shown in Fig. 2. Reported Cyber Experience Level by Skill.

Testing Facility and Equipment. The experiment was conducted in JHU/APL's Behavior and Human Performance in Advanced Environments (BeHAVE) lab, configured to engage participants in the scenario. A clock was used to countdown the time remaining in each Trial, posters were mounted with key scenario information and propaganda, and music was available if participants desired. Participants worked from on a desktop PC that had a connection to JHU/APL's virtual environment hosting the experimental simulation. They were provided Cobalt Strike software and the Kali operating system to conduct attacks on the fictional victim (Liberal Democratic Idealists (LDI)) network.

Participants filled out demographic information, task questions, and the NASA TLX (cognitive workload measure) using a separate windows desktop that accessed the Qualtrics software. While conducting the task, participants were outfitted with the

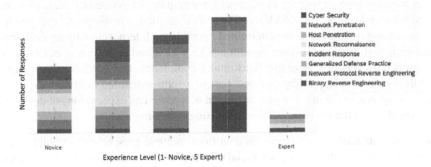

Fig. 2. Reported cyber experience level by skill

NIRSport system (NIRx, Germany) fNIRS device to collect brain imaging data. The fNIRS device provides relative change in hemoglobin levels, calculated using a modified Beer-Lambert law.

- Oxygenated hemoglobin change: delta O2Hb (μmol/L)
- Deoxygenated hemoglobin change: delta HHb (μmol/L)
- Total hemoglobin change: delta cHb (μmol/L)

Measurement is taken from NIR light sources, placed directly onto a participant's scalp, to the detectors. A 16-channel NIRSport fNIRS device with a sampling rate of 7.812 Hz was used to measure hemodynamic response. A total of 16 (sources = 8, detectors = 8) fNIRS optodes were distributed evenly over the left prefrontal and right prefrontal cortices. The optodes were secured within individually sized EEG caps to ensure proper spacing and stability of the optodes during data collection. Plastic supports were placed between each source/detector pair to maintain a 3-cm channel length for all participants.

Procedure. Participants individually completed the two sessions between one and two weeks apart. Within each session, participants role-played a nefarious attacker executing a cyberattack mission of a political party's computing network. During Session 1, participants were instructed to complete four exfil attacks (experimental trials) and during Session 2, attempt two exfil and website content manipulation attacks (experimental trials). Participants executed their attacks using Cobalt Strike beacon running on a "pre-compromised" Windows desktop machine in the test environment with a Kali virtual machine and Cobalt Strike against the target network simulation. Each trial had a slightly modified network [change in Internet Protocol (IP) addresses, location of insertion point]. The network complexity and density were consistent across trials such that all trials had equal network environment difficulty. Participants were provided a network map for each trial identifying their established insertion point and key terrain; they were not informed of the potential presence of cyber maneuvers. They were allotted 20 min to complete each attack in Session 1, and 30 min in Session 2. A countdown timer was displayed prominently near the participant's workstation to provide continuous time-remaining status and to increase performance pressure.

In addition to executing the cyberattacks, participants responded to status inquires, called Status Update Reports (STURs). These STURs queried participants' current mission status and confidence at predetermined intervals via Internet chat during each trial. After each trial, participants completed the NASA TLX and at the end of each session questions on levels of uncertainty, frustration, confidence, and surprise. Lastly, upon completing Session 2, participants took part in a semi-structured interview exploring general response to the mission task, detection of maneuvers, expectations of deception on networks, and their typical TTP in conducting red team missions.

Findings. Our methodology captures data from multiple perspectives to build a converging analysis pointing to the beneficial effects of cyber maneuvers and the cognitive mechanisms that underlie their success. Measures include the following:

- Adversary behavior
- Change in participant cognitive state (e.g., confidence, frustration, perceived workload)
- Adversary perception (and attribution) of the maneuver (to defender action)
- Attack success (content exfilled, website defacement)
- Attacker brain activity (exploratory)

This initial study was conducted as a pilot to demonstrate the ability to measure behavioral and cognitive effects on cyber attackers. It is an early step to developing empirical approaches to more comprehensively integrate human considerations into cybersecurity. Therefore, while we considered findings across participants for self-reported workload, cognitive state, and adversary perception, our analysis for the comprehensive set of data was conducted with a case study approach looking in detail on an individual participant (CM012). Selection of the participant for detailed analysis involved consideration of a few factors. We considered the experience reported by each participant both in terms of red teaming and in use of the toolset. Once we had determined which participants had the highest skill level, we considered the completeness of data ensuring we had at least one participant with a complete data set. Long duration fNIRS data is challenging to collect and we encountered instances of signal loss or poor-quality connection across many participants. We had five participants who were skilled with the toolset and task data. Of these, participant CM012 had the highest quality fNIRS data set. Our detailed analysis and evaluation of the data collection tools will be used to hone data collection tools for use in follow-on experiments. We present initial data to show the efficacy of measuring behavioral and cognitive response to maneuvers.

Behavioral Effects. Analysis of adversary behavior was evaluated from activity on the network measured by machine load and tool interactions captured with Filebeat and Metricbeat sensors. Analytic scripts placed on the attacker's Kali tracked total machine load, interactions with the Cobalt Strike tool, and specific human interactions with the tool. The activity shows tool use over time providing indication of participants' proficiency and effectiveness of tool use and insight into behavioral effects.

Session 1: The ***stimulate a response*** maneuver (reboot and revert actions) resulted in increased activity on the target machine. Figure 3 shows the activity load from Cobalt

Strike (desktop) and the types of commands over the course of the four Trials. Time across the entire session (all four Trials) runs along the x-axis and total machine load along the y-axis. The participant takes additional actions using task-oriented commands (such as port scans, taking screenshots, downloading and performing other commands) during the two Trials with maneuvers (2 and 3) compared to the Trials without maneuvers (1 and 4) (Fig. 3).

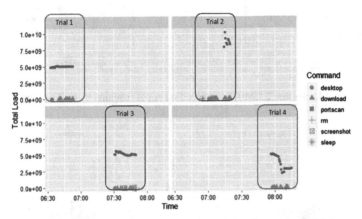

Fig. 3. Session 1 CM012 machine load by trial and command and time

Session 2: The ***stimulate a response/leverage deception/decoy*** combination maneuver resulted in a higher machine load and activity than the no maneuver (Trial 1). Inspection of types of commands used by CM012 in Trial 1 versus Trial 2 shows fewer listing of files and downloads and more use of PS exec and Pass the Hash attempts (Fig. 4). This indicates multiple attempts to complete the task and upload the defaced webpage. The machine load data is insufficient to determine which maneuver is driving the increased activity. Consideration of other cognitive performance related experimental data along with the machine load is required to interpret the results.

Cognitive Effects. The impact of maneuvers on cognitive processing was measured with STURs, NASA TLX, task questions, and fNIRS imaging. The NASA TLX results include the individual factors and an overall workload calculated by a weighted score. Across all participants there were no significant differences in overall workload between Trials (Fig. 5). The No Maneuver 1 Trial always occurred first, as seen in the figure, this Trial has the highest average workload. This is likely attributed to learning effects and participants gaining familiarity with the toolset and task. This effect was anticipated and we included an additional 'no maneuver' Trial at the end to better understand the impacts of the maneuver apart from gaining experience with the task and task environment. The No Maneuver 2 Trial has the lowest average workload further suggesting that there were indeed learning effects associated with the performance of Trial 1.

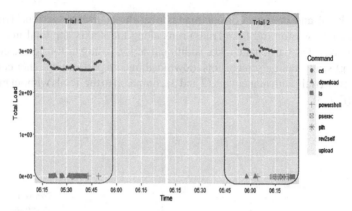

Fig. 4. Session 2 CM012 total load on target machine by trial and time

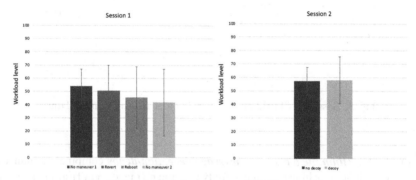

Fig. 5. Session 1 & 2 average workload by condition

Participant CM012 reported notable increases in the time/effort associated with exfiltration of the target files in the reboot condition, as reported in NASA TLX (Fig. 6). This figure shows the reported workload (y-axis) over Trial condition (x-axis) of no maneuver, revert, reboot, and no maneuver for session 1 and decoy, no-decoy for session 2. Analysis of the adversary command-line activity logs supports this interpretation: the *stimulate a response* maneuver increased the attacker workload by requiring the participant to re-acquire access to the file and reinitiate exfil, which increased the time and effort associated with exfil actions. The *decoy* (content) action had no apparent effect on subjective workload; the task was equally difficult in both Trial conditions.

Session 1: Thematic analysis conducted of the STURs showed individual participant STUR summaries to be consistent with NASA TLX data; indicating that participants were learning the task environment over time. Confidence in performance varied across participants. Some were quite confident and able to complete the exfil mission, others had low confidence and performance throughout. Interestingly, CM012 had high confidence across Trials except for the last STUR in Trial 3 which is also the Trial with the highest self-report workload condition. Results from the end of session questionnaire measuring confusion, confidence, frustration, and surprise across all participants show that they

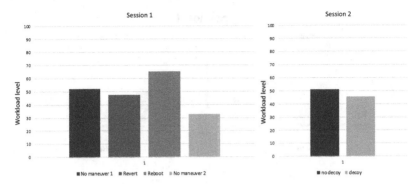

Fig. 6. CM012 session 1 & 2 workload by condition

were sometimes confused and relatively split on confidence with regard to how they were doing (Fig. 7). Despite expectations that exposure to the reset action would introduce increased frustration, we did not observe higher frustration levels in the maneuver. Post-hoc interview response analysis indicates participants did not attribute reset actions to proactive defender behavior (no participant responded that they noticed the maneuver) and they were not very frustrated or surprised in Session 1.

Session 2: During Session 2, each time the target webpage was modified and launched a STUR was sent to the participant. Thematic analysis of STURs across participants in Session 2 showed decreased confidence in mission completion over the two Trials as a result of the revert maneuver. The presence of decoys did not appear to impact participants; they were not identified as deception and the effect of the revert maneuver garnered almost exclusive attention. Results from the post-session task questions shown in Fig. 7 are consistent with the STURs. The post-session questions show that participants' level of confusion was relatively low, but they experienced more frustration in Session 2 than in Session 1. Confidence increased and participants were less surprised. During post-experiment interviews, participants were asked about their experiences. When asked about a low surprise self-report, at least one participant responded: *"Because I knew you were going to do something; I just didn't know what."* This could arguably be perceived as increasing the confidence in knowing defensive mechanisms occurred, while also lowering their confidence in completing the task successfully.

Neural Analysis Our study included a proof-of-principal investigation to demonstrate the feasibility of collecting neural imaging data over long duration complex cyber tasks. We were able to collect data from participants through all Trials in both sessions; however, we found there was signal loss over time and not all participants had full data sets. The participant who comprises our case study did have the most complete data set and, as described below, we found indications that there are differences in neural activity at times when maneuvers were occurring and at the end of the Trials. This suggests that there is orienting to the network changes and that there were cognitive impacts possibly due to time pressure associated with completing the mission prior to the end of Trial [22].

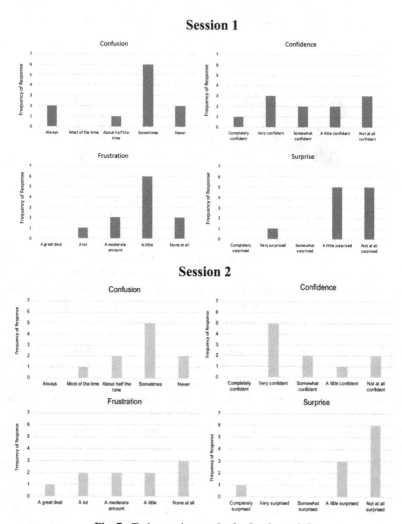

Fig. 7. Task question results for Session 1 & 2

Exploratory analysis of CM012's fNIRS data was conducted for mental activity along specified blocks of time in Sessions 1 and 2. NIRsLab was used to pre-process the raw fNIRS data by excluding excessive noise from channels, removing irrelevant time intervals, and deleting data artifacts (e.g., irrelevant frequency bands) through filtering. Hemodynamic states were computed using both path length dependent and wavelength parameter settings, revealing the color-coded images. These visualizations are represented as computed hemodynamic time series responses, or simply blood flow activation for that temporal period. The level of brain activity (cognitive processing) is inferred from this from blood flow activation shown with color coding – dark blue is low and dark red is high level of activity Fig. 8).

Low level
Oxygenation
Change

High level
Oxygenation
Change

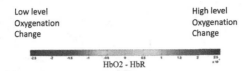

HbO2 - HbR

Fig. 8. 9 Scale of average oxygenation change (HbO2 - HbR)

Our current analysis is at the overall neural activity level. Future analysis will investigate specific channels in the fNIRS that align to brain areas corresponding to specific cognitive functions (e.g., Lateral Prefrontal Cortex for workload [27]). Heatmaps of the participant's prefrontal cortex activity during blocks of time were developed for each Trial. Time blocks with higher levels of oxygenation change are circled in red.

Session 1: The time blocks for this session were consistent across all Trials with scheduled maneuvers; for the no-maneuver condition we broke the Trial into the same intervals to allow for consistency of blocks across all Trials. The blocks are defined events of the Trial as follows:

- Beginning of the Trial until STUR 1
- STUR 1 to timed maneuver (revert) 1
- Maneuver 1 to maneuver 2
- Maneuver 2 to STUR 2
- STUR 2 to end of Trial

Visual inspection of imaging data from the fNIRS can provide insights into processing across and within a Trial. Note that there was some loss of channel signal in Trials 1 and 2; adjustments made between yielded improved signal in Trials 3 and 4. Trial (Fig. 9), had a relatively consistent and moderate level of activity across the Trial. Considered with the STUR and post session interview data, this suggests that the participant was orienting to the task and environment. The visual heatmap of Trials 2, 3, and 4 suggests that there are higher levels of mental activity change in the experiment timeline when the maneuvers begin and during the last few minutes of the Trial (when time is running out). In Trial 3, the maneuver started at minute 7 and there were no maneuvers in Trial 4. These time blocks are illustrated by the red circles in Fig. 9, 10 and 11.

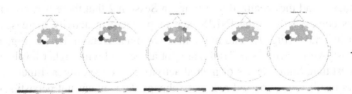

Fig. 9. Mapping of brain activity to trial 1 timeline Session 1 – *neural activity level was fairly constant across the Trial, showing moderate levels of activity.*

Fig. 10. Mapping of brain activity to trial 2 timeline Session 1 - *neural activity level was more variable across the Trial, with two time blocks showing higher levels than the others.*

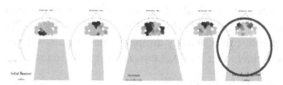

Fig. 11. Mapping of brain activity to trial 4 timeline Session 1 - *neural activity level was relatively constant across the Trial at a somewhat low-moderate level of activity until the final 5 min of the Trial which had higher level of activity.*

Fig. 12. Mapping of brain activity to trial 1 timeline Session 2 - *neural activity level was relatively constant across the Trial at a moderate level of activity until the final 5 min of the Trial which had higher level of activity*

Exploratory data analysis of CM012's fNIRS data for Session 2 was conducted in blocks of time between either scheduled STURs (when no maneuver had yet occurred) or maneuvers. In Session 2, the revert actions occurred in both Trials and were in direct response to the participant uploading a modified webpage; therefore, there is a different number of blocks between Trials. The heat maps were also considered with post-experiment interview data to get a qualitative understanding of how maneuvers effected cognitive processing. The revert maneuvers were executed every time the attacker uploaded the manipulated webpage; as such, the pattern was quickly determined by the attacker and they realized mid-point in Session 2 that there was no winning the Trial. This corresponds to the fNIRS heat map where in activity increases after the maneuver in Trial 1 (Fig. 12) and in the first few maneuvers of Trial 2 (Fig. 13). However, the last two maneuvers in Trial 2 are not associated with higher levels of activity. This suggest that, higher levels of mental activity in the experiment timeline when the maneuvers result in unexpected results (webpage defacement not persisting) but once the result is expected the change does not create additional load. Our study is an early research step towards addressing some and the analysis of the data is exploratory and preliminary. It is a promising first step to implementing objective neural measures into cyber experimentation. Future research is required to unpack these findings and provide deeper understanding of the underlying cognitive processes.

Fig. 13. Mapping of brain activity to trial 2 timeline Session 2 - *neural activity level was more variable across the Trial, with multiple blocks showing high levels of activity*

5 Discussion

Our enhanced cyber maneuver framework elaborates Allen's [2] concept by adding the cognitive mechanisms underlying response to the defensive cyber actions aimed to shape adversary behavior. Leveraging current research on cyber deception and network change effects on shaping adversary behavior [31–37], we constructed a technical methodology that facilitates the design and implementation of maneuvers and the collection of interpretable technical data to assess the efficacy of specific maneuvers within the proposed framework and cognitive data to verify the cognitive processes mitigating those effects.

This initial study addresses two maneuvers (stimulate a response and leverage deception) from our framework. Our initial results demonstrate the ability to capture data directly related to the measurement of cyber maneuver effects on attacker behaviors and cognition. Table 2 presents a summary of findings from across Session 1 and 2 data sets (VM logs, observer notes, workload measures, session questionnaire response, and post-interview data) aligned to the cyber maneuvers. Through a use case study of CM012 we found evidence that the stimulate a response maneuver increased workload and behavioral activity, increased frustration, was not detected as a purposeful system action or cyber maneuver, and was effective in interrupting exfil downloads. In Session 1, the experience with the task environment may have contributed more to the results than the impact of the maneuver, likely related to learning the environment. Disruption to file downloads was not noticed or recognized. We attribute this null effect to CM012's failure to connect diminished progress to defender behavior. That is, for them, the slow progress felt like "business as usual." This could potentially be related to cognitive biases, where the participant is focused on executing the task, not noticing network changes and believing any disruption to their efforts is due to error, not an intentional defensive action. Comments related to task performance highlight this focusing of attention: "When you have fingers on keyboard, you don't care about other stuff. You are focused on your task."

Session 2 actions (revert and decoy) were more noticeable and showed some interesting cognitive effects. Workload was impacted by the revert action as in Session 1. We found that while these actions were detected, they were not attributed to purposeful defender actions leading to confusion and frustration, as implied in the post-experiment interviews. Interesting perceptions from the participants included the following:

1. *"Wow. I don't know what I am doing wrong now. Got the change posted, but out of time first Trial. Second Trial, It's not there! Did you wipe it out? After all the work I did? ... That's not fair! I never questioned the network. Just kept pushing the script on screen."*

2. *"Uploaded files and it worked. Then it reverted. "It fixes itself. How do you respond to that? What's going on?"*
3. *"On 2nd Trial, I make a change, and it eradicates it. I see it on my screen. I ask myself, 'Did I update?'" Did not question the network.*
4. *"I tried to log onto the webserver to figure out what was going on—to figure out how to work around the maneuver. The server was being refreshed or reverted somehow. I made the changes first. Then I reloaded the page and it reverted. Then I reloaded it again, and realized it would be a losing battle." [He tried a second time] "Because maybe I had done something wrong. I second-guessed myself."*

Table 2. Summary cyber maneuver effects

Cyber maneuver	Cyber action	Technical finding	Cognitive finding	Behavioral finding
Stimulate a response	Reboot Session 1	Download interrupted	Increased workload, reduced confidence	Increased adversary activity on network
	Revert Session 1 SharePoint reverted Session 2 Web server reverted	Participant's changes did not persist	Increased frustration and reduced confidence, added some confusion (Session 2)	Increased activity to redo changes made
Leverage deception	Decoy content Session 2		Confidence, attention, decision-making, heuristics and bias	80% exfiltrated or tried to exfiltrate fake content; may confuse adversary regarding content validity

The decoy content for the leverage deception maneuver did not elicit a strong effect. However, as seen in other cyber deception research [17, 18, 31], when people encountered decoys, they interacted with them. Suggesting that, if designed properly, decoy content can be effective at drawing the attention of cyberattackers.

The results from this initial study demonstrate the ability to collect data within a rapidly configured and consistently deployable experimentation environment. One of the most nascent aspects of this research is that of the neural evidence of information processing. This is driven in part by the expense and time limitations of conducting neurophysiological research. Further, cyber operation tasks are complex and long in duration, making interpretation of the fNIRS data challenging. We were able to collect data from participants through all Trials in both sessions. Research is needed to mature the use of fNIRs as a measure of cognitive impacts from cyber maneuvers. We will continue to refine this environment to make these experiments more efficient.

5.1 Limitations

This study was designed to mature a methodology for evaluating cyber maneuvers. We found that the experimental approach and measures were useful for evaluating the effects of the maneuver on cyberattackers. However, there are some limitations, which will be addressed in follow-on experiments. Recruiting representative participants is key to effective experimentation. Although familiar with red teaming and the types of tasks in the study, the participants in this study had a wide variety in recency of conducting similar tasks and skills related to the toolset. We observed differences across participants with regard to their familiarity with Cobalt Strike and the commands availability to them. Broadening our sample population is planned for future studies.

A key driver of the experimental design was to develop a task that could be executed within a tight time window to allow for repeated trials of the task under different conditions (cyber maneuvers). To achieve this goal, a simplification of the exfil and web defacements tasks was needed; specific files to target and scripts on pushing the website page change were provided. The ecological validity of the completion of the task could be called into question because steps to successfully complete the mission may not fully reflect adversary TTPs. Refinement of the experimental task is ongoing and will be reviewed by subject matter experts. Additionally, the time required to complete a mission and the number of trials for conditions is under consideration.

5.2 Future Work

The experimentation shows that technical and cognitive effects from cyber maneuvers can be systematically evaluated. Future work will expand this research to test other cyber maneuvers and the evaluation methodology. Due to the participant limitations highlighted above, future work will also seek opportunities with offensive cyber operations-representative subjects and experiments should include in-depth training sessions to ensure all participants have the same basic training necessary to complete the tasks.

6 Conclusion

While maneuver as a military concept has been in existence for thousands of years, it is relatively nascent in cyber. Cyber maneuver as a concept to gain advantage over an adversary is a promising approach to cyber operations (defensive and offensive). Current frameworks only partially address cyber actions that would comprise a maneuver [15–17]. These existing frameworks support design, development, and evaluation of cyber deception and are useful for consideration and leveraging for cyber maneuver.

We presented an enhanced cyber maneuver framework based on existing cyber frameworks [18] and sound principles and theory of influence and behavior change. We have shown that it is useful to enhance the frameworks with specification of adversary desired behavior and the cognitive mechanisms by which the behavior is shaped. These cognitive mechanisms can be exploited based on theories of persuasion, like the ELM [23] and the interplay of cognitive biases [24], where biases can be identified and used to steer a cyber actor to central or peripheral processing. By leveraging cyber attacker objectives of stealth and speed, cyber maneuvers can be deployed that lead attackers to believe the network and their actions on it are leading them to mission completion.

Designing implementation of cyber actions and network system response to elicit predicted adversary behavior is possible. Behavioral response is predictable in part from understanding and measuring cognitive effects of cyber actions. The study demonstrated a holistic and systematic way to evaluate cyber-maneuver technical and cognitive effects on adversaries. The study contributes to the development of a methodical cyber maneuver framework by demonstrating an effective experimental protocol and simulated network environment to achieve specific effects based on selected actions of cyber maneuver.

Acknowledgements. This work was partially supported by the Department of Homeland Security (DHS) Cybersecurity and Infrastructure Security Agency (CISA).

References

1. FireEye: Highly evasive attacker leverages solar winds supply chain to compromise multiple global victims with SUNBURST backdoor (2020)
2. Allen, P.: Cyber Maneuver and Schemes of Maneuver. Cyber Def. Rev. 79–96 (2020)
3. Applegate, S.D.: The principle of maneuver in cyber operations. In: 2012 4th International Conference on Cyber Conflict (CYCON 2012), pp. 1–13. IEEE (2012)
4. Huang, C.: Towards Effective Techniques For Cyber Maneuver Defenses. The Pennsylvania State University (2015)
5. Schoka, A.: Training cyberspace maneuver. Small Wars J. (2018)
6. Beraud, P., Cruz, A., Hassell, S., et al.: Using cyber maneuver to improve network resiliency. In: Proceedings - IEEE Military Communications Conference MILCOM, pp. 1121–1126 (2011)
7. Clay, P.: A modern threat response framework. Netw. Secur. **2015**, 5–10 (2015)
8. Hart, B.H.L.: Strategy. Praeger, New York (1954)
9. Chiang, C.Y.J., Venkatesan, S., Sugrim, S. et al.: On defensive cyber deception: A case study using SDN. In: Proceedings - IEEE Military Communications Conference MILCOM. Vol. 2019-October, pp. 110–115. Institute of Electrical and Electronics Engineers Inc. (2019)
10. Sengupta, S., Chowdhary, A., Sabur, A. et al.: A survey of moving target defenses for network security. IEEE Commun. Surv. Tutorials **22**(3), 1–34 (2019)
11. Carroll, T.E., Crouse, M., Fulp, E.W. et al.: Analysis of network address shuffling as a moving target defense. In: IEEE ICC 2014 - Communication and Information Systems Security Symposium. IEEE (2014)
12. Carroll, T.E., Grosu, D.: A game theoretic investigation of deception in network security. Secur. Commun. Networks **4**, 1162–1172 (2011)
13. Fugate, S., Ferguson-Walter, K.: Artificial intelligence and game theory models for defending critical networks with cyber deception. AI Mag. **40**(1), 49–62 (2019)
14. Wang, S., Zhou, Y., Li, Y., et al.: Quantitative analysis of network address randomization's security effectiveness. In: International Conference on Communication Technology Proceedings, ICCT. Vol. 2019-October, pp. 906–910. Institute of Electrical and Electronics Engineers Inc. (2019)
15. Brantly, A.F.: Strategic cyber maneuver. Small Wars J. (2015)
16. Duan, Q., Al-Shaer, E., Islam, M. et al.: CONCEAL: A strategy composition for resilient cyber deception– framework, metrics and deployment. In: 2018 IEEE Conference on Communications and Network Security (CNS). IEEE (2018)

17. Almeshekah, M.H., Spafford, E.H.: Cyber Security Deception. Cyber Deception: Building the Scientific Foundation, pp. 1–312 (2016)
18. Allen, P.: Cyber Maneuver and Schemes of Maneuver: Preliminary Concepts, Definitions, Categorizations and Examples: AOS-19–0941 (2019)
19. Paul, C., Clarke, C.P., Schwille, M., et al.: Lessons from Others for Future U.S. Army Operations in and Through the Information Environment RAND Corporation (2018)
20. JP 3-13: Joint Publication 3-13.2, Psychological Operations (2010)
21. Dykstra, J., Paul, C.L.: Cyber Operations Stress Survey (COSS): Studying Fatigue, Frustration, and Cognitive Workload in Cybersecurity Operations. In: 11th USENIX Workshop on Cyber Security Experimentation and Test (CSET 2018) (2018)
22. Chowdhury, N.H., Adam, M.T.P., Skinner, G.: The impact of time pressure on human cyber-security behavior: An integrative framework. In: ICS Eng 2018:26th International Conference on Systems Engineering: Conference Proceedings, Sydney, Australia (2018)
23. Petty, R.E., Cacioppo, J.T.: The elaboration likelihood model of Persuasion. ACR North American Advances (1984)
24. Kahneman, D.: Thinking, Fast and Slow. Macmillan (2011)
25. Ferguson-Walter, K., Shade, T.B., Rogers, A. et al.: The Tularosa study: An experimental design and implementation to quantify the effectiveness of cyber deception. In: Proceedings of the 52nd Hawaii International Conference on System Sciences (2019)
26. Hart, S.G.: NASA-TASK LOAD INDEX (NASA-TLX); 20 YEARS LATER. In: Proceedings of the Human Factors and Ergonomics Society Annual Meeting, vol. 50, No. 9, pp. 904–908. Sage Publications, Los Angeles (2006)
27. Ayaz, H., Shewokis, P.A., Bunce, S., et al.: Optical brain monitoring for operator training and mental workload assessment. Neuroimage **59**, 36–47 (2012)
28. McCulloh, I.: Neuroscience of influence. In: Spitaletta, J. (ed.) Bio-Psycho-Social Determinants of Behavior. Office of Secretary of Defense, Washington DC (2016)
29. Strom, B.E., Applebaum, A., Miller, D.P., Nickels, K.C., Pennington, A.G., Thomas, C.B.: MITRE ATT&CK^{TM}: Design and Philosophy (2018)
30. Nossiter, A., David Sanger, N.P.: Hackers Came, but the French were prepared - The New York Times. *New York Times.* https://www.nytimes.com/2017/05/09/world/europe/hackers-came-but-the-french-were-prepared.html?emc=edit_tnt_20170509&nlid=72077760&tnt email0=y&_r=0. Published 9 May 2017. Accessed 29 March 2020
31. Heckman, K.E., Walsh, M.J., Stech, F.J., et al.: Active cyber defense with denial and deception: A cyber-wargame experiment. Comput. Secur. **37**, 72–77 (2013)
32. Farar, A., Bahşi, H., Blumbergs, B.: A case study about the use and evaluation of cyber deceptive methods against highly targeted attacks. In: 2017 International Conference On Cyber Incident Response, Coordination, Containment & Control (Cyber Incident) (2017)
33. Ferguson-Walter, K.J., Lafon, D.S., Shade, T.B.: Friend or faux: Deception for cyber defense. Source J. Inf. Warf. **16**, 28–42 (2017)
34. Yahyaoui, A., Rowe, N.C.: Testing simple deceptive honeypot tools. Cyber. Sens. **9458**, 945803 (2015)
35. Bellekens, X., Jayasekara, G., Hindy, H. et al.: From cyber-security deception to manipulation and gratification through gamification. In: HCI for Cybersecurity, Privacy and Trust: First International Conference, HCI-CPT 2019, Held as Part of the 21st HCI International Conference (2019)
36. Pal, P.P., Lageman, N.J., Soule, N.B.: Disrupting adversary decision logic: An experience report. J. Inf. Warf. **17**, 78 (2018)
37. Shade, T.B., Rogers, A.V., Ferguson-walter, K.J. et al.: The Moonraker study: An experimental evaluation of host-based deception the Moonraker study. In: Hawaiian International Conference on System Science (HICSS) (2019)

Studies on Usable Security in Intelligent Environments

A User Study to Evaluate a Web-Based Prototype for Smart Home Internet of Things Device Management

Leena Alghamdi(✉), Ashwaq Alsoubai, Mamtaj Akter, Faisal Alghamdi, and Pamela Wisniewski

University of Central Florida, Orlando, FL 32816, USA
{leenaalghamdi,atalsoubai,mamtaj.akter,faisal.ramzi}@knights.ucf.edu,
pamwis@ucf.edu

Abstract. With the growing advances in the Internet of Things (IoT) technology, IoT device management platforms are becoming increasingly important. We conducted a web-based survey and usability study with 43 participants who use IoT devices frequently to: 1) examine their smart home IoT usage patterns and privacy preferences, and 2) evaluate a web-based prototype for smart home IoT device management. We found that participants perceived privacy as more important than the convenience afforded by the IoT devices. Based on their average scores of the privacy vs. convenience importance, participants with low privacy and low convenience significantly reported less privacy control and convenience preferences than participants with high privacy and high convenience. Overall, all participants were satisfied about the proposed website prototype and their actual usability evaluation demonstrated good understanding of the website features. This paper provides an empirical examination of the privacy versus convenience trade-offs smart home users make when managing their IoT devices.

Keywords: IoT device management · Prototype evaluation · Web-based prototype · Privacy management

1 Introduction

According to MediaPost [17], 69% of households in the United States own at least one smart Internet of Things (IoT) device, while 12% of those (about 22 million homes) own multiple devices. Despite the widespread proliferation of IoT smart home technologies, there are several concerns around the data privacy and management of these IoT devices. For example, people do not feel comfortable with third-parties using their sensitive data [20]. However, people use third-party platforms to manage their smart IoT devices, even though these platforms invade users' surroundings and capture their sensitive information without permission [4]. The reasons behind this is that people may not understand the extent of the data collection by the third party, or people may think the trade-off is worth it for the added convenience [19]. In other cases, some people may not care enough about their personal privacy to be concerned about data leakages [19]. Thus, it is important to further understand the trade-off between privacy and convenience in the context of smart home IoT device management.

There are various platforms that already exist that aim to provide a centralized management platform for IoT devices. For example, Silva et al. [25], proposed a system management tool for devices and networks in IoT with user interface (M4DN.IoT), and this system provides information about connected devices and networks. It supports both automatic IoT networks management and user interface. Although the existing systems provide a management platform for IoT devices, they come with certain limitations. For example, some of the platforms are proposed for smart devices controlling purposes only, they do not preserve the users privacy and provide no mechanisms for protecting sensitive information. At the same time, though, it remains unclear whether a privacy-focused IoT device management platform is actually improving IoT users' privacy perceptions by sufficiently helping them to manage their smart home IoT devices based on their privacy preferences and convenience of usage. Consequently, we asked the following high level research questions:

- **RQ1:** *Do smart home IoT device users generally value their privacy versus convenience more?*
- **RQ2:** *Based on their preference towards privacy versus convenience, how does this influence their decisions to protect their privacy?*
- **RQ3:** *Does this preference influence how they evaluate a web-based prototype for centralized IoT smart home management?*

To address these research questions, we first developed a web-based prototype as a centralized location for users to manage their IoT smart home devices. This prototype is intended to enable IoT users to gather all of their smart devices into a single platform and effortlessly manage them, while protecting their privacy based on their preferences when managing their devices. We gave participants several tasks to complete using the prototype. We then conducted a web-based survey with 43 adults to evaluate the prototype and answer survey questions about their preferences towards privacy versus convenience, as well as their privacy control, privacy preference, convenience preferences and their website satisfaction.

Overall, we found that the majority of our participants valued both privacy and convenience (RQ1). Most participants (37.2%, N = 16) valued both privacy and convenience, followed by convenience over privacy (27.9%, N = 12), neither privacy nor convenience (23.3%, N = 10), and privacy over convenience (11.6%, N = 5). However, within-subjects, we found significant differences between privacy and convenience importance. Specifically, participants were more concerned about privacy than convenience when using IoT devices. For RQ2, we found significant differences based on the privacy vs. convenience profiles, such that participants who were in the low privacy/low convenience group significantly reported less Privacy Control and Convenience Preferences than the group of high privacy/high convenience. For RQ3, participants generally were satisfied about our website with the website organization, ease of website navigation, and the user-interface when they experience it. Participants' responses towards the website satisfaction also reflected on their website usage. Most of our participants ($N = 35, 92.11\%$) could follow our website usage instructions and could navigate to the website pages to perform the activities that we asked them to do. This gave us the further understanding of how our website design appeared easy to learn and use to our participants.

This study contributes to the field of IoT smart home management by evaluating users' perception of using one platform to manage IoT devices while protecting their privacy based on their preferences, as IoT device management platform ensure that users' privacy requirements are met. Also, it provides a clear ideas about privacy and convenience preferences of smart home users when using such a platform. This paper is organized as follows: Sect. 2 reviews the background of smart home IoT privacy issues, then outlines some of the research contributions to overcome these issues, also, it discusses some of the IoT devices management mechanisms. Section 3 describes the process of designing and implementing our proposed prototype. Section 4 describes our methodologies with the details regarding our analysis approach. Section 5 highlights the findings, and Sect. 6 discusses the key findings, outlines the limitations and provides an outlook of the future work that needs to be conducted in this area. Finally, Sect. 7 concludes the research.

2 Related Work

A Pew research [2] reported that 55% of the smart device users find it unacceptable that smart home devices collect their sensitive personal information (e.g., precise location, communication patterns, physical movements, and so on). Although smart devices bring conveniences and monetary benefits for home, many recent work reported that these devices have become cause of concerns to the users [1,16,18,31]. For example, Arabo et al. in [3] studied how smart home network users' online security, safety and privacy can be compromised. They summarized the threats in several categories, i.e., identity theft, social threat, online safety, data security, cyber attacks. Some other research works also reported that users in general are not aware of these privacy threats since they are not informed how and to what extent their personal information is being accessed [11,14,23,31]. Additionally, smart home users often share their devices with trusted people who live outside of their home [27]. Thus, researchers have suggested to design IoT management tools that allow users to have a transparency on the data that get collected by their smart home devices [16,23,31]. To this end, Yan et al. designed a smart home device data monitoring mechanism titled RestThing [30] that enabled users to monitor the status of their physical and technological resources including their collected information. Moreover, Delicato et al. [9] proposed a web-based paradigm (EcoDiF) that aims to offer a platform that provides users a real-time data monitoring and visualization. Although these proposed solutions combined physical devices with IoT networks and provided web services to users to monitor; some recent work revealed that IoT management tools still require to be more user centric so that users can have the agency over their own privacy management and this self privacy management may benefit them to become more aware and confident about their data privacy management.

Many researchers have proposed solutions to allow IoT users to manage their devices via web pages or web/mobile applications. For example, Piyare in [22] proposed a low cost, flexible, and Web-server-based solution to smart home device control. However, their system is only for switching and controlling home appliances and devices through an Android-based app that can work only by using Android Smartphone or Android Tablet, and their system did not help users in preserving their privacy. Similar to this work, [15] and [24] also designed and developed Android based web apps that allowed users to control the smart home devices through it and interact with devices remotely using Android Smartphones and it provides voice command functionalities, security, and save energy as well. Similar to the Piyare's system, this system is an Android-based app that works only on Android smartphones. While all these research focused on allowing users to monitor and control the data collected by the smart home devices on specific platform (Android), we identified that there are more research needed to understand how users would be benefited if we could design a web application (that can be accessed from web browsers) for such mechanisms. It is also important to know how users' privacy perception, sense of privacy importance impact on their behavior towards such management tool. Our research makes a contribution to this end by developing a web-based prototype as a centralized platform for users to remotely manage and review the data collected by their IoT smart home devices and evaluating this prototype from participants' perception of privacy concern and convenience of usage. In the next section, we provide a detailed overview of the design of our developed web prototype.

Fig. 1. The login page

3   Design of an IoT Device Management System

We designed and developed a web-based IoT device management interface that acted as a centralized portal for IoT device management. The website included the following webpages and capabilities:

3.1   Account Login

The Account Login (Fig. 1) page allowed users to log in to their accounts by signing up as a new user with the following required information: Email Address and Password. The purpose of this page was to ensure users that the website was secure and that sensor-based information presented by the website would not be accessible to the public.

3.2   Device Categories Page

Next, the Category Page (Fig. 2) was organized into seven categories of IoT device types (i.e., home, health, agricultural, automobile, wearable, energy, and industrial). These categories were selected based on several factors, including importance to user's daily life and their coverage on a large number of IoT devices and sensors. For the purposes of this study, we only implemented a temperature and pressure sensor under the 'Home' category.

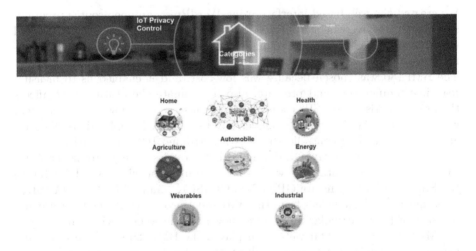

Fig. 2. The category page

3.3   IoT Device Management Page

This prototype allowed users to interact with an IoT device that measured the room temperature and air pressure. On the IoT Device Management Page for the temperature and pressure sensor, users were able to: 1) review the device status and history, and 2) control the device. Our web-based prototype retrieved the temperature readings the database and displayed them in a human-readable format to our participants in the Temperature and Pressure Sensor page under the Home category (Fig. 3). Through this page, users also could turn on or off the device. Lastly, a Home Page allowed users to navigate to all other pages.

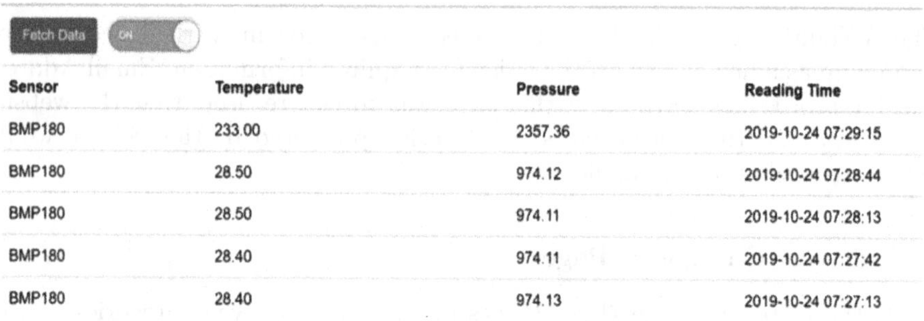

Sensor	Temperature	Pressure	Reading Time
BMP180	233.00	2357.36	2019-10-24 07:29:15
BMP180	28.50	974.12	2019-10-24 07:28:44
BMP180	28.50	974.11	2019-10-24 07:28:13
BMP180	28.40	974.11	2019-10-24 07:27:42
BMP180	28.40	974.13	2019-10-24 07:27:13

Fig. 3. An IoT device (Temperature and Pressure Sensor) page

3.4 System Architecture

We created the web-based interface using WordPress, an open-source program, as a Content Management System (CMS) that includes plugin architecture and template system features. We also implemented a sensor (BMP180) that was connected to an ESP32 controller board and communicated with a mySQL database. The BMP180 was chosen because was low-cost, and it enabled us to measure real-time temperature and pressure, also to estimate the altitude that affects the pressure. Also, the ESP32 was chosen because it was a low-powered system with integrated Wi-Fi, which is universally used for IoT applications. We programmed the ESP32 controller board with Arduino IDE, using a PHP script to insert data into our MySQL database that provides enough storage capacity to store the needed data. The wires that were used for wiring the BMP180 to the ESP32, the I2C pins are GPIO 22: SCL (SCK), and GPIO 21: SDA (SDI). Consequently, all the values from the BMP180 sensor, such as temperature and pressure of that particular area, were shown on the website via connecting to the MySQL database. Our website displayed the BMP180 sensor readings and timestamps from the database to allow data visualization on the website, as shown in (Fig. 3).

4   Methods

Below, we provide an overview of our study methodology, the details regarding our analysis approach, and then explain our recruitment strategy.

4.1 Study Overview

The primary purpose of our study was to understand participants' perception of digital privacy versus convenience and to evaluate our prototype keeping these preferences in mind. Therefore, we designed our user study to include two distinct phases: 1) A Web-based survey that included a questionnaire regarding convenience and privacy perceptions for smart device usage, 2) A guided exploration of the prototype with pre-defined tasks.

4.2 Study Procedure

The study started with asking the participants to answer the eligibility screening questions (whether they were at least 18 years old) and sign the statement of informed consent. Participants then provided their demographic information (e.g., age, education level). Next, a web-based survey that consisted of newly developed measures related to their perception of privacy and convenience of smart device usage (Table 10, 11, 12, 13, 14 and 15 in Appendix A and B). Participants were then asked to perform a specific set of tasks using different pages of our web prototype. Participants were instructed to browse to our web application from their web browsers using any device (e.g., smart phones, tablets, or computers). Since we aimed to evaluate participants' actual usage of the website prototype, the participants were asked to log into the website as a user. Next, we asked the participants to complete the following tasks: 1) Discover how many smart devices are connected to this website, 2) Turn on the temperature and pressure sensor and review the temperature readings, 3) Turn off the temperature and pressure sensor to pause collecting information and review the temperature readings. Once the participants' interactions with the prototype were completed, participants were then asked to complete another set of survey questions regarding their level of satisfaction on the web prototype usability. Participants took between thirty minutes to one and a half hours to complete the study. Next, we describe the survey measured created for this study.

4.3 Privacy and Convenience Constructs

In this study, we developed survey constructs to measure the importance and preferences aspects of privacy and convenience when using IoT devices. All measures were based on a 5-point Likert scale from 1 to 5 (scale 1 = Not important at all, scale 5 = Very Important). All measures reported satisfactory (higher than 0.7) Cronbach's alpha, which measures the internal consistency of survey constructs [7] as listed in the descriptive statistics (Table 2). The following subsections will describe each measure in more detail.

Privacy Importance. Privacy is one of the most concerning factors that affect users' decisions to adopt and/or use IoT devices [28]. Therefore, we were interested to measure the users' perception about their privacy in the context of IoT devices to compare it with their perceptions about the convenience afforded by these devices. Therefore, a Privacy Importance measure was developed to measure users' perception about the importance of protecting their privacy when using smart devices. This measure included one question for the participants to rate how important their privacy when they use IoT devices.

Convenience Importance. IoT users consider the tradeoffs between privacy and convenience when using smart devices [28]. Therefore, for this study, we included these two constructs to understand the participants' perceptions for privacy vs. convenience based on their rates for privacy and convenience constructs. As such, the Convenience Importance construct quantifies how important the convenience that IoT devices afford to their users. This measure has one direct question for the participant to rate the importance of convenience for them when using smart devices.

Privacy Control. Using IoT devices generally increases the risks associated with the sensitive personal data transmission, acquisition, and utilization with/ without users knowledge [28]; therefore, it is critical for users to be able to manage their personal information that IoT devices collected. The Privacy Control construct measured IoT users' ability to control their personal information that are collected by smart devices. This measure has three questions for participants to rate the importance of enabling them to know when and what type of personal information was collected and the importance to require users' permissions prior any data collection by the devices. We used this measure to uncover differences between the participants in terms of their ability to take actions in order to manage the collection of personal information when using smart devices.

Privacy Preferences. Although IoT have potential benefits, it is also associated with concerns related to recording data of people who does not own the IoT device [13]. The Privacy Preferences measure was developed to quantify users' privacy preferences. This measure has three questions for users to rate the importance of three reactions (not saying anything, hide themselves, or use applications to hide their identity) to protect their privacy in case of a security camera in another place (e.g., friend's house) was recording their audio or video. Thus, we used this measure to examine the participants' differences regarding the importance of their reactions to an IoT device that they do not own, but collected data about them.

Convenience Preferences. IoT users usually find it difficult to effectively control multiple smart devices [8]. Therefore, the Convenience Preferences measure was used to measure users' convenience preferences to manage their smart devices. This measure has three questions for users to rate strategies to manage IoT devices by having one platform, use website, or implement centralized monitoring. Therefore, this measure was important for this study to examine differences on what users would prefer for managing multiple smart devices.

Website Satisfaction. The Website Satisfaction construct measured participants satisfaction about the proposed website prototype to manage multiple IoT devices. This construct quantifies participants' satisfaction based on: 1) prototype organization, 2) ease of navigation, and 3) user-friendly interface. Measuring users' satisfaction was important to us to evaluate any differences between the participants' regarding their feedback on the website prototype. This measure was also useful to recommend future recommendations that will be discussed in the discussion section.

4.4 Data Analysis Approach

To answer RQ1, we first conducted a dependent t-test for paired samples (i.e., within subjects) to examine if there was a significant difference between the importance of privacy and convenience based on participants self-reported scores. We hypothesized the following difference would be detected:

- **H1:** *Participants will rate their Privacy as more important relative to their Convenience.*

We then used a mean split to divide the participants into four quadrants based on their scores on the privacy and convenience importance measures. We did this by calculating the mean of the Privacy and Convenience Importance measures, which are listed in Table 2. Participants who had higher scores than the mean scores were assigned to the high (privacy or convenience) groups, while participants who reported scores lower than the mean scores were assigned to the low (privacy or convenience) groups.

To answer RQ2, we calculated the between group differences on our privacy and convenience preference constructs (i.e., Privacy Control, Privacy Preferences, and Convenience Preferences) based on the four groups. We hypothesized the following between-group differences.

- **H2:** *Participants with low Privacy/low Convenience Importance will rate a) Privacy Control and b) Privacy Preference lower than participants with high Privacy/high convenience Importance.*
- **H3:** *Participants with low Privacy/Convenience Importance will rate a) Convenience Preference lower than participants with high Privacy/Convenience Importance.*

We investigated the differences in the self-reported measures between the generated quadrant groups by conducting ANOVA tests [26]. In order to compare individual groups with one another, we conducted post-hoc analyses [12] for the significant differences found. These identified differences demonstrate a holistic understanding of the distinct patterns between the privacy/convenience groups regarding a series of privacy control and convenience preferences.

4.5   The Prototype Usability Evaluation

Based on the tasks described above, we coded whether the participants were able to successfully complete each task or not (0 = Incomplete; 1 = Complete). In the results section, we present the percentages of the correct and wrong answers regarding these tasks. We also assessed between-group differences on the Website Satisfaction measure based on the Privacy and Convenience Importance groups as a grouping variable (Website Satisfaction). We hypothesized the following significant difference:

- **H4:** *Participants with low privacy/high convenience will be more satisfied about the website prototype than participants with high privacy/low convenience Importance.*

In the next section, we describe how we recruited participants and summarize their demographic profiles.

4.6   Participant Recruitment and Demographics

Overall, we recruited 43 participants who completed the study voluntary without a compensation, which was stated in the informed consent prior participating to the study. We recruited participants who are over 18 years old. We advertised through word of mouth, recruitment emails, and by posting the flyers on social media. The study took place online where the participants were given the web URL to interact with the prototype and complete the surveys. Three of the participants answered the survey questions but skipped completing the tasks. Since our informed consent allowed participants to skip questions, we retained their survey data for the RQ1 and RQ2 analyses. Therefore, 38 out of the 43 participants completed the tasks and answered the related questions.

A diverse sample of participants participated in this study, where 60%, $N = 26$ were between 25–34, 14%, $N = 6$ of them were 18–24, 14% were 35–44, and 12% were 45–54 years old. In terms of education, most of our participants completed their bachelor's degree (49%, $N = 21$) or master's (33%, $N = 14$) degree programs. Almost all participants (98%, $N = 42$) owned more than two smart home devices. The most frequently chosen device were smartphones with a percentage of 90.70%, followed by smart watch and smart TV with an equal percentage of 55.81%.

5   Results

In Table 2, we report the descriptive statistics of our survey measures. As shown in the table, all measures demonstrated adequate construct validity (Cronbach's alpha >0.70). A general trend we observed was that the means for the privacy-related constructs were typically higher than those associated with convenience-related measures. Further, we note that all constructs were rated relatively high with means ranging from 3.6 to 4.2 on a 5-point scale (Table 1).

Table 1. Participants' demographic information ($N = 43$)

Demographic	Number	Percentage
Age		
18–24	6	13.95%
25–34	26	60.47%
35–44	6	13.95%
45–54	5	11.63%
Educational background		
High school	6	13.95%
Bachelor's degree	21	48.84%
Master's degree	14	32.56%
Ph.D. or higher	2	4.65%
Smart devices owned		
Smartphone	39	90.70%
Smartwatch	24	55.81%
Activity tracker	10	23.26%
Smart refrigerator	4	9.30%
Smart speaker	7	16.28%
Smart thermostat	3	6.98%
Smart TV	24	55.81%
None	1	2.33%

Table 2. The constructs' descriptive statistics

Constructs	Number of items	Cronbach's alpha	Mean	SD
Privacy importance	1.00	N/A	4.16	0.94
Convenience importance	1.00	N/A	3.88	0.82
Privacy control	3.00	0.75	4.15	0.80
Privacy perferences	3.00	0.76	3.60	1.19
Convenience preferences	3.00	0.80	3.85	0.86
Website satisfaction	3.00	0.83	4.20	0.79

5.1 Privacy over Convenience (RQ1)

A dependent t-test for paired samples yielded a significant difference between users in terms of Privacy Importance and Convenience Importance ($p = 0.01$). Users' perceived privacy ($m = 4.23$) as more important than ($p = 0.01$) than their desire for convenience ($m = 3.86$) as shown in Table 3. This results supports our H1.

Table 3. Privacy versus convenience

	Mean	SD
Privacy	4.23	0.92
Convenience	3.86	0.89

The privacy/convenience quadrant groups resulted in: A) high privacy/high convenience group, B) high privacy/low convenience group, C) low privacy/high convenience group, and D) low privacy/low convenience group. Table 4 showed the participants' distribution across the quadrant groups. The largest group among the quadrants was participants who reported both high privacy and high convenience ($N = 16, 37\%$) while the smallest group was participants who reported high privacy, but low convenience ($N = 5, 12\%$).

Table 4. The distribution of privacy/convenience quadrant groups. The percentages out of the total number of participants ($N = 43$).

	High convenience	Low convenience	Total
High privacy	N = 16, 37%	N = 5, 12%	N = 21, 49%
Low privacy	N = 12, 28%	N = 10, 23%	N = 22, 51%
Total	N = 28, 65%	N = 15, 35%	

To some extent, our results highlight that the trade-off between privacy and convenience may be a false dichotomy, as the majority of our participants felt that both were important. When there was a discernible trade-off, participants tended to prefer convenience over privacy (between-groups), which conflicted with our earlier within-subject findings that individuals tended to rate privacy as more important than convenience when making comparative decisions.

5.2 Differences in Privacy Control, Privacy Preferences, and Convenience Preferences (RQ2)

This section presents the between-group results to examine the differences between the four groups of privacy/convenience importance in terms of Privacy Control, Privacy Preferences, Convenience Preferences, and Website Satisfaction. Table 5 listed the means and standard deviations of these measures for the four groups. Table 6 showed significant differences in terms of Privacy Control and Convenience Preferences measures based on ANOVA tests. We will discuss the results of this ANOVA tests in the following subsections.

Table 5. Mean and standard deviation of Privacy Control, Privacy Preferences, Convenience Preferences by the privacy/convenience quadrants

Groups	Privacy control		Privacy preferences		Convenience preferences		Website satisfaction	
	M	SD	M	SD	M	SD	M	SD
High-privacy/high-convenience	4.17	0.44	3.92	0.90	4.31	0.74	4.25	0.64
High-privacy/low-convenience	4.33	0.67	3.80	1.02	4.33	0.62	4.47	0.38
Low-privacy/high-convenience	3.94	0.68	3.50	1.05	3.53	0.77	4.03	0.70
Low-privacy/low-convenience	3.43	0.50	3.10	0.86	3.27	0.90	4.20	0.74

Privacy Control. An ANOVA yielded significant differences between the privacy/ convenience groups regarding their Privacy Control ($F(3, 43) = 11.75, p < 0.001$) as shown in Table 6. Post-hoc tests (Table 7) demonstrated that users in the low privacy/convenience group ($m = 3.43$) reported significantly less Privacy Control than the group of high privacy/convenience ($m = 4.71$) and the group of high privacy/low convenience ($m = 4.33$). Based on this result, the hypothesis **H2** was supported. We also found that IoT users in the group of low privacy and high convenience ($m = 3.43$) had significantly less Privacy Control than the group of high privacy and convenience ($m = 94$) as shown in Table 5. This partially supported the **H2** hypothesis since the group of low privacy/ high convenience has only one low privacy group. The group of low privacy/convenience reported less than the average score of the Privacy and Convenience Importance constructs, which align well with their low Privacy Control as well.

Table 6. ANOVA results for the Privacy Control, Privacy Preferences, Convenience Preferences by the privacy/convenience groups. There were significant differences found between the groups in terms of Privacy Control and Convenience Preferences. Bold values denote significant difference results.

Constructs	F	df	$p-value$
Privacy control	**11.75**	**3**	**<0.001**
Privacy preferences	1.67	3	0.18
Convenience preferences	**5.11**	**3**	**0.004**
Website satisfaction	0.57	3	0.63

Privacy Preferences. Regarding Privacy Preferences, an ANOVA did not yield any significant differences between the four groups ($F(3, 43) = 1.67, p = 0.18$) as shown in Table 6. The mean scores of these groups listed in Table 5. This suggests that all groups were fairly high, in the range of "Neutral" to "Somewhat important" in the Privacy Preferences scale. Therefore, this may be why we did not detect significant differences. Based on this non-significant result, hypothesis **H2** could not be supported.

Table 7. Post-hoc tests to identify the significant differences between the privacy/convenience groups.

Constructs	Significant pairwise differences (mean)	p-value
Privacy control	Low Priv./Low Conv. < High Priv./High Conv.	<0.001
	Low Priv./Low Conv. < High Priv./Low Conv.	0.004
	Low Priv./High Conv. < High Priv./High Conv.	0.02
Convenience pref.	Low Priv./Low Conv. < High Priv./High Conv.	<0.001
	Low Priv./High Conv. < High Priv./High Conv.	0.05

Convenience Preferences. There were significant differences between the privacy/convenience groups in terms of their Convenience Preferences ($F(3, 43) = 5.11, p = 0.004$) as shown in Table 6. Post-hoc analysis showed (Table 7) that the group of low privacy/convenience ($m = 3.27$) reported significantly less Convenience Preferences than the group of high privacy/convenience ($m = 4.31$). Thus, hypothesis **H3** was supported. Additionally, the group of low privacy/high convenience ($m = 3.53$) were significantly lower on the Convenience Preferences scale than the group of high privacy/convenience ($m = 4.31$) as shown in Table 5. This result partially supported the **H2** hypothesis. Generally, we found that the participants' self-reported Importance of Privacy and Convenience were fairly aligned with their Convenience Preferences since the group who reported low Privacy and Convenience Importance had the lowest Convenience Preferences.

5.3   Participants' Evaluation of the Website Usability (RQ3)

Website Satisfaction Survey. There were no significant differences between the groups based on their website satisfaction ($F(3, 43) = 0.57, p = 0.63$) as shown in Table 6. Thus, we could not support **H4** hypothesis because of the non-significant difference. Generally, most participants were satisfied with the website as shown in Table 8, where all mean scores on the individual items as well as the overall construct (Table 5) were higher than 4, which were between "Very Satisfied" and "Satisfied" on the scale.

Table 8. The means and standard deviation of the individual scale items for website satisfaction.

Website satisfaction items	Mean	SD
Website organization	4.07	0.80
Ease of website navigation	4.23	0.81
User friendly interface	4.30	0.64

Since we did not find significant differences between the privacy/convenience groups based on Website Satisfaction construct, we went beyond the high satisfaction on the website to evaluate their actual usability of the website prototype, which will be discussed in the next section.

Task Completion. Next, we present participants' responses to the tasks we assigned to them to evaluate their understanding of the website. In the first task, participants were asked to determine the number of currently connected devices on the website account, 35 out of 38 participants (92.11%) answered this question correctly. Where the correct answer was six devices.

The second task contained instructions for the participants, where they were asked to turn on the sensor readings function for the temperature and pressure sensor (IoT device). Then, they were asked to determine the number of current readings available for the temperature and pressure sensor. Most participants 36 out of 38 (94.74%) were able to follow the instructions and answer the question correctly. Where the correct answer was five temperature and pressure readings. Participants were also asked to determine the temperature readings for a specific date and time. All participants ($N = 37, 97.37\%$) answered this question correctly, except for one participant.

6 Discussion

In this section, we describe the implications of our findings in relation to prior work and provide design implications of smart home IoT device management systems.

6.1 Smart Home IoT Trade-Offs Between Privacy and Convenience

Previous works have investigated the factors that may affect people's opinions about IoT adoption [21]. In the same direction, we investigated our participants' views on the importance of privacy and convenience when using smart devices. While previous works such as [6,10], emphasized on the privacy as the reason behind the abandonment of technology from users, Our findings from the H1 hypothesis test confirms the importance of privacy for IoT devices, showing that privacy is more important than convenience for the smart devices users. This implies that users would avoid using IoT devices due to the compromise of user privacy in the way of collecting sensitive personal data. However, based on our results when examining the privacy/convenience quadrants groups, we found that the largest group among the quadrants was participants who valued both high privacy and high convenience. Thus, our results confirm that the trade-off between privacy and convenience creates a false dichotomy, given that most of our participants valued both privacy and convenience. Existing research on IoT mainly focuses on the importance of privacy for IoT users [21]. Therefore, we urge future research to leverage both users' privacy and convenience in order to understand the perceptions of smart IoT devices users toward their privacy concerns and convenience preferences when using IoT devices.

6.2   Implications for the Design of Smart Home IoT Device Management Systems

Our findings demonstrated that in general most participants were satisfied with our prototype (website) since they found it to be well-organized, easy to use, and user-friendly. This result indicates that the proposed prototype could an easily accessible platform, and it could be used easily by IoT user with different levels of education and without much technical experience (based on our diverse participants demographics). Having a website to manage IoT devices while preserving users' privacy is key to IoT devices [5]. Therefore, we recommend that developer would base their user-centered website designs on our prototype since we showed that the website would be useful in fulfilling IoT requirements in terms of privacy and convenience.

By showing the quadrant groups of privacy and convenience, which demonstrated different levels (i.e., high and low) of privacy and convenience. This suggests that different design solutions should be designed based on these groups' privacy concerns or convenience preferences. This is important because by estimating how much users value their privacy or convenience, IoT developers can predict appropriate features that may become sources of competitive advantage in IoT device management platforms. Therefore, we recommend that IoT designers to take into account that users may not perceive privacy and convenience at the same level. This highlights the importance of creating personalized privacy experiences for IoT users based on either initial survey questions to report their preferences or trained machine learning algorithms that would predict users privacy and convenience preferences similar to smart phone personalized permission management algorithms [29].

6.3   Limitations and Future Work

This section outlines limitations of our study that inform future work in the space of smart home IoT. We studied younger adults, where 60% of our participants were between 25 and 34 years old. Therefore, our results could not be generalized to older adult populations who may have a different privacy versus convenience calculus. Therefore, future studies should further study smart home IoT users' preferences towards privacy versus convenience. In our study, participants were asked to imagine themselves in a hypothetical situation, where they explored our IoT smart home device management website that was connected to a temperature and pressure sensor that was located in the first-author's home. While it was not feasible for us to test our system in the homes of our actual participants, future studies that leverage existing smart home sensors in participants' homes or install such sensors for the purpose of the study would increase the ecological validity of our results. Finally, our web-based prototype, while functional, had limited capabilities. Future studies that build upon our work could go in more depth in regards to feature design that optimizes users' privacy and convenience when managing their IoT smart home devices.

7   Conclusion

A large number of smart home IoT devices demands management and control solutions. Moreover, the growing number of connected devices and their inherent constraints motivate the need for efficient smart home IoT device management that focus on users privacy-preserving. Therefore, we conducted a web-based survey and usability study with 43 participants who use IoT devices frequently to: 1) examine their smart home IoT usage patterns and privacy preferences, and 2) evaluate a web-based prototype for smart home IoT device management. The findings confirmed that privacy is more important for the users than convenience when using smart devices, Moreover, based on our prototype evaluation, we found that all participants were generally satisfied with our website prototype and their actual usability evaluation demonstrated that they understand the functionality of the website. Overall, this study provided a rich picture of privacy and convenience preferences of smart home IoT users when using smart home IoT device management website.

A Appendix A

(See Table 9).

Table 9. Survey items of IoT device usage

Which Internet of Things (IoT) device(s) do you own. (Select all that apply)
1. Smart phone
2. Smart watch
3. Activity tracker
4. Smart refrigerator
5. Smart speaker
6. Smart thermostat
7. Smart TV
8. None
9. Other (Please specify)
How many hours per week do you use IoT devices?
0 h
4–6 h
7–10 h
11–14 h
15–20 h
20+ h
For what purposes do you use IoT devices? (Select all that apply)
1. Smart Home
2. Smart energy monitoring system
3. Vehicle Tracking
4. Entertainment
5. Lifestyle
6. Health monitoring
7. None (do not have an IoT device)
8. Other (please specify)
Which of the following applications do you use to manage your IoT devices?
1. Wink
2. SimpliSafe Home Security
3. Yonomi
4. ADT Control
5. Olisto
6. None
7. Do not have an IoT device
8. Other (please specify)

Table 10. Survey items of prototype satisfaction

Based on your experience in our website http://iotprivacycontrol.com/, *how satisfied are you with the following. (1 = Not Satisfied at all, 5 = Very Satisfied)*

---

1. Website organization

2. Ease of website navigation

3. User friendly interface

B   Appendix B

Table 11. Survey items of privacy concern

In general, how concerned are you about your privacy in the daily activities as the following? (1 = Not at all concerned, 5 = Very concerned)

---

1. People knowing your private and personal information

2. Walking in a public place which is full of sensors such as, private security camera, traffic microwave radar sensor, etc.

3. To be in the background of photos that are taken by strangers

4. To be in the foreground of photos that are taken by strangers

---

Table 12. Survey items of importance of privacy and convenience

---

Rate how important privacy (e.g., protecting your personal information) is to you when you are using smart devices. (1 = Not important at all, 5 = Very important)

Rate how important convenience (e.g., completing a task such as, increasing the thermostat temperature) is to you when you are using smart devices. (1 = Not important at all, 5 = Very important)

Table 13. Survey items of privacy actions for protecting personal information

If you were using some IoT devices, e.g., Smart Thermostat, Smart TV, and Smart phone, what type of information do you think would be captured by these devices? Select all that apply
1. Personal Information (e.g., name, address, bank information, etc.)
2. Biometric Information (e.g., Fingerprint, Facial Pattern, Voice, etc.)
3. Location Information
4. Weather Information (e.g., temperature degree)
5. Audio recordings
6. Video recordings
7. Health Information (e.g., medical histories, test and laboratory results, mental health conditions, etc.)
8. Other (please specify)
How important to you are each of the following actions in terms of protecting your personal information that is captured by IoT devices: (1 = Not important at all, 5 = Very important)
1. Enabling you to control what information is being collected about you by IoT devices
2. Informing you when personal information about you is being collected by IoT devices
3. Requesting your permission to collect your information by IoT devices before it is collected.
Assume you are at your friend's house and they have a security camera which is recording audio and video that is kept for one week. How important to you are each of the following actions in terms of protecting your personal information that is captured by that IoT device. (1 = Not important at all, 5 = Very important)
1. I would be very careful of what I do (e.g., act differently)
2. I would be very careful of what I say
3. I would sit in blind spots where I am not captured by the security camera
4. I would use technical methods if applicable (e.g., applications, websites) to hide my identity

Table 14. Survey items of privacy preference

Rate the extent to which you agree or disagree with the following actions and statements if you were in this situation: You live in a Smart home that contains different IoT devices and sensors which are: Smart Tv, Smart light, Smart Thermostat, and Smart watch) that capture various types of your information (e.g., your personal information, room temperature degree, your heart rate, your TV watching preferences, etc.), and you want to manage your devices, and reduce the risk of privacy breaching: (1 = Strongly disagree, 5 = Strongly agree)

1. I am concerned about the privacy of data sensed about me when using IoT devices

2. I prefer to use ONE platform (e.g., website) to manage all my IoT devices

3. I prefer to use website to manage my IoT devices rather than a particular application

4. For each device I prefer to use its related application for management purposes

5. I prefer to implement centralized monitoring for my IoT devices to manage privacy and security issues

6. I prefer to update my IoT devices with regular software updates

---

Table 15. Survey items of privacy measures

Rank the following statements in order of importance from 1 to 5. (1 = Not important at all, 5 = Very important)

1. Governments should provide new rules and laws to regulate IoT devices to protect our privacy when using them

2. IoT devices' manufacturers need to provide software updates and new features constantly for IoT devices to protect our privacy when using them

3. IoT devices' users need to use platforms (e.g., websites and applications) to manage their IoT devices to protect their privacy

---

References

1. Living in a glass house. In: Proceedings of the 13th International Conference on Ubiquitous Computing. https://dl.acm.org/doi/10.1145/2030112.2030118

2. Smart homes, comfort and data capture, January 2016. https://www.pewresearch.org/internet/2016/01/14/scenario-home-activities-comfort-and-data-capture/

3. Arabo, A., Brown, I., El-Moussa, F.: Privacy in the age of mobility and smart devices in smart homes. In: 2012 International Conference on Privacy, Security, Risk and Trust and 2012 International Confernece on Social Computing, pp. 819–826, September 2012. https://doi.org/10.1109/SocialCom-PASSAT.2012.108

4. Balliu, M., Bastys, I., Sabelfeld, A.: Securing IoT apps. IEEE Secur. Priv. **17**(5), 22–29 (2019). https://doi.org/10.1109/MSEC.2019.2914190

5. Boeckl, K., et al.: Considerations for managing internet of things (IoT) cybersecurity and privacy risks. Technical report NIST IR 8228, National Institute of Standards and Technology, Gaithersburg, MD, June 2019. https://doi.org/10.6028/NIST.IR.8228, https://nvlpubs.nist.gov/nistpubs/ir/2019/NIST.IR.8228.pdf

6. Clawson, J., Pater, J., Miller, A., Mynatt, E., Mamykina, L.: No longer wearing: investigating the abandonment of personal health-tracking technologies on craigslist, pp. 647–658 (2015). https://doi.org/10.1145/2750858.2807554

7. Cronbach, L.J., Meehl, P.E.: Construct validity in psychological tests. Psychol. Bull. **52**(4), 281 (1955)

8. Dehury, C.K., Sahoo, P.K.: Design and implementation of a novel service management framework for IoT devices in cloud. J. Syst. Softw. **119**, 149–161 (2016)

9. Delicato, F., Pires, P., Avila Barros, T., Batista, T., Costa, B.: A platform for integrating physical devices in the internet of things (2014). https://doi.org/10.1109/EUC.2014.42

10. Epstein, D.A., Caraway, M., Johnston, C., Ping, A., Fogarty, J., Munson, S.A.: Beyond abandonment to next steps: understanding and designing for life after personal informatics tool use. In: Proceedings of the 2016 CHI Conference on Human Factors in Computing Systems, CHI 2016, pp. 1109–1113. Association for Computing Machinery (2016). https://doi.org/10.1145/2858036.2858045

11. Gupta, S.D., Kaplan, S., Nygaard, A., Ghanavati, S.: A two-fold study to investigate users' perception of IoT information sensitivity levels and their willingness to share the information. In: Meng, W., Katsikas, S.K. (eds.) EISA 2021. Communications in Computer and Information Science, pp. 87–107. Springer International Publishing, Cham (2022). https://doi.org/10.1007/978-3-030-93956-4_6

12. Hilton, A., Armstrong, R.A.: Statnote 6: post-hoc ANOVA tests. Microbiologist **2006**, 34–36 (2006)

13. Jayaraman, P.P., Yang, X., Yavari, A., Georgakopoulos, D., Yi, X.: Privacy preserving internet of things: from privacy techniques to a blueprint architecture and efficient implementation. Futur. Gener. Comput. Syst. **76**, 540–549 (2017)

14. Kröger, J.L., Gellrich, L., Pape, S., Brause, S.R., Ullrich, S.:Personal information inference from voice recordings: user awareness and privacy concerns. Proc. Priv. Enhanc. Technol. **2022**(1), 6–27 (2021). https://doi.org/10.2478/popets-2022-0002, https://www.sciendo.com/article/10.2478/popets-2022-0002

15. Kunal, D., Tushar, D., Pooja, U., Vaibhav, Z., Lodha, V.: Smart home automation using IoT. Int. J. Adv. Res. Comput. Commun. Eng. **5**(2), 3. https://doi.org/10.17148/IJARCCE.2016.52131

16. Lau, J., Zimmerman, B., Schaub, F.: Alexa, are you listening? Privacy perceptions, concerns and privacy-seeking behaviors with smart speakers. Proc. ACM Hum.-Comput. Interact. **2**(CSCW), 102:1–102:31 (2018). https://doi.org/10.1145/3274371

17. Martin, C.: Smart home technology hits 69% penetration in U.S. https://www.mediapost.com/publications/article/341320/smart-home-technology-hits-69-penetration-in-us.html

18. McCreary, F., Zafiroglu, A., Patterson, H.: The contextual complexity of privacy in smart homes and smart buildings. In: Nah, F.F.-H.F.-H., Tan, C.-H. (eds.) HCIBGO 2016. LNCS, vol. 9752, pp. 67–78. Springer, Cham (2016). https://doi.org/10.1007/978-3-319-39399-5_7

19. Molla, R.: People say they care about privacy but they continue to buy devices that can spy on them, May 2019. https://www.vox.com/recode/2019/5/13/18547235/trust-smart-devices-privacy-security

20. Naeini, P.E., et al.: Privacy expectations and preferences in an IoT world, pp. 399–412 (2017). https://www.usenix.org/conference/soups2017/technical-sessions/presentation/naeini

21. Page, X., Bahirat, P., Safi, M.I., Knijnenburg, B.P., Wisniewski, P.: The internet of what? Understanding differences in perceptions and adoption for the internet of things 2(4), 183:1–183:22 (2018). https://doi.org/10.1145/3287061

22. Piyare, R., Tazil, M.: Bluetooth based home automation system using cell phone. In: 2011 IEEE 15th International Symposium on Consumer Electronics (ISCE), pp. 192–195, June 2011. https://doi.org/10.1109/ISCE.2011.5973811. iSSN 2159-1423

23. Saeidi, M., Calvert, M., Au, A.W., Sarma, A., Bobba, R.B.: If this then that: exploring users' concerns with IFTTT applets. Proc. Priv. Enhanc. Technol. 2022(1), 166–186 (2021). https://doi.org/10.2478/popets-2022-0009, https://www.sciendo.com/article/10.2478/popets-2022-0009

24. Shrestha, B., Mali, S., Joseph, A., Singh, K.J.: Web and android based automation using IoT, p. 4 (2017)

25. Silva, J.D.C., Rodrigues, J.J.P.C., Saleem, K., Kozlov, S.A., Rabelo, R.A.L.: M4DN.IoT-a networks and devices management platform for internet of things. IEEE Access 7, 53305–53313 (2019). https://doi.org/10.1109/ACCESS.2019.2909436, https://ieeexplore.ieee.org/document/8681396/

26. St, L., Wold, S., et al.: Analysis of variance (ANOVA). Chemom. Intell. Lab. Syst. 6(4), 259–272 (1989)

27. Tabassum, M., Kropczynski, J., Wisniewski, P., Lipford, H.R.: Smart home beyond the home: a case for community-based access control. In: Proceedings of the 2020 CHI Conference on Human Factors in Computing Systems, pp. 1–12. Association for Computing Machinery, New York, April 2020. https://doi.org/10.1145/3313831.3376255

28. Weinberg, B.D., Milne, G.R., Andonova, Y.G., Hajjat, F.M.: Internet of things: Convenience vs. privacy and secrecy. Bus. Horiz. 58(6), 615–624 (2015)

29. Wisniewski, P., Safi, M.I., Patil, S., Page, X.: Predicting smartphone location-sharing decisions through self-reflection on past privacy behavior. J. Cybersecur. 6(1), tyaa014 (2020)

30. Zhang, P., Vasilakos, A.: A survey on trust management for internet of things. J. Netw. Comput. Appl. 42, 120–134 (2014). https://doi.org/10.1016/j.jnca.2014.01.014

31. Zheng, S., Apthorpe, N., Chetty, M., Feamster, N.: User perceptions of smart home IoT privacy. Proc. ACM Hum.-Comput. Interact. 2(CSCW), 200:1–200:20 (2018). https://doi.org/10.1145/3274469

What Makes IoT Secure? A Maturity Analysis of Industrial Product Manufacturers' Approaches to IoT Security

Laura Lynggaard Nielsen[(⊠)]

Alexandra Institute, Åbogade 34, 8200 Aarhus N, Denmark
laura.nielsen@alexandra.dk

Abstract. The Internet of Things (IoT) carries enormous potential but also exposes products to new security threats. Even though recent years have seen several costly breaches and security experts advocate for a more proactive approach, security is often not up to par with technological innovations. But why is this so? Whereas a lot of research has been dedicated to describing technical security issues, there is a lack of research into product manufacturers' practices of securing IoT; what challenges do they face in developing, manufacturing, and selling secure IoT products, and what resources do they have for overcoming them? Without knowledge of these empirical perspectives, initiatives to further IoT security grope in the dark.

Employing a theory of change to unfold organizational aspects of IoT security, this paper seeks to explore the socio-technical factors that shape IoT security in practice. Based on a qualitative interview study with 52 informants from 26 companies making products for industrial enterprises and critical infrastructures, this paper not only offers insights into the real-world challenges in working with IoT security, but also presents a maturity model based on three necessary conditions for companies' ability to handle IoT security.

Keywords: Internet of Things · IoT security in practice · Organizational maturity · Interview study · Maturity analysis

1 Introduction

As connected solutions are becoming ever more ubiquitous, IoT is making its way into industrial and critical sectors. This not only brings new potentials but also creates attack surfaces that are different from those of traditional industrial products [1–7]. Even though the security issues of IoT are widely recognized, there is a lack of research around the dynamics of securing IoT (cf. [6, 8]); what challenges do companies face in developing, manufacturing, and selling secure IoT products, and what resources do they have for overcoming them? As cybersecurity is a rather technology-dominated field, the importance of organizational factors is often overlooked [8, 9]. By studying the field empirically, this work is a step towards addressing the challenges companies experience in their efforts to secure their IoT solutions.

© The Author(s), under exclusive license to Springer Nature Switzerland AG 2022
A. Moallem (Ed.): HCII 2022, LNCS 13333, pp. 406–421, 2022.
https://doi.org/10.1007/978-3-031-05563-8_25

In this paper, we present a qualitative maturity analysis of Danish industrial product manufacturers' ability to handle the security challenges that come with transitioning into IoT. Based on an interview study with 52 informants from 26 companies, our research explores the socio-technical factors that shape the practices around IoT security in organizations. Employing a theory of change [10] to analyze these interviews, we further point to three necessary conditions for IoT security maturity within organizations and elaborate on these conditions in a maturity model containing four different approaches to IoT security. Finally, we analyze general challenges that appeared across the interviews and exemplify how they are approached depending on the maturity level of the companies.

The study described in this paper was conducted as part of *Cybersecure IoT in Danish Industry* (CIDI) [11] – a project aimed at enabling industrial companies to strengthen their IoT security. As manufacturers of products for industrial enterprises and critical infrastructures (e.g., the energy sector), these companies have typically been structured around mechanical products. Transitioning into IoT increases the complexity of those products, and companies have to cope with new elements that were not previously part of their development and service, e.g., data protection, life cycle management etc. [7]. These changes do not only give rise to technical concerns but also require that the companies fundamentally change their mindset and the way they work with products.

2 Related Work

Wash [12] and Squires and Shade [13] have conducted interviews underscoring the importance of understanding the ways people perceive risks in cybersecurity. Wash [12] analyzes the mental models of private users regarding security threats and Squires and Shade [13] explore the perceptions of risk in three different communities of practice within an educational organization. Both papers point out that the way security advice is received is highly dependent on people's understanding of how cyberattacks work. Our research is complementary to these studies in surveying how understandings of risk and security in industrial companies affect decisions regarding IoT security.

In their ethnographic and interview-based studies Palombo et al. [14] and Assal and Chiasson [15] explore the ways development teams balance security against other requirements. Palombo et al. [14] point out that lacking security cannot be ascribed solely to technological or human capacities. Rather, security depends on developers' strategies for navigating in technical and human demands. Analyzing human vulnerabilities, Morgan et al. [16] similarly stress that technology alone is not enough to reduce cyber risk. A more human-centric approach is needed. Assal and Chiasson [15] describe six central factors affecting security practices: division of labor, security knowledge, company culture, resource availability, external pressure, and experiencing a security incident. Similar points are made in Heeager and Nielsen's [17] research on the development of safety critical software. We supplement these studies by focusing on the wider organizational context to deepen the understanding of the dynamics around IoT security in companies. Also, as opposed to the cases of [14, 15, 17], working with software development is often rather new to the companies in our research, traditionally having mechanical products as their core business. Finally, our interviews did not only center on the development process but also on the implementation, operation, and maintenance of the IoT products.

Through a survey of existing standards and guidelines for IoT security, Bellman and van Oorschot [18] illustrate a lack of best practice regarding IoT security. In our research, we explore how this affects companies working to secure their IoT products and the steps the companies take to navigate in the lack of clear directions for IoT security.

Organizations' practices and perceptions in relation to IoT security have been researched in Sweden – a context in many ways comparable to Denmark. Asplund and Nadjm-Tehrani [5] conducted an interview study to identify information security requirements for critical infrastructures. Two key findings of this research were that there are large variations in risk perceptions regarding IoT and that IoT security transverses existing roles and competencies in companies, which leads to lack of ownership. Through interviews with industrial companies, Höst et al. [19] studied challenges and procedures regarding IoT security updates. They found that navigating in the vast amount of vulnerability reports and recommended updates can be rather difficult, especially for small companies who lack the resources and competencies to survey and assess these. Furthermore, Höst et al. recount that few companies have formalized update procedures. In this paper, we point to similar findings, but also nuance the ways IoT security is practiced and perceived depending on organizational maturity.

Georgiadou et al. [8] have created a cybersecurity culture framework for assessing organizational readiness. In this methodology, the awareness and competencies of individual employees are the central unit for evaluation and improvement. In our research, we take a different approach, viewing individual behavior only as a subset of organizational capability. Moreover, we do not define variables such as awareness to be increased to achieve the goals of IoT security. Rather, taking the stance of equifinality, this analysis focuses on identifying necessary conditions for organizational maturity [20, 21].

Approaching security from a cultural and management perspective, Ruighaver et al. [9] list a number of dimensions that affect security in organizations. Based on previous case studies, they describe how contextual factors have a significant influence on individual and group behaviors, leading them to emphasize that studies of security culture must consider the wider organizational culture and that initiatives to improve security culture cannot be focused on individuals. The link between organizational culture and security culture is also explored by Lim et al. [22]. We build on this approach by addressing security as a matter of organizational maturity rather than individual awareness and competencies. Also, whereas [9] and [22] focus on the field of information security, our research centers on IoT security.

3   Background: Studying IoT Security from a Maturity Perspective

Forming the scope and method of this research is the notion of maturity. As de Bruin and Rosemann state, the purpose of maturity models is to "assess the maturity (i.e. competency, capability, level of sophistication) of a selected domain based on a more or less comprehensive set of criteria" [23]. In doing so, maturity models "allow users to cognitively simplify a complex environment by highlighting commonalities, allowing comparisons and providing holistic understanding [...]" [20].

There is a tendency for cybersecurity maturity models to focus on the technical and formal organizational aspects of securing, e.g., IoT (cf. [24–28]). This paper takes a more holistic approach, exploring the socio-technical factors that shape IoT in practice. In this, we follow Nadler and Tushman in their definition of maturity as a matter of "aligning an organization's people, culture, structure, and tasks to compete effectively by taking advantage of opportunities enabled by technological infrastructure, both inside and outside the organization" [29]. Whereas other maturity models within security typically evaluate security initiatives against specific goals, our approach furthermore focuses on developing organizations' ability to handle IoT security regardless of the criticality of their products. Hence, this model centers around complex connections and necessary conditions rather than average effects [20].

3.1 Scoping Maturity: Developing a Theory of Change

Viewing the companies in this study as being in the process of developing and improving their practice of IoT security, the maturity model of this study is constructed around a theory of change. This framework originates from Petersen and Dinesen [10] whose work draws upon systemic and constructionist organizational theory, including both macro and micro level parameters. The theory of change contains six categories:

- **Resources:** What resources are necessary for companies to handle IoT security? (e.g., competencies, suppliers, procedures)
- **Activities:** What activities need to take place for the organization to reach its goals for IoT security? (e.g., risk-assessments, governance, building security into IoT solutions)
- **Contexts:** What internal and external factors frame the work with IoT security in the given company context? (e.g., age, size, and type of company, culture, how efforts are organized, relevant standards)
- **Mechanisms:** What underlying mechanisms are affecting the practices around IoT security? (e.g., risk awareness, perceptions about IoT security, support from management, finances)
- **Results:** What are the goals for IoT security? (e.g., implemented procedures for IoT security, appropriate level of security, new customers)
- **Outcomes:** What outcome values can the results within IoT security produce for different stakeholders? (e.g., competitive parameters, risk management, new business cases for IoT)

By taking the theory of change as our point of departure, we avoid the pitfall of an essentialist analysis treating the companies as carriers of static behaviors, perceptions, and values. Rather, this study is set up to identify necessary conditions for maturity in IoT in order to stimulate reflection and inspire development [20].

The first step in constructing a theory of change was gathering relevant parameters and terminology from reports, guidelines, existing maturity models, academic papers, and popular science articles (cf. [1–6, 24–26, 30–37]). This input was condensed into a theory of change which was then consolidated through feedback and additional input from the technical IoT security experts in our project team.

The theory of change formed the backbone of the study going forward, supplying the categories for the interview guide as well as the analyses of our empirical findings.

4   Interviews: Exploring IoT Security in Practice

4.1   Semi-structured Interviews

A key goal of our research was to go beyond best practices, pre-understandings, and formalistic security terms. Wanting to gain insight into how the companies perceive and work with IoT security, we chose to conduct our research as a qualitative interview study. Qualitative research focuses on the ways phenomena unfold in different contexts; exploring the practices around the phenomena and looking for meaning rather than facts [38–40].

The interviews were conducted in a semi-structured manner as we wanted informants to talk about IoT security in their specific context and convey in their own words how they perceive and approach it [38, 41]. In the interviews we asked questions about topics such as design and security of the IoT solution, attack surfaces and worst-case scenarios, procedures around IoT security, previous experiences with breaches, culture and organization around IoT security, management's attitude towards IoT security, and customers' views on IoT security. Through the semi-structured format new subjects, reflections and findings came up in the interviews that we could not have anticipated. The interviews typically lasted an hour and a half.

Interviews were conducted from February to September 2019 with two additional interviews taking place in the beginning of 2020. All interviews but one was carried out in Danish – this interview was in English. Quotes in this article have been translated into English by the author.

4.2   Informants

In total, informants from 26 companies making products for industrial enterprises and critical infrastructures were interviewed. This sampling was based on the criterion of saturation – the point at which the same information starts to be repeated [38, 39]. The participating companies fall into three categories (Table 1):

Table 1. Companies according to category.

Category	Companies in study
Established companies working to integrate IoT into existing products	15
Start-ups and spinouts building new products based on IoT	6
Suppliers and consultancies developing IoT components for customers	5

The first category is the most predominant, with a variance in experience ranging from companies that are just starting to explore the possibilities of IoT to companies that have been working with connected products for many years, only without them being on the internet.

Besides recruiting companies from different places in the supply chain, we also made sure to include SMEs as well as large companies to secure diversity in our sample. See Table 2 for companies categorized in accordance with European standards for company size [42].

Table 2. Companies according to size.

Category	Companies in study
Micro: <10 employees	7
Small: <50 employees	4
Middle-sized: <250 employees	5
Large: 250 < employees	10

When setting up the interviews, we asked for participants with technical as well as business-oriented backgrounds to be able to cover all aspects of IoT security within the organization. Hence, our informants have profiles such as software developer, architect, engineer, business developer, CEO, owner-manager, CTO, head of development, etc. The number of informants in each interview ranged from one to five people, totaling up to 52 people being interviewed. None of the informants were given an incentive.

4.3 Research Ethics

Our institution has no review board, but we are obligated to follow the *Danish Code of Conduct for Research Integrity* [43] as well as the European *General Data Protection Regulation* [44]. In addition, we adhere to The American Anthropological Association's *Principles of Professional Responsibility* [45]. Therefore, informants and companies have been anonymized.

4.4 Coding and Analysis: Identifying Necessary Conditions

As a first step towards a qualitative analysis, the transcribed interviews were loaded into NVivo where they were coded according to our model of change with its six dimensions and nodes for each subdimension [20, 38, 39, 41, 46]. The coding allowed us to identify factors that were central to the companies' ways of working with IoT security. Based on these parameters, a series of clustering and matrix analyses [47] were made, exploring common characteristics between the companies, while at the same time checking the clusters against the empirical data as a whole. In this way, challenges with IoT security were identified and hypotheses about necessary conditions for maturity in IoT security were generated and tested [38].

5 Results

In this section, the results of the interview study and the maturity analysis will be pre-sented. First, we outline three necessary conditions that define how companies approach and handle IoT security. Next, we present a maturity model of four different approaches, showing how the necessary conditions manifest themselves in practice. Finally, we describe general challenges that appeared across the interviews and, when relevant, exemplify how they are approached depending on the maturity level of the companies.

5.1 Necessary Conditions for IoT Security Maturity

In analyzing what separates the more capable companies from the less capable compa-nies, three necessary conditions for IoT security maturity were identified in this study. These necessary conditions are not an indication of a company's security level as such, but rather its ability to handle IoT security. The necessary conditions identified are:

1. **The level to which IoT security is rooted within the organization:** For IoT security to be on the agenda in an organization, there must be a strategic focus from man-agement as well as efforts to embed IoT security through procedures and division of responsibility.
2. **The organization's mindset towards IoT security:** For companies to work con-tinually on improving IoT security, it must be viewed as a matter of implementing and maintaining procedures – not just as a technical issue which can be solved once and for all.
3. **The organization's awareness of risk:** Whether the company and its products are viewed as potential targets of cybercrime is central to the willingness to invest resources in IoT security; is IoT security seen as business critical, a necessary evil, or irrelevant to the company and its products?

Based on these necessary conditions, we now scored each of the interviewed companies which resulted in four approaches to IoT security, reflecting four levels of maturity.

5.2 Maturity Analysis and Four Approaches to IoT Security

Through categorization based on the necessary conditions, we identified four approaches to IoT security amongst the interviewed companies: Optimistic, Gradual, Integrated, and Managed. These approaches represent different degrees of maturity, with Optimistic being the least mature and Managed being the most mature. There is an even distribution in the number of companies in each category, with most suppliers and consultancies falling into the Integrated category. In this section we provide a brief characteristic of each of the four approaches, empirically unfolding the three abovementioned necessary conditions (Table 3).

Table 3. Four levels of maturity

Maturity level	Necessary conditions		
	Rootedness	**Mindset**	**Risk awareness**
Optimistic *The optimistic companies are characterized by the basic assumption that suppliers take care of security as part of assuring the quality of the products.*	IoT devices and systems are bought from suppliers. There are no in-house IoT security competencies. IoT security is seen as something best left to suppliers who are assumed to have the expertise and take the proper measures. The companies do not have procedures around IoT security but act on what they view as 'common sense'.	IoT security is mainly viewed as a technical issue; IoT security is thought of as something that is built into the product and that depends on the overall quality of the technical design.	The risk and potential consequences of a cyberattack are viewed as rather insignificant. The companies cannot see what anyone could gain from getting access to their system. IoT security is perceived as a necessary evil – something that needs to be addressed to sell IoT to customers.
Gradual *At this level, security is viewed as something that must be handled gradually as the IoT products are matured and become part of the companies' core business.*	The companies are new to IoT, but they do have knowledge of other technical aspects like engineering or IT security which can sometimes be drawn upon. Instead of outsourcing IoT security completely, they try to be as involved as possible, preferring to collaborate with their suppliers and make an effort to learn as much about IoT security as they can.	For the time being, IoT security is handled as a technical issue. The companies have made sure to implement basic, technical security measures to make the products fit for the market. There is an expectation that more systematic and formal processes around IoT security will be implemented once the connected products are scaled up and become part of the core business, making e.g., operational reliability business critical.	There is an awareness that IoT security is important, but as IoT currently only plays a minor role for the business, the companies are wary of over-investing in IoT security. E.g., there is an idea that making risk assessments would be premature as the product will undergo further iterations before reaching the final version.

(continued)

Table 3. (*continued*)

Maturity level	Necessary conditions		
	Rootedness	Mindset	Risk awareness
Integrated *Perceiving IoT security to be business critical, this approach is characterized by integrating IoT security into the development process on par with other quality parameters.*	In-house competencies within IoT make the companies capable of making and to some degree securing their own products. IoT security is discussed and handled during the development of the products. It mainly happens towards the end of the process, but the companies are working on setting up specific goals for security in the gates of their development models.	IoT security is seen to depend on processes as well as technology. Procedures, functions, and security boards are being established to make IoT security less dependent on individual priorities and competencies and more streamlined across teams, setting internal standards for IoT security.	IoT security is seen as vital to maintain and expand the companies' market position. There is an awareness amongst developers and architects that security breaches come in many different shapes and sizes. Consequently, IoT solutions are designed to withstand not only targeted but also scattered attacks as well as human errors.
Managed *Wanting to secure a high level of security in all products and business areas, these companies make sure that IoT security is managed throughout the organization.*	IoT is part of the core business and, having in-house security expertise, the companies handle all aspects of developing and securing IoT products. Not only aware what they do know, but also what they *do not* know, companies prioritize in- and outsourcing critical tasks that require in-depth expertise, such as testing or building certain components.	IoT security is perceived to be a moving target and companies seek to be proactive, taking a process-oriented, risk-based approach to IoT security. A lot of effort is put into stream-lining practices and procedures as well as creating a shared language across the organization. E.g., reference architectures and standard frameworks for risk assessment are implemented.	IoT security is vital to the companies' brand and market position. Securing a high level of IoT security, is key to harnessing the potentials of IoT and even the smallest breach is unacceptable. Expecting it to pay off in the long run, companies invest considerable resources into being front-runners and set the standard for IoT security.

5.3 Challenges with IoT Security

We have now presented the three necessary conditions and the four approaches resulting from the maturity analysis. This forms the backbone of this study and sheds light on the companies' ability to handle IoT security. This section will analyze general challenges that appeared across the interviews and compare them to findings from other fields of security and, when relevant, exemplify how they are approached depending on the maturity level of the companies.

5.3.1 IoT Security is Fundamentally Different from the Companies' DNA

Having typically been in the domain of manufacturing and selling mechanical products, the companies are challenged by the new tasks and problems that IoT security entails. As an informant puts it:

"We are used to working with iron, steel, bolts and screws. This is a whole new world for us to navigate in!"

IoT security is in many ways a hybrid field, cutting across the traditional structures of the organization. Simply put, the companies have an IT department taking care of internal IT security and one or more engineering departments in charge of functionality – and maybe, in some cases, a compliance department. There may be relevant competencies in all these departments, but no one department has all the insights and competencies necessary to handle IoT security. An informant describes the problematics in this fragmentation:

"This means that we do not have people with the necessary expertise. Because one person down here knows one thing and another person down there knows another. Together they may have nearly 100%, but you cannot be sure. Everyone has small fragments of knowledge – it is very hard to get that organized and to get an overview".

The fact that knowledge is fragmented within the companies does not only complicate the process of getting the right resources for a project; it also complicates the matter of embedding IoT security within the organization. As it is often not possible to locate a person or team both willing and able to handle IoT security, companies are unsure where to place responsibility for this area – an issue that is also pointed out by Asplund and Nadjm-Tehrani [5]. Especially in the less mature companies, this leaves the question of who has the mandate and who is responsible for IoT security unresolved. Depending on their size, the more mature companies might set up a new department to handle IoT security, but more often, responsibility is delegated across departments with the simultaneous task of coordinating between themselves e.g., through a cross-functional board. In smaller companies, the responsibility often falls, formally or informally, on a specific person.

5.3.2   There are No Agreed-Upon Standards and Guidelines for IoT Security

As with other kinds of cybersecurity, there is no universal standard for the level at which IoT is sufficiently secured. Regardless how many layers of security are built into a solution, there will always be a residual risk. It is therefore up to the individual companies to decide on their risk appetite vis-a-vis the intended applications of the IoT solutions. Even though several standards and guidelines around IoT security exist to help guide these assessments, there is no single agreed-upon standard that IoT products aimed at industrial enterprises and critical infrastructures must comply with. Furthermore, the informants criticize the existing range of standards for being unspecific in only stating overall goals without specifying how these are to be met. As an example, an informant refers to a standard requiring that companies have procedures in place to make sure their solutions are secured without in any way specifying what these procedures should be. This echoes Bellman and van Oorschot's survey of best practices for IoT security [18]. In analyzing guidelines such as The British Code of Practice for Consumer IoT Security [28] they find that these often state desired outcomes – and sometimes vaguely so – rather than providing actionable guidelines on how to secure IoT.

In practice, a lot of the decisions regarding IoT security are made informally by individual employees and teams, which results in a lack of consistency across departments and products. An informant explains that this creates insecurity around security:

"If you ask three architects and ten developers what 'secure' is, they will have thirteen different answers. This requires us to establish a baseline, and we could use some help for that. We think that what we have is good enough – but basically, we have no idea".

Because of the lacking standards, informants feel that it is up to them and their coworkers to assess what level of security is necessary for their IoT solutions as well as evaluate if the task of securing them has been sufficiently resolved. The informants express that it is difficult to make qualified decisions without anything to base them on. This is especially challenging for the less mature companies who do not have in-house IoT security competencies and have limited resources for identifying critical security measures and standards.

Informants liken the current conditions around IoT security to a Wild West scenario where everyone can do what they find best. Even when the companies converge internally on a security level for their products, it can be difficult for them to assess whether it is sufficient for specific areas of application – and even more difficult to convince customers that this is the case. Informants experience challenges in communicating with customers about IoT security as they are often very nervous about the increased risk IoT might induce, and some preclude connected solutions altogether. Generally, informants point to the need for authoritative guidelines on IoT security as these would aid them in their dialogue with customers and be a starting point for internal discussions:

"But if we could learn that the level is on a scale from 1 to 100 and that we have the resources to upgrade to 70 – for many customers that would be enough and for a few it would not be. [...] The waterworks has to test for pesticides; they only find what they are looking for. It is kind of the same thing we are up against. We need something to base these conversations on".

These findings on the insecurity amongst companies and customers point to a general lack of a common understanding of what IoT security implies and a shared language for communicating about the risks and measures taken. This makes it difficult for the companies to get a grasp of what IoT entails and which initiatives should be prioritized.

5.3.3 Risk Assessments Are Based on Intuition

According to Gordon and Lob [48] three parameters factor into risk assessments: potential losses resulting from a breach, the probability of a threat occurring, and vulnerability if a threat were to be realized. These parameters and the way they impact each other are also seen in our research. In this section we will analyze the way companies perceive different risks in relation to IoT.

Regardless of their maturity level, all companies have an uncompromising approach to safety; in designing their IoT products, they make sure that safety functionalities stay mechanical and are kept separate from the features requiring connectivity. Another aspect that is pivotal for the companies is how IoT affects the operational reliability of their products. E.g., one informant holds the view that the risk of breakdowns should not be higher than in mechanical products:

"We need to have the same risk as before IoT; back then you could also smash parts or break the functionality. But if someone were able to suddenly discontinue a thousand products, that would probably be the end of our company".

Availability is highlighted as the most important objective for IoT in industrial and critical domains, as also described by Sadeghi et al. [3] and Asplund and Nadjm-Tehrani [5]. Many informants, however, do not view this as a security concern. Rather, they describe it as part of making and selling a quality product.

Discussing the information security of their IoT solutions, we asked informants about risk scenarios in relation to data. Informants from companies with the Optimistic, Gradual, and Integrated approaches did not see this as an issue. They told us that they knew attacks and breaches were possible but argued that this was not problematic for their products and business cases. Oftentimes the first response to the question of data sensitivity was to point to the fact that the companies' IoT products do not handle any personal data – only operational data. In many cases, the risk assessment does not go any further after making this conclusion as the companies consider operational data non-critical. Informants expressed the view that a breach on these data would be rather harmless as they themselves could not think of any ways for outsiders to misuse them, making statements like: "We do not have the imagination to come up with anyone who could possibly have an interest in that". Generally, the least mature companies consider risk against data to be a question of whether confidentiality is critical for their product. Not being able to find any relevant scenarios in this category, they often dismiss data breaches as an issue.

As opposed to the risk of data being compromised, an area that is viewed with great concern across maturity levels is the risk of devices being used as a backdoor to access customers' systems. Informants from all types of companies reflected on the fatal consequences that this kind of misuse could have for their business and the outlook of IoT in their field. When it came to the likelihood of an attack, however, the less mature companies were also less concerned. For instance, after listing what motivations different types of intruders might have for breaking into their customers' systems, an informant reflected on the probability of this actually happening:

"On a scale from one to five, I would probably rate it as a one in likelihood – so the lowest rating possible".

Another informant simply relied on the belief that breaking into their system would not be worthwhile:

"We do not have any alarms if someone tries to get in – not even if the lid is removed. But we also kind of feel that if someone has gotten that far, they should almost get the credit".

What this last quote also shows is that the companies with the Optimistic and Gradual approaches are inclined to perceive themselves as being too insignificant for anyone to be interested in attacking them. This stems from an idea that their data, field of application, company profile, etc. do not have sufficient status to be attractive for adversaries. In short: the companies see themselves as small fish that no one could hope to gain a profit from attacking. This is similar to a finding by Squires and Shade [13] in their interview study of users' risk perceptions. In this, they point to a perception that "no one really cares what I'm doing" as a rational basis for a lack of precaution. This perception is linked to a mental model of how cyberattacks happen. As Wash [12] explains, mental models are an important basis for decisions on security as they constitute people's ideas of how things work. In our study, we found that the less mature companies have a mental model of cyberattacks as a process where hackers single out attractive companies or IoT products and target their efforts, time, and resources into compromising them. The informants do not reflect on the fact that their companies can be targeted because of their role in the supply chain or that many attacks happen in a less targeted way through, e.g., opportunistic port sweeping or phishing attacks [1]. At the opposite end of the spectrum, the more mature companies become, the more informants are aware that everything can be hacked and that nothing can be left to chance.

As this paragraph shows, working with IoT security requires that industrial product manufacturers gain knowledge and develop a new mindset regarding risk in relation to their products. As IoT security is hybrid in nature, companies cannot handle these challenges by inducing neither safety nor IT security logics onto this area.

6   Conclusion and Further Research

By conducting a maturity analysis of Danish companies making IoT products for industrial enterprises and critical infrastructures, this paper has identified necessary conditions for IoT security maturity and demonstrated how these unfold in practice. The maturity model can be used in two ways. Firstly, companies can use it to identify their own level of maturity – an insight that provides an informed starting point for working strategically with IoT security and can create new dialogue around security in companies. Secondly, initiatives aimed at furthering IoT security – like the CIDI project that we were part of – can take these factors into consideration when scoping and designing their activities.

In describing IoT security from a socio-technical perspective, this paper further provides an important contribution to the understanding of the challenges that companies face in working with IoT security. A basic problem for the companies is that securing IoT is fundamentally different from the kinds of quality and safety controls as well as IT security that they have traditionally worked with. Furthermore, there is a general lack of a best practice and shared language for IoT security inhibiting the efforts to settle on the right level of security for specific products and fields of application. Generally, a new mindset around risk is necessary for companies transitioning into IoT.

The study described in this paper is limited to a very specific scope; IoT products in a Danish context. Researching the same types of companies in other countries could improve the generalizability of the results. Moreover, looking into other aspects of these findings, further research could explore challenges and maturity patterns in other sectors learning to overcome the challenges of IoT security such as companies making consumer IoT products or companies from other parts of the industrial supply chain, i.e., manufacturing companies implementing IoT into their operations.

Qua our holistic approach, this research also contributes to the body of organizational perspectives on cybersecurity. Further qualitative studies into how security is perceived, prioritized, and practiced at different organizational levels could elaborate these findings.

References

1. Chen, K., et al.: Internet-of-Things security and vulnerabilities: Taxonomy, challenges, and practice. J. Hardw. Syst. Secur. 2(2), 97–110 (2018)
2. Vorakulpipat, C., Rattanalerdnusorn, E., Thaenkaew, P., Hai, H.D.: Recent challenges, trends, and concerns related to IoT security: An evolutionary study. In: 20th International Conference on Advanced Communication Technology (ICACT), 2018, pp. 405–410 (2018)
3. Sadeghi, A.-R., Wachsmann, C., Waidner, M.: Security and privacy challenges in industrial internet of things. In: 2015 52nd ACM/EDAC/IEEE Design Automation Conference (DAC), pp. 1–6 (2015)
4. OWASP: OWASP IoT Top 10 2018 (2018). https://owasp.org/www-pdf-archive/OWASP-IoT-Top-10-2018-final.pdf. Accessed 21 Feb 2021
5. Asplund, M., Nadjm-Tehrani, S.: Attitudes and perceptions of IoT security in critical societal services. IEEE Access 4, 2130–2138 (2016)
6. Alaba, F.A., Othman, M., Hashem, I.A.T., Alotaibi, F.: Internet of Things security: A survey. J. Netw. Comput. Appl. 88, 10–28 (2017)
7. Miloslavskaya, N., Tolstoy, A.: Internet of Things: information security challenges and solutions. Clust. Comput. 22(1), 103–119 (2018). https://doi.org/10.1007/s10586-018-2823-6
8. Georgiadou, A., Mouzakitis, S., Bounas, K., Askounis, D.: A cyber-security culture framework for assessing organization readiness. J. Comput. Inf. Syst., 1–11 (2020)
9. Ruighaver, A.B., Maynard, S.B., Chang, S.: Organisational security culture: Extending the end-user perspective. Comput. Secur. 26(1), 56–62 (2007)

10. Petersen, C.K., Dinesen, M.S.: Essensen af Innovativ evaluering. Dansk Psykologisk Forlag (2013)
11. CIDI consortium: CIDI project. https://marketing.alexandra.dk/acton/media/35392/cidi
12. Wash, R.: Folk models of home computer security. In: Proceedings of the Sixth Symposium on Usable Privacy and Security, pp. 1–16 (2010)
13. Squires, S., Shade, M.: People, the weak link in cyber-security: Can ethnography bridge the gap?. In: Ethnographic Praxis in Industry Conference Proceedings, vol. 2015, no. 1, pp. 47–57 (2015)
14. Palombo, H., Tabari, A.Z., Lende, D., Ligatti, J., Ou, X.: An ethnographic understanding of software (In) security and a co-creation model to improve secure software development. In: Sixteenth Symposium on Usable Privacy and Security ({SOUPS} 2020), pp. 205–220 (2020)
15. Assal, H., Chiasson, S.: Security in the software development lifecycle. In: Fourteenth Symposium on Usable Privacy and Security ({SOUPS} 2018), pp. 281–296 (2018)
16. Morgan, P.L., Asquith, P.M., Bishop, L.M., Raywood-Burke, G., Wedgbury, A., Jones, K.: A new hope: Human-centric cybersecurity research embedded within organizations. In: Moallem, A. (ed.) HCII 2020. LNCS, vol. 12210, pp. 206–216. Springer, Cham (2020). https://doi.org/10.1007/978-3-030-50309-3_14
17. Heeager, L.T., Nielsen, P.A.: Meshing agile and plan-driven development in safety-critical software: A case study. Empir. Softw. Eng. 25(2), 1035–1062 (2020). https://doi.org/10.1007/s10664-020-09804-z
18. Bellman, C., van Oorschot, P.C.: Best practices for IoT security: What does that even mean? arXiv Prepr. arXiv2004.12179 (2020)
19. Höst, M., Sönnerup, J., Hell, M., Olsson, T.: Industrial practices in security vulnerability management for IoT systems–an interview study. In: Proceedings of the International Conference on Software Engineering Research and Practice (SERP), pp. 61–67 (2018)
20. Lasrado, L., Vatrapu, R., Andersen, K.N.: A set theoretical approach to maturity models: guidelines and demonstration. In: Thirty Seventh International Conference on Information Systems (2016)
21. Dul, J.: Identifying single necessary conditions with NCA and fsQCA. J. Bus. Res. 69(4), 1516–1523 (2016)
22. Lim, J.S., Chang, S., Maynard, S., Ahmad, A.: Exploring the relationship between organizational culture and information security culture. In: Australian Information Security Management Conference (2009)
23. De Bruin, T., Rosemann, M., Freeze, R., Kaulkarni, U.: Understanding the main phases of developing a maturity assessment model. In: Australasian Conference on Information Systems (ACIS), pp. 8–19 (2005)
24. Jason Christopher, D.G., Muneer, F., Fry, J. et al.: Cybersecurity Capability Maturity Model (C2M2) (2014)
25. Shire, C.: IoT Security Compliance Questionnaire. IoT Security Foundation (2018)
26. IoT Security Maturity Model: Description and Intended Use (2018). https://www.iiconsortium.org/smm.htm
27. Le, N.T., Hoang, D.B.: Can maturity models support cyber security?. In: 2016 IEEE 35th International Performance Computing and Communications Conference (IPCCC), pp. 1–7 (2016)
28. Code of Practice for consumer IoT security (2018). https://www.gov.uk/government/publications/code-of-practice-for-consumer-iot-security/code-of-practice-for-consumer-iot-security. Accessed 21 Feb 2010
29. Nadler, D.A., Tushman, M.L.: A model for diagnosing organizational behavior. Organ. Dyn. 9(2), 35–51 (1980)
30. Fågelstedt, E.: Virksomheders uvidenhed om IoT-sikkerhed er en samfundsrisiko, Version 2 (2018)

31. Christopher, J.: The cybersecurity maturity model: A means to measure and improve your cybersecurity program. Forbes Technol. Counc. (2018)
32. Tannenbaum, A.: Why do IoT companies keep building devices with huge security flaws?. Harv. Bus. Rev. **27** (2017)
33. Lewis, K.: IoT security vs. IT security: What's the difference?. IBM (2016). https://www.ibm.com/blogs/internet-of-things/security-iot/
34. Almuhammadi, S., Alsaleh, M.: Information security maturity model for NIST cyber security framework. Comput. Sci. Inf. Technol. (CS IT) **7**(3), 51–62 (2017)
35. Mortensen, H.: Vejledning: Sikkerhed i Internet of Things. https://www.danskindustri.dk/viradgiver-dig-ny/di-dokumenter-for-virksomhed/it--og-datasikkerhed/sikkerhed-i-internet-of-things/
36. Bær dit brand sikkert med over i den digitale verden. The Alexandra Institute (2015)
37. IoT Security Guidelines for Service Ecosystems. GSM Association (2016).
38. Runeson, P., Höst, M.: Guidelines for conducting and reporting case study research in software engineering. Empir. Softw. Eng. **14**(2), 131–164 (2009)
39. Ladner, S.: Practical Ethnography: A Guide to Doing Ethnography in the Private Sector. Left Coast Press (2014)
40. Michrina, B.P., Richards, C.: Person to Person: Fieldwork, Dialogue, and the Hermeneutic Method. SUNY Press (1996)
41. Bernard, H.R.: Research Methods in Anthropology: Qualitative and Quantitative Approaches. Sage, London (1994)
42. SMV Portalen: http://www.smvportalen.dk/Om-smvportalen/definition-af-smv. Accessed 21 Feb 2010
43. The Danish Code of Conduct for Research Integrity: Ministry of Higher Education and Science (2014). https://ufm.dk/publikationer/2014/the-danish-code-of-conduct-for-research-integrity
44. The European Parliament: General Data Protection regulation. https://eur-lex.europa.eu/eli/reg/2016/679/oj
45. Principles of Professional Responsibility: American Anthropological Association (2012). http://ethics.americananthro.org/category/statement/
46. Thomas, D.R.: A general inductive approach for analyzing qualitative evaluation data. Am. J. Eval. **27**(2), 237–246 (2006)
47. Miles, M.B., Huberman, A.M., Saldaña, J.: Qualitative data analysis: A methods sourcebook. Sage Publications, London (2018)
48. Gordon, L.A., Loeb, M.P.: The economics of information security investment. ACM Trans. Inf. Syst. Secur. **5**(4), 438–457 (2002)

Users, Smart Homes, and Digital Assistants: Impact of Technology Experience and Adoption

Michael Shlega[✉], Sana Maqsood, and Sonia Chiasson

Carleton University, Ottawa, ON, Canada
michaelshlega@cmail.carleton.ca

Abstract. Smart Homes are becoming the norm, with manufacturers including connectivity within many home electronics and appliances by default; and these are often controllable through voice-activated digital assistants. Using an online survey of 212 participants, we explore how users' self-reported Technology Experience relates to their perceptions of the data protection done by Smart Home devices, their security and privacy concerns towards Smart Home digital assistants, and their likelihood of adopting mitigation techniques for digital assistants. We found no relation between self-reported Technology Experience and our dependent variables. We also compared adopters to non-adopters to explore differences between the two groups. We found that adopters of Smart Home technology had a higher level of perceived data protection and less overall concern towards the assistants.

Keywords: Usable security · Smart Homes · Digital assistants · Technology adoption · User study · Survey

1 Introduction

Recent statistics suggest that there are currently over 258 million "Smart Homes" worldwide [18]. According to estimates, 40% of US households have adopted Smart Home technology [19]. Even more popular, there are an estimated 4.2 billion voice digital assistants deployed worldwide [17]. Smart Home devices are now commonly combined with digital assistants to provide convenience and usability for consumers.

Despite these trends, some researchers project that the Smart Homes market is stalling, partly because of resistance in adoption due to perceived privacy and security risks [9]. Further research carried out by Barbossa et al. categorized factors that impact user adoption into blockers and motivators [3], with motivators promoting adoption and blockers impeding adoption. Of the blockers found, the more impactful ones can be grouped into user concerns and user perceptions.

Within this paper, we use the following definitions.

Smart Homes: Smart Homes are equipped with systems and appliances that can be operated remotely using a computer or mobile phone. Examples of

Smart Homes are homes that include appliances/systems such as thermostats, fridges, locks, light switches, TVs, sound systems, or security cameras that can be controlled by the user through a computer or phone.

Digital Assistants: Digital assistants are digital AI, within Smart Home technology, meant to assist a user by carrying out voice commands. When this paper talks about digital assistants, it refers to devices such as the Amazon Alexa, Google Assistant, SmartThings, Siri, and other voice-controlled assistants. These assistants can perform tasks such as search the web, control other smart devices, play music, set timers, check the weather, make phone calls, or run other voice-controlled apps.

As discussed in Sect. 2, researchers have previously investigated end user perceptions of data protection of Smart Home devices, end user concerns, and the mitigation techniques users take to protect themselves from the risks facing them. Our paper extend this work by analyzing the differences between users who have more Technology Experience and those who do not. To our knowledge, this analysis has not been done before and may provide insight into why users differ on their perceptions, concerns, and mitigation methods. Thus, our first research question is:

RQ1: What is the relationship between users' self-reported Technology Experience and users' perceived protection of data by Smart Home devices, their security and privacy concerns towards Smart Home digital assistants, and their mitigation technique implementation decisions?

Prior research (e.g., [1,2,7,8,20,25]) on users' perceptions and concerns towards Smart Homes has been primarily focused on users who have already adopted Smart Home devices. This leaves out a significant proportion of users: those who have chosen to avoid these types of devices. Investigating their perspective will enable a more complete understanding of the differences between adopters and non-adopters and the range of perceptions and concerns towards Smart Home digital assistants. Our second research question is:

RQ2: What are the differences between adopters and non-adopters of Smart Homes in terms of users' Technology Experience, their perceived protection of data by Smart Home devices as well as their security and privacy concerns towards Smart Home digital assistants?

To explore our research questions, we conducted an online survey with 212 participants. Our analysis revealed no relationship between the Technology Experience of respondents and (i) their perception of data protection with respect to Smart Home devices, (ii) the privacy and security concerns users harbor about Smart Home digital assistants, (iii) nor users' protection implementation strategies. When comparing adopters to non-adopters, we found that adopters had significantly more positive views on data protection in Smart Homes, had fewer privacy and security concerns about Smart Home digital assistants, and had higher level of Technology Experience. Furthermore, we found that adopters of Smart Homes rarely implemented proposed mitigation measures that would help protect their privacy or security.

2   Background

For context, we review recent research on Smart Homes and Smart Home digital assistants related to user perceptions, concerns, and mitigation strategies, organized by relevance to our two Research Questions.

2.1   Effect of Technology Experience

End User Perceived Protection of Data. Based on recent research, users' perceptions on data protection by Smart Homes and Smart Home digital assistants vary considerably. Georgiev et al. [7] showed that users had differing beliefs about how well Smart Home devices protect users' private data. The authors specifically noted that participants had different levels of technology understanding, but this was not explicitly assessed as a factor. Other papers [1,11,13,22,23,25] have similarly noted differences in technology understanding in their participant samples, however to our knowledge, none have explicitly tested its relationship to users' assessment of the perceived data protection offered by Smart Homes.

End User Concerns. Users' concerns relating to Smart Home devices have also been investigated. A qualitative interview study with 15 adopters of Smart Homes found that participants exhibited a varied understanding of the Smart Home threat model and did not share a common set of concerns [24]. The authors noted that participants' described threat models often depended on the sophistication of their technical mental models. Moreover, the concerns held by users were said to be different from the concerns held by security experts [24]. Others have also noted a potential correlation between users' degree of technical understanding and concern levels [5,6,11,23] though none explicitly tested for it. The literature on concerns has highlighted several common types of concern shared amongst users, with privacy and security being the most prominent categories [5,6,11,23,24]. It has been demonstrated that users who originally had few concerns showed increased concern immediately after being educated on the security and privacy issues arising from Smart Home devices, suggesting a potential connection between knowledge and the concerns of users [14]. Together, these studies indicate a potential link between the technical understanding of users and their concern level, however, no studies have directly investigated this relationship.

End User Mitigations. Users tend to adopt a variety of mitigation strategies, with no clear pattern emerging [8,11,20,24]. Mitigation strategies adopted by users have ranged from covering the microphone of a Smart Home digital assistant, to moving the Smart Home to a less sensitive room, to deleting Smart Home collected data. Zeng et al.'s interview study, mentioned above, found that users' understanding of the Smart Home threat model influenced their mitigation responses, however, it was not determined if a relationship exists between how advanced a users' mental model is and their likelihood of implementing a mitigation technique. Furthermore, Tabassum et al. [20] found that participants who had more advanced mental models showed more awareness about the mitigation strategies available for the Smart Home, yet it was unclear if this awareness led to higher likelihood of using mitigation strategies. Other academic work investigating mitigation strategies has suggested a link between *awareness* of mitigation strategies and users' overall understanding of Smart Homes, but has not determined whether this awareness leads users to adopt mitigation strategies [8,11,20,24].

2.2 Comparison of Adopters and Non-adopters

End User Perceived Protection of Data. Previous research has primarily analyzed perceptions of Smart Home data protection from the perspective of current users of Smart Home devices, but few studies have explored the perceptions of non-adopters.

One notable exception is a recent survey conducted by Barbossa et al. [3] which investigated both adopters and non-adopters, looking at their decision-making process for adopting or not adopting Smart Home devices. They suggest that user perceptions can be categorized into 'motivators' and 'blockers' of adoption. Participants who had more blockers, or had more highly weighed blockers, such as privacy or security relating towards their personal data, were less likely to adopt Smart Home technologies.

Similarly, Lau et al. [11] analyzed both adopters and non-adopters in an interview study with 17 participants, where they found motivators for adoption such as perceived convenience, and non-motivators for adoption, such as perceived privacy and security concerns relating to their personal data.

Most other academic research in this area is primarily qualitative and has also mainly targeted adopters' of Smart Home technologies [1,5–8,12,15,20,24,25].

End User Concerns. End user concerns have also been primarily investigated from the adopters' point of view. A number of studies have examined the concerns held by adopters and demonstrated that adopters of Smart Home technology generally hold disparate concerns [1,5–8,20,24,25]. Several studies have suggested that adopters' concerns about Smart Home devices may depend on the sophistication of their technical mental models of Smart Homes [11,24]. Most often, research has demonstrated that adopters' are primarily worried about privacy and security; however, this has been shown to not necessarily be a result of their knowledge of the risks, but rather their awareness of media reports surrounding privacy breaches or other Smart Home security violations [6,11,20,26].

2.3 Research Gap

While research has suggested a likely link between technical literacy and a user's perception and usage of Smart Home technology, this relationship has not been explicitly explored. Furthermore, most research has focused on adopters and this may under-report the prevalence of concerns relating to Smart Home technologies.

3   Methodology

Our study was reviewed and cleared by our institution's ethics review board. From November 2020 until April 2021, we conducted an online survey with participants to determine their: (1) Level of Technology Experience; (2) Concerns related to Smart Homes digital assistants; (3) Perceived protection of data by Smart Home devices; (4) Security and privacy behaviors relating to digital assistants within Smart Homes. We use this data to address our two research questions.

For this study, we define *Technology Experience* as an aggregate measure of users' understanding of various aspect of cybersecurity, their level of comfort and experience with using internet technology, their familiarity with privacy and security options online, and their education/work experience in the field.

3.1   Recruitment

Participation was open to anyone over 18 years of age who could complete a survey in English. Recruitment material was distributed through word of mouth, online research study groups, and the survey distribution site Survey Circle[1]. We also distributed our study through the online recruitment site Prolific[2], which is a crowd sourcing platform specifically meant for research studies. 250 participants (89 through Prolific, and 161 through other means) responded to the survey which took on average 10 min to complete. We excluded data from 38 participants because they did not press the final 'submit responses' button indicating their consent, had obvious patterns in their answers (e.g., $\{1, 2, 3, 4, 5\}$ or $\{1, 1, 1, 1,\}$). After cleaning the data, we had 212 valid responses. Participants who completed the survey on Prolific were paid £1.43. Participants who were recruited through other avenues were offered the chance to enter a raffle at the end of the survey for one of two $50 Amazon gift cards.

3.2   Participants

Participants' were between 18–70 years old; 43% identified as men, 55% women, 1% non-binary, and the remaining preferred not to say. With regards to education, 12% had completed up to high school, 5% had completed trade/poly-technical training, 28% had some undergrad (College/University), 27% finished undergrad, 14% some graduate school (e.g., Masters, PhD, Medical), and 14% completed graduate school. Geographically, 41% of participants resided in North America, 48% in Europe, 5% in Asia, and the rest were spread among the Middle East, Southern Africa, and Australia.

We asked participants whether they had adopted Smart Home technologies in their home: 49% (N = 103) of participants were *adopters*, and 51% (N=109) were *non-adopters*. Of the adopters, 55 used Google devices, 43 used Amazon devices,

---

[1] https://www.surveycircle.com/en/.
[2] https://www.prolific.co/.

and others used Apple (37), Samsung (17), and Microsoft (15) devices. A few (13) used brands not included on our list. Participants could select more than one option. With regards to security and privacy, 73 out of 103 adopters (74%) and 88 out of 109 non-adopters (81%) had previously encountered a privacy breach of their data.

3.3 Survey

We hosted the survey on the online survey platform Qualtrics[3]. The survey (available in Appendix A) consisted of 41 questions, including two definition confirmation questions. Prior to starting the survey questions, participants were informed that the term "digital assistant" refers to digital assistants that are specifically within Smart Homes. Participants were then provided definitions for 'Smart Homes' and 'Digital Assistants' to ensure that all respondent had a uniform understanding. The terms were described as follows:

This survey applies to *digital assistants* within *Smart Homes*

Smart Homes: Smart Homes are equipped with systems and appliances that can be operated remotely using a computer or mobile phone. Examples of Smart Homes are homes that include appliances/systems such as thermostats, fridges, locks, light switches, TVs, sound systems, or security cameras that can be controlled by the user through a computer or phone.

Digital Assistants: Digital assistants are digital AI meant to assist a user by carrying out voice commands. When this survey talks about digital assistants, it refers to devices such as the Amazon Alexa, Google Assistant, SmartThings, Siri, and other voice-controlled assistants. These assistants can perform tasks such as search the web, control other smart devices, play music, set timers, check the weather, make phone calls, or run other voice-controlled apps.

Following these definitions, two attention questions were posed: one asked participants to identify Smart Home technologies from a given list, and the other asked participants to identify examples of digital assistants. Participants had to correctly answer these two questions to proceed to the remainder of the survey. Those who failed could re-read the definitions and re-attempt the attention check questions until correct.

The remaining 43 questions consisted of 22 five-point Likert scale questions with two extra options for not understanding the question, or not knowing the answer. The remaining questions consisted of yes/no questions, questions with matrix table rankings, and questions with multiple choice answers. Our survey asked questions within the following five categories:

Understanding Definitions (2 Questions): Questions to double check participants' understanding of the provided definitions.

Demographics (8 questions): We asked about participants' age, education, gender, geographic location, work experience in cyber security, and the adoption of Smart Homes technology in their homes.

---

[3] https://www.qualtrics.com/.

Understanding of data collection (3 questions): We asked participants' perceptions of data collection practices on Smart Home devices.

Perceived protection of data by Smart Home devices (2 questions): Participants were asked their views on Smart Home data collection and their trust of companies holding user data.

Security and Privacy Concerns (10 questions): Participants ranked their level of concern for a set of privacy and security risks. The questions were modeled off claims used by Deursen et al. [21] which are based on truth statements ('Very true of me', 'Not at all true of me', 'Not very true of me', etc.). Deursen et al. showed that the wording of this scale led to objective responses from participants. We included additional options for not understanding the question and being unsure of an answer.

Experience with Technology (15 questions): We assessed participants' comfort and Experience with technology and cybersecurity. Four questions were based on the Internet Skills Scales test [21] which analyzed the five basic categories of internet skills: navigational, operational, social, creative, and mobile. Of these five skills, the operation and information navigation skills were most relevant to our study. The remaining 11 questions were devised by us to analyze Technology Experience by asking the participants to identify their knowledge level about various aspect of cybersecurity, familiarity with privacy and security options online, and their education/work experience in the field.

Security and Privacy Behaviors (3 questions): Participants who had adopted Smart Home technology were further prompted to identify whether they used certain mitigation techniques to minimize the risks associated with a Smart Home digital assistant. The techniques provided on the survey were based on multiple studies which had identified various common mitigation techniques that users took to defend themselves from risk [8,23,24]. We asked about the three most used strategies. These mitigation techniques were related to security and privacy as well as personal data management.

Table 1. Internal consistency across the various scales used.

Reliability statistics		
Scale category	Chronbach's alpha	Number of items
Technology experience	0.821	15
Privacy and security concerns	0.896	10
Perceived protection of data	0.708	2

We analyzed the inter-reliability of our scales (Table 1) to ensure the survey questions were assessing similar concepts in their respective categories, and found acceptable levels of agreement for all three categories.

Table 2. Statistical analysis of participants' perceived protection of data, protective strategies, and security and privacy concerns across two factors: Experience and adoption of Smart Home devices. Bold and * indicates statistically significant result at $p < .05$.

Measure	Factor	
	Experience	Adoption
Perceived protection of data	$(r = -.006, p = .933)$	$(t\ (205) = -3.63, p = .001)*$
Protective strategies (only asked of adopters)	$(r = -.182, p = .65)$	–
Concerns	$(F = 0.412, p = .522)$	$(U = 7034, p = .00005)*$
Experience	–	$(t\ (210) = 2.253, p = 0.025)*$

4 Results

We provide an overview of participants' understanding of data collection practices on Smart Home devices, and then analyze the survey data to answer our two research questions:

RQ1: What is the relationship between users' self-reported Technology Experience and users' perceived protection of data by Smart Home devices, their security and privacy concerns towards Smart Home digital assistants, and their mitigation technique implementation decisions?

RQ2: What are the differences between adopters and non-adopters of Smart Homes in terms of users' Technology Experience, their perceived protection of data by Smart Home devices as well as their security and privacy concerns towards Smart Home digital assistants?

A summary of the inferential statistics results discussed in the following sections can be found in Table 2.

4.1 Understanding of Data Collection

We asked participants three questions (Q11–Q13) to assess their current understanding of data collection practices on digital assistants. Specifically, we asked them about the (i) types of data collected, (ii) manufacturer's purpose for collecting data, (iii) perceived likelihood of the manufacturer being able to identify the user.

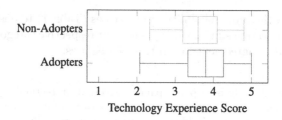

Fig. 1. Experience scores for adopters and non-adopters of Smart Home devices. Higher scores indicate higher Experience.

Participants were asked to pick from a pre-defined list of data they believed was collected by digital assistants. Participants could select multiple options, including "Other" to provide free-form feedback. We found that most participants correctly identified that digital assistants commonly collect searches and commands (n = 177), users' voice patterns (n = 140), and everything users say (n = 139).

A few participants incorrectly identified that digital assistants collect medical (n = 46) and banking (n = 48) information, suggesting that they may over-estimate the data collection practices in digital assistants and have mental models that reinforce (and possibly over-estimate) the surveillance or tracking capabilities of the technology. This was also reflected in the free-form feedback provided by a small number of participants (n = 15). These participants explained that digital assistants collected specific types of data (e.g., hardware IDs, location) or collected "everything" once triggered by a command (e.g., "Ok, Google"). As one participant explained:

> "They will collect anything that they have sensors to collect. If it is in or connected to a smart watch it may collect blood oxygen level. If it is connected to something with GPS it will track where you have been".

With regards to the purpose of data collection on digital devices, participants were asked to select from a pre-defined list of choices. They could pick multiple choices, including "Other" to provide free-form feedback. Most thought that the manufacturer's main objective of data collection was to build a digital profile of users for advertising purposes (n = 159), or to sell their data to third parties (n=106). Approximately half (n = 122) thought that it was for improving the quality of service.

On a 5-point Likert-scale (1 = not at all, 5 = very likely), we asked participants if they believed that companies could identify the current user of a digital assistant. A Mann-Whitney test found non-adopters ($M = 4.14$, $Md = 4$, $SD = 1.00$) were more likely to believe that companies could identify users of a digital assistant than adopters ($M = 3.79$, $Md = 4$, $SD = 1.07$), ($U = 3234$, $n1 = 92$, $n2 = 87$, $p = .020$. two-tailed).

4.2   Addressing RQ1: Effect of Experience

We computed participants' *Experience Score* by averaging their responses to the 15 *Experience with Technology* Likert-scale questions (Q19-Q33). Their *Experience Score* was out of 5 (M = 3.71, Md = 3.73, SD = 0.625), with 1 indicating the least Experience and 5 indicating the most Experience. Of the 3180 data points (212 participants * 15 questions), 36 responses were either 'I do not know' or 'I don't understand the question'; we coded these to align with the most negative Likert-scale response, since if one cannot understand the question or is unsure, this implies a lack of concept knowledge.

Experience and Perceived Protection of Data. We asked participants two 5-point Likert-scale questions (Q14–Q15) to assess their views on Smart Home data protection. Specifically, we asked them whether they (i) trusted companies which held their digital assistant data; (ii) believed that Smart Home devices are well protected in terms of security and privacy. We averaged participants' responses to these questions to give them a perceived protection score out of 5 ($M = 3.32$, $Md = 3.00$, $SD = 1.01$). A higher score indicated a more positive perception, while a low score was indicative of negative perception. A Pearson product-moment correlation found no linear correlation between participants' Experience and their views on Smart Home device data protection ($r = -.006$, n = 211, p = .933), indicating no linear relationship between the two measures.

Experience and Protective Strategies. Of the participants who had adopted Smart Home devices, we asked three 5-point Likert-scale questions (Q16–Q18) assessing their likelihood of using certain protective strategies on digital assistants. Specifically, we asked of their likelihood of: (i) covering the Smart Home digital assistants' microphone to prevent eavesdropping; (ii) regularly deleting data collected by the Smart Home digital assistant; (iii) covering the Smart Home digital assistants' camera to prevent unauthorized video recordings. As shown in Fig. 5, we found that most adopters of Smart Home devices did not implement common strategies to protect their security and privacy in relation to the digital assistants.

We further explored whether there was a relationship between participants' Experience and their likelihood of using protective strategies on their Smart Home digital assistants. To do this, we averaged their scores on the three 5-point Likert-scale (1 = always implemented, 5 = never implemented) questions assessing their likelihood of using certain protective strategies. A Pearson product-moment correlation found no linear relationship between participants' Experience and their likelihood of using protective strategies on their Smart Home digital assistants ($r = -.182$, $n = 103$, $p = .065$).

Experience and Security and Privacy Concerns. Participants' security and privacy concerns about Smart Home digital assistants were measured using 10 Likert scale questions (Q34–Q43). We averaged their scores on these questions to compute a *Concern* score out of 5 (M = 3.43, Md = 3.60, SD = 1.00), where a higher score indicated higher security and privacy concerns about Smart Home digital assistants. To explore the existence of a relationship between participants' Experience and their security and privacy concerns, we computed a Pearson product-moment correlation, which found no correlation between the two ($r =$ .065, $n = 212$, $p = .348$).

4.3   Addressing RQ2: Difference Between Adopters and Non-adopters of Smart Home Devices

As indicated by responses to Q7, 103 of the 212 survey respondents had adopted at least one type of Smart Home device. We explored the relationship between adoption and participants' Technology Experience, perceived protection of data by Smart Home devices as well as security and privacy concerns towards Smart Home digital assistants.

Adoption and Experience. Figure 1 shows the Technology Experience of adopters and non-adopters. Using an independent samples t-test, we found that adopters ($M = 3.80$, $Md = 3.80$, $SD = .614$) of Smart Home devices had more Technology Experience compared to non-adopters ($M = 3.61$, $Md = 3.63$, $SD = .626$) $(t\ (210) = 2.253,\ p = 0.025)$. Normality and equal variance assumptions for the t-test were checked using the Shapiro-Wilk and Levene's tests respectively.

Adoption and Users' Perceived Protection of Data by Smart Home Devices. We investigated whether adopters and non-adopters had different levels of perceived protection of data in Smart Home devices, using the same questions as in the previous section (Q14–Q15). We averaged participants' responses to these questions to give them a perceived protection of data score out of 5 ($M = 3.32$, $Md = 3.00$, $SD = 1.01$). Figure 2 shows the distribution of responses. An independent-samples t-test found that compared to non-adopters, adopters perceived protection of data Smart Home devices more in terms of the companies which collected data on these devices, and believed that Smart Home devices are well protected in terms of their security and privacy $(t\ (205) = -3.63,\ p = .001)$. Normality and equal variance assumptions for the t-test were checked using the Shapiro-Wilk and Levene's tests respectively (Fig. 3).

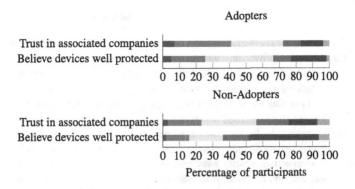

Fig. 2. 5-point Likert Scale responses to participants' perceived protection of data by Smart Home devices. 1 = 'True of me', represented in dark green; and 5 = 'Not true of me', represented in dark red. An answer of "Not Sure" or "I don't know" was represented in grey. (Color figure online)

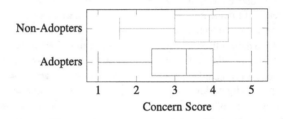

Fig. 3. Adopters and non-adopters' security and privacy concerns on Smart Home digital assistants; higher scores indicate a higher degree of concern.

Adoption and Security and Privacy Concerns Towards Digital Assistants. Participants' security and privacy concerns about Smart Home digital assistants were measured using 10 Likert scale questions (Q34–Q43). Figure 4 illustrates the distribution of responses for adopters and non-adopters. We see that non-adopters expressed high levels of concern for all privacy questions. Adopters were least concerned about image collection and voice data collection. We note smaller differences between the two groups on all security questions, although in each case non-adopters expressed more concern. We conducted an independent samples t-test to compare the concern score (comprised of the privacy and security questions) of adopters and non-adopters.

We found that adopters ($M = 3.19$, $Md = 3.30$, $SD = 1.02$) are less concerned about Smart Home digital assistants than non-adopters ($M = 3.65$, $Md = 3.90$, $SD = 0.94$), ($t\ (210) = -3.483$, $p = 0.001$). Normality and equal variance assumptions for the t-test were checked using the Shapiro-Wilk and Levene's tests respectively.

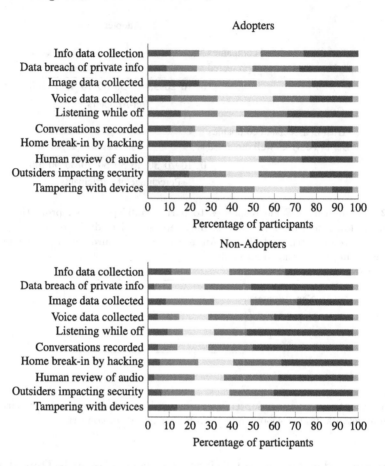

Fig. 4. 5-point Likert Scale responses to participants' Concerns relating to Smart Home digital assistants. 1 = 'Not at all concerned', represented in dark green; and 5 = 'Very Concerned', represented in dark red. An answer of "Not Sure" or "I don't know" was represented in grey. (Color figure online)

4.4 Post-hoc Analysis

Adopters had more Technology Experience, more positive views on the perceived protection of data by Smart Homes, and were less concerned about Smart Home digital assistants. However, we did not find any relationships between Technology Experience and perceived protection of data, nor with security and privacy concerns of Smart Home digital assistants. Given this, we conducted post-hoc analysis to determine whether the observed differences between adopters and non-adopters were due to other factors, such as geographical location, gender, or age.

Covering microphone of digital assistant
Covering camera of digital assistant
Regularly deleting data collected

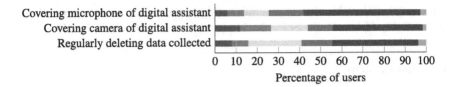

0   10   20   30   40   50   60   70   80   90   100
Percentage of users

Fig. 5. 5-point Likert Scale responses to participants' the likelihood of adopters using protective strategies on their Smart Home devices. 1 = 'All the Time', represented in dark green; and 5 = 'Never', represented in dark red. An answer of "Not Sure" or "I don't know" was represented in grey. *Note: The deleting data question was missing the 'rarely' (4) option for approximately the first one third of participants. (Color figure online)

Geographical Location. Most of our participants were from Europe or North America. Adopters consisted of 50 North Americans and 44 Europeans, and non-adopters consisted of 37 North Americans and 57 Europeans. We explored whether there was a difference between the two geographical areas in terms of Technology Experience and participants' likelihood of adopting Smart Home devices.

A Kruskal-Wallis H test found no statistically significant differences in Technology Experience scores between European ($M = 3.70$, $Md = 3.73$, $SD = 0.60$) and North American ($M = 3.68$, $Md = 3.73$, $SD = 0.66$) participants ($\chi^2 (1) = 0.012$, $p = 0.913$).

We conducted a Mann-Whitney test, which found no relationship between geographical location and likelihood of adopting Smart Home devices ($U = 3782.5$, $n1 = 87$, $n2 = 101$, $p = .058$ two-tailed).

Gender. We further explored the role of gender in the differences observed between adopters and non-adopters. A Kruskal-Wallis H test found a statistically significant difference in Technology Experience between men ($M = 3.93$, $Md = 3.97$, $SD = 0.57$) and women ($M = 3.52$, $Md = 3.60$, $SD = 0.61$), with men having a higher Technology Experience ($\chi^2 (1) = 20.833$, $p = 0.000005$).

We then conducted a Mann-Whitney test and found no relationship between gender and likelihood of adopting Smart Home devices ($U = 5140.0$, $n1 = 92$, $n2 = 116$, $p = .600$ two-tailed).

Age. Prior work has shown a potential relationship between participants' age and their mental models of Smart Home devices, with older users having less complete mental models [6]. Thus, we explored whether participants' age could be a factor in the differences observed between adopters and non-adopters.

A Pearson product-moment correlation, found no linear relationship between participants' Technology Experience and age ($r = .015$, $n = 212$, $p = .824$). We then conducted an independent samples t-test to see if there was a difference in age between adopters and non-adopters. We found that adopters ($M = 30.51$,

$Md = 26.0$, $SD = 11.34$) were significantly younger compared to non-adopters ($M = 37.41$, $Md = 34.00$, $SD = 13.54$) (t $(210) = -4.005$, $p = 0.025$).

5   Discussion

5.1   Answering RQ1

Returning to our first research question, we expected to find a relationship between Technology Experience and each of our dependent variables. However, this was not the case and we found no statistically significant results for this research question. This leaves two possibilities: that there is no relationship, or that our instrument was unable to detect it.

Let us first assume that our results are in fact correct, and consider its implications. First, we see quite a range of responses from participants, so it may be that another trait, besides Experience, is at play. For example, previous research has found that emotion had a stronger effect on concerns and trust [10] than knowledge of the subject matter. Thus, there may be other unexplored traits that together with Experience, or alone, are more closely related to the concern of users' and their behaviour.

Contrary to our findings, other researchers have pointed to a likely connection (see Sect. 2), and it would seem plausible that a connection exists between Technology Experience and perceived protection of data, behaviours, and concerns. Although we carefully created our Technology Experience measure as an aggregate score of questions covering several areas, we may have failed to capture the relevant aspects of Technology Experience. Similarly, we may have failed to measure the right elements relating to perceived protection of data, concerns, or behaviours. Given that many other works identify a possible link used qualitative methods, perhaps the relationship between Experience and behaviours, perceived protection of data, and concerns is too nuanced to be captured in a quantitative survey.

5.2   Answering RQ2

On this research question, we have identified some statistically significant results. It may be that adoption is a more relevant differentiator than Experience.

We found that adopters held more positive views towards data protection within Smart Home devices and held a higher self reported trust in the associated companies, adopters also expressed fewer concerns related to privacy and security, and they generally had more Technology Experience. In post-hoc analysis, we further found that adopters were younger than non-adopters.

These findings highlight the importance of considering non-adopters in research related to Smart Home technologies. It is possible that their reluctance in engaging with this technology stems in part from significant privacy and security concerns (i.e., note the proportion of non-adopters saying they are very concerned in Fig. 4). As Smart Home technologies become ubiquitous, it will be increasingly difficult for non-adopters to purchase 'non-smart' devices even if that is their preference. Non-adopters must already cope with Smart Home technology as bystanders or unknowing users when they visit other homes, or even within their own homes if another occupant chooses to adopt Smart Home devices.

We also note that although adopters had fewer concerns than non-adopters, this did not mean that they were wholly comfortable with the technology. The proportion of adopters who expressed *no* concern was roughly equivalent to the proportion of adopters expressing *a high degree* of concern. This high variability is interesting and suggests that other factors play an important role in users' decisions to adopt Smart Home technology. Despite their concerns, our adopters were very unlikely to use any of the three listed mitigation strategies that had been most commonly identified in the literature.

Furthermore, we see that two privacy risks relating to eavesdropping and surveillance were especially concerning. The concern of digital assistants listening while turned off and the concern about conversation being recorded were the highest rated concerns amongst both adopters and non-adopters.

5.3 Relationship to Previous Work

Haney et al. [8] found that while users expressed concerns, this did not deter them from adopting Smart Home technologies, with mitigation measures. Our work also suggests that adopters had significant concerns but few reported using common mitigation strategies. Our work extends previous findings by putting them into perspective: we demonstrate that the levels of concern expressed by adopters are significantly lower than for non-adopters. Participants in studies about security and privacy may be primed to express such concerns simply because the study brings this topic to the forefront. By surveying non-adopters as well, we supply context for the responses of adopters; any over-estimates would be present in both groups, thus the relative levels of concern can still offer insight. Barbosa et al.'s MTurk survey [4] had a mix of adopters and non-adopters, but their questions focused on hypothetical scenarios. Despite our different approach, our results do closely align with Barbosa et al.'s findings.

5.4 Limitations

In an attempt to minimize inattention, our survey was relatively short and focused mostly on closed types of questions. Such self-reported data may not entirely reflect users' actual behaviours and concerns. We tried to briefly cover the most important topics but it is possible that we missed some. In particular, our Technology Experience score may not adequately capture the actual Experience of individuals. We also note that our survey does not consider other reasons why users might not adopt Smart Homes technology, besides privacy and security. For example, recent work by Hong et al. [9] and Barbosa et al. [4] found that monetary considerations may negatively impact such decisions.

Furthermore, it is important to note that due to this being an online survey, participants may have skimmed the definition questions in which we note that the digital assistants discussed within the survey are in relation to Smart Home devices. Therefore, some may have considered all digital assistants in their responses. In terms of age, 91% of our participants were between the ages of 18–40, meaning that our study results may not accurately represent the older population. Despite this limitation, our results may reflect typical users as adoption have been shown to be primarily done by adults ranging from the ages of 18–50 [16]. Lastly, our survey did not explore *how* users became adopters. Adopters may have unwittingly become adopters due to a member of their residence purchasing a Smart Home device. Rather, than simply asking if one has adopted a device, we recommend future studies more closely differentiate between an active adoption and a passive adoption.

6   Conclusion

Through an online survey of 212 participants, we compared responses of adopters and non-adopters in relation to Smart Home digital assistants. We explored privacy and security concerns, security and privacy behaviors, and Technology Experience levels of participants. Our results showed that adopters were more optimistic about the perceived protection of data by Smart Home devices, had fewer concerns towards Smart Home digital assistants, and self-reported a higher level of Technology Experience than non-adopters. Nevertheless, many adopters still reported being very concerned about several security and privacy issues relating digital assistants. Adopters were also unlikely to use mitigation techniques to alleviate their concerns. Non-adopters expressed significant concern related to security and privacy. Our results further showed no relationship between Technology Experience score and our dependent variables, suggesting that adoption may be a better differentiator. There is, therefore, a definitive need for considering the perspectives of non-adopters in relation to Smart Home technologies.

A   Survey Questions

A.1   Understanding of Definitions

- This survey applies to *digital assistants* within *Smart Homes*.
- Smart Homes are equipped with systems and appliances that can be operated remotely using a computer or mobile phone. Examples of Smart Homes are homes that include appliances/systems such as thermostats, fridges, locks, light switches, TVs, sound systems, or security cameras that can be controlled by the user through a computer or phone.
- Digital assistants are digital AI meant to assist a user by carrying out voice commands. When this survey talks about digital assistants, it refers to devices such as the Amazon Alexa, Google Assistant, SmartThings, Siri,

and other voice-controlled assistants. These assistants can perform tasks such as search the web, control other smart devices, play music, set timers, check the weather, make phone calls, or run other voice-controlled apps.

1. Please select all examples of Smart Homes devices.
   - LG Smart TV; Ecobee voice controlled thermostat; Amazon Echo Speaker; Microsoft Cortana Speaker; Tesla Autopilot car; TP-Link mobile light switch; Voice controlled home security system
2. Please select all examples of voice-controlled digital assistants within Smart Homes.
   - Microsoft Cortana; Amazon Alexa; Siri; Microsoft Office spellcheck; Google Voice Assistant; Samsung Bixby

A.2   Demographics

3. What is your age?
4. Which of these best describes you
   - Male; Female; Non binary; Prefer to self-describe (please specify); Prefer not to say
5. In what region do you reside?
   - North America; Europe; Middle East; Southern Africa; Northern Africa; South America; Asia; Australia; Prefer to self-describe (please specify); Prefer not to say
6. What is the highest level of education you have completed?
   - Less than secondary school (e.g., up to grade 8); Some of secondary school (e.g., between grade 8 and 12); Completed secondary school (e.g., completed grade 12); Trade/Technical/Polytechnic; Some undergraduate(College/University); Completed undergraduate; Some graduate or professional degree (e.g., Masters, PhD, medical); Completed graduate or professional degree (e.g., Masters, PhD, medical)
7. Have you adopted Smart Home technology into your home?
   - Yes; No
8. If yes, which brand of Smart Home have you adopted?
   - Google; Amazon; Samsung; Wink; Other (Please specify)
9. Have you ever encountered a privacy breach of your data?
   - Yes; No; Not Sure
10. Please rate these topics in order of importance to you (1 = least important, 4 = most important)
    - Usability; Being connected; Privacy of data; Security of data.

A.3   Understanding of Data Collection

11. What type of data do you think digital assistants collect
    - Medical information; Everything you say; Banking information; Voice patterns; Your searches/commands; Other (please specify); None
12. What is manufacturers' main purpose when collecting data through digital assistants
    - Building a digital profile of you for advertising purposes; Improving the quality of service provided; Selling your data to third parties; Other (please specify); Not sure
13. On a scale of 1 (not at all) to 5 (very likely), how likely is it that the manufacturer can identify the current user of the digital assistant?

A.4   Perceived Protection of Data

Questions in this section have the following options:

- *True of me; Mostly true of me; Halfway true of me; Slightly untrue of me; Not true of me; Not sure what the question entails; I don't know.*

14. You trust the companies that hold your data
15. You believe that Smart Home devices are well protected in terms of security and privacy.

A.5   Use of Protective Strategies

Questions in this section have the following options:

- *All the time; Most of the time; Sometimes; Rarely; Never; Not sure what the question entails; I don't know*

16. You cover the microphone of the digital assistant to prevent 'eavesdropping'
17. You cover the camera of the digital assistant to prevent video recording
18. You regularly delete the data that the digital assistant has collected.

A.6   Technology Experience

Questions in this section have the following options:

- *True of me; Mostly true of me; Halfway true of me; Slightly untrue of me; Not true of me; Not sure what the question entails; I don't know*

19. You find it hard to decide what the best keywords are to use for online searches
20. You find it hard to find a website you visited before
21. You have an education related to cybersecurity or work experience in cybersecurity

22. All the different website layouts make working with the internet difficult for you
23. You find it hard to verify the accuracy of information you have retrieved online
24. You are comfortable using and understanding technology
25. You understand the impact of changing privacy settings online
26. You are comfortable navigating your computer/mobile device
27. You are comfortable working with the internet router in your home
28. You understand how cookies work on the web
29. You are comfortable configuring the firewall on your home network
30. You follow news stories relating to data leaks and privacy threats
31. You have customized the privacy settings on your browser or on your device
32. You have customized your devices or browser to limit ad trackers
33. You believe that you have a good understanding of how your data is being used online.

A.7   Security and Privacy Concerns

34. You are concerned about the way digital assistants collect information about you
    – True of me; Mostly true of me; Halfway true of me; Slightly untrue of me; Not true of me; Not sure what the question entails; I don't know

The following questions have answer options on a scale of 1 (not all concerned) to 5 (very concerned). How concerned are you about the following in relation to digital assistants?

35. Data breach of private info gathered by the voice assistant
36. Image data collected by the voice assistant
37. Voice data collected by the voice assistant
38. Voice assistant listening while turned off
39. Conversations recorded by the voice assistant
40. Outsiders changing settings or interfering with home devices (thermostats, fridge, etc.)
41. Outsiders using your Smart Homes to open locks or turn off security systems
42. Human review by the manufacturer of audio recordings revealing sensitive information (bank info, lock code, medical info, etc.)
43. Someone breaking into your home by hacking the home device.

References

1. Abdi, N., Ramokapane, K.M., Such, J.M.: More than smart speakers: security and privacy perceptions of smart home personal assistants. In: Fifteenth Symposium on Usable Privacy and Security ({SOUPS} 2019) (2019)
2. Adams, R.J.: 'Alexa, how can we increase trust in you?': an investigation of trust in smart home voice assistants. B.S. thesis, University of Twente (2019)

3. Barbosa, N.M., Zhang, Z., Wang, Y.: Do privacy and security matter to everyone? Quantifying and clustering user-centric considerations about smart home device adoption. In: Sixteenth Symposium on Usable Privacy and Security ({SOUPS} 2020), pp. 417–435 (2020)
4. Barbosa, N.M., Zhang, Z., Wang, Y.: Do privacy and security matter to everyone? Quantifying and clustering user-centric considerations about smart home device adoption. In: Sixteenth Symposium on Usable Privacy and Security (SOUPS 2020), pp. 417–435. USENIX Association, August 2020. https://www.usenix.org/conference/soups2020/presentation/barbosa
5. Emami-Naeini, P., Dixon, H., Agarwal, Y., Cranor, L.F.: Exploring how privacy and security factor into IoT device purchase behavior. In: Proceedings of the 2019 CHI Conference on Human Factors in Computing Systems, pp. 1–12 (2019)
6. Frik, A., Nurgalieva, L., Bernd, J., Lee, J., Schaub, F., Egelman, S.: Privacy and security threat models and mitigation strategies of older adults. In: Fifteenth Symposium on Usable Privacy and Security ({SOUPS} 2019) (2019)
7. Georgiev, A., Schlögl, S.: Smart home technology: an exploration of end user perceptions. Innovative Lösungen für eine alternde Gesellschaft: Konferenzbeiträge der SMARTER LIVES 18(20.02) (2018)
8. Haney, J.M., Furman, S.M., Theofanos, M.F., Fahl, Y.A.: Perceptions of smart home privacy and security responsibility, concerns, and mitigations. In: Symposium on Usable Privacy and Security. USENIX (2019)
9. Hong, A., Nam, C., Kim, S.: What will be the possible barriers to consumers' adoption of smart home services? Telecommun. Policy 44(2), 101867 (2020)
10. Lahno, B.: On the emotional character of trust. Ethical Theory Moral Pract. 4(2), 171–189 (2001)
11. Lau, J., Zimmerman, B., Schaub, F.: Alexa, are you listening? Privacy perceptions, concerns and privacy-seeking behaviors with smart speakers. Proc. ACM Hum.-Comput. Interact. 2(CSCW), 1–31 (2018)
12. Liao, Y., Vitak, J., Kumar, P., Zimmer, M., Kritikos, K.: Understanding the role of privacy and trust in intelligent personal assistant adoption. In: Taylor, N.G., Christian-Lamb, C., Martin, M.H., Nardi, B. (eds.) iConference 2019. LNCS, vol. 11420, pp. 102–113. Springer, Cham (2019). https://doi.org/10.1007/978-3-030-15742-5_9
13. Lin, H., Bergmann, N.W.: IoT privacy and security challenges for smart home environments. Information 7(3), 44 (2016)
14. Manikonda, L., Deotale, A., Kambhampati, S.: What's up with privacy? User preferences and privacy concerns in intelligent personal assistants. In: Proceedings of the 2018 AAAI/ACM Conference on AI, Ethics, and Society, pp. 229–235 (2018)
15. Singh, D., Psychoula, I., Kropf, J., Hanke, S., Holzinger, A.: Users' perceptions and attitudes towards smart home technologies. In: Mokhtari, M., Abdulrazak, B., Aloulou, H. (eds.) ICOST 2018. LNCS, vol. 10898, pp. 203–214. Springer, Cham (2018). https://doi.org/10.1007/978-3-319-94523-1_18
16. Statista: Smart home technology ownership rates by age in the U.S. (2016). https://www.statista.com/statistics/756519/united-states-smart-home-survey-demographic-adoption-rates-by-age/
17. Statista: Number of digital voice assistants in use worldwide from 2019 to 2024 (in billions) (2021). https://www.statista.com/statistics/973815/worldwide-digital-voice-assistant-in-use/
18. Statista: Smart home - statistics & facts (2021). https://www.statista.com/topics/2430/smart-homes/

19. Statista: Smart homes (2021). https://www.statista.com/outlook/279/109/smart-home/united-states
20. Tabassum, M., Kosinski, T., Lipford, H.R.: "I don't own the data": end user perceptions of smart home device data practices and risks. In: Symposium on Usable Privacy and Security ({SOUPS}. USENIX (2019)
21. Van Deursen, A.J., Helsper, E.J., Eynon, R.: Development and validation of the internet skills scale (ISS). Inf. Commun. Soc. **19**(6), 804–823 (2016)
22. Williams, M., Nurse, J.R., Creese, S.: Privacy is the boring bit: user perceptions and behaviour in the internet-of-things. In: 2017 15th Annual Conference on Privacy, Security and Trust (PST), pp. 181–18109. IEEE (2017)
23. Yao, Y., Basdeo, J.R., Mcdonough, O.R., Wang, Y.: Privacy perceptions and designs of bystanders in smart homes. Proc. ACM Hum.-Comput. Interact. **3**(CSCW), 1–24 (2019)
24. Zeng, E., Mare, S., Roesner, F.: End user security and privacy concerns with smart homes. In: Thirteenth Symposium on Usable Privacy and Security (SOUPS 2017), pp. 65–80 (2017)
25. Zheng, S., Apthorpe, N., Chetty, M., Feamster, N.: User perceptions of smart home IoT privacy. Proc. ACM Hum.-Comput. Interact. **2**(CSCW), 1–20 (2018)
26. Zimmermann, V., Bennighof, M., Edel, M., Hofmann, O., Jung, J., von Wick, M.: 'Home, smart home'-exploring end users' mental models of smart homes. In: Mensch und Computer 2018-Workshopband (2018)

Privacy in the Smart Household: Towards a Risk Assessment Model for Domestic IoT

Markus Frogner Werner$^{(\boxtimes)}$, Ida Ness, and Cristina Paupini🅱

Oslo Metropolitan University, 0890 Oslo, Norway
markus.werner93@gmail.com

Abstract. There has been an overwhelming increase of connected Internet of Things (IoT) devices on the market in recent years, and the number is rapidly growing. The applications for IoT are nearly endless, and the emergence of house assistants made IoT available for the masses and everyday consumers. With this exponential growth come challenges, and one of the most pressing is perhaps the risk of privacy breach. These small IoT devices rarely have any real computing power, and therefore are rarely equipped with antivirus software or other safeguards. Most IoT devices rely on the same communication protocols that they have always used, and with the evolution of the internet of things, and the internet in general, there are revealed new vulnerabilities everyday due to little or no effort to update or patch the existing software in these devices. Even the companies that publish their device specifications and information, leave it almost impossible for the user to understand, or even find said information. With the Risk Assessment model, this research aims to give the users of smart devices a tool to determine the potential risks that are involved with the internet of things and the many different smart devices.

Keywords: Internet of Things · Privacy · Smart household

1 Introduction

The Internet of Things (IoT) has emerged as one of the most important areas of technology, with an incredible potential for impact and growth. For the purpose of this paper, IoT is defined as a network of computers that look like everyday objects and are connected to the internet [1]. This definition includes smart devices such as house appliances, phones and tablets, sensors and control units which are connected to the internet and interact with both the user and other smart devices. This creates a network of devices that share information via various communication protocols and technologies. The purpose of IoT and smart devices is to increase the level of comfort, efficiency, and automation for the users [2].

The number of smart devices is rapidly increasing, and research predicts their number will reach 84 billion by 2024, which will be a 130% increase from the 35 billion connected devices in 2020 [3]. According to Kandaswamy and Furlonger (2018) western Europe, North America and China are the largest driving forces for this growth, although the use of IoT applications is increasing in all parts of the world [4].

A. Moallem (Ed.): HCII 2022, LNCS 13333, pp. 444–454, 2022.
https://doi.org/10.1007/978-3-031-05563-8_27

As IoT and smart devices rapidly become predominant in our society, a number of concerns arise, especially when it comes to privacy and security risks. According to Hassija et al. (2019), securing IoT devices is significantly more challenging than securing non-smart technological devices. As a result, IoT devices often present vulnerabilities that create fertile ground for cyber threats of various kinds [2]. For instance, adversaries can gain access to home and corporate networks through unsecure gateways, and thus get hold of private data. Furthermore, the heterogeneity and complexity of IoT devices makes ensuring security protocols even more challenging [5]. Additionally, not counting smartphones and tablets, most smart devices do not possess the computing power, storage, and network capacity to accommodate proper security. This leaves many units vulnerable to hacking and can potentially compromise sensitive data [6].

Moreover, the numerous security concerns are only one part of the problem. An even more pressing concern is represented by the users of IoT devices. Smart devices are now widely used in homes, controlling appliances, and keeping surveillance. Inexperienced users are interacting on a daily basis with microphones, cameras, and other sensors of which the potential danger is oftentimes not recognized or acknowledged [7]. According to Ahlmeyer and Chircu (2016) the lack of consumer awareness is due to the insufficient education and information available [8].

Through the current research project, work has been carried out to identify the primary security concerns of smart home devices, which have then been adapted into a risk assessment tool. The model presented in this article is a 15-items questionnaire designed to unveil the risks of cyber criminality, privacy violation and information shortage for domestic IoT devices. Questions are designed to explore different aspects of the IoT devices, including connectivity, protocols, encryption mechanisms, authentication, operating systems information and update procedures, data storage and protection, licenses, and risk estimates. The purpose of the risk assessment is to provide IoT users with a tool to assess the security of their current and future devices, in order to make more informed choices about the risk of application.

The Risk Assessment model has been tested by four different teams over the course of two years. The teams evaluated the smart devices from ten different smart homes to identify strengths and weaknesses of the model, and thereby improve upon it. Improvements and changes have been applied continuously throughout the duration of the project, such as reviewing each question for validity and relevance, and rephrasing some of the questions to make them more understandable and accessible to inexperienced users as well. This paper describes and deliberates the validity and useability of the Risk Assessment Model: from how it was created and improved upon, to its current state and suggestions for further developments.

2 State of the Art

The internet of things can be considered a network of "things" that are fitted with many different types of technology, like sensors and AI-software, which can communicate with other devices to exchange data over a network. Today, many people own smart assistants like Alexa or Google, which can help automate certain mundane tasks around the house, as well as provide some useful utilities. Different industries can, thanks to the development of IoT devices, connect monitoring systems and sensors in places that are hard to reach for humans. Consequently, inspections are made a lot easier, cheaper, and safer. Industrial IoT devices are however not limited to this area, but also exist for the purpose of several other uses [9]. These two areas of use are just scratching the surface of what the world of IoT offers, and the field is expanding like never before [10].

Most IoT devices need sensors to measure and record all sorts of telemetry, and in recent years there has been a massive growth of cheap to manufacture, low power cost sensors that make these IoT devices more affordable and thus accessible [11]. While more and more smart devices flood the markets, corporations are, seemingly, just now starting to improve the security of their products. Research shows that 48% of people are unaware of the potential risks to their own privacy when it comes to IoT-devices [12]. In general terms, risk can be regarded as the potential for an event to occur. In relation to the IoT, we are talking about the risk of exposure to technical, ethical, security and privacy breaches due to weaknesses of the device and/or network. Considering this, risk can be derived from the assets that are collected on these devices or networks like personal data and other recorded information.

Privacy is becoming a growing concern in the evolution of the internet, and therefore, also with the evolution of the IoT. People have become more aware that their personal data is being used by giant corporations to track consumer habits, location, behavior and much more. However, a survey by Deloitte (2016) revealed that 91% of people agree to the terms and conditions without reading them, and for people aged 18–34 the rate is at a staggering 97% [13].

The information these devices collect, share and stream to hubs and servers are primarily used to enhance the experience of using the device, but as with any other type of information, it has a double edge. The way these devices are manufactured leaves very little thought to security. They are designed to be easy to connect and to use, and they contain very little computing power. This leads to them often not being equipped with sufficient firewalls or even antivirus software [14].

Smart devices are rapidly increasing in number worldwide, and with the aforementioned prediction of around 84 billion connected devices within 2024, one can only speculate on the increase in breaches of privacy if the manufacturers of said devices neglect developing adequate safeguards. According to Zhang, Cho, Wang, Hsu, Chen, and Shieh (2014), the high risk of security breaches of IoT devices is mainly a result of heterogeneity and the large scale of objects. Given that each of these encounters' different security problems, they can be divided into two categories, namely: the diversity of the "Things" and the communication of the "Things". A contributing factor for these security risks is the somewhat careless program design which results in IoT devices being left vulnerable to malware attacks, and unwanted installations through open "back doors" [5].

Furthermore, Zhang et al. (2014), claim the growth of IoT leads to an increase in security issues. This is often the case with technology. More devices mean more connections, and with more connections comes more ways for attackers to exploit weaknesses in the design. Combine all this with the limited computing power in many IoT devices, and they can become risky to use, even for the average person [5].

The lack of existing methods of detecting vulnerabilities in smart devices is one of the main reasons for this research and paper. The risk assessment questionnaire and accompanying scale has the potential to be a great asset for users of everyday, household smart devices.

3 Methods

3.1 Initial Development

The development of the first prototype of the Risk Assessment Model was carried out by four international students, completing the European Project Semester (EPS), under the supervision of five internal and external supervisors. The work was carried out in collaboration with the Relink – Relinking the weak link project during the second half of 2019.

In the initial stages of the project, the team investigated smart home devices available in the Norwegian market. This included getting an overview of available and commonly owned devices. In addition, the group researched security features of these devices and the potential threats they can cause. Theories, academic literature, worst case scenarios and experience set the basis for the development of the model. Furthermore, specialists within the field of IoT and cyber security were consulted on account of the state of the art and the group's initiative. This groundwork led to the identification of three types of risk: Privacy Violation, Information Shortage and Cyber Criminality. Consequently, it became apparent these three categories of risk would have to be reflected in the model.

During the research stage, the group identified five different criticalities that would have to be implemented in the model in order to assess a device's level of risk as accurately and in depth as possible. These are: connectivity and protocols for connection, encryption mechanisms, authentication, information about the operating system, and finally licenses and protocols for data storage and protection. As such, questions were developed within these categories, covering the aforementioned criticalities. As such the model goes further than the global lines of systems security (Authorisation, authentication, and accounting). This is a key feature of the model, as cyber criminality acts beyond user interface's limits. Finally, an impact question was added to estimate the level of risk due to an accident caused by the device.

The development stage consisted of adjusting the model over and over based on results from testing the questions on different IoT devices. Specifically, 26 different devices were used to test the different questions. This helped identify which questions should be implemented, changed, or discarded. Additionally, it led to rephrasing of the questionnaire items.

As a result, the group ended up with a first draft of the risk assessment model: A 15-item questionnaire, where the first 14 questions ask about the specifics of the device and manufacturer, and the 15th asks the user to provide impact scores of both physical and digital breaches in security. The answer to these questions leads to a score between 0 to 100, which is used to imply the level of risk the assessed device poses.

3.2 Testing and Improvements

From the first prototype of the model, continuous testing and improvements have been applied. Specifically, three rounds of testing have been carried out since the first draft of the model was completed. The testing aimed to identify weaknesses of the model and to assess its usability. Results and findings from the testing were used to make changes to the model, with the goal to both improve upon the usability of the model and its accuracy and ability to identify risk.

The testing was carried out by using the model to evaluate a range of different smart home devices to get a feel of which aspects of it worked well, and which would have to be improved upon. Devices the model was tested on included different smart home devices available in the Norwegian market, as well as devices from 10 different smart homes, part of RELINK's fieldwork. Resources used to complete the evaluations included digital resources such as company websites, forums, academic papers etc.

The test procedure consisted of researching the IoT devices online to collect the relevant information needed to complete the Risk Assessment Model. Measures were taken to use reliable resources such as the manufacturer's websites. Nevertheless, lack of transparency from said manufacturers resulted in having to gather information from forums and other channels. When this occurred, the group found several sources stating the same information to safeguard the correctness of the information. If no corroborating sources were found, the device would receive a point in the risk assessment model, with a stipulation that the information could not be located.

Through filling out the questions and doing research on the devices, it became obvious which questions did not serve their intended purpose, were unspecific or simply irrelevant. In addition, the research of devices led to realizations about other questions which had to be implemented into the model for it to fulfill its purpose and represent a broad analysis of the given risks involved in using the IoT device.

First Round of Testing. The first round of testing was completed by the EPS-group, the same group of people that developed the model, during the fall of 2019. The group consisted of four testers. The model was tested on 12 different devices from four different types of IoT devices: smart speakers, smart light bulbs, smart fire alarm systems and smart outdoor cameras. Changes made included adding a question about Global Data Protection Rules (GDPR) and sub-questions to ensure a more accurate assessment of the technical questions.

Second Round of Testing. The second round of testing was carried out during the autumn of 2020. The newest, and updated version of the Risk Assessment Model was used. Devices used to test the model were part of the fieldwork RELINK performed in the Norwegian smart households during the year 2020. During this round of assessment, the model was tested on a total of 31 IoT devices and led to the decision of implementing another sub-question to the model. Specifically, "Can the user access the logs" was added to question 11. "Are there system logs?" This, because whether the users can actually access the system logs is important towards the control they have on their privacy related to the device.

Third Round of Testing. The final round of testing was completed during the spring of 2021, by two groups with three testers in each group. Group A tested the model on 30 different devices from three different households, whilst group B assessed the model by testing it on 20 devices from three different households. Through joint discussion, the two groups decided to change the wording of question 3 from "transmission over internet" to transmission over network" as not all devices use internet such as Wi-Fi/ethernet, but they all use a form of network. Additionally, sub two sub questions were added. Lastly, group B made improvements to the layout of the model to improve its readability and usability.

4 Results

As a result of continuous testing and improvements, this paper presents the newest version of the Risk Assessment Model: a 15-item questionnaire, consisting of questions designed to examine multiple characteristics of smart home devices in order to unveil risks of cyber criminality, privacy violation and information shortage. The questions are designed to examine multiple characteristics of the device: the first three questions (Q1–Q3) explore connectivity, and the protocols used for local and distant connections. The following two questions (Q4–Q5) analyze data transmissions to verify encryption mechanisms. Next, two questions (Q6–Q7) explore authentication. The model then moves onto an overview of the Operating System information along with its update procedures (Q8–Q9). The next steps concern data storage, data protection guarantees and end user license, guide & procedures (Q10–Q14). The questionnaire ends with a subjective open question made to estimate the impact of an accident caused by the device over the house and on its owner, from the risk analyzer's point of view (Fig. 1).

4.1 Guidelines

- Every question should be answered with yes or no (except 15)
- Questions that cannot be answered are considered a risk, and graded accordingly
- The answer "yes" typically implies danger, unless the opposite is stated
- If a question has sub questions, grade the sub questions before the main one.
- the score of one question is the sum of sub-questions that are ticked.
- meaning: the 1 point of that question is divided by the number of sub-questions it has. The sub-questions' scores are then summed to give the final score of the question
- Each question will be scored with a score between 1 and 0 points, where 1 implies risk and 0 implies safe
- The 15th question consists of two parts (to underline the degree of exposure). give a grade from 1–5. an average within the outputs.
- Bringing the results to a scale from 1 to 100.

#	Question	Yes/No	Score
Name of device			
1	Is the device connected with other smart devices?		
	Wired:		
	Wi-Fi:		
	Is it possible to connect it to 3G, 4G, 4G+, 5G?		
	Are there different connection/communication protocols available on it (Bluetooth, IrDA, Z-Wave, etc)?		
	Does this device control other devices?		
2	Does it use a custom network for initial configuration?		
3	Is the data transmission over the network encrypted by default (Answer no is a danger)?		
	is there an option to encrypt the data transmission (Answer no is a danger)?		
	Is the option easy to find?		
4	Does it generate/record/collect any private data?		
5	Does it stream or upload data? (Even local-only streaming is dangerous)		
6	Is the authentication uncontrolled? (ID/Password in the App is accepted)		
	Does the manufacturer force to change the default password and login? (Answer no is a danger)		
7	Is multiple-factor authentication the default? (Answer no is a danger)? Only answer subquestions if NO		
	is there an option to enable multiple-factor authentication? (Answer no is a danger)? Is the option easy to find?		
8	Is the OS based on an unknown kernel?		
9	Does the current version of the OS have known vulnerabilities?		
	Are software upgrades & security patches applied automatically? (Answer no is a danger)		
	Can up-to-date OS versions or release notes easily be found? (Up-to-date means the last update or patch was included during the past 9 months.) (Answer no is danger)		
10	Is the device designed to be controlled from a remote network?		
11	Are there system logs?		
	Are they stored on the cloud?		
	Are they in clear text?		
	Can the user access the logs?		
12	Does the manufacturer collect personal data?		
	Does the company claim to follow GDPR's requirements? (Answer no is a danger)		
	Is personal data shared with third parties (even partners)?		
13	Are user information and operational data merged?		
14	Is the end user licence agreement published? (Answer no is a danger)		
	and if so, does it include a security guide or notes & warnings? (Answer no is a danger)		
Score of question 1-14			
15	1 = Low impact → 5 = High impact	Impact	Score
	Rate from 1 to 5 the potential impact of a data breach/leak from this device.		
	Rate from 1 to 5 the physical impact of a malfunction or a defect of the device.		
Total score (sum of question 1-14 × average of question 15) brought up to a scale of 1-100			

Fig. 1. The Risk Assessment Model's questions and score module.

5 Discussion

The Risk Assessment Model, with its questions and grading system, has been made with careful deliberation. To make an effective and reliable tool for risk assessment of IoT devices, it was not only important that the questions collectively could cover a broad spectrum of different possible risk factors, but also that they would have to be of such nature that the users could actually be able to access information about them. Covering a broad area of security factors, the questions touch upon a great range of security and privacy features. Simultaneously, the questions in the model must be asked in a way that makes it possible for the user to answer them. The required information has to be easily obtainable. As of today, the questions making up the model should all be possible to answer in the presence of manufacturer transparency. However, there are likely some additional questions that would result in a more accurate assessment, but the technical nature of some information makes it difficult to pose the questions in a way that is understandable for everyone. This would in turn make the risk assessment model a tool that only those with extensive IoT knowledge could use, which negates its original purpose. Not to mention, some of these questions may also be impossible to answer by actual professionals. Thus, making the model useless.

Building on that, a further point for discussion is whether to adjust the model to either maintain usability for the average user or improve the accuracy of the risk assessment. The goal of this project is to develop a tool that can be used by everyone, and not only those with extensive IT experience and knowledge. As of today, the model is possibly too complicated for the average user, as some of the questions require the user to have a certain amount of technical knowledge. As such, assessing the questions and making them "easier" may make the model more usable for everyone. However, that would result in the loss of both content and depth, and thus affect the accuracy of the assessment tool. On that same note, we also have to acknowledge the 15 questions the model consists of today may not go sufficiently in depth to carry out a comprehensive risk assessment. This, despite touching upon several different themes of IoT security. Yet, it is impossible to touch upon every topic within only fifteen questions. However, by adding more questions, usability of the model will likely decrease.

With the evolution of the internet of things comes new ways to exploit vulnerabilities in the software. IoT devices often contain little computing power and therefore they cannot be fitted with the most sophisticated anti-virus protection or protective software. Zhang et al. (2014) claims that the growth of IoT devices in the markets, and their increasing use in the world opens up many doors for malicious intent. The more connections being made leave more doors for attackers to enter through. Given that companies rarely patch the software used in their IoT devices, known vulnerabilities remain unfixed, leaving the device and all its connections in jeopardy. This fact makes the risk assessment model obsolete if not revised and improved as time passes.

As a result, the teams of testers have continuously made changes to the model based on their acquired results from the testing, which are believed to have improved the accuracy and relevance of the model. The changes consist mostly in adding more sub-questions, rephrasing the questions in a more understandable manner, and thereby improving upon the model's authenticity and area of use. The purpose of both these types of changes was to make the model more applicable, even for household devices.

Specifically, rephrasing was carried out to clarify questions, and sub-questions were added to aid in how to assess the main questions.

For instance, during the first round of testing, a sub-question on GDPR ("Does the company claim to follow GDPR's requirements?") was added to help answer question 12: "Does the manufacturer collect personal data?" GDPR and the processing of personal data is something both businesses and private households are concerned with. While many businesses collect a lot of information about their customers, they now have to process the collected data according to set, very strict laws, and are eligible for major financial or legal consequences if they do not abide by these laws (Burgess, 2018). Since these laws are applicable to every organization that handles personal data, it may seem redundant to have to include it in the model, however research performed during the testing of the model show that many organizations hide, or neglect to inform properly, their stance on the matter. Some companies even completely refrain from acknowledging it.

Moreover, the sub-question "Can the user access the logs?" was added under question 11 "Are there system logs?" during the second round of testing. This, because it is not only important to consider whether a device has system logs, but also whether the user can access them. In the third round of testing, the changes to the questions were carried out in order to achieve a more accurate assessment of smart devices of different natures. The new questions 3 and 7 allows for a more accurate evaluation of devices in which encryption and multiple-factor authentication is optional. For instance, question 3 in the original assessment form asked "Is the data transmission over the internet in clear text?". It was quickly realized that many of the assessed devices had encryption as an option rather than the default. Similarly, question 7 asked "Does it use a multiple factors method for authentication?". It was found that many devices let the user set up multiple-factor authentication as an option rather than it being the default. As such it was decided to change the two questions and add sub-questions to accommodate these options.

The final improvement made to the Risk Assessment Model was to redesign the layout of the form to improve readability. Originally, the questionnaire was just a list of questions with no clear space to put the score. As such, it was suggested to make a template for the questions, with separate columns for the scores - making the model clearer and more readable. However, it is acknowledged the model's layout still contains room for improvement. The new layout makes it somewhat easier to keep track of points from questions and the total point score by providing a column for these. However, it does not make it easier to calculate the total score, which we will get back to.

The testing of the model, and in particular the risk assessment of IoT devices, proved that such devices offer a wide array of services and fulfill many different tasks in our homes. Due to these devices having such varying qualities and capabilities, one can ask whether all the questions of the Risk Assessment Model are appropriate for all kinds of devices. In example, question six inquiries about the possibility to change the default password, where in fact some devices do not require any password at all, without that necessarily being a risk factor. For instance, certain smart light bulbs can be controlled by an included remote control. Unless it is also connected to a gateway, the device does not require controlled authentication. Due to the structure of the model, the fact that a password is not needed negatively affects the overall score. This, regardless that the device, in this state, is more or less unconnected and offers little or no security threat at all. Thus, further investigation into whether questions like these are appropriate to evaluate all different types of smart home devices needs to be evaluated.

Furthermore, the questionnaire does not take into account unavailable information and lack of manufacturer transparency. During the testing, a couple of the devices received a high score due to the information being unavailable. In such cases, this automatically affected the score of these questions negatively although it may not actually be the accurate score. For instance, one of the motion detectors used to test the model received the highest scores of all the assessed devices. One can question how a motion detector gets a higher score than for instance a surveillance camera and smart hubs, which actually records the user. The main reason for this issue is the lack of transparency on security concerns from certain companies, along with the fact some of the questions are not optimal to accommodate the different types of devices. When the required information is hard to find, it may result in artificially high final scores. That being said, it is possible that the assessment is correct, and the motion sensor is more of a risk to use, but logic dictates it is not.

Finally, the method of calculating the scores is somewhat complicated. During the rounds of testing, the groups found it troublesome to calculate the scores and often made errors. This makes us believe the method of calculating the scores is too complex and will most likely result in wrong assessments by users who might interpret the method incorrectly.

6   Conclusion and Future Work

As introduced in this paper, a risk assessment model for IoT devices has been designed, tested, and improved through a time period spanning 2 years. The proposed model is not a finished product and needs continuous improvements to adapt to future advancements in technology, stay up to date and function as intended. Throughout the process of creating the model, several changes to the questions and layout have been adapted. This includes changes to the phrasing of questions in order to make them more understandable, the addition of sub-questions to help guide the user in answering the main questions, and changes to the layout to improve readability and usability. Although the model today can be used to assess the risk of IoT devices with discrete accuracy, it is also acknowledged there is still a great potential for improvement. Nevertheless, an advantage to the given design of the model is that it can, at any time, be expanded and improved - either it be due to assure more accurate risk assessments, to keep the model relevant or functional along the advancements of technology, or to improve its usability.

In the context of future work on the model, further advancements should focus on finding a way in which the integrity and accuracy of the model can be maintained, if not improved, whilst simultaneously improving its usability. One potential approach for succeeding with this, could be making the model a digital tool where points are automatically calculated according to the inputs of the user, and questions vary depending on the nature of the device. Taking this to the next level, with enough data about several different devices and manufacturers, one can create a database that is accessible for consumers via a web application. This, so that they do not have to answer all the questions for themselves, but rather get an instant risk assessment of the given device.

Acknowledgments. The research this paper is based on is part of the RELINK - Relinking the "weak link". Building resilient digital households through interdisciplinary and multilevel exploration and intervention project. The research project is funded by the Research Council of Norway, IKTPluss, grant no. 288663, and is headed by Consumption.

Special thanks to the teams that contributed to the development and testing of the Risk Assessment Model: Anthony G. Giannoumis, Terje Gjøsæter, Caroline Gau, Eray Kip, Eren Sensoy, Edjinam Siliadin, Martin Bang, Adrian Gåsøy, Bernt Ferner, Martin Walberg Nicolaysen and Lars Erik Viken.

References

1. Angrishi, K.: Turning internet of things (IoT) into internet of vulnerabilities (IoV): IoT botnets. arXiv preprint arXiv:1702.03681 (2017)
2. Hassija, V., et al.: A survey on IoT security: Application areas, security threats, and solution architectures. IEEE Access **7**, 82721–82743 (2019)
3. Smith, S.: IoT connections to reach 83 billion by 2024, Driven by maturing industrial use cases, vol. **10**, p. 2021. Accessed Apr 2020
4. Kandaswamy, R., Furlonger, D.: Blockchain-based transformation: A gartner trend insight report. Gartner IT Glossary (2018)
5. Zhang, Z.-K., et al.: IoT security: Ongoing challenges and research opportunities. In: IEEE 7th International Conference on Service-Oriented Computing and Applications. IEEE (2014)
6. Khan, M.A., Salah, K.: IoT security: Review, blockchain solutions, and open challenges. Futur. Gener. Comput. Syst. **82**, 395–411 (2018)
7. Zheng, S., et al.: User perceptions of smart home IoT privacy. Proc. ACM Hum.-Comput. Interact. **2**(CSCW), 1–20 (2018)
8. Ahlmeyer, M., Chircu, A.M.: Securing the Internet of Things: A review. Iss. Inf. Syst. **17**(4) (2016)
9. Lee, S.K., Bae, M., Kim, H.: Future of IoT networks: A survey. Appl. Sci. **7**(10), 1072 (2017)
10. Xia, F., et al.: Internet of things. Int. J. Commun Syst **25**(9), 1101 (2012)
11. Buntak, K., Brlek, P., Cesarec, B.: The impact of the Internet of Things and artificial intelligence on the supply chain. Bus. Logist. Mod. Manage. **21**, 369–383 (2021)
12. McGuire, D.: Security challenges with the commercialization of the Internet of Things. Cardiff Metropolitan University (2017)
13. Deloitte, U.: Global mobile consumer survey: Us edition. Deloitte US (2016)
14. Meneghello, F., et al.: IoT: Internet of threats? A survey of practical security vulnerabilities in real IoT devices. IEEE Internet Things J. **6**(5), 8182–8201 (2019)

The Impact of the Covid-19 Pandemic on Cybersecurity

Demarcating the Privacy Issues of Aarogya Setu App in Covid-19 Pandemic in India: An Exploration into Contact Tracing Mobile Applications from Elaboration Likelihood Model

Nirmal Acharya[1]([✉]) [iD] and Abhishek Sharma[2] [iD]

[1] University of Southern Queensland, Toowoomba, Australia
nirmal.nilu007@gmail.com
[2] Swinburne University of Technology, Melbourne, Australia

Abstract. Demand for contract tracing applications is significantly increasing as governments across the globe are relying on these mobile apps to help combat the spread of the COVID-19 virus. However, while this technology has a potential benefit, there is widespread concern that consumers' fears around privacy and data protection prevent them from downloading such apps. By focusing on this emerging crisis, in this study, we investigate the potential obstacles imposed by privacy concerns (i.e., the perceived risk of accepting the app permission, the perceived risk of providing the information). This study also investigates the popularity of Aarogya Setu, the Indian government's COVID-19 app. In doing so, we examine privacy concerns through the theoretical lens of the Elaboration Likelihood Model and explore the download intentions of new users. Using the above dimensions of privacy, we then propose a conceptual framework that depicts the influence of privacy concerns over the download intention of new users. Lastly, this paper provides suggestions to allow the Aarogya Setu to improve its perceived reliability among its users and increase downloads.

Keywords: Privacy concerns · COVID-19 · Aarogya Setu · Elaboration likelihoodmodel · Download intention · Mobile applications

1 Introduction

On the 11th March 2020, COVID-19 was declared a global pandemic by the World Health Organisation (WHO) (Cucinotta and Vanelli 2020; Zwitter and Gstrein 2020) Originating in the Hubei province of China, by December 2019, the virus had begun to spread to other Asian countries such as Japan and South Korea (Singhal 2020; Wang et al. 2020; Zwitter and Gstrein 2020). By April 2020, India had only 84 COVID-19 cases (WHO 2020). However, as of October 2021, India has more than 34 million cases, which is among the highest number of people affected by COVID-19 of any country across the world (Worldometers 2022).

In order to tackle the pandemic, decisive measure were taken by countries across the world, including vigorous enforcement of social distancing rules and contact tracing

A. Moallem (Ed.): HCII 2022, LNCS 13333, pp. 457–468, 2022.
https://doi.org/10.1007/978-3-031-05563-8_28

applications (Cho et al. 2020; Liu et al. 2020). Gradual advancements in artificial intelligence and blockchain technology have provided contact tracing apps with the capacity to help deal with this emergency (Sharma 2021). With GPS and Bluetooth enabled technologies, these contact tracing applications can determine the movement of individuals and inform them about any infected individuals nearby (Cho et al. 2020; Gu et al. 2017). Based on these notions, on the 1st April 2020, the Indian government launched the Aarogya Setu application to help fight the spread of the COVID-19 virus throughout the country (Dhar 2020; Garg et al. 2020). Although the application was developed with the foundational pillars of contact tracing and risk assessments, there is still currently a spirited debate ongoing in India on the privacy issues it presents (Gu et al. 2017; Jung and Park 2018; Tang et al. 2020; Wang et al. 2019; Wottrich et al. 2018).

By focusing on these emerging issues, this study briefs on the potential obstacles imposed by privacy concerns (i.e., the perceived risk of accepting the app permission, the perceived risk of providing the information) and the perceived popularity of the app. In doing so, this article first discusses the privacy concerns of users using the Aarogya Setu app. Secondly, by drawing on the Elaboration likelihood model, we discuss the role of perceived risk with permission, information justification and perceived app popularity over the download intention within the new users. Thirdly, based on these set of ideas, we propose a conceptual model on how the privacy issues of contact tracing apps can influence the download intention of the new users. Lastly, we discuss the modifications that can enhance reliability and the download intention of the Aarogya Setu app users.

2   Background of the Study

2.1   India's Aarogya Setu App

With the growing number of COVID-19 cases worldwide, every country seemed to rely on contact tracing apps to restrict the upsurge in the transmission of this infection. These apps were developed with a fusion of artificial intelligence and Bluetooth technologies to detect the transmission of the virus by their smartphones (Cho et al. 2020; Liu et al. 2020). Moreover, to enhance this cutting-edge technology, individuals who did not own a smartphone relied on an interactive voice response system (IVRS) to trace the virus transmission. For example, Singapore launched the contact tracing app Trace Together to combat this pandemic, which runs on Bluetooth technology (Cho et al. 2020). This mobile app (i.e., Trace Together) was proven to be very reliable as it depends on limited data collection and shows transparency on data destruction (Cho et al. 2020).

Likewise, India's Aarogya Setu app was launched with similar intentions. The application seemed to seek extra access for a person's constant location tracking with the help of Google maps. However, recent research made by MIT Technology highlights the fact that monitoring someone's location seems to be deemed unnecessary and violates the rules of an individual's privacy (Degirmenci 2020; Nagori 2021). Additionally, the reviews made by MIT experts criticized apps such as Aarogya setu for not having clear guidelines on how the data is collected, stored and destructed by the governing body (Nagori 2021).

This contact tracing app had 50 million users within just two weeks of its launch, making it the fastest app to reach the highest downloads within the world (Arevalo

2020). However, it was heavily criticized for risk issues and was ranked lower in privacy parameters (See Fig. 1) (Krehling and Essex 2021). The app exchanges information through Bluetooth and GPS tracking facilities (Cho et al. 2020; Liu et al. 2020). The contact tracing features notify users if they have contacted infected individuals. The app refreshes the information within its servers in 15 min (Hindu 2020; Liu et al. 2020) and stores users' contact details and travel history for the previous three months (Cho et al. 2020). Users must first register with a mobile phone number and authenticate it using an OTP to use the app. Although millions of people are already using the app, the number of downloads seems to be negligible compared to the current population of India (i.e., 1.38 billion) (Basu 2021; Nagori 2021).

Country	App Name	Meets Privacy Requirements			Score	Rank
		Yes	Partial	No		
Australia	COVIDSafe	4	6	0	7	Medium
Austria	Stopp Corona	3	4	3	5	Medium
Azerbaijan	e-Tabib	0	1	9	0.5	
Bahrain	BeAware Bahrain	0	0	10	0	
Bangladesh	Corona Tracer BD	1	4	5	3	
Canada	Covid Alert	7	3	0	8.5	
China	Health Code	2	0	8	2	
Colombia	CoronApp	0	5	5	2.5	
Czech Republic	eRouška (eFacemask)	4	4	2	6	Medium
Denmark	Smittestop	3	3	3	3.5	Medium
Ecuador	ASI (SOS)	1	5	4	3.5	
Estonia	Hoia	6	1	3	6.5	Medium
Ethiopia	Debo	0	1	9	0.5	
France	TousAntiCovid	3	5	2	3.5	Medium
Fiji	careFIJI	4	2	4	5	Medium
Finland	Koronavilkku	3	4	3	5	Medium
Germany	Corona-Warn-App	7	2	1	8	
Ghana	GH Covid-19 Tracker App	0	0	10	0.5	
Gibraltar	Beat Covid Gibraltar	2	0	8	2	
Guatemala	Alerta Guate	0	0	10	0	
Hungary	VirusRadar	2	2	6	3	
Iceland	Rakning C-19	6	1	3	6.5	Medium
India	Aarogya Setu	3	5	4		
Ireland	COVID Tracker	5	4	1	7	Medium
Israel	HaMagen	3	3	4	4.5	
Italy	Immuni	5	3	2	6.5	Medium
Japan	COVID-19 Contact Confirming Application	6	2	2	7	Medium
Jordan	AMAN APP—Jordan	3	2	5	4	
Kazakhstan	eGovhizbingemäz mobile app	4	2	4	5	Medium
Kuwait	Shlonik	0	1	9	0.5	
Latvia	Apturi Covid	4	2	4	5	Medium
Malaysia	MyTrace	1	5	4	3.5	
Netherlands	CoronaMelder	5	2	3	6.5	Medium
New Zealand	NZ COVID Tracer	2	5	3	4.5	
North Macedonia	Stop Korona!	3	1	6	3.5	
Northern Ireland	StopCOVID NI	5	1	1	7	Medium
Norway	Smittestopp	1	2	7	3	
Poland	ProteGO Safe	3	4	3	5	Medium
Portugal	STAYAWAY COVID	4	4	2	6	Medium
Qatar	Ehteraz App	0	0	10	0	
Russia (Moscow)	Social Monitoring Service	0	2	8	1	
Russia	Contact Tracer	1	0	9	1	
Saudi Arabia	Tabaud	3	3	4	4.5	
Scotland	Protect Scotland	3	3	2	6.5	Medium
Singapore	TraceTogether	3	5	2	5.5	Medium
Slovenia	#OstaniZdrav	4	2	4	6.5	Medium
South Africa	COVID Alert South Africa	4	2	4	5	Medium
Spain	Radar COVID	6	2	2	7	Medium
Switzerland	SwissCovid App	6	2	2	7	Medium
United Kingdom	NHS COVID-19	3	3	4	4.5	
United States	Co6pi	1	3	6	2.5	
United States	CovidSafe/CommonCircle Exposures	3	4	4		
United States (Ariz.)	Covid Watch	3	3	4	4.5	
United States (Calif.)	California COVID Notify	3	0	5	5	Medium
United States (N.Dak. and Wyo.)	Care19 Alert	3	2	8	4	

Fig. 1. Privacy ranking of contact tracing apps. Source – (Krehling and Essex 2021)

Currently, privacy is a major concern for both existing and new users of the Aarogya setu app (Basu 2021; Krehling and Essex 2021). The app primarily deals with a user's personal information, such as name, age, occupation, foreign travel history in the previous 30 days, and other profiling data. Additionally, there exists a "Self-Assessment Test" function that collects information about a user's current health conditions and then assesses the profile and displays the risk level for the user in different colour codes based on the responses. Precisely, there exists three major colour codes (i.e., orange, yellow and green) that assess a user's profile. Based on a user's profile, the app displays various colours (i.e., Orange for High risk, Yellow for Moderate risk, Green for No risk) depending upon their exiting risks they possess within the society. Additionally, based on these assessments, the app also proposes specific steps that can be performed to prevent the transmission of COVID-19, such as social isolation, hygiene, and remaining at home as safeguards.

However, the sensitive nature of the data and the obligatory prescription for using the app raises concerns about privacy issues (Basu 2021). Invasion of people's privacy in health records can have disastrous consequences for a person's social status and can lead towards discriminatory outcomes. Through digital methods, India witnessed the indiscriminate sharing of lists of people infected with the COVID-19. A breach of privacy can have serious consequences, including the abuse of personally identifiable information (Basu 2021). State-level authorities are revealing user information such as name, home address, and phone number to those who have been quarantined, which has resulted in illicit data sharing. This shows that issues such as data minimization, openness, and accountability are all violated by the app's massive collection of personal information (Gupta et al. 2020). As a result, investigations into the privacy concerns of contract tracing apps (i.e., Aarogya Setu app) requires severe attention. As a result, the following subsections examine the concepts of privacy through the lens of the Elaboration Likelihood Model (ELM).

3 Literature Review

During the pandemic, contact tracing apps have gained popularity across the globe. Despite the usefulness of contact tracing applications in helping to limit the spread of COVID-19, most of existing its users have deeper concerns on the notions of privacy; in particular, most users are concerned about their data protection and its privacy (Alanzi 2021; Krehling and Essex 2021). Based on these lines of arguments, this study explores three significant privacy concerns, using the Elaboration Likelihood Model (ELM) as the theoretical foundation of the study. To begin with, we discuss perceived risks associated with app permissions settings, personal information and the popularity of an app. Later, based on these dimensions of risk perceptions, we discuss the download intention of new users through the theoretical lens of ELM.

3.1 Perceived Risk with Mobile User's Permissions

The concepts of information privacy with mobile users (MUIPC) were first coined by Xu et al. (2012), Gupta (2012), which were based on the notions of concerns for information privacy (CFIP) and internet user's information privacy (IUIPC). The base foundation of MUIPC relied on three major dimensions; the collection of data, having improper permission to access the data and unauthorized access to use secondary information of data (Degirmenci 2020; Gupta and Jithendranathan 2012). Besides this, Malhotra et al. (2004) investigated user privacy concerns through the lens of social contract and justice theories aligned with the IUIPC notions. With the classification of the above dimensions of privacy, it is argued that gathering private information is linked with distributive justice. In contrast, owing control on one's personal information and awareness of information privacy process is seen to be connected with procedural, interactional and informational justice, respectively (Degirmenci 2020; Malhotra et al. 2004).

By analyzing the Aarogya Setu app from the point of view of the MUIPC framework, users' privacy concerns can be grouped into three categories; perceived surveillance, perceived intrusion and secondary use of personal information (Degirmenci 2020; Gupta and Jithendranathan 2012). Within the contact tracing apps, location tracking functions that employ GPS and Bluetooth technologies are seen as a form of surveillance (Cho et al. 2020; Liu et al. 2020). Although most app users believe that the location tracking function enhances the search feasibilies, these sensory tracking activities can have privacy risks as they might lead to information disclosures (Liu et al. 2020; Krehling and Essex 2021). Thus, we hypothesize:

Hypothesis 1: Mobile users' permissions sensitivity positively influences privacy concerns.

3.2 Perceived Risk with Mobile User's Information Justification

In addition to prior perceived privacy of the users, information justification and permission requests play a vital role in risk assessments of a mobile app. Both aspects have distinct characteristics. However, there are many growing concerns related to privacy issues with the user's information (Degirmenci 2020; Liu et al. 2020). Regarding permission sensitivity, seeking access to a user's location is considered a high-risk permission request. Most of the apps nowadays collect personal information and seek permission for live locations (Gu et al. 2017; Degirmenci 2020). However, users seem to be highly conscious when some apps with the desired set of necessary functions ask for live location tracking. With recent research data, it is seen that more than 100,000 mobile applications in Google Play Store are seen collecting users' data and their live location data which goes beyond desired application tasks (Degirmenci 2020). On similar lines of arguments, India's Aarogya Setu app is seen to be very debatable as it asks for live location access, even though its primary function can be resolved by Bluetooth facilities (Dhar 2020; Times 2020). Therefore, it can be argued that privacy-related permissions and information justification related to mobile applications are critical concerns of a user. Hence, we hypothesize:

Hypothesis 2: Mobile user's information justification positively influences the privacy concerns of a user.

3.3 Perceived Risks with Mobile App Popularity

Nowadays, users seem to download a mobile app based on their popularity among their peer members (Gu et al. 2017; Lowry et al. 2012). Based on privacy calculus theory (PCT), it can be argued that a user's download intention depends on their cost-benefit analysis done on the privacy issues related to the mobile app (Lowry et al. 2012; Xu et al. 2012). This behaviour of users can be depicted in a simple example of TikTok, a video-sharing app developed by Byte Dance which is primarily made to exchange short videos on social media platforms (Jennings 2019). Tiktok has been one of the fastest-growing apps globally, with more than 400 million active users until May 2020 (Susilo 2020). Although TikTok has been heavily criticized for privacy issues and banned in India & US. Still, people worldwide are seen to use it because of its popularity and its benefits.

Due to this tendency of mindsets among the users, an individual's intention to download an app is seen to be related to its popularity among its users. Further, this argument is seen to be in line with the scenario of the Aarogya Setu app, where being one of the riskiest contact tracing apps allowed itself to become the highest downloaded app across the globe in just two weeks (Dhar 2020). This further proves that in a pandemic situation, users tend to prioritize the app benefits & its popularity over its privacy concerns. Hence, we hypothesize:

Hypothesis 3: Mobile app popularity negatively influences privacy concerns.

3.4   Elaboration Likelihood Model (ELM)

Elaboration Likelihood Model (ELM) provides a valuable theoretical perspective to explore the privacy concerns of the Aarogya Setu app. ELM sheds light on the effect of how an app user processes messages. The Elaboration Likelihood model is one of the frequently mentioned models of persuasion (Petty and Cacioppo 1996, 2012); it describes how shaping attitudes also shapes behaviours. ELM is a dual-process theory that argues that persuasion occurs via central or peripheral route and that the person's processing depth determines the relative effectiveness of those processes informing the attitude (Angst and Agarwal 2009; Gu et al. 2017). Simply put, when an individual receives a message in various contexts, the recipients will depend upon the amount of cognitive energy they devote to the message (Petty and Cacioppo 1996).

By looking at the processing depth of a user, it is seen that privacy concerns, along with to download an app, fade over time. Precisely, an app user is seen to undergo three significant phases (i.e., download, installation and runtime) from decision-making till the process of installing on their smartphones (Degirmenci 2020; Wottrich et al. 2018). Users tend to have a deep concern over their information and data privacy before they decide to download. Hence, in the upcoming sections, we describe the two pathways (i.e., central-route and peripheral route) of ELM through which a user processes information before making a final decision.

Centre-Route of Processing for Privacy Evaluation. Central-route processing happens when users carefully scrutinize the arguments related to the message and are influenced by argument quality (Bhattacherjee and Sanford 2006). The reaction to the information to which a user is exposed depends upon the underlying elaboration process entails in developing one's thoughts (Tam and Ho 2005). In some cases, the content of the message is read, processed cognitively and taken into account, while in other situations, message contents are entirely ignored.

Perceived permission sensitivity is an integral part of the users' privacy concerns in the Aarogya Setu app at the intention to download stage. Existing studies on information privacy literature strongly suggests that collected information can lead to the induction of different degrees of sensitivity perceptions and affect the privacy concerns of users (Bansal and Gefen 2010; Dinev et al. 2013; Malhotra et al. 2004). According to Bansal et al. (2010), individuals using web-based healthcare services are anxious to reveal information relating to their wellbeing, where they perceive that the data is sensitive.

It would be fundamental to the privacy consideration of an individual as perceived permission sensitivity is directly linked to privacy concerns. Through this point of view, perceived permissions sensitivity would potentially trigger the information processing via the central route when raising concerns about privacy (Degirmenci 2020; Gu et al. 2017). As Aarogya Setu app permission requests are explicitly communicated in public, the sensitivity of the permission requests is likely to be evaluated by the users. Individuals with high permission sensitivity would be most bothered about the possible harm caused by accidental information leaks and misuse.

Permission justification is a direct indication of an application's information privacy practice; therefore, it invokes central-route processing (Gu et al. 2017). Permission justification informs the Aarogya Setu app users who can access their data and how the data collected will be used. Past studies indicate that the availability of privacy justification for data collection will mitigate the privacy concerns of online customers (Gu et al. 2017; Kelly et al. 2019; Spears 2013). For example, Gu et al. (2017) indicated that justifying permission just makes app adopters with a less mobile experience less concerned about their privacy. In Spears (2013), it is found that online customers seem to perceive a higher degree of privacy assurance if they are informed of the information practices of a collector. As reported by Kelley et al. (2009), explaining the purpose of information collection is an appropriate approach to address consumer privacy concerns. Based on these notions, it can be argued that information disclosures and information justification in an app can mitigate users' privacy concerns. However, looking at the dimensions of privacy from both the central and peripheral routes of processing is necessary. Therefore, the upcoming sub-section briefs on how the peripheral route of processing influences the privacy evaluation within users' mindsets.

Peripheral-Route of Processing for Privacy Evaluation. Peripheral route processing is mainly seen to occur at a superficial level. When users process information through the peripheral route, secondary factors such as presentation, visual appeal, and source credibility is seen to affect their attitude. In this scenario, users would support an argument as they believe in the source (Angst and Agarwal 2009).

By drawing ideas from ELM, we argue that the heuristic assessment of perceived app popularity can influence customers' privacy concerns. As stated earlier, the Aarogya Setu app's popularity can be reflected by 50 million adopters within two weeks of its launch (Duan et al. 2009). Previous studies have proposed it as a peripheral cue in persuasion (Bhattacherjee and Sanford 2006; Park et al. 2007). The perceived popularity of an app is not considered an inherent attribute of privacy as it does not disclose any practice of gathering and storing app adopters' personal information. Nonetheless, users follow a "popular app" hypothesis in which they tend to make decisions based on past adopters. The latter have evaluated this app through the lens of trust and privacy (Duan et al. 2009). In this sense, although perceived popularity is not a core attribute in privacy concerns, we still contend that adopting a peripheral route mitigates privacy concerns. Therefore, we hypothesize:

Hypothesis 4: Users' privacy concerns positively influence users' download intentions.

Moderating Effect of Processing Depth. As noted earlier, the ELM postulates that the persistence of risk is linked with an individual's processing depth in forming the attitude

(Petty and Cacioppo 1996; Haugtvedt and Petty 1989). A person generates a series of thoughtful, problem-related arguments for examination if the processing depth is high, such as when processing a message through the central route. The argument scheme is contrasted several times with the problem-related schema previously stored in the memory for careful analysis (Krosnick 1995; Sengupta and Johar 2002). Further, processing leads to greater access to memory schemes, resulting in more robust connections between previously saved problem-related schemas and the new argument schema (Priester and Petty 2003). Therefore, the perception of privacy concerns is more by deeper processing of the message.

In contrast, a person relies on simple cues when low processing depth, such as when processing a message through the peripheral route. These cues provide relatively simple inferences or provide some efficient associations on the acceptability of advocacy (Sengupta and Johar 2002). The inference or effect generated by the peripheral cue may be ample by accessing the problem-related scheme once. Additionally, it involves significantly less cognitive effort than on the central route for forming an attitude (Petty and Cacioppo 1996). Besides, the peripheral schema may invoke a "wrong" schema in the memory, which is irrelevant to the peripheral cue assessment (e.g., is the design of the app good?) (Krosnick 1995). Therefore, the persistence of attitude is less by the shallower processing of the message. Through this point of view, we anticipate that if the Aarogya Setu app user carefully elaborates perceived permissions sensitivity and permission justification, it is likely that they will develop a more persistent attitude towards privacy issues. Hence, we hypothesize:

Hypothesis 5: *Processing depth moderates the effects of mobile users' permissions on privacy concerns.*

Hypothesis 6: *Processing depth moderates the effects of mobile users' information justification on privacy concerns.*

4   Conceptual Framework

To address the above-mentioned knowledge gaps, the objective of this current paper is to carve out a conceptual model that is developed by using the perspectives of both the MUPIC (Mobile user's information privacy concerns) framework and ELM (Elaboration Likelihood model) to demonstrate the effects of privacy on download intention of the new users. The model proposes that user's permission, information justification for the users and app popularity among users play a pivotal role in the privacy concerns of existing and new users. Further, in this model, we also look at the moderating effects of processing depth on a user's permission and the justification provided to a user when downloading a mobile application. Drawing on the literature reviewed above, we propose a conceptual framework in Fig. 2 applied in the current study.

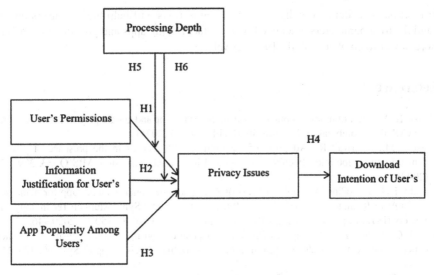

Fig. 2. Conceptual framework

5   Research Implications and Conclusion

Although contact tracing applications require access to live tracking facilities to control the spread of the COVID-19 virus, there are deeper concerns about its impact on privacy and data protection. Therefore, based on the logic presented above, we suggest that the government and research agencies who have access to the private data of billion people across India need to develop strategies to combat the threat of viruses by safeguarding our private information. The gradual evolution of artificial intelligence (AI) and machine learning (ML) techniques has the power to keep track of the live location of positive infected patients.

Traditional devices, such as security cameras in public places, can be used to monitor people's movements during lockdown orders if used for a limited time period. However, if such movement is tracked with contact tracing applications that use GPS or Bluetooth technology for no discernible reason, surveillance concerns may arise. The government must be mindful of the rights of users who are affected by contact tracing technologies. When developing a policy relating to new technologies, the fundamental principles of data protection should be taken into account.

A key limitation of this study is that we did not empirically validate the proposed conceptual model. The next step of our study is to test our hypothesis experimentally. This study aimed to fill some of the existing information gap related to the potential obstacles' privacy concerns imposed on downloading the Aarogya setu app. Therefore, it can serve not only as a foundation for making decisions relating to the design, adoption, and implementation of contract tracing apps but also can serve as a basis for future study. Furthermore, by adhering to the above arguments, we suggest that the Indian government make specific improvements to the Aarogya Setu app, providing a transparent understanding of secure data storage, entities who have access to this data, and the data destruction procedures. Finally, the above suggestions will help the new users understand the trust parameters associated with contact tracing apps and give the government more power to combat COVID-19 effectively.

References

Alanzi, T.: A review of mobile applications available in the app and google play stores used during the COVID-19 outbreak. J. Multidiscip. Healthc. **14**, 45 (2021)

Angst, C.M., Agarwal, R.: Adoption of electronic health records in the presence of privacy concerns: the elaboration likelihood model and individual persuasion. MIS Q. **33**, 339–370 (2009)

Arevalo, F.N.: Decoding the public interest of Aarogya Setu, contact tracing app for managing the COVID19 pandemic in India. In: 2020 IEEE International Symposium on Technology and Society (ISTAS), pp. 508–512 (2020). https://doi.org/10.1109/ISTAS50296.2020.9462225

Bansal, G., Gefen, D.: The impact of personal dispositions on information sensitivity, privacy concern and trust in disclosing health information online. Decis. Support Syst. **49**, 138–150 (2010)

Basu, S.: Effective contact tracing for COVID-19 using mobile phones: an ethical analysis of the mandatory use of the aarogya setu application in India. Camb. Q. Healthc. Ethics **30**, 262–271 (2021)

Bhattacherjee, A., Sanford, C.: Influence processes for information technology acceptance: an elaboration likelihood model. MIS Q. **30**(4), 805–825 (2006)

Cho, H., Ippolito, D., Yu, Y.W.: Contact tracing mobile apps for COVID-19: privacy considerations and related trade-offs. aXiv preprint arXiv:2003.11511 (2020)

Cucinotta, D., Vanelli, M.: WHO declares COVID-19 a pandemic. Acta Bio-Med.: Atenei Parmensis **91**, 157–160 (2020)

Degirmenci, K.: Mobile users' information privacy concerns and the role of app permission requests. Int. J. Inf. Manage. **50**, 261–272 (2020)

Dhar, T.: Aarogya Setu-carrying your privacy in your hands? Available at SSRN 3614506 (2020)

Dinev, T., Xu, H., Smith, J.H., Hart, P.: Information privacy and correlates: an empirical attempt to bridge and distinguish privacy-related concepts. Eur. J. Inf. Syst. **22**, 295–316 (2013)

Duan, W., Gu, B., Whinston, A.B.: Informational cascades and software adoption on the internet: an empirical investigation. MIS Q. **33**(1), 23–48 (2009)

Garg, S., Bhatnagar, N., Gangadharan, N.: A case for participatory disease surveillance of the COVID-19 pandemic in India. JMIR Public Health Surveill. **6**, e18795 (2020)

Gu, J., Xu, Y.C., Xu, H., Zhang, C., Ling, H.: Privacy concerns for mobile app download: an elaboration likelihood model perspective. Decis. Support Syst. **94**, 19–28 (2017)

Gupta, M., Abdelsalam, M., Mittal, S.: Enabling and enforcing social distancing measures using smart city and its infrastructures: a COVID-19 use case. arXiv preprint arXiv:2004.09246 (2020)

Gupta, R., Jithendranathan, T.: Fund flows and past performance in Australian managed funds. Account. Res. J. **25**, 131–157 (2012)

Haugtvedt, C.P., Petty, R.E.: Need for cognition and attitude persistence. ACR North American Advances (1989)

Hindu. Data | How safe is Aarogya Setu compared to COVID-19 contact tracing apps of other countries? (2020)

Jennings, R.: TikTok, Explained. Vox (2019)

Jung, Y., Park, J.: An investigation of relationships among privacy concerns, affective responses, and coping behaviors in location-based services. Int. J. Inf. Manage. **43**, 15–24 (2018)

Kelley, P.G., Bresee, J., Cranor, L.F., Reeder, R.W.: A "nutrition label" for privacy. In: Proceedings of the 5th Symposium on Usable Privacy and Security, pp. 1–12 (2009)

Kelly, L., Kerr, G., Drennan, J., Fazal-E-Hasan, S.M.: Feel, think, avoid: testing a new model of advertising avoidance. J. Mark. Commun. 27(4), 343–364 (2019). https://doi.org/10.1080/135 27266.2019.1666902

Krehling, L., Essex, A.: A security and privacy scoring system for contact tracing apps. J. Cybersecur. Priv. 1, 597–614 (2021)

Krosnick, J.: Attitude strength: an overview. In: Petty, R.E., Krosnick, J.A. (eds.) Attitude Strength: Antecedents and consequences. Erlbaum, Hillsdale (1995)

Liu, J.K., et al.: Privacy-preserving COVID-19 contact tracing app: a zero-knowledge proof approach. IACR Cryptol. ePrint Arch., 2020, 528 (2020)

Lowry, P.B., Moody, G., Vance, A., Jensen, M., Jenkins, J., Wells, T.: Using an elaboration likelihood approach to better understand the persuasiveness of website privacy assurance cues for online consumers. J. Am. Soc. Inform. Sci. Technol. 63, 755–776 (2012)

Malhotra, N.K., Kim, S.S., Agarwal, J.: Internet users' information privacy concerns (IUIPC): the construct, the scale, and a causal model. Inf. Syst. Res. 15, 336–355 (2004)

Nagori, V.: "Aarogya Setu": the mobile application that monitors and mitigates the risks of COVID-19 pandemic spread in India. J. Inf. Technol. Teach. Cases 11, 66–80 (2021)

Park, D.-H., Lee, J., Han, I.: The effect of on-line consumer reviews on consumer purchasing intention: the moderating role of involvement. Int. J. Electron. Commer. 11, 125–148 (2007)

Petty, R.E., Cacioppo, J.T.: Attitudes and Persuasion: Classic and Contemporary Approaches. Westview Press, Boulder (1996)

Petty, R.E., Cacioppo, J.T.: Communication and Persuasion: Central and Peripheral Routes to Attitude Change. Springer, Heidelberg (2012)

Priester, J.R., Petty, R.E.: The influence of spokesperson trustworthiness on message elaboration, attitude strength, and advertising effectiveness. J. Consum. Psychol. 13, 408–421 (2003)

Sengupta, J., Johar, G.V.: Effects of inconsistent attribute information on the predictive value of product attitudes: toward a resolution of opposing perspectives. J. Consum. Res. 29, 39–56 (2002)

Sharma, A.: The role of IoT in the fight against Covid-19 to restructure the economy. In: Stephanidis, C., et al. (eds.) HCII 2021. LNCS, vol. 13097, pp. 140–156. Springer, Cham (2021). https://doi.org/10.1007/978-3-030-90966-6_11

Singhal, T.: A review of coronavirus disease-2019 (COVID-19). Indian J. Pediatr. 87, 1–6 (2020)

Spears, J.L.: The effects of notice versus awareness: an empirical examination of an online consumer's privacy risk treatment. In: 46th Hawaii International Conference on System Sciences, pp. 3229–3238. IEEE, Hawaii (2013)

Susilo, D.: Unlocking the secret of E-loyalty: a study from Tiktok users in China. Int. J. Econ. Bus. Entrep. (IJEBE) 3, 37–49 (2020)

Tam, K.Y., Ho, S.Y.: Web personalization as a persuasion strategy: an elaboration likelihood model perspective. Inf. Syst. Res. 16, 271–291 (2005)

Tang, J., Akram, U., Shi, W.: Why people need privacy? The role of privacy fatigue in app users' intention to disclose privacy: based on personality traits. J. Enterp. Inf. Manage. (2020)

Times, T.E.: Aarogya Setu's not all that healthy for a person's privacy (2020)

Wang, D., et al.: Epidemiological characteristics and transmission model of Corona Virus Disease 2019 in China. J. Infect. 80, e25 (2020)

Wang, L., Hu, H.-H., Yan, J., Mei, M.Q.: Privacy calculus or heuristic cues? The dual process of privacy decision making on Chinese social media. J. Enterp. Inf. Manag. 33 (2019)

WHO. World Health Organization - India Situation Report (2020)

Worldometers. Worldometer: Coronavirus Cases (2022). https://www.worldometers.info/corona virus/: Worldometers. Accessed 21 Oct 2021 2020

Wottrich, V.M., van Reijmersdal, E.A., Smit, E.G.: The privacy trade-off for mobile app downloads: the roles of app value, intrusiveness, and privacy concerns. Decis. Support Syst. **106**, 44–52 (2018)

Xu, H., Teo, H.-H., Tan, B.C.Y., Agarwal, R.: Research note—effects of individual self-protection, industry self-regulation, and government regulation on privacy concerns: a study of location-based services. Inf. Syst. Res. **23**, 1342–1363 (2012)

Zwitter, A., Gstrein, O.J.: Big data, privacy and COVID-19–learning from humanitarian expertise in data protection. **5**, 4 (2020)

The Importance of Strengthening Legal Concepts in Overcoming Cybercrime During the Covid-19 Pandemic in Indonesia

Ardiansyah[1]([✉]), M. Rafi[2], and Pahmi Amri[1]

[1] Universitas Islam Riau, Pekanbaru, Indonesia
ardiansyah@law.uir.ac.id
[2] Universitas Muhammadiyah Yogyakarta, Yogyakarta, Indonesia

Abstract. This study aims to analyze the importance of strengthening legal concepts in overcoming cybercrime during the Covid-19 pandemic in Indonesia. The Covid-19 pandemic that hit Indonesia made some people lose many things in various aspects of their lives due to multiple types of cybercrimes that often occur in society, such as malware attacks, trojan activities, and information leaks. The Electronic Information and Transactions Law (ITE) Number 11 of 2008 and the revised version of the ITE Law Number 19 of 2016 have historically been the legal basis for regulating cyber security in Indonesia. However, this regulation does not include essential parts of cybersecurity such as information and network infrastructure and human resources with cybersecurity experience. Thus, it is necessary to know how important it is to strengthen legal concepts in overcoming cybercrime during the Covid-19 pandemic in Indonesia. This study uses a qualitative approach. The data sources are from various online news media and relevant research journals and analyzed using the NVivo12 Plus application. Based on the results of the analysis, this study found that the acceleration of the ratification of the Personal Data Protection Bill, the establishment of special regulations related to cybersecurity and cybercrime, the creation of a multi-sectoral cyber security management ecosystem, as well as increasing awareness and capacity of human resources in the cyber security sector are alternative policies that must be considered and realized to strengthen the concept of law in overcoming various cyber crimes during the Covid-19 pandemic in Indonesia.

Keywords: Covid-19 pandemic · Cybercrime · Legal concepts

1 Introduction

Today, information and communication technology (ICT) has positively contributed to global economic growth and competitiveness in the public sector [1–3]. However, as government institutions, businesses, and society are increasingly connected in cyberspace, the new challenges posed by cyber threats require more attention to develop robust cybersecurity [4, 5]. Then, the existence of the Covid-19 pandemic as an unprecedented phenomenon has changed the life patterns of billions of people globally in terms of social

© The Author(s), under exclusive license to Springer Nature Switzerland AG 2022
A. Moallem (Ed.): HCII 2022, LNCS 13333, pp. 469–479, 2022.
https://doi.org/10.1007/978-3-031-05563-8_29

norms that experience a series of circumstances related to cybercrime [6]. Where when humans experience increased anxiety due to the Covid-19 pandemic in public spaces, on the other hand, the possibility of cyber attacks also increases with a significant increase in the number [7–9].

Furthermore, after the Covid-19 pandemic in Indonesia, some people have lost many opportunities in various aspects of life due to various types of crimes that occur regularly [10]. According to data from the National Cyber and Crypto Agency (BSSN), Indonesia's number of cyber attack cases increased significantly, with 888,711,736 cyber-attacks occurring between January and August 2021, with the most common cyber-attacks being malware attacks, trojan activity attacks, and information leaks [11]. Of course, this is a problem that Indonesian law enforcement agencies must face and address to provide assurances for cybersecurity in the public arena [9, 12].

Historically, the Electronic Information and Transactions Law (ITE) Number 11 of 2008 and the revised version of the Electronic Information and Transactions Law (ITE) Number 19 of 2016 have become the legal basis for regulating cyber security in Indonesia. This legal concept regulates the distribution of prohibited content, data breaches, unauthorized access to computer systems to collect information, and illegal computer eavesdropping on other electronic systems. However, the regulation does not cover essential parts of cyber security such as information and network infrastructure and competent human resources in dealing with cybercrimes [13, 14]. In addition, law enforcement authorities' handling of cybercrime cases has not been able to be tried effectively due to non-specific regulations and the scarcity of experts to handle these cases [15]. Therefore, this research is important and exciting because the various phenomena of the many cybercrime cases during the Covid-19 pandemic in Indonesia have confused the public about the lack of specific legal frameworks in Indonesia. Thus, this study aims to answer how important it is to strengthen legal concepts in overcoming cybercrime during the Covid-19 pandemic in Indonesia.

2   Literature Review

2.1   The Phenomenon of Cybercrime During the Covid-19 Pandemic

Today, almost the entire world relies on the Internet and computer systems to manage all parts of its daily life [16]. Of course, the interconnection of the Internet and advances in technology around the world can allow criminals to abuse the potential of these networks [1, 17, 18]. Fundamentally, the Covid-19 pandemic is not just a medical problem, evidenced by the rise of cybercrime during the pandemic phase [19]. Then, various cyber crimes that continue to increase during the Covid-19 pandemic also affect digital activities to become so dominant that each individual carries out them [9, 20]. As a result, this condition continues to be exploited by cybercriminals to carry out missions that tend to harm the public sector [10, 21].

Furthermore, depending on the type of crime, the presence of the Covid-19 pandemic will impact victimization [22]. The public's tendency to engage in daily digital-based activities has increased the risk of becoming a victim of cybercrime [23]. As a result of the Covid-19 pandemic, various cybercrime phenomena have emerged, posing a considerable threat to people's safety and the global economy around the world [24].

Thus, Cybercrime phenomena during a pandemic must be analyzed to find fundamental principles for overcoming and responding to current and future cybercrime events [25].

2.2 Legal Concepts in Cybercrime

Cybercrime is conceptually an act of crime committed through ICT and is a significant threat today. The threat is not only to individuals but also to government organizations and businesses [26]. Cybercrime is still a new phenomenon because criminals no longer need to be close to their victims but can attack and steal from a distance [27]. The impact of cybercrime causes financial and intangible losses. It even impacts the risk of global peace and security [28]. In particular, the first provision as an international response is the cybercrime legal convention. The substance of the Cybercrime Convention includes material criminal law, procedural law, business accountability, and international cooperation [29]. Currently, Indonesia's position in regulation has not ratified the international cybercrime legal convention. However, only adopting cybercrime legal conventions are substantially broader and not specific in Law Number 11 of 2008 concerning Information and Electronic Transactions and Law Number 19 of 2016 concerning Amendments to Law Number 11 of 2008 concerning Information and Electronic Transactions [30].

In the process, the weak concept of law enforcement is a factor causing the increase in cybercrime cases that occur [31]. So, security policies in legal products must be improved to deal with all types of questionable cybercrime activities [32]. Then, strengthening the concept of cybercrime law must be carried out effectively in advances in technology and information [33, 34]. In addition, in times of disturbance and uncertainty, each future regulatory actor should also be involved in a more recursive and reflective analysis to increase responsiveness [35]. Therefore, several research reviews have concluded that strengthening the concept of cybercrime law should be a top priority for all governments [36].

3 Research Methods

This study uses a qualitative approach to analyze various phenomena from secondary data, including government websites, books, journals, proceedings, and national online news media content such as tribunnews.com, kompas.com, and detik.com. Then, data collection techniques will focus on various legal concept literature and cybercrime phenomena during the Covid-19 pandemic in Indonesia's national online media. The Nvivo 12 Plus application performed crosstab analysis on the qualitative data [37, 38]. Furthermore, there are five stages in using Nvivo 12 Plus: data collection, data entry, data coding, data classification, and data display. The processed data through Nvivo will then proceed to visualize the qualitative analysis.

4 Result and Discussions

In Indonesia, various cybercrime incidents have always been a trending issue in the public space since the onset of the Covid-19 pandemic on March 2, 2020-December 23,

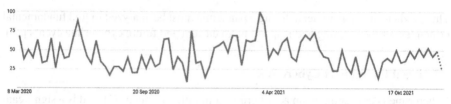

Fig. 1. Trends in cybercrime issues during the Covid-19 pandemic in Indonesia. Source: [39]

2021. The trend in question is the threat of cybercrime that can harm the public sector (Fig. 1).

Then, in the process, various cybercrime phenomena are growing over time. During the covid-19 pandemic, it has emphasized and visualized that Indonesia needs to strengthen legal concepts to minimize the occurrence of cybercrime, which is increasingly happening in public spaces.

4.1 The Phenomenon of Cybercrime During the Covid-19 Pandemic in Indonesia

Currently, various countries face cybercrime phenomena amid the Covid-19 pandemic, which has also changed the global cyber threat landscape. Hackers take advantage of the desire for information and online transactions to launch attacks and gain illegal profits in an all-digital culture. Cybercriminals target billions of vigilant people and have a crucial role in reacting to the pandemic, such as governments and other relevant organizations, without regard to ethics. Cybercriminals also use network security weaknesses to attack companies whose employees must work from home due to the Covid-19 pandemic [10]. Then based on data processing through the Nvivo 12 Plus software on the specified online media, there are several types of cybercrime attacks during the Covid-19 pandemic in Indonesia, namely:

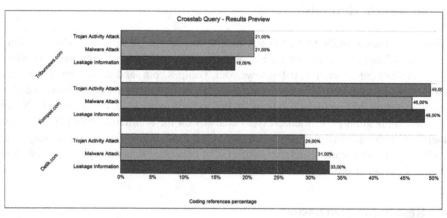

Fig. 2. Crosstab analysis on cyber crime attacks during the Covid-19 pandemic in Indonesia

Figure 2 shows that during the Covid-19 pandemic in Indonesia, there were numerous assaults, including trojan-activity attacks, malware attacks, and information leaking. Then, the most dominant online media in highlighting the issue of trojan-activity attacks is kompas.com (49.18%), followed by detik.com (29.51%) and tribunnews.com (21.31%). Malicious software that can harm a system or network is a Trojan activity attack. Trojans are not detectable like viruses and worms. However, they are challenging to discover since they often look like common apps or files, such as mp3 files, free software, phony antivirus, and free games. There are various types of Trojan malware, namely AllAple, ZeroAccess, WillExec, Glpteba, and CobaltStrike. The purpose of a trojan-activity attack is to steal information from the victim, such as passwords, log data, credentials, and other sensitive information. Trojan exploits pose a severe threat to victims if hackers gain access to the system and gain access to sensitive data. As a result, based on monitoring data from the Indonesian National Cyber Security Operations Center throughout 2020, Trojans became the anomaly with the highest number [40].

Furthermore, kompas.com (48.33%) is the most dominating online media in highlighting information leakage, followed by detik.com (33.33%) and tribunnews.com (18.34%). Another cyber-attack has happened, this time involving a data breach at the Health Social Security Administering Body (BPJS). Due to hacking, information belonging to 279 million Indonesians was stolen and sold on internet forums (dark web). The information transferred includes full name, PIN, date of birth, email, and mobile number. The information is then traded for 0.15 bitcoin, equivalent to 81.6 million Indonesian rupiahs [41]. The phenomenon of data leakage is certainly hazardous because vulnerable to abuse for various cybercrimes, such as bank account hijacking and fake online loans.

In the aspect of malware attacks, the most dominant online media highlighting this type of attack is kompas.com (46.67%), followed by detik.com (31.61%) and tribunnews.com (21.66%). The type of malware attack in question has long been a broad multidirectional attack because cybercriminals will exploit information systems using software containing viruses, trojans, worms, or ransomware. Malware attacks that encrypt files and demand ransom and Distributed Denial of Service (DDoS) are two types of cyber attacks that are increasing and worrying [42]. Then, most malware attacks have common targets that can harm a more comprehensive system. As a result, individual cybersecurity knowledge and assistance from authority figures in the pandemic era are critical to building a safe environment in remote work [10]. Several cybercrime attacks in Indonesia during the COVID-19 pandemic exposed the vulnerability of the Indonesian state to digital security systems due to the lack of adequate protective measures and particular legal concepts.

4.2 The Importance of Strengthening Legal Concepts in Overcoming Cybercrime During the Covid-19 Pandemic in Indonesia

Currently, the Information and Electronic Transactions (ITE) Law Number 11 of 2008 and Law Number 19 of 2016 are the legal basis for regulating cyber security in Indonesia. The ITE law prohibits various offenses, including distributing prohibited content, breaches of data protection, unauthorized access to other computer systems to collect information, and unauthorized interception of computer systems or other electronic systems. Substantially, the ITE Law protects the contents of electronic systems and electronic transactions legally. However, the ITE Law does not address critical cybersecurity areas such as information and network infrastructure and human resources [5].

Based on the 2016 ITE Law, the Government stipulates technical regulations in Government Regulation Number 71 of 2019 concerning the Implementation of Electronic Systems and Transactions. As stated in Government Regulation Number 71 of 2019, updating cyber security in electronic systems and transactions has set more stringent laws for personal data and information security and website authentication to avoid fake and fraudulent sites. Furthermore, Government Regulation No. 71 of 2019 emphasizes the importance of developing a national cybersecurity plan to prevent harm to the public interest caused by misuse of information and electronic transactions such as data misuse, illegal electronic signatures, and the spread of viruses and malicious codes. However, the ITE Law and Government Regulation Number 71 of 2019 do not provide adequate protection for ever-changing cyber threats, especially those affecting critical infrastructure in the government sector.

After that, the Minister of Defense Regulation No. 82 of 2014 provides cyber defense principles to deal with cyber threats to national security. This rule then de-fines cyber security, referring to all government actions to protect information and technology. This regulation explains that cyber-attacks are every statement or action of any party that damages national security, sovereignty, and territorial integrity. Unlike the ITE Law, this regulation includes critical infrastructure as cybersecurity objects, such as financial and transportation networks. However, this regulation only enhances the military's cyber defense capabilities created and implemented for the Indonesian National Armed Forces (TNI). For non-military cyber threats, only refer to the regulations in the ITE Law.

In the process, the rules and regulations of cyber security in Indonesia resulted in the division of tasks between several ministries. Of course, this becomes ineffective in preventing cybercrime. As a result, specific cyber security regulations have become very important for state security in Indonesia. The following is a design for strengthening the legal concept in overcoming cybercrime during the Covid-19 pandemic in Indonesia (Table 1).

Table 1 illustrates that perfecting legal concepts is very important to overcome cybercrime during the covid-19 pandemic in Indonesia. Alternative policies can be implemented by: First, accelerating the ratification of the Personal Data Protection Bill. Second, pass specific laws related to cybersecurity and cybercrime. Third, create a cybersecurity ecology. Furthermore, Fourth, to increase the capacity of human resources.

5   Conclusions

Various cybercrime attacks throughout the pandemic have shown that Indonesia still does not have an adequate protection system, and the legal concept is not yet specific. This study concludes that the draft for strengthening the legal concept can start by accelerating the ratification of the Personal Data Protection Bill. Then, pass special laws related to cyber security and cybercrime. Furthermore, create a cybersecurity ecology. The last

Table 1. Design of strengthening legal concepts in overcoming cybercrime attacks during the Covid-19 pandemic in Indonesia. Source: [43].

Number	Policy alternative	Legal concept design
1	Accelerate the passage of the Personal Data Protection Bill	Based on the availability of security policy documents, legal certainty in cyber security can regulate all information security procedures. Therefore, the discussion of the Personal Data Protection Bill must be realized immediately and maintain an anticipatory premise in the increasingly rapid development of technology. Then, the Personal Data Protection Bill must also be based on various government actors, the private sector, and the people's consultative council (DPR-RI). It aims to unify all existing regulations to be more integrated into all types of personal data, data owner rights, data processing, data controllers, data transfer, dispute resolution, and the imposition of administrative and criminal sanctions
2	Establish special regulations dealing with cyber-security and cyber-crime	The complexity of the threat of cyber attacks in the public, government, and private sectors necessitates the development of two regulatory products that tightly regulate domestic and worldwide cyber security and cybercrime. Cybersecurity legislation should address the concerns of protecting critical infrastructure from cyberattacks and cross-sectoral coordination. In addition, Indonesia needs an autonomous institution to foster cross-sectoral cooperation in handling cyber cases in the public, private, and government sectors. Strict rules must emphasize the phenomenon of cybercrime in behavioral problems and types of cybercrime as well as steps to combat it on a national and global scale

(*continued*)

Table 1. (*continued*)

Number	Policy alternative	Legal concept design
3	Creation of a multisectoral cybersecurity management ecosystem	Cybercrime threats are increasingly complex and widespread in various sectors in the pandemic era, requiring optimal coordination and synergy between various stakeholders. The stakeholders in question are the National Cyber and Crypto Agency, Cybercrime Police, the Ministry of Communication and Information, and the State Intelligence Agency. The sectoral ego that is still happening so far has made cyber handling in Indonesia stagnating, so sweeping changes must be made. Then, the Government of Indonesia can also build cross-sectoral ecosystem collaboration by following the approach used in the UK and other European countries by involving independent non-profit organizations
4	Increase awareness and capacity of human resources in the field of cyber security	During the Covid-19 pandemic in Indonesia, various government organizations must immediately organize online webinars in various media to educate the public about various types of cybercrime attacks. The organizations in question are the Ministry of Communication and Information, the National Cyber and Crypto Agency, the Financial Services Authority, and Bank Indonesia. Then, the National Cyber and Crypto Agency must also provide support to various companies throughout the Indonesian industry to improve the security of information systems and networks. In addition, the Government must also address the issue of human resource capabilities, especially for the younger generation to be directly involved in career paths and training in cyber security

step increases the capacity of human resources. The limitation of this study is that it only uses data from online news sources and focuses on analyzing the phenomena and significance of increasing the concept of cybercrime law during the pandemic. Therefore, we recommend that further research be conducted on the Penta helix to strengthen the concept of cybercrime law in Indonesia.

References

1. Thomas, A.M.B., Holt, J.: The Palgrave Handbook of International Cybercrime and Cyberdeviance. Springer, Switzerland (2020). https://doi.org/10.1007/978-3-319-78440-3
2. Shalaginov, A., Shalaginova, M., Jevremovic, A., Krstic, M.: Modern cybercrime investigation: technological advancement of smart devices and legal aspects of corresponding digital transformation. In: IEEE International Conference on Big Data, Big Data, pp. 2328–2332 (2020). https://doi.org/10.1109/BigData50022.2020.9378224
3. Koto, I.: Cyber crime according to the ITE law. Int. J. Reglem. Soc. 2(2), pp. 103–110 (2021). http://jurnal.bundamediagrup.co.id/index.php/ijrs/article/view/124
4. Djanggih, H., Thalib, H., Baharuddin, H., Qamar, N., Ahmar, A.S.: The effectiveness of law enforcement on child protection for cybercrime victims in Indonesia. J. Phys. Conf. Ser. 1028(1), 1–8 (2018). https://doi.org/10.1088/1742-6596/1028/1/012192
5. Anjani, N.H.: Cybersecurity protection in Indonesia. Cent. Indones. Policy Stud. 1(9), 1–12 (2021). https://www.cips-indonesia.org/post/policy-brief-cybersecurity-protection-in-ind onesia
6. Buil-Gil, D., Zeng, Y., Kemp, S.: Offline crime bounces back to pre-COVID levels, cyber stays high: interrupted time-series analysis in Northern Ireland. Crime Sci. 10(1), 1–16 (2021). https://doi.org/10.1186/s40163-021-00162-9
7. Umanailo, M.C.B., et al.: Cybercrime case as impact development of communication technology that troubling society. Int. J. Sci. Technol. Res. 8(9), 1224–1228 (2019). https://doi.org/10.5281/zenodo.3457420
8. Wijaya, M.R., Arifin, R.: Cyber crime in international legal instrument: how Indonesia and international deal with this crime? IJCLS (Indonesian J. Crim. Law Stud. 5(1), pp. 63–74 (2020). https://doi.org/10.15294/ijcls.v5i1.23273
9. Lallie, H.S.: Cyber security in the age of Covid-19: a timeline and analysis of cyber-crime and cyber-attacks during the pandemic. Comput. Secur. 105, 102248 (2021). https://doi.org/10.1016/j.cose.2021.102248
10. Amarullah, A.H., Runturambi, A.J.S., Widiawan, B.: Analyzing cyber crimes during Covid-19 time in Indonesia. In: 3rd International Conference on Computer Communication and the Internet (ICCCI), pp. 78–83 (2021). https://doi.org/10.1109/ICCCI51764.2021.9486775
11. Cnnindonesia.com, BSSN: Ada 888 Juta Serangan Siber Sepanjang 2021 (2021). https://www.cnnindonesia.com/nasional/20210913131225-12-693494/bssn-ada-888-juta-serangan-siber-sepanjang-2021. Accessed 20 Dec 2021
12. Rachh, A.: A study of future opportunities and challenges in digital healthcare sector: Cyber security vs crimes in digital healthcare sector. Asia Pacific J. Heal. Manag. 16(3), 7–15 (2021). https://doi.org/10.24083/apjhm.v16i3.957
13. Makarim, E.: Privacy and personal data protection in indonesia: the hybrid paradigm of the subjective and objective approach. In: Kiesow Cortez, E. (ed.) Data Protection Around the World. ITLS, vol. 33, pp. 127–164. T.M.C. Asser Press, The Hague (2021). https://doi.org/10.1007/978-94-6265-407-5_6
14. Hicks, J.: A 'data realm' for the Global South? Evidence from Indonesia. Third World Q. 42(7), 1417–1435 (2021). https://doi.org/10.1080/01436597.2021.1901570

15. Cortez, E.K.: Data Protection Around the World: Privacy Laws in Action, 3rd edn. Asser Press, The Hague (2021). https://www.asser.nl/asserpress/books/?rId=13963
16. Paat, Y.F.: Digital crime, trauma, and abuse: Internet safety and cyber risks for adolescents and emerging adults in the 21st century. Soc. Work Ment. Health 19(1), 18–40 (2021). https://doi.org/10.1080/15332985.2020.1845281
17. Perrone, G.: Online crimes as a result of a digital interconnection system. A cyber criminological reflection. Rass. Ital. di Criminol. 15(3), 239–247 (2021). https://doi.org/10.7347/RIC-032021-p239
18. Miguel, C.S.: Online victimization, social media utilization, and cyber crime prevention measures. Asia-Pacific Soc. Sci. Rev. 20(4), 123–135 (2020). https://www.scopus.com/inward/record.uri?partnerID=HzOxMe3b&scp=85097731756&origin=inward
19. Gryszczyńska, A.: The impact of the Covid-19 pandemic on cybercrime. Bull. Polish Acad. Sci. Tech. Sci. 69(4), 1–9 (2021). https://doi.org/10.24425/bpasts.2021.137933
20. Olofinbiyi, S.A.: The role and place of covid-19: an opportunistic avenue for exponential world's upsurge in cyber crime. Int. J. Criminol. Sociol. 9, 221–230 (2020). https://doi.org/10.6000/1929-4409.2020.09.20
21. Boussi, G.O.: A proposed framework for controlling cyber- crime. In: ICRITO 2020 - IEEE 8th International Conference on Reliability, Infocom Technologies and Optimization (Trends and Future Directions), pp. 1060–1063 (2020). https://doi.org/10.1109/ICRITO48877.2020.9197975
22. Hawdon, J., Parti, K., Dearden, T.E.: Cybercrime in America amid COVID-19: the initial results from a natural experiment. Am. J. Crim. Justice 45(4), 546–562 (2020). https://doi.org/10.1007/s12103-020-09534-4
23. Akdemir, N.: Exploring the human factor in cyber-enabled and cyber-dependent crime victimisation: a lifestyle routine activities approach. Internet Res. 30(6), 1665–1687 (2020). https://doi.org/10.1108/INTR-10-2019-0400
24. Díaz, R.M.: Cybersecurity in the time of Covid-19 and the transition to cyberimmunity. FAL Bulletin 382: Economic Commission for Latin America and the Caribbean (ECLAC), no. 6, Latin America and the Caribbean, pp. 1–17 (2020). https://www.cepal.org/en/publications/46511-cybersecurity-time-covid-19-and-transition-cyberimmunity
25. Vienna: Cybercrime and Covid-19: Risks and Responses. United Nations Office on Drugs and Crime, Wina (2020). https://www.unodc.org/documents/Advocacy-Section/UNODC_-_CYBERCRIME_AND_COVID19_-_Risks_and_Responses_v1.2_-_14-04-2020_-_CMLS-COVID19-CYBER1_-_UNCLASSIFIED_BRANDED.pdf
26. Cordova, J.G.L., Álvarez, P.F.C., De Jesús Echerri Ferrandiz, F., Pérez-Bravo, J.C.: Law versus cybercrime. Glob. Jurist 18(1), 1–9 (2018). https://doi.org/10.1515/gj-2017-0024
27. John Bandler, A.M.: Cybercrime Investigations: A Comprehensive Resource for Everyone, 1st edn. CRC Press, New York (2020). https://doi.org/10.1201/9781003033523
28. Christou, G.: The challenges of cybercrime governance in the European Union. Eur. Polit. Soc. 19(3), 355–375 (2018). https://doi.org/10.1080/23745118.2018.1430722
29. Maillart, J.-B.: The limits of subjective territorial jurisdiction in the context of cybercrime. ERA Forum 19(3), 375–390 (2018). https://doi.org/10.1007/s12027-018-0527-2
30. Bunga, D.: Legal response to cybercrime in global and national dimensions. Padjadjaran Jurnal Ilmu Hukum (J. Law) 06(01), 69–89 (2019). https://doi.org/10.22304/pjih.v6n1.a4
31. Zharova, A., Elin, V.: On the using datamessage as evidence of cybercrime. IOP Conf. Ser. Mater. Sci. Eng. 1069(1), 012037 (2021). https://doi.org/10.1088/1757-899x/1069/1/012037
32. Shalaginov, A.: Big data analytics and artificial intelligence for cyber crime investigation and prevention. Futur. Gener. Comput. Syst. 109, 702–703 (2020). https://doi.org/10.1016/j.future.2020.04.007
33. Maskun: Qualifying cyber crime as a crime of aggression in international law. J. East Asia Int. Law, 13(2), 397–418 (2020). https://doi.org/10.14330/jeail.2020.13.2.08

34. Sikos, L.F.: AI in digital forensics: ontology engineering for cybercrime investigations. WIREs Forensic Sci. **3**(3), 1–11 (2021). https://doi.org/10.1002/wfs2.1394
35. Walker-Munro, B.: A case for the use of cyber-systemics to combat financial crime in Australia. Kybernetes **50**(11), 3082–3105 (2021). https://doi.org/10.1108/K-09-2020-0581
36. Koziarski, J., Lee, J.R.: Connecting evidence-based policing and cybercrime. Polic. An Int. J. **43**(1), 198–211 (2020). https://doi.org/10.1108/PIJPSM-07-2019-0107
37. Hai-Jew, S.: "NVivo 12 plus's new qualitative cross-tab analysis function. Kansas State University (2020). https://scalar.usc.edu/works/c2c-digital-magazine-fall-2018--winter-2019/nvivo-12-plus-new-qual-cross-tab-analysis-function
38. Sotiriadou, P., Brouwers, J., Le, T.: Choosing a qualitative data analysis tool: a comparison of NVivo and Leximancer. Ann. Leis. Res. **17**(2), 218–234 (2014). https://doi.org/10.1080/11745398.2014.902292
39. Google.com: Trends in cyber crime issues during the Covid-19 pandemic in Indonesia (2021). https://trends.google.com/trends/explore?date=2020-03-022021-12-23&geo=ID&q=CyberCrime. Accessed 23 Dec 2021
40. Tribunnews.com, BSSN: Ada Tren Peningkatan Serangan Siber Malware Pencuri Informasi di Awal Pandemi (2021). https://www.tribunnews.com/nasional/2021/03/01/bssn-ada-tren-peningkatan-serangan-siber-malware-pencuri-informasi-di-awal-pandemi?page=3. Accessed 24 Dec 2021
41. Kompas.com, Kronologi Kasus Kebocoran Data WNI, Dijual 0,15 Bitcoin hingga Pemanggilan Direksi BPJS (2021). https://tekno.kompas.com/read/2021/05/22/09450057/kronologi-kasus-kebocoran-data-wni-dijual-0-15-bitcoin-hingga-pemanggilan?page=all. Accessed 24 Dec 2021
42. Detik.com, BSSN dan BPS Kerja Sama Perkuat Keamanan Data dari Serangan Siber, (2021). https://inet.detik.com/security/d-5767571/bssn-dan-bps-kerja-sama-perkuat-keamanan-data-dari-serangan-siber?_ga=2.51210796.46083478.1640343522-756276621.1635146417. Accessed 25 Dec 2021
43. Wicaksana, R.H., Munandar, A.I., Samputra, P.L.: A narrative policy framework analysis of data privacy policy: a case of cyber attacks during the Covid-19 pandemic. J. Ilmu Pengetah. dan Teknol. Komun. **22**(2), 143–158 (2020). https://doi.org/10.33164/iptekkom.22.2.2020.143-158

Exploration of Privacy, Ethical and Regulatory Concerns Related to COVID-19 Vaccine Passport Implementation

Abhishek Sharma[(⊠)] [iD], Chandana Hewege, and Chamila Perera

Swinburne University of Technology, Melbourne, Australia
sharmaabhishek570@gmail.com, {chewege,chamilaperera}@swin.edu.au

Abstract. As countries emerge from lockdowns, vaccine passports are being implemented around the world to allow unrestricted movement of people. However, the implementation of vaccine passports has proven to be a double-edged sword that can compromise an individual's privacy in manifold ways. This paper provides a comprehensive review of the privacy, ethical, and regulatory issues associated with the implementation of vaccine passports. It also engages in a theoretical analysis incorporating the concept of ethical data governance and the health belief model (HBM) with a view to making sense of the technological adoption of vaccine passports. Finally, key ethical and legal issues that may arise following the implementation of vaccine passports and the necessary policy implications are discussed.

Keywords: Vaccine passports · Covid-19 · Privacy · Ethics · Regulatory issues · Health-pass · Health belief model · Ethical data management

1 Introduction

The Covid-19 pandemic has been spreading at an increasing rate over the years, resulting in over 4 million deaths to date (Worldometers 2022). To protect against these transmissions, governments around the world are implementing mass vaccination programs and considering the use of vaccine passports to ensure the smooth operations of international travel (Sharma, 2021). However, restricting an individual's travel movement on the basis of Covid-19 immunity is highly questioned (Tsoi et al. 2021; Wilford et al. 2021; Paris 2021). The speed with which using the COVID-19 vaccine passports were agreed upon and implemented suggests that there was insufficient time to fully consider the risks, benefits or develop policy around subsequent regulations (Wilford et al. 2021, Rosen et al. 2021).

Concerns about the efficacy of vaccines and irregularities in vaccine distribution and production capacity are among the major issues raised about the implications of vaccine passports (Brown et al. 2020; Wilford et al. 2021). Furthermore, the exclusion of people who are unable to obtain vaccines due to medical reasons and people who are vaccine-hesitant has also been criticized (Wilford et al. 2021; Rosen et al. 2021). Data sharing, privacy, and the storage of information of each individual is very sensitive and has been a source of debate in terms of privacy violation (Radic et al. 2021; Mitchell 2021). While fewer studies raise concerns about the implementation of vaccine passports, less attention has been paid to the privacy, ethical, and regulatory issues associated with vaccine passport implementation. Therefore, this study aims to understand the key privacy, ethical and regulatory issues of information disclosure required within vaccine passport implementation in light of individuals' travel intentions.

The paper is organized into seven sections. Following the introduction in the first section, Sect. 2 provides an overview of the study's key objectives and parameters of vaccine passport implementation. In Sect. 3, key theoretical concepts associated with the vaccine passport implementation are discussed. Next, a brief discussion of the methodological approach adopted in this study is provided in Sect. 4. Section 5 presents a review of key selected literature on the key opportunities and challenges associated with the implementation of the vaccine passports. Section 6 then briefly discusses the findings that are gathered as part of this review. Finally, Sect. 7 concludes with practical contributions and policy implications that can assist policymakers and governments in understanding the risks, benefits and privacy concerns associated with mandatory COVID-19 vaccination as a prerequisite for international travel.

2 Background

The implementation of 'vaccine passports' is currently a heatedly debated topic. However, vaccination certificates are not a new concept. Historically, individuals were required to show proof of yellow fever vaccination in order to visit certain destinations. Furthermore, individuals travelling to the Hajj were also needed to show proof of polio/ meningococcal vaccinations in certain circumstances (Schlagenhauf et al. 2021). In the year 2005, International Health Regulations had expanded the scope of critical diseases to all "events which may constitute public health emergencies of international concern" (Baker and Fidler 2006). As a result, it is clear that the framework for data sharing for Vaccine Passport implementation has already been documented. Vaccine passports are typically implemented using blockchain technology (Tsoi et al. 2021; Wilford et al. 2021) which enables data collection and sharing of electronic health records through a system infrastructure, as demonstrated in Fig. 1. Each building block of the framework includes permissioned blockchain, which allows certain types of actions to be performed only through certain authorized departments. These authorized departments will include immigration authorities, who will be in charge of verifying an individual's vaccination status using a QR code stamped on an electronically verified document (Tsoi et al. 2021; Haque et al. 2021).

Prior to the introduction of vaccine passports, contact tracing apps (e.g., Ehteraz in Qatar, Staysafe in the Philippines, COVID Safe in Australia, Aarogya Setu in India) were used to combat Covid-19 by identifying the contacts of each carrier with the infection (Sun et al. 2021; Dar et al. 2020). Within these technologies, data sharing is viewed as one of the critical steps required to combat Covid-19; however, the issue of privacy and the processes used for the safe storage of personal data are heavily criticized (Jahmunah et al. 2021, Liu et al. 2020; Cho et al. 2020). Despite the fact that vaccine passports and

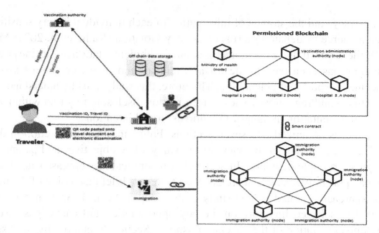

Fig. 1. An architecture framework for vaccine passport implementation Source- Haque et al. (2021)

Internet of Things (IoT) technologies have provided long-term tracking technologies to combat pandemic, only a few studies have addressed the usage, privacy, ethical, and regulatory aspects of vaccine passport implementation. Therefore, the present study investigates the key opportunities and challenges associated with the implementation of vaccine passports. The following research questions guide the study:

(a) What are the key theoretical models that will assist in the implementation of vaccine passports?
(b) What are the key privacy, risk, ethical, and regulatory issues associated with the implementation of vaccine passports?

3   Review of Theoretical Models Underpinning Vaccine Passport Implementation

3.1   Implementing a Data Governance and Ethical Data Management Framework

Privacy and ethics are the most important considerations when developing data governance frameworks. In the tourism and hospitality industries (THOs), such frameworks must ensure that widespread ethical concerns about travellers' digital data and information, which are collected in various structured and unstructured ways, are addressed in order to ensure travellers' safety and data security. According to Yallop et al. (2021), ethical data governance and management are made up of four distinct pillars that serve as the foundation for processing and governing data in tourism and hospitality organizations (THO) (See Fig. 2). These four pillars are concerned with (a) data privacy and ethics, (b) data social legitimacy and trustworthiness, (c) fair and transparent exchange of data and private information, and (d) ethical compliance in the disclosure of data sets and their storage. These all work together to promote the integration of trustworthy ethics with legal compliance in the context of data governance.

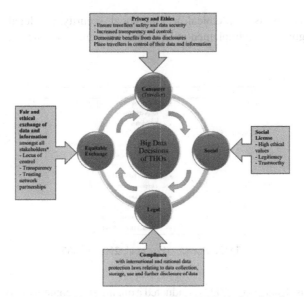

Fig. 2. Data governance and ethical data management in THOs industries Source- (Yallop et al. 2021, p. 8)

Firstly, the tourism and hospitality industries (THOs) must ensure that data collection, use, storage, and disclosures are carried out in accordance with legal and compliance standards within a data governance framework (THOs) (Yallop et al. 2021; Yallop and Seraphin 2020). For example, it should be ensured that data collection within the Vaccine passport implementation adheres to GDPR regulations and principles of lawfulness, fairness, and transparency (Masseno and Santos 2018, Yallop et al. 2021). Secondly, from an ethical perspective, the tourism and hospitality industries must implement appropriate procedures to ensure that data collection and disclosures adhere to the requirements of the vaccine passport implementation. According to Masseno and Santos (2018), organizations must be clear about why data is being collected and how data will be used in accordance with GDPR regulations and principles such as lawfulness, fairness, and transparency, as well as how data will be used. Thirdly, from a societal perspective, it should be ensured that trust and belief are maintained among stakeholders and travellers in the tourism and hospitality industries through the concept of social licence (SLO). The notion of social license is not new; however, the term "Social license" has grown in popularity (Gehman et al. 2017; Yallop et al. 2021). This approach provides a broader perspective on the social considerations and responsibilities of tourism and hospitality organizations that are solely related to accepted societal norms and standards. Lastly, tourism and hospitality organizations must ensure a fair and ethical exchange of travelers' data and information among all stakeholders as a key component of their data governance systems designed to protect their travelers' privacy and data security.

Toward these discussions, Foy et al. (2022) highlighted that there are a number of factors that must be taken into account when determining how effectively data governance is conducted within vaccine passport implementation. Furthermore, the study shed light on how various aspects (i.e., ethical, technological, security, and legal) will allow for a strong data governance implementation within the context of vaccine passports (See Fig. 3).

Analysis Facet	Data Governance Aims
Ethical	• Prevents discrimination
	• Respects Privacy
	• Establishes Trust
Technical	• Scalability
	• Low Cost – Financial and Temporal
	• Available technology
	• Low Energy Usage
Security	• Protects Personal Data
	• Tamper-resistant
	• Ensures Data Integrity
Legal	• GDPR Compliant
	• Cross Jurisdiction Compatibility
	• Upholds Human Rights

Fig. 3. Source- (Foy et al. 2022, p. 665)

Besides this, Khan et al. (2022) conducted a quantitative content analysis on a Twitter data set to better understand an individual's attitudes towards vaccine passport implementation. According to the study, perceived barriers, benefits, predisposition & knowledge, and cues to action are key factors related to vaccine passport implementation when viewed through the lens of the health belief model (HBM) and Theory of planned behaviour (TPB). The colour coding in Fig. 4 below illustrates how several constructs have either a positive (i.e., Green Colour) or a negative (i.e., Red Colour) influence on an individual's attitude towards vaccine passport implementation (See Fig. 4).

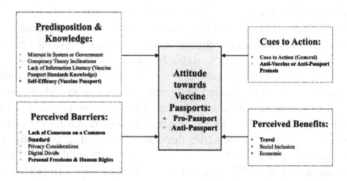

Fig. 4. Factors influencing attitudes towards vaccine passport implementation Source- (Khan et al. 2022, p. 6)

Based on these notions, the present study seeks to explore how ethical data governance and management (i.e., ethical, technical, security, legal) are preserved in the vaccine passport implementation. In response to these discussions, several researchers have adopted the health belief model (HBM) to better understand the importance of getting vaccinated before undertaking an international travel (Wong et al. 2020; Tadesse et al. 2020; Suess et al. 2022). As a result, the following sub-section provides a brief discussion of the key aspects of vaccine passport implementation from the theoretical perspective of the health belief model (HBM).

3.2 Application of Health Belief Model in Vaccine Passport Implementation

For more than two decades, the Health Belief Model (HBM) has served as one of the most widely used theoretical foundations in health behaviour research, both to explain change and maintenance of health-related behaviours (Suess et al. 2022; Wong et al. 2020; D'Souza et al. 2011). The fundamental constructs of the HBM include perceived vulnerability, perceived severity, perceived rewards, perceived barriers, self-efficacy to engage in a behaviour, and cues to action. Though HBM has previously been considered to explain a variety of diseases, both infectious and noninfectious, the current study focuses on explaining the role of the HBM in explaining vaccination passport implementation (See Fig. 5).

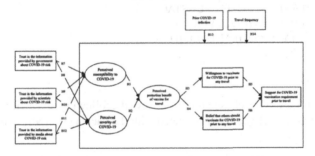

Fig. 5. Health belief model in vaccine passport implementation Source- (Suess et al. 2022, p. 5)

As per Suess et al. (2022), vaccine passports implementation is dependent on several key parameters, including (a) trust in information provided by government/media/scientists (Tadesse et al. 2020; Suess et al. 2022), (b) perceived susceptibility and severity of Covid-19 (D'Souza et al. 2011; Suess et al. 2022), (c) perceived protection and benefit of vaccination (Wilson and Chen 2020; Suess et al. 2022), (d) willingness to be vaccinated (Wong et al. 2020; Suess et al. 2022), (e) belief that others should be vaccinated (Suess et al. 2022; Wong et al. 2020), and (f) support for Covid-19 requirement (Chung et al. 2020; Suess et al. 2022).

Though, it is evident from the above two theoretical perspectives (i.e., HBM & TPB) that several parameters contribute to the vaccine passport implementation, it remains unclear how many of these notions have been implemented in the real-world scenario. Therefore, a review is carried out in the following subsections to provide in-depth insights on articles relating to vaccine passport implementation's privacy, trust, risks, and ethical acceptability issues, which could aid in the effective development of the framework.

4 Methodology

To accomplish the objectives of the paper, an extensive literature review search is conducted upon designated databases such as Scopus, ProQuest and Google Scholar. Based on this review, articles relating to the privacy, trust, risks, and ethical acceptability issues of vaccine passport implementation are chosen. Several keywords shown in Table 1 below were selected to conduct this review.

Table 1. Search results from designated databases

Keywords	Scopus	Google scholar	ProQuest
("Vaccine Passports" OR "Health Pass") AND (bioethics OR ethic OR consent OR "e-consent*" OR autonomy OR empowerment OR privacy OR confidential OR "data protection" OR "de-identification" OR security OR trust OR transparent OR fairness OR justice OR legitimation OR governance) AND (LIMIT-TO (PUBSTAGE, "final")) AND (LIMIT-TO (DOCTYPE, "ar") OR LIMIT-TO (DOCTYPE, "re")) AND (LIMIT-TO (LANGUAGE, "English"))	47	514	62

Based on the keywords chosen for this review, the following subsection discusses the key opportunities and challenges associated with the vaccine passport implementation.

5 Key Opportunities and Challenges Associated with Vaccine Passport Implementation

In addition, Table 2 shows the critical pieces of literature that are screened within this review.

Table 2. Key opportunities and challenges associated with vaccine passport implementation

Domain	Key opportunities & challenges	Type of study	Related literatures
Vaccine Passport Implementation	Real Time Data Sharing	Quantitative/Qualitative	Tsoi et al. (2021); Platt (2021), Buckner (2021); Clark (2021)
	Accurate & Precise Information	Quantitative/Qualitative	Ljungholm and Olah (2021), Sotis et al. (2021)
	Trust & Privacy Issues/ Vaccine Hesitancy	Quantitative	Mitchell (2021), Mitchell et al. (2021), Robinson et al. (2021), Gstrein (2021), (2021), Porat et al. (2021), Tsung-Ling (2021), Hu et al. (2021), Radic et al. (2021)
	Ethical Acceptability	Quantitative/Qualitative	Clark (2021), (Buckner, 2021), (Ljungholm and Olah, 2021), Mitchell et al. (2021), Kirkman (2021), Platt (2021), Phillips et al. (2021), Walker (2021), Wilford et al. (2021), Haque et al. (2021), Ljungholm and Popescu (2021), Sotis et al. (2021), Rosen et al. (2021), Suess et al. (2022), Huang et al. (2021)
	Counterfeit Production of Vaccine Passport	Quantitative	Liew and Flaherty (2021), Shah et al. (2021), Buckner (2021), Kosciejew (2021)

6   Findings

Based on the above review, several arguments can be drawn. According to Table 2, there are a number of challenges and opportunities that can be addressed in the field of vaccine passport implementation. In a broader sense, privacy and trust concerns, as well as ethical acceptability concerns, continue to be major challenges in the vaccine passport implementation.

Firstly, the rapid growth of information and communication technologies has resulted in an increase in the amount of personal data being collected on a daily basis. Healthcare, educational institutions, the supply chain industry, and agriculture are all becoming increasingly digitalized, and as a result, data protection and privacy issues are of critical concern in the current scenario (Yousif et al. 2021). As a result, it is proposed that GDPR (General Data Protection Regulation) be implemented throughout the world in order to make issues such as data security, verifiability, authentication, and traceability easier to manage (Haque et al. 2021; Masseno and Santos 2018).

Secondly, it is recommended that an expanded compliance-based approach be implemented within tourism and hospitality organisations so that officials have a greater ability to respond to consumers' concerns about personal data and information in a more ethical manner (Yallop et al. 2021). Additionally, it must be ensured that consumers are given the freedom to choose which data they want to share, as well as access to their stored data and the ability to delete data with permission on the grounds of special security concerns (Mitchell, 2021, Mitchell et al. 2021; Porat et al. 2021).

Thirdly, working on effective real-time data sharing could ensure and promote an accurate and precise flow of information, which is one of the key directions that need to be improved within the vaccine passport implementation framework. This real-time data sharing can help to stop the spread of the Covid-19 virus and help officials identify the counterfeit production of vaccine passports (Buckner 2021).

Lastly, support for the mandate must begin with the population's willingness to be vaccinated to travel and enforce vaccine requirements necessitates government-level strategies (Suess et al. 2022). Hence, it must be ensured that government strategies reflect and promote the concept of "vaccine passports" through key subsidiaries such as embassies and consulates by providing registration options.

7   Conclusion and Policy Implications

Digital aided vaccine passports are a complex concoction of technologies that are difficult to regulate. However, understanding its implementation needs to coincide with the privacy, ethical and regulatory aspects of society. Therefore, the current review intends to provide a deeper understanding of the dynamics that may enable the success of important health-related travel policy and ideas for investigating future health-related travel behaviour. In addition to the above contributions, the review provides a brief overview of several policy implications that the government should pursue in order to address concerns about the ethical deployment of vaccine passports (See Table 3).

Table 3. Policy implications in the context of vaccine passport implementation

Concerns about the ethical deployment of vaccine passports	Policy implications
Anonymity and Privacy with Data Sharing	Providing different authorities/governing bodies with selective data access
Counterfeit Production of Vaccine Passports	Standardization of vaccination certificates
Increasing Costs with higher levels of testing	Government/state/employer-sponsored schemes to lower the costs associated with certifications
Reliability & accuracy with tests in terms of evolving variants of Covid-19	Improving quality assurance and end-user testing, as well as testing for standard compliance and interoperability with other systems

References

Baker, M.G., Fidler, D.P.: Global public health surveillance under new international health regulations. Emerg. Infect. Dis. **12**, 1058 (2006)

Brown, R.C., Savulescu, J., Williams, B., Wilkinson, D.: Passport to freedom? Immunity passports for COVID-19. J. Med. Ethics **46**, 652–659 (2020)

Buckner, K.: Would it be ethically problematic to introduce mandatory vaccination for COVID-19? Linguist. Philos. Inv. **20**, 55–64 (2021)

CHO, H., Ippolito, D., Yu, Y.W.: Contact tracing mobile apps for COVID-19: Privacy considerations and related trade-offs. arXiv preprint arXiv:2003.11511 (2020)

Chung, G., Lanier, P., Wong, P.Y.J.: Mediating effects of parental stress on harsh parenting and parent-child relationship during coronavirus (COVID-19) pandemic in Singapore. J. Fam. Violence, 1–12 https://doi.org/10.1007/s10896-020-00200-1 (2020)

Clark, A.: Ethical acceptability of COVID-19 immunity certification. Linguist. Philos. Inv. **20**, 105–114 (2021)

D'Souza, C., Zyngier, S., Robinson, P., Schlotterlein, M., Sullivan-Mort, G.: Health belief model: evaluating marketing promotion in a public vaccination program. J. Nonprofit Public Sect. Mark. **23**, 134–157 (2011)

Dar, A.B., Lone, A.H., Zahoor, S., Khan, A.A., Naaz, R.: Applicability of mobile contact tracing in fighting pandemic (COVID-19): issues, challenges and solutions. Comput. Sci. Rev. **38**, 1–14 (2020)

Foy, M., Martyn, D., Daly, D., Byrne, A., Aguneche, C., Brennan, R.: Blockchain-based governance models for COVID-19 digital health certificates: a legal, technical, ethical and security requirements analysis. Procedia Comput. Sci. **198**, 662–669 (2022)

Gehman, J., Lefsrud, L.M., Fast, S.: Social license to operate: legitimacy by another name? Can. Public Adm. **60**, 293–317 (2017)

Gstrein, O.J.: The EU digital COVID certificate: a preliminary data protection impact assessment. Eur. J. Risk Regul. Forthcoming **12**, 370–381 (2021)

Haque, A., Naqvi, B., Islam, A., Hyrynsalmi, S.: Towards a GDPR-compliant blockchain-based COVID vaccination passport. Appl. Sci. **11**, 6132 (2021)

Hu, M., Jia, H., Xie, Y.: Passport to a mighty nation: exploring sociocultural foundation of chinese public's attitude to COVID-19 vaccine certificates. Int. J. Environ. Res. Public Health **18**, 10439 (2021)

Huang, J., Kwan, M.-P., Kim, J.: How culture and sociopolitical tensions might influence people's acceptance of COVID-19 control measures that use individual-level georeferenced data. ISPRS Int. J. Geo Inf. **10**, 490 (2021)

Jahmunah, V., et al.: Future IoT tools for COVID-19 contact tracing and prediction: a review of the state-of-the-science. Int. J. Imaging Syst. Technol. **31**, 455–471 (2021)

Khan, M.L., Malik, A., Ruhi, U., Al-Busaidi, A.: Conflicting attitudes: analyzing social media data to understand the early discourse on COVID-19 passports. Technol. Soc. **68**, 101830 (2022)

Kirkman, J.: Would COVID-19 testing and vaccination status certificates erode civil liberties? Linguist. Philos. Inv. **20**, 65–74 (2021)

Kosciejew, M.R.H.: COVID-19 immunity (or vaccine) passports: a documentary overview and analysis of regimes of health verification within the coronavirus pandemic. J. Documentation, 463–484 (2021)

Liew, C.H., Flaherty, G.T.: Immunity passports to travel during the COVID-19 pandemic: controversies and public health risks. J. Public Health **43**, e135–e136 (2021)

Liu, J.K., et al.: Privacy-preserving COVID-19 contact tracing app: a zero-knowledge proof approach. IACR Cryptol. ePrint Arch. 2020, 528, 1–26 (2020)

Ljungholm, D.P., Olah, M.L.: Implementing digital vaccine passports to control the spread of COVID-19: law, rights, and ethics. Linguist. Philos. Inv. **20**, 35–44 (2021)

Ljungholm, D.P., Popescu, V.: Is It ethically and legally acceptable for governments to require citizens to be vaccinated against COVID-19? Rev. Contemp. Philos. **20**, 71–80 (2021)

Masseno, M.D., Santos, C.: Privacy and data protection issues on smart tourism destinations–a first approach. Intelligent Environments 2018. IOS Press (2018)

Mitchell, K.: COVID-19 threat perceptions and willingness to get vaccinated: efficacy, safety, and trust concerns. Rev. Contemp. Philos. **20**, 93–104 (2021)

Mitchell, K., Grupac, M., Zauskova, A.: Ethical management and implementation of COVID-19 immunity passports and vaccination certificates: lawfulness, fairness, and transparency. Linguist. Philos. Inv. **20**, 45–54 (2021)

Paris, E.: Applying the proportionality principle to COVID-19 certificates. Eur. J. Risk Regul. **12**, 287–297 (2021)

Phillips, A., Suler, P., Rowland, Z.: Behavioral responses and inequalities in vaccine uptake against COVID-19. Linguist. Philos. Inv. **20**, 75–84 (2021)

Platt, C.: Public legitimacy of vaccine passports: Ethical and Regulatory Issues Raised by COVID-19 Immunity Certificates. Linguist. Philos. Inv. **20**, 135–144 (2021)

Porat, T., et al.: "Vaccine passports" may backfire: findings from a cross-sectional study in the UK and Israel on willingness to get vaccinated against COVID-19. Vaccines **9**, 902 (2021)

Radic, A., Koo, B., Gil-Cordero, E., Cabrera-Sánchez, J.P., Han, H.: Intention to take COVID-19 vaccine as a precondition for international travel: application of extended norm-activation model. Int. J. Environ. Res. Public Health **18**, 3104 (2021)

Robinson, R., Zvarikova, K., Sosedova, J.: Restricting human rights and increasing discrimination through COVID-19 vaccination certificates: necessity, benefits, risks, and costs. Linguist. Philos. Inv. **20**, 115–124 (2021)

Rosen, B., Waitzberg, R., Israeli, A., Hartal, M., Davidovitch, N.: Addressing vaccine hesitancy and access barriers to achieve persistent progress in Israel's COVID-19 vaccination program. Isr. J. health policy res. **10**, 1–20 (2021)

Schlagenhauf, P., Patel, D., Rodriguez-Morales, A., Gautret, P., Grobusch, M.P., Leder, K.: Variants, vaccines and vaccination passports: challenges and chances for travel medicine in 2021. Travel medicine and infectious disease (2021)

Shah, H., Shah, M., Tanwar, S., Kumar, N.: Blockchain for COVID-19: a comprehensive review. Personal and Ubiquitous Computing, 1–28 (2021)

Sharma, A.: The role of IoT in the fight against Covid-19 to Restructure the Economy. Cham. Springer International Publishing, 140–156 https://doi.org/10.1007/978-3-030-90966-6_11 (2021)

Sotis, C., Allena, M., Reyes, R., Romano, A.: Covid-19 vaccine passport and international traveling: the combined effect of two nudges on americans' support for the pass. Int. J. Environ. Res. Public Health 18, 8800 (2021)

Suess, C., Maddock, J., Dogru, T., Mody, M., Lee, S.: Using the health belief model to examine travelers' willingness to vaccinate and support for vaccination requirements prior to travel. Tour. Manag. 88, 104405 (2022)

Sun, X., Wandelt, S., Zhang, A.: Vaccination passports: challenges for a future of air transportation. Transp. Policy 110, 394–401 (2021)

Tadesse, T., Alemu, T., Amogne, G., Endazenaw, G., Mamo, E.: Predictors of coronavirus disease 2019 (COVID-19) prevention practices using health belief model among employees in Addis Ababa, Ethiopia, 2020. Infect. Drug Resist. 13, 3751 (2020)

Tsoi, K.K., Sung, J.J., Lee, H.W., Yiu, K.K., Fung, H., Wong, S.Y.: The way forward after COVID-19 vaccination: vaccine passports with blockchain to protect personal privacy. BMJ Innovations, 7 (2021)

TSUNG-LING, L.: COVID-19 vaccination certificates and their geopolitical discontents. Eur. J. Risk Regul. 12, 321–331 (2021)

Walker, A.: Would COVID-19 immunity passports undermine the right to health of individuals? Linguist. Philos. Inv. 20, 95–104 (2021)

Wilford, S.H., et al.: The digital network of networks: regulatory risk and policy challenges of vaccine passports. Eur. J. Risk Regul. 12, 393–403 (2021)

Wilson, M.E., Chen, L.H.: Re-starting travel in the era of COVID-19: preparing anew. J. Travel Med. 27, taaa108, 1–5 (2020)

Wong, L.P., Alias, H., Wong, P.-F., Lee, H.Y., Abubakar, S.: The use of the health belief model to assess predictors of intent to receive the COVID-19 vaccine and willingness to pay. Hum. Vaccin. Immunother. 16, 2204–2214 (2020)

Worldometers: Worldometer: Coronavirus Cases (2022). https://www.worldometers.info/coronavirus/ :Worldometers. Accessed 21 Oct 2020–2021

Yallop, A., Seraphin, H.: Big data and analytics in tourism and hospitality: opportunities and risks. J. Tourism Futures, 257–262 (2020)

Yallop, A.C., Gică, O.A., Moisescu, O.I., Coroș, M.M., Séraphin, H.: The digital traveller: implications for data ethics and data governance in tourism and hospitality. J. Consum. Market. (2021)

Yousif, M., Hewage, C., Nawaf, L.: IoT technologies during and beyond COVID-19: a comprehensive review. Future Internet 13, 105 (2021)

Attitudes Towards the Use of COVID-19 Apps and Its Associated Factors

Tian Wang(✉) and Masooda Bashir

University of Illinois, Champaign, IL 61820, USA
tianw7@illinois.edu

Abstract. Since early 2020, the COVID-19 pandemic has been significantly changing people's daily lives as social activities are limited to slow down the spread of the novel coronavirus. New technologies, especially mobiles apps, have been widely applied to help with reducing the spread of the pandemic. However, although these apps bring many benefits, it also raises privacy issues given the amount of user information being collected and shared. The goal of this study is to understand individuals' attitudes towards the privacy concerns on using COVID-19 apps, and their expectations on the privacy protections. By conducting the survey and collecting responses, results found that majority of the participants expressed privacy concerns on COVID-19 apps, and participants with different socioeconomic status may have different levels of willingness to use the app. Results from this study not only provide guidance for the government and app service providers on the implementation of appropriate safeguards, but also address on the needs of privacy protections for the vulnerable groups.

Keywords: COVID-19 apps · Privacy protections · Socioeconomic factors

1 Introduction

The COVID-19 pandemic, which became a serious global challenge since 2020, has impacted individuals' daily routines in negative ways. Besides the physical health being threatened, people are also forced to limit their social connections and start to self-quarantine because of the lockdown and distance restrictions. Dealing with situations like working from home, temporary unemployment, or lack of physical contact with family and friends, it is expected that people's lifestyles change a lot due to the pandemic, and most of the activities may be more relied on the usage of technologies. As the spread of the COVID-19, many governments and health organizations around the world began to take actions towards combating the pandemic and one strategy was to develop and use relevant mobile applications. The goal and the utilization of COVID-19 related apps was to address the urgent need for healthcare workers and for public health systems to be able to begin contact tracing, health information dissemination and symptom checking [1].

While there were many utilities that the COVID-19 apps could provide in controlling the spread of the outbreak and bringing in-time healthcare, there were also serious concerns about the use of these apps and the privacy vulnerabilities it may pose. COVID-19

A. Moallem (Ed.): HCII 2022, LNCS 13333, pp. 492–501, 2022.
https://doi.org/10.1007/978-3-031-05563-8_31

apps often collected and shared users' sensitive and personal data [2], thus the need for adequate privacy protections became a critical issue. In addition, a related study reported that both information accuracy and privacy protections influence people's willingness to install a COVID-19 app [3]. Similarly, another study revealed that users' trust, willingness, and preferences in the context of COVID-19 app development are important factors for app design and development [4].

Especially, it is important to have structures in place to help the vulnerable populations so that they stand a better chance to have information privacy protections when using relevant apps during the COVID-19 pandemic. The vulnerable groups include but are not limited to racial minorities, children and the elderly, socioeconomically disadvantaged groups, and people from rural communities. Since the disadvantaged groups often suffer from a lack of information and barriers to access [5], it is possible that they may be more concerned and reserved on the new developed apps, especially if such app is linked to their personal health information. Therefore, it is necessary to accurately understand their needs and expectations on the privacy protections provided by COVID-19 apps, in order to encourage them to use such apps.

The goal of this study is to examine individual's attitudes towards the COVID-19 apps and their expectations for privacy protections provided by these apps. Specifically, the study aims to answer the following research questions:

1. Are people's attitudes towards the COVID-19 apps related to individual differences such as gender, age, and ethnicity?
2. Does one's socioeconomic factors such as education, occupation, and income relate to a person's willingness to use such apps and their expectations for the privacy protections?

We believe that the results from this study could be helpful to raise public awareness on the importance of information privacy protections when using relevant apps during a crisis like the COVID-19 pandemic, especially for the vulnerable populations such as racial minorities and lower socioeconomic groups. Considering the possibility of inequities exposed in this global pandemic, this study encourages the government and app service providers to take responsibility not only to provide better and more efficient privacy protections when developing the app, but also to ensure the needs on the privacy protections for the vulnerable groups are satisfied.

2   Literature Review

Although the usage of new technologies like mobile applications has been beneficial to help with controlling the spread of the COVID-19 pandemic, it also brings privacy risks given the amount of information being collected and shared. For example, while the embedded sensors could be used for tracing the spread of certain diseases, it could also disclose private information of the users and then becomes a threat to user's privacy [6]. A previous review on the current COVID-19 apps [7] found that most of the apps use central server to store and manage users' data, which leads to different types of privacy risks (i.e., data manipulation, compromising, or stealing). Therefore, it becomes the app developers and providers' responsibilities to come up with efficient and effective approaches to protect user's privacy.

On the other hand, users become aware of potential privacy violations when using the COVID-19 apps, and they are demanding powerful protections on their personal information. One of the reasons that individuals are against the use, download, and adoption of any contact tracing app is the potential invasion of personal privacy [8], thus such concerns could limit the acceptability of tracing apps in the general population [9]. Besides the privacy considerations, it is important to build trust with the users to encourage them to use relevant apps. Research found that if it reveals to users that their data were not properly secured, it will reduce their trust in the service providers, and then negatively impact their adoption of the tracing apps [10].

It is especially important to emphasize the privacy protections for the vulnerable groups during the pandemic. COVID-19 has had a variety of effects on individuals, with socioeconomic factors being one possible explanation for the difference. For example, a review article by Singu et al. [11] examined the impact of social determinants of health (SDOH) on the COVID-19 pandemic, and it found that the education level determines an individual's income level, which further impacts the type of healthcare he or she is eligible for. Differences on the socioeconomic status may not only result health disparities, but also bring privacy risks to the vulnerable groups. Previous research stated that the vulnerable groups are at particular risk in the society at large, especially for the online privacy violations. Furthermore, such privacy risk has not been fully considered when designing technologies since the risks and potential harms are not fully understood [12]. Therefore, it is necessary to accurately understand the needs of the vulnerable groups on the privacy protections in order to encourage them to use the technologies.

3   Method

To learn more about individuals' preferences and concerns on the COVID-19 apps and privacy protections, we analyzed the data collected from a survey study that included questions on assessing individuals' attitudes toward using COVID-19 tracing app (an app that is used to trace the contacts of people who have been diagnosed with COVID-19 and document the places that people have been to) and status app (an app that is used to track the user's status, including the test results and other indicator like temperature). The survey was conducted in June 2020 and involved a representative sample of 1790 participants from a midwestern state in the United States. The full version of the survey included a comprehensive set of questions: participants' demographic information, COVID-19 experiences questions, COVID technology questions (including participants' views on the COVID-19 apps and their expectation for privacy protections), income issues, and food security questions.

After pre-processing the data, only participants who fully completed the survey with valid responses were included in this study. Also, to have accurate results for the data analysis, we focused on the responses that clearly expressed their views in the questionnaire, while answers like "Other" or "Not Sure" without further explanation were ignored. Descriptive statistical analysis was conducted to summarize the characteristic of the dataset, and the statistical significances were tested as well. For this study, we especially focused on the data related to participants" privacy preferences and their attitudes on the privacy protections for the COVID-19 tracing and status apps.

The study was approved by the Institutional Review Board (IRB) at the university, and no personal identifiable information was collected or stored.

4 Results

To understand individual's attitudes toward the COVID-19 apps related to privacy protections, we focused on the three aspects:

- Privacy concerns: individual's privacy concerns on using COVID-19 mobile apps (Question: In general, how concerned you are, regarding your privacy on mobile apps are these days?)
- Willingness: individual's willingness on using COVID-19 mobile apps (Questions: Would you be willing to use an app like the one described above that traces who you have been around for the last two weeks? Would you be willing to use a COVID-19 status app like the one described above?)
- Attitudes towards privacy protections/regulation: how should the COVID-19 apps be regulated, or what kinds of privacy protections are necessary (Questions: If you could be guaranteed that you could completely delete all your data from this app at any time, would that make you more likely to use it? If such a COVID-19 app were available, would it matter to you who offered the status app and controlled your data?)

The following subsections show the results of each aspect. Data visualizations (pie charts and tables) are applied to display the distributions, and chi-square test was conducted to test the hypotheses.

4.1 Privacy Concerns

Overall, majority of the participants (91.41%) expressed at least some level of concerns on their privacy when using the COVID-19 apps. It is interesting to find that 55 participants were aware of potential privacy issues, but they were not actually concerned on this situation (choosing "I know I should be concerned but I'm not). The detailed distribution is shown in Table 1.

To have better understanding on individual's concerns, we tested if people's privacy concern towards the COVID-19 apps relate to individual differences such as gender, age, race, education, income, employment status, working from home status, self-quarantine status. The statistical significances were found in age, race, education, income, and employment status, while there was no statistical significance in gender, working status, or self-quarantine status.

Especially, people with different age, race, or income level would have different level of concerns on the privacy protections of the apps. For example, as shown in Fig. 1, participants over 45 years (47.16%) old are more likely to be very concerns on the app privacy comparing to people under 45 years old (31.36%), as the young adults tend to be less concerned on this situation.

Table 1. Level of concern regarding the privacy on COVID-19 apps

Level of concern	Number of participants
Very concerned	617 (38.71%)
Somewhat concerned	526 (33.00%)
A little concerned	314 (19.70%)
Not at all concerned	82 (5.14%)
I know I should be concerned, but I'm not	55 (3.45%)

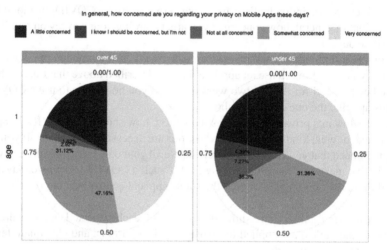

Fig. 1. Age and the level of privacy concerns on COVID-19 apps.

4.2 Willingness

In the survey, we introduced two types of COVID-19 apps, the tracing app and the status app, and asked participants if they willing to use an app like the one described. The distributions of the answers are shown in Table 2.

Table 2. Willingness on using the tracing and status apps

Willingness to use the app	Tracing app	Status app
Yes	658 (38.84%)	717 (43.53%)
No	657 (38.78%)	611 (37.10%)
Maybe	379 (22.37%)	319 (19.37%)

As shown in the table, the percentage of participants who are willing to use the tracing app (38.84%) is almost equal to the percentages of the ones who don't want to use such app (38.78%). For the willingness to use the status app, number of participants who chose "Yes" was slightly larger than the number of participants who chose "No". However, for both apps, about 20 percent of the participants were unsure if they would like to use such app or not. It is reasonable since we only provided the scenarios in the survey instead of an actual application, and participants may prefer to make the decision based on the real-world cases.

The results revealed that the willingness to use the apps is related to age and gender. Participants who are over 45 years old and identified themselves as Whites are more willing to use such apps. Also, participants who have higher education level (above college) or higher income level (over $50,000), currently have a job, and those who were staying home for self-quarantining (following the government's regulation) showed more positive attitudes towards using the COVID-19 apps. For example, as shown in Fig. 2 and Fig. 3, participants with above college level of education or currently holding a job are more willing to use the status app described in the survey, comparing with the ones who are below college or currently unemployed. This may imply that individuals in the higher socioeconomic groups are more willing to accept such apps while individuals from the disadvantaged groups may be more reserved to adopt the apps due to privacy vulnerabilities.

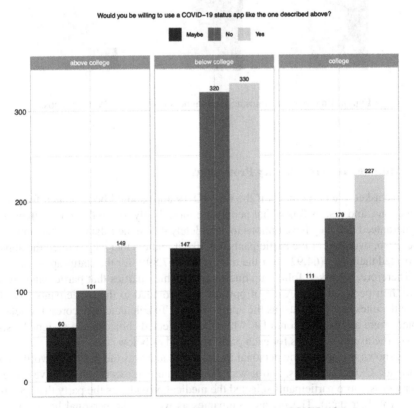

Fig. 2. Education level and willingness to use the COVID-19 apps.

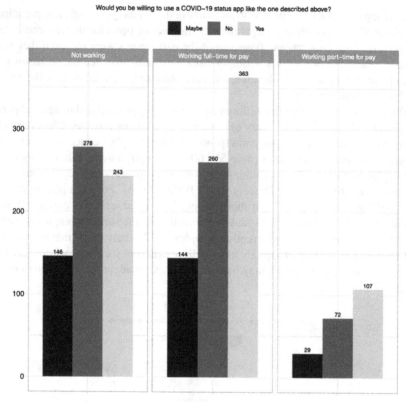

Fig. 3. Employment status and willingness to use the COVID-19 apps.

4.3 Attitudes Towards Privacy Protections

First, we asked the participants if the COVID-19 apps should be regulated for privacy protections, and results found that people are more likely to use the apps if they could be guaranteed that they have options to completely delete their data from the app at any time. Also, over half of the participants feel like it matters that who offered the app and controlled their data (64.92% for the tracing app, 67.89% for the status app).

Therefore, we asked follow-up questions on which parties that participants trust to share their personal data. A list of options was provided to the participants, and they chose the ones that they trust as the app providers. To calculate the scores, the selected choices were assigned a score of 1, while the unselected choices were assigned a score of −1. The averages scores for each party are listed as below.

As shown in Table 3, the personal medical provider was the most trustworthy party to provide COVID-19 apps, and it was the only one that received a positive score (in other words, more participants selected the medical provider as the party that they trust to control their data). The private companies as well as the personal health insurers also received higher level of trust over other parties. However, there were also a lot of

Table 3. Scores for each app provider

App provider	Tracing app	Status app
My Medical Provider	0.0474339	0.01084337
Private Company	−0.0526953	−0.1026201
My Health Insurer	−0.0720859	−0.0741176
Local Government	−0.1258318	−0.1412095
Public Research University	−0.1513255	−0.1616972
Private Research University	−0.1528288	−0.1716981
My Employer	−0.1560886	−0.1744537
Non-Profit Organization	−0.1833705	−0.1907255
Federal Government	−0.2030872	−0.2076588
Not Anyone	−0.0943542	−0.086516

participants indicated that they don't trust anyone to offer the app and control their data, which means that they are more cautious and reserved to use such an app that involves large amount of personal information.

5   Discussion

Overall, results from this study found that individuals are concerned about their privacy when using COVID-19 apps to share personal information. A previous survey study focused on college students found that majority of the young adults in the university are willing to use COVID-19 related apps if certain privacy and security protections are designed and implemented [13]. Results from this study also found similar pattern in the elder adults that although they expressed privacy concerns on the COVID-19 apps, they are still willing to use such apps during the pandemic. It may imply that individuals are open to the COVID-19 apps to trace and share their personal information if privacy protections are guaranteed. Also, people tend to trust more on the parties that they are more familiar with (i.e., personal medical provider or health insurer) instead of the governments to provide the apps and control their personal data. It is understandable since individuals have more connections with their personal medical providers, thus they are able to easily communicate with the service providers if they have any privacy concerns on the COVID-19 apps.

Our study results also reveal that vulnerable groups, which include minority ethnicity groups, people with lower income or education levels, and people who are unemployed, are significantly more likely to express their concerns on the privacy protections provided by the apps, and they show more negative attitudes towards using the COVID-19 apps. While a previous study found the association between socioeconomic status and individual's health conditions [14], results from this study imply that socioeconomic factors may also influence individual's attitudes towards usage of technology and their perspectives of privacy protections. The differences on the individuals' attitudes may imply the existence of disparities and that the vulnerable groups may be at higher risk of privacy violations when using COVID-19 apps.

In conclusion, results from this study underscore that providing appropriate privacy protections is important when developing the COVID-19 related apps, and especially the vulnerable groups' needs on privacy should be emphasized and satisfied. It is well-documented that the services of local libraries benefit members of vulnerable groups [15]. An increase in community resources, for example, by having social workers or staff at libraries to help individuals to be familiar with the apps' privacy protections, could potentially encourage more people to use relevant apps. Meanwhile, this study also raises public awareness of protect information privacy when using COVID-19 apps during the crisis. Ideally, there would be a coordinated effort between the government and app service providers to ensure that vulnerable groups' personal information is well protected. It has been said that a society is only as strong as its weakest members. Vulnerable groups should receive the same attention as more privileged groups, and our goal is to accomplish it. The higher level of privacy concerns from the vulnerable groups suggests that more efforts are needed as a community in order to address the privacy considerations when developing and applying the COVID-19 apps.

6 Limitations and Future Works

One of the study limitations is that the survey was conducted during the early stage of the COVID-19 pandemic. It is possible that individual's attitude towards COVID-19 apps could be positively or negatively impacted by any events occurred in the later stages of the outbreak. Another limitation is that results of this study were based on an anonymous survey. As a result, we were unable to observe how individual's attitude changes over time during the COVID-19 pandemic.

For the future works, one of the directions is to compare how individual's attitude towards COVID-19 app privacy changes in different time periods, and if such attitude is affected by any significant event or regulation. Also, we will continue analyzing different types of COVID-19 related apps developed during the later stages of the pandemic, thus learn more on how the latest apps protect individuals' privacy.

Results from this study and future related works are expected to provide guidance to governments, health organizations, and app developers in understanding people's expectations for these apps and more importantly the factors that is critical in their adoption of these apps especially for those in vulnerable groups. The results can also provide direction on the implementation of privacy features and protections that can be included in the COVID-19 tracing and status apps.

References

1. Davalbhakta, S., et al.: A systematic review of smartphone applications available for corona virus disease 2019 (COVID19) and the assessment of their quality using the mobile application rating scale (MARS). J. Med. Syst. 44(9), 1–15 (2020). https://doi.org/10.1007/s10916-020-01633-3

2. Gerke, S., Shachar, C., Chai, P.R., Cohen, I.G.: Regulatory, safety, and privacy concerns of home monitoring technologies during COVID-19. Nat. Med. **26**(8), 1176–1182 (2020)
3. Kaptchuk, G., Goldstein, D.G., Hargittai, E., Hofman, J., Redmiles, E.M.: How good is good enough for COVID19 apps? The influence of benefits, accuracy, and privacy on willingness to adopt. arXiv preprint arXiv:2005.04343 (2020)
4. Sharma, T., Dyer, H.A., Bashir, M.: Enabling user-centered privacy controls for mobile applications: Covid-19 perspective. ACM Trans. Internet Technol. (TOIT) **21**(1), 1–24 (2021)
5. Peters, D.H., Garg, A., Bloom, G., Walker, D.G., Brieger, W.R., Hafizur Rahman, M.: Poverty and access to health care in developing countries. Ann. N. Y. Acad. Sci. **1136**(1), 161–171 (2008)
6. Azad, M.A., et al.: A first look at privacy analysis of COVID-19 contact-tracing mobile applications. IEEE Internet Things J. **8**(21), 15796–15806 (2020)
7. Arifeen, M.M., Al Mamun, A., Kaiser, M.S., Mahmud, M.: Blockchain-enable contact tracing for preserving user privacy during COVID-19 outbreak (2020)
8. Chan, E.Y., Saqib, N.U.: Privacy concerns can explain unwillingness to download and use contact tracing apps when COVID-19 concerns are high. Comput. Hum. Behav. **119**, 106718 (2021)
9. Altmann, S., et al.: Acceptability of app-based contact tracing for COVID-19: cross-country survey study. JMIR Mhealth Uhealth **8**(8), e19857 (2020)
10. Hargittai, E., Redmiles, E.M., Vitak, J., Zimmer, M.: Americans' willingness to adopt a COVID-19 tracking app. First Monday, **25**(11) (2020) online
11. Singu, S., Acharya, A., Challagundla, K., Byrareddy, S.N.: Impact of social determinants of health on the emerging COVID-19 pandemic in the United States. Front. Public Health **8**, 406 (2020)
12. McDonald, N., et al.: Privacy and power: acknowledging the importance of privacy research and design for vulnerable populations. In: Extended Abstracts of the 2020 CHI Conference on Human Factors in Computing Systems, pp. 1–8 (2020)
13. Wang, T., Guo, L., Bashir, M.: COVID-19 apps and privacy protections from users' perspective. Proc. Assoc. Inform. Sci. Technol. **58**(1), 357–365 (2021)
14. Cameron, L., Williams, J.: Is the relationship between socioeconomic status and health stronger for older children in developing countries? Demography **46**(2), 303–324 (2009). https://doi.org/10.1353/dem.0.0054
15. Moxley, D.P., Abbas, J.M.: Envisioning libraries as collaborative community anchors for social service provision to vulnerable populations. Practice **28**(5), 311–330 (2016)

Correction to: The Dimensionality of the Cyber Warrior

Morgan L. Ferretti, Timothy Richards, Jessica G. Irons,
and Kirsten Richards

Correction to:
Chapter "The Dimensionality of the Cyber Warrior" in:
A. Moallem (Ed.): *HCI for Cybersecurity, Privacy and Trust,*
LNCS 13333, https://doi.org/10.1007/978-3-031-05563-8_21

In the originally published version of chapter 21, the name of the author Kirsten Richards and the affiliation of all the authors were presented incorrectly. This has been corrected.

The updated version of this chapter can be found at
https://doi.org/10.1007/978-3-031-05563-8_21

Author Index

Printed in the United States
by Baker & Taylor Publisher Services

Printed in the United States
by Baker & Taylor Publisher Services